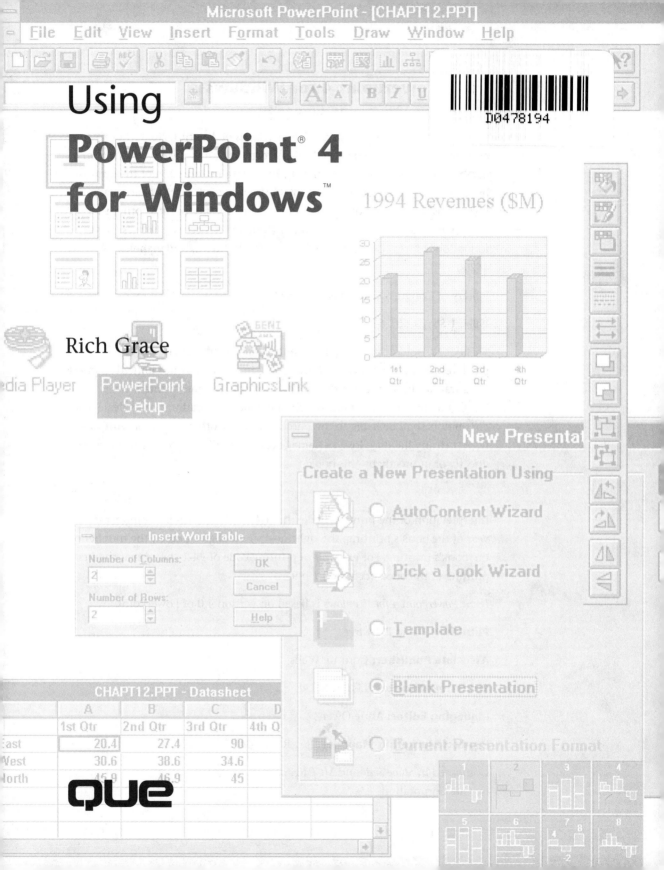

Using PowerPoint 4 for Windows

Copyright © 1994 by Que® Corporation

Library of Congress Catalog No.: 94-65143

ISBN: 1-56529-651-6

97 96 95   6 5

Interpretation of the printing code: the rightmost double-digit number is the year of the book's printing; the rightmost single-digit number, the number of the book's printing. For example, a printing code of 94-1 shows that the first printing of the book occurred in 1994.

Using PowerPoint 4 for Windows is based on version 4.0 of PowerPoint.

Publisher: David P. Ewing

Associate Publisher: Corinne Walls

Publishing Director: Lisa A. Bucki

Managing Editor: Anne Owen

Product Marketing Manager: Ray Robinson

Composed in *Stone Serif* and *MCPdigital*
by Que Corporation

Dedication

This book is humbly dedicated to:

*My mother, **Carol Grace**, without whom this book could not have been written, and my Grandmother, **Mary Langan**, who has helped me so much over the years.*

About the Author

Author, journalist, and scholar, **Rich Grace** has been bumping around the computer industry for years. He's written dozens of articles for computer publications, and his work has appeared in *InfoWorld Direct*, *MicroTimes*, *Windows User*, *Mac Home Journal*, *PC Home Journal*, *PC Today*, *Electronic Engineering Times*, and *Imaging Magazine*. He is also the author of Que's *Word 6 for Windows Quick Reference*. The proud owner of a highly checkered academic career, Rich hopes to eventually get a real job, perhaps in real estate or mercenary combat. He can be reached at CompuServe ID# 72672,2266.

Acknowledgments

Thanks to Microsoft Corporation, without which this project would not have been possible. Thanks also for Microsoft's excellent press relations support, represented by the professionals at Waggener Edstrom in Seattle, Portland, and San Jose. They are an extremely helpful and enthusiastic group of people to work with, particularly Phil Missimore at the San Jose office.

Without Pantone's wonderful ColorUp program for both Windows and the Macintosh, it would have been much harder to write intelligently about the basic mechanics of color and the use of color in PowerPoint. For anyone who needs to learn more about color, Pantone's ColorUp is a necessity.

Brenda Bennett at Western Digital, in Irvine, California, was gracious enough to provide me with an additional 420M Caviar hard disk for this book project. The Caviar 2420 is inexpensive, reliable, and capacious enough for almost any appetite.

Diamond Computer Technologies provided me with their spectacular Viper VLB Windows accelerator card, which proved invaluable on many levels for this book. Thanks to Scott Kim for his generous support.

KFC USA, Inc of Costa Mesa, California, was kind enough to furnish one of their 15-inch CA 1507 multisync monitors for the duration of this project.

During my normal mid-project hardware crisis, Striker Langston, of Essence Group in Fountain Valley, California, was crucial in aiding one very panicked writer to resolve a serious hard-disk controller problem.

Ralph Bond of Intel Corporation went far out of his way to provide me with crucial information on handling video and sound objects in PowerPoint presentations. He's a good friend, and I appreciate his efforts on my behalf.

Thanks to all my friends and relatives for putting up with my frantic mood swings and panic fits. Thanks especially to Alice Zenns, Marc Busch, John DeHaan, Rick Reardon, Rick White, Mark Woodward, Craig Bobchin, my agent Matt Wagner of Waterside Productions, and my wonderful and beautiful sister, Catherine.

Que's editors have been a crucial part of the success of this project, particularly Heather Kaufman, Kathie-Jo Arnoff, and Patrick Kanouse, whose incisive criticisms on the advanced chapters were a crucial part of whatever success I realized in writing them. I'd especially like to thank Tom Godfrey at Prentice Hall Computer Publishing, who was patient enough to stick by me until the PowerPoint 4 project became a reality.

I also want to thank the writers who chipped in with important chapters during the brutal holiday-time working schedule. Bryan Pfaffenberger contributed the chapter on printing and output (chapter 16); David Nesbitt wrote the chapters on using clip art and on customizing PowerPoint (chapters 10 and 22); Jean Knight wrote the chapters on handling and formatting text (chapters 6 and 7); and Jeffry Byrne contributed the chapters on table creation and on the basic handling of objects (chapters 8 and 9). While I labored under difficult circumstances, their work was important and appreciated.

Trademarks

All terms mentioned in this book that are known to be trademarks or service marks have been appropriately capitalized. Que Corporation cannot attest to the accuracy of this information. Use of a term in this book should not be regarded as affecting the validity of any trademark or service mark.

Microsoft and PowerPoint are registered trademarks and Windows is a trademark of Microsoft Corporation.

Genigraphics is a registered trademark and GraphicsLink is a trademark of Genigraphics Corporation.

Contents at a Glance

Contents

4 Setting Up Your New Presentation   123

7 Creating Speaker's Notes, Handouts, and Outlines   223

17 Working with Color   481

VI Advanced PowerPoint 4   511

18 Using Links to Other Applications   513

19 Using Advanced Charting Features   541

Introduction

Microsoft PowerPoint is among the leaders in a competitive and growing category of computer software: graphics presentations. PowerPoint 4, in particular, is appropriately named because the program combines the most powerful features of not one program category, but several:

Drawing. PowerPoint 4 offers a wide selection of drawing and art creation features that rival dedicated drawing programs. While PowerPoint can never replace, for example, CorelDRAW!, many presentation artists may find that PowerPoint is all they need. An extensive clip art library offers instant art content to the presentation creator.

Charting. PowerPoint 4 offers a highly flexible and feature-rich charting and graphing capability. You type the numeric data you want to present (sales for a company department for the four quarters of the year, for example) into a simple spreadsheet, and then choose from among the many dozens of chart styles. PowerPoint 4's charting and graphing capabilities have been substantially enhanced.

Outlining and Word Processing. PowerPoint offers an easy and intuitive Outlining feature in which you can add any amount of text, choose your favorite fonts and typeface sizes, and quickly create bulleted lists. Spell checking is provided, as is Search and Replace. You can construct an entire presentation and study its logic in Outline view.

An Artist's Palette. PowerPoint utilizes the graphics power of the Windows platform to offer you thousands of professionally created color schemes for your slide shows, and hundreds of predefined graphic backgrounds for various presentation motifs. If a predefined scheme doesn't please you, it's remarkably easy to create your own.

An Output Program. PowerPoint gets the most from your output devices. PowerPoint handles color printing and slide output with aplomb. You can easily create overhead transparencies. If you want professional color output, use the GraphicsLink program to send your files to Genigraphics Corporation, a service bureau that makes the slide output for you.

Corporate Communications. PowerPoint 4's mission, ultimately, is to empower and expand your delivery of corporate communications. All the tools listed above are placed in the service of providing you with the most efficient, integrated program available for making your corporate communications ring with conviction and authority.

Unlike a drawing or charting package, in which one screen at a time is created, programs like PowerPoint enable you to create extensive multiple-slide presentations at once. You can create as many slides as the memory on your system can contain. PowerPoint 4 has perhaps the greatest flexibility of any program in its field for this purpose.

If you have multiple slides in your presentation file, you can make use of PowerPoint's handy Slide Sorter to rearrange slides by simply dragging and dropping. You can delete and add slides in the Sorter, and change the entire color scheme of the presentation at once. You can also apply different color schemes to individual slides. You can quickly and easily add any type of data to your presentation that your computer can support—including sounds, movie clips, and photo-realistic pictures.

How does PowerPoint 4 work? This book attempts to answer that question.

PowerPoint 4 represents a big jump in capabilities from its previous version, particularly in how the program actually works. Every capability and feature in PowerPoint is, for the first time, integrated into a seamless, interdependent whole. Not only that: PowerPoint also associates more closely with fellow Microsoft applications programs than ever before.

You may need to create a presentation from scratch: define a color scheme; create a common background for your slide show; create the titles and basic outline for the slides in your show; write the body text for your slides; and create 3-D pie and column charts from company sales data. You may need to import Lotus 1-2-3 or Excel spreadsheets on which to base those charts. Add film clips and sounds from the "firing line:" the sales force. Define a specific font: perhaps 40-Point Arial, for all the titles in your presentation. Define another font for your body text and bulleted points. Add framing effects to all your objects for a custom effect. Arrange the objects on your slides for a clean, organized appearance. Add a company logo to all the slides in the presentation. Import bitmap pictures. Create tables. Spell check your presentation. Save and print your file in color transparencies.

And it all has to be done yesterday!

If you had to specify each step in the presentation process by name, you would never get it done. Fortunately, with PowerPoint 4, you don't have to. Just point and click with the mouse. With a couple of mouse clicks, even the most complex-sounding features can be mastered rapidly.

When you point to the desired feature or object and select it, you're using a Graphical User Interface (GUI, or goo-ey), a front-end for a program or even for an entire computer system, which uses the mouse and a color display to simplify the use of your computer. Windows, of course, is a popular example of a GUI. The advantage of using Windows and other GUIs (such as the Macintosh, for example) is the offering of another acronym that defines another advanced capability—WYSIWYG, or "What You See Is What You Get." When a slide show or document appears on your computer screen, WYSIWYG ensures that it bears close resemblance to what you see on paper— or, in PowerPoint's case, the on-screen slide show, color transparencies, or color slides.

Thanks to the GUI, PowerPoint 4 is more powerful and easier to use than ever before. You don't have to be a graphics designer to use PowerPoint. On the contrary, PowerPoint is designed for those users who need to apply their expertise—corporate communications—to a visual presentation; and to do it quickly and effectively. To this end, PowerPoint offers over 160 different sample templates for the quick creation of appealing and effective slide shows. PowerPoint's templates offer many of the basic elements of an outstanding slide show, such as attractive color schemes, title fonts, placement of graphic objects, and the logical flow and basic content of the presentation.

PowerPoint 4's new Wizards offer an intelligent and speedy way to create several different styles of content for presentations—anything from communicating bad news to progress reports. You can change the words, the outline, and the content of your presentation at will, and craft a slide show with a top-notch professional appearance. PowerPoint frees you from having to sweat the basic details of using the program and lets you focus on what's most important—what to say and what images you want to convey.

PowerPoint 4 combines vast power in a friendly and approachable package. You can become a power user almost as soon as you begin, and using the program will soon become second nature. At first, however, you can profit by reading about the program. PowerPoint 4 offers such a depth of features that you're likely to miss some of them unless you take a little time to seek them out. Helping you discover PowerPoint 4's possibilities for your corporate communications is the mission of this book.

What Is in This Book

Like the PowerPoint software itself, *Using PowerPoint 4 for Windows* endeavors to make the power of the program easily accessible. The book opens with basic features and functionality and gradually moves to more advanced and complex topics. It's recommended that you start by learning the basics, and when you feel at home with the fundamentals, you can progress to more advanced topics. Be reassured, though: Even the most complex features of PowerPoint are surprisingly straightforward and accessible most are accomplished with a couple of mouse clicks.

This book is divided into six parts that split the PowerPoint 4 program into several discrete areas of study: PowerPoint Basics, Text, Drawing, Charts, Output and Color, and Advanced PowerPoint 4.

Part I, "PowerPoint 4 Basics," introduces you to the basic features of PowerPoint 4. The chapters in Part I are as follows:

Chapter 1, "An Overview of PowerPoint 4 for Windows," offers a quick road map of many of PowerPoint 4's most significant upgrades and enhancements, including PowerPoint's new toolbars, Wizards, drag and drop, and other features.

Chapter 2, "Getting Acquainted with PowerPoint 4," describes how to work with the mouse and keyboard, to work with the menus, to get help, and to understand the new features of PowerPoint 4's user interface that help speed you on the way to successful presentations.

Chapter 3, "Quick Start: Creating a First Presentation," ties many of PowerPoint's most important features together in a basic exercise for creating your first presentation in PowerPoint 4.

Chapter 4, "Setting Up Your New Presentation," describes the interlocking tools of PowerPoint 4 that cooperate in helping you create the best possible presentation: PowerPoint's Masters and Views.

Chapter 5, "Using and Creating Templates," describes how to work with the fundamental building block of any presentation: PowerPoint's templates.

Part II, "Text," covers all of PowerPoint's text handling and text entry features:

Chapter 6, "Working with Text," describes basic text entry techniques, text object manipulation (including PowerPoint's enhanced drag and drop capabilities), and using fonts and text styles.

Chapter 7, "Creating Speaker's Notes, Outlines, and Handouts," shows how to produce the other elements of your presentation: your personal notes for the slide show, working with your presentation outline, and audience handouts.

Chapter 8, "Working with Tables," shows you how to create, edit, and format tables of text data with Word 6 for Windows and then bring those tables into PowerPoint.

Part III, "Drawing," approaches the subject of drawing and creating art objects in PowerPoint:

Chapter 9, "Drawing Objects," shows you how to use PowerPoint's numerous drawing tools.

Chapter 10, "Adding Clip Art and Scanned Art," shows you how to work with PowerPoint's extensive clip art library, how to place clip art into your slide show, and how to work with photo-realistic images in PowerPoint.

Chapter 11, "Selecting, Editing, and Enhancing Objects," describes the process of using, moving, aligning, and changing object placeholders on PowerPoint slides.

Part IV, "Charts," describes how to create and use charts and organizational charts in PowerPoint:

Chapter 12, "Working with Datasheets," shows you how to edit the building blocks of every chart you'll ever create—the numeric datasheet.

Chapter 13, "Creating Basic Charts," summarizes how to choose chart types, the various elements of a chart, and how to change various elements on a chart.

Chapter 14, "Customizing Charts," digs deeper into the process of changing your chart's appearance, offers more detailed discussions of changing chart elements, drawing objects, and adding custom colors to charts, among other subjects.

Chapter 15, "Creating Organizational Charts," introduces you to the process of creating organizational charts to depict a corporation's or department's structure.

Part V, "Output and Color," focuses on an essential part of PowerPoint: the final output and its appearance.

Chapter 16, "Printing and Other Kinds of Output," describes printing the various elements of a presentation, including handouts, notes, and slides, and using the Genigraphics service bureau for final color slide output.

Chapter 17, "Working with Color," discusses basic color theory and how color really works in PowerPoint, as well as some topics on applying color to PowerPoint objects.

Part VI, "Advanced PowerPoint 4," discusses advanced topics and techniques for getting the most out of the program:

Chapter 18, "Using Links to Other Applications," discusses how object linking and embedding (OLE) works and how it can help you work more effectively with other data types and application programs.

Chapter 19, "Using Advanced Charting Features," further explores sophisticated chart types and chart customizing techniques.

Chapter 20, "Advanced Presentation Management," offers discussions on adding special effects to presentations and working with multimedia data types.

Chapter 21, "Using Advanced Color, Text, and Drawing Features," touches on operations such as scaling objects for different screen resolutions, importing custom color palettes, and recoloring pictures.

Chapter 22, "Customizing PowerPoint," details how to create custom toolbars and change PowerPoint's user interface to your liking.

Appendix A, "Installing PowerPoint 4 for Windows," shows you how to install PowerPoint.

Appendix B, "Gallery of Presentation Examples," offers a dozen examples of complex and customized PowerPoint slides that demonstrate how you can extend the capabilities of the program.

Who Should Use This Book

Why read a book about PowerPoint 4 if the software is so "intuitive?" Virtually every feature in PowerPoint can be used and activated with a few mouse clicks—even advanced features such as changing color schemes or rotating charts. PowerPoint doesn't require you to know sophisticated commands or memorize an arcane set of keystroke combinations. Nor is it necessary to know graphic arts.

This book is aimed at anyone who wants to create more effective communications. Read this book to become acquainted with the myriad possibilities contained in the PowerPoint software package. You can easily copy a presentation template or any of its default elements and make them your own. To use a presentation template, however, you must know that it's available for your use. Creating effective and attractive charts is easy in PowerPoint. But how do you know what types of charts to use? Any book about PowerPoint, like this one, is more a catalog of possibilities than a simple how-to instruction manual. This is the approach attempted throughout this book, eschewing whenever possible the practice of simply rewording the program's documentation.

Even the most advanced chapters in this book don't plumb the full depths of PowerPoint 4. Instead, they provide signposts pointing you in creative directions. If you start using PowerPoint 4 and never read a word about it, it's quite possible to produce serviceable presentations. Over time, you may make many discoveries. You could continue to make them for interminable periods of time. What do you do if you need to harness advanced features but don't have the time to fish around in the software? Much of the program's power will certainly be lost to you, because there's so much to offer.

This book is aimed at beginning and intermediate users and any Windows user who appreciates an alternative way to use graphics on his or her computer. It isn't aimed at graphics specialists or software experts, though either can profit by reading it. Graphics specialists can learn about an alternative use of computer graphics in the workaday business world, and thus understand more about the needs of the business community. A software expert can gain insight and advice about creating high-quality graphics.

Using PowerPoint 4 for Windows is also written for corporate communications specialists and business presenters who want to create their own presentations. This book shows you how to use the program in step-by-step, task-oriented examples. Guidelines, explanations, margin tips, and highlighted notes keep you firmly on course and help you get the most out of PowerPoint 4 in the shortest period of time. Liberal quantities of illustrations aid in depicting features and procedures in the program.

How to Use This Book

PowerPoint is not hard to use. Microsoft has gone to great lengths to make the program more accessible than ever before. You do need to know, however, what the program's features are and to understand what its panoply of features can do for you. (A Slide Sorter, for example, is a great idea, but you must know what it is and how to use it. That's where this book comes in.)

You probably won't read this book as you would a novel, from beginning to end. Keep it available as a reference for real-world tasks whenever you use the program. You may use some features frequently, and others seldom. *Using PowerPoint 4 for Windows* can serve you as a reference for features you only partially remember. Even if you use features often, this book can still be a source of tips, notes, techniques, shortcuts, and troubleshooting. A feature-rich program, no matter how accessible, merits a feature-rich book to accompany it on your desktop.

Tips for using Microsoft PowerPoint more effectively are included in the page margins. The margin tips can assist you in becoming more proficient with the program.

Notes are included in highlighted boxes. Notes are important information about program features and can contain warnings about avoiding certain mistakes in the program.

Short troubleshooting sections, included after many sections of the book, try to answer commonly asked questions about the program.

Regardless of the program's ease of use, you must still follow step-by-step instructions to perform even basic operations. This book is no exception. Skipping a step can cause headaches and force you to retrace your steps. When you read a Que book such as *Using PowerPoint 4 for Windows,* you learn all the right steps to follow and the exact sequence in which to follow them.

Conventions Used in This Book

Some conventions are used in this book to help you quickly learn to use Microsoft PowerPoint 4. Book conventions are as follows:

You can choose menu names, commands, and dialog box options with either the mouse or a keystroke combination (such as Alt+T). In this book, the instructions are written so that you can use the method with which you are most comfortable.

When you see an instruction such as "From the **E**dit menu, choose the **C**opy command," you can use the mouse to pull down the Edit menu and then click on **C**opy; or you can use the key combination Alt+E to display the **E**dit menu and then press C to choose the **C**opy command.

Keyboard shortcuts are often given when they are available. For example, Ctrl+C is a shortcut for choosing **C**opy from the **E**dit menu. There are a number of standard Windows keyboard shortcuts that are common to most Windows applications, such as Ctrl+C for Copy or Ctrl+V for Paste, and they are mentioned where applicable.

"Clicking" on a button or menu option is done with the mouse on your computer. The word "click" or "clicking" indicates that you should press the left mouse button once over the indicated option.

Several chapters in this book deal with the process of creating and customizing charts. PowerPoint uses a separate program, Microsoft Graph, to create charts for use in PowerPoint slides. In the chapters dealing with the subject (primarily chapters 12, 13, 14, and 19), the word *chart* is used when describing such objects as bar charts, pie charts, column charts, and so on. Although PowerPoint's graphing and charting application is named Microsoft Graph, all its menu commands, options, and help menus use the word chart in their commands, so that standard is used throughout this book except when specifically referring to the Microsoft Graph program by name.

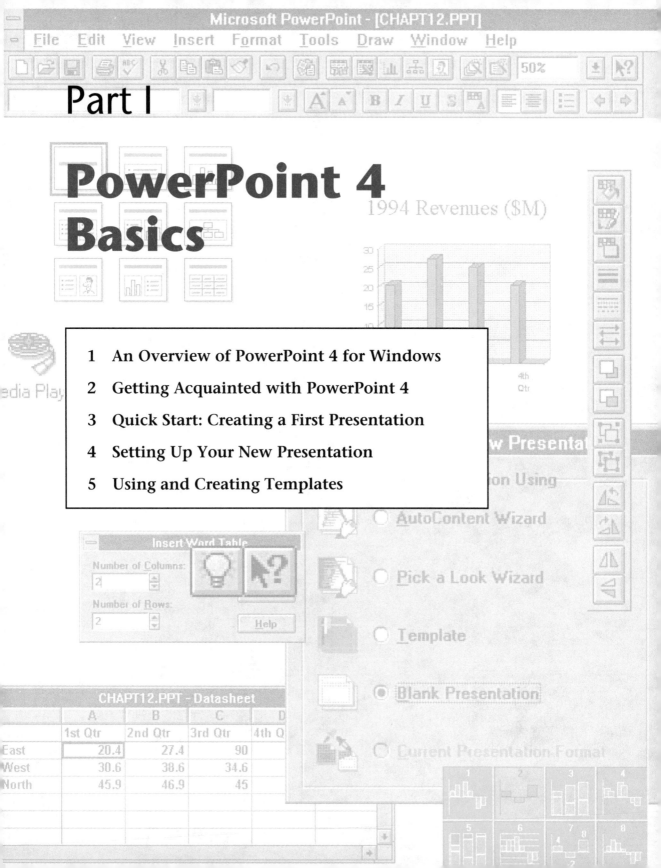

Part I

PowerPoint 4 Basics

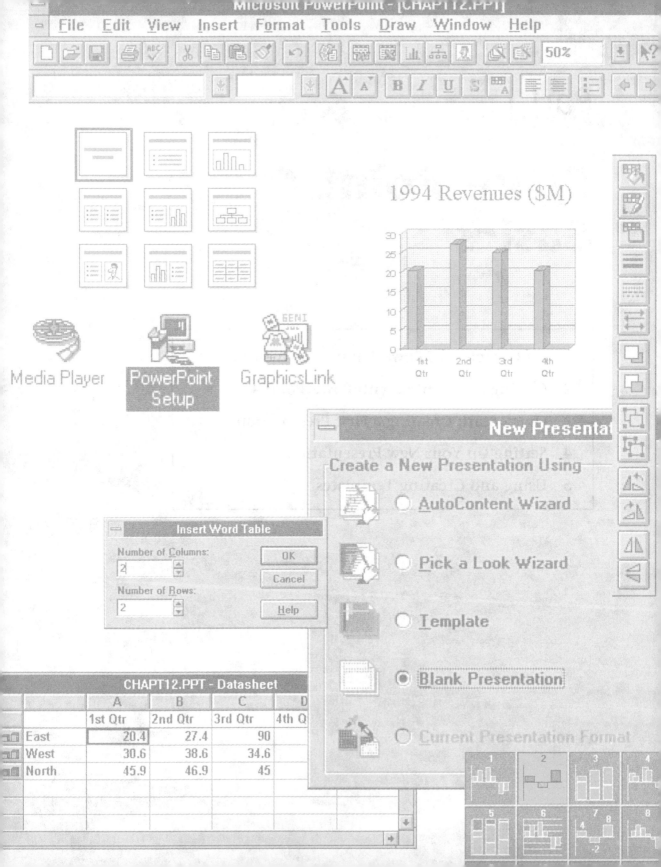

Chapter 1

An Overview of PowerPoint 4 for Windows

PowerPoint 4 for Windows represents a major upgrade from the previous version, PowerPoint 3. While in many ways the program offers the same functions and methods as its predecessor, Microsoft's presentation package has undergone a facelift and boasts added functionality in many areas. A few of the most important areas of improvement in PowerPoint 4 are:

■ A dramatically enhanced interface, including an expanded set of toolbars

■ Toolbars can be customized with new tools and the user can also create new and custom toolbars

■ PowerPoint 4's menu bars and standard toolbars offer nearly identical functionality with its companion programs, Word 6 for Windows and Excel 5 for Windows, as part of the Microsoft Office application suite

■ Drastically improved and expanded charting capability, including greater integration with the PowerPoint main program, an expanded selection of chart types, and easier creation of custom chart types

■ AutoContent and Pick a Look Wizards enable quick and easy creation of the basic elements of a presentation

There's a lot more, but this short list describes the major feature enhancements that most users probably look for.

This chapter gives you an overview of PowerPoint 4's features, including:

■ New enhanced productivity and ease-of-use features

■ Enhanced and integrated charting features

■ Organizational charting feature

■ Improved drawing features

■ Enhanced color features

■ Presentation rehearsal and annotation

■ Table creation and use of Excel spreadsheets

Tip
A presentation
is composed of
many interrelated
elements: the slide
show, outline,
notes, and
handouts.

PowerPoint is widely considered to be among the leaders in a new and grow-ing field of computer applications software—presentations. Almost everyone who works in a corporate environment is familiar with the idea of a presenta-tion: A presentation, for most people, is a slide show that is delivered by a speaker to help illustrate points in his or her talk. The production of slide shows is the core of the PowerPoint program. Nonetheless, you can easily make a distinction between a *slide show* and a *presentation*. A slide show is only one part (though a very important one) of the presentation process. A presentation is a slide show combined with hard-copy elements such as speaker's notes, audience handouts, and outlines, which are used to build the structure of the presentation.

Many elements can be included in a slide show: point-by-point arguments, called bulleted lists or body text, that form the backbone of the discussion; charts of various kinds, such as bar charts, pie charts, column charts, and many other types, which are used to illustrate statistics and data trends; tables, which deliver the actual statistics and categorical explanations; graphics and clip art; and, finally, the various types of hard copy that are used to support and round out the presentation.

The tools offered in PowerPoint 4 are designed to make the presentation design and production process easier than ever before. All the elements of a presentation—the slide show itself, as well as the various forms of hard copy and the outlining tools used to help build it—are united into a seamless whole in the new version of PowerPoint. All the various parts of the program are closely linked into a highly cooperative and collaborative process that, when used properly, can help you inform and persuade your audience.

The rest of this chapter is devoted to a brief discussion of some of PowerPoint 4's most important new features. In later chapters, you will also notice cover-age of many of the new features in PowerPoint that are small incremental upgrades to capabilities that have long been in the program. These small upgrade changes are not mentioned here.

Enhanced Productivity and Ease-of-Use Features

Though PowerPoint 4 offers many improvements and enhancements, any user of PowerPoint 3 should immediately feel at home with it. Many features have been added to streamline the process of using simple and complex

program features, such as shortcut menus, Cue Cards, Wizards, Chart
AutoLayouts, expanded and customizable toolbars, and much more.

Shortcut Menus

Many areas of the program are more accessible than ever before with a
startlingly simple feature: clicking the right mouse button.

Whenever you click the right mouse button on an object on the PowerPoint
screen, such as a slide background, a drawing, a chart, or a slide title, you
display a special shortcut menu similar to the one shown in figure 1.1.

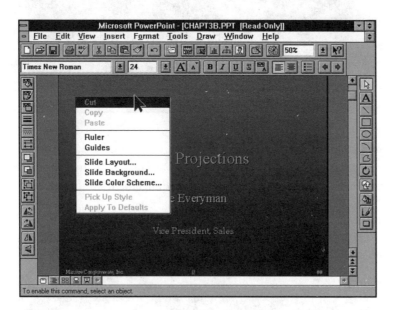

Fig. 1.1

The shortcut menu
displays options
for changing a
slide background.
Choose any
options that are
in black text.
Ghosted options
are unavailable.

What is the biggest advantage to using the right mouse button? Ever get tired
of constantly reaching up with the mouse to pull down a menu? Or hunting
for the right menu option? If you click the right mouse button over the
desired object on the screen, that extra work is over.

Additional Toolbars

PowerPoint is one of a new generation of Windows applications that allows
you to define exactly how you want your program screen to appear.
PowerPoint 4 offers an expanded toolbar set, any or all of which can be
displayed on the program screen at any time, as shown in figure 1.2.

PowerPoint 4 Basics

Fig. 1.2
PowerPoint's
toolbar set.

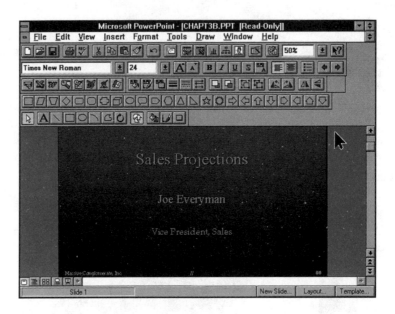

Of course, a toolbar arrangement such as the one in figure 1.2. is probably
not to your taste. Not many users would appreciate having half the screen
occupied by frivolous icons. How does the arrangement in figure 1.3
compare?

Fig. 1.3
The same
PowerPoint
toolbars
rearranged.

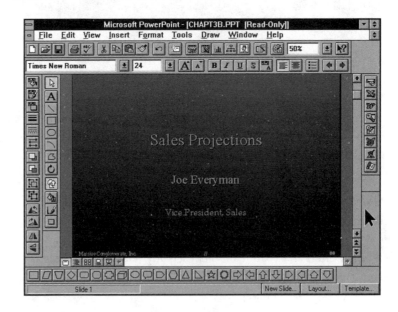

PowerPoint's toolbar set can be moved and rearranged at will. Any toolbar can be moved to any margin of the screen and toolbars can also "float" over the PowerPoint screen, as in figure 1.4.

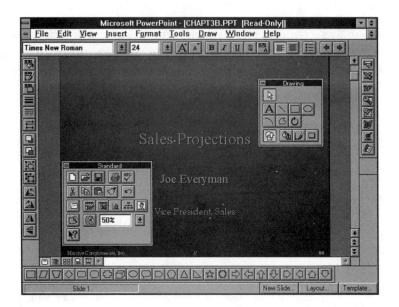

Fig. 1.4
More toolbar madness.

As you can see, there's much more flexibility than before in how you can tailor your PowerPoint screen. Figure 1.4 also displays another interesting feature of the program: the capability to display and work with more than one presentation at a time.

Among PowerPoint's new toolbars is a Microsoft toolbar that enables you to start any Windows-based Microsoft application program with a mouse click on a tool. Programs supported include FoxPro, Publisher, Project, Schedule Plus, Access, and Microsoft Mail, as well as PowerPoint's Microsoft Office companions Word and Excel.

Any PowerPoint function can be placed on a toolbar by choosing from PowerPoint's generous selection of toolbar icons for assignment to each function. The user can change any existing toolbar to suit his own needs or add any desired number of new toolbars.

Status Bar, Standardized Menus, ToolTips, and Dialog Box Hints
PowerPoint 4's ease-of-use enhancements don't stop with mere toolbars and icon collections. PowerPoint's front end now provides help every step of the way, from the most basic procedures to the most complex. It all begins with

I

PowerPoint 4 Basics

PowerPoint's status bar. Any action you perform, any menu option you select, or any button, icon, or tool that you pass the mouse over displays a helpful message on the status bar at the bottom of the PowerPoint screen succinctly describing the exact action you're about to perform.

PowerPoint uses a standard menu arrangement that bears a very close resemblance to those in Microsoft Word and Excel. In fact, only one menu heading is different between PowerPoint and Microsoft Word, two seemingly very different applications, as shown in figure 1.5.

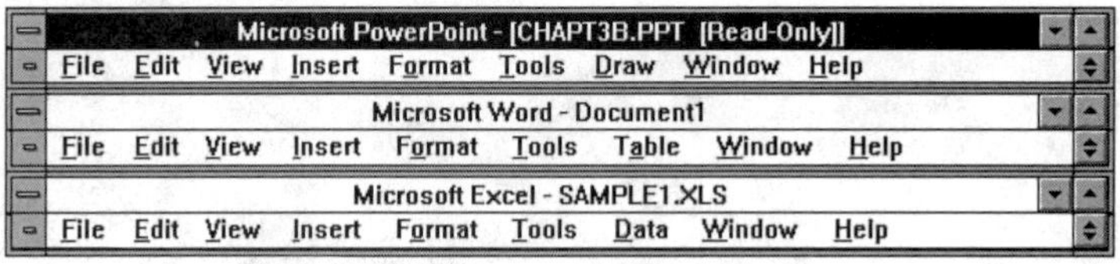

Fig. 1.5
The Word and
PowerPoint menu
bars.

All of PowerPoint's dialog boxes provide a running narrative of the actions you perform and the options you select. There's never a chance to get lost inside PowerPoint.

ToolTips is an intelligent and unobtrusive feature that displays a small yellow text balloon when you pass the mouse over any button on a toolbar. Even advanced users will appreciate the security of knowing exactly what that foreign-looking icon is on the crowded custom toolbars they created.

Wizards for Template and Style Selection and Outlining

For many situations in your workplace, you are forced to produce a presentation on a very tight schedule. In other situations, you may be forced to do so without having any substantial previous experience in making presentations.

That's where PowerPoint 4's handy Wizards come in. PowerPoint offers two Wizards to help you get a running start in producing a complete presentation: the Pick a Look Wizard and the AutoContent Wizard. Both are important, and using both Wizards in succession ensures that you not only create a consistent and attractive look for your presentation, but also that the content, style, and structure of your new presentation are reasonably complete and organized in every way before you enter your actual content and graphic elements.

The Pick a Look Wizard provides a nine-step process for choosing a *template* to define the artistic appearance of your slide show (see fig. 1.6). A template tells PowerPoint how the various elements of your slide show are supposed to look—with specific colors assigned to the various parts of your slides. The Pick a Look Wizard also helps you decide what other parts of a presentation you want to produce: slide printouts, printer outlines, audience handouts, and speaker's notes to help you keep track of your show while you deliver it.

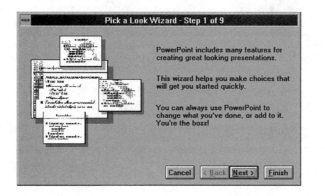

Fig. 1.6
The Pick a Look
Wizard.

The AutoContent Wizard provides a four-step procedure to define what the basic message of your presentation is going to be (see fig. 1.7). Stepping through this quick process helps you decide what you're going to say and how you're going to say it, as illustrated in figure 1.8.

Fig. 1.7
The AutoContent
Wizard.

Fig. 1.8
The AutoContent Wizard helps you define your message.

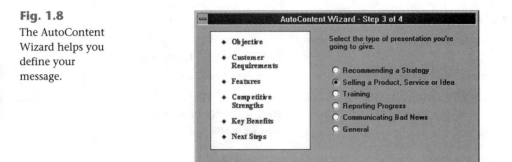

Cue Cards Speed Complex Tasks

PowerPoint's Cue Cards, available on the program's Help menu, are a set of easy-to-follow procedures that describe how to perform more difficult tasks within the program. A lengthy list of common but somewhat complex tasks is offered, including adding a company logo or text to every slide, branching to other presentations, changing colors in a color scheme, editing PowerPoint clip art, and more. Figure 1.9 illustrates how the basic Cue Card feature appears.

Fig. 1.9
Selecting from PowerPoint's Cue Cards to perform tasks.

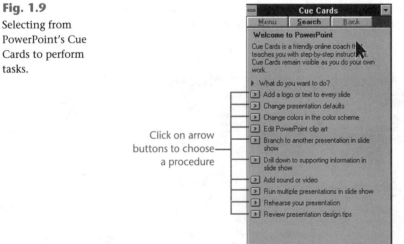

Cue Cards "coach" you through all the steps required to perform an important task in PowerPoint. You select a Cue Card by clicking on one of the small right-arrow buttons shown in the list. A step-by-step procedure with a detailed description appears (see fig. 1.10).

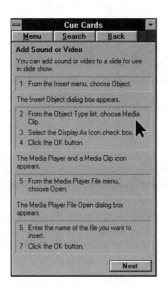

Fig. 1.10
Stepping
through a Cue
Card procedure.

AutoLayouts for Quick Slide Layouts

Instead of having to design slides yourself, PowerPoint 4 offers 21 slide AutoLayouts that combine just about every possible combination of basic slide layouts (see fig. 1.11). AutoLayouts bring together five different basic slide elements in various combinations: charts, tables, titles, body text, and objects. Choosing a slide AutoLayout is as simple as a double-click with the mouse.

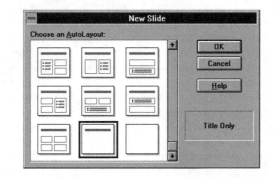

Fig. 1.11
PowerPoint's
AutoLayout
feature.

Any slide layout can, of course, be modified by the user to suit his or her own needs.

Tighter Application Integration with OLE 2.0

PowerPoint is not just a remarkably powerful application program—it's also part of an even greater product called Microsoft Office, which combines

Microsoft Word for Windows, Microsoft Excel, and PowerPoint into a closely integrated "super-app" that eases the process of creating powerful complex documents. Complex documents combine many types of data: charts, spreadsheets, databases, formatted word processing text and layouts, graphics and clip art, and even multimedia elements such as movie clips and sound files. Many office workers will never in their lives create a document with all these elements, yet the power is there to tap into at any time.

PowerPoint, along with all the new Microsoft Office products, supports a powerful new concept called *in-place editing*. It's a system in which the various programs in the Microsoft Office suite can be made to work in one program window, without the need to open up several programs and tediously swap back and forth between them. If you're working in PowerPoint and you need to use Word 6 to create a table and then paste the table onto a slide, all you need to do is click a button on the toolbar. The PowerPoint screen remains, but the PowerPoint toolbars and menus disappear and are replaced by those for Microsoft Word, as shown in figure 1.12.

Fig. 1.12
When you use OLE 2.0 to integrate Windows applications, Word menus and toolbars replace those of PowerPoint on the PowerPoint screen.

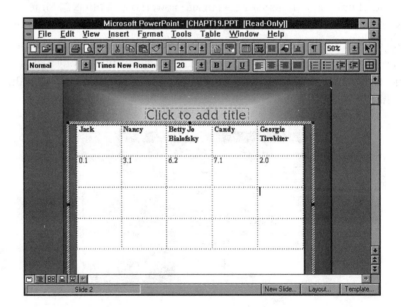

The feature that makes this possible is Microsoft's OLE 2.0—Object Linking and Embedding, version 2.0. It allows you to copy and paste virtually any type of data between any application program that supports OLE 2.0, and to bind the applications that create your data types into a seamless, potent, mutually supportive mega-application program. All the programs in the new version of Microsoft Office—PowerPoint 4, Word 6, and Excel 5—offer this powerful inter-application capability.

PowerPoint's use of objects, and its definition of an object, has been greatly expanded. Anything that's placed on a slide is now considered a PowerPoint object—even another presentation from PowerPoint or any other presentation program. Any data type that's supported as an object by Microsoft Windows can be embedded or linked into a PowerPoint slide show.

Enhanced and Integrated Charting Features

Perhaps one of PowerPoint's greatest improvements is in its charting capabilities. PowerPoint offers a new version of Microsoft Graph, the separate charting program that has traditionally been bundled with PowerPoint. The new version of Graph takes full advantage of OLE 2.0 to integrate itself much more closely to the main program, offering complete consistency between itself and the parent PowerPoint application. Thus, for the first time, PowerPoint's color palettes and color schemes are fully supported in Graph. In fact, most users won't even realize that Graph is a separate application program, because it works so closely with PowerPoint 4.

Dozens of New Chart Types

PowerPoint's new Graph application offers several new chart types, including a spectacular new 3-D surface chart (see fig. 1.13), which enables you to literally build topographical maps based on altitude numbers, as well as to add a new dimension to statistical analysis.

Fig. 1.13
A 3-D surface
chart.

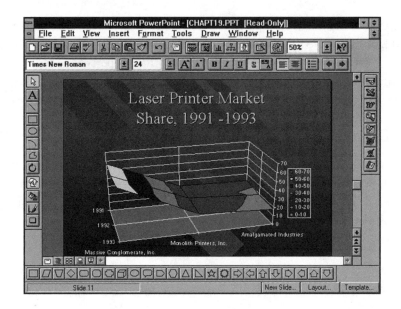

Radar, or "spider," charts are another new chart type that is well suited as a different style of comparative chart (see fig. 1.14).

Fig. 1.14
A typical radar
chart.

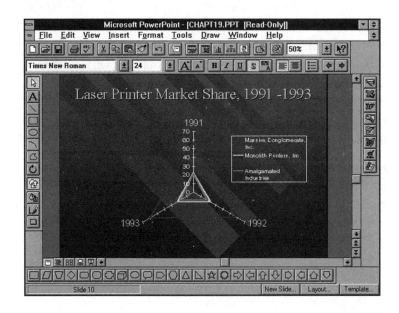

A new doughnut chart type is offered, creating a new variation on the pie charts that are so prevalent in corporate presentations. All the previous chart types are also supported, including bar, pie, column, area, and line charts in 2-D and 3-D types. All the chart types offered also have new variations included in their basic sets, and PowerPoint 4 offers a remarkably straightforward method for adding your special charts as new types. You can also easily adopt a preferred chart as your new default chart.

Direct Manipulation of Chart Labels, Legends, and Captions

For the first time, Graph allows you to drag chart elements with the mouse—including axis titles, chart legends, and chart captions that previously could only have set locations defined within the program. As a result, you have greater convenience and ease in manipulating various objects when you're editing a chart.

Organizational Charting

PowerPoint also offers a special easy-to-use organizational chart application that enables you to quickly draw flow charts of a company's or department's employees and their relationships to one another (see fig. 1.15).

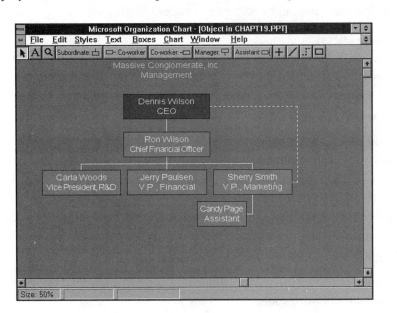

Fig. 1.15
PowerPoint's organizational chart program.

Improved Drawing Features

PowerPoint 4 offers expanded drawing features that put greater artistic power in your hands, without having to resort to a drawing program to create simple artwork. Many different types of polygons can be quickly drawn, including squares and rectangles, circles and ellipses, and 24 different hard-to-draw AutoShapes that allow a fast starburst, thought balloon, or other complex shape to be drawn quickly with a couple of mouse clicks. Other new tools include drop-down color palettes for lines, object fills, and shadows. PowerPoint 4 offers a special text rotation feature, and axis labels can now be rotated 90 degrees in the Microsoft Graph application.

Also notice that many drawing features in PowerPoint are replicated in Microsoft Graph. Any shape drawn in PowerPoint or Graph can be filled with colors, shading, and patterns in many different ways.

Freehand Drawing Tools

A major addition to PowerPoint's drawing capabilities is the Freehand tool. With it, you can draw a shape of any complexity without any restrictions on how the shape must look. A freehand shape can be edited by simply dragging a point to change the shape, without tedious redrawing. Freehand lines are also supported, and can be edited and changed in the same way.

Editable Curves

PowerPoint's Arc tool not only enables you to draw basic curves, but any arc can be edited after it's drawn by selecting it and choosing PowerPoint's new Edit Object command. By dragging any corner or side of a curve, its shape can be changed, shortened, or lengthened to suit the user's needs.

Expanded Clip Art Library

PowerPoint's Clip Art library has been expanded to over 1,400 pieces, all of which are drawn by the graphics professionals at Genigraphics Corporation. The clip art is organized into 26 separate categories. PowerPoint offers an improved ClipArt Gallery (see fig. 1.16) that organizes the categories of clip art into easy-to-view thumbnails, enabling the user to preview any piece of artwork before she decides to include it in the presentation.

Any piece of clip art can also be completely changed and edited using PowerPoint's drawing tools.

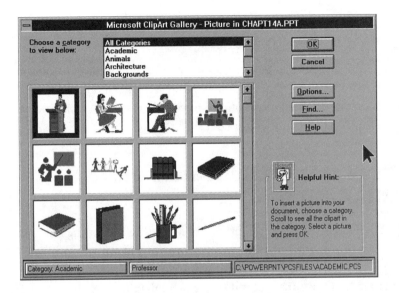

Fig. 1.16
PowerPoint's
ClipArt Gallery.

Support for 24-Bit True Color Pictures

For the first time, PowerPoint includes support for 24-bit "true-color" graphics in a presentation. Depending on the color depth supported by your Windows screen, PowerPoint now accepts hi-color and true-color pictures as easily as any other object type (see fig. 1.17).

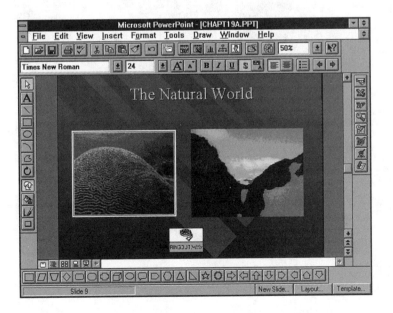

Fig. 1.17
Importing a
16-million color
bitmapped picture.

Incidentally, PowerPoint now directly imports 22 different graphics file formats, including direct support for CorelDRAW! files.

PowerPoint also offers intelligent color scheme modification: the capability to assign a single background color and title text and automatically have several sets of preferred colors offered to you, dramatically easing the process of creating custom color sets for your slide show.

Presentation Rehearsal and Annotation

PowerPoint 4 eases the crucial process of rehearsing and setting the timing of events of your presentation with its improved Slide Show capabilities. By simply watching a digital clock and pressing the mouse button during a presentation, all events that occur during a presentation can be triggered at specific times, so that running your presentation in front of your audience goes off like clockwork.

During your presentation, a member of the audience may ask a question. If this happens, you can use the Annotate tool on the presentation screen to help illustrate your point (see fig. 1.18).

Fig. 1.18
PowerPoint's presentation Annotate tool.

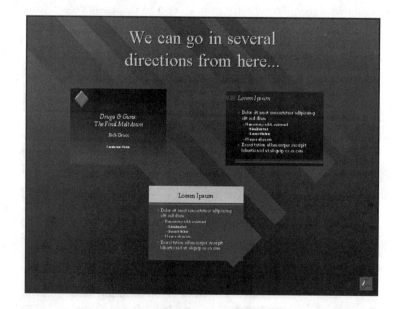

Clicking on the tool in the bottom right corner pauses the presentation and allows you to draw and handwrite with the mouse directly on the presentation screen.

Hidden Slides and Branching Between Presentations

You can easily hide individual slides or any number of them with PowerPoint 4's new Hide Slide command. PowerPoint 4 also takes advantage of object linking and embedding to allow an innovative method of branching between presentations. Figure 1.19 shows three different presentations that have been loaded as objects into a parent presentation.

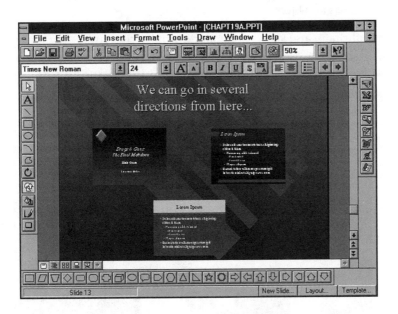

Fig. 1.19
Three presentations loaded as objects into another presentation.

Branching offers tremendous advantages to the user, because any number of presentations can be combined into a super-presentation offering numerous tangents and different tracks that can be requested by the audience at appropriate times during the show.

PowerPoint also offers the capability to build a Play List for running several presentations in sequence.

Integrated Table Creation and Use of Excel Spreadsheets

Along with PowerPoint 4's improved OLE support, tools are offered for automatic use of other Microsoft applications to create specific data types for use in your slide show. Particularly for those who already own Excel and Word, or the entire Microsoft Office application suite, it has never been easier to justify spending hard-earned dollars on application programs. Clicking on a toolbar button enables the PowerPoint user to take advantage of Excel's powerful spreadsheet capabilities and to easily insert them into a slide.

Another toolbar button enables owners of Word 6 for Windows to avail themselves of that program's sophisticated table creation capabilities and to place them as an object.

Microsoft Graph also allows the importing of Excel datasheets for direct use in generating new charts in PowerPoint. Excel charts can also be imported for use in PowerPoint slides. When doing so, the chart's datasheet information is also automatically imported, as shown in figure 1.20.

Fig. 1.20

An Excel chart and datasheet imported directly into Microsoft Graph. The chart is directly imported from Excel; the datasheet comes along for the ride.

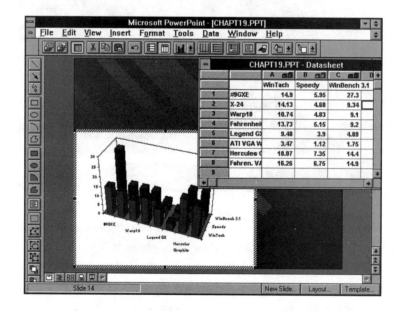

From Here...

From here, you start the task of learning PowerPoint. As noted earlier, the basics are covered in the first few chapters, dealing primarily with providing the large view of using PowerPoint 4 to quickly create a serviceable presentation. Each section beyond that digs into specific areas of the PowerPoint application in steadily increasing detail. Nonetheless, even the most advanced chapter in this book is very easily accessible to anyone. Here's what you'll see in the first few chapters:

- Chapter 2, "Getting Acquainted with PowerPoint 4," describes the basic mechanics of working with the program, including the numerous nuances of working with a mouse, the basics of working in the Windows environment, and the nuts and bolts of getting around in the program.

- Chapter 3, "Quick Start: Creating a First Presentation," takes you through a test drive of PowerPoint 4 by helping you create a first presentation.

- Chapters 4 and 5 delve more deeply into many areas of the PowerPoint 4 program that were introduced in earlier chapters. Chapter 4, "Setting Up Your New Presentation," discusses using PowerPoint's various Views and Masters for effective presentation creation. Chapter 5, "Using and Creating Templates," relates the process of using and creating PowerPoint templates.

Chapter 2

Getting Acquainted with PowerPoint 4

Windows applications offer you many advantages. A key advantage is that once you know how to use one major Windows application, you know how to activate and use most of the basic features of many other Windows software packages.

In this chapter, you take a look at the standard Windows features offered in PowerPoint 4 and also examine many of the program's most important user interface features, including new toolbars, ToolTips, PowerPoint's Status Bar, and many other elements of the PowerPoint 4 screen.

In this chapter, you learn the basic how-to's of PowerPoint 4:

- Using the mouse

- Choosing menu options

- Using PowerPoint's toolbars

- A quick overview of PowerPoint's screen elements and key features

> **Note**
>
> Windows offers many basic features common to all applications—clicking and dragging objects with the mouse, choosing menu options and program features by using the mouse or keyboard, changing the size of windows, minimizing and maximizing windows, and many more. If you aren't already familiar with these basic Windows operations, refer to your Windows 3.1, Windows for Workgroups, or Windows NT user's manual for complete explanations of basic Windows features before you move ahead with this chapter.

Using the Mouse

To perform many PowerPoint actions, you can use either a mouse or a keyboard command; however, because many sophisticated PowerPoint actions can be performed only with a mouse, a mouse is required to use PowerPoint. In many cases, keyboard commands may be more convenient to use and can offer handy shortcuts.

Choosing vs. Selecting

When you *choose* rather than *select* an item, you start a program action. To *choose* an item, you double-click it with the left mouse button. For instance, you start PowerPoint 4 by double-clicking its icon in Windows Program Manager.

To *select* an item in PowerPoint 4, you click that item only once with the left mouse button. For example, a single click on the PowerPoint 4 icon in Windows Program Manager selects that icon. *Selecting* is often referred to as *highlighting* because selected items appear highlighted on-screen. Once an item is selected, you can perform many different operations on it, like formatting text or changing an object's color, discussed in later chapters.

Normally, you can use the mouse to start a PowerPoint feature, especially when the feature is a dialog box option. Click the option once to select it, and then click OK to run the feature. Alternatively, you can double-click the option to run the feature. Using the mouse this way speeds up the process of using program features. Using PowerPoint's menus and dialog boxes is covered a little later in this chapter.

In many situations, you may need to *drag* the mouse. For example, you may need to move items from one place to another or to select a group of objects. To drag the mouse, you click and hold down the left mouse button and then move, or "drag," the mouse to a new position on-screen.

Selecting Multiple Objects and Scrolling

In many situations while using PowerPoint, dragging the mouse defines a box, which changes size as you move the mouse, and drawing a box around several objects in the program selects all those objects at once. You can also, in some situations, hold down the Shift key while you click the left mouse button on several successive objects; they will all be selected and remain highlighted when you select each successive object.

Using the mouse, you can move to any area visible on-screen by moving the pointer to that position and clicking. Sometimes, however, your PowerPoint slide or program window may not be entirely visible on-screen, particularly if you've been moving and resizing windows. To scroll through a slide or program window, use the *scroll bars,* which lie on the right side and bottom of each window. Each scroll bar contains two *scrolling arrows* and a *scroll box* that enable you to see hidden portions of the window.

I

The Changing Mouse Pointer

The mouse pointer can assume several different shapes while you use it. The *arrow pointer* is the most common shape. Use the arrow for pointing, choosing from menus, selecting objects, and so on. When the pointer changes to an *I-beam* (resembling an uppercase *I*), use it to highlight text or to tell PowerPoint that you want to enter new text. As you type, your position is indicated by a vertical bar called the *insertion point*.

For drawing shapes such as rectangles, ellipses, lines, and freeform polygons, and for some other functions in the program, the mouse pointer appears as a *crosshair*. When the program is completing a job and you have to wait, the pointer turns into an *hourglass*. When you are resizing windows, the pointer appears as a *two-headed arrow*. The two-headed arrow is diagonal when you are resizing horizontally and vertically at the same time. In some situations, a *four-headed arrow* allows you to move items with the keyboard rather than drag them with the mouse.

Using the Right Mouse Button

New Windows applications such as PowerPoint 4 offer expanded mouse functionality. In many situations in the program, you can now use the right mouse button to access program features. Clicking once with the *right* mouse button on many different kinds of items in the PowerPoint screen displays a special menu called the *shortcut menu* (see fig. 2.1). The features and commands on the shortcut menu depend on the type of item or object selected on-screen.

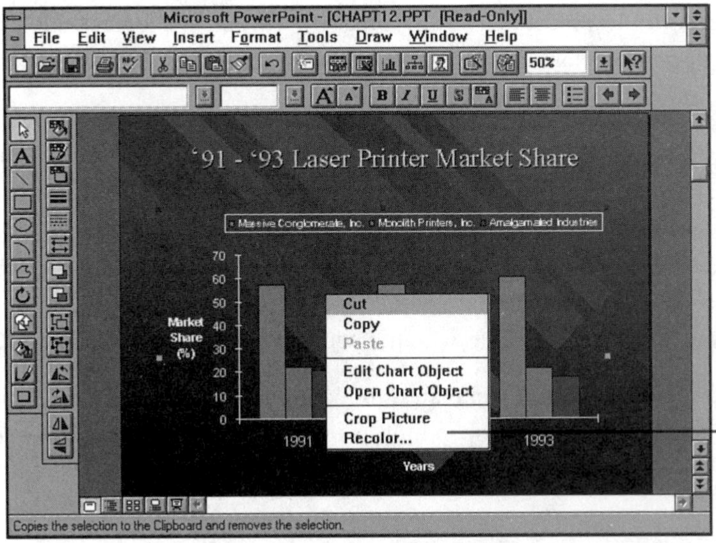

Fig. 2.1
The shortcut menu is activated with the right mouse button.

Shortcut menu

To display an object's shortcut menu, you do not have to select the object first by clicking the left mouse button. By right-clicking on a PowerPoint object or screen area, you automatically select it at the same time that the shortcut menu pops open. The shortcut menu offers a way to avoid moving the mouse to the top of the screen to choose menu options, allowing you to perform fast changes on objects.

Manipulating Windows

PowerPoint 4 conforms to all the Windows standards for minimizing, maximizing, moving, and resizing windows.

PowerPoint 4 also offers the ability to have multiple documents open at once within the program, called *Multiple Document Interface* (MDI). If you have a presentation file open in PowerPoint, you can open a second and a third file and then minimize and maximize their windows, just as you can in Windows.

The *Minimize button* and *Maximize button,* which respectively shrink and enlarge windows, are located at the top right corner of open windows. There are two pairs of Minimize and Maximize buttons: one pair for the program (PowerPoint) window, and one pair for each presentation window that's open in PowerPoint (see fig. 2.2). The buttons for the program window are located at the far right end of the PowerPoint title bar.

Maximizing a window causes it to fill all the available space on-screen. Minimizing a window reduces it to an icon at the bottom of the screen. If a program or presentation window is minimized, the task is still running and the file is still open and active.

The *Control menu button* is for general Windows application management tasks. This menu provides another way to minimize and maximize a window. Double-clicking the Control menu button in a presentation closes that file. Double-clicking the Control menu button in the program window enables you to exit the PowerPoint program. If you haven't saved the file you're working on, PowerPoint asks whether you want to do so before exiting.

You can use PowerPoint commands to manipulate windows in other ways— open and close a window, open multiple files, arrange windows, and so on. These procedures are described in later sections of this chapter.

PowerPoint Control menu   PowerPoint Minimize button

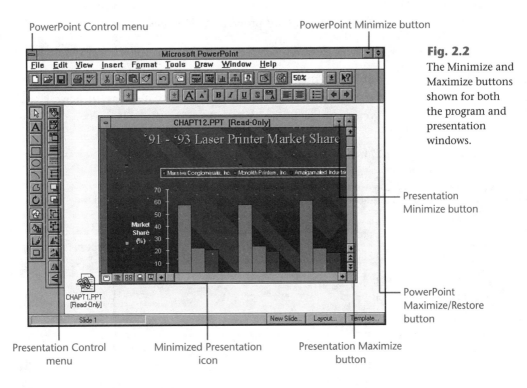

Fig. 2.2
The Minimize and
Maximize buttons
shown for both
the program and
presentation
windows.

Presentation
Minimize button

PowerPoint
Maximize/Restore
button

Presentation Control   Minimized Presentation   Presentation Maximize
menu   icon   button

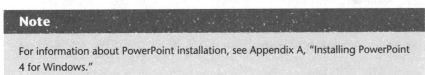

Starting PowerPoint

Since PowerPoint is a Windows application program, you can use it only
within Windows. (PowerPoint 4 requires Windows 3.1 and runs under Win-
dows NT and Windows for Workgroups.) When you install PowerPoint, the
Microsoft PowerPoint 4 group window is created in the Windows Program
Manager. The window contains six icons: Microsoft PowerPoint, PowerPoint
Setup, Media Player, PowerPoint Viewer, PowerPoint Readme Help, and
GraphicsLink. The Microsoft PowerPoint icon starts the program.

Note

For information about PowerPoint installation, see Appendix A, "Installing PowerPoint
4 for Windows."

PowerPoint 4 Basics

To start up the PowerPoint program, follow these steps:

1. At the DOS prompt, type **win** and press Enter to start Windows.

   Windows Program Manager appears. Your screen should resemble (but may not be identical to) figure 2.3, which displays the PowerPoint group window inside Program Manager. If the PowerPoint group window is not open, you see a minimized group icon labeled *Microsoft PowerPoint,* like the ones at the bottom of the figure.

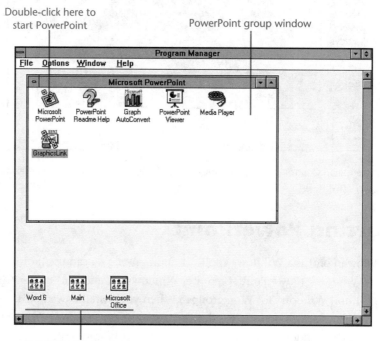

Fig. 2.3
The Windows Program Manager displaying the Microsoft PowerPoint group window.

2. If the Microsoft PowerPoint icon isn't visible, double-click on the Microsoft PowerPoint group icon to open its window.

3. In the Microsoft PowerPoint group window, double-click the Microsoft PowerPoint icon.

   The PowerPoint program starts. If you're starting the program for the first time, PowerPoint's Quick Preview screen appears. Figure 2.4 shows the basic PowerPoint opening screen.

Fig. 2.4
The PowerPoint 4
Quick Preview
opening screen.

Click here to start
the Quick Preview

Click here   Click here
to quit   to get help

The Quick Preview is a simple five-minute step-through that helps the new user understand some of PowerPoint 4's most important features.

4. You can run the Quick Preview by clicking the Click to **S**tart button. To leave the Quick Preview, click the **Q**uit button.

5. If you choose the Click to Start button in the Quick Preview screen, the next Preview screen appears. You can step forward and backward through each Preview screen by clicking the Next and Back buttons, respectively. They're shown in figure 2.5.

6. If you quit the Quick Preview, the next thing you see during your first PowerPoint 4 session is the New Presentation dialog box. This is where you select a Wizard to help you create a new presentation.

The New Presentation dialog box options are briefly listed below:

AutoContent Wizard	Quickly design the types of slides you want for your new presentation
Pick a Look Wizard	Quickly design the visual appearance for a new presentation
Template	Select a template for a presentation

Blank Presentation   Create a new, blank presentation

Current Presentation   Open a new presentation by using the
Format   template for a currently displayed
                                     presentation. This option is ghosted
                                     whenyou start the program for the
                                     first time.

Fig. 2.5
Stepping through
the PowerPoint 4
Quick Preview.

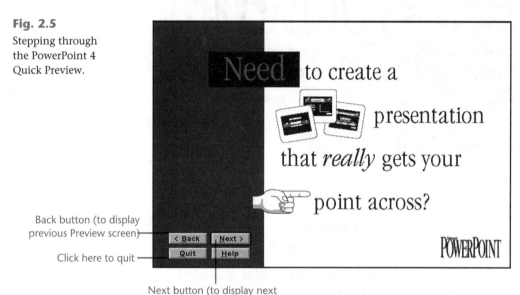

Back button (to display
previous Preview screen)

Click here to quit

Next button (to display next
Preview screen)

Fig. 2.6
The New Present-
ation screen.

Option buttons

The process of creating a presentation is described in the following sections of
this chapter.

The next dialog box to appear when you start the program for the first time is the Tip of the Day (see fig. 2.7), which offers a set of simple tips for easier use of the program.

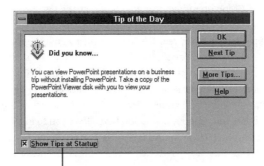

Fig. 2.7
The Tip
of the Day.

Show Tips on Startup check box

The Tip of the Day can be displayed whenever you start the program by clicking the Show Tips at Startup check box. (It's enabled as its default.) If you don't want to see it, click the check box again to remove the x. Click the OK button to quit the Tip of the Day dialog box and go to the basic PowerPoint screen.

When you quit the Tip of the Day, you see the PowerPoint screen displaying several toolbars and other default screen elements (see fig. 2.8).

Standard toolbar   Menu bar   PowerPoint title bar

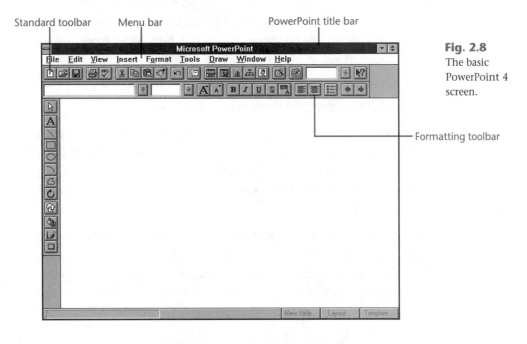

Fig. 2.8
The basic
PowerPoint 4
screen.

Formatting toolbar

Troubleshooting

When I try to start Microsoft Graph, the program doesn't start.

Unfortunately, if Graph doesn't appear after you click the Insert Graph button on the PowerPoint Standard toolbar or after you double-click the chart icon on a new Graph slide, you will probably have to reinstall PowerPoint. You may be able to get away with installing only the Graph application program. PowerPoint's Setup program allows you to create a custom installation. *It also allows you to install components of the program that were missed before.* Simply double-click on the PowerPoint Setup icon in your PowerPoint group under Windows Program Manager and follow the instructions it offers you. Choose the option that allows you to install missing components. (Start by clicking the **A**dd/Remove button during Setup.)

Getting Familiar with the PowerPoint Screen

In this section, you look over the PowerPoint screen and the elements that make it unique. PowerPoint is a Windows program, but it offers many tools and screen elements that necessitate some brief explanation.

The title bar at the top of the PowerPoint program window displays the title *Microsoft PowerPoint.* If a file is open in the program, the title bar also displays the name of that file, as figure 2.9 illustrates. The menu bar rests just below the title bar, displaying the menu choices **F**ile, **E**dit, **V**iew, **I**nsert, **F**ormat, **T**ools, **D**raw, **W**indow, and **H**elp.

If the active presentation file isn't maximized in PowerPoint, its own window title bar appears below the menu bar (see fig. 2.9).

PowerPoint's screen offers a number of features to help you get started. When you start up PowerPoint, a set of toolbars is displayed at the top of the screen just below the menu bar. Another toolbar sits on the left side of the PowerPoint window, called the *Drawing toolbar.* (Toolbars are discussed in more detail later in this chapter.)

At the bottom of the PowerPoint screen is the *status bar,* in which *Slide 1* appears at the left end. The message displayed in the status bar changes whenever you do something with the program or display another slide. If you ever "get lost" while using a program feature, the status bar always tells you where you currently are in PowerPoint.

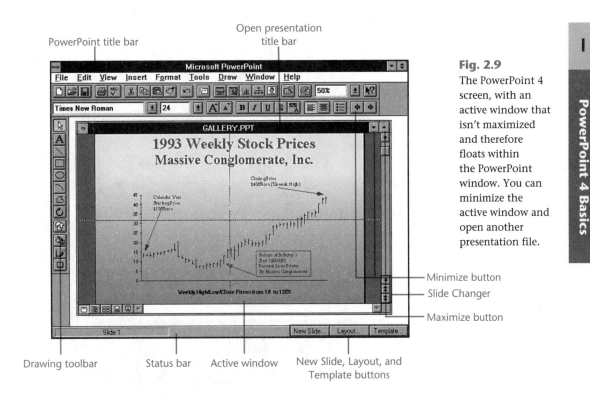

PowerPoint title bar

Open presentation
title bar

Fig. 2.9
The PowerPoint 4
screen, with an
active window that
isn't maximized
and therefore
floats within
the PowerPoint
window. You can
minimize the
active window and
open another
presentation file.

PowerPoint 4 Basics

Minimize button
Slide Changer
Maximize button

Drawing toolbar   Status bar   Active window   New Slide, Layout, and
Template buttons

At the right end of the status bar are three buttons—*New Slide, Layout,* and
Template—that perform the following tasks:

New Slide   Inserts a new slide into the presentation

Layout   Enables you to select a new slide layout

Template   Allows you to select a new template for your presentation

The far right side of the PowerPoint screen is occupied by the *Slide Changer*
and its scrolling buttons (which show as double Up and Down arrows). Clicking on the scrolling buttons moves you through each slide in your presentation. The Slide Changer also works like a regular Windows scroll bar, except
that as you drag up or down on the scroll bar, new slides appear.

Using the Wizards

The PowerPoint Wizards are tools meant to help both beginners and sea-
soned professionals design a presentation from scratch quickly, from the first
slide to the last, and to quickly design its look. The *AutoContent Wizard* steps

through four short processes to help you create all the slides in your new file and to assign a basic theme for the presentation (see fig. 2.10). The *Pick a Look Wizard* helps you select or design a look for your presentation (see fig. 2.11).

Fig. 2.10
The AutoContent Wizard (step 1).

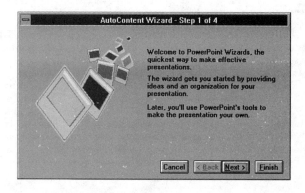

Fig. 2.11
The Pick a Look Wizard (step 1).

Using wizards is very simple: Choose from the options displayed in each step and then click the Next button to move to the next design step, click the Back button if you change your mind and want another option in a previous step, or click the Finish button if you want PowerPoint to make the most of the design decisions for you. Wizards, as simple as they are, can save many steps in the basic creation of a presentation. Much more about wizards is discussed in the next chapter.

Using the Tip of the Day

The *Tip of the Day* is a dialog box that automatically opens when you start the program (see fig. 2.12). It offers simple, useful information about program features and workarounds for complex tasks.

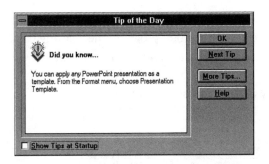

PowerPoint 4 Basics

Fig. 2.12
The Tip of the Day
dialog box.

Tips of the Day usually consist of keyboard or mouse shortcuts, tips
about basic program operation, or hints about major program functions.
PowerPoint has a database of tips you can flip through by clicking the **N**ext
Tip button. If you get tired of seeing the Tip of the Day every time you start
the program, click in the **S**how Tips at Startup check box to remove the X.

Understanding the Toolbars

Toolbars are one of the most important parts of the PowerPoint program.
Version 4 of PowerPoint adds an expanded and heavily customizable set of
toolbars. When you start up PowerPoint for the first time, three toolbars are
displayed: two at the top of the screen and one on the left side (see fig. 2.13).

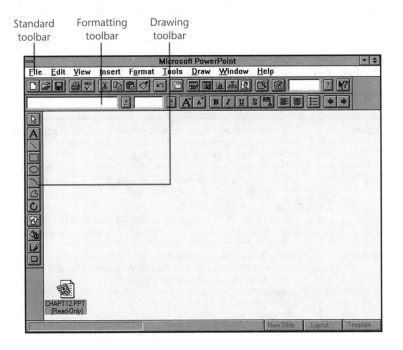

Fig. 2.13
The toolbars
displayed after
the first start up
of PowerPoint.

The three toolbars shown in figure 2.13 are offered for all phases of PowerPoint's operation: the main program, the charting facilities, the Equation Editor, the Slide Sorter, and other areas. The main PowerPoint screen itself has a default set of seven different toolbars, any or all of which you can display at any time (see fig. 2.14).

Fig. 2.14
The PowerPoint screen with the seven default toolbars displayed.

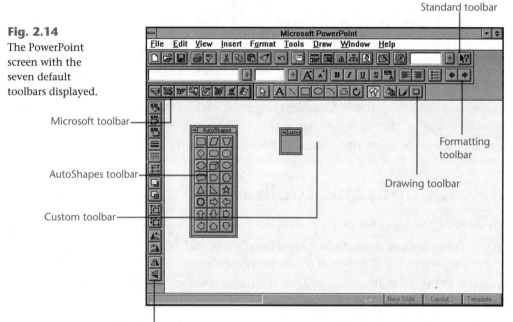

Standard toolbar

Microsoft toolbar

AutoShapes toolbar

Custom toolbar

Formatting toolbar

Drawing toolbar

Drawing+ toolbar

Here is a description of the toolbars shown in figure 2.14:

Toolbar	Description
Standard	Offers many standard PowerPoint program functions such as opening, saving, and printing files; handling files; and cutting, copying, and pasting
Formatting	Provides text formatting functions such as bold, italic, justification, and font selection
Custom	Allows you to add your own buttons (it is blank until you add buttons)
Drawing	Offers basic drawing functions such as drawing basic shapes, arcs, and curves; applying color fills; and grouping drawn objects

Toolbar	Description
Drawing+	Provides extra and advanced drawing functions, such as applying fill colors to objects and lines, applying line styles, adding arrowheads, grouping and ungrouping, and other functions
Microsoft	Activates other Microsoft applications such as Excel and FoxPro (particularly applicable to Microsoft Office owners)
AutoShapes	Provides automatic drawing of 24 polygon shapes, including stars, speech balloons, sunbursts, and other hard-to-draw objects

Using the Toolbars

The toolbars pictured in the preceding section offer fast access to most of the crucial features of the PowerPoint 4 program. You can use the toolbars only with a mouse or a similar pointing device. To use the toolbars, click the tool (button) that represents the command or program function you want to execute.

As you've noticed, not all the toolbars are displayed when you first start the program. You decide which toolbars you want to display and where they will appear on-screen. Toolbars are always accessible, regardless of where they are, because they always float above your presentation windows.

To display or remove toolbars from the PowerPoint screen, follow these steps:

1. From the **V**iew menu, choose **T**oolbars.

2. The Toolbars dialog box appears (see fig. 2.15).

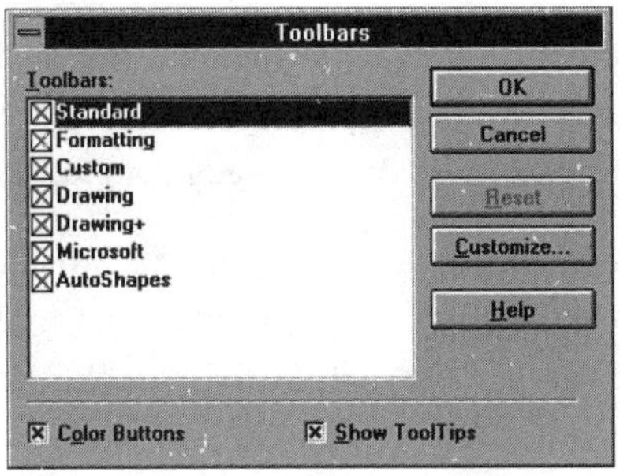

Fig. 2.15
Choosing the toolbars to be displayed on the PowerPoint screen.

3. Under the **T**oolbars list, the seven check box options are listed. Clicking on any empty check box places an x inside it, resulting in the display of the desired toolbar in the program. Clicking on any check box that has an x inside it removes the toolbar from the screen.

Tip
For quick help on any toolbar function, press Shift+F1 and click the mouse on any tool.

4. To show color buttons on the toolbars, click the Color Buttons check box. (It's enabled as the default, so you may not have to do this.) Another check box, **S**how ToolTips, also appears. The ToolTips feature is described a bit later.

5. To display the toolbars, choose OK or press Enter.

Another button is offered in the Toolbars dialog box: the **C**ustomize button. Clicking this starts up PowerPoint's toolbar customization feature. Describing this capability is beyond the scope of this chapter, but if you want to learn more, see chapter 22, "Customizing PowerPoint."

When you need help on using a particular tool, click the Question Mark tool on the Standard toolbar and then click the tool with which you need help. If the Question Mark tool isn't available, press Shift+F1 and then click on the tool you need help with. PowerPoint displays a Help window to show you how to use the tool in question. Choose the **F**ile E**x**it command or press Alt+F4 to close the Help window.

Using Floating Toolbars

Floating toolbars are toolbars you can detach from their normal places at the top or side of the PowerPoint screen so that they "float" above the presentation. Any toolbar in the PowerPoint program can be detached from the edges of the screen and placed on the screen as a floating toolbar (see fig. 2.16). To do so, simply click and hold the mouse button on any gray area of the toolbar that isn't occupied by a tool button (such as the top or bottom end of a toolbar) and drag it. The toolbar changes shape as you drag it around the screen. Drag the toolbar where you want it and release the mouse.

Tools in a floating toolbar work exactly the same way as they otherwise would, and you can drag them to any margin of the PowerPoint screen to relocate them there. You can also drag any edge of a toolbar to reshape it.

When you place toolbars in new locations on-screen or display new toolbars, PowerPoint automatically displays them in their new arrangements when you start the program again. PowerPoint's toolbars thus allow you to arrange the screen exactly as you see fit.

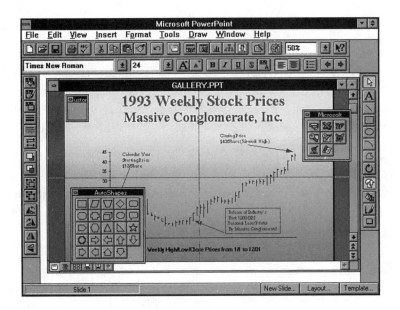

PowerPoint 4 Basics

Fig. 2.16
A PowerPoint
screen showing
several floating
toolbars. One
toolbar has also
been dragged to
the right edge of
the PowerPoint
screen.

Note

The PowerPoint screen can get a little crowded if you want to display all your
toolbars, particularly if you're running VGA mode. If your monitor and computer's
video card support it, you can run Windows at higher screen resolutions and thus
significantly relieve the crowding. If your system supports it, run Windows at
800x600 or 1024x768. You should then have plenty of room for your toolbars.
Consult your Windows documentation or the manual for your computer's video
card for more information if you're not sure how to do this.

Using ToolTips

ToolTips are a simple and unobtrusive form of "balloon help" that help you
quickly understand the functions of the tools on the various PowerPoint
toolbars. Given the propensity of new programs like PowerPoint 4 to succumb to "iconitis"—the practice of subjecting every possible program function to an icon or a tool button—you may find it hard to keep all the tools
straight. ToolTips are a remarkably easy and convenient way to navigate all
the button functions without getting lost or, even worse, doing something
in the program that you didn't intend to do.

If the ToolTips feature is enabled (as it is by default), a small yellow box with
text appears as you pass the mouse over any toolbar tool on the screen. If you

compare the ToolTip and the status bar at the bottom of the PowerPoint screen, you'll notice that their messages are the same.

To turn on the ToolTips feature, open the **V**iew menu and choose **T**oolbars. The Toolbars dialog box appears listing the toolbars available in the program (as noted, PowerPoint has a default list of seven toolbars, but you're not limited to those by any means). Click the **S**how ToolTips check box at the bottom of the dialog box to place an X in it.

Choose OK or press Enter to start up the ToolTips feature. The ToolTips function whether you're in PowerPoint, in the Graph screen, or in any of the program's views, such as Outline view or the Slide Sorter. (PowerPoint's various views and screens are discussed later in this chapter.)

Troubleshooting

I can't find the text formatting tools on PowerPoint's toolbar.

You probably need to display more toolbars on the screen—namely, the Formatting toolbar. To do so, from the **V**iew menu, choose **T**oolbars and the Toolbars dialog box appears. Click in the Formatting check box to place an X. Then, choose OK or press Enter. The text formatting tools appear on the PowerPoint screen.

Using PowerPoint's Menus

PowerPoint's menu bar is a complement to the toolbars and offers access to literally every function of the program. Earlier, you learned the basic menu names and where they are located on the PowerPoint screen; now you get into them in somewhat more detail. Bear in mind that this is an overview chapter and that all the options and functions mentioned here are discussed comprehensively in other chapters.

While the toolbars offer fast access to many of PowerPoint's basic features, the menu bar, with its many options, allows you to attend to every possible detail of program management in PowerPoint.

Choosing Menu Commands

Each PowerPoint menu, as in any other Windows application, opens when you click on its menu name in the menu bar. Clicking a menu name displays a *pull-down menu,* so-called because the menu is normally "pulled," or dragged, downward from the menu bar at the top of the screen.

Some menu options have a submenu that pops out slightly to the side of the originally selected menu. This menu is called a *cascading menu* (see fig. 2.17).

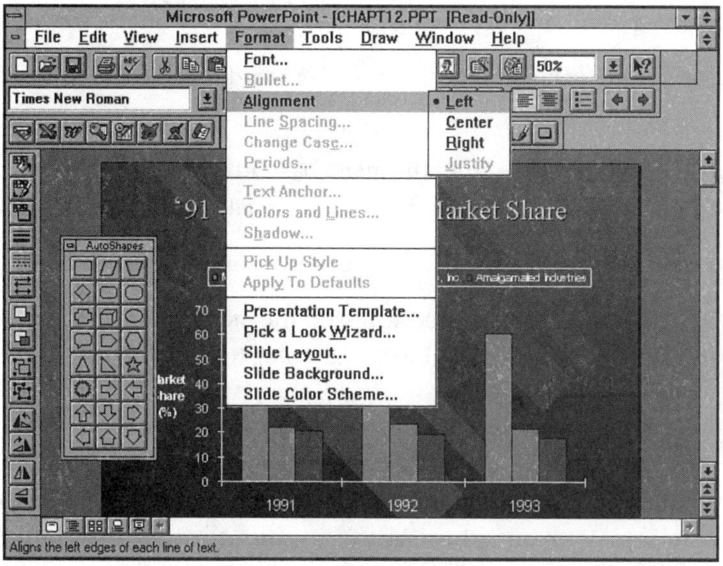

I

PowerPoint 4 Basics

Fig. 2.17
A cascading menu, subordinate to the original pull-down menu.

As you can see, further options are offered on cascading menus. Cascading menus are indicated on the pull-down menu by a small black arrow on the right edge of the menu.

This book discusses menu options in a very specific way. Whenever you have to choose a menu command, the language is as follows:

> From the F**o**rmat menu, choose **F**ont.

Notice that you choose rather than select menu options. Also notice that certain letters in the preceding example are boldfaced in both the menu name and the menu option. The boldfaced letters indicate keyboard mnemonics. *Mnemonics* are keyboard shortcuts that allow you to avoid having to reach for the mouse, move it across the screen, and pull down a menu just to execute a command.

Tip
Keyboard mnemonics are a good way to save time. Look for underlined letters on the PowerPoint menu options and dialog boxes, and use the Alt key to activate them.

On the PowerPoint screen, mnemonics are indicated by underlined letters. Dialog boxes and their options (discussed later) also have underlined mnemonics, and they work the same way. This book indicates mnemonics in boldface rather than underlining for greater visibility on the page.

To access a menu command by using the keyboard mnemonics, you need to follow three steps:

1. Pull down the menu from the menu bar with an Alt+*keystroke* command, such as Alt+F to pull down the **F**ile menu.

2. Press the appropriate key for the menu option you want to run.

3. If there is a dialog box associated with the menu command, use the Alt key in combination with the dialog box option.

The Alt+*keystroke* combination is the trick to using keyboard access to the menu bar. To access a keyboard mnemonic, simply hold down the Alt key and type the underlined letter (mnemonic) of the menu you want to access. The menu pops down onto the screen.

For example, to pull down the F**o**rmat menu with the keyboard, press the Alt+O key combination (uppercase or lowercase—it doesn't matter). You don't press the plus sign that you see in the Alt+O combination; it simply indicates that you hold down the Alt key while you press the O (or other) key.

Reviewing PowerPoint's Menus

Another advantage of using PowerPoint with other Windows applications (especially other Microsoft applications) is that its set of menus closely mirrors those of other applications. You almost always see the File and Edit menus in every Windows application program. Other Microsoft programs, such as Word 6.0 for Windows and Excel 5.0, offer other common menus—Insert, Window, and Help, for example. Of course, there are differences (*major* ones), but the basics are the same between most programs.

The basics of PowerPoint's menus are described in table 2.1. The table offers the big picture about which menu on the menu bar governs which program features.

PowerPoint 4 Basics

Table 2.1	The PowerPoint Main Menu Bar
Menu	**Description**
File	The File menu lists PowerPoint's file-handling options, such as Open (loading a file), Close, create a New file, Print, Saving files, Finding files, Exiting the program, and a list of previously opened files that allows you to open files again quickly.
Edit	The Edit menu offers access to many of PowerPoint's most important editing features, such as Cut and Paste, Paste Special (object linking and embedding functions), clearing and deletion, and Find and Replace.
View	The View menu offers access to the various views and screens within PowerPoint, including the default Slide view, the Slide Sorter, Outline view, and notes pages; you also can enable the current Slide Show presentation from this menu.
Insert	The Insert menu offers access to program features for inserting new entities of various types into a presentation—anything from inserting a new slide into a presentation to placing new objects of various descriptions onto a slide, such as pictures, clip art, charts, video clips, and others.
Format	The Format menu controls every possible feature for changing and defining the look and appearance of every aspect of your presentation, including font changes, presentation templates, color handling, bulleted text, text alignment, picking up formats from objects and applying them to other objects of the same type, and many others.
Tools	The Tools menu controls many of PowerPoint's most powerful add-on features, such as the Spelling checker, transition timing for special effects in a presentation, customizing toolbars, and using or disabling Smart Quotes and Smart Cut and Paste, among other program options.
Draw	The Draw menu controls most of PowerPoint's basic graphics handling features, such as grouping and ungrouping objects, layering drawn objects (Sending to Back and Sending to Front), setting precise sizes and scales of objects, and rotation and flipping of objects.
Window	The Window menu lets you arrange PowerPoint's presentation windows on the screen: Tiling, Cascading, and Fitting the current presentation window onto the screen.
Help	The Help menu offers many different kinds of help, including a comprehensive on-line Help system; a fast Help Index and Search capability; the Tip of the Day, Quick Preview, Technical Support information, and Cue Card features; and program version and system information.

Choosing Dialog Box Options

Tip

An ellipsis (...) after a menu option indicates that a dialog box appears when you select that option.

When you pull down any menu, you'll notice a pattern. Each menu has certain options that are followed by an ellipsis (...), such as New or Open on the File menu. Whenever you see an ellipsis after a pull-down menu option, selecting that option brings up a dialog box that displays other options for the program—options that directly relate to the menu's program function you've just chosen.

> **Note**
>
> If a menu option doesn't have the ellipsis, it simply means that when you select that menu command, it is performed immediately. For example, if you select the Date command from the Insert menu, the current date is inserted as a text object.

A pair of fairly typical dialog boxes are shown in figures 2.18 and 2.19; together they show the various dialog box elements you need to work with in PowerPoint.

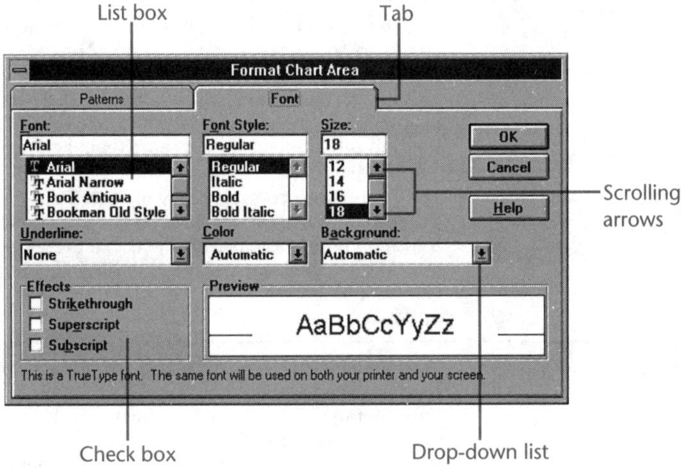

Fig. 2.18
A dialog box containing tabbed sections with list boxes, check boxes, and drop-down lists.

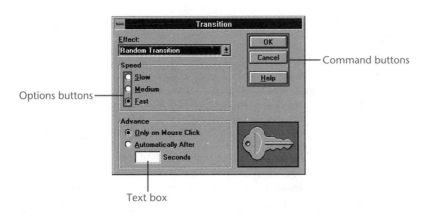

Fig. 2.19
A dialog box
containing a text
box, option
buttons, and
command buttons.

As you can see, dialog boxes contain a substantial number of items. The
nature of each item type and how you use it in the program is described in
the text that follows:

- *Tab.* Multiple sections of a dialog box. Only one group of options is
  displayed at a time, and each group contains related options.

  To open a tab in a dialog box, simply click on the tab at the top; the
  new group appears (not all dialog boxes have tabs).

- *Text Box.* A box in which you can type and edit text, dates, and
  numbers.

  To use a text box, click the mouse inside it. A blinking bar, or *insertion
  point,* appears. You can use the Del and Backspace keys in these boxes.
  To select a word in a text box, drag the mouse across the word(s) or
  double-click on it.

- *Option Button.* A button that gives you one choice from a group of
  options. Each option has a button. They also are sometimes called
  radio buttons, but not in this book.

  To choose an option button, click on it.

- *Check Box.* A square box that can be turned on or off. An X in the box
  means that the option is enabled.

  To select or deselect a check box, click the mouse inside it.

PowerPoint 4 Basics

- *List Box.* A list or drop-down list that scrolls to display available alternatives.

  To select and use a list box, either click on the list item if it's visible, or click on the scroll arrow to scroll down the list to view other items and then click on the desired list item.

- *Command Button.* A button that completes or cancels a command; some command buttons also provide access to additional options.

Now that you are familiar with PowerPoint's basic operation, it's time to turn to a description of some of PowerPoint's most important and basic features.

Understanding PowerPoint Slides

Presentations are composed of *slides,* the core of PowerPoint. All the objects you create for your 35mm slides, your overhead transparencies, or your on-screen shows are placed and arranged on slides.

As mentioned earlier in this chapter, you can scroll through slides by using the Slide Changer, which occupies the right edge of the PowerPoint screen when you're working with a presentation file. You can view slides full-screen or in zooms of up to 400 percent magnification. Slides can be cut, pasted, and rearranged at will, and can quickly have new color schemes and complete *templates* applied to them with a few mouse clicks.

Templates are files that define the appearance of a presentation. They're discussed a bit later in this chapter, and more extensively later in this book.

Each slide in a presentation has a specific purpose—to deliver a message, or an aspect of a message, efficiently and effectively. Slides have specific designs, depending on the type of slide you want. When you want to add a new slide to a presentation, you are given a selection of choices to pick from, as shown in the dialog box in figure 2.20.

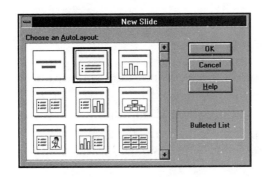

Fig. 2.20
Creating a new
slide from
predefined slide
types.

The next chapter describes how to pick and create new slides, along with the complete process of creating a basic presentation. For now, take a look at figure 2.20. Several small thumbnails are displayed in the dialog box, each of which represents a slide layout. Each layout has a specific purpose and is intended to have certain kinds of content. Some of the thumbnails depict a slide containing charts, while others depict a bulleted list of points, or an argument, to be made on the slide. Other slides may offer combinations of both. Thus, the message conveyed in each slide is framed in its context or design.

The AutoContent Wizard, briefly discussed earlier in this chapter (and in the next chapter), helps you govern how the content of your new presentation is structured. It determines the text contents of your slides, and thus can be an important step in creating slides.

Troubleshooting

I can't edit the title on a slide. The program doesn't allow me to select and edit the title on a slide.

You probably have edited and placed a title on the Slide Master, perhaps mistakenly thinking it was a slide. It isn't. It defines the common elements in the slides in your presentation. Anything that shows up in all your slides is part of the Slide Master and cannot be directly edited on a slide. To fix this problem, from the **V**iew menu, choose **M**asters, and then **S**lide Master. The Slide Master appears, very likely displaying the recalcitrant title that was resisting your efforts to edit it. Click once on the title and delete it by hitting the Del or delete key. It doesn't need to be there unless you want the same title to be on all your slides.

Go back to Slide view by choosing **S**lides from the **V**iew menu. Page down to the desired slide. You should now be able to edit the title to your heart's content.

Understanding PowerPoint Templates

Templates, another crucial aspect of creating a presentation and a powerful time-saving feature in PowerPoint 4, are the graphical "look" of your presentation. They are separate from the actual slide type or content, which can change from slide to slide. In general, a template is the same throughout all slides in a presentation. It determines the appearance of your slides.

Why a template? If you're a busy person and suddenly have to pull together a sales pitch for an important meeting in only one hour, you definitely don't want to fight through the process of creating your own graphic arts layout for your slide show. If you're not a professional artist or colorist, or if you're just pressed for time, PowerPoint's substantial array of predefined templates provide you with a sharp, attractive color background on which you can then build your pitch.

You can apply a template to an existing presentation, or you can create a new presentation by using the template of an existing one. If you have time, you also can create your own templates.

Choosing PowerPoint Template Files

PowerPoint offers a wide variety of templates for quick use. Each template was designed for a specific type of output and is therefore grouped into three template categories:

- Black-and-white overheads

- Color overheads

- On-screen (video screen) slide show presentations

These categories, which are simply directories of files on your disk drive, each contain 57 templates. The directories of each set of templates are normally as follows:

Templates	Directory
Black-and-White Overheads	C:\POWERPNT\TEMPLATES\BWOVRHD
Color Overheads	C:\POWERPNT\TEMPLATES\CLROVRHD
Slide Show Presentations	C:\POWERPNT\TEMPLATES\SLDSHOW

Each set of 57 templates is based on a certain theme, and the same theme is repeated across each template in each directory. For example, one of the templates in the SLDSHOW directory is titled BLUDIAGS.PPT. The template displays blue diagonal lines in the slide background. In the black-and-white overhead directory (BWOVRHD), the same template is named BLUDIAGB.PPT, and the color overhead template directory contains a file named BLUDIAGC.PPT.

To browse through the templates in any of the directories, follow these steps:

1. From the **F**ile menu, choose **N**ew.

   The New Presentation dialog box appears.

2. Click the **T**emplate option button.

3. Choose OK or press Enter.

   The Presentation Template dialog box appears.

4. In the **D**irectories list box, double-click the TEMPLATE directory.

5. Double-click a subdirectory, such as SLDSHOW.

   The **F**ile Name list displays the template files available in the directory. (Template files are named with the extension PPT, just as a normal presentation file is.)

6. Click on any of the files listed. The dialog box displays a thumbnail preview of the template you select (see fig. 2.21).

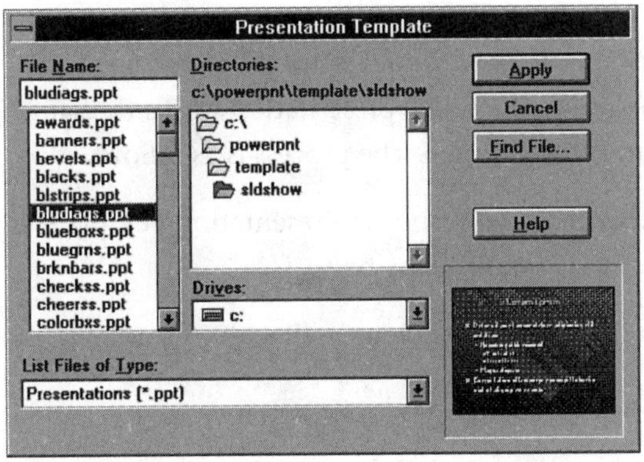

Fig. 2.21
Browsing templates in the Presentation Template dialog box.

7. To return to the presentation without applying a new template, click Cancel or press Esc.

Note

At times, the thumbnail preview of templates in the Presentation Template dialog box may be inadequate to really see their quality. To view the template on an actual slide, follow the steps in the next section. Be aware, however, that if you don't like the template you've selected, you can't use the Undo feature to change back to the template you previously used. You need to go back to the Format Presentation Template dialog box to reload the template. Fortunately, the thumbnail should be adequate for identifying the previously used template, even if you don't know its exact name.

When you create a new presentation, you also can use the Pick a Look Wizard to help you make a choice between templates.

There's one more element of templates that you need to know about: the *Slide Master*. Every template has one. Slide Masters are used to define common objects that may appear in all your slides, such as a company logo and company name, the time and date the presentation was created, a border, or a specially drawn graphic object.

At the same time, the Slide Master provides access to the basic elements in your template and can be used to change existing elements and to define new ones. In other words, the Slide Master is where you modify a template. Slide Masters are discussed in greater detail later in this chapter and elsewhere in this book.

Using and Applying PowerPoint Template Files

Applying a template to the active presentation works the same way as previewing it, until the last step. The process is as follows:

1. From the Format menu, choose **P**resentation Template to display the Presentation Template dialog box.

2. In the **D**irectories list box, double-click the TEMPLATE directory.

3. Double-click a subdirectory.

4. Click on any of the template files listed.

5. To apply the selected template to the current presentation, click on the **A**pply command button. The dialog box disappears and the presentation is reformatted for the new template.

Bear in mind that templates don't affect the content of the presentation or the actual slide layout; they change the artistic appearance of the slides' background.

Troubleshooting

I can't find my custom template file.

It's easy to misplace files after you save them. You may decide to save the file in a different directory. There are two easy ways to recover files that you've lost. First, check the file name listing on PowerPoint's File menu. At the bottom of the menu, a short list of the files you opened most recently is displayed. If the desired file isn't there and you can't find it in the normal PowerPoint Template directories, you can use the Find File feature, which is available when you want to open a file. Simply choose **O**pen from PowerPoint's **F**ile menu and click the **F**ind File button in the Open dialog box. PowerPoint's Search dialog box appears. In the Search For section of the Search dialog box, type the name of the file you want to search for in the **F**ile Name text box and choose the drive to search through in the **L**ocation text box. Click the Include Su**b**directories check box to make sure you search the entire drive for your desired file. Then choose OK or press Enter. A prompt screen pops up showing you the directories as the program searches through them. If you have more than one drive in your system, you may have to search through all of them to find your file.

If and when your file turns up and the program is finished searching, the Find File dialog box appears, displaying your file name and the directory in which it's located. If the file doesn't turn up, the Find File dialog box will read `No matching files found`. If that's the case, try another drive. Using this method, you should eventually find it (assuming it hasn't been accidentally deleted).

Understanding PowerPoint Masters

You've already been introduced to the Slide Master, which defines the contents of the template. Templates also have a few more, different masters that control various parts of a presentation. The *Outline Master,* the *Notes Master,* and the *Handout Master* all have a role to play in producing effective, powerful messages.

Introducing the Slide Master

Slide Masters control the background in a slide show and define the styles of the text and titles that appear in your presentation. They also can contain any objects you want in every slide of a presentation, such as a company logo or graphic objects.

To view the Slide Master, follow these steps:

1. Open the presentation whose master you want to view. You can also simply open a template.

2. From the **V**iew menu, click on the **M**aster menu option. A cascading menu appears. Choose **S**lide Master. Your current presentation's display is replaced by its Slide Master. An example of a Slide Master is shown in figure 2.22.

Fig. 2.22
The Slide Master.

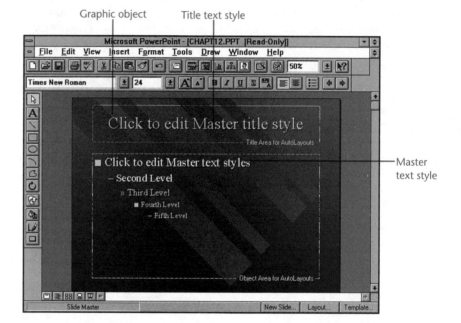

This figure shows the way slides for the current presentation will appear when you add text statements and bulleted lists to them. Notice also that the Slide Master provides several levels of bullets. You can apply new fonts or any other available text style to the titles and text, even though the statement Click to edit Master title style doesn't actually appear in any of your slides. That statement is just a placeholder to contain the styles for slide titles and their accompanying formatting information. The graphic object at the top left corner is a typical PowerPoint drawing object, which you can edit and change in any way that's normally available for objects drawn in PowerPoint.

Introducing the Outline Master

The Outline Master has one key purpose: to help format and structure the printed outline of your presentation. An illustration of a typical Outline Master is displayed in figure 2.23.

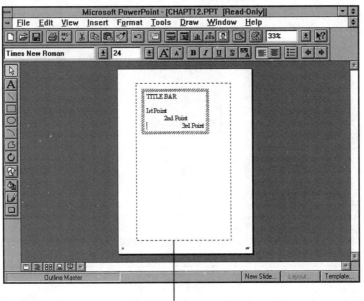

Fig. 2.23
The Outline Master.

Outline placeholder

A box drawn in dashed lines, called a *placeholder,* holds the contents of your outline and any other objects you add. Like the Slide Master, the Outline Master enables you to add a company logo, date and time information, and other items that you want displayed on every page of your outline.

To view the Outline Master, follow these steps:

1. Open the presentation you want to edit.

2. From the **V**iew menu, click on the **M**aster menu option. A cascading menu appears. Choose **O**utline Master. Your current presentation's display is replaced by its Outline Master.

Introducing the Notes Master

PowerPoint's Notes Master offers an extremely handy way for speakers to organize their notes for an upcoming presentation. Combining a miniaturized view of each slide in your presentation with the contents of each slide's text, the Notes Master enables the user to create notes pages to organize your talk without being forced to gaze at the screen whenever you need to make a point. A typical Notes Master is shown in figure 2.24.

Fig. 2.24
The Notes Master.

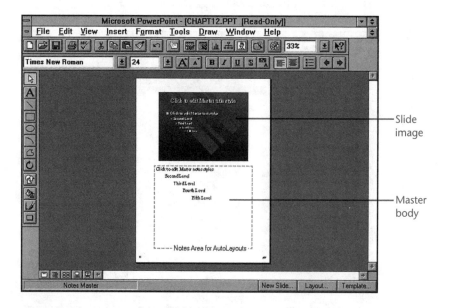

The Notes Master defines the appearance and organization of each notes page. You can add page numbers to the Notes Master that correspond to the slides in your presentation, and you can apply color schemes to the notes. In the *master body* (refer to fig. 2.24), you can format your notes just as you do normal text—with fonts, text styles, centering, and so on. You then print your notes pages with the slide images and each slide's notes.

To view the Notes Master, follow these steps:

1. Open the presentation you want to edit, or create a new presentation by using the Wizards or by opening a new template. (You must have an active presentation open to view any of its masters.)

2. From the **V**iew menu, click on the **M**aster menu option. A cascading menu appears. Choose **N**otes Master. Your current presentation's display is replaced by the notes master.

Introducing the Handout Master

The Handout Master is similar to the Outline Master but is used to format the handouts you want to pass out to your audience. The Handout Master displays several slide image placeholders, which are the overlapping boxes shown in figure 2.25.

Rulers

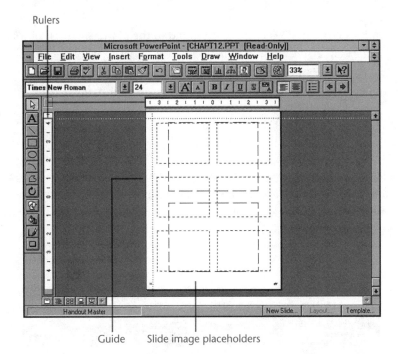

Fig. 2.25
The Handout Master.

Guide   Slide image placeholders

As with all the other masters, you can add background page numbers, dates and times, and graphic objects to your handout pages. You must place them outside the placeholders on the master handout page. The text you type in the Handout Master is included on every page of your handout.

Also shown are *guides* and *rulers,* which can help you design and measure items in every Master and View in PowerPoint. Guides are a tool that may be familiar if you've used desktop publishing programs; they can aid in object placement and layout for slides, handouts, and any other View and Master in PowerPoint.

To view the Handout Master, follow these steps:

1. Open the Presentation you want to edit. (A presentation must be open and active to view the Handout Master.)

2. From the **V**iew menu, click on the **M**aster menu option. The cascading menu appears. Choose Han**d**out Master. Your current presentation's display is replaced by its Handout Master.

Understanding PowerPoint Views

The various views in PowerPoint correspond to the Masters. PowerPoint has an *Outline view,* a *Slides view,* a *Notes Pages view,* and a special *Slide Sorter.* Several of these views interact with each other and offer some unique convenience features that put additional power in your hands.

Using the View Buttons

PowerPoint's views also include a Slide Changer feature, which allows you to preview your slide show with the click of a mouse. Several view buttons are displayed just above the status bar, in the bottom left corner of the screen (see fig. 2.26). Each button, when clicked, displays a different view in the program. In fact, the view buttons allow you to access not only the various views, but also the Masters.

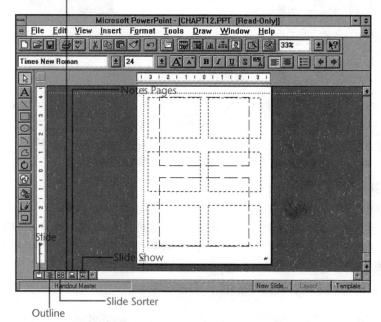

Fig. 2.26
The Slide Changer and the view buttons.

Clicking on the Outline button displays the entire outline for the presentation, showing all the actual text with the proper indents for each slide. The Slide Sorter is a drag-and-drop view that allows you to rearrange slides, somewhat like a deck of cards when you're playing Solitaire. The Notes Pages view allows you to look at and page down all the notes pages that correspond to each slide in your presentation.

In PowerPoint 3, you could use the view buttons to toggle between Masters and the views. (Yes, they are different, as you see later in this section.) In PowerPoint 4, to access the Masters for each type, you must hold down the Shift key while you click the button. The view buttons are described in table 2.2.

Table 2.2   The View Button Functions

Action	Displayed Result
Slide View	Individual slides view
Shift+Slide View	Slide Master
Notes	Notes Pages view
Shift+Notes	Notes Master
Outline	Outline view
Shift+Outline	Outline Master
Slide Sorter	Slide Sorter view
Shift+Slide Sorter	Handout Master
Slide Show	Run the slide show
Shift+Slide Show	Specifies slides to use in show, rehearses timing, and runs slide show

Note

Watch the status bar while you pass the mouse over each button. Then press the Shift key with the mouse over each button. The status bar tells you the function of each button. Also, if ToolTips is enabled, the ToolTips change as you move the mouse over each button, both when you are holding down Shift and when you aren't.

Viewing Slides

If you're creating presentations, you are spending most of your time in the Slide view. You can page through each individual slide by using the Slide Changer at the right side of the screen, as shown earlier in figure 2.26.

You can use the Slide Changer in several ways. For example, you can page up or down through each slide by clicking the scrolling arrows at the bottom of the Changer, or you can drag the scrolling icon up or down on the Slide Changer. When you do so, a small slide number pops up next to the Changer (see fig. 2.27). You also can page down the slides by clicking in the vacant area of the Slide Changer.

Fig. 2.27
The Slide Changer showing the slide number indicator.

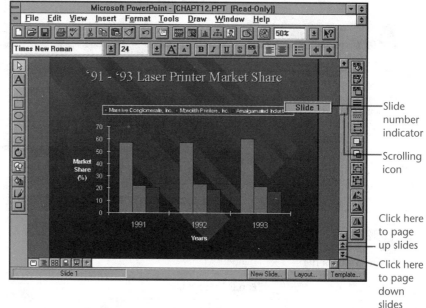

You will do most of your creative work for slides in Slide view. Many of the major creative features of PowerPoint, including chart creation, drawing, table creation, and text editing, are performed here.

Viewing the Slide Sorter

The Slide Sorter is a quick and dirty method for moving slides around and changing their order. As seen in figure 2.28, the Slide Sorter displays rough thumbnails of the slides in your presentation.

Slide Sorter toolbar

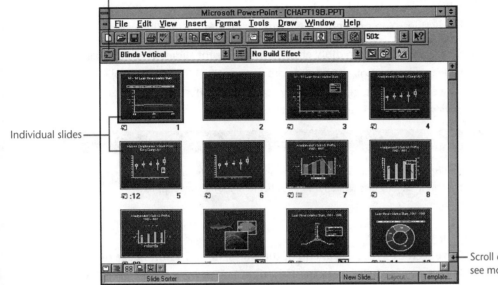

Individual slides

Fig. 2.28
The Slide Sorter
displaying
a typical
presentation.

Scroll down to
see more slides

To view the Slide Sorter, simply click the Slide Sorter button, just above the
status bar at the bottom left corner of the screen.

When you enter the Slide Sorter, PowerPoint displays the Slide Sorter toolbar,
which offers several key functions you can apply to any slide in your presentation. Two drop-down lists allow you to apply special effects—transitions
and builds—to any displayed slide. Although these subjects are discussed in
much greater depth later in this book, they do bear a brief introduction.

Transitions are special effects that set up different ways for slides to appear
and disappear during a slide show. You can apply 45 transitional effects to
any slide, including various fades, wipes, and explodes. You can set them to
appear randomly, or you can assign one specific effect to a slide. When you
apply any transition to a slide in the Sorter, a small icon appears at the bottom of the thumbnail for that slide, indicating that you have applied an
effect to it.

As opposed to transitions, which govern how an entire slide will appear,
builds are special effects you can apply to individual text elements in a slide.
PowerPoint offers 30 builds, including effects that make body text objects fly
onto the slide from the left, right, top, or bottom, or dissolve onto the slide.

In the Slide Sorter, you apply builds from another drop-down list. You cannot apply builds to graphic objects like charts or graphics drawn in PowerPoint, or to slide titles. You can apply them only to entries in the slides' body text.

The Slide Sorter is an incredibly effective manager for slides. You can drag any slide to any position in the slide order; the other slide changes places with the one you're dragging. You also can delete slides from the Slide Sorter view, as well as from the Slide view.

> **Note**
>
> Although the Standard toolbar is displayed in the Slide Sorter, some of its functions work only in other views. Watch the status bar for information about tool functions.

Viewing Notes Pages

As you've seen from the discussion of the Notes Master, a notes page displays a slide in the upper half of a page; the second half of the page displays any notes and narrative you enter for that slide in your presentation.

Notes pages are especially helpful when you have a lot of content to communicate for any particular slide; however, you cannot crowd a slide with too much information. In fact, a good design rule is to limit the amount of information you convey in any particular slide. In the notes pages, you can place information, statistics, and narrative that amplify and elaborate on a slide's contents.

To view the notes pages, simply click on the Notes Pages button at the bottom of the PowerPoint screen, just above the status bar. The Notes Pages view is displayed (see fig. 2.29).

To edit notes in Notes Pages view, click the mouse inside the notes area on the page. You enter, format, and edit notes like you do for any other text element in PowerPoint.

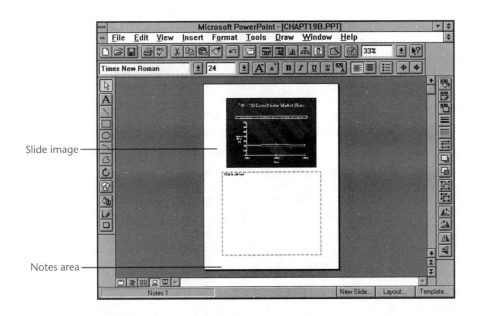

PowerPoint 4 Basics

Slide image

Notes area

Fig. 2.29
In Notes Pages view, the Notes area can be edited.

Viewing Outlines

Outline view provides powerful and handy interaction capabilities with other views in the program, notably the Slide view. In Outline view, you can add and delete slides, and you can edit, format, and alter their text content. You can rearrange slides, along with body text elements, at the click of a mouse, and indent text (called *promoting* and *demoting*). In fact, until you run the actual slide show, you hardly have to look at anything else besides Outline view, because many key program functions are available here (see fig. 2.30).

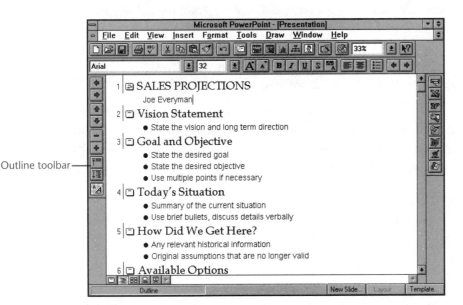

Outline toolbar

Fig. 2.30
The Outline view.

There's much more about Outline view that is discussed later in this book. In brief, Outline view is a good place to plan your presentation and to look at the logical progression of your arguments in the presentation.

Viewing the Slide Show

The Slide Show button allows you to preview or rehearse the results of your masterpiece. Simply click on the Slide Show button above the status bar to start the show at the currently selected or displayed slide. The PowerPoint screen disappears, replaced by a full-screen display of each slide.

Once you start the slide show, click the mouse or press the spacebar or Enter to display each successive slide. If you have build effects in each slide, PowerPoint displays those with each mouse click or keystroke.

To end the slide show at any time, press the Esc key.

The depth of features offered in Slide Show view is substantial and goes far deeper than the space available in this chapter. Slide timing and rehearsals, rearranging, using transitions, and many other features are discussed in detail later in this book.

Getting Help

PowerPoint 4 sports an expanded on-line Help system you can access by using the mouse to pull down the Help menu, by pressing Alt+H, or by pressing the F1 key (see fig. 2.31). The Help system provides concise descriptions and procedures on virtually every possible PowerPoint topic. Every feature and view is explained, and the Help system also offers suggestions regarding how to most effectively use the features in the program. Also, every dialog box in PowerPoint offers a Help button that provides access to a quick explanation of the features and options you're about to use.

The mouse pointer changes shape in certain areas of the Help system. Throughout Help's narrative are many terms that appear in green, underlined text. When you move the mouse over this text, the pointer changes shape to a hand with its index finger extended.

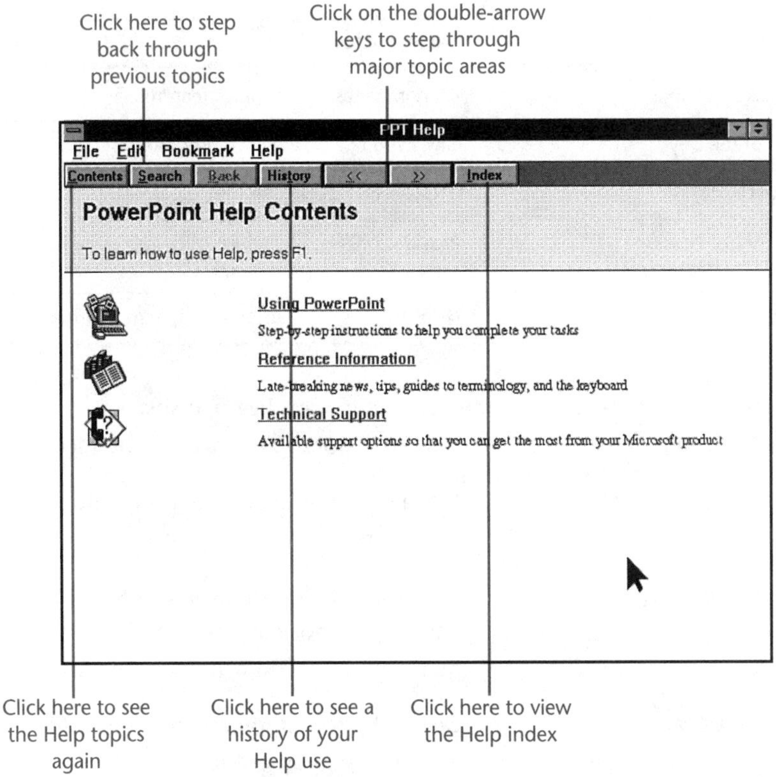

Click here to step
back through
previous topics

Click on the double-arrow
keys to step through
major topic areas

Fig. 2.31
The Help Contents
screen showing
the three key help
facilities.

Click here to see
the Help topics
again

Click here to see a
history of your
Help use

Click here to view
the Help index

Clicking the mouse on these terms allows you to "jump" to helpful text on that topic. This system is often called *hypertext,* because the subject matter changes dynamically whenever a new idea or point of question crosses your mind. (To move back to the previous topic, you can click the **B**ack button.)

Also, many terms in PowerPoint are in green with a dotted underline. Clicking on these terms displays a pop-up definition. Clicking outside the definition removes it.

Using Help Menu Options
The Help menu offers eight different options:

Option	Description
Contents	Shows a table of contents for the Help system. This option displays the main Help screen.
Search for Help On	Enables a search for specific terms and features in PowerPoint.
Index	Provides an alphabetical index of Help topics.

Option	Description
Quick Preview	Demonstrates PowerPoint's features.
Ti**p** of the Day	Gives you tips on effective program operation.
Cue Cards	Displays on-screen, step-by-step procedures.
Technical Support	Provides information about Microsoft technical support.
About Microsoft PowerPoint	Displays program version and system information.

Contents. The Contents option, where many users begin, displays the PowerPoint Help screen, which lists three major topic areas and their icons:

Using PowerPoint   Information on specific features and procedures

Reference Information   Vital information on program, keyboard, and mouse shortcuts; an overview of menu, toolbar, and window commands

Technical Support   Detailed information about Microsoft technical support services

Search for Help On. The help menu's Search for Help On command (see fig. 2.32) automatically brings up one of Help's most detailed and useful levels: the Search level.

PowerPoint Help's **S**earch feature allows you to specify any specific topic covered in the on-line Help system, from specific menu commands and common PowerPoint terms to procedures for doing things in the program. The hypertext capabilities allow for fast jumps between almost any conceivable topic (by clicking on text that is colored and underlined in green), and the **B**ack button allows you to return to any previous level of Help that you may have used. The double arrows (<< and >>) allow you to move rapidly through each successive level of Help, from the most general to the most specific.

The Search list covers almost every conceivable topic in the PowerPoint program. You must carry out two steps in the Search process: specifying a command or word pertaining to the subject you need information on, and then displaying the topic that contains that information.

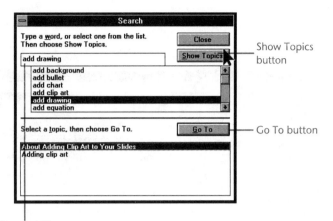

Fig. 2.32
Using the Search
for Help On
listings to obtain
detailed help
on specific
PowerPoint
features and
commands.

Show Topics
button

Go To button

Specify a word here

To find a specific topic, the easiest method is to type in a name of a feature or
a command. The Search list automatically adjusts to display the closest match
for the name or command you specify. You can also, of course, scroll down
the list to find your desired topic.

Click on the word in the list and then click on the Show Topics button. (You
can also double-click the word to do the same thing.) In the topics box occupying the bottom of the Search dialog, the main PowerPoint topic or topics
containing the information you need appear.

Click on the topic to select it. It is highlighted in blue. Then, click the Go To
button. A new Help screen comes up, displaying the topic information that,
very likely, contains the tips and information you're looking for. Information
displayed here can be lengthy, and you may need to scroll through the text
by using the PgDn key or the arrow keys or the scroll bar. The Back button,
double arrow buttons, and other tools enable you to move.

Index. PowerPoint's Help Index offers another powerful way to reference any
topic in the program in an even more direct way than with Search. Figure
2.33 shows the Help Index.

Click on any button
to bring up an
alphabetical section

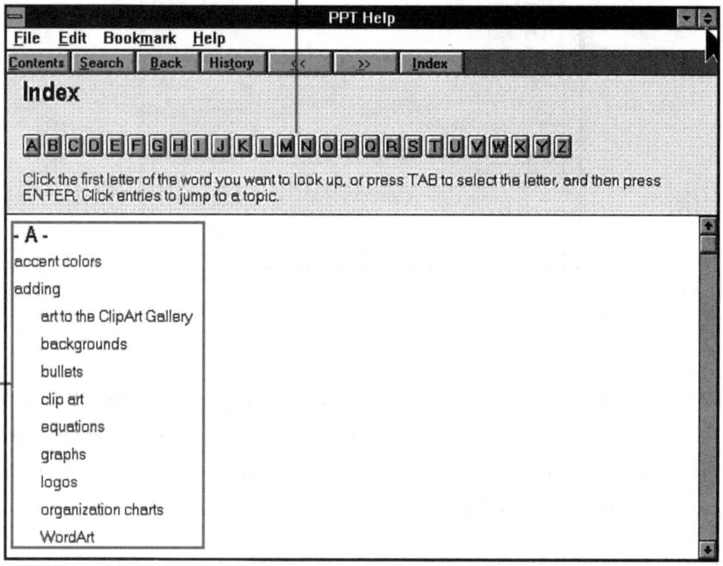

Fig. 2.33
Using the Search
for Help On
listings to obtain
detailed help on
specific
PowerPoint
features and
commands.

PPT Help

File   Edit   Bookmark   Help

Contents | Search | Back | History | << | >> | Index

Index

A B C D E F G H I J K L M N O P Q R S T U V W X Y Z

Click the first letter of the word you want to look up, or press TAB to select the letter, and then press
ENTER. Click entries to jump to a topic.

- A -

accent colors

adding

    art to the ClipArt Gallery

    backgrounds

    bullets

    clip art

    equations

    graphs

    logos

    organization charts

    WordArt

Click on any
displayed index
item and its Help
screen appears

PowerPoint 4's Help index offers a set of alphabetized push buttons that offer
a way to avoid scrolling through the very long index to find topics. Clicking
on a letter brings up the index section containing the alphabetized entries
under that letter.

To make effective use of the Help Index, follow these steps:

1. Click the button of the first letter of the topic you want to reference,
   from A to Z.

2. Scroll down the list until you locate your topic, and click on an index
   entry. The Help information for that entry appears.

Quick Preview. PowerPoint's Quick Preview, as described earlier in this chapter, offers a tour of some of PowerPoint's most important features. It shows
up the first time you run the program, but can also be accessed from the Help
menu at any time if desired.

Tip of the Day. As mentioned earlier in this chapter, the Tip of the Day can be displayed automatically whenever you start the program. You also can access it from the Help menu whenever you're curious about what it has to offer.

Cue Cards. Even for advanced presentation artists, the *Cue Cards* feature can prove extremely handy. For anyone else, they can be a godsend. Cue Cards are a fairly short list of crucial tasks that normally require tedious menu and point-and-click navigation to master (see fig. 2.34).

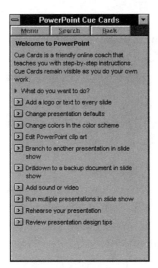

Fig. 2.34
Cue Cards offer a handy guide to traditionally difficult tasks.

To activate Cue Cards, follow these steps:

1. Create a new presentation or open up an existing one.

2. From the **H**elp menu, choose C**u**e Cards. The Cue Cards list appears.

3. Click on one of the arrow buttons (>) from the Cue Card list.

4. Follow the instructions as they appear.

5. If another step is available or implied in the instructions, click the Next button at the bottom of the Cue Card. Click the **M**enu button on top if you want to reference another Cue Card. Click the **B**ack button if you need to review an instruction.

> **Note**
>
> One very nice feature of Cue Cards is their interactivity with the main PowerPoint program. You can read each step and perform it in the program while keeping the Cue Card displayed on the screen.

Technical Support About Microsoft PowerPoint. Help's About Microsoft PowerPoint menu option simply displays a dialog box showing the version of the program and the user information entered when you first installed the program.

Click OK or press Enter to close the dialog box. If you click the System Info button, however, PowerPoint displays the System Information dialog box, where you can find out a great deal more about your system.

 The System Information dialog box offers a tremendous amount of information about the inner workings of your Windows machine. Each selection from the drop-down list displays a new collection of information about your system.

Exiting Help

To exit Help, double-click the Control menu button or press Alt+F4. The Help system is a separate program in a window you can minimize, maximize, or resize, as you can with any other Windows program. The Help system can still run even if PowerPoint is turned off.

From Here...

Only the most basic aspects of PowerPoint have been covered in this chapter. Chapters 1 and 2 gave you the guided tour of PowerPoint 4's new features and the basic functionality of the program. From here, you can go in many different directions.

■ Chapter 3, "Quick Start: Creating a First Presentation," lets you take a pretty thorough test drive of PowerPoint 4 by helping you create a first presentation.

- Chapters 4 and 5 delve more deeply into many areas of the PowerPoint 4 program that were first introduced in this chapter. Chapter 4 discusses using the Views and Masters for effective presentation creation, and chapter 5 relates the process of using and creating PowerPoint templates.

- Chapter 7 discusses the creation and use of speaker's notes, outlines, and handouts.

Chapter 3

Quick Start: Creating a First Presentation

In the last chapter, you were introduced to many of the tools you use to create presentations. Now, it's time to cut to the chase and actually make a presentation.

For many people, this chapter might be all they need for their day-to-day work, because all the basics are covered. This chapter can also be considered a jumping-off place, however, for when you plunge into PowerPoint 4, you may find that the features you explore here trigger many ideas and reveal many patterns to you that fire your desire to learn more.

Using Wizards

As you learned in chapter 2, when you start PowerPoint you are greeted by the Tip of the Day dialog box. Click the OK button to get it out of the way. The next thing that appears is the New Presentation dialog box (see fig. 3.1).

In this chapter, we use both Wizards in succession to start a presentation. First, we use the AutoContent Wizard to choose and set up the specific type of presentation (i.e. the type of message and argument to be conveyed), and then we use the Pick A Look Wizard to define the overall appearance of the presentation.

The following subjects are covered in detail in this chapter:

- The use of Wizards to create a fast presentation design

- Adding common background elements (such as a date or company name) to a template for a presentation

- Creating and working with slides in a presentation

- Adding text and other objects to a presentation

- Creating a chart

- Saving and printing a presentation

Fig. 3.1
The New Presentation dialog box, which normally appears on PowerPoint startup. The top two options in this dialog box are AutoContent Wizard and Pick a Look Wizard.

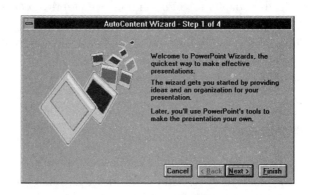

Developing an Outline with the AutoContent Wizard

To start creating the presentation, click the **A**utoContent Wizard option button in the New Presentation dialog box pictured in figure 3.1. The first dialog box of the AutoContent Wizard appears. It shares a few common elements with all the other ones in the Wizard's dialog box sequence. Its elements are displayed in figure 3.2.

Fig. 3.2
The AutoContent Wizard showing the first of four dialog boxes. Notice the buttons at the bottom right: Cancel, Back, Next, and Finish.

The four buttons displayed on the bottom of the dialog box are used to move through the Wizard. After you make your choice from the options offered by the Wizard at each step, click the **N**ext button to go to the next box. The **B**ack button (which is ghosted in the first dialog box) enables you to backtrack if you change your mind and want another option. Clicking Cancel ends the Wizard outright without implementing its previous choices. The **F**inish button cuts the Wizard short, but implements the presentation's design based on the information it already has.

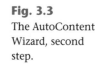

The title bar at the top of the dialog box shows the step of the Wizard that you are currently in. At each step, the title increments. The figure shows that you're in the first of four steps of the AutoContent Wizard.

The first AutoContent screen is simply an introduction. The following step-by-step example shows you, with illustrations, how to create a structured outline with a specific type of content for your first presentation:

1. With the first AutoContent screen displayed, click the **N**ext button. The second of the four AutoContent screens appears, as shown in figure 3.3.

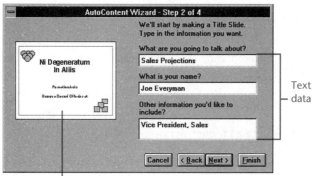

Fig. 3.3
The AutoContent Wizard, second step.

Title slide sample preview

Text boxes for data entry

Three text boxes are shown that may require typing on your part. Figure 3.3 shows three text boxes with sample entries:

What are you going to talk about?	*Sales Projections*
What is your name?	*Joe Everyman*
Other information you'd like to include?	*Vice President, Sales*

2. Click the mouse inside each text box to enter your own data.

3. Click the **N**ext button to go to the next step. The third AutoContent screen appears (see fig. 3.4).

Fig. 3.4
The AutoContent
Wizard, third step.

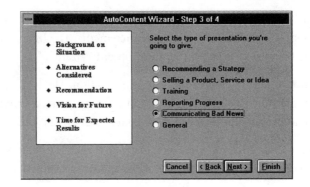

The third step of the AutoContent Wizard is the most complex (but still quite simple), and requires a choice among six different logical sketches for your presentation. Six option buttons are displayed, each of which displays a general content proposal:

■ Recommending a Strategy

■ Selling a Product, Service, or Idea

■ Training

■ Reporting Progress

■ Communicating Bad News

■ General

A preview box is shown to the left of the option buttons. The preview roughly shows the slide-by-slide outline of each sample content proposal. As seen in figure 3.4, the Communicating Bad News option button is selected, and five bulleted statements are shown—each roughly corresponding to a slide in the proposed presentation. Each of the six options shows a different preview.

4. Choose the content option you want by clicking its option button.

5. Click the Next button again to go to the next step.

You actually just finished the AutoContent Wizard (see fig. 3.5). The basic content and outline of your new presentation has been created. It's up to you, of course, to refine the titles and text of each slide to convey your specific message.

Fig. 3.5
The AutoContent
Wizard, final step.

PowerPoint 4 Basics

6. Click the **F**inish button to conclude the Wizard.

The PowerPoint screen reappears, this time displaying a very important part of the program: Outline view. Before proceeding further, take a moment to glance at the Outline view's contents (see fig. 3.6).

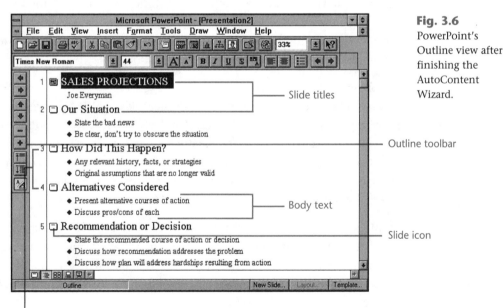

Slide
numbers

Fig. 3.6
PowerPoint's
Outline view after
finishing the
AutoContent
Wizard.

Note

After running each Wizard, PowerPoint displays its Cue Cards feature, which "coaches" you through important and complex procedures in the program. You do not run or use Cue Cards for the current examples. Click on the Cue Card title bar and press Alt+F4 to close the Cue Cards feature. Bear in mind that the Cue Cards are always available from the Help menu.

Each slide is numbered and is also marked with a small icon. The slide title is in large type, and body text outlines for each slide are shown in bullets and smaller indented text under each slide title. All the text under each title through each lower level of indented text represents the contents of each slide.

You're not married to this outline structure, however. Any statement in the outline can be made into a slide title in its own right. In many cases, bulleted statements in the outline may merit a slide of their own, because the level of detail and amount of information under consideration may be substantial. For now, though, the content is relatively unimportant; it's time to turn to the process of creating a look for your presentation.

Choosing a Look

You can start creating a presentation with the Pick a Look Wizard just as easily as you can by using the AutoContent Wizard. The two Wizards are not dependent on each other and address different aspects of creating a presentation. One is devoted to determining the content; the other, Pick a Look, is devoted to helping you pick a template or graphic design for your new presentation.

At this point, if you followed the previous example, all you have is an outline. You could design a template from scratch, but why? Unless you have a large time budget for creating the presentation (and is there ever such a thing in the business world?), you need to get the job done fast and effectively. It's time to use the Pick a Look Wizard.

You can use the Pick a Look Wizard by choosing it from the Wizard requester box or you can activate it from a tool button on the Powerpoint toolbar. That's the procedure you use in the following example.

1. Click the Pick a Look Wizard button on the PowerPoint toolbar.

2. The Pick a Look Wizard's first screen appears, as shown in figure 3.7.

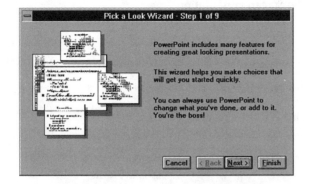

Fig. 3.7
The Pick a Look Wizard showing the first of nine dialog boxes. Notice the buttons at the bottom right: Cancel, Back, Next, and Finish.

This wizard works exactly the same way as the AutoContent Wizard—the function buttons at the bottom are the same, and you flip through each screen of the Wizard in the same way. Nonetheless, the Pick a Look Wizard has nine steps to go through, whereas the AutoContent has only four. When you use Pick a Look, you're not only defining how the slides are going to look—you are also setting up your notes pages, your handouts, and your Slide Master.

3. Click the **N**ext button to go to the next step.

4. The second of the Wizard's nine screens appears (see fig. 3.8).

This is the first one where a decision is made: What kind of output do you want? Four options are offered, all of which are supported by PowerPoint 4.

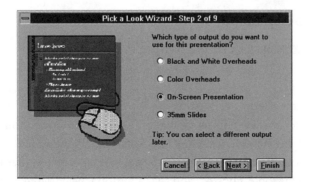

Fig. 3.8
The Pick a Look Wizard, second step.

■ Black and White Overheads

■ Color Overheads

■ On-Screen Presentation

■ 35mm Slides

5. For our example, click the On-Screen Presentation option button.

6. Click the **N**ext button.

The third Wizard screen appears (see fig. 3.9).

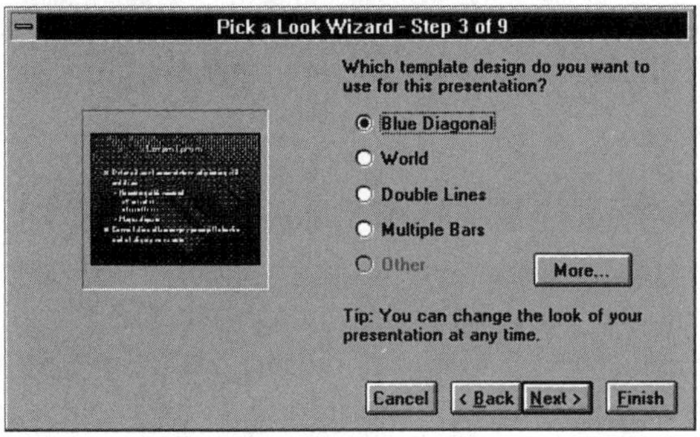

Fig. 3.9
The Pick a Look
Wizard, third step.
Notice that the
More button
enables you to
choose among all
the other tem-
plates offered in
PowerPoint.

7. The third Wizard screen is where you choose the actual appearance for
   your slide show. PowerPoint offers 57 different templates for immediate
   use as a visual design; the third Wizard screen offers you five concrete
   choices in option buttons, as follows:

   ■ Blue Diagonal

   ■ World

   ■ Double Lines

   ■ Multiple Bars

   ■ Other

   A preview window rests alongside the option buttons. Clicking any of
   the four template choices changes the preview to show a thumbnail
   view of the new choice. Therefore, you always have an idea of the template you select before you actually apply it. Notice also that the Other
   option button is ghosted, and that a button labeled More is located
   next to it.

8. Before you make your choice, click the More button on the Wizard screen. Since there are many more template choices, let's have a quick glance at them before we move on.

   Clicking the More button in the third Pick a Look Wizard screen brings up the Presentation Template dialog box (see fig. 3.10).

   The on-screen (or slide show) templates that are available are shown in the scroll-down list under the File **N**ame text box. Any of the displayed names can be clicked on to select them, and the list can be scrolled down to reveal more choices.

Tip
Remember, when an ellipsis (...) appears on a menu command or a command button, it means a dialog box is brought up when the command or button is selected.

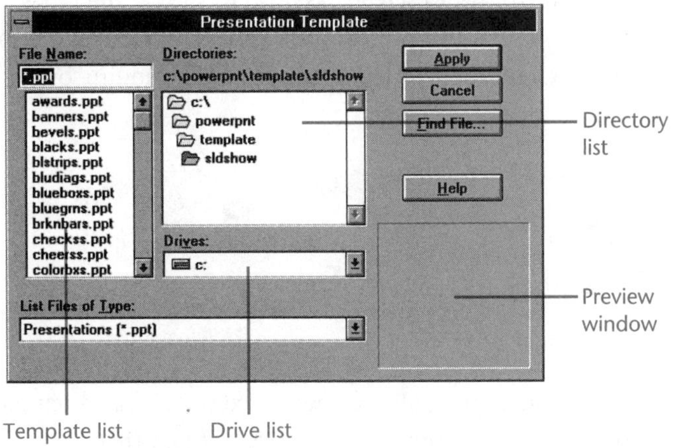

Fig. 3.10
The Presentation Template dialog box from which more templates can be selected.

   When you click on any template name in the File **N**ame list, the preview window in the bottom right corner of the dialog changes to show the appearance of the selected template. If one of the new templates appeals to you, you can select it and choose **A**pply or press Enter.

9. For now, choose the Cancel button or press the Escape key. (It doesn't matter what template you select—they all work the same. For now, to prevent confusion, we bypass using a new template.)

   The third Wizard screen reappears.

10. Click on the Blue Diagonal option button. The preview window on the left shows the template's appearance.

11. Choose the Next button. The fourth Wizard screen appears (see fig. 3.11).

Fig. 3.11

The Pick a Look Wizard, fourth step.

Option check boxes

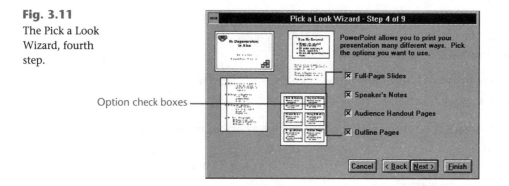

The fourth Wizard screen asks you to specify the types of printouts you want to use in this presentation. Four check boxes are shown, any or all of which can be selected or deselected depending on what your needs are.

■ Full-Page Slides

■ Speaker's Notes

■ Audience Handout Pages

■ Outline Pages

In the illustration, all the check boxes have xs, which means they're all selected. For the time being, we leave them that way, since specifying all the options offers a quick look at many of the other key hard-copy elements of a presentation. In particular, speaker's notes (also known as notes pages), audience handout pages, and outline pages can be valuable tools for use during a presentation, and they're relatively little trouble to create.

12. Choose the **N**ext button. The fifth Wizard screen appears, as shown in figure 3.12.

The fifth Wizard screen is titled Slide Options. This is where you specify some basic common background elements to be placed on your slide template: date, page number, name, company, or other text entry. All the check box options are selected and the company name text box is blank when the Wizard screen initially appears. The illustration above simply shows a sample company name.

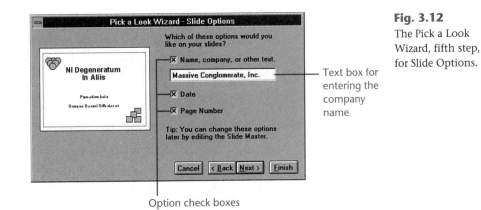

Fig. 3.12
The Pick a Look
Wizard, fifth step,
for Slide Options.

All the check box options and text entry that you specify here are
placed on the Slide Master (about which you learn more later on) and
can be changed later, as mentioned in a tip below the check boxes.

13. For our example, all the check boxes should be selected (have Xs in
    them). Click the **N**ext button to move to the next step. The sixth Wiz-
    ard screen, Notes Options, appears, as shown in figure 3.13.

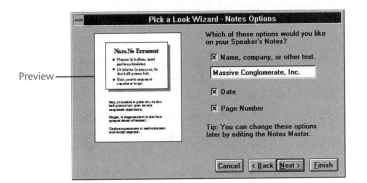

Fig. 3.13
The Pick a Look
Wizard, sixth step,
for Notes Options.

The Notes Options screen displays the same options and check boxes
as those on the previous Slide Options screen. The company name or
other information you entered in the previous text box is also displayed, as shown in figure 3.13. The figure above shows that all the
check boxes are selected, and for the example they should be left that
way.

The preview shows a typical notes page. The top half of the preview
shows a slide (though it only bears a very rough resemblance to one).
Each notes page, as a default, uses the top half of the page for a picture

of the slide and the bottom half of the notes page is used for the actual speaker's notes. (Chapter 7, "Creating Speaker's Notes, Outlines, and Handouts," describes speaker's notes, handouts, and outlines in greater detail.)

14. Type the company name (or other information) in the text box if it isn't correct. If the check boxes aren't all selected, click on them to select them.

15. Click the **N**ext button to proceed to the next step. The wizard's Handout Options screen appears (see fig. 3.14).

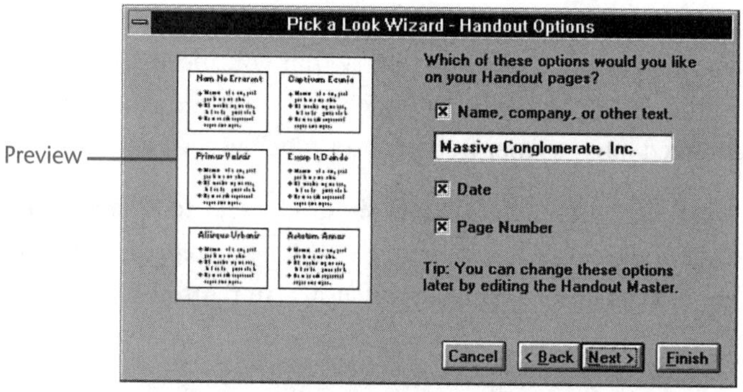

Fig. 3.14
The Pick a Look Wizard, seventh step, for Handout Options.

As you see in the previous two Wizard screens, the same check box options are offered for attaching the page number, company name or other information, and date, this time to the audience handout sheets. It's often a good idea to provide your audience with hard copy, especially if you have a large number of people witnessing your show. Handouts in PowerPoint are generally split into multiple sections, each of which contains a small representation of each slide. The dashed lines shown on the handout template indicate several layout choices: two, three, or six slides per page on the handout. (This is specified when you print the presentation.) Audience handouts can be structured to have space for taking notes (though not in this quick example).

For the current example, all the check box options in the Handout Options screen should be enabled, as they appear in figure 3.14. Click in any vacant check boxes to enable them.

You're almost done with the Pick a Look Wizard, but a couple of short steps remain.

16. Click **N**ext to move to the next step.

The Outline Options screen appears, as shown in figure 3.15.

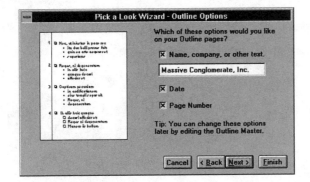

PowerPoint 4 Basics

Fig. 3.15
The Pick a Look Wizard, eighth step, for Outline Options.

The options for the presentation outline, around which the entire presentation is automatically organized, are the same as for the three previous steps. The options offered are the page number, name, company or other text, and date; the check boxes for the current example should all be selected. Click in any vacant check boxes to enable them.

The outline is one of the most important aspects of PowerPoint because it represents the organization of the entire presentation in text form. Every slide can be edited and its text contents changed in this view. Points and arguments made in each slide can be promoted or demoted in the outline, and slides can be rearranged in the outline as well. Even if you prefer working in Slide view, it's a good idea to refer to the outline on a regular basis because it provides a larger view of the presentation, making it easier to see flaws in the argument and to see its logical flow. As with the other elements in your first presentation, the Outline Master can be used to edit the options at any time.

17. Click **N**ext to go to the last step.

18. Click the **F**inish button to finish creating the presentation template. The program accesses the hard disk for a moment and returns to the Outline view.

19. From the **V**iew menu, choose **S**lides.

A Slide view of the first slide in your presentation appears. If, as in the example, you selected the Blue Diagonal template background, the display will resemble figure 3.16.

Fig. 3.16
The finished presentation template showing the first slide.

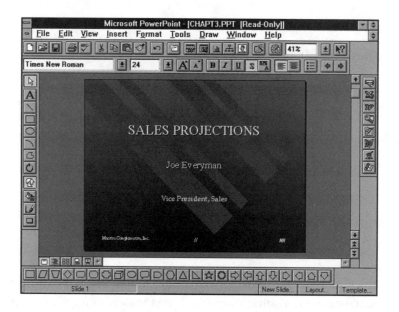

Glancing at PowerPoint's Templates

Now that you have created the basis for your first presentation, it may be useful to turn back briefly to sum up the components of templates offered in PowerPoint 4 and how they affect your work in the program.

As mentioned earlier, 57 pre-designed templates are offered as part of the PowerPoint package. Each template is offered in three types: On-screen Presentation (one of which you just created), Black and White Overhead, and Color Overhead. Each template has certain common elements, contained on Master pages, that are used in every presentation:

■ *Slide Master.* The Slide Master sets up the design of every slide in the presentation. Text and objects that you place on the Slide Master appear on all the slides in your presentation. For more information, see the section "Understanding the Slide Master" in chapter 4.

■ *Outline Master.* The Outline Master organizes each outline page of the presentation. See chapter 7 for more information on outlines.

■ *Notes Master.* Speaker's notes pages for a slide provide a reduced image of the slide at the top of the page and your edited notes about the slide and its contents at the bottom of the page. Slide images are resizable in the Notes Master, thus notes can be as detailed as necessary. The Notes Master contains the elements that appear on every notes page. Chapter 7 discusses notes pages in more detail.

■ *Handout Master.* Handouts can be produced for distribution to the audience. The Handout Master defines the format and appearance of handout pages and the elements that appear on each handout page, including a company name, date, or logo. When handouts are printed and given to the audience, they can be laid out with two slides per page, three slides per page, or six slides per page. Chapter 7 also talks about handouts in more depth.

When you choose the Pick a Look Wizard, each of the four masters is automatically set up. If you don't want to set up all these masters immediately, you can choose a **T**emplate from the New Presentation dialog box. You can also apply a new template to the current presentation or even create a new presentation with a totally blank template— a blank canvas upon which every element of the design is decided by you.

Now that the basic framework is in place by using the Wizards, the next part of this chapter deals with the process of adding the actual content—charts and text.

Working with Slides

Whether you use a Wizard or template to set up your presentation, or you start with a blank presentation, many new elements need to be added. You might want to add a new slide to the presentation. (Your presentation outline is automatically expanded as you add new slides to a presentation.) The text for each slide may need to be edited to suit your specific subject matter and formatted to suit your aesthetic taste. You might want to add a logo or other custom chart or element to your slides and draw artwork into a single slide. You may also need to add charts to your slide show to add impact to statistical comparisons.

Back in figure 3.16, the first slide in your new presentation was displayed in Slide view. The Slide view is not a static display; objects can be edited and added at will while providing immediate visual feedback on the results. If something doesn't look right, you know it immediately. Take another look at the first slide, shown in figure 3.17.

The lines of text in the first slide are, quite simply, objects. The slide title and the name and job description (the body text) are all flexible, editable units that can be changed, reformatted, and moved around.

Fig. 3.17
The first slide
introducing the
presentation topic.

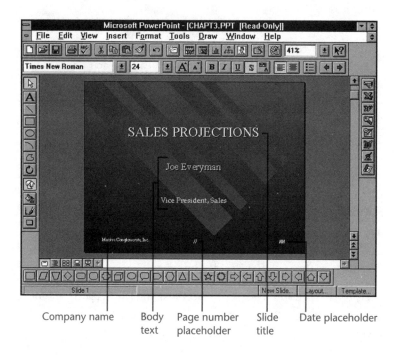

Company name   Body   Page number   Slide   Date placeholder
                text   placeholder   title

Tip
In Slide view, the
date and page
numbers are
shown in hash
marks. They dis-
play properly
during the slide
show.

At the bottom of the slide are the elements that were previously placed in the Slide Master when you used the Pick a Look Wizard. They include the company name, a page number, and a date. The page number and date are shown in hash marks in Slide view. The proper values appear normally, however, when you run your slide show. The hash marks are placeholders for the Master values.

Eight slides are placed in the presentation as you've created it. Nonetheless, say you discover that you need another slide—this one to announce on the most essential level that the company is facing some rough times. The new slide is inserted between the current first and second slides in your presentation, Sales Projections and Where We Are Today, and is titled A Time of Change. Unlike running a company, it's a simple matter to accomplish this task.

Adding a New Slide
AutoLayouts are predefined slide layouts that are based on the typical objects and data types that are laid onto slides during the course of creating a presentation. The New Slide dialog box provides a scrollable list of AutoLayout thumbnails that, when you look them over, pretty much cover every possible combination of charts, bulleted lists, clip art, and slide titles that you could think of. As you can see from figure 3.18, some AutoLayouts offer simpler

slide types than others. Some combine a title with only a chart or bulleted list of argument points, while others offer two columns below the title, combining a chart with a bulleted list.

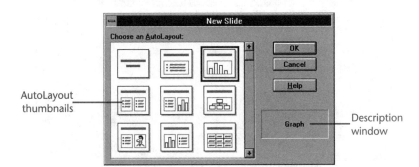

AutoLayout thumbnails

Description window

PowerPoint 4 Basics

Fig. 3.18
Adding a new slide with the Insert New Slide command. Select the top right thumbnail for our example.

Whenever you see a slide layout with chart or clip art elements or any object type that is offered in an AutoLayout, bear in mind that they *are* simply objects. They don't contain any data that directly relates to your subject matter; they are items that you edit to construct and illustrate your own logical procession of ideas. The AutoLayout thumbnails are displayed in rows of three.

A description window on the right side of the New Slide dialog box displays the type of layout that's selected. Keep an eye on this for the next step.

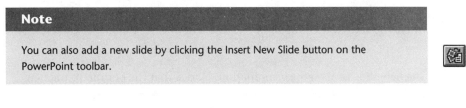

Note

You can also add a new slide by clicking the Insert New Slide button on the PowerPoint toolbar.

To add a new slide to your sample presentation, perform the following steps:

1. Display the first slide in your presentation.

2. From the **I**nsert menu, choose New **S**lide; or press Ctrl+M.

   The New Slide dialog box appears.

3. The top row of the **A**utoLayout thumbnail list shows the first three slide layouts. Click on the thumbnail on the top right, as shown in figure 3.18. The description window reads Graph.

4. Choose OK or press Enter.

A new slide is inserted into your presentation. Its appearance should resemble figure 3.19.

Fig. 3.19
The new slide with
a chart object.

Title to be edited ——————

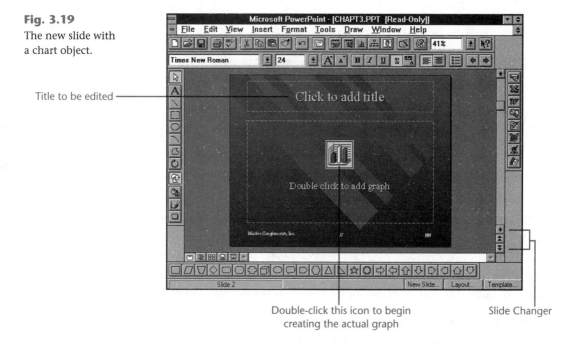

Double-click this icon to begin
creating the actual graph

Slide Changer

The new slide is inserted after the first slide, which was the one you displayed when you started the process of creating a new slide. Whenever you create a new slide, it is inserted *after the currently displayed* slide.

The new slide bears some examination. Notice that the bottom of the new slide contains the Massive Conglomerate company name, along with the placeholders for the date and the page number. Two other elements are present: a slide title, which is nothing unusual since all your other slides have them also; and a new item called a *chart object*. The chart itself hasn't been created yet; as with all the other elements in your presentation, you need to edit it for content to round your presentation into shape. Even now, only the framework for your presentation has been created.

Moving from One Slide to Another

Now that you have created a new slide, how do you get back to the first one? Navigating a presentation can be a bit confusing for those just starting out. There are several straightforward methods for doing so, however.

First of all, you can use the PgUp and PgDn keys. Pressing PgUp displays the *previous* slide. Pressing PgDn displays the *next* slide in the presentation sequence.

You can also use the Slide Changer, as pointed out in figure 3.19. Clicking the doubled up arrow or doubled down arrow icons moves you up or down through the slide sequence in the same way as using the PgUp or PgDn keys.

The Slide Changer can also be used in another way. Dragging the scroll icon in the Slide Changer moves you up or down the slide sequence. As a bonus, the Changer also displays a slide number indicator as you drag the mouse.

Working with Text

Working with text in an actual slide is a simple process. Nonetheless, many powerful features are available to the user. With both title text and body text, you can change fonts, select new font styles and effects (any text font that is available under Windows can be used in your slides), change the font size, and much more.

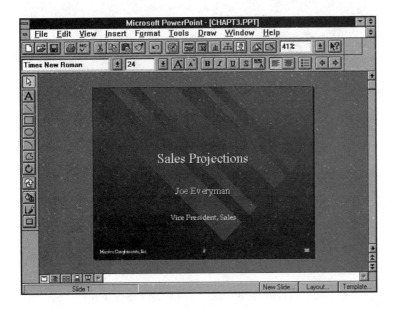

Fig. 3.20
Your new presentation displaying the introductory slide.

Adding and Editing Text

In the next exercise, you expand on your knowledge of working with text to actually perform some basic text editing. Figure 3.20 shows the first slide in your new presentation, which is your starting point for the steps below.

1. With your presentation displayed in Slide view and showing the introductory title slide Sales Projections, use the Slide Changer to page down to the next slide.

   The new chart slide that you created earlier in this chapter should appear, as shown in figure 3.21.

Fig. 3.21
Preparing to edit
the chart slide.

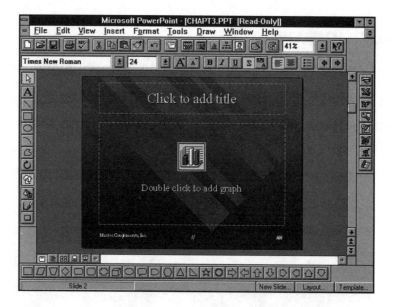

2. Click on the slide title above the chart object, which reads `Click to add title`.

   The text `Click to add title` disappears and is replaced by a blue highlight bar with the blinking insertion point in the middle.

3. Type **Yearly Sales Figures, 1991-1994**.

4. Click the mouse pointer anywhere outside the title text. The slide should appear as in figure 3.22.

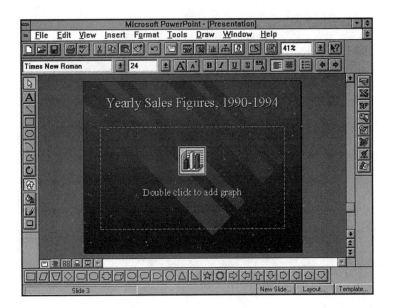

Fig. 3.22
The edited title on
the chart slide.

PowerPoint 4 Basics

5. Although you just edited the title for the chart slide, body text works
   much the same way. Use the Slide Changer to move to the next slide,
   slide 3, titled *Where We Are Today,* or press the PgDn key.

6. Click the mouse inside the text reading Discuss subject background.
   Notice that the body text in this slide is in the form of a bulleted list,
   and that you clicked on the upper of the two bulleted items.

7. Backspace or use the Delete key to erase the text Discuss subject
   background and type **Our 1994 sales have not met expectations**.

8. Using the arrow keys, move the blinking insertion point to the next
   line, include history, facts, or strategies to be considered.

9. Backspace or use the Delete key to erase the text and type **After years
   of uninterrupted growth, Massive Conglomerate is faced
   with a stalled economy and declining durable goods
   purchases**.

10. Click anywhere outside the text block you just edited. The results
    should appear as shown in figure 3.23.

Fig. 3.23
The edited body
text on the third
slide.

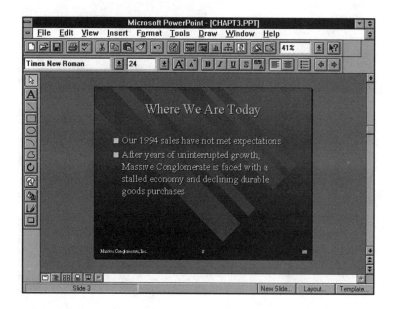

Selecting and Editing Techniques

As you have seen from the examples above, it's easy to edit text in the Slide view. There are many convenient ways to speed the editing of text in a presentation. PowerPoint supports a wide variety of simple keystroke combinations for selecting and editing text. The same is true for using the mouse—a significant number of mouse actions are supported for editing and selecting.

Titles and body text, when clicked on, show the blinking insertion point, which is used to delete and enter text in the item. When the blinking insertion point appears in a text object, you can use the keystrokes listed below to carry out many different editing and selection procedures without using the mouse. Below is a summary of basic keystrokes and mouse actions that can be performed on titles and body text in Slide view:

■ Editing Keystrokes

Del or Delete	Deletes the character after the blinking insertion point
Backspace	Deletes the character before the blinking insertion point
Ctrl+Del or Ctrl+Delete	Deletes the word after the blinking insertion point
Ctrl+Backspace	Deletes the word before the blinking insertion point

■ Selecting with Keystrokes

Shift+left arrow	Selects the next character before the insertion point
Shift+right arrow	Selects the character after the insertion point
Shift+up arrow	Selects the line above the insertion point
Shift+down arrow	Selects the line below the insertion point
Ctrl+Shift+ left arrow	Selects the next word before the insertion point
Ctrl+Shift+ right arrow	Selects the word after the insertion point

■ Selecting with the Mouse

Single-click	Places the insertion point in sentence or line of text
Double-click	Places the insertion point and selects word
Triple-click	Places the insertion point and selects entire paragraph
Click and drag	Selects any text with left mouse button held down
Drag & Drop	Select and drag with the mouse
Drag & Drop Copy	Press and hold Ctrl and select and drag with the mouse

You can also drag the mouse to select any or all parts of a sentence in body text or a title, or all the text in a title or body text.

> **Note**
>
> Another efficient way to alter and edit text is to use PowerPoint's Outline view. In Outline view, all the text contained in the presentation is displayed, ready for editing, and there's no need to flip back and forth through slides to make changes or to select each individual text object in order to edit it. All text can also be formatted in Outline view. Press Ctrl+A to select all the text in Outline view.

Formatting Text

In this section, you format text items in Slide view. If you want to know more about using Outline view to edit slide text, chapter 7 discusses the subject in detail.

To format text, you select it with the mouse or keyboard as described in the preceding section and then apply the formatting with a command or toolbar tool. The quickest way to format text on a slide is by using the mouse and the PowerPoint Formatting toolbar. The Formatting toolbar simplifies many tedious text formatting tasks and, in many ways, simplifies the process.

PowerPoint's Formatting toolbar contains many tools for formatting text:

Times New Roman ⬇	Drop-down list for selecting a font
24 ⬇	Drop-down list for selecting a font size, or a new font size in points can be entered with the keyboard
A▲	Tool for increasing font size to the next predefined point size (from 32 to 36 points, and so on)
A▼	Tool for decreasing font size to the next predefined point size (from 36 to 32 points, and so on)
B	Tool for applying **Boldface** style to selected text
I	Tool for applying *Italic* to selected text
<u>U</u>	Tool for applying <u>Underlining</u> to selected text
S	Tool for applying shadowing to selected text
A	Drop-down palette for applying new colors to selected text

Aligns selected text to left margin of placeholder

Aligns selected text to center of placeholder

Adds or deletes bullets from selected sentence

Promotes selected text sentence (decreases its indent level)

Demotes selected text sentence (increases its indent level)

Notice that for any toolbar button, such as Bulleting or Boldfacing, the formatting that is added to selected text can also be removed by clicking the proper button again.

PowerPoint's Format menu also offers the same range of choices and options as the Formatting toolbar. Chapter 6 in this book discusses formatting techniques in greater detail.

Here's a short list of keystrokes you can apply for text formatting:

Ctrl+B	Boldfaces selected text
Ctrl+I	Italicizes selected text
Ctrl+U	Underlines selected text
Ctrl+=	Subscripts selected text
Ctrl+Shift+=	Superscripts selected text

Tip
The last four key combinations can unselect in their opposite directions as well. All the key combinations can toggle their formatting on and off as well.

Here's how to apply any formatting tool to selected text:

1. Click once inside the text box on the slide and select the text or paragraph you want to format.

2. Click the toolbar button that you want to use for the desired format.

Adding Bullets to Text

Bullets can be added to paragraphs in a slide, can be of several different types, and can change according to the indenting level of the bulleted statement.

In PowerPoint, a *paragraph* is any length of text that is ended by a carriage return. A paragraph can be one word, a few words, a short sentence, or a sequence of sentences of any length—just like a word processor. The act of pressing Enter at the end is what creates the paragraph. By definition, bullets are added only to paragraphs.

To add bullets to text, simply select the paragraph(s) you want and click the Bullet button on the Formatting toolbar.

A fun feature of bullets is their flexibility of character type; in other words, bullets can look like just about anything you want. The bullets in figure 3.23 are square blocks, but any character can be used. Generally, a bullet is culled from "Dingbats," or a font that contains a bunch of oddball characters. Here's how to choose a new bullet style for a bulleted list in a slide:

1. Select the bulleted list whose style you want to change, such as that pictured in figure 3.23.

2. From the Format menu, choose **B**ullet.

   The Bullet dialog box appears (see fig. 3.24) displaying the following options:

   - **U**se a Bullet: When selected, uses bullets on selected paragraphs and removes them if the X is removed

   - **B**ullets From: List of fonts available from which bullets can be chosen

   - Special **C**olor: Drop-down palette of colors that can be applied to bullets

   - **S**ize: Up and Down Size adjuster box to determine the size of the bullet in relation to the point size of the paragraph's font

3. Any bullet character from the displayed font can be clicked on the grid in the dialog box. A small Zoom pops up, showing a close-up of the bullet character you chose.

4. After choosing the bullet and its formatting, choose OK or press Enter. Your new bullet characters are applied and displayed on your slide.

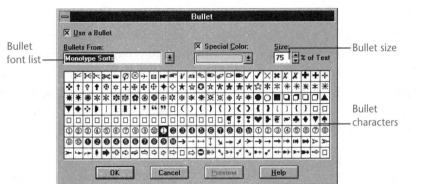

Bullet font list

Bullet size

Bullet characters

Fig. 3.24
The Bullet dialog box.

PowerPoint 4 Basics

Working with Objects

The idea of an object is probably one of the most alien things you deal with in PowerPoint—and in other Windows applications as well. What *is* an object, exactly?

Even though the entire computer press industry tends to drown the word object in reams of verbose terminology (while, in a seemingly deliberate way, intimidating the business or beginning user), it is a straightforward concept. In PowerPoint 4, an *object* is simply any type of data item, such as a picture you draw, a chart you create in Excel or PowerPoint, a sound that you record with your Sound Blaster sound card and save as a file, or a piece of pre-recorded music, that can be cut and pasted between applications and documents or moved around on a slide or between slides.

If you draw a simple graphic in PowerPoint, that's an object. If you create a chart, that's an object too. Pieces of clip art are considered objects.

Drawn and Text Objects

You can create surprisingly sophisticated drawings in PowerPoint and group them to form, if you will, a meta-object composed of numerous simpler drawn objects. The how-to's of basic drawing in PowerPoint are covered in chapter 9, "Drawing Objects."

Although they're not usually discussed this way, text items in PowerPoint slides can also be considered objects, because they have many of the same simple properties. They can be cut and pasted, altered, moved around, and deleted in the same way. They also have a large selection of formatting options available to them, as you know by now.

Objects Created in Other Programs

In Windows, any type of data file or data item is potentially an object—a Microsoft Word table, an Excel spreadsheet, a PowerPoint chart, even a PowerPoint presentation. Objects of any kind are selected and moved around. Objects like this are cut and pasted in two ways: they can be cut, copied, and pasted in the conventional way; or, more important and more powerfully, a process called Paste Special can be used to *embed* an object in a document for special use.

 When an object is embedded in your presentation, it has special properties. The object can still be edited by the original application that created it, even though the object may be something you created in an entirely different program than PowerPoint. An example of this is the charts that you create for use in PowerPoint—bar charts, column charts, and other business charts that are introduced to you a little later in this chapter. Those charts aren't created in PowerPoint, but in a separate program called Microsoft Graph, which appears on top of the main PowerPoint package to let you create the object (chart).

What's going on? It's called *Object Linking and Embedding.* It's used to link PowerPoint, Word, Excel, and other programs into something like a "super-app"—whose document parts are used interchangeably and in which use of all the very powerful separate applications programs is managed by using just one window. Thus, cutting and pasting between packages is made easier and more interactive than ever.

When you edit the object and click outside it, the object is then *embedded into your slide.* The PowerPoint toolbars and screen elements rapidly reappear. Then, if you need to edit the chart again, all you do is double-click on the object—and it truly is an object—and the Graph program appears again. It's almost as if, to use PowerPoint to its fullest extent, you also have to buy Microsoft Word and Excel to be able to create tables and use datasheets effectively. (Microsoft Office users, of course, can relax. They already have all that stuff.)

Adding Objects to a Slide

It's a lot to absorb. For now, you won't be dealing with the use of objects created in Microsoft Word or Excel or other Windows programs. For now, objects are any class of data that you create and use in PowerPoint: drawn artwork, charts, clip art, and so on. They can all be added, selected, changed, and manipulated.

Working with Placeholders

You've been using and manipulating placeholders all along. Placeholders are used particularly when you create a new presentation using the Wizards that were described earlier in this chapter. Placeholders of various types, like the ones shown in figure 3.25, are used to set aside spaces on a slide for a specific purpose.

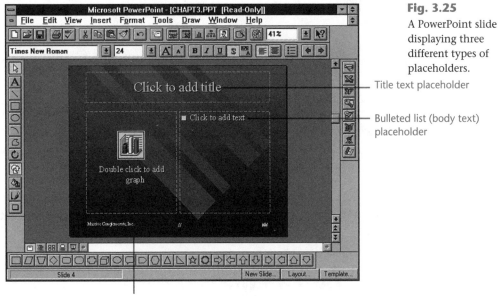

Fig. 3.25
A PowerPoint slide displaying three different types of placeholders.

— Title text placeholder

— Bulleted list (body text) placeholder

Graph placeholder

Whenever you create a new slide, particularly using the AutoLayouts, placeholders are set up to aid in the layout and proper placement of objects in the slide. After that's done, it's up to you to define each placeholder's content.

Inserting a Placeholder or Object

You can also insert a placeholder of a different type into any slide in your presentation. In fact, you've already done so in many earlier exercises. There are five Insert toolbar buttons that allow you to place different types of objects on a slide. They are briefly described in the text that follows:

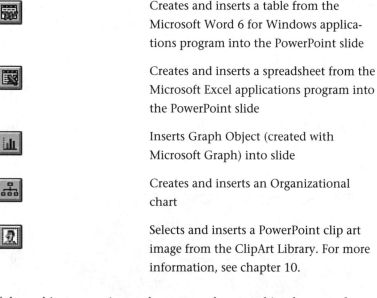

Creates and inserts a table from the Microsoft Word 6 for Windows applications program into the PowerPoint slide

Creates and inserts a spreadsheet from the Microsoft Excel applications program into the PowerPoint slide

Inserts Graph Object (created with Microsoft Graph) into slide

Creates and inserts an Organizational chart

Selects and inserts a PowerPoint clip art image from the ClipArt Library. For more information, see chapter 10.

Any of these objects, once inserted, act not only as an object but as a place-holder, because double-clicking any of them enables you to change, alter, or substitute for the particular item using the program feature or application program that created it.

Right now, this is only a quick glance at the possibilities. Various chapters later in this book deal with every aspect of inserting and changing the different types of objects available to you.

Creating a Chart

Creating charts is one of the more important operations you perform in PowerPoint. An entire section of this book is devoted to the process of creating charts out of statistical data, and only the simplest basics are touched upon here.

Charts are a commonly used tool to illustrate statistics of many kinds. Charts are used to support points in a presentation, to present sales figures, to show market shares between companies in a specific business realm, and to indicate long-term trends in the fortunes of a business. Charts can be used to show the progress of a company's stock prices. Charts can be used in combination to illustrate sales figures or company earnings in conjunction with other figures such as a company's long-term growth or stock price. In this section, you start digging into the basics of chart creation.

Understanding Microsoft Graph

PowerPoint employs a separate charting program called Microsoft Graph 5.0 for creating charts. In Microsoft Graph, you deal with two specific elements when you make a chart: the chart itself, which is the graphical representation of your data, and the *datasheet*, which contains the actual statistics used to generate the chart.

> **Note**
>
> PowerPoint's nomenclature for Graph is confusing. The charting application in PowerPoint is called Microsoft Graph, but every command in the program uses the word *chart*. Because of this, we use the word *chart* almost exclusively in this book, except when reference is made to the program Microsoft Graph. Also, when you create a new slide from AutoLayouts, one AutoLayout type is called Graph as well. In no other area of PowerPoint (including Help) is the word Graph used—the word *chart* is used to describe features.

Spreadsheet users are very familiar with the concept of a datasheet, which is essentially rows and columns of numbers under specific headers that are used to describe the categories of the data. Figure 3.26 shows a picture of a typical datasheet.

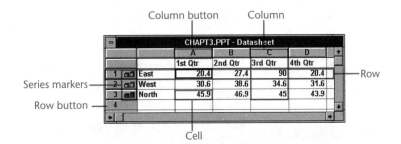

Fig. 3.26
A typical datasheet displayed in PowerPoint's Microsoft Graph application.

All of Graph's datasheets work essentially the same way: you type in rows and columns of numbers that are structured to fit into one or more *series* for display in a chart. Each column and row is numbered with a 3-D button on the edge of the datasheet that can be clicked on to select the entire row or column.

Notice the small colored markers on the row buttons 1, 2, and 3. They're *series markers,* indicating that the data displayed in the sheet and in the chart is organized in three *series* of data. This small fact can have major implications in a datasheet and on a chart, as you see in later chapters.

Each rectangular space in a datasheet is called a *cell.* In the default datasheet, there are three rows of four cells each. You click the mouse inside any cell on a datasheet to enter a new value or to edit an existing one.

Starting Up Graph

Charting is one of the most important features of the PowerPoint 4 program. But how do you start it? What steps do you execute to perform basic chart creation? This section shows you how by using the charting and graphing "applet," or mini-application program bundled with PowerPoint, Microsoft Graph.

Graph is a separate program from PowerPoint, but when you use the program it doesn't appear that way. When you start the Graph application, a new toolbar appears at the top of the PowerPoint window and the menu bar also changes. For the current section, we use the chart slide you created earlier in this chapter as our example.

1. Use the Slide Changer (or press the PgUp key) to move to slide #2 in your presentation, which you previously titled *Yearly Sales Figures, 1991-1994* (see fig. 3.27).

Fig. 3.27
The Sales Figures slide.

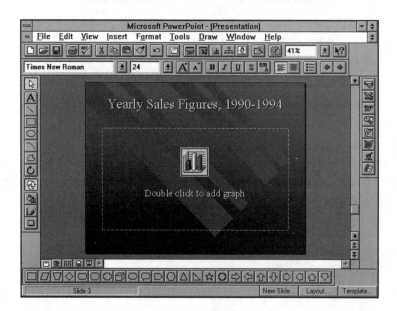

2. Double-click the chart icon, as shown in figure 3.27.

The Microsoft Graph application toolbar and menu bar appears with a default chart and datasheet (see fig. 3.28).

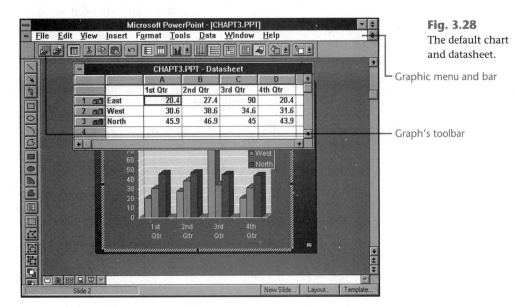

Fig. 3.28
The default chart and datasheet.

— Graphic menu and bar

— Graph's toolbar

Graph starts up. To create a new chart, it's only necessary to enter a new set of data values and labels (in other words, to edit the datasheet) and to select a new chart type if necessary.

Entering and Deleting Data

Here's a short list of keystrokes you can use to edit datasheets:

Left arrow	Move to the next cell to the left
Right arrow	Move to the next cell to the right
Down arrow	Move to the next row down
Up arrow	Move to the next row up
Shift+left arrow	Selects each successive cell to the left
Shift+right arrow	Selects each successive cell to the right
Shift+down arrow	Selects each successive cell down through the column

Shift+up arrow	Selects each successive cell up through the column
Delete or Del	Erases the cell's contents
Backspace	Erases the previous digit in the cell when directly editing a cell's contents. If the entire contents of the cell are selected, pressing Backspace deletes the contents.

To enter and delete data in a Graph datasheet, follow these simple steps:

1. Click on the first cell (Row 1, Column 1) in the default datasheet shown in Graph.

2. Type in the numeric value **25.4** to replace the value 20.4.

3. Using the keystrokes listed above, enter in the rest of the 12 data values as shown below:

1991	1992	1993	1994
25.4	22.1	23.5	21.8
54.3	57.1	57.3	60.2
22.1	20.8	19.2	18.0

4. For the *1st Qtr, 2nd Qtr, 3rd Qtr,* and *4th Qtr* labels at the top of the data sheet, substitute **1991**, **1992**, **1993**, and **1994** respectively. Leave the *East, West,* and *North* labels alone for this exercise.

The new datasheet and chart should look like figure 3.29.

Selecting and Changing the Graph Type

Now, you choose a new chart type. This task is done in Microsoft Graph, not in PowerPoint. You use Graph's toolbar and menu options to perform such operations, and that's the objective of the example below. To keep it simple, while still showing where the various chart types are chosen, you choose a simple 2-D chart type.

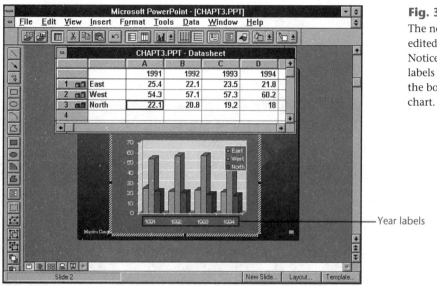

Fig. 3.29
The new chart and edited datasheet. Notice the new labels for years at the bottom of the chart.

Year labels

PowerPoint 4 Basics

Note

There are two key types of charts—2-D and 3-D. Two-dimensional charts are easier to format and work with because they're not as complex, but 3-D charts can be more visually attractive. The default chart type is a 3-D column chart.

1. Click inside the chart to select it. The datasheet disappears.

2. Click the Chart Type down arrow button on the Graph toolbar.

A drop-down list appears displaying 14 icons showing the different basic chart types (see fig. 3.30).

The chart types, listed as they appear in the drop-down list, are as follows:

2-D Area	3-D Area
2-D Bar	3-D Bar
2-D Column	3-D Column
2-D Line	3-D Line

2-D Pie	3-D Pie
Scatter	3-D Surface
Doughnut	Radar

Fig. 3.30
The Graph Type
drop-down icons.

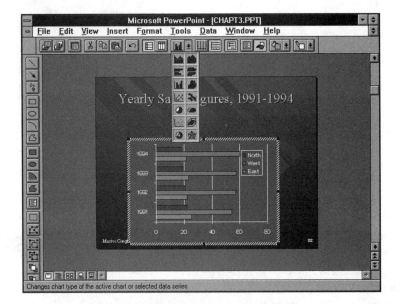

> **Note**
>
> Chapters 13, 14, and 19 discuss the numerous chart types and how to customize them in greater detail.

3. For the current example, click the 2-D Bar Graph button on the drop-down list.

The chart now appears similar to figure 3.31.

As you can see, you haven't even scratched the surface of PowerPoint's charting features. Charts can have tremendous amounts of custom effects applied to them. The large number of chart types and variations can be quite confusing, and to make things more confusing, certain chart types can't be used except for specific types of data. Those issues, of course, are dealt with in other parts of this book. For now, you only see the basics.

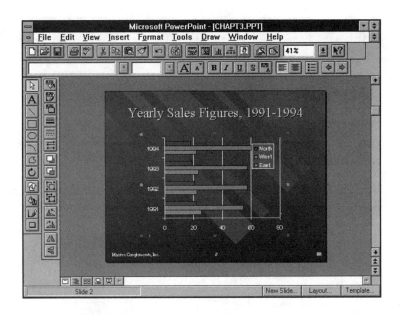

PowerPoint 4 Basics

Fig. 3.31
The new 2-D bar
chart. Horizontal
bars display the
data series.

Pasting the Graph into the Slide

When you've finished creating the basic chart in this section, it's a very
simple matter to paste the new chart into the Sales Figures slide:

■ Click anywhere outside the highlighted chart.

The Graph toolbar and menu bar disappear and are replaced by the more
familiar PowerPoint screen elements. The chart has now been embedded into
the slide.

To start up Graph and edit the chart again, simply double-click it on the
slide. The Graph screen elements appear and the chart and datasheet display,
ready for editing.

Saving Your Presentation

Saving your presentation is, needless to say, a very simple but very important
operation. Any time you create something new in your PowerPoint presentation, you should save your work. Here's how to do so:

> **Note**
>
> A good rule of thumb for saving your work is to save every five minutes. Frequent saving minimizes the risk of losing important work.

1. With your presentation displayed (the view in which it's displayed—Outline, Slide view, or whatever—doesn't matter), from the **F**ile menu, choose **S**ave.

Tip
For a quick save, press Ctrl+S.

If you're saving a new file for the first time, the Save As dialog box appears, as shown in figure 3.32.

Fig. 3.32
The Save As dialog box.

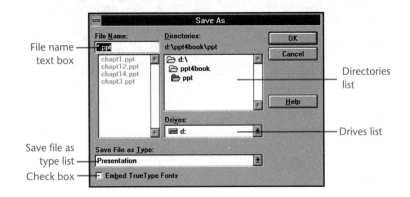

File name text box — Directories list — Drives list — Save file as type list — Check box

2. Click the mouse inside the File **N**ame text box and type the file name you want: **FIRSTONE.PPT**, for example. Backspace or delete any other characters in the text box.

3. The Save File As **T**ype list should show, as its default, Presentation. That's what you want, so it's fine the way it is.

4. You may want to save your file in a different directory and even a different drive. Select the new drive and directory from their respective lists (the Dri**v**es list is a drop-down list).

5. Choose OK or press Enter.

Printing a Presentation

A substantial number of printing options are offered for the well-appointed presenter. If you're planning to use several elements during your presentation, such as an on-screen slide show, audience handouts, and your own set of notes pages, you need to print all those items out before you give your talk.

To print a presentation, you need to decide which of the various parts you want to use as output. There are six different types of output you can specify:

- Slides

- Notes pages

- Handouts (2 Slides Per Page)

- Handouts (3 Slides Per Page)

- Handouts (6 Slides Per Page)

- Outline View

To print your presentation, follow these steps:

1. From the **F**ile menu, choose **P**rint to display the Print dialog box (see fig. 3.33).

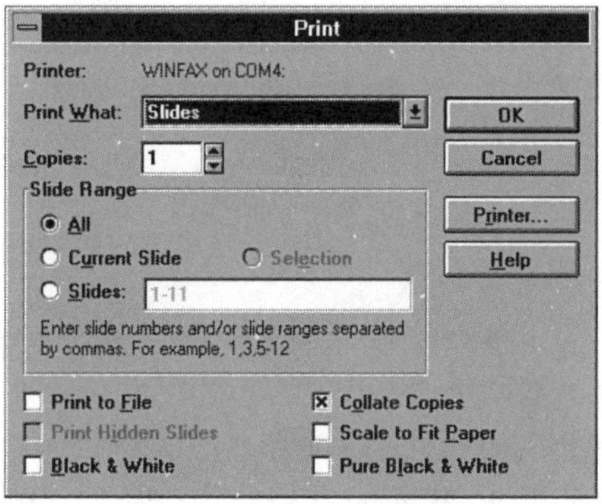

Fig. 3.33
The Print dialog box.

The Print dialog box displays the following options:

- Print **W**hat   Specifies the type of output

    Slides

    Notes Pages

    Handouts (2 Slides Per Page)

Handouts (3 Slides Per Page)

Handouts (6 Slides Per Page)

Outline View

■ **C**opies	Specifies the number of copies of the page or document to print (type in a number or use the up- or down-arrow icons to increase or decrease the value)
■ Slide Range	Specifies which or how many
All Current Slides	Slides to print: All, the Current Slide, or separate slides and separate ranges of slides
■ Print to **F**ile	Sends output to a file
■ Print H**id**den Slides	Enables printing of hidden slides
■ **B**lack & White	Output of slides in black-and-white
■ C**o**llate Copies	Prints collated copies
■ Scale to Fit **P**aper	Scale slide output to paper size
■ Pure B**l**ack & White	Converts gray scale to Black & White

   2. Select the options you want, and click OK or press Enter.

As is very clear, this is only a very basic introduction to the output process. Chapter 16, "Printing and Other Kinds of Output," discusses every major aspect of printing and of many related subjects such as setting up your presentation for special printing output, setting up your printer, troubleshooting printing problems, and more.

Exiting PowerPoint

When you finish working on your presentation, it's a good time to save your work again before you exit the PowerPoint program:

Tip
For a fast exit, press Alt+F4.

   1. From the **F**ile menu, choose **S**ave; or press Ctrl+S.

   2. After the presentation file is saved, from the **F**ile menu, choose E**x**it; or press Alt+F and then X.

From Here...

A tremendous amount of ground has been covered in this chapter. It's been a brief look and overview at almost every major part of PowerPoint 4. You segued from the first phases of designing and creating a presentation to adding new slides, to the beginnings of understanding not only how templates work, but looking at all their components. You took the briefest of glances at how objects of various kinds work in PowerPoint and found out exactly what objects are. You typed in text and created charts. You also saved and printed your presentation file. Not a bad day's work.

- To understand more about the basic parts of your presentation (including slides, handouts, notes, and outlines), simply go on to the next chapter, chapter 4, "Setting Up Your New Presentation."

- Template creation and customizing is explained in greater detail in chapter 5, "Using and Creating Templates."

- An extensive discussion of text formatting and creation is found in chapter 6, "Working with Text."

- To find out more about creating and working with speaker's notes, notes pages, outlines, and handouts, see chapter 7.

- An entire book could be written just on PowerPoint's charting features. Chapters 12, 13, 14, and 19 discuss that subject in much greater detail than could be mentioned in this chapter.

- Chapter 16, "Printing and Other Kinds of Output," discusses all the related issues of printing slides and presentations, plus outlines, notes pages, and other elements.

Chapter 4

Setting Up Your New Presentation

As you saw in the last chapter, there are several major components of a presentation: notes pages, the outline, the handouts, and finally the slides. The slides, while seen as the flashy part of the whole business, should be considered as only a part of the whole production. If you focus all your attention on working with slides and ignore most of the other phases of working with PowerPoint 4, you are cheating yourself out of some of the program's most helpful and powerful productivity features.

Understanding the Presentation Process

PowerPoint 4 can be considered the most flexible and powerful presentation and slide show package currently on the market. But PowerPoint isn't just about slides. It's about organizing ideas and arguments into the most effective presentation. In many situations, you are not just displaying pretty pictures to dazzle your client—you are trying to persuade them that your proposed course of action is the best or that they should buy your product.

While it is possible to produce a presentation by working exclusively in Slide view, doing so defeats the purpose of 90 percent of PowerPoint 4's features. In fact, if you want to save yourself a lot of work, the wisest move for creating the basics of a brand-new presentation is to use the Slide Master, one of several Masters available in the program. After you create the look and basic format for your new presentation with the Slide Master, there are other masters you can use to rapidly expand and change many elements of your presentation. You learn the basics of these techniques in this chapter.

In this chapter, you explore the following aspects of working with PowerPoint 4:

- A more detailed look at the process of starting a new presentation

- A closer look at PowerPoint's various views

- A closer look at PowerPoint's Masters and how they interact with each other

Starting a New Presentation

It is not necessary to use any templates at all to create a new presentation. If you are the sort of person who just has to do everything for yourself, this is the chapter where you begin to do so.

You can start a new presentation in several ways: by using a Wizard, by simply selecting a template, or by creating your own blank presentation. Since the previous chapter dealt with Wizards in considerable detail, we focus here on starting from scratch. Although it sounds difficult, it is actually remarkably easy to build a new presentation from scratch in a few simple steps. Doing so, you begin to see the myriad possibilities for exercising your own creativity.

To begin a new presentation, follow these steps:

1. From the **F**ile menu, choose **N**ew. The New Presentation dialog box appears (see fig. 4.1).

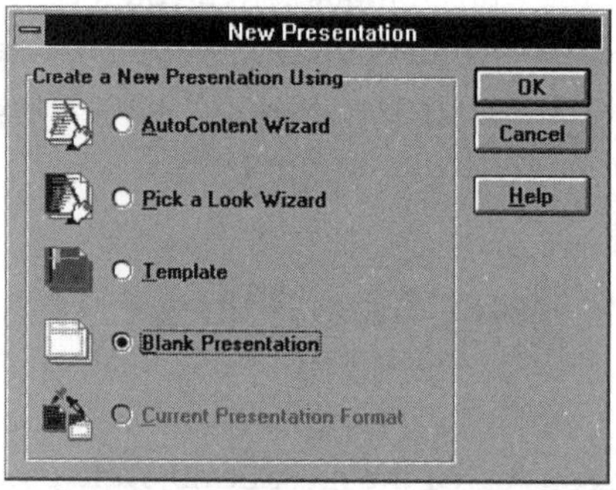

Fig. 4.1
The Wizard requester, which normally appears on PowerPoint startup.

You have seen this screen before, especially if you read the last chapter. This is where you select the Wizards for a complete presentation layout. You can also select from three other option buttons:

Template

Blank Presentation

Current Presentation Format

2. For the current exercise, choose **B**lank Presentation by clicking the option button and clicking OK or pressing Enter.

   Next, you are prompted to choose the AutoLayout for the first slide, as shown in figure 4.2.

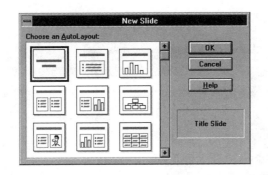

Fig. 4.2
Using the New Slide dialog box to help create a new presentation.

You have seen this dialog box before, too. This time, you are not using the New Slide AutoLayouts to add a slide to an existing presentation—you are using it to create a new presentation from scratch.

3. Click the Title Slide thumbnail (it should be the upper left AutoLayout).

4. Choose OK or press Enter. The results should appear as shown in figure 4.3.

Fig. 4.3
The new presentation.

The new title slide appears. The slide has no formatting.

5. From the **V**iew menu, choose **M**aster, and then choose **S**lide Master. The Slide Master appears displaying the blank title slide (see fig. 4.4).

Fig. 4.4
The unformatted
slide displayed in
the Slide Master.

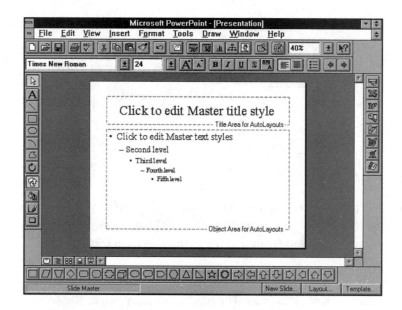

Just for fun, let's do a couple of simple formatting tricks.

6. From the **F**ormat menu, choose Slide Back**g**round.

   The Slide Background dialog box appears. As you saw in chapter 3, "Quick Start: Creating a First Presentation," this is where you decide on the color backgrounds and shading patterns for the entire presentation. The current presentation is blank and the Shade Styles section shows that the **N**one option button is selected.

7. Click the **V**ertical option button under Shade Styles.

8. In the Var**i**ants dialog box section, choose the shading on the top right, which shows a dark-to-light shading from top to bottom.

9. Choose Appl**y** or press Enter. The results should resemble figure 4.5.

   You can even add shading effects to a blank template. Because color has not even been added yet, the text (particularly the title) is not readable against the background. Since you are in the Slide Master, it's a simple matter to fix this so that all your slides are readable.

10. From the **E**dit menu, choose Select A**ll**; or press Ctrl+A.

    If you want to change the color of just one text item, such as the title, here's how you select it:

Click inside the title text. The insertion point appears.

Triple-click the mouse to select the entire text of the title. (You could also drag the mouse over the text for the same purpose.)

Then proceed with the formatting.

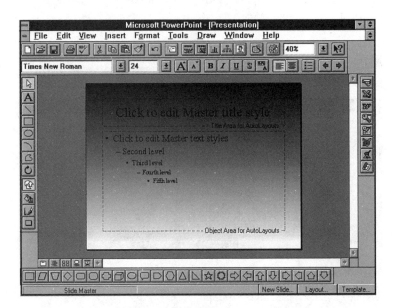

Fig. 4.5
The Slide Master showing the effects of shading on a previously blank template.

11. From the F**o**rmat menu, choose **F**ont.

The Font dialog box appears, as shown in figure 4.6.

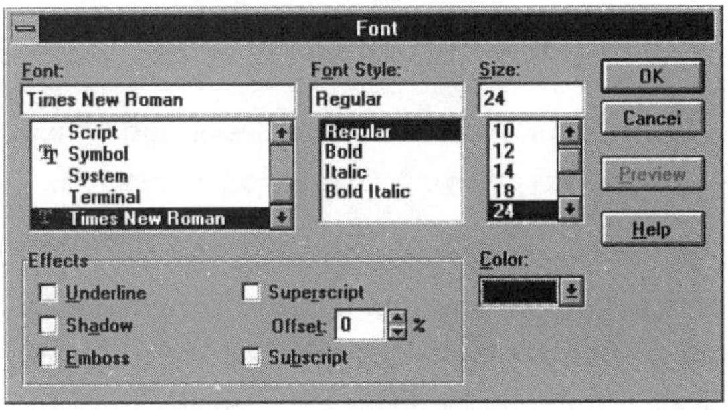

Fig. 4.6
Using the Font dialog box to change the color of text elements in the Slide Master.

12. Click the **C**olor drop-down list button. The eight-color default palette appears, along with the Other Color option and a box displaying the currently selected "other color."

13. Choose Other Color from the Color drop-down list. The Other Color dialog box appears, displaying the 90-color palette as shown in figure 4.7.

Fig. 4.7
Changing the color of text elements in the Slide Master.

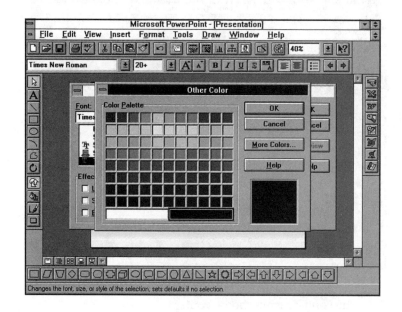

Tip
Watch the status bar while you perform just about any action in PowerPoint 4.

14. Click the Yellow #8 color from the palette. If it is hard to distinguish colors, look at the status bar as you click a color.

15. Choose OK or press Enter. The Other Color dialog box disappears.

16. Click the App**ly** All button in the Slide Background dialog box. The dialog box disappears and your changes are carried out.

Now the title text is much more visible against the dark background. Nonetheless, as you can see from figure 4.8, there is still a problem at the bottom of the Slide Master sample, because yellow text doesn't show up well against the white background. The background still needs to be altered. It's probably best to apply a specific color, such as a shade of blue that matches the yellow text.

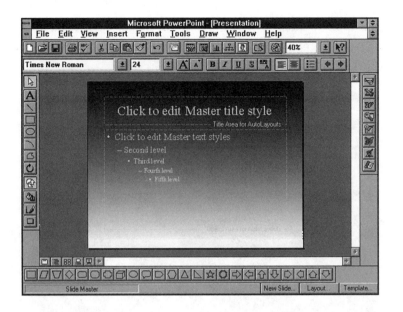

Fig. 4.8
The template is still imperfect, so the background color can be changed in the Slide Master.

17. From the Format menu, choose Slide Background. The Slide Background dialog box reappears.

18. Click the Change Color button. The Background Color dialog box, which looks identical to the Other Color dialog box shown in figure 4.7, appears.

19. For this example, choose Blue #4.

20. Choose OK or press Enter.

21. Choose Apply All from the Slide Background dialog box.

22. From the View menu, choose Slides (see fig. 4.9).

You have literally created a new presentation from scratch. All the other slides you add to the presentation are the same format that you defined in this exercise.

There is one key point to carry away from this section: the importance of the Slide Master. When creating a new presentation with your own specifications, this is where it should all happen. More Slide Master tips and information can be found later in this chapter.

Save your work by choosing **S**ave from the **F**ile menu, specifying a file name for your new presentation, and clicking the OK button. Proceed to the next section.

Fig. 4.9
You have success-
fully started a new
presentation.

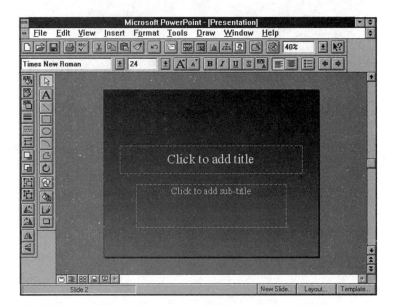

Understanding the View Options

Views and Masters bear considerable similarities to one another. Each primary functional area of PowerPoint 4—slides, outlines, handouts, and notes pages—has both a Master and a view.

Using the View Buttons on the PowerPoint Status Bar

PowerPoint's View buttons are not located on a toolbar—they are located at the bottom of the screen, just above the status bar, as shown in figure 4.10. Each View button is described in table 4.1.

Table 4.1 PowerPoint 4's View Buttons

Button	Name	Action
▢	Slide View	Changes the view to directly edit a slide
▤	Outline View	Changes the view to show the title and body text from all slides

Button	Name	Action
88	Slide Sorter View	Changes the view to show miniatures of all slides
🖳	Notes Pages View	Changes the view to edit speaker's notes
🖥	Slide Show View	Runs or rehearses a slide show

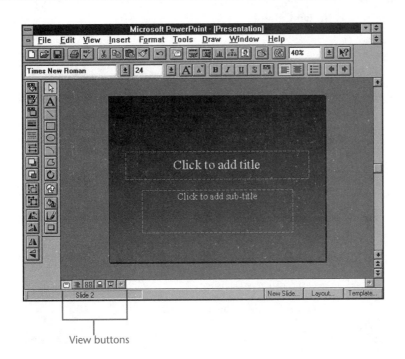

Fig. 4.10
The PowerPoint
screen displaying
the View buttons
at the bottom of
the screen.

View buttons

PowerPoint 4 Basics

Clicking on any of the five View buttons displays their respective sections of
the program.

Viewing Slides

Clicking the Slide View button brings up the screen in which you edit,
change, and add elements on the currently displayed slide. The Slide Changer
can be used to page through each slide in your presentation, or the PgUp and
PgDn keys can also be used. Virtually every possible operation that can be
performed on slide objects, such as charts, drawn graphics, placing clip art,
entering and formatting text, and so on, can be performed here. All these
issues are discussed in later chapters.

Viewing the Outline

PowerPoint 4 offers greater flexibility than the competition because of the various tools it offers—in particular, its notes pages, the handout feature, and especially its powerful and straightforward outlining capabilities. Outlining, in particular, is the key feature for organizing your ideas and critiquing your argument for logical flow and impact. A single slide view can never provide such a viewpoint.

The outline is one of the hidden sources of power in PowerPoint 4. A sample Outline view is shown in figure 4.11.

Fig. 4.11
The Outline view showing a typical outline.

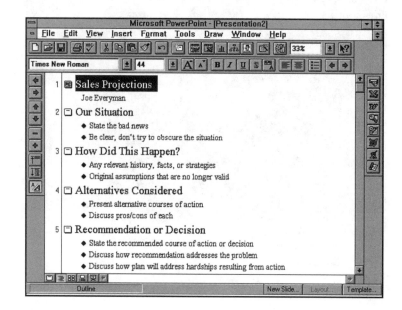

The outline view offers intelligent tools for rearranging and editing an entire presentation at a glance. Each slide in the presentation is numbered, and clicking any slide's number selects it. When a slide is selected, as Slide #5 is in figure 4.11, it can be dragged with the mouse, deleted, copied, cut and pasted, and the slide's text can be formatted.

One key element of Outline view is the slide icons shown in figure 4.11. The slide icons can be dragged and dropped at any location in the outline, thus providing an easy way to rearrange slides. Clicking any slide icon also selects the entire text contents—title and body text—available in the slide for formatting and editing functions.

A special toolbar is provided that covers most of the key functions for working with an outline. The buttons are described in order from top to bottom in table 4.2.

Table 4.2 PowerPoint 4's Outline View Toolbar Buttons		
Button	**Name**	**Action**
⬆	Move Up	Moves selected slide up the slide sequence
⬇	Move Down	Moves selected slide down the slide sequence
➖	Collapse Selection	Hides body text from the outline view of the selected slide or slides (does *not* delete it)
➕	Expand Selection	Restores any body text in selected slides to the outline view
⬆≣	Show All	Shows all slide titles and body text for each slide in the outline
⬇≣	Show Titles	Shows only slide titles in the outline
ᴬ𝐴	Show Formatting	Toggle to show text formatting for titles and body text. If formatting is off, text is shown in standard sans serif characters without boldfacing or different sizes

You can insert new slides in Outline view, as the presence of the New Slide button at the bottom right of figure 4.11 indicates. However, you have no control over slide layout in Outline view, so any new slide that is added is a blank slate, defaulting to a standard title and body text slide.

Placing the text insertion point at the end of a title line and pressing Enter creates a new slide. Placing the insertion point at the end of a bulleted point and pressing Enter creates a new bulleted point in the body text for that slide. Selecting any text for editing enables the use of all the standard text formatting tools on the PowerPoint Formatting toolbar. Formatting that is added to any text in Outline view is shown in the presentation. Some text formatting, such as adding colors to text, is not available in Outline view.

Individual argument points in a slide can be promoted or demoted. Such an action is also reflected in the presentation (see fig. 4.12).

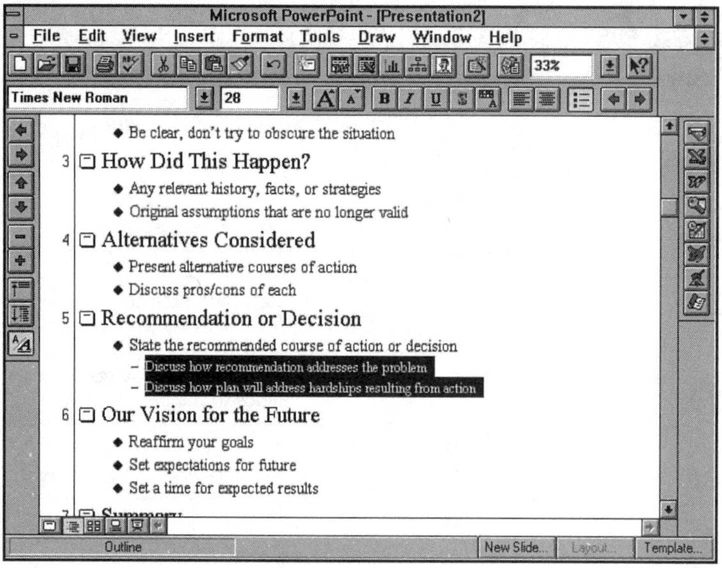

Fig. 4.12
Demoting
argument points
in Outline view.

Viewing the Slide Sorter

The Slide Sorter is a very powerful convenience feature in PowerPoint 4. As mentioned in chapter 3, "Quick Start: Creating a First Presentation," the Slide Sorter enables fast rearranging of slides to any order—just drag and drop and the slide is in its new place. It's also easy to apply various special effects to the contents of a slide, including transition effects determining how a slide appears and disappears on-screen and build effects determining how body text elements (in particular, bulleted text items) appear on each slide. Simply knowing where these two powerful special effects classes can be applied to your presentation allows a wide scope for experimenting.

Applying Special Effects in the Slide Sorter

To apply transition or build effects in the Slide Sorter, follow these steps:

1. With your presentation displayed, from the **V**iew menu, choose Sli**d**e Sorter.

2. Click the slide to which you want to apply special effects.

3. With the slide selected, choose either the Transition drop-down list or the Build drop-down list, and choose the effect you want. (For a fast choice, choose Random Effects from either list.)

4. As the effect is applied, the slide shows a brief demonstration of the applied effect.

When you apply effects to a slide, notice that small icons are placed under each slide thumbnail that has the respective effects applied to it (see fig. 4.13). The icons correspond to the Transition tool and Build tool icons shown on the toolbar and indicate whether one, the other, or both classes of effects have been applied to the slide.

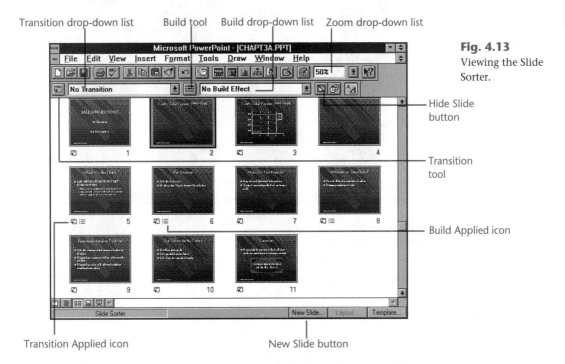

Fig. 4.13
Viewing the Slide Sorter.

To view the slide sorter from the currently displayed view, use either of these techniques:

■ Click the Slide Sorter button on the PowerPoint screen.

■ From the **V**iew menu, choose Sli**d**e Sorter.

Tip
Double-clicking
any slide in the
Sorter displays
that slide in Slide
view, ready for
editing and
changes.

Unlike Outline view, you can add new slides to a presentation and have full
access to the AutoLayouts for determining what type of slide you want to
insert by clicking the New Slide button at the bottom of the PowerPoint
screen.

The Slide Sorter offers a powerful Zoom feature that enables you to make the
slide thumbnails as large or as small as desired (see fig. 4.14).

Fig. 4.14
Zooming in the
Slide Sorter.

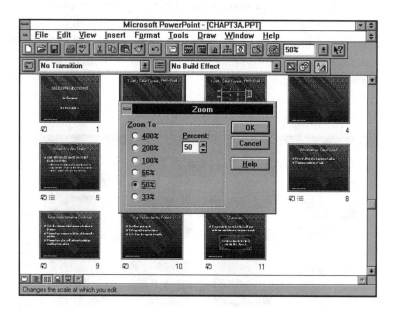

Viewing Notes Pages (Speaker's Notes)

Notes pages offer a valuable tool to the speaker: the capability to write and
print out extensive speaker's notes for each slide in the presentation, allowing for greater ease and confidence while conducting a slide show for your
viewers.

As noted in chapter 3, notes pages generally have one slide printed on each
page, occupying the top half of the page, with space for text provided in the
bottom half. Figure 4.15 shows a typical notes page layout.

Notes pages can have special information placed on them, such as company
names, dates, logos, and any other appropriate information. That task is done
in the Notes Master, which is discussed later in this chapter.

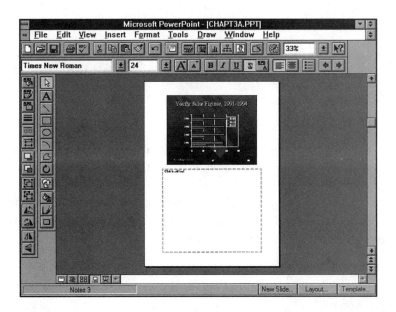

Fig. 4.15
Viewing the notes
pages.

PowerPoint 4 Basics

> **Note**
>
> A distinction must be made between the Notes Master and the Notes view. You enter your speaker's notes in the Notes view. The Notes Master simply defines the general layout of the notes pages when you print them out, including any common elements for notes pages such as page numbering, logos, etc.

In Notes view, each notes page shows a slide. Below the slide, notes for each page can be entered and edited by the user. To do so, follow these steps:

1. Click inside the Notes text area (also called a placeholder) for the desired page. The insertion point appears inside the placeholder.

2. If you want to have a closer look at your edits, use the Zoom feature until the view is comfortable for typing text. (66 percent view from the Zoom drop-down list is a good place to start.)

3. Begin typing your notes. The Notes Master determines the basic format of your text, but that is just the beginning. You can use the Promote and Demote buttons on the Formatting toolbar and add bullets to your text.

   To execute further formatting on your text, such as hanging indents, continue with these steps.

Tip
Double-clicking the slide shown on any notes page in the Notes view brings up that slide in Slide view.

4. From the **V**iew menu, choose **R**uler.

   PowerPoint's Ruler appears. The Ruler's gadgets can be dragged to create hanging indents and standard indents. This is especially handy for bulleted text.

5. Select the text that you want to format.

6. Drag the ruler gadgets until the text is formatted the way you want. Add tabs if necessary between bullets and their associated text.

For a more detailed discussion of text formatting, see chapter 6, "Working with Text." Chapter 7, "Creating Speaker's Notes, Outlines, and Handouts," also discusses editing notes in greater detail.

Viewing the Slide Show

Viewing the slide show is simply a matter of clicking the Slide Show button above the Status bar.

Several keystrokes can be used for various purposes in the slide show:

Keystrokes	Action
Enter, Space bar	Advances to next slide
Enter, Space bar	Executes next build effect (appearance of next bulleted point in slide, *if builds are applied*)
Page Up	Back to previous slide
Page Down	Advances to next slide

Bear in mind that presentation rehearsals can be done that set the precise timing of all events that occur in each slide. The keystrokes listed above are used when you are manually advancing the slide show and the build effects (if any) applied to each slide.

Simply clicking the Slide Show button, however, somewhat limits your access to control features in the slide show. Choosing the Slide Sho**w** option from the **V**iew menu (regardless of the view you are currently in) affords you a few more options, as figure 4.16 shows.

Fig. 4.16
The Slide Show
dialog box
showing the
available options.

PowerPoint 4 Basics

The options available for running your slide show are listed below:

■ Slides

All	When clicked on, enables show of all slides
From: **T**o:	Specify range of slides to show

■ Advance

Manual Advance	When clicked on, enables manual control of when each slide and effect is displayed
Use Slide Timings	Use slide timings built into presentation
Rehearse New Timings	Create new timings for slide show, using keystrokes (for more information about rehearsing timings, see chapter 20)

■ Run **C**ontinuously Until Esc	Check box option: Continuous slide show until Escape is pressed

To run the slide show after setting your options, choose OK or press Enter.

Understanding the Master Views

As you saw in chapter 2, "Getting Acquainted with PowerPoint 4," the Master Views are the place where the *common elements* of all the parts of your presentation are created and applied. A presentation template has several Masters that are part of the whole package, as you discovered when you used the AutoContent and Pick a Look Wizards. The Master Views enable you to access all the components of your template and to change them for any preference, from a company name appearing on your handouts (via the Handout Master) to a company logo appearing on your slides (via the Slide Master), and the layout of all your Notes Pages (via the Notes Master).

Understanding the Slide Master

The Slide Master provides the basis for the visual appearance of your presentation. Your template's color scheme, graphic objects, and other common elements of each slide are based here and can be edited and changed here.

In this short section, you perform some minor reformatting chores in the Slide Master, play around with a few of its elements to get used to working with them, and explore the elements that compose it.

Using the Slide Master

To display the Slide Master for your presentation, perform the following steps:

1. From the **V**iew menu, choose **M**aster.

   A cascading menu pops up, offering four menu choices: **S**lide Master, **O**utline Master, Han**d**out Master, and **N**otes Master.

2. Choose **S**lide Master.

   The Slide Master appears (see fig. 4.17).

   Notice that the template used is the "Blue Diagonal" template, named BLUEDIAG.PPT, located in the C:\POWERPNT\TEMPLATE\SLDSHOW directory. This is the template you use in the current exercise. Use the **O**pen command under the **F**ile menu to locate the template and open it. Then display its Slide Master using the two steps above and proceed to the next step below.

   Now, it's time to play with some of the objects that compose the Slide Master. The Slide Master is the basis for the entire visual look of your presentation, and you see why in the following steps.

3. Click the blue diagonal graphic on the slide background in the top left corner, *making sure not to click any of the text objects*.

   The graphic object is highlighted, showing small, square pressure points around it.

4. Drag the diagonal down the Slide Master about a half-inch with the mouse by clicking and holding the mouse on any area of the graphic *except* the pressure points. *Do not perform any other actions yet.* The master looks something like figure 4.18.

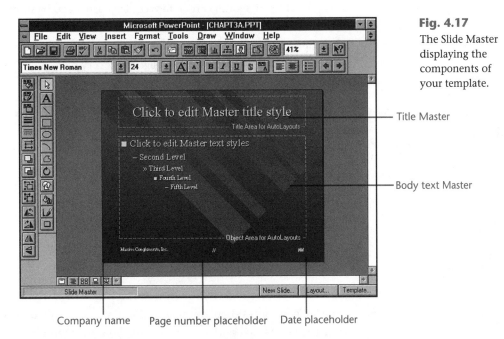

Fig. 4.17
The Slide Master displaying the components of your template.

Title Master

Body text Master

Company name   Page number placeholder   Date placeholder

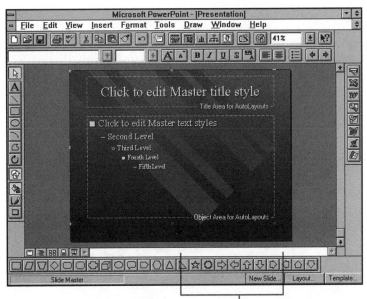

Fig. 4.18
The Slide Master after moving the blue diagonal.

Pressure points

5. From the **E**dit menu, choose **U**ndo.

You really do not want to mess up your template just yet, so the **U**ndo command was used to efface the previous action. Nonetheless, this is a very important exercise. The blue diagonal can be moved. Because it can be moved, it can have many other things done to it as well. It can have its color changed, be reshaped, and be deleted should you so desire. The implications are vast. The Slide Master is where you can design your very own graphically styled templates.

Chapter 5, "Using and Creating Templates," discusses in detail the process of creating custom templates.

Adding and Changing Elements in the Slide Master

We'll do three things to the current Slide Master:

- Change the color and pattern fill of the Slide Master background

- Change the color and fill of the diagonal graphic

- Change the font in the title and body text of the Master

The following steps are presented to show you the essentials of working with elements in the Slide Master. When you master them, you have the tools you need to work with Slide Master and to start creating your own templates.

To change the color of the Slide Master background:

1. From the **F**ormat menu, choose Slide Back**g**round. The Slide Background dialog box appears, as shown in figure 4.19.

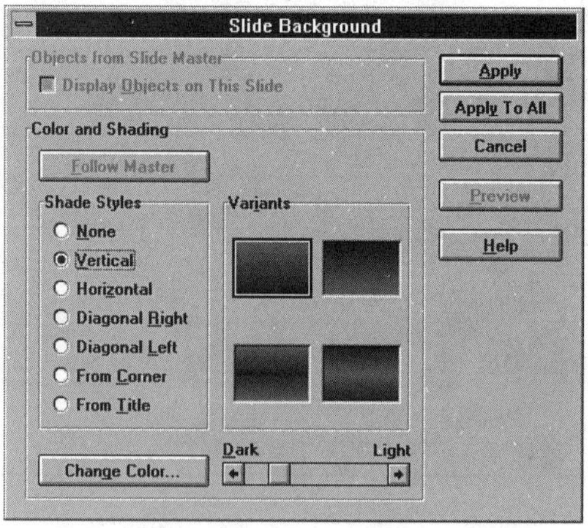

Fig. 4.19

Using the Format Slide Background command to change the Slide Master.

There are several tools that can be used to change your slide background: the Shade Styles option button list; the shading Variants, which displays four thumbnails showing different orientations for the same fill type; the Change Color button, which gives you access to a 90-color palette from which you can choose any color for the background; and the **D**ark-Light slider bar, which enables you to change the visual aspect of the Slide Master background.

While the possibilities are almost endless and changing the Slide Master background has been made simple and actually fun, you select some straightforward changes here just to show the possibilities.

2. From the Shade Styles list, click the Diagonal **R**ight option button.

3. In the Variants area, click the top left thumbnail.

4. Click the **A**pply button. The dialog box disappears, and the results appear, as shown in figure 4.20.

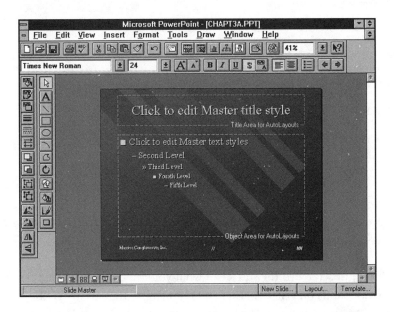

Fig. 4.20
Viewing the new Slide Master background. Notice that the background has been changed to a diagonal pattern, matching the blue diagonal graphic stripes.

To change the color of the diagonal graphic stripes, follow these steps:

1. Click the diagonal graphic in the Slide Master. If you cannot select it, or if you select a text object instead, click the diagonal outside of any other objects.

PowerPoint 4 Basics

2. With the diagonal stripes selected, from the Format menu, choose Colors and **L**ines.

The Colors and Lines dialog box appears, as shown in figure 4.21.

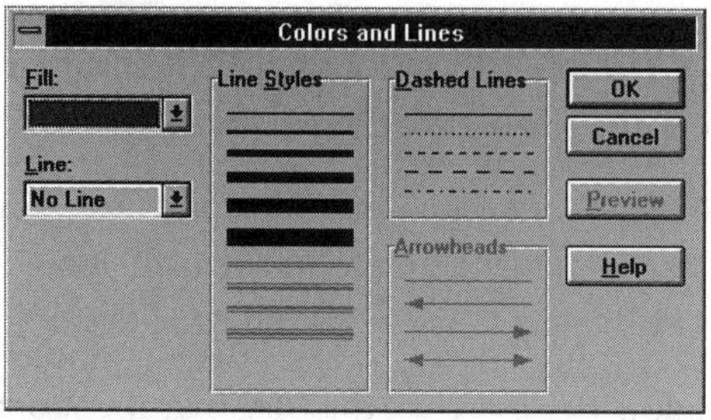

Fig. 4.21
Changing the
diagonal graphic
with the Colors
and Lines dialog
box.

3. To keep it simple, apply a shaded fill to the diagonal.

4. Click the down-arrow icon for the **F**ill drop-down list. Its options are displayed.

5. Choose Shaded, and the Shaded Fill dialog box appears.

6. From the Shade Styles list, choose Diagonal **R**ight.

7. In the Variants list, click the top right thumbnail.

8. Choose OK or press Enter.

9. Choose OK or press Enter again. The Slide Master appears again. The results of the changes should resemble figure 4.22.

10. From the **F**ile menu, choose Save **A**s to save your template changes to a new PowerPoint file, and specify a new file name and directory to save your file in. *Do NOT simply save your work, or PowerPoint will erase your original template* and substitute your changes in it!

You have just scratched the surface of what you can do with graphic elements and backgrounds on a Slide Master and template. Now, we change the font of the Slide Master title text and the body text:

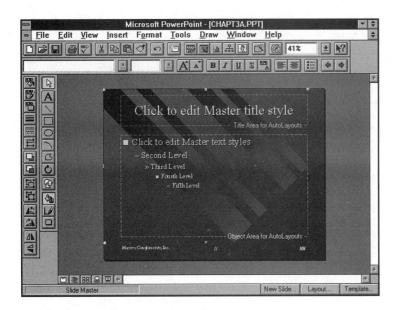

Fig. 4.22
The new fill
applied to the
diagonal graphic
stripes.

1. Click once on the Title text to select it.

2. From the Format menu, choose Font to display the Font dialog box
   (see fig. 4.23).

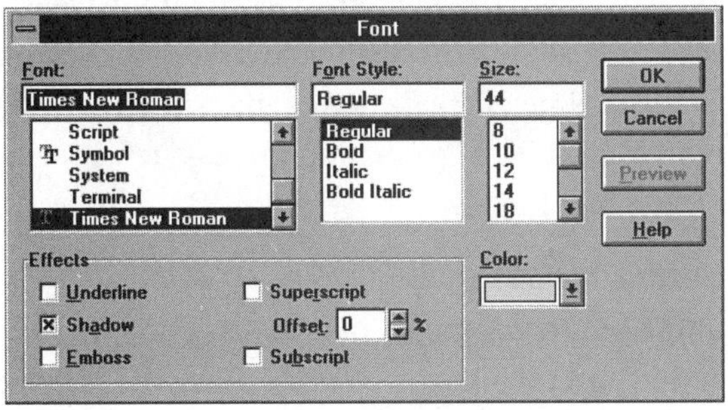

Fig. 4.23
Choosing a new
font style from the
Font dialog box.

3. Choose Bold from the Font Style list.

4. Choose OK or press Enter.

Your new Slide Master should appear similar to figure 4.24.

Fig. 4.24
The final appearance of the Slide Master after the various changes. The title text is now in boldface, making it easier to read across the background.

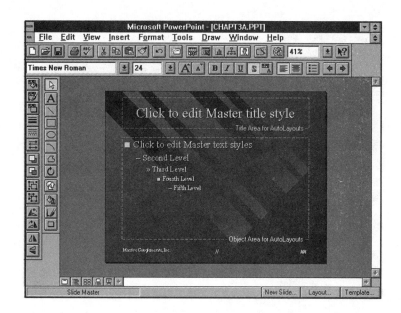

Understanding the Outline Master

The Outline Master differs significantly from Outline view. The Outline Master is used only to format your printed outline, which can differ significantly from the Outline view in your presentation. The Outline view shows only your outline based on the contents of all your slides. The Outline Master displays none of the outline's actual content, but shows the elements that would be common to printed pages of an outline—such as company names, page numbers, logos, and the like.

Viewing the Outline Master

To view the Outline Master for the current presentation, from the **V**iew menu, select **M**aster, and then choose **O**utline Master to display the screen shown in figure 4.25.

Using the Outline Master

Using the Outline Master is as straightforward as viewing it. For example, to add a date marker to the outline, follow these steps:

1. Display the Outline Master as described in the preceding section.

2. From the **I**nsert menu, choose **D**ate.

   A date marker appears in the middle of the sample outline page, as shown in figure 4.26.

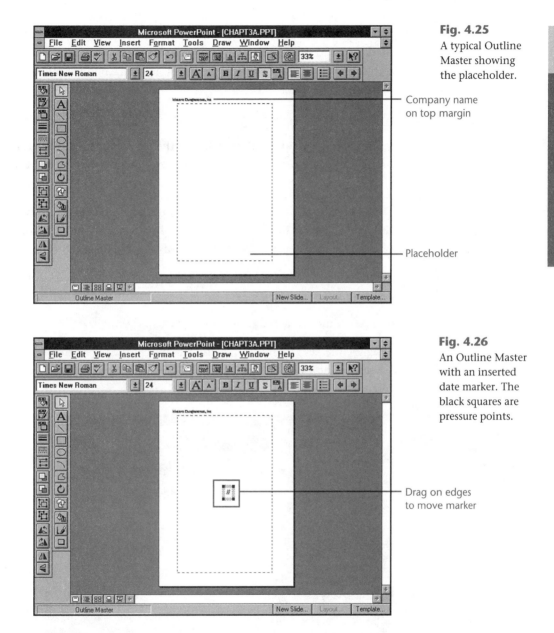

Fig. 4.25
A typical Outline Master showing the placeholder.

Company name on top margin

Placeholder

Fig. 4.26
An Outline Master with an inserted date marker. The black squares are pressure points.

Drag on edges to move marker

3. Drag the date marker to an appropriate location on the margins of the page. You can use the placeholder margins as a guide if necessary.

Now, you insert a page number marker and format it for convenient placement on the page.

4. From the **Insert** menu, choose Page N**u**mber. (Click *outside* of the date marker first to deselect it—otherwise, the page number marker is inserted into the same object as the date.) A new page number marker is placed onto the Slide Master.

Now, you resize the page number marker to make it more legible.

5. Grab a pressure point on the left side of the page number marker and drag it to the left margin of the placeholder. The page number marker is resized.

6. Drag a pressure point on the right side of the page number marker to the right margin. The marker should now be sitting on the left margin of the page, and be resized to the width of the page margin.

7. With the marker object selected, click the Center button on the Formatting toolbar; or press Ctrl+E.

The page number marker is centered on the page.

8. Drag the marker object (by dragging any part of the object that is not a pressure point) to the top or bottom of the page. The results should resemble figure 4.27.

Fig. 4.27
An Outline Master with an inserted date marker and page number marker.

Date marker

Page number marker

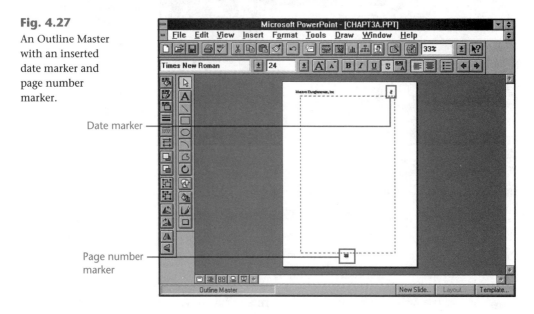

PowerPoint 4 Basics

> **Note**
>
> When you enter date and page number markers on your Handout Master, a date marker is denoted by a single hash mark. A page number marker is denoted by a double hash mark.

If you want to print outlines with standard elements like the ones you just did, it is almost absurdly easy. Just make sure, as you did in this exercise, that you place inserted objects out of the way of possible printed matter on your outline. For more information about placing graphics (such as logos or clip art) on the Outline Master, see chapter 7, "Creating Speaker's Notes, Outlines, and Handouts."

Understanding the Handout Master

The Handout Master is almost as simple as the Outline Master, and it is a lot simpler than it appears. Although the appearance of the slide image placeholders on the Handout Master seems complex, the only time they ever come into play is when you print the Handout Master. That, as you may recall, is done with the **P**rint command from the **F**ile menu. It's as simple a matter to add dates, page numbers, and other elements to the Handout Master as it is to other masters.

Viewing the Handout Master

To view the Handout Master for the current presentation, from the **V**iew menu, select **M**aster, and then choose Han**d**out Master. Figure 4.28 shows a typical Handout Master.

Using the Handout Master

To insert some background objects into the Handout Master, follow these steps:

1. From the **I**nsert menu, choose D**a**te.

   A date marker is placed in the middle of the Handout Master page.

2. Drag the date marker to an appropriate location on the margins of the page. You can use the placeholder margins as a guide if necessary.

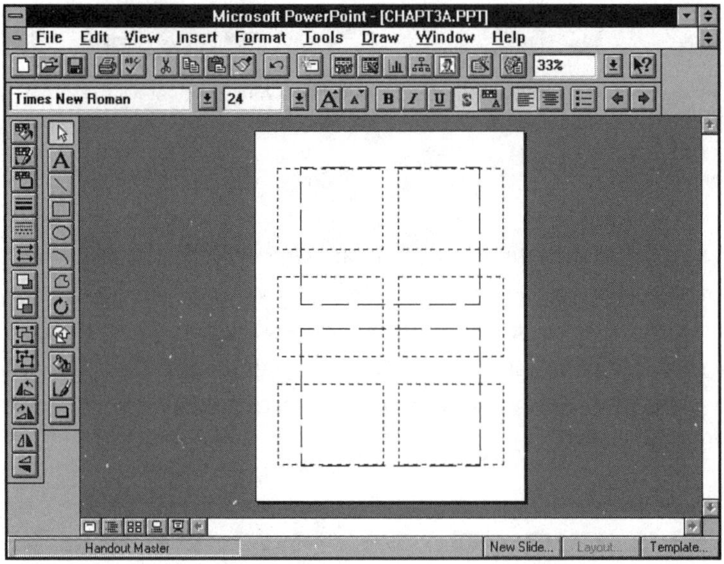

Fig. 4.28
A Handout Master
with placeholders
for 2, 3, or 6 slide
images.

3. From the **I**nsert menu, choose Page Number. (Click outside of the date marker first to deselect it—otherwise, the page number marker will be inserted into the same object as the date.) A page number marker is placed on the Handout Master.

   The page number marker can be resized for more convenient formatting and text entry.

4. To resize the page number marker, grab a pressure point on the left side of the page number marker and drag it to the left margin of the placeholder. The page number marker is resized.

5. Drag a pressure point on the right edge of the marker object to the right margin. The marker should now be sitting on the left margin of the page.

6. With the marker object selected, click the Center button on the Formatting toolbar; or press Ctrl+E.

   The page number marker is now centered on the page.

7. Drag the marker object (by dragging any part of the object that isn't a pressure point) to the top or bottom of the page. The results should resemble figure 4.29.

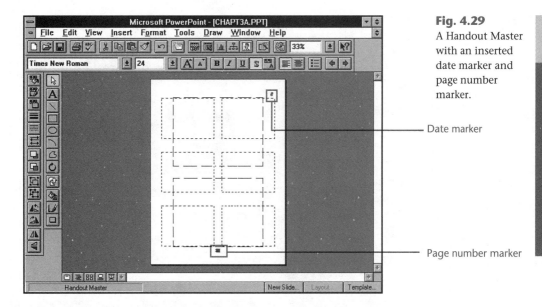

Fig. 4.29
A Handout Master
with an inserted
date marker and
page number
marker.

Date marker

Page number marker

PowerPoint 4 Basics

Understanding the Notes Master

The Notes Master, because it automatically contains some graphic elements
(namely, images of a slide on each notes page), offers more room for creativity than some of the other masters. The slide image on each notes page can
be resized with the mouse, as can the placeholder for notes text. As you can
see in figure 4.30, the Notes Master bears a very close resemblance to the
Notes view discussed earlier in this chapter.

Viewing the Notes Master
To view the Notes Master, from the **V**iew menu, select **M**aster, and then
choose **N**otes Master. The Notes Master appears; it should look similar to
figure 4.30.

Using the Notes Master
Using the Notes Master is quite similar to working in Notes Pages view. In
fact, since you don't enter notes in the Master, it is actually simpler.

To resize the slide image to a smaller size and reformat the Notes Master text,
follow these steps:

   1. Click on the slide image in the Notes Master to select it.

Fig. 4.30
A typical Notes Master showing a slide image and a notes text placeholder.

Slide image ———

Notes text ——
placeholder

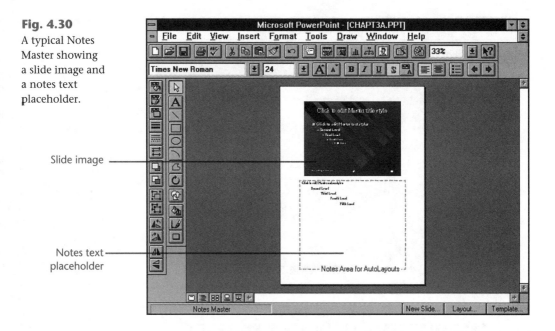

Tip
Use the guides. From the **View** menu, choose **G**uides to help you resize and place the slide image where you want it.

2. With the mouse, grab a corner pressure point and drag it to shrink the slide image. The slide is resized symmetrically and retains its visual proportion.

3. Drag the slide to a centered place on the page.

To reformat the sample text in the Notes Master text placeholder, follow these steps:

1. Click inside the text placeholder.

2. To reformat all the placeholder text, click and drag the mouse to select the placeholder's contents. The text is highlighted.

3. Use the tools on the Formatting toolbar, such as Fonts, Font Size, Boldface, and so on, to format the text in the desired way. You can also Zoom and use the Ruler to aid in effective formatting for indents.

The result should look similar to figure 4.31.

As with the other masters you worked with, dates, times, page numbers, and other items can quickly and easily be placed on the Notes Master. The method is the same as for the other masters you looked at. For example, to place a date on a Notes Master, follow these steps:

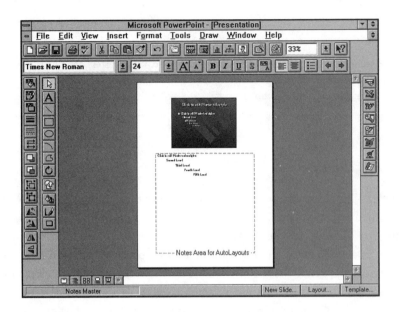

PowerPoint 4 Basics

Fig. 4.31
A Notes Master
showing a resized
slide image and
reformatted text.
The slide image is
shrunk and guides
are used to help
place it properly.

1. From the **I**nsert menu, choose **Da**te.

   A date marker is placed in the middle of the Notes Master page.

2. Drag the date marker to an appropriate location on the margins of the
   page. You can use the placeholder margins as a guide if necessary.

Troubleshooting

I can't display any of the Masters.

Make sure you have a presentation open and currently active.

My outline text doesn't show its formatting in Outline view.

Click the Show Formatting tool button on the Outlining toolbar. In its default, the
Outlining toolbar is displayed on the right side of the PowerPoint screen when you're
in Outline view. The Show Formatting tool is the bottom button on that toolbar.

My notes pages don't have any text placeholders or slides on them.

There's an easy way to fix this. Display your Notes Master (not an individual notes
page, but the Notes Master for your presentation), and choose Master Layout from
the Format menu. Two check boxes appear in the Master Layout dialog box: **A**dd
Slide Image and Add Notes Text. Click both check boxes to place an X in each of
them. Then choose OK or press Enter. Your Notes Master now displays the proper
elements for your notes pages.

(continues)

(continued)

This technique is common to all the Masters. If any of your Masters don't have a standard element, check the Format Master Layout command. The odds are that you'll be able to fix many problems here.

From Here...

Chapter 4 has been more of a specialized chapter than the previous ones, focusing more on how to manage information and formatting on the various views and Masters of PowerPoint. There have also been a few surprises, such as the capability to edit and format text in notes pages (which stands to reason, considering that you are responsible for the contents of notes pages in the first place). The next chapter, chapter 5, builds on some of the things you learned in this chapter and more deeply addresses the issue of using templates in PowerPoint.

- Chapter 5, "Using and Creating Templates," discusses the use and development of custom templates in more detail than could be offered in the last two chapters.

- Chapter 6, "Working with Text," discusses using PowerPoint's Ruler, and the fine points of working with text in all of PowerPoint's Views, in greater detail.

- Chapter 7, "Creating Speaker's Notes, Handouts, and Outlines," attacks the complete production process of those elements of a presentation.

Chapter 5

Using and Creating Templates

Templates are the foundation of every presentation you make. Without a good understanding of templates, it's difficult to understand everything that's going on during the presentation process. Fortunately, as with just about everything else in the program, templates are easy to understand and use effectively.

In the course of this chapter, Wizards are not used when creating or using presentation templates. Therefore, this chapter goes a little more behind the scenes to discover how things work.

Reviewing Template Elements

Templates consist of four discrete Master components, all of which take part in the building of a complete presentation. While chapter 4, "Setting Up Your New Presentation," discusses the various Masters in more detail, their roles in the overall creation of a presentation bear repeating here.

Slide Master: Defines the appearance of your slide show. While it's possible to have individual slides in your presentation that use a different color scheme from the Master, the Slide Master is the visual basis for your slide show. Common slide elements, such as a company logo, company name, dates, and page numbers, are placed here.

Among the other information in this chapter, you discover:

- How to apply templates to new and existing presentations

- How to inspect the contents of PowerPoint 4's sample presentations and templates

- How to define your own default template

- How to add company names and logos to your template

Outline Master: Tracks the entire text content of your presentation. In this way, the Outline Master functions very much like a word processor, with indenting of text entries, font formatting, and many other basic word processing functions. It's a good idea to use the Outline Master frequently to study the logical flow of your arguments.

Notes Master: The Notes Master enables you to create a set of speaker's notes for your presentation. Notes are a valuable tool for presenters to maintain control of a slide show and of their speech even if the slide show screen isn't directly viewable by them. Each default notes page has a print of one slide occupying the top half of the page with text notes entered below. Notes pages can be rearranged, with text boxes and slide images resized, to suit the user.

Handout Master: Defines a basic layout of audience handouts. A single handout page can have two, three, or six slides printed on it. The Handout Master displays several dashed boxes, which are simply indicators for where the different quantities of slides would be printed. The user does not edit or interact with the Handout Master; handouts are created by specifying the type of handouts that will be printed.

The Slide Master is the core of any slide show. It has items placed on it called *placeholders,* which are the building blocks of your slide show. Every slide you create also has placeholders of various kinds on it, which are used to define the basic size and location of objects on your slides. In a later section, you look at placeholders and see how to use them to define any slide layout.

Using Templates

Templates are used in two different ways: to create a new presentation, or to change the appearance of an existing presentation.

Selecting a Template to Create a New Presentation
Selecting a template, without using a Wizard, is identical to the process of selecting a presentation file to edit. In fact, you're doing the same thing. Loading a template is simply loading a presentation file that needs to have content added to it.

To load a new template, follow these steps:

1. From the **File** menu, choose **O**pen.

    The Open dialog box appears, as shown in figure 5.1.

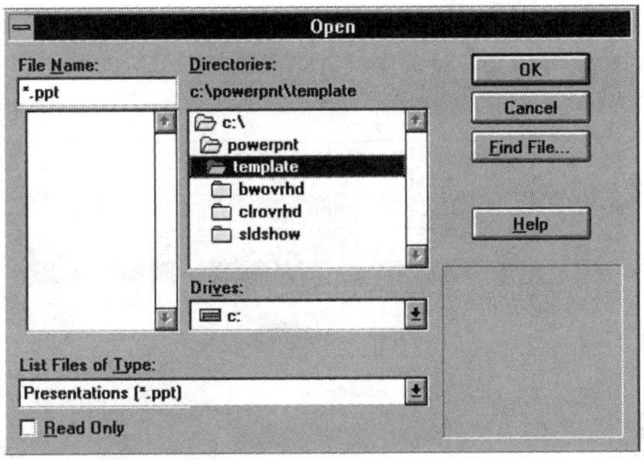

Fig. 5.1
Opening a new template file, which is functionally identical to opening a new presentation file.

PowerPoint 4 Basics

2. If you have more than one drive or drive partition on your system, locate it in the Drives drop-down list.

3. Locate the PowerPoint 4 directory on your hard disk (the default when you install PowerPoint is C:\POWERPNT, unless you specified another directory and/or drive) in the **D**irectories list.

   The PowerPoint directory has a subdirectory titled TEMPLATE.

4. Double-click the TEMPLATE subdirectory in the **D**irectories list. A new set of subdirectories appears.

   The TEMPLATE directory has another subdirectory titled SLDSHOW.

5. Double-click the SLDSHOW subdirectory in the **D**irectories list.

   A lengthy list of PowerPoint files appears in the File **N**ame list, as shown in figure 5.2.

6. Scroll down the File Name list until you see the file name FLAGS.PPT. (You can, however, choose any other file you want. It's just an example.)

7. Click on the file FLAGS.PPT.

8. Choose OK or press Enter.

A new PowerPoint presentation window pops up, displaying the FLAGS.PPT name in a new presentation, as shown in figure 5.3.

You've just opened a new template, and in the process created a new presentation without using a Wizard. Opening a template is literally the same thing as opening a new presentation—the only difference is that you do not name

Tip
Use the Save As command to change the current FLAGS.PPT file to another name and continue using the template.

the file yourself. Use the Save As command if you want to do so and prevent accidentally overwriting the original template file.

Fig. 5.2
The list of
files in the
C:\POWERPNT\
TEMPLATE\
SLDSHOW
directory.

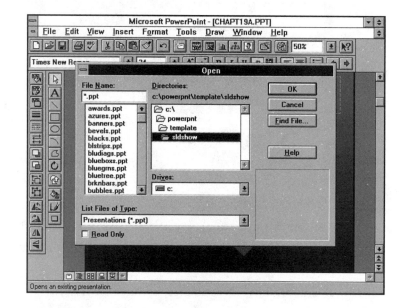

Fig. 5.3
Using the
FLAGS.PPT file
to create a new
presentation.

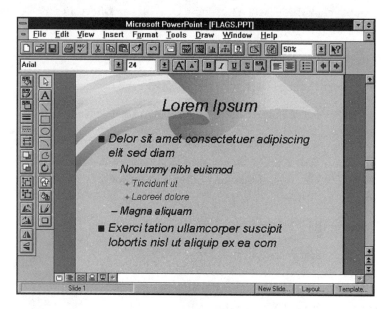

> **Note**
>
> *Avoid saving over existing template files.* The best and easiest way to do this is to click the **R**ead Only check box in the Open dialog box when you load a new template. If you place an X in this check box, you avoid any possibility of accidentally overwriting a PowerPoint original template file.

Modifying an Existing Presentation by Applying a Template

If you have a presentation open and you're not satisfied with how it looks, you can apply any other template to the existing file by following these steps:

1. Display the presentation that you want to change.

2. From the F**o**rmat menu, choose **P**resentation Template.

   The Presentation Template dialog box appears, as shown in figure 5.4.

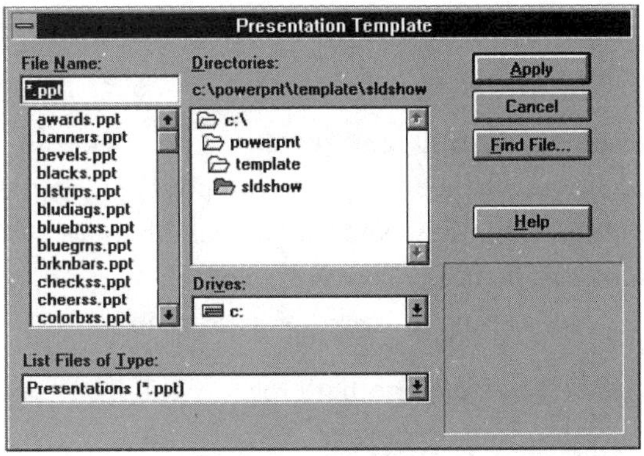

Fig. 5.4
Initiating the process of applying a template to an open presentation with the Presentation Template command.

3. If you have more than one drive or drive partition on your system, locate it in the Dri**v**es drop-down list.

4. Locate the PowerPoint 4 directory on your hard disk (the default when you install PowerPoint is C:\POWERPNT, unless you specified another directory and/or drive) in the **D**irectories list.

   The PowerPoint directory has a subdirectory titled TEMPLATE.

5. Double-click the TEMPLATE subdirectory in the **D**irectories list. A new set of subdirectories appears.

   The TEMPLATE directory has another subdirectory titled SLDSHOW.

Tip
The **A**pply button does duty for the OK button you normally see in PowerPoint dialog boxes. Selecting **A**pply applies the chosen template to the current presentation.

6. Double-click the SLDSHOW subdirectory in the **D**irectories list.

   A list of PowerPoint template files appears in the File **N**ame list.

7. Scroll down the File Name list until you see a template that looks interesting. Use the thumbnail in the bottom right corner to help you pick it out.

8. Click on the desired template file.

9. Choose **A**pply or press Enter.

The dialog box disappears and the currently displayed presentation begins to undergo its facelift. If you have any charts in the presentation, a message is displayed on-screen:

```
Charts are being updated with the new color scheme
```

After a moment or two, the process is complete and your presentation gets its new look. Text, default object colors, slide backgrounds, and charts all have a new color scheme.

Importing Templates from Other Presentation Packages

PowerPoint 4 supports the direct importing of presentation files from Lotus Freelance for DOS and Windows and Harvard Graphics for DOS and Windows. PowerPoint automatically converts color schemes, objects, and charts to its own format. It's a straightforward process to do so.

To import a presentation from another program, follow these steps:

1. From the **F**ile menu, choose **O**pen.

   The Open dialog box appears, as shown in figure 5.5.

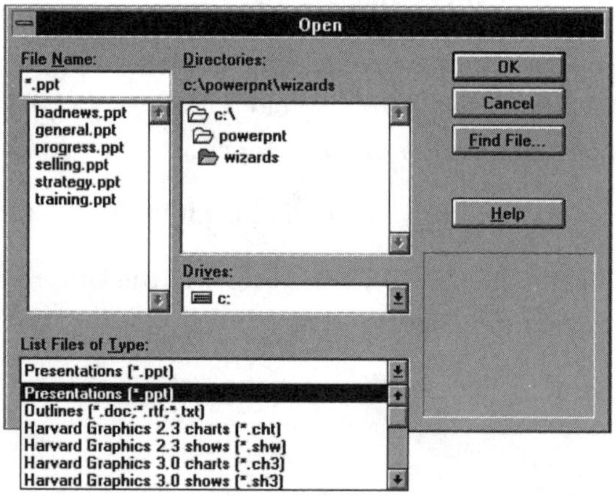

Fig. 5.5
Importing a presentation file or a chart from another package. A drop-down list shows the file types available for importing.

2. Click the down arrow in the List Files of **T**ype drop-down list.

3. If you have more than one drive or drive partition on your system, locate it in the Dri**v**es drop-down list.

4. Locate the directory on your hard disk that contains the presentation files you want to import in the **D**irectories list.

5. Choose the presentation file you want to import from the File **N**ame list. It must be a file that is specifically supported under the List Files of **T**ype list.

   Notice that several chart file types are available for importing. As you see later in this book, it's quite easy to import Microsoft Excel charts and datasheets as well, although they're not displayed in the list shown in figure 5.5. Other features are used in PowerPoint for that purpose, primarily in Microsoft Graph, the charting package that's bundled with PowerPoint.

6. Choose OK or press Enter.

After a moment, the imported presentation file is converted in PowerPoint, retaining its original color scheme, data, and charts.

PowerPoint 4 Basics

Note

You can also import outlines in several text formats by using the File Open dialog box. Along with the various presentation formats supported in the preceding example, the list also includes Outline, with four different file formats directly supported for text importing of outlines for a presentation:

*.DOC Microsoft Word for Windows

*.MCW Microsoft Word for DOS

*.RTF Rich Text Format (export format supported by many word processors)

*.TXT Standard ASCII text file format

Clicking on the Outline option enables you to locate the desired outline file. Importing the outline automatically converts it to a PowerPoint outline with slide titles and body text placed appropriately. For more information on this feature, see chapter 7, "Creating Speaker's Notes, Outlines, and Handouts."

Using PowerPoint's Sample Presentations and Templates

Browsing the Directories

As you have already seen in this chapter, the PowerPoint directory has a fairly complex directory structure. Everything in the PowerPoint program has a specific place, and PowerPoint relies on the files to be where they belong in order to run properly. Let's take a brief look at the contents of the PowerPoint directory, starting with its structure:

```
POWERPNT
        PCSFILES
        SAMPLES
        SETUP
        TEMPLATE
                BWOVRHD
                CLROVRHD
                SLDSHOW
        WIZARDS
        XLATORS
```

Of course, the PowerPoint directory name may change depending on whether you specified a different one during installation, but all of PowerPoint's subdirectories bear the names that are shown here. *Don't change them.* As mentioned, PowerPoint expects those directories to be named and placed exactly where they are. If they're changed, the program will probably not work at all.

> **Note**
>
> Don't change the names of any of PowerPoint's subdirectories. At the very least, the program will not be able to find important features. PowerPoint depends on its files and accompanying applets to be where it expects them to be. Almost every Windows program besides PowerPoint does pretty much the same thing, so this is a good rule of thumb for most programs you have on your system.

What are the contents of each directory? If you've worked with some of the earlier chapters in this book, you already have some idea of a few of them. Here's a complete breakdown:

POWERPNT   Contains the PowerPoint executable program plus support files and the Default template, which can be the default originally set by the program or a default set by the user.

PCSFILES

A subdirectory of the C:\POWERPNT directory containing PowerPoint's clip art files.

SAMPLES

A subdirectory of the C:\POWERPNT directory containing several sample PowerPoint presentation files for special applications, such as timeline graphics, flowcharting, and other tasks.

SETUP

The setup files directory, a subdirectory of the C:\POWERPNT directory, contains PowerPoint's Setup utility, which enables you to install or remove various parts of the program.

TEMPLATE

The template directory, a subdirectory of the C:\POWERPNT directory, contains three subdirectories; each holds a set of presentation templates that are tailored for a specific purpose.

BWOVRHD

This directory, a subdirectory of the C:\POWERPNT\TEMPLATE directory, contains template files that are specifically tailored for black-and-white overhead presentations.

CLROVRHD

This directory, a subdirectory of the C:\POWERPNT\TEMPLATE directory, contains template files that are specifically tailored for color overhead presentations.

SLDSHOW

This directory, a subdirectory of the C:\POWERPNT\TEMPLATE directory, contains template files that are specifically tailored for on-screen slide show presentations.

WIZARDS

This directory, a subdirectory of the C:\POWERPNT directory, contains several more Wizard-used sample presentations that are drawn upon by the Wizards and offered as alternatives for special messages for your presentation.

XLATORS

This directory, a subdirectory of the C:\POWERPNT directory, contains PowerPoint's support files for translating presentations of other formats for importing into PowerPoint.

Viewing PowerPoint's Sample Presentations

Two PowerPoint subdirectories, the C:\POWERPNT\SAMPLES directory and the C:\POWERPNT\WIZARDS directory, contain a small set of sample presentations that can be drawn upon (as can any of the many templates the program offers) for various graphic elements.

Whenever you decide to open another template or finished presentation file, you have the capability to preview any files before you apply them or open them. It's done by simply viewing the thumbnail preview window in the Open dialog box, as shown in figure 5.6.

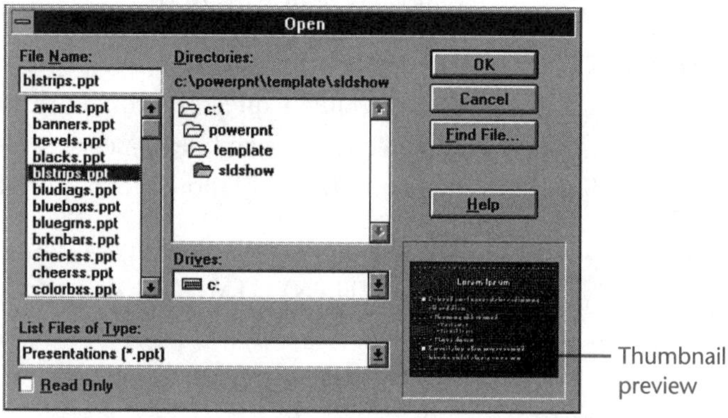

Fig. 5.6

Studying template types with the thumbnail preview. The thumbnail on the bottom right corner shows the appearance of each template as you click on it.

Thumbnail preview

Clicking once on each template name displays a color thumbnail view of the template's appearance. When a template appears that looks good to you, choose OK or press Enter, or double-click on the file name to load it.

To load a PowerPoint Sample Presentation, follow these steps:

1. From the **F**ile menu, choose **O**pen.

2. Locate the C:\POWERPNT\SAMPLES directory, or the C:\POWERPNT\WIZARDS directory, on your hard disk.

   Bear in mind that you may have installed PowerPoint in another directory and/or drive. If that's the case, simply select that drive and directory instead.

   The SAMPLES directory contains five sample presentations:

   CALENDAR.PPT
   FLOWCHRT.PPT
   PRINTME.PPT

    TABLES.PPT

    TIMELINE.PPT

The WIZARDS directory contains six more sample files:

    BADNEWS.PPT

    GENERAL.PPT

    PROGRESS.PPT

    SELLING.PPT

    STRATEGY.PPT

    TRAINING.PPT

3. Choose a sample presentation, such as PROGRESS.PPT.

4. Click the **R**ead Only check box in the bottom left corner of the Open dialog box.

5. Choose OK or press Enter.

The sample presentation is displayed in Outline view, as shown in figure 5.7.

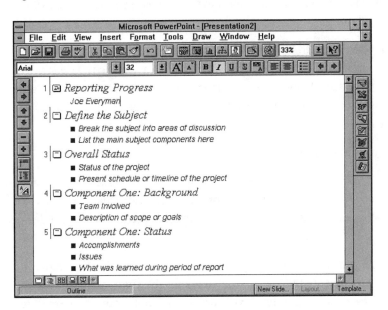

Fig. 5.7
The sample presentation displayed in Outline view.

6. From the **V**iew menu, choose **S**lides.

The sample presentation appears in Slide view and displays the various graphic elements of the template, as shown in figure 5.8.

Fig. 5.8

The sample
presentation
PROGRESS.PPT
displaying the
title slide.

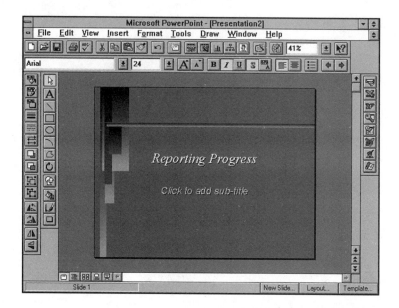

Feel free to explore the other sample presentations available. Many of them, particularly those in the C:\POWERPNT\SAMPLES directory, display some of the substantial graphic capabilities that you can take advantage of in PowerPoint.

Reviewing Sample Presentation Slides

Each sample presentation actually conforms to a specific type: a series of body text slides that when strung together, as in the samples, constitute a line of argument or a series of points made to deliver a specific message, such as a progress report like the framework used in PROGRESS.PPT.

To look at the slides in the sample presentation, follow this:

1. To advance to a body text slide, click the Next Slide icon (the double down-arrow button on the bottom of the Slide Changer). If you've loaded PROGRESS.PPT, as in the preceding steps, the next slide appears as in figure 5.9.

   As you can see, the sample doesn't provide the actual content, but it does provide the logical framework for the argument you want to present. Clicking the Next Slide icon again displays the next slide in the sequence, as shown in figure 5.10.

Any sample presentation can be studied in the same way. To close the sample presentation file, simply choose **C**lose from the **F**ile menu.

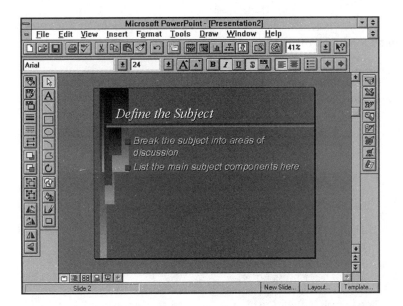

Fig. 5.9
The sample presentation PROGRESS.PPT displaying the next body text slide.

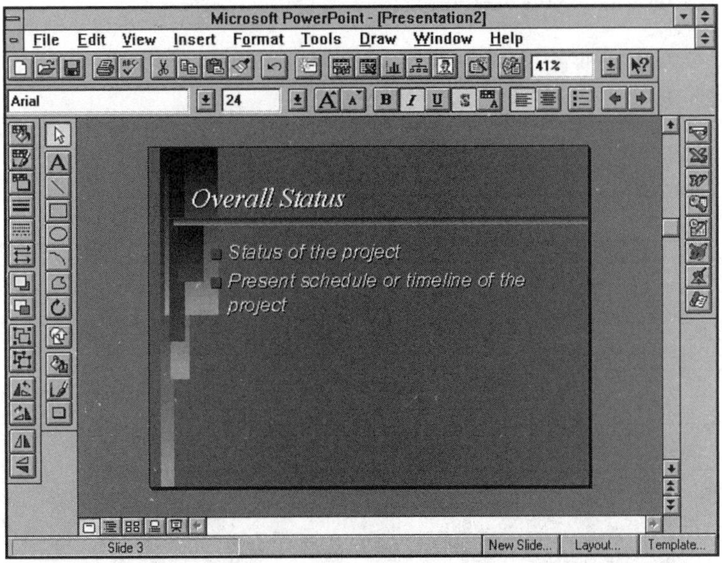

Fig. 5.10
The sample presentation PROGRESS.PPT displaying the third slide in sequence.

Using Elements from Sample Presentations and Templates

Because so many templates are offered with the program, why not use some of their graphic elements to embellish your own presentations? It's actually a simple process—essentially, a matter of copying and pasting. The key is understanding how to use the template properly. First, you display a template that offers some graphic objects that could be desirable in another presentation by following these steps:

1. From the **F**ile menu, choose **O**pen.

2. Locate the C:\POWERPNT\TEMPLATES\SLDSHOW directory on your hard disk.

   The list of templates appears in the File **N**ame list.

3. From the file list, choose the template file ISLANDS.PPT.

4. Click the **R**ead Only check box in the Open dialog box.

   This ensures that you won't cause any changes to the original template file.

5. Choose OK or press Enter.

   The template file is displayed. Now, to access the graphics elements of the template, you need to display the Slide Master.

6. From the **V**iew menu, select **M**aster. A submenu appears. Choose **S**lide Master.

   The Slide Master for the chosen template appears, as shown in figure 5.11.

Fig. 5.11
The template ISLANDS.PPT displaying the Slide Master.

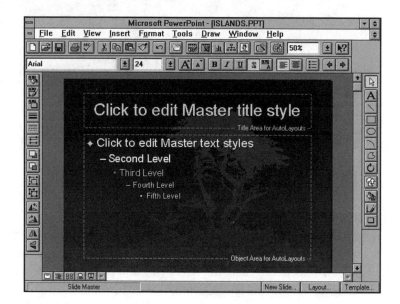

7. Click anywhere outside the placeholders on the Slide Master. The graphic object (a large tree on an island) is selected.

8. From the **E**dit menu, choose **C**opy; or press Ctrl+C.

   The Island graphic object has now been copied to the Windows clipboard.

9. Display the presentation to which you want to add the new graphic object.

10. From the **V**iew menu, select **M**aster. A submenu appears. Choose **S**lide Master.

    The Slide Master for the presentation to which you want to paste the graphic object appears.

11. If you want to paste the graphic only on one slide instead of on all of them, display the desired slide in the presentation.

12. From the **E**dit menu, choose **P**aste; or press Ctrl+V.

    The graphic copied from the template's Slide Master appears in the other presentation, as shown in figure 5.12.

Tip
When you paste a graphic from one presentation to another, the graphic automatically adjusts to the new color palette.

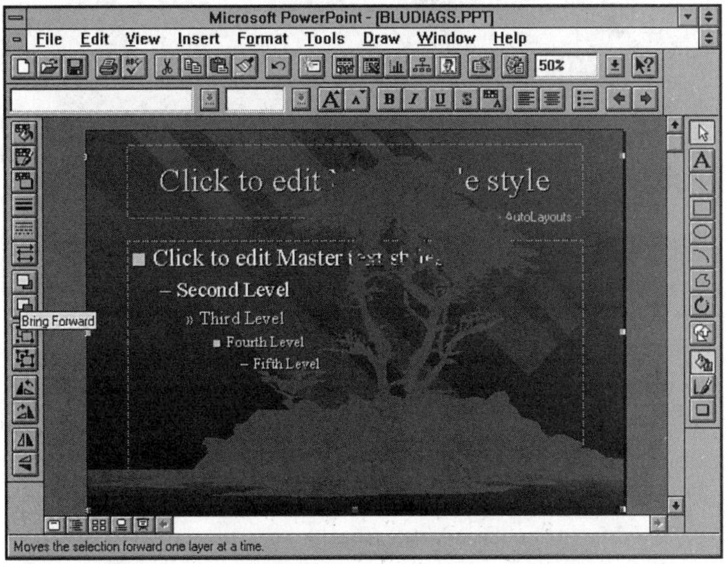

Fig. 5.12
The Island graphic displayed in an existing presentation's Slide Master.

Notice that the pasted graphic automatically conforms to the color palette of the presentation it's pasted into. Also notice that the pasted graphic needs some rearranging for a better placement on the Slide Master. The body text object and slide title object are obscured by the pasted graphic.

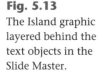

13. With the pasted graphic still selected, from the **D**raw menu choose Send **B**ackward. Or, click the Send Backward tool on PowerPoint's Drawing+ toolbar.

    The graphic is sent back one layer in the Slide Master.

14. With the pasted graphic still selected, from the **D**raw menu choose Send **B**ackward again.

    The graphic is now layered behind both text objects in the Slide Master, as shown in figure 5.13.

Fig. 5.13
The Island graphic layered behind the text objects in the Slide Master.

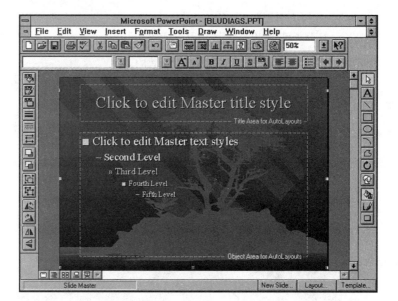

This example should be enough to point out some of the possibilities in working with graphic objects and other elements from different presentations. Items can be mixed, matched, and rearranged at will. The blue diagonal graphic, which is still layered behind the island graphic, could be deleted from the Slide Master, and if you do so (by clicking on the blue diagonal graphic and choosing the Cle**a**r command from the **E**dit menu), you have substantially changed the look of your template.

15. Save your new template by choosing Save **A**s from the **F**ile menu and following the normal steps for saving a file.

The next section expands on this powerful concept—the capability to create your own templates.

Creating Your Own Templates

In the preceding text, you learned some of the basics of working with template elements and applying them to other presentation files. By doing so, you have moved a long way down the road to creating your own special template.

If you like the look of the presentation file you created, it's a simple matter to create it as a template for future use.

> **Note**
>
> Don't save an existing presentation containing a bunch of slides as a template. The intended template file will be huge and contain a set of unwanted slides. The average PowerPoint template file is about 50K to 60K in size.

To create your own template, follow these steps:

1. Display the presentation whose appearance you want to create as a new template.

2. From the **V**iew menu, select **M**aster, and then choose **S**lide Master.

The current presentation's Slide Master appears.

3. From the **E**dit menu, choose Select A**l**l.

4. From the **F**ile menu, choose **N**ew.

The New Presentation dialog box appears, as shown in figure 5.14.

5. Choose the **C**urrent Presentation Format option button.

6. Press Enter or choose OK.

The New Slide dialog box appears displaying the slide AutoLayouts.

Tip
Press Ctrl+A to select the contents of a slide or Slide Master.

7. Choose the Title Slide AutoLayout.

8. Choose OK or press Enter.

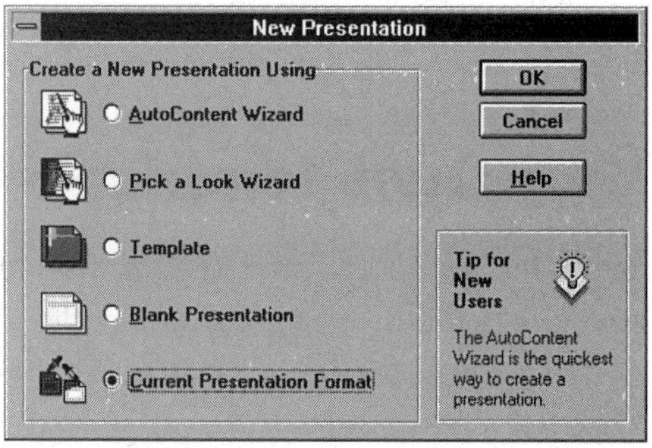

Fig. 5.14
Using the New
Presentation
dialog box to
help create a
new presentation
template.

To save the new presentation as a slide show template for later use, follow these steps:

1. From the **F**ile menu, choose Save **A**s.

   The Save As dialog box appears.

2. In the File Name text box, type in the name you want, such as **bluetree.ppt**.

3. Locate the C:\POWERPNT\TEMPLATE\SLDSHOW directory if it is not already displayed.

4. Choose Save or press Enter.

5. If the Summary Info dialog box appears, choose OK or press Enter again.

The new file is saved as a template. It is also a reasonable size, around 50–60K. You just created and saved a new template without affecting the contents of the existing presentation on which the new template was based.

Using Placeholders

Placeholders are homes for all the object types on your slides. Titles, body text, graphs, tables, clip art, movie clips, and sounds all reside in placeholders. As noted earlier, they are the building blocks of your presentation. Whenever you create a new slide, placeholders of specific types are automatically added to it by PowerPoint. That's why new slide types are called AutoLayouts by the program.

For example, when you create a Graph slide type, a chart object is added to a new slide, as is seen in figure 5.15.

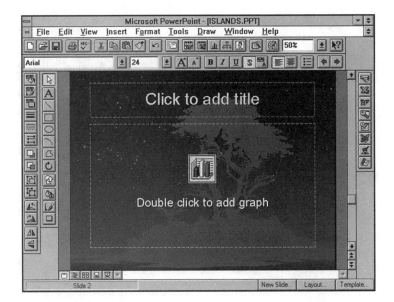

Fig. 5.15
The new chart slide displays a chart object.

Double-clicking on the Graph icon in the placeholder starts the Microsoft Graph application, which PowerPoint uses to create charts.

Nonetheless, that chart object is only a placeholder, and doesn't have to hold a chart. It can hold any other object type available in your system. All that has to be done is to select the placeholder and choose a different type of object to be placed in it. For example, you can insert a piece of clip art into the chart placeholder by following these steps:

1. Click inside the placeholder to select it.

2. From the **I**nsert menu, choose **C**lip Art.

    After a moment, the ClipArt Gallery appears.

3. Choose a category of art from the Choose a **c**ategory list.

4. Click on an art thumbnail.

5. Choose OK or press Enter.

The new artwork is inserted into the placeholder and assumes the shape of the placeholder (see fig. 5.16). The Graph icon disappears.

Fig. 5.16
Inserting a piece of artwork into a placeholder with the ClipArt Gallery.

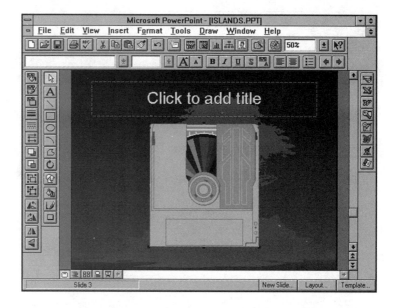

Tip
Placeholders are generic items on your slides that can have their contents changed with a few mouse clicks.

Placeholders are generic items on a slide. As you can see, they are capable of holding any object you can use in PowerPoint. They can be resized, cut and pasted, copied and reproduced, and deleted. They are totally flexible and changeable to the needs of the user.

Figure 5.16 shows a piece of clip art inside a placeholder. The clip art sizes itself to the size and shape of the placeholder, and may not automatically appear the way you want it to. In figure 5.16, the art has a distorted aspect ratio. Grab a corner or side pressure point to resize and reshape the clip art until it looks the way you want.

Adding a Company Logo and Company Name to a Template

Through most of this chapter, you used the Slide Master as the tool for applying and changing templates in the program. The Slide Master is also the key tool for another important task: adding a company name and logo to every slide in your presentation. Of course, since PowerPoint doesn't offer a selection of company logos as part of its clip art collection, you very likely have to draw your own by using PowerPoint or another drawing program. For the example, a simple logo can be created using a small text object and a piece of clip art.

To place a company logo in your presentation, follow these steps:

1. From the **V**iew menu, select **M**aster, and then choose **S**lide Master.

   The Slide Master is where the company logo is placed.

2. Import the picture containing your company logo (from the **I**nsert menu, choose **P**icture) or use PowerPoint's drawing and clip art tools to create a logo yourself.

3. Place the graphic object in an acceptable place in your Slide Master (in a corner of the Slide Master, for instance), as shown in figure 5.17.

Tip
For a precise placement of your logo, display PowerPoint's Rulers and use the Zoom feature.

PowerPoint 4 Basics

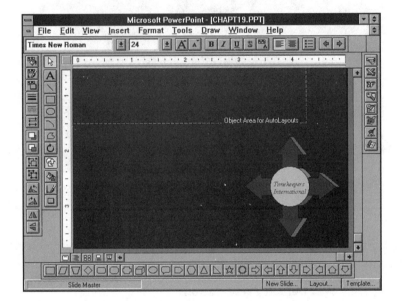

Fig. 5.17
Using the Slide Master to place a company logo on all the slides of your presentation.

The logo appears in the bottom right corner of every slide.

To add a company name to the Slide Master, follow these steps:

1. Click the Text tool in the Drawing toolbar.

2. Click the mouse in the approximate location on the Slide Master where the company name can be placed (near the bottom, perhaps). A text object appears, ready for editing.

3. Type in the company name.

4. Change the font size by clicking the Font Size drop-down list and choosing a different font size.

5. If you want, change the color of the company name by clicking the Text Color tool on the Standard toolbar and choosing another color (make sure it's a color that stands out well against the Slide Master background).

The end results should resemble figure 5.18.

Fig. 5.18
A logo and company name have been placed on the Slide Master.

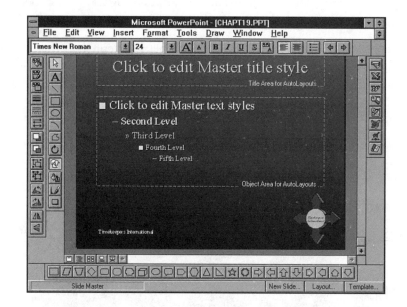

The logo and company name appear on every slide in the current presentation, providing consistency and identification to the slides (see fig. 5.19).

Saving Your Own Default Presentation

When you add special elements to a template, such as a company logo, it may be desirable to save that template as the default. Doing so ensures consistency in the image that anyone's presentation conveys. Or, perhaps you just crafted a presentation template that is very pleasing to you, and it would be a smashing way to start out any presentation.

Fortunately, it's almost shamefully easy to create a new default presentation using the current template. The advantage to doing so is that a preferred presentation format can be used by many employees—for example, several people in a corporate P.R. department could be required to use a presentation template that uses the company's specific color scheme. Here's how:

1. Display the presentation that the default is to be modeled after.

2. From the **F**ile menu, choose Save **A**s.

   The Save As dialog box appears.

3. Use the **D**irectories and Dri**v**es lists to move to the PowerPoint application directory (for example, C:\POWERPNT).

4. In the File Name text box, type the name **default.ppt**.

5. Choose OK or press Enter.

That is all there is to it. To check your default, simply create a new presentation.

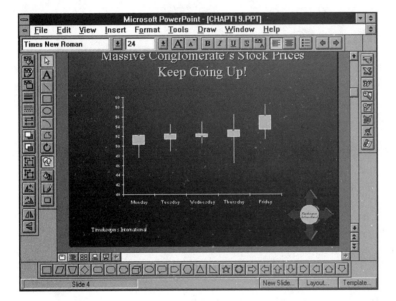

Fig. 5.19
All slides bear the logo and company name.

PowerPoint 4 Basics

Troubleshooting

I made a mistake and overwrote one of my original template files.

It isn't a big deal. In the end, all you have to do is copy the original compressed file from the installation disks. (Save your changed file under another name in case you want to use it later.) Whenever a file is compressed on an installation floppy disk, it has an underline (_) character at its end, such as BLUEDIAG.PP_ or BADNEWS.PP_. You have to locate your template file this way. The name of your template file will be the same except for the underline. The underline denotes a compressed file. You have to then uncompress it to make it work.

(continues)

(continued)

You may have to search through several floppies before you find the file you're looking for; in MS-DOS, do a DIR A: command for each of the PowerPoint installation floppies until you find the desired file. Then, make sure you're in the C:\POWERPNT\TEMPLATE directory, and execute the following MS-DOS command:

        EXPAND A:*TEMPLATE*.PP_

where *TEMPLATE* represents the name of the file you want. The DOS EXPAND command reads the file off the floppy disk and automatically places the file's uncompressed version in your current directory.

From Here...

In the last several chapters, you've worked with many critical areas in the PowerPoint program. You learned how to create a basic presentation and glanced at many features that bear deeper study in later chapters, such as artwork, working with text, and looking at the various Masters in PowerPoint.

- Chapter 6, "Working with Text," discusses using PowerPoint's Ruler and the fine points of working with text in all of PowerPoint's Views in greater detail.

- Chapter 7, "Creating Speaker's Notes, Handouts, and Outlines," shows you how to produce and work with those important elements of a presentation.

- Chapter 9, "Drawing Objects," describes how to use PowerPoint's flexible and powerful drawing features.

- Chapter 11, "Selecting, Editing, and Enhancing Objects," shows how to change and edit objects of various types in greater detail.

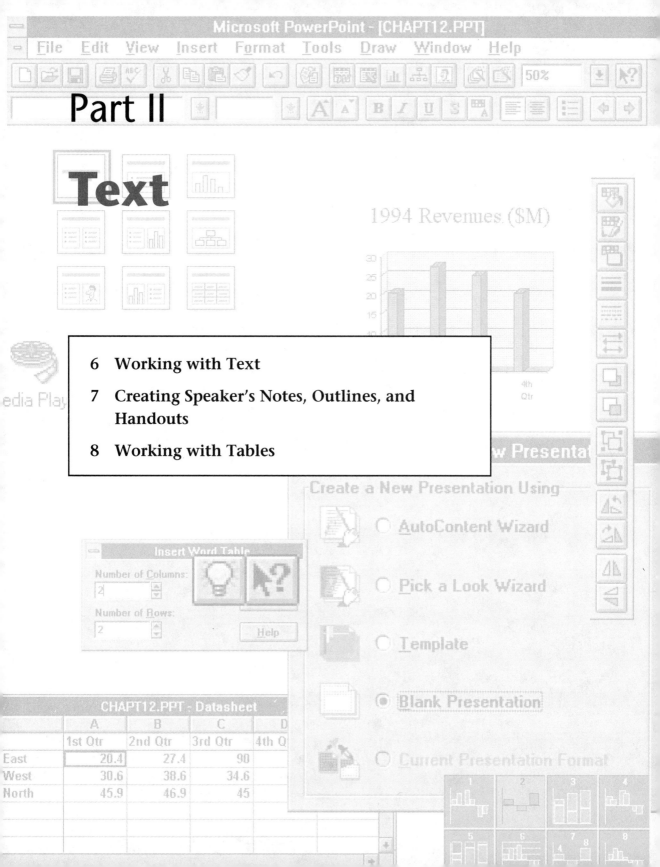

Part II

Text

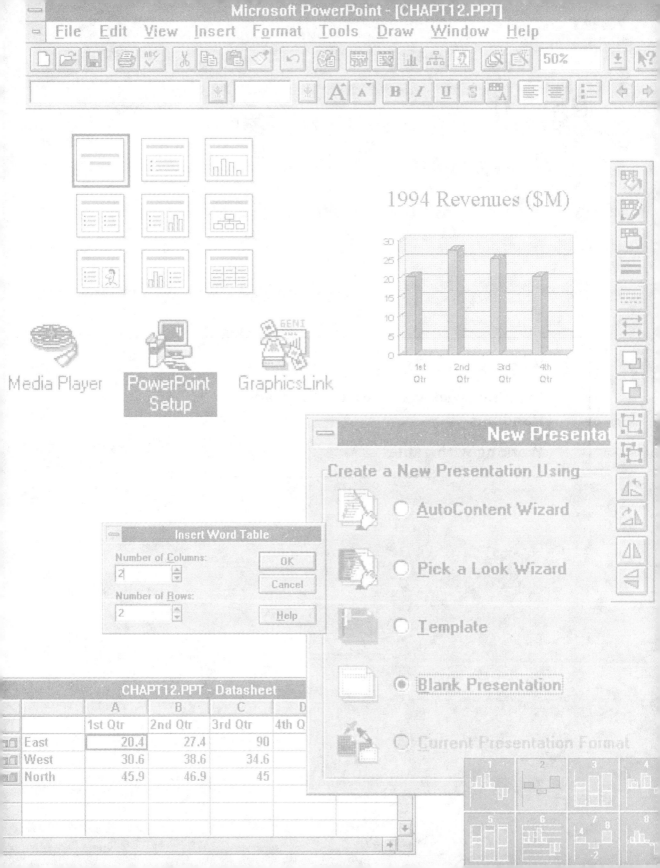

Chapter 6

Working with Text

In most presentations, bulleted lists and other text charts predominate. Fortunately, PowerPoint makes it easy to create text charts and to automatically apply a consistent format to all text charts in a presentation. Features such as Smart Cut and Paste and Automatic Word Selection simplify common tasks such as copying and moving text. In addition, you can use the following features to eliminate many common inconsistencies in text charts:

Major topics
in this chapter
include:

■ Creating text

■ Deleting,
copying, and
moving text

■ Formatting text

■ Using the spell-
ing checker

■ Manipulating
and enhancing
text placeholders

- *The Slide Master,* which enables you to set the basic format—font, type color, bullet shape, tabs, and so forth—for title and body text in all slides in a presentation.

- *The Change Case command,* which enables you to change selected text to uppercase, lowercase, title case (capitalizes initial letters), or sentence case (capitalizes the initial letter of the first word).

- *The Period command,* which enables you to add or delete periods from the end of selected paragraphs, such as bulleted list items.

- *The Spelling Checker,* which enables you to check the spelling of all text in your presentation.

In this chapter, you learn how to create and manipulate text on a slide. You also learn many shortcuts for working with text. In addition to the basics of entering, editing, and formatting text, it addresses the special features noted above, except for the Slide Master, which is discussed in chapter 4, "Setting Up Your New Presentation."

Understanding Text Placeholders

In PowerPoint, you enter all text in text placeholders, such as those shown in figure 6.1.

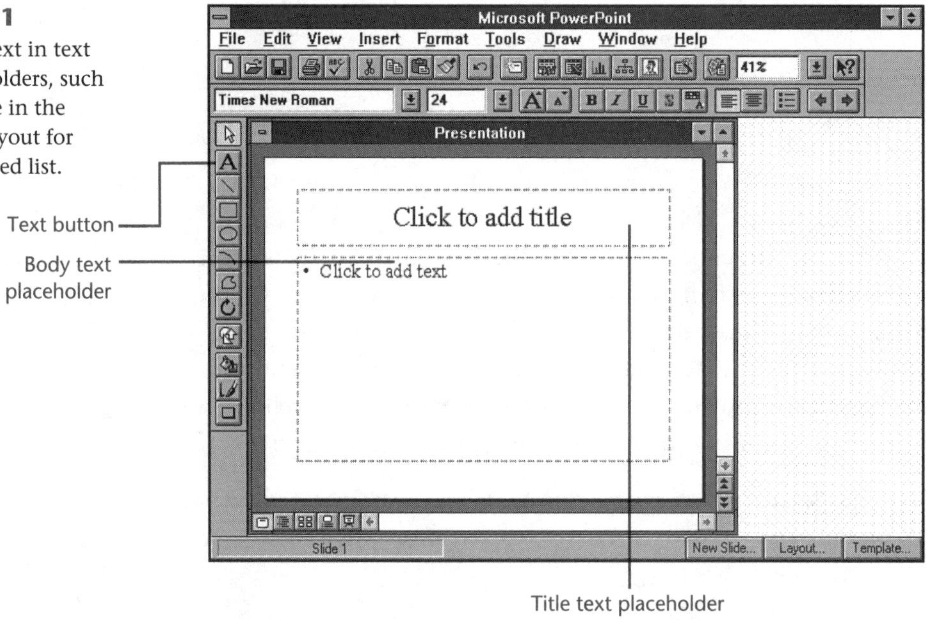

Fig. 6.1
Enter text in text placeholders, such as these in the AutoLayout for a bulleted list.

Text button

Body text placeholder

Title text placeholder

PowerPoint has two types of text placeholders:

- Preset text placeholders, such as those that appear in AutoLayouts. As shown in figure 6.1, these placeholders initially contain the prompt Click to add title (for title placeholders) or Click to add text (for body text placeholders). Once you add text, the prompt disappears.

- Placeholders that you create using the Text button (refer to fig. 6.1). You might use such placeholders, for example, to create labels or other text outside the preset placeholders. Text created using the Text button does not appear in Outline view.

Creating Text

Creating text is as simple as clicking in a text placeholder and typing the text. If you are entering title or body text, PowerPoint has already created the text placeholders for you. If you are creating a label or other special text, you must create the placeholder before you can type the text. This section describes both of these procedures.

Creating Title and Body Text

When you create a slide, one of your first steps is selecting the AutoLayout for the type of slide you are creating. As described in chapter 3, AutoLayouts set up the general layout for each type of slide. The AutoLayout for a bulleted list, for example, includes a placeholder for the chart title and a placeholder for the bulleted list (refer to fig. 6.1). When you initially click in the bulleted list placeholder, a bullet appears; thereafter, a new bullet automatically appears whenever you press Enter to start a new list item. (For more information on AutoLayouts, see chapter 3, "Quick Start: Creating a First Presentation.")

In all AutoLayouts, PowerPoint automatically creates a text placeholder for the title, and if the chart is a text chart, a second text placeholder for the subtitle or body text. Figure 6.2, for example, shows the AutoLayout for a title slide, and figure 6.3 shows the AutoLayout for a chart. These AutoLayout placeholders are often the only text placeholders you need.

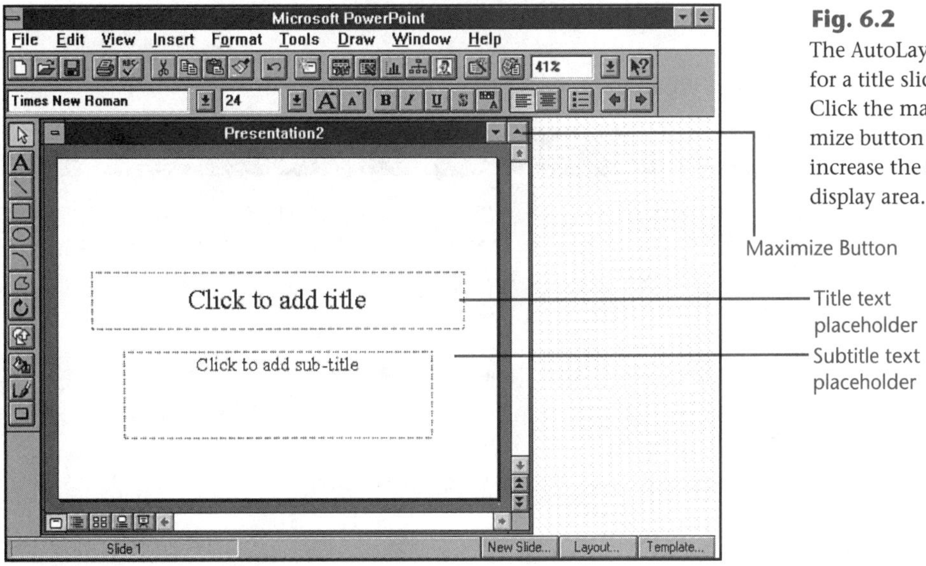

Tip

To maximize the area of the slide on-screen, click the Maximize button, shown in figure 6.2. Figure 6.3 shows a slide with maximum area displayed.

Fig. 6.2
The AutoLayout for a title slide. Click the maximize button to increase the slide display area.

Maximize Button

Title text placeholder

Subtitle text placeholder

Fig. 6.3
The AutoLayout
for a chart.

Title text
placeholder

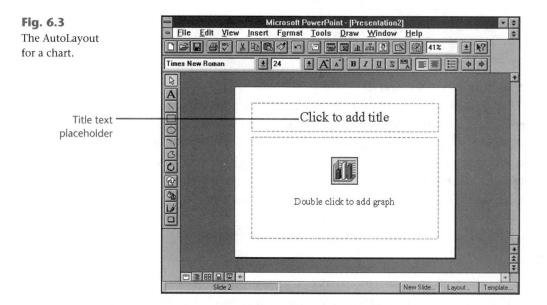

To enter text in an AutoLayout placeholder, follow these steps:

1. Click inside the placeholder. The blinking text insertion point appears.

2. Type the text.

Later in this chapter, you learn how to edit and format the text.

> **Note**
>
> The shape of the mouse pointer differs depending on the type of operation you are performing. Within a text placeholder, the mouse pointer looks like an I-beam. This indicates you are in an area where you can enter and edit text.

Creating Labels and Other Special Text

To label an object in a slide or to add special text, such as the date, use the Text button. This lets you add text anywhere on a slide.

The procedure for using the Text button depends on whether you want text exceeding a certain width to automatically wrap to a new line. For short text such as labels, this isn't a concern. You add such text by following these steps:

1. Display the slide in Slide view.

2. Click the Text button, shown in figure 6.4.

3. Move the mouse pointer where you want the new text to begin.

4. Click the left mouse button to fix the text insertion point at that location. The gray outline of a text placeholder appears with the text insertion point inside (see fig. 6.4).

5. Type the text. The text placeholder expands to accommodate the text.

6. To start another line, press Enter. The text box automatically expands to include the next line. Type the text for that line.

Tip
To automatically add the date, time, or slide number to all your slides, insert a date, time, or page number code on the Slide Master. See chapter 4, "Setting Up Your New Presentation," for more information.

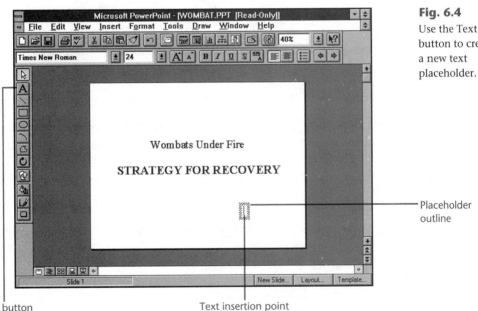

Text button

Text insertion point

Fig. 6.4
Use the Text button to create a new text placeholder.

Placeholder outline

> **Note**
>
> If an AutoLayout title or body text placeholder is not used (that is, if the placeholder still displays the prompt `Click here to add...`), you cannot use the Text button inside that box. If you don't need that placeholder, you can just delete it; then you can use the Text button. If you want to keep the placeholder and place a label inside it, create the label anywhere *outside* the existing placeholder and then move the label inside the text placeholder. To move the label, click on the label to display the gray outline of the placeholder, place the mouse pointer on the gray outline, press and hold the left mouse button, drag the outline to the correct location, and release the mouse button.

Tip

You can also add labels to notes pages, handouts, and outlines. Such labels appear only on those pages— not on the slide. See chapter 7, "Creating Speaker's Notes, Outlines, and Handouts," for details.

The procedure just given is suitable for short labels, where automatic word wrapping isn't necessary. You can also use the Text button, however, to create a text placeholder of a specific size, where text automatically wraps to the next line when it exceeds the placeholder width. To do so, follow these steps:

1. Display the slide in Slide view.

2. Click the Text button.

3. Move the mouse pointer where you want the new text to begin.

4. Press *and hold* the left mouse button. This sets the left edge of the new text placeholder.

5. Still pressing the left mouse button, drag the mouse pointer to where you want to fix the right edge of the new placeholder (notice that as you drag the mouse pointer, the outline of a text placeholder appears and expands as you move the pointer) and release the left mouse button.

   When you release the mouse button, PowerPoint creates a text placeholder that is the selected width and one line long. The text insertion point appears inside the placeholder.

6. Type the text. Any text that exceeds the width of the placeholder automatically wraps to a new line, and the text placeholder automatically expands to include the new line.

You can resize any text placeholder, as explained later in this chapter in "Manipulating Text Placeholders." The text within automatically rewraps to fit the new size. If you used the first procedure—which doesn't enable word wrapping—to add text to a slide, you can later enable word wrapping simply by resizing that text placeholder.

Moving the Insertion Point within Text and Between Text Placeholders

In a text placeholder, the text you type is entered at the location of the insertion point, which is a vertical bar that blinks on and off. You can move the insertion point by placing the mouse pointer where you want the insertion point to appear and clicking the left mouse button. You can also use the following keys and key combinations to move the insertion point:

Press...	To Move the Insertion Point...
→	Right one character
←	Left one character
↑	Up one line
↓	Down one line
Ctrl+→	Right one word
Ctrl+←	Left one word
Ctrl+↑	Up one paragraph
Ctrl+↓	Down one paragraph
Home	To the beginning of the line
End	To the end of the line

To move to another text placeholder, just click in that placeholder. You also can move to the next placeholder by pressing Ctrl+Enter. (If you press Ctrl+Enter in the last text placeholder on a slide, PowerPoint creates a new slide and moves to the first text placeholder on the new slide.)

Selecting Text

For many operations involving text, you must begin by selecting the text. To make existing text italic, for example, you select that text and then choose

Tip

To enable word wrapping in any text placeholder, choose Format from the main menu, select Text Anchor, choose Word-wrap Text in Object, and then choose OK.

Italic (see "Changing Text Attributes" later in this chapter). Selected text is highlighted on-screen in reverse video.

Like most Windows programs, PowerPoint allows you to use the keyboard or the mouse to select text. This section describes the most common selection techniques.

Mouse Techniques

You can use the mouse to select a single word, a paragraph, or a text block of any length.

To select a word or paragraph, use these techniques:

To Select	Do This
A word	Double-click anywhere in the word.
A paragraph	Triple-click anywhere in the paragraph.

To select a block of text, you can use either of two methods. The first method uses the mouse:

1. Place the mouse pointer where you want the selection to begin.

2. Press and hold the left mouse button.

3. Drag the mouse pointer to where you want the selection to end.

4. Release the left mouse button.

The second method for selecting a block uses the mouse and the Shift key:

1. Place the mouse pointer where you want the selection to begin.

2. Click the left mouse button.

3. Place the mouse pointer where you want the selection to end.

4. Press the Shift key while clicking the left mouse button again.

Note

If Automatic Word Selection is on, PowerPoint selects an entire word if one letter of the word is selected (see "Using Automatic Word Selection" later in this section).

Keyboard Technique

To use the keyboard to select text, follow these steps:

1. Place the insertion point where you want the selection to begin.

2. Press *and hold* the Shift key.

3. Press the arrow keys to move the highlight to the end of the text you want to select.

4. Release the Shift key.

> **Note**
>
> The Automatic Word Selection feature, which automatically selects a word when any letter in that word is selected, does not work with the keyboard technique. See the next section for information on this feature.

Using Automatic Word Selection

PowerPoint's Automatic Word Selection feature automatically selects a word when any letter of that word is selected with the mouse. It also selects the space following a word or a period. Automatic Word Selection often speeds editing, because it eliminates the need to carefully position the mouse pointer at the precise beginning and end of text you want to select; instead, you place the mouse anywhere in the first and last words you want to select. If you've ever had too many cups of coffee and the consequent jittery hands, you know how valuable this feature can be.

By default, Automatic Word Selection is turned on. To turn it off, follow these steps:

1. From the main menu, choose **T**ools. The **T**ools menu appears.

2. From the **T**ools menu, choose **O**ptions to display the Options dialog box.

3. Select the Automatic **W**ord Selection check box.

4. Choose OK.

Tip

Even when Automatic Word Selection is on, you can still select a portion of a word by using the keyboard technique described in the preceding section.

Editing Text

No slide presentation is perfect on the first try. In fact, chances are you will edit the text several times before you're satisfied. This section teaches not only basic text editing techniques, but also PowerPoint shortcuts that can simplify the editing process. If you use a Windows word processing program, many of the editing techniques described in this section will be familiar.

Inserting Text

To insert text in an existing text placeholder, place the insertion point where you want to insert the text and type the text. Remember that you can use the arrow keys or the mouse to move the insertion point. To use the arrow keys, just press them (see "Moving the Insertion Point within Text and Between Text Placeholders" earlier in this chapter). To use the mouse, place the mouse pointer where you want the insertion point and click the left mouse button.

Deleting Text

Use the Delete or Backspace key to delete text. To delete characters one by one, follow these steps:

1. Place the insertion point where you want to begin deleting text.

2. To delete the character to the *right* of the insertion point, press the Delete key. To delete the character to the *left* of the insertion point, press the Backspace key.

To delete a block of text, select the block and then press Delete or Backspace. You can also replace a selected block with new text. To do so, just select the block and then type the new text; PowerPoint automatically deletes the original text and inserts the new text at that location.

Moving or Copying Text

You can move or copy text within a text placeholder and between text place-holders—even between placeholders on different slides. The procedure is the same for each case.

To move text, follow these steps:

1. Select the text you want to move.

2. Use one of the following methods to cut the text from its current location:

■ Press Ctrl+X.

■ From the main menu, choose **E**dit to display the **E**dit menu. From the **E**dit menu, choose Cu**t**.

■ Click the Cut button (see fig. 6.5).

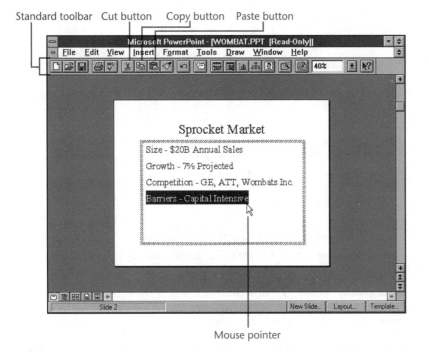

Fig. 6.5
The Standard toolbar contains buttons for cutting, copying, and pasting text.

3. Place the insertion point where you want to insert the text.

4. Use one of the following methods to paste the text in its new location:

■ Press Ctrl+V.

■ From the main menu, choose **E**dit to display the **E**dit menu. From the **E**dit menu, choose **P**aste.

■ Click the Paste button (refer to fig. 6.5).

To copy text, follow these steps:

1. Select the text you want to copy.

2. Use one of the following methods to copy the text from its current location:

   ■ Press Ctrl+C.

   ■ From the main menu, choose **E**dit to display the **E**dit menu. From the **E**dit menu, choose **C**opy.

   ■ Click the Copy button (refer to fig. 6.5).

3. Place the insertion point where you want to insert the copy of the text.

4. Use one of the following methods to paste the copy in its new location:

   ■ Press Ctrl+V.

   ■ From the main menu, choose **E**dit to display the **E**dit menu. From the **E**dit menu, choose **P**aste.

   ■ Click the Paste button (refer to fig. 6.5).

 With PowerPoint's drag-and-drop feature, you can also move or copy selected text to a new location within the text placeholder simply by dragging the text to the new location. You can use the drag and drop feature in Slide, Notes, and Outline views. The procedure is the same in each case:

1. Select the text you want to move or copy.

2. Place the mouse pointer over the selected text. The pointer should look like the arrow shown in figure 6.5; if it doesn't, move it over the selection until it does.

3. To *move* the selected text, press and hold the left mouse button. To *copy* the text, press and hold both the Ctrl key and the left mouse button.

   In both cases, a "shadow" pointer and a box representing the text appear by the mouse pointer and move as you move the mouse pointer. If you are copying the text, a plus sign (+) also appears next to the mouse pointer.

4. Move the mouse pointer until the shadow pointer is where you want to insert the text. If the selected text includes a space, you can place the shadow pointer between words but not within words.

5. Release the mouse button to insert the text at that location.

When you move or copy text, PowerPoint's Smart Cut and Paste feature automatically adjusts the spaces before and after words. The Smart Cut and Paste feature appears as an option in the Options dialog box. To display this dialog box, select **T**ools from the main menu, and then select **O**ptions. By default, PowerPoint selects the Use **S**mart Cut and Paste option. To disable this feature, clear the Use **S**mart Cut and Paste check box and choose OK.

Moving List Items Up and Down

To simplify editing further, PowerPoint enables you to quickly move list items up or down in the list by following these steps:

1. Click anywhere in the bulleted list.

2. Move the mouse pointer left of the list item until the pointer looks like a four-sided arrow.

3. Press and hold the left mouse button. The list item is highlighted.

4. Drag the mouse pointer where you want to insert the item. As you drag the pointer, it changes to a double-sided arrow. A horizontal line indicates the pointer's location in the list.

5. Release the left mouse button.

Changing the Case of Text

If many persons are involved in a presentation, inconsistencies in the text are common. Inconsistent use of letter case is one of the most frequent problems. It also used to be one of the most time-consuming to fix because you had to retype the text in the correct case. Not any more. PowerPoint includes an automated Change Case feature that enables you to change selected text to any of the following cases:

- Lowercase: these are lowercase letters.

- Uppercase: THESE ARE UPPERCASE LETTERS.

- Title case: Title Case Uses Initial Capital Letters, As Shown Here.

- Sentence case: Sentence case capitalizes only the initial letter of the first word, as in a sentence.

You can also toggle the cases in selected text so that lowercase letters change to uppercase and uppercase letters change to lowercase.

Tip
You can quickly
toggle among the
cases by pressing
Shift+F3.

To change the case of text, follow these steps:

1. Select the text you want to change.

2. From the main menu, choose F**o**rmat. The F**o**rmat menu appears.

3. From the F**o**rmat menu, choose Change Cas**e** to display the
   Change Case dialog box.

4. Select the case you want.

5. Choose OK.

Adding or Removing Periods at the End of List Items

Another common inconsistency is the use of periods at the end of list items.
Inevitably, some lists do not conform to your convention. As you may have
guessed, PowerPoint also simplifies the task of fixing this problem. You can
quickly add or remove periods from the end of list items by following these
steps:

1. Select the items you want to change.

2. From the main menu, choose F**o**rmat. The F**o**rmat menu appears.

3. From the F**o**rmat menu, choose Pe**r**iods to display the Periods
   dialog box.

4. Select **A**dd Periods or **R**emove Periods.

5. Choose OK.

Finding and Replacing Text

PowerPoint's Find feature and Find and Replace feature enable you to search
for text and replace it with different text. To quickly display a slide, use the
Find feature to search for text that appears only on that slide.

To search for text, follow these steps:

1. Open the slide presentation you want to search.

2. Press Ctrl+F. Alternatively, choose **E**dit from the main menu to display
   the **E**dit menu; from the **E**dit menu, choose **F**ind. The Find dialog box
   appears, as shown in figure 6.6.

Fig. 6.6
The Find
dialog box.

3. In the Find What text box, type the text you want to find.

4. To find only text that matches the case you entered, select the Match Case check box. If you enter **CAMP** in the Find What text box and select Match Case, for example, PowerPoint finds only *CAMP*. If you don't select Match Case, PowerPoint finds *CAMP, Camp, camp,* and all other instances of the word *camp*.

5. To find only whole words that match the text you entered, select the Find **W**hole Words Only check box. PowerPoint finds only instances where the text is preceded and followed by a space or punctuation.

6. Choose **F**ind Next. PowerPoint goes to the first instance of text that matches the Find criteria.

7. To find the next instance, repeat step 6.

8. When you finish searching, choose Close.

To search for text and replace it with different text, follow these steps:

1. Open the slide presentation you want to search.

2. Press Ctrl+H. Alternatively, from the main menu, choose **E**dit to display the **E**dit menu; from the **E**dit menu, choose R**e**place. The Replace dialog box appears.

3. In the Find What text box, type the text you want to find.

4. To find only text that matches the case you entered, select the Match Case check box. To find only whole words that match the text you entered, select the Find **W**hole Words Only check box.

5. In the Re**p**lace With text box, type the text you want to replace the original text.

Tip
To display the last four words for which you searched, click the Find What button in the Find or Replace dialog box.

6. To replace *all* instances of the original text with the new text, choose Replace **A**ll. PowerPoint does not prompt you to confirm that you want the text replaced.

   To choose the instances where the new text replaces the original text, select **F**ind Next. PowerPoint goes to the first instance of text that matches the Find criteria. If you want to replace that text, select **R**eplace. To find the next instance, repeat the steps in this paragraph.

7. When you finish, choose Close.

Replacing Fonts

Suppose you develop a presentation for several of your company's offices, and then find that some of the offices cannot print the fonts you use. With PowerPoint, you can quickly replace these fonts with other fonts the office *can* print. To do so, follow these steps:

1. Open the presentation you want to change.

2. From the main menu, choose **T**ools. The **T**ools menu appears.

3. From the **T**ools menu, choose Replace **F**onts to display the Replace Fonts dialog box.

4. Click the Re**p**lace button to list the fonts used in the presentation, and then select the font you want to replace.

5. Click the **W**ith button to list available fonts; then select the replacement font.

6. Choose **R**eplace. PowerPoint replaces all instances of the font throughout the presentation.

Troubleshooting

Is there a fast way to delete all text in a placeholder?

With the insertion point in the placeholder, press Ctrl+A. This selects all text in the placeholder. Then press the Delete or Backspace key.

To conserve space, I want to use " and ' as symbols for inch and foot (or second and minute); but whenever I press the " and ' keys, I get real quotation marks. How can I get inch and foot (second and minute) symbols?

Disable the Smart Quotes feature, which automatically enters true double and single quotation marks when you press the " and ' keys.

To disable the feature, choose **T**ools from the main menu and then choose **O**ptions. In the Options dialog box, clear the Replace Straight **Q**uotes with Smart Quotes check box and choose OK. This won't change true quotation marks already in the presentation—only quotation marks you subsequently enter. If you later need true quotation marks, just reselect the Replace Straight **Q**uotes with Smart Quotes check box.

How can I select part of a word, rather than the whole word?

The easiest way is to use the keyboard: Place the insertion point where you want the selection to begin and then press and hold the Shift key while pressing the arrow keys to extend your selection; when you're finished selecting text, release the Shift key. (You couldn't select part of a word because you were using the mouse to select it. By default, PowerPoint automatically selects whole words when you use the mouse to select more than one word. For more information on this feature, including how to disable it, see "Using Automatic Word Selection" earlier in this chapter.)

Formatting Text

The Master Slide sets the default format for the title and body text in a slide. This includes the text font, size, and color; the bullet shape, size, and color; and the tabs, line spacing, and justification. If you want a format to affect all slides in your presentation, set the format in the Master Slide (see chapter 4). PowerPoint automatically reformats all slides according to the new Master Slide format.

To change the characteristics of individual words or paragraphs in a slide, however, you must make the changes on the slide itself. A common example is when you emphasize key words by making them boldface or by changing their color. Formats you enter on individual slides are preserved even if you change the format for the corresponding text in the Master Slide.

Changing Text Attributes

PowerPoint provides you great flexibility in choosing the appearance of your text, allowing you to change the following text characteristics:

■ *Font.* In PowerPoint, a *font* is a type family, such as Times New Roman or Switzerland Condensed (see fig. 6.7). You can select one of the TrueType fonts installed with PowerPoint or any other font installed on your system.

■ *Font style.* You can make text plain, bold, italic, or both bold and italic. As shown in figure 6.8, plain text is the upright, medium-weight text you normally see. Bold text is darker than plain text. Italic text slants to the right.

■ *Font size.* Font size is expressed in *points,* with one point equaling 1/72 inch. The size of the font you are reading now, for example, is nine points.

■ *Color.* Color is one of the most powerful graphic elements in a slide. You can select from predefined colors or from custom colors you create.

■ *Special effects.* You can also underline, superscript, subscript, shadow, or emboss text (see fig. 6.9). Shadowed text appears to have a drop shadow behind it. Embossed text appears raised.

Fig. 6.7
Sample fonts.

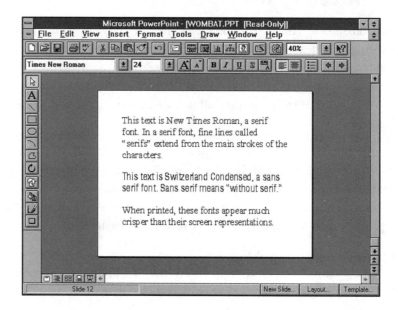

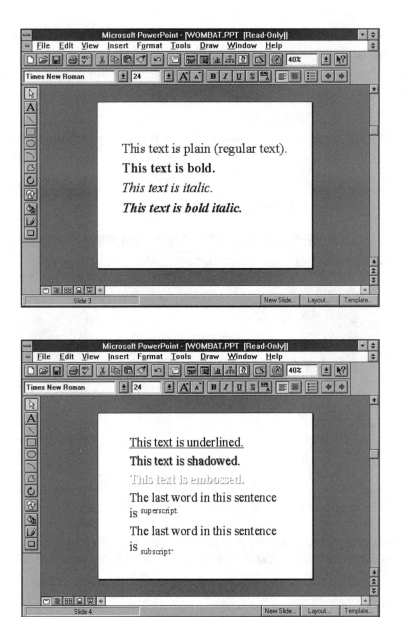

Fig. 6.8
Font styles.

Fig. 6.9
Special text effects.

With so many possibilities, you might be confused about their appropriate use. The cardinal rule of presentation design is "Keep it simple." If you remember this as you design your slides, you create a more effective presentation, where the audience focuses on the presentation content—not a busy design. For help in designing your presentation, try the Pick a Look Wizard (see Chapter 3) or one of PowerPoint's many professionally desined templates (see Chapter 5).

PowerPoint lets you use menus, the Formatting toolbar, or keystroke short-cuts to change text characteristics. The toolbar and keystroke shortcuts are the fastest methods, but they cannot be used to select some special effects, such as embossing and superscript. To select these special effects, you must use menus.

Table 6.1 describes each of the buttons on the Formatting toolbar, shown in figure 6.10. To use a button to format text, select the text and then click the button.

Fig. 6.10
The Formatting toolbar.

Standard toolbar

Formatting toolbar

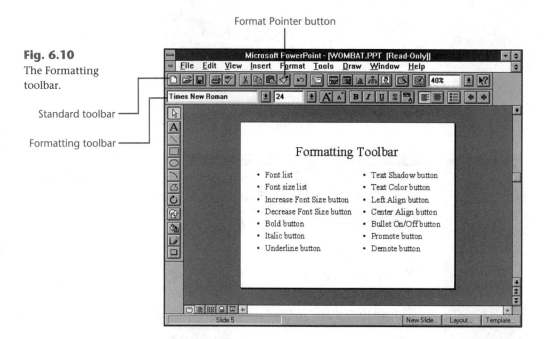

Tip
If the Formatting toolbar doesn't appear on-screen, from the main menu, choose **V**iew, select **T**oolbars, choose Formatting, and choose OK.

Table 6.1 Buttons That Change Text Appearance

Button	Name	Use
Times New Roman	Font list box	Click the down arrow to display a list of fonts and then select a font. The four most recently used fonts appear at the top of the list.
24	Font Size list box	Click the down arrow to display a list of font sizes and then select a size. Alternatively, type the size in the box.
A	Increase Font Size button	Click on this button to incrementally increase the font size.

Button	Name	Use
A	Decrease Font Size button	Click on this button to incrementally decrease the font size.
B	Bold button	Click on this button to toggle between adding and removing bold style.
I	Italic button	Click on this button to toggle between adding and removing italic style.
U	Underline button	Click on this button to toggle between adding and removing underlining.
S	Text Shadow button	Click on this button to toggle between adding and removing the drop shadow effect.
A	Text Color button	Click on this button to display a color menu; then select a color.

Table 6.2 lists the keystroke shortcuts. To use these to format text, select the text and then press the keys designated in table 6.2.

Table 6.2 · Keystroke Shortcuts for Changing Text Appearance

To Select This Style	Press
Bold	Ctrl+B
Italic	Ctrl+I
Underline	Ctrl+U

You can use the menu to change any text characteristics by following these steps:

1. Select the text that you want to change.

2. From the main menu, choose Format. The Format menu appears.

3. From the Format menu, choose Font to display the Font dialog box.

4. Make your changes. If you select Superscript or Subscript, enter in the Offset box the percentage you want the super- or subscript text offset; for subscript text, enter a negative number. To choose a different color, select the **C**olor button to display a palette, and then select a color.

5. Select OK.

Copying Text Styles

After you format text—for example, as red 30-point italic Times New Roman—you can copy the text style to any other text. Copying text styles not only saves you steps, it also saves you from having to remember detailed styles.

To use the Standard toolbar to copy a style, follow these steps:

1. Select any word that has the format you want to copy.

2. From the Standard toolbar, click the Format Painter button, which is designated by a paintbrush icon (see fig. 6.10). To apply the format to more than one selection, double-click the button.

3. Select the text you want to format according to the new style.

4. Click the left mouse button.

5. If you are applying the format to more than one selection (that is, if you double-clicked the button in step 2), repeat steps 3 and 4. When you are finished, click the Format Painter button.

To use menus to copy a style, follow these steps:

1. Select any word that has the format you want to copy.

2. From the main menu, choose F**o**rmat. The F**o**rmat menu appears.

3. From the F**o**rmat menu, choose Pic**k** Up Text Style.

4. Select the text you want to format according to the new style.

5. From the F**o**rmat menu, choose Appl**y** Style.

Changing Bullet Characteristics

You can also change the shape, color, and size of the bullets you use in bulleted lists. Bullet size is given as a percentage of the text size. A bullet size of 80 percent, for example, means the font size used for the bullet is 80 percent of the text font size.

To change bullet characteristics, follow these steps:

1. Select all items whose bullets you want to change.

2. From the main menu, choose F**o**rmat. The F**o**rmat menu appears.

3. From the F**o**rmat menu, choose **B**ullet. The Bullet dialog box appears, as shown in figure 6.11.

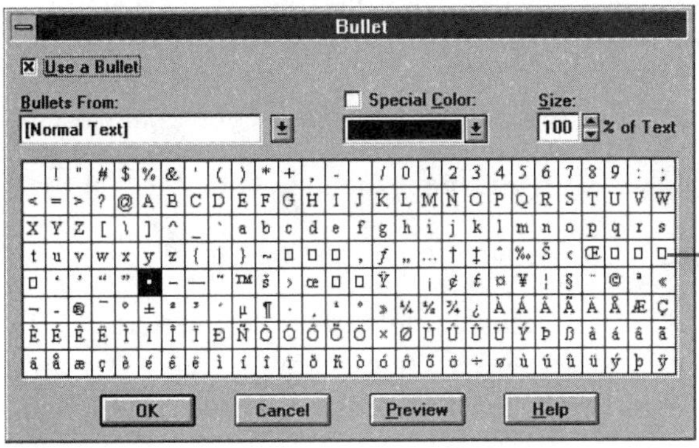

Fig. 6.11
The Bullet
dialog box.

Character palette

4. To change the bullet character, select the desired character in the character palette (see fig. 6.11). To choose a character from a different font, select the **B**ullets From button to list the fonts and select a font; when the characters in that font appear in the character palette, select the character you want.

5. To change the bullet color, select the color beneath the Special **C**olor check box to display a color palette and then select the new color.

6. To change the bullet size, type a new size percentage in the **S**ize box, or click the Size increment buttons to increase or decrease the percentage shown.

7. Save your changes by choosing OK.

Setting Tabs and Indents

Tabs and indents enable you to control how text aligns in a chart. If your presentation includes columns of text, you can use tabs to set up the column format—the location of the columns and the alignment of text within the columns. To set up a bulleted or numbered list, where you want text to align at a point inside the left margin, use a paragraph indent. The AutoLayouts for bulleted lists, for example, use indents to set the placement of bullets and the text aligned to the right of the bullets.

Understanding the Ruler. You set tabs and indents with the PowerPoint ruler, which you can display in Slide or Notes Page view. To display the ruler for a paragraph, place the insertion point in the paragraph, choose **V**iew from the main menu, and then choose **R**uler. The ruler appears just below the main menu bar and any toolbars that are displayed.

As shown in figure 6.12, the ruler has the following features:

■ *Tab Type button.* Click the Tab Type button to cycle through the four tab types:

     L   Left: aligns the left end of text at the tab.

     ⌐   Right: aligns the right end of text at the tab.

     ⊥   Center: centers text on the tab.

     ⊥•   Decimal: centers text on a period.

Tip

Use decimal tabs to set up numbered lists. A decimal tab makes the numbers align left of the period and the text align right of the period.

■ *Tab markers.* The default tabs, which are left tabs spaced at one-inch intervals, are marked by ticks at the bottom of the ruler (see fig. 6.12). Tabs that you set are shown on the ruler by the icon for that tab type (left, right, center, or decimal, as shown earlier).

■ *Paragraph indent markers.* The top marker shows the indent for the first line of text in the selected paragraph (see fig. 6.12). The bottom marker shows the indent for the rest of the paragraph. When both markers are aligned, all lines of text in a paragraph are equally indented. For most text placeholders, the default setting for both markers is zero inches; that is, there is no indent so that all text in paragraphs aligns at the left margin of the placeholder. In the AutoLayouts for bulleted lists, default indents are set for the bulleted list items.

Changing the Default Tabs. You can change the default tabs for a placeholder to any evenly spaced intervals, enabling you to quickly set up evenly spaced columns across a chart. Remember, the default tabs are always left tabs. If you want a different type of tab—for example, a decimal tab to align numbers around a decimal point—you must set a specific tab of that type, as described in the next section.

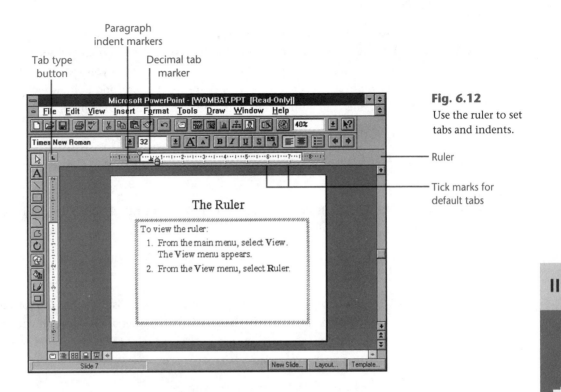

Tab type
button

Paragraph
indent markers

Decimal tab
marker

Fig. 6.12
Use the ruler to set
tabs and indents.

Ruler

Tick marks for
default tabs

To change the default tab interval, follow these steps:

1. Place the insertion point anywhere in the placeholder you want to change.

2. If the ruler isn't displayed, from the main menu, choose **V**iew, and then choose **R**uler.

3. Place the mouse pointer directly on the first tick mark and drag the tick mark to where you want the first tab. When you release the mouse button, the other tick marks adjust to be evenly spaced at the interval determined by the first tick mark.

Note

If in step 3 the mouse pointer isn't directly on the tick mark, you insert a tab rather than reset the default interval. If you accidentally insert a tab, you can delete it by dragging it off the ruler.

II

Text

Setting Specific Tabs. You can override the default tabs by setting your own. The tab type can be left, right, center, or decimal. When you set a tab, PowerPoint ignores all default tabs preceding that tab. If you set a tab at three inches, for example, pressing Tab once moves the insertion point directly to the three-inch tab, rather than to the first default tab at one inch.

Tip
To select all text in a placeholder, place the insertion point anywhere in the placeholder and press Ctrl+A.

To set individual tabs, follow these steps:

1. Place the insertion point in the paragraph you want to change, or select two or more paragraphs.

2. If the ruler isn't displayed, from the main menu, choose **V**iew, and then choose **R**uler.

3. Depending on the changes you want to make, follow one or more of these procedures:

   To add a tab: Click the Tab Type button until it displays the icon for the type of tab you want, and then click on the ruler at the location where you want the tab. To insert more than one tab of that type, click every location where you want a tab.

   To move a tab: Drag it to the new location.

   To delete a tab: Drag it from the ruler.

4. To hide the ruler, from the main menu, choose **V**iew, and then choose **R**uler (the ruler toggles on and off). Hiding the ruler doesn't affect the tab settings.

Setting Indents. PowerPoint lets you choose one indent for the first line of a paragraph and another indent for subsequent lines in the paragraph. You can set up the indents so that the first line begins either to the right or the left of the subsequent lines. In the first example below, the first line begins to the right; this is a standard paragraph indent. In the second and third examples, the first line begins to the left; this is called a *hanging indent.*

Example 1:

The first line in this paragraph is indented. Subsequent lines in the paragraph automatically begin at the normal left margin.

Example 2:

> This is a hanging indent. Notice that the first line begins to the left of
> subsequent lines.

Example 3:

> ■ This is also a hanging indent. The bullet, which is the beginning of the
> first line, begins to the left of subsequent lines. In bulleted lists, the first
> line of text automatically moves right, so that it aligns with other text
> in the paragraph.

To change paragraph indents, follow these steps:

1. Place the insertion point in the paragraph you want to change, or select
   two or more paragraphs.

2. If the ruler isn't displayed, from the main menu choose **V**iew, and then
   choose **R**uler.

3. Depending on the changes you want to make, follow one or more of
   these procedures:

   To change the indent for the first line of text in the selected paragraphs: Drag
   the top indent marker to where you want the text to align on the left.

   To change the indent for the remaining text in the selected paragraphs: Drag
   the bottom indent marker to where you want the text to align on the
   left.

   To use the same indent for all lines of text in the selected paragraphs: Align
   the top and bottom indent markers and then drag the lower (square)
   half of the bottom marker to move both indent markers to where you
   want the text to align on the left.

Note

PowerPoint allows up to five indent levels in a text placeholder. Each level is defined
by one set of indent markers. To display the indent markers for the levels already
used in a placeholder, place the insertion point in any paragraph in the placeholder
and display the ruler. To display the indent markers for a level that isn't yet used,
place the insertion point in an empty line and press Alt+Shift+right arrow or click the
Demote button to demote the line to that level. The right-most indent markers on
the ruler define the settings for that indent level.

Moving to Tab and Indent Stops. In most placeholders, press Tab to move to a tab stop. In placeholders containing a bulleted list, however, you must press Ctrl+Tab; in those placeholders, pressing Tab indents the text. In any placeholder, press Backspace to move back one tab stop.

To move the insertion point to the next indent, press Alt+Shift+right arrow or click the Demote button. (In bulleted lists, you can also press Tab.) In AutoLayouts for bulleted lists, this inserts a bullet, as well as indents the text. To move the insertion point back an indent, press Alt+Shift+left arrow or click the Promote button. (In bulleted lists, you can also press Shift+Tab.)

Tab settings do not affect indents: When you indent list items by pressing Alt+Shift+right arrow or by selecting the Demote button, the insertion point moves only to indent stops, ignoring tab stops. Similarly, if you set up indents to automatically indent the first line of a paragraph, the first line begins at the indent, regardless of whether you set a tab before that indent.

Indent settings, however, do affect tabs: When you press Tab, the insertion point moves to the next tab or indent stop.

Setting Margins

Margins within a text placeholder are similar to margins on a page: all text lies between the margins, which are measured from the edge of the placeholder. In PowerPoint, you can change the left and right margins jointly, but not separately. Similarly, you can change the top and bottom margins jointly, but not separately.

To change the margins in a text placeholder, follow these steps:

1. Click the text placeholder you want to change.

2. From the main menu, choose Format. The Format menu appears.

3. From the Format menu, choose Text Anchor. The Text Anchor dialog box appears.

4. To change the left and right margins, type a new measurement (in inches) in the top text box in the Box Margins area. Alternatively, you can click the increment buttons to the right of the text box to increase or decrease the measurement in 0.05-inch increments.

5. To change the top and bottom margins, type a new measurement (in inches) in the bottom text box in the Box Margins area. Alternatively,

you can click the increment buttons to the right of the text box to increase or decrease the measurement in 0.05-inch increments.

6. Choose OK. The dialog box closes.

Aligning Text

You can align text on the right, on the left, on both the right and the left (fully justified), or in the center. Generally, lists are best aligned left. Full justification, however, may be used to give a more formal appearance. Titles and subtitles may be left-aligned, right-aligned, or centered.

To change the alignment of text, follow these steps:

1. Select the paragraphs you want to change.

2. From the main menu, choose Format. The Format menu appears.

3. From the Format menu, select Alignment. The Alignment cascading menu appears.

4. Choose Left, Center, Right, or Justify.

A paragraph cannot have more than one type of alignment.

Setting Line and Paragraph Spacing

Line spacing is the distance from the baseline of one line of text to the baseline of the next line of text. Paragraph spacing is additional space you can add before and after paragraphs. To change line or paragraph spacing, follow these steps:

1. Select the paragraphs you want to change.

2. From the main menu, choose Format. The Format menu appears.

3. From the Format menu, choose Line Spacing. The Line Spacing dialog box appears.

4. To change line spacing, type a new measurement in the Line Spacing text box. Alternatively, click the increment buttons to increase or decrease line spacing by 0.05-line increments.

   The default unit of measure is lines. If you prefer to use points as the unit of measurement, click the drop-down button displaying Lines and then select Points.

Tip
You can also select left or center alignment by clicking the Left Alignment or Center Alignment button on the Formatting toolbar.

II

Text

5. To change paragraph spacing, type a new measurement in either or both of the **B**efore Paragraph and **A**fter Paragraph text boxes. Alternatively, click the increment buttons to increase or decrease spacing by 0.05-line increments.

6. Choose OK. The dialog box closes and the text is reformatted.

Using True Quotation Marks

With PowerPoint's Smart Quotes feature, pressing the " or ' key inserts true quotation marks (" ", ' ') rather than straight quotation marks (" ", ' '). PowerPoint is even smart enough to recognize when the quotation mark should be an opening or closing quotation mark. There may be occasions, however, when you want straight quotation marks—for example, as symbols for inch or foot. For these cases, disable the Smart Quotes feature as follows:

1. From the main menu, choose **T**ools. The **T**ools menu appears.

2. From the **T**ools menu, choose **O**ptions. The Options dialog box appears.

3. Clear the check box named Replace Straight **Q**uotes with Smart Quotes.

4. Choose OK.

Disabling this feature won't affect any true quotation marks already typed.

Bulleting a List

If a text placeholder contains a simple list (that is, a list without bullets), you can change the list to a bulleted list as follows:

1. Select all items in the list.

2. From the main menu, choose F**o**rmat. The F**o**rmat menu appears.

3. From the F**o**rmat menu, choose **B**ullet. The Bullet dialog box appears.

4. Select the **U**se a Bullet check box.

5. If desired, change the bullet character (the default for first-level list items is a round bullet), Special **C**olor, or **S**ize. For details, see the section "Changing Bullet Characteristics" earlier in this chapter.

6. Choose OK. The dialog box closes and bullets precede each of the selected items.

7. If necessary, change the indent settings to adjust the space between the bullets and the text. Setting indents is discussed in the section "Setting Tabs and Indents" earlier in this chapter.

If you intend to use the default bullet character, color, and size, you can change to a bulleted list even more quickly. Just select the list items and then select the Bullet On/Off button from the Formatting toolbar (see fig. 6.13). To remove the bullets, reselect the items and then reselect the Bullet On/Off button.

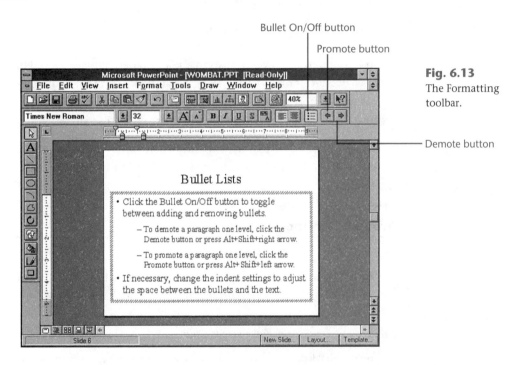

Bullet On/Off button

Promote button

Fig. 6.13
The Formatting toolbar.

Demote button

After you have a bulleted list, you can use the Promote and Demote buttons to add sub-items beneath the main items. To list secondary items beneath a main item, follow these steps:

1. Place the insertion point at the end of the item to which you are adding the new list.

2. Press Enter to insert a new line. A bullet automatically appears.

3. Press Tab or Alt+Shift+right arrow, or click the Demote button (refer to fig. 6.13). PowerPoint automatically indents the bullet beneath the preceding line. If the text is in a placeholder you created, the bullet character does not change. (You can change it later, as described in the section "Changing Bullet Characteristics" earlier in this chapter.) Also, the indent may not be correct; in placeholders you create, for example, there typically is no space between the bullet and the text. To fix this,

you must create a hanging indent, as explained earlier in this chapter in "Setting Indents."

4. Type the text for the item and press Enter when you are finished. The insertion point moves to a new line that is automatically indented the same as the preceding item.

5. Continue adding items until the list is finished.

You can have up to five levels of lists in a placeholder, but you should limit yourself to two levels on the same slide. An audience can't digest much more than this in the short time a slide is shown. If you must add more levels, the procedure is the same as that just described for adding a secondary list.

To promote an item up one level, click anywhere in the item and then press Shift+Tab or Alt+Shift+left arrow, or click the Promote button (refer to fig. 6.13).

Troubleshooting

When I press Tab, PowerPoint inserts a bullet and indents the text. How do I just tab?

You are getting an indent because you are in a bulleted list. In bulleted lists, pressing Tab has the same effect as clicking the Demote button. To tab in bulleted lists, press Ctrl+Tab.

How do I make text automatically wrap to a new line?

In most placeholders, this happens automatically. In some placeholders created with the Text button, however, word wrapping is not automatic. To enable word wrapping, choose **F**ormat from the main menu, choose **T**ext Anchor, choose **W**ord-wrap Text in Object, and then choose OK. For more information on word wrapping, see "Creating Labels and Other Special Text" earlier in this chapter.

How can I increase or decrease the space between the text and the edge of the placeholder (or between text and a border I created around the text)?

Change the placeholder margins. For instructions, see "Setting Margins" earlier in this chapter.

What's the best way to emphasize text in a slide?

In color slides, make the text a warm color, such as red or yellow (but don't mix red with green, since some people are red-green color blind). In black-and-white slides, make the text bold or italic; bold provides a greater degree of emphasis than does italic. Some designers also use underlining for emphasis. Don't use other special effects, such as shadow or embossing, unless they fit well with the slide design.

Using the Spelling Checker

Always check the spelling in a presentation before the audience sees it. Few things are more embarrassing than an 18-inch-high typo. To check the spelling, use PowerPoint's spelling checker, which checks both spelling and letter case.

> **Note**
>
> By default, PowerPoint suggests corrections when it detects a potential error. If your spelling checker is slow, you can speed it up by disabling this feature. To do so, from the main menu choose **T**ools; then **O**ptions, deselect **Al**ways Suggest, and choose OK.

To use the spelling checker, follow these steps:

1. Open the presentation you want to check.

2. Press F7. Alternatively, from the **T**ools menu, choose **S**pelling.

PowerPoint begins checking the spelling. If it detects a potential error, the Spelling dialog box appears. As shown in figure 6.14, the potential error appears at the top left of the dialog box.

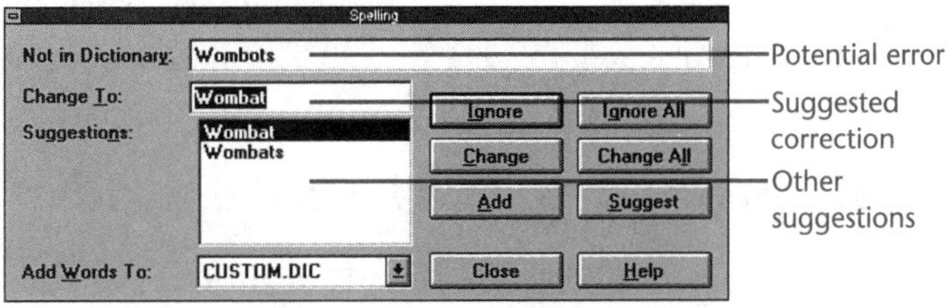

Fig. 6.14
The Spelling dialog box.

A suggested spelling or case appears in the Change **T**o text box (unless you have disabled the Always Suggest feature). Beneath this suggestion, there may be a list of additional suggestions. You can take one of the following actions:

■ To continue without correcting the word, choose **I**gnore.

■ To ignore this and all further instances of this word, choose **Ig**nore All.

- To correct only this instance of the word, choose one of the suggested alternatives, or type the correction in the Change **T**o text box, and choose **C**hange.

- To correct this and all further instances of the word, choose one of the suggested alternatives, or type the correction in the Change **T**o text box, and then choose Change A**ll**. PowerPoint doesn't prompt you to confirm the changes.

- To add the word in the Change **T**o text box to the dictionary listed in the Add **W**ords To text box, choose **A**dd. If the word differs from the word highlighted in the slide, PowerPoint also replaces the highlighted word with the correct word. To select a different dictionary, select the Add **W**ords To text box to list available dictionaries and then choose a dictionary.

- If the Always Suggest feature is disabled, to have PowerPoint suggest a correct spelling, choose **S**uggest.

After you make your selection, the spelling checker continues checking the presentation. When it has finished checking the entire presentation, it displays a message to that effect. Choose OK to close the message box.

After using the spelling checker, carefully proof the presentation for errors that a spelling checker can't detect. No spelling checker can tell you, for example, that "Sales Sour in 1994" should be "Sales Soar in 1994."

Manipulating Text Placeholders

A text placeholder is an object in PowerPoint. As such, you can treat it like any other object. You can resize, move, or copy it. And you can enhance it with a border or a different background to visually separate text areas on the slide. This section describes the basics of manipulating text placeholders as objects. You can find additional information in chapter 11, "Selecting, Editing, and Enhancing Objects."

Resizing a Text Placeholder

After you enter text in a placeholder, you may find that it appears unbalanced or has awkward line breaks—for example, a bulleted list item may wrap so that only one word is on the last line. You can sometimes improve the appearance by resizing the text placeholder, forcing the words to wrap at a different location, or even not at all. In the examples shown in figures 6.15 and 6.16, widening the placeholder allows all items to fit on one line. In figures 6.17 and 6.18, narrowing the placeholder forces the long item to wrap to another line so that all list items have an approximately equal width.

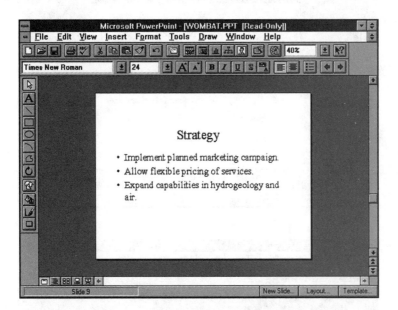

Fig. 6.15
Before: In this chart, one word in the last item wraps to a new line, taking precious space.

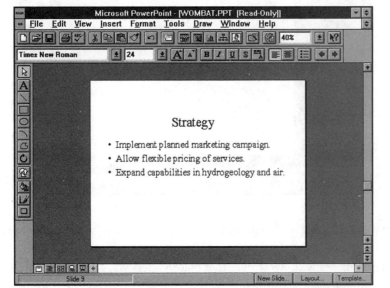

Fig. 6.16
After: By widening the placeholder slightly, the item now fits on one line.

Fig. 6.17
Before: In this
chart, the one
long item has
destroyed the
balance in the
chart.

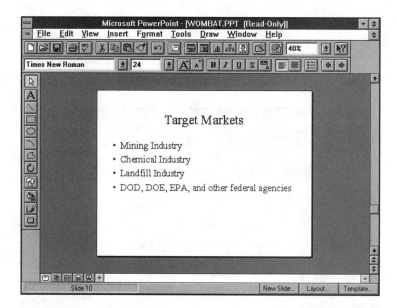

Fig. 6.18
After: By reducing
the placeholder
width, we forced
the long item
to wrap to two
approximately
equal lines.

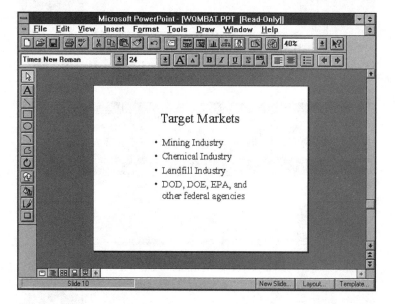

You can also resize the length of a placeholder. You might leave additional
space, for example, to indicate to a colleague the approximate space allotted
for entering her text. Remember that placeholders you create automatically
adjust their length to fit the text. You must disable this feature before you
can change the length of such a placeholder. To do so, follow these steps:

1. Click anywhere inside the text placeholder.

2. From the main menu, choose F**o**rmat. The F**o**rmat menu appears.

3. From the F**o**rmat menu, choose **T**ext Anchor. The Text Anchor dialog box appears.

4. Select the check box named Adjust Object Size to **F**it Text.

5. Choose OK.

The preset text placeholders in AutoLayouts already have this option disabled.

To resize a text placeholder, follow these steps:

1. To display the gray outline of the text placeholder, click anywhere in the text within that placeholder.

2. Click the gray placeholder to select it. Sizing handles appear, as shown in figure 6.19.

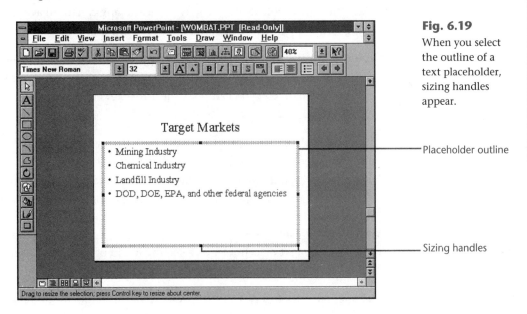

Fig. 6.19
When you select the outline of a text placeholder, sizing handles appear.

Placeholder outline

Sizing handles

3. Place the mouse pointer over the sizing handle on the side or corner you want to move in or out. The pointer changes to a double-sided arrow (refer to fig. 6.19).

4. Drag the sizing handle in or out to shrink or expand the text placeholder.

Moving or Copying a Text Placeholder

Moving and copying a text placeholder is similar to moving and copying text. You just select the placeholder and use the mouse to move or copy the original to the new location. When you move or copy a text placeholder, all text inside also is moved or copied.

Follow these steps to move or copy a text placeholder:

1. Display the gray outline of the text placeholder by clicking anywhere in the text within that placeholder.

2. Click the gray placeholder to select it.

3. Place the mouse pointer on the gray outline, being careful to avoid the sizing handles. The mouse pointer *must* look like a single-headed arrow.

4. To *move* the placeholder, press and hold the left mouse button, drag the placeholder to the new location, and then release the left mouse button. Alternatively, you can press the arrow keys to move the placeholder.

   To *copy* the placeholder, press and hold the Ctrl key. Notice that a plus sign appears next to the mouse pointer. With the Ctrl key still depressed, press and hold the left mouse button, drag the copy to the new location, and then release the left mouse button and the Ctrl key.

Deleting a Text Placeholder

You can delete any text placeholder by selecting it and pressing the Delete key. Text in the placeholder is also deleted.

If you accidentally delete a placeholder, you often can restore it—and its text—by using the Undo command, which reverses the last edit made. To use Undo, press Ctrl+Z (Undo); or, from the main menu, choose **E**dit and then choose **U**ndo.

Creating a Border for Text

To emphasize or visually separate a text area from the rest of a slide, you can create a border around the text. The border appears just inside the boundaries of the text placeholder. Figure 6.20 illustrates several line styles you can use for borders. You can also select the border color.

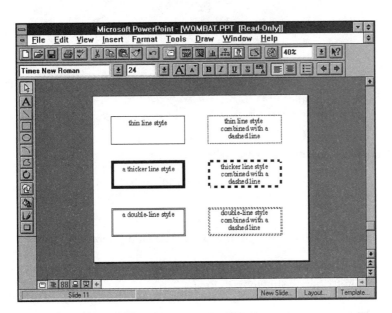

Fig. 6.20
Sample line styles for text borders.

To create a border, follow these steps:

1. Click anywhere in the text around which you want to create the border. The gray placeholder outline appears.

2. Click the gray placeholder outline to select it.

3. From the main menu, choose Format. The Format menu appears.

4. From the Format menu, choose Colors and Lines. The Colors and Lines dialog box appears, as shown in figure 6.21.

5. Beneath Line Styles, select one of the line styles shown.

6. To make the line dashed as well, select one of the styles beneath Dashed Lines.

7. To change the border color (the default is black), select the Line box to display the color selections, and then select a color.

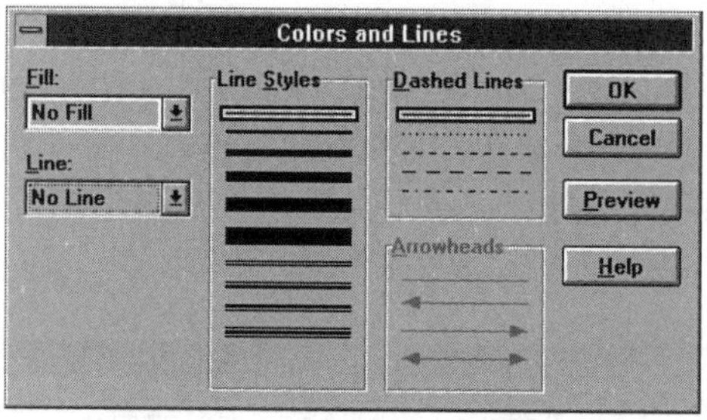

Fig. 6.21
The Colors and
Lines dialog box.

8. Choose OK. The dialog box closes and the border appears just inside the text placeholder.

The default shape for a border is a rectangle, but you can change the shape to be any AutoShape by following these steps:

1. Create the border as described earlier in this section.

2. If the text placeholder isn't selected, select it.

3. From the main menu, choose **D**raw. The **D**raw menu appears.

4. From the **D**raw menu, choose **C**hange AutoShape. PowerPoint displays the AutoShapes, shown in figure 6.22.

Fig. 6.22
The AutoShapes
appear when you
choose **C**hange
AutoShape from
the **D**raw menu.

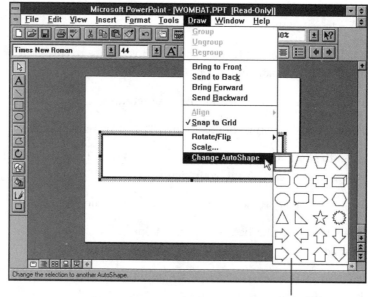

Autoshapes

5. Select the AutoShape you want. The border changes to the new shape. (The outline of the text placeholder remains rectangular; this doesn't affect the border.) Text automatically rewraps to fit the new shape. If the text can't fit within the shape, it extends below it.

For information on editing AutoShapes, see chapter 11, "Selecting, Editing, and Enhancing Objects."

Changing the Background Color of the Text Placeholder

To further emphasize a text area, you can change the background color of the text placeholder. If you have limited experience with combining colors, review chapter 17, "Working with Color," for tips on when and how to use color effectively. If you then decide that a different background color is appropriate for the text, follow these steps to add the new color:

1. Click anywhere in the text for which you want to change the background color. The gray outline of the text placeholder appears.

2. Click on the gray placeholder outline to select it.

3. From the main menu, choose F**o**rmat. The F**o**rmat menu appears.

4. From the F**o**rmat menu, choose Colors and **L**ines. The Colors and Lines dialog box appears (refer to fig. 6.21).

5. Select the **F**ill box to display the color selections, and select a color.

6. Choose OK. The dialog box closes, and the background color appears inside the text placeholder.

Troubleshooting

I resized a text placeholder and now the title and body text placeholders no longer align. How do I realign them?

Align text placeholders the same way you align graphic objects. Select one placeholder by clicking its gray border. Then place the mouse pointer over text in the other placeholder and press and hold the Ctrl and Shift keys while clicking the left mouse button. This selects the second placeholder and keeps selected the first placeholder. Release the keys. From the main menu, choose **D**raw and then choose **A**lign. In the cascading menu that appears, choose the alignment (for example, Lefts).

The text in a placeholder extends beyond the placeholder. How do I fix it?

(continues)

(continued)

You have several options: you can reduce the font size, resize the placeholder, or edit the text so it fits. If you can edit the text without compromising clarity, this is the best method (in slide presentations, text should be as concise as possible). If you reduce the font size, make sure the audience at the back of the room can read the smaller text. To resize the placeholder so it automatically fits the text, click in the placeholder. From the main menu, choose **Fo**rmat and then choose **T**ext Anchor. In the dialog box that appears, select the check box named Adjust Object Size to **F**it Text, and choose OK.

From Here...

In this chapter you learned the basics of working with text and many time-saving features for editing text. For related topics, review the following chapters:

- Chapter 8, "Working with Tables," describes how to create Microsoft Word tables.

- Chapter 11, "Selecting, Editing, and Enhancing Objects," shows how you can place text inside objects.

- Chapter 13, "Creating Basic Charts," explains how to add legends and labels to charts.

- Chapter 21, "Using Advanced Color, Text, and Drawing Features," describes the special equation editor.

Chapter 7

Creating Speaker's Notes, Handouts, and Outlines

An effective slide presentation flows logically from one slide to the next, with each slide illustrating a few key points. To help you prepare and give an effective presentation, PowerPoint offers some powerful aids: outlining, speaker's notes, and handouts.

Outlining helps you organize and focus your thoughts. And because PowerPoint lets you create slides directly from your outline, following the outline is a snap. After you complete a draft presentation, you can revisit the outline—which automatically reflects any changes to the presentation—and modify, rearrange, or delete slides as necessary.

Speaker's notes, called *notes pages* in PowerPoint, are pages that display a slide and any notes you have for that slide. You may add notes, for example, to remind you of the key points illustrated by the slide. Such notes help you focus during your presentation and reduce the chance that you might accidentally skip an important topic.

You can make your presentation even more effective by providing your audience with *handouts*, which are printouts of the slides. Handouts relieve your audience of the need to take extensive notes, so that they can focus on your presentation instead. Handouts also provide a common reference for participants in question and answer sessions.

In this chapter, you learn how to:

- Create and print speaker's notes and handouts

- Develop an outline for a slide presentation

- Create a slide presentation from an outline

II

Text

In this chapter, you learn how to create and print speaker's notes, handouts, and outlines and how to use an outline to develop a presentation. You also learn how to use the master pages (Notes Master, Handout Master, and Outline Master), which enable you to globally change the layout of speaker's notes, handouts, and outlines. The presentation aids you learn in this chapter will improve the effectiveness of any slide presentation.

Creating Speaker's Notes

You can create speaker's notes for any slide in a presentation. As shown in figure 7.1, a notes page displays the slide at the top of the page. Beneath the slide is a notes box in which you can type notes on that slide. Notes typically are most useful for bar, pie, and other graphical slides that have no text to explicitly state the main points illustrated by the slides. In those cases, you can use the notes pages to list the points you want to make. Although text charts, such as bullet charts, usually state the key points in the text itself, you may find it helpful to add notes regarding subthemes or the transition to the next slide.

Fig. 7.1
Speaker's notes display the slide at the top of the page and a notes box at the bottom.

Slide image

Notes box

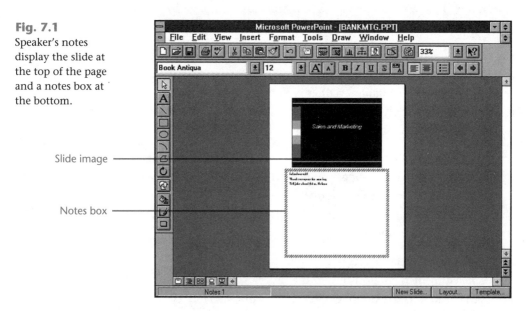

Creating a Notes Page for a Slide
To create a notes page for a slide, follow these steps:

1. Display the slide for which you want to create a notes page.

2. From the main menu bar, choose **V**iew and then choose **N**otes Pages; or click the Notes Pages View button shown in figure 7.2. PowerPoint displays the notes page for the slide, as shown in figure 7.3.

3. Click the notes box, shown in figure 7.3. The insertion point appears in the notes box.

Tip
To enlarge the view of the typing area, increase the zoom percentage to 75 percent (see fig. 7.3).

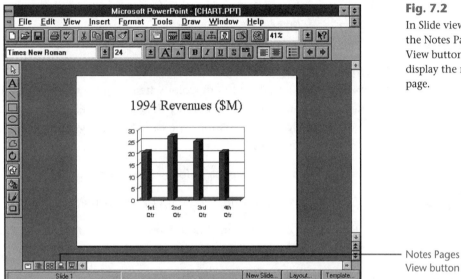

Fig. 7.2
In Slide view, click the Notes Pages View button to display the notes page.

Notes Pages View button

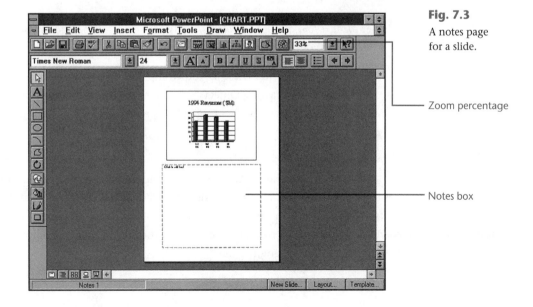

Fig. 7.3
A notes page for a slide.

Zoom percentage

Notes box

II

Text

4. Type your notes.

5. From the **File** menu, choose **S**ave to save your notes page. The page is saved with your presentation.

Note

If this is a new presentation, the Save As dialog box appears. In the File **N**ame text box, type a file name and then choose OK.

Modifying Notes Pages

PowerPoint provides a default font, color scheme, and layout for the notes pages. You can change these for an individual notes page, or globally change all notes pages in your presentation. You can also modify individual or all pages to include graphics and labels.

To modify an individual notes page, follow these steps:

Tip
If you don't like your text changes, you can revert to the default text settings by selecting Format, Notes Layout, **R**eapply Master, OK.

1. Display the slide for which you want to modify the notes page.

2. From the main menu bar, choose **V**iew and then choose **N**otes Pages; or click the Notes Page View button.

3. Depending on what you want to modify, follow one or more of the procedures described in the text that follows.

To change the text font, format, or color: Modify text on a notes page as you would text on a slide. For details, see chapter 6, "Working with Text."

To add labels or a graphic: Add these as you would add them on a slide. For details, see chapter 9, "Drawing Objects"; chapter 10, "Adding Clip Art and Scanned Art"; and the section "Creating Labels and Other Special Text" in chapter 6.

To move the slide or notes box to a different position: To select the slide, click it; to select the notes box, click in the text area to display the gray border of the notes box, and then click the gray border. A selection box encloses the slide or notes box, as shown in figure 7.4. Place the pointer inside the selection box and drag the slide or notes box to the new location. Be careful not to place the pointer on a sizing handle.

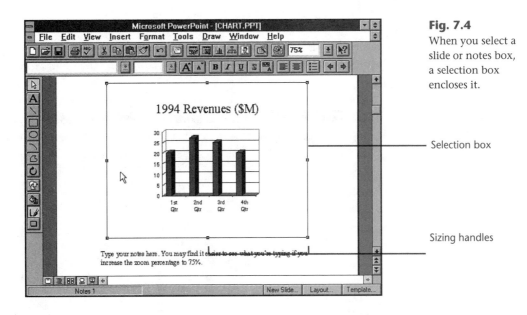

Fig. 7.4
When you select a slide or notes box, a selection box encloses it.

Selection box

Sizing handles

To resize the slide or notes box: To select the slide, click it; to select the notes box, click in the text area to display the gray border of the notes box and then click the gray border. The selection box appears. Place the pointer on a sizing handle, as shown in figure 7.5, and drag the handle until the slide or box is the correct size. Notice that the pointer becomes a double-headed arrow when it is on a sizing handle.

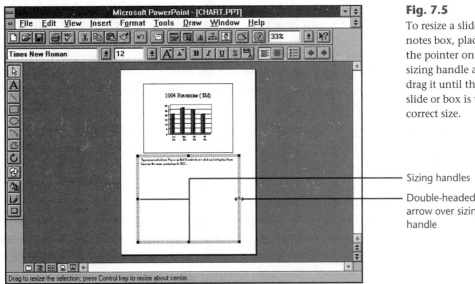

Fig. 7.5
To resize a slide or notes box, place the pointer on the sizing handle and drag it until the slide or box is the correct size.

Sizing handles

Double-headed arrow over sizing handle

To crop the slide: Click the slide. The selection box encloses the slide. From the **T**ools menu, choose Crop **P**icture. The crop pointer appears, as shown in figure 7.6. Place the pointer over any sizing handle and drag it to crop the picture.

Fig. 7.6
To crop a slide image, place the crop pointer over a sizing handle and drag it to crop the image.

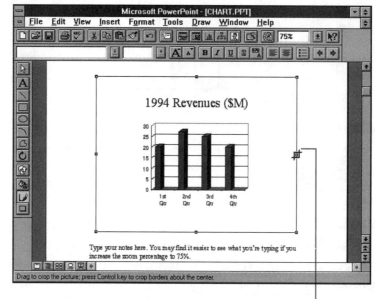

Crop pointer

To add a border or shadow around the notes box or slide image: Add these as you would add them on a slide. For details, see "Manipulating Text Placeholders" in chapter 6 or see chapter 11, "Selecting, Editing, and Enhancing Objects."

To change the background color of the notes box: Change the color as you would change it for any text placeholder. For details, see "Manipulating Text Place-holders" in chapter 6.

To change the background design on the notes page: From the **Fo**rmat menu, choose Notes Back**g**round. The Notes Background dialog box appears, as shown in figure 7.7. You can use this dialog box to change or shade the back-ground color of the notes pages:

■ To change the background color, select Chan**g**e Color. In the Back-ground Color dialog box that appears, choose a color from the Color **P**alette and then choose OK. (To display more colors, from the Back-ground Color dialog box choose **M**ore Colors.)

■ To use a shaded background, choose the direction of shading (for example, **V**ertical or Diagonal **R**ight) from the Shade Styles box. If that
style has one or more variations, they appear in the Variants box; in
this case, choose the variation that you want. To adjust the lightness or
darkness of the shading, drag the scroll bar beneath the Variants box.
To darken (add more black to) the shading, drag the scroll bar left. To
lighten (add more white to) the shading, drag the scroll bar right.

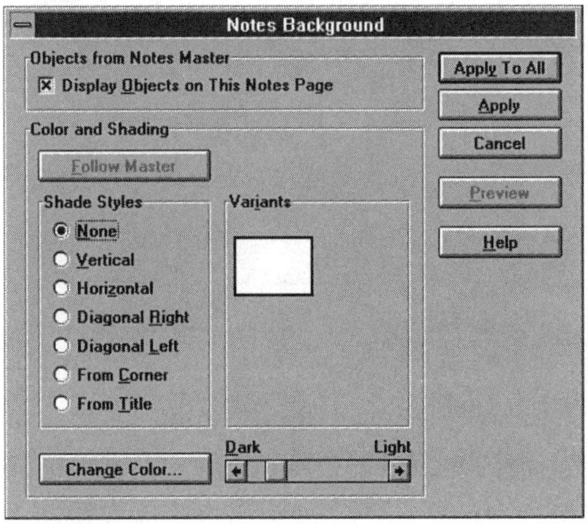

Fig. 7.7
The Notes
Background
dialog box.

You can also use the Notes Background dialog box to hide graphic objects,
including any text added with the Text button. To do so, deselect the Display
Objects on This Notes Page check box.

After you've made your changes in the Notes Background dialog box, you can
apply the changes to the single notes page or to all notes pages in the presentation. To apply the changes to only the displayed notes page, choose **A**pply.
To apply the changes to all notes pages, choose Appl**y** To All. To cancel the
changes, select Cancel.

You can revert at any time to the default color and shading settings (those
set by the Notes Master page) by choosing **F**ollow Master in the Notes
Background dialog box.

To change the notes color scheme: From the F**o**rmat menu, choose Notes **C**olor
Scheme. The Notes Color Scheme dialog box appears, as shown in figure 7.8.
The **C**hange Scheme Colors palette in this dialog box shows the current colors for the title text, the background, and other items in a notes page. In this
palette, the *Accent* colors refer to additional fill colors, such as those used for

additional bars in bar charts. To change a color, double-click on the color or select the color and then choose Change Color. In the dialog box that appears, choose a color from the color palette (or choose **M**ore Colors and complete the More Colors dialog box and then choose OK). You return to the Notes Color Scheme dialog box, where the new color scheme is previewed in a thumbnail sketch at the lower left of the dialog box.

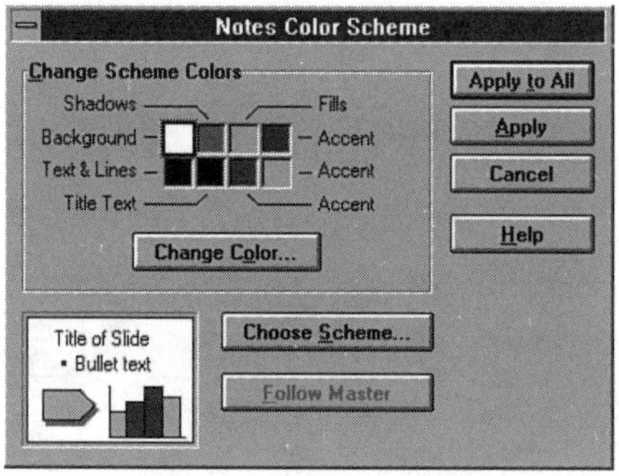

Fig. 7.8

The Notes Color Scheme dialog box.

If you aren't comfortable creating your own color scheme, you can let PowerPoint suggest one. In the Notes Color Scheme dialog box, select Choose **S**cheme. The Choose Scheme dialog box appears. In the **B**ackground Color box, select a color for the notes background. Based on your choice, compatible colors for the body text and the chart lines appear in the **T**ext and Line Color box. Choose one of these colors. Based on your selections, PowerPoint displays four suggested color schemes in the **O**ther Scheme Colors box. To choose one of these schemes, select it and then choose OK. You return to the Notes Color Scheme dialog box, which now reflects the new color scheme.

After you've made your changes in the Notes Color Scheme dialog box, you can apply the changes to the single notes page or to all notes pages in the presentation. To apply the changes to only the displayed notes page, choose **A**pply. To apply the changes to all notes pages, choose Apply **T**o All. To cancel the changes, choose Cancel. You can revert at any time to the default color scheme (set by the Notes Master page) by choosing **F**ollow Master in the Notes Color Scheme dialog box.

To change the font, color scheme, or layout for all notes pages in a presentation, use the Notes Master. This enables you to make the changes just once—to the Notes Master page. The changes to the Notes Master page automatically apply to all notes pages in that presentation, giving the pages a consistent appearance. You can also use the Notes Master to add graphics or text, such as the date or page number, that you want to apply to all notes pages in your presentation.

To use the Notes Master, follow these steps:

1. Open the presentation for which you want to modify the Notes Master.

2. From the main menu bar, choose **V**iew. The **V**iew menu appears.

3. From the **V**iew menu, select **M**aster, and then choose **N**otes Master. The Notes Master page appears, as shown in figure 7.9.

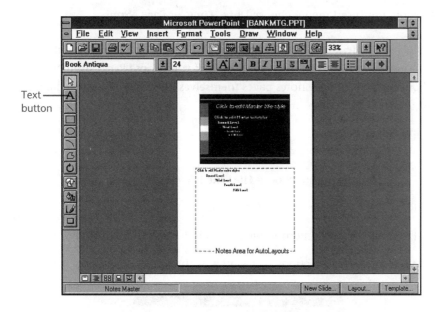

Text button

Fig. 7.9
The Notes Master page.

4. Follow one or more of the procedures given earlier for modifying individual notes pages. If you want to move or resize the notes box, you can select the notes box on the Notes Master page simply by clicking the dashed border of the box.

5. From the **F**ile menu, choose **S**ave to save the new format. The new master page is saved with your presentation, and all notes pages in the presentation are modified according to the new settings in the master page.

Tip
You can change
the type size and
font of the Date,
Time, and Page
Number symbols
on the Notes
Master page just as
you do other text.

Inserting the Date, Time, and Page Number

To have the date, time, or page number automatically appear on all notes pages, you must use the Notes Master. The steps are as follows:

1. To insert the date, time, or page number *within* the notes box, position the insertion point in the notes box where you want the date, time, or page number to appear. To insert the date, time, or page number *outside* the notes box, click the Text button (shown in fig. 7.9), position the insertion point where you want the date, time, or page number to appear, and then click the left mouse button to create a text placeholder.

2. From the main menu, choose **I**nsert. The **I**nsert menu appears.

3. From the **I**nsert menu, choose D**a**te, **T**ime, or Page N**u**mber.

If you choose D**a**te, the symbol // appears at the insertion point location; if you choose **T**ime, the symbol :: appears; and if you choose Page N**u**mber, the symbol ## appears. In the notes pages themselves, these symbols are replaced with the actual date, time, or page number.

Printing Notes Pages

To print your notes pages, follow these steps:

1. From the main menu, choose **F**ile. The File menu appears.

2. From the **F**ile menu, choose **P**rint. The Print dialog box appears.

3. From the Print **W**hat drop-down list, select Notes Pages (see fig. 7.10).

4. Make any other selections you want and choose OK.

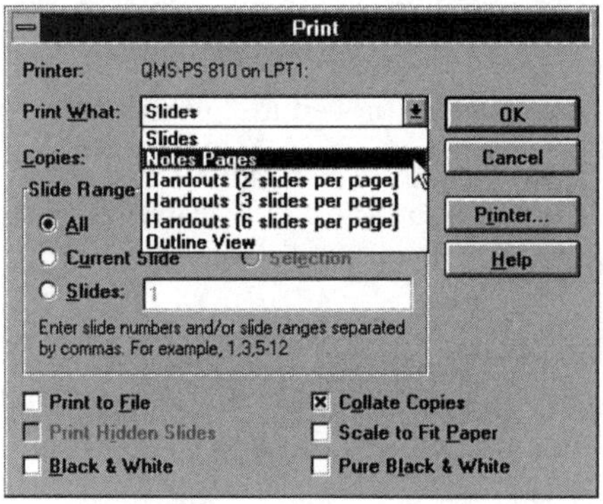

Fig. 7.10
The Print
dialog box.

Troubleshooting

I accidentally deleted the slide image or notes box. Can I restore it?

You can restore the slide image or notes box at any time as follows: from the F**o**rmat menu, choose Notes Lay**o**ut. In the Notes Layout dialog box that appears, choose **A**dd Slide Image or Add Notes **T**ext (or both) and then choose OK. If the notes box you deleted contained text, it won't be restored. Slide images, however, are restored.

If the deletion was your last action, you can also use Undo, which reverses your last action. To use Undo, press Ctrl+Z; or from the **E**dit menu, choose **U**ndo.

I changed the background and color scheme of a notes page. Can I change it back to the default format used by other notes pages?

Yes. Restore the default background color and shading as follows: from the F**o**rmat menu, choose Notes Back**g**round. In the Notes Background dialog box that appears, choose **F**ollow Master and then choose **A**pply. (To restore the default background for all notes pages in a presentation, choose Appl**y** To All.)

To restore the default color scheme, from the F**o**rmat menu, choose Notes **C**olor Scheme. In the Notes Color Scheme dialog box that appears, choose **F**ollow Master and then choose **A**pply. (To restore the default color scheme for all notes pages in a presentation, choose Apply **T**o All.

*I selected **P**review in the Notes Background dialog box, but nothing happened. What is wrong?*

The Notes Background dialog box is probably hiding the preview image. To move the dialog box, place the mouse pointer over the dialog box title and drag the dialog box to the lower right corner of your screen. (You can drag it so that most of it is off the screen.)

Creating Handouts

By providing your audience with handouts of the slides, you enable your audience to focus on your presentation, rather than on taking notes. Handouts can display two, three, or six slides per page. You select the layout when you print the handouts, as discussed later in this section. To allow room for notes on handouts, choose the three-slide layout.

Adding Text and Graphics to Handout Pages

Tip

To insert the date, time, or page number, use the Text button to create a text placeholder as described in step 5; then, from the **I**nsert menu, choose D**a**te, **T**ime, or Page N**u**mber.

You can add text and graphics to handout pages by using the Handout Master. Use the Handout Master, for example, to add the company logo and the date of the presentation to handouts. Any text or graphics added to the Handout Master appears on every handout page. Unlike notes pages, you cannot edit handout pages in PowerPoint individually.

To add text or graphics to the Handout Master, follow these steps:

1. Open the presentation for which you want to modify the Handout Master.

2. From the main menu, choose **V**iew. The View menu appears.

3. From the **V**iew menu, select **M**aster, and then choose Han**d**out Master. The Handout Master page appears, as shown in figure 7.11. Placeholders on the page show the layout for two, three, and six slides per page. (For three slides per page, the layout is shown by the three slides on the left side.)

Fig. 7.11
The Handout Master page.

Text button

Slide placeholders

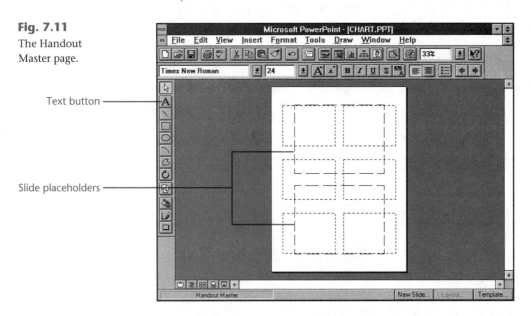

4. Add graphics, draw, or import artwork as you would on any slide. For details, see chapter 9, "Drawing Objects," and chapter 10, "Adding Clip Art and Scanned Art."

5. To add text, click the Text button (shown in fig. 7.11), position the insertion point where you want the text to appear, click the left mouse button to create a text placeholder, and type the text. You can format the text as you would text in any slide.

Be sure to place any graphics and text outside the placeholders for the layout you intend to use; otherwise, the slide images print over the graphics and text.

Printing Handouts

To select the number of slides per handout and print the handouts, follow these steps:

1. From the main menu, choose **F**ile. The File menu appears.

2. From the **F**ile menu, choose **P**rint. The Print dialog box appears.

3. From the Print **W**hat drop-down list, select one of the following:

    Handouts (2 slides per page)

    Handouts (3 slides per page)

    Handouts (6 slides per page)

4. Make any other selections you want and choose OK.

Working with Outlines

The first step in planning a presentation is preparing an outline. PowerPoint provides you with all the tools necessary to create and manipulate an outline—and even enables you to create slides directly from the outline.

Creating an Outline

To create an outline, you use Outline view. To display this view, from the **V**iew menu choose **O**utline, or click the Outline View button on the status bar, shown in figure 7.12. If you are starting a new presentation, Outline view displays the number 1 and a slide icon in the left margin, as shown in figure 7.13.

Tip

To maximize the area of the Outline view window, as shown in figure 7.14, click the Maximize button.

Fig. 7.12
In Slide view, click
the Outline View
button to display
Outline view.

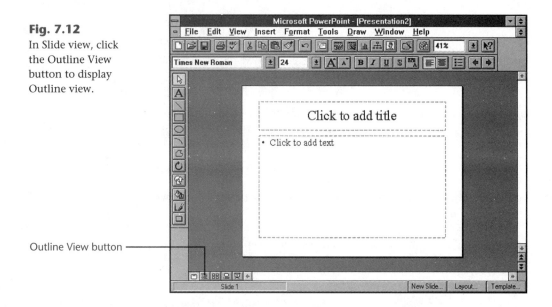

Outline View button ————

Fig. 7.13
Outline view for a
new presentation.

Slide icon ————

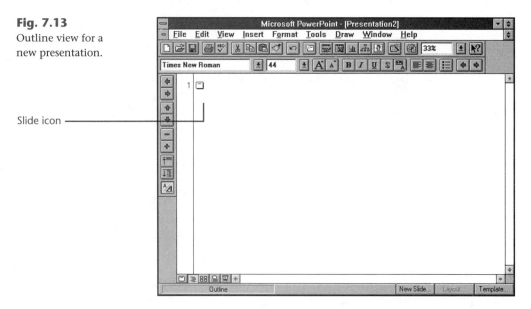

To create an outline for a new presentation, follow these steps:

1. Type the title of the first slide in your presentation and press Enter.
A slide icon appears for slide 2.

2. To enter a bullet point beneath the title, keep the insertion point on the line for slide 2. Then, click the Demote button, shown in figure 7.14; or press Alt+Shift+right arrow. PowerPoint automatically indents the line and inserts a bullet.

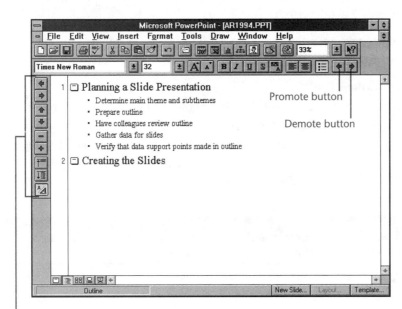

Outlining toolbar

Fig. 7.14
Use the Demote and Promote buttons to decrease and increase the level of an outline item. Notice that the buttons appear on both the Standard and the Outlining toolbars.

3. Type the text for that bullet point.

4. To add another bullet point, press Enter. PowerPoint automatically indents the next line and inserts the bullet. Repeat steps 3 and 4 until you have entered all the bullet points.

> **Note**
>
> An outline can have up to five levels beneath each slide title. Each level is indented from the previous level. To demote an item one level, place the insertion point on the item and click the Demote button; or press Alt+Shift+right arrow. To promote an item one level, click the Promote button; or press Alt+Shift+left arrow.

Tip
To insert a new line at the same level as the previous line but without a bullet, press Shift+Enter.

5. At the end of the last bullet point for the slide, press Ctrl+Enter to create the next slide.

6. Type the title of the next slide.

7. Repeat steps 2 through 6 to complete your outline.

You can also use Outline view to review the outline of an existing presentation. Just open the presentation and click the Outline View button in the status bar. The slide presentation appears as an outline, with the title and main text displayed for each slide. The outline does not show graphic objects or text you entered with the Text button.

Once you have an outline, you can use it to create, delete, modify, and rearrange slides. The next sections describe how.

Using Outline Tools

Outline view includes a special toolbar, shown in figure 7.14, that makes creating, modifying, and reviewing an outline easy. (If the toolbar isn't displayed, from the **V**iew menu, choose **T**oolbars. When the Toolbars dialog box appears, select the Outlining check box and then choose OK.) Table 7.1 describes each of the tools on this toolbar.

Table 7.1	Outlining Toolbar	
Tool	**Name**	**Action**
	Promote (Indent less)	Promotes one level the paragraph containing the insertion point. This moves the paragraph left one indent and changes the bullet character to match other bullets at that level.
	Demote (Indent more)	Demotes one level the paragraph containing the insertion point. This indents the paragraph more and changes the bullet character to match other bullets at that level.
	Move Up	Moves the paragraph containing the insertion point above the preceding item.
	Move Down	Moves the paragraph containing the insertion point below the next item.
	Collapse Selection	Collapses all levels of text for a slide, so that only the slide title appears. A line below the slide title indicates the text is collapsed. To use this tool, place the insertion point anywhere in the text for that slide (can be at any level of text), and click the tool button.

Tool	Name	Action
⊕	**Expand Selection**	Expands text that has been collapsed. To use this tool, place the insertion point in the slide title text and click the tool button.
↓≣	**Show Titles**	Collapses all levels of text for all slides, so that only slide titles appear. The insertion point can be anywhere in the outline to use this tool.
↑≣	**Show All**	Expands the outline so all levels of text for all slides appear. The insertion point can be anywhere in the outline to use this tool.
ᴬ⁄𝐀	**Show Formatting**	A toggle that lets you choose to display actual character formatting (for example, font and type size) or plain text. Using plain text, which is a smaller type size, enables you to see more of the outline on-screen. The insertion point can be anywhere in the outline to use this tool.

Using Outline View to Create Slides

When you create an outline, PowerPoint automatically creates slides with the titles and text you entered in the outline. To view one of the slides in Slide view, place the insertion point on the slide title in Outline view. Then choose **S**lides from the **V**iew menu; or click the Slide View button in the status bar. To display the next or previous slide in the outline, click the Next Slide or Previous Slide button; these are near the bottom of the right-hand scroll bar (the Next Slide button displays a double arrowhead pointing down; the Previous Slide button displays a double arrowhead pointing up).

In Slide view, you can edit the slide as you would any slide. Outline view automatically adjusts to reflect any changes you make in Slide view, so you need not worry about having different versions of the presentations. After you edit slides in Slide view, you may want to redisplay the presentation in Outline view to obtain an overall view of the changes.

You can also create a presentation from an imported outline. To import the outline, follow these steps:

1. From the main menu, choose **F**ile. The File menu appears.

2. From the **F**ile menu, choose **O**pen. The Open File dialog box appears.

3. From the List Files of **T**ype drop-down list, select Outlines. PowerPoint lists files that you can open as outlines.

4. Select the outline file you want to import.

5. Choose OK.

Manipulating Text in Outline View

You can edit text (except labels) in Outline view just as in Slide view. To make text italic, for example, select the text and then click the Italic button on the toolbar. (For details on working with text—including formatting, copying, and moving text—see chapter 6, "Working with Text.") Any changes you make to text in Outline view appear on the slide.

You cannot add graphics or labels in Outline view. To add these to a slide, you must first change to Slide view.

Rearranging and Deleting Slides in Outline View

Outline view enables you to easily rearrange and delete slides in your presentation. To select a slide to move or delete, click the slide icon for that slide. PowerPoint highlights the icon and all outline text associated with that slide.

To move the slide, drag the slide icon up or down to the new position in the presentation. PowerPoint automatically reorders the other slides. To delete the slide, just press Delete. When you move or delete a slide, PowerPoint moves or deletes the entire slide, including all text and graphics on the slide.

Adding Text and Graphics to Outline Pages

Use the Outline Master to add text and graphics objects that you want to appear on all outline pages, by following these steps:

1. Open the presentation for which you want to modify the Outline Master.

2. From the main menu, choose **V**iew. The View menu appears.

3. From the **V**iew menu, select **M**aster, and then choose **O**utline Master. The Outline Master page appears, as shown in figure 7.15. A placeholder on the page shows the text area for the outline.

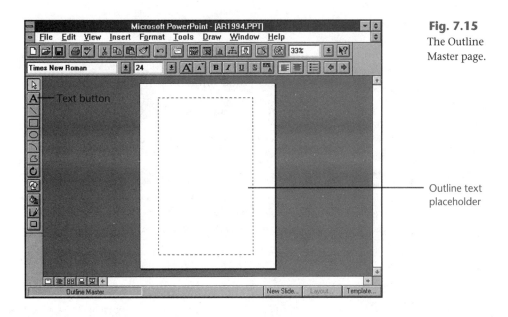

4. Add graphics, draw, or import artwork as you would on any slide. For details, see chapter 9, "Drawing Objects," and chapter 10, "Adding Clip Art and Scanned Art."

5. To add text, click the Text button (refer to fig. 7.15), position the insertion point where you want the text to appear, click the left mouse button to create a text placeholder, and type the text. You can format the text as you would text in any slide.

Be sure to place any graphics and text outside the placeholder for the outline text; otherwise, the outline text may print over the graphics and text.

Printing an Outline

An outline prints as it appears in the Outline view screen. If you have selected plain text and have collapsed the entries, for example, the printed outline is also plain text with collapsed entries. The outline also prints at the same scale as the zoom scale in the Outline view. Before you print an outline, therefore, make sure the Outline view has the settings you want for the printed handout.

Tip
To insert the date, time, or page number, use the Text button to create a text placeholder, as described in step 5; then, from the **I**nsert menu, choose **D**ate, **T**ime, or Page N**u**mber.

To print an outline, follow these steps:

1. From the main menu, choose **F**ile. The File menu appears.

2. From the **F**ile menu, choose **P**rint. The Print dialog box appears.

3. From the Print **W**hat drop-down list, select Outline view.

4. Make any other selections you want and choose OK.

Troubleshooting

I changed the indent or tab settings in my text chart, but Outline view doesn't reflect those changes. Can I change the tab or indent settings in Outline view?

No. Outline view has default tab and indent settings that cannot be changed. When you return to Slide view, however, your charts retain the tab and indent settings you selected.

I used the Text button to add text to my chart, but it doesn't appear in Outline view. How can I display it in Outline view?

You cannot. Outline view doesn't show text created with the Text button or any graphic objects.

From Here...

For other information relating to speaker's notes, handouts, and outlines, review the following chapters:

- Chapter 6, "Working with Text," covers most aspects of creating and editing text, including selecting, editing, and formatting text, searching and replacing text, and using the spelling checker.

- Chapter 9, "Drawing Objects," chapter 10, "Adding Clip Art and Scanned Art," and chapter 11, "Selecting, Editing, and Enhancing Objects," describe how to add graphics to a slide. The procedures also apply to adding graphics to master pages.

Chapter 8

Working with Tables

Using tables is a way to effectively communicate some types of information. A table can be used to list a group of specific points with short, explanatory notes beside them. While you can show this same information by using a text box and tabs for spacing, the table makes your job much easier by enabling you to easily place your text and format it as needed. By using a table you can easily align text into perfectly aligned rows and columns, enabling you to display information in a form that can be quickly grasped by your audience. From within PowerPoint you can use the power of Word's capability to create and manipulate tables and the information in them.

For you to use the Microsoft Word table option you must have Word 6 for Windows installed on your computer. If you do not, then this feature is not active. PowerPoint and Microsoft Word for Windows are capable of working together. When you want to place a table on a slide, clicking the Table button activates Word and places a table frame on your slide. You actually use Word and Word's menus and functions to create the table and then insert it in PowerPoint.

Starting Table Creation

Inserting a table onto your slide could not be easier. The only requirement is that you must have Microsoft Word 6 for Windows installed on your computer's hard disk before you can use the table function. When you use the Table command, you are actually inserting a table into your PowerPoint presentation from Microsoft Word for Windows.

In this chapter, you learn to create and work with a Microsoft Word for Windows table inside of PowerPoint to:

- Open the Word table function and select the table size

- Enter, format, and edit information in the table

- Adjust column and row widths in the table

- Add borders to the table

- Paste the table to the slide

II

Text

When you insert a table into PowerPoint from Word, you see the menus and most of the tools on-screen change from the PowerPoint menus and tools to the Word menus and tools. Some tools remain on the main toolbar but are not selectable until you have created your table and inserted it onto your slide. There are two basic methods that you use to insert a table from Word to your PowerPoint slide: by using the menus and by using the toolbar. The end result is the same for either method; you have a table displayed on your slide.

Starting Table Creation from the Menus

By using the menus, you can more easily create a larger table. To use the menus to create a table, follow these steps:

1. Display the slide on which you want to insert a table.

2. From the **I**nsert menu, choose Microsoft **W**ord Table. You see the Insert Word Table dialog box on-screen, as shown in figure 8.1.

Fig. 8.1

You use the Insert Word Table dialog box to select the number of rows and columns to be displayed in your table.

3. Enter the number of columns that you need for your table in the first text box named Number of **C**olumns. For example, enter **3** columns. You can also click the up- or down-arrow buttons to the right of the text box to increase or decrease the number of columns.

   The maximum number of columns that you can insert when you first create your table is 15. You can add additional columns later.

4. Enter the number of rows that you need for your table in the second text box labeled Number of **R**ows. For example, enter the number of rows as **4**. Again, you can type the number of rows needed or click the up- and down-arrow buttons to increase or decrease the number of rows.

   The maximum number of rows that you can insert from this dialog box is five. Again, you can add additional rows later if necessary.

5. Choose OK. PowerPoint automatically accesses Word's table function and displays a blank table within a table box. Figure 8.2 displays a table that is three columns by four rows.

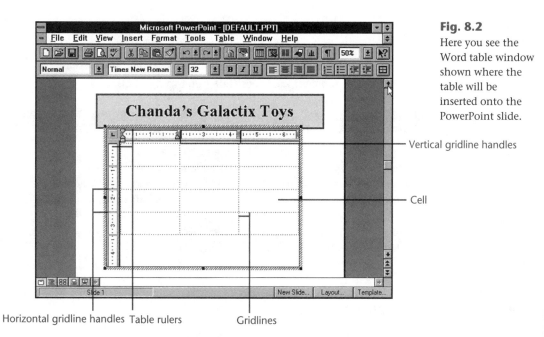

Fig. 8.2
Here you see the Word table window shown where the table will be inserted onto the PowerPoint slide.

Vertical gridline handles

Cell

Horizontal gridline handles   Table rulers   Gridlines

Starting Table Creation with the Toolbar

The main toolbar contains a tool named the *Insert Microsoft Word Table*, and that is what it does. To use this tool to insert a table, follow these steps:

1. Place the mouse pointer on the Insert Microsoft Word Table button and click. You see the grid box appear, as shown in figure 8.3.

Fig. 8.3
Here you see the grid box displayed beneath the Insert Microsoft Word Table button. You use this grid box to select the row and column format for your table.

2. Click and drag the mouse pointer across the grid box to indicate the number of columns and rows that you want in your table. Create a three row and four column table.

As you drag across the grid boxes from the upper left corner, you see the word Cancel at the bottom of the grid box replaced with 1 x 1 Table. The first number indicates the number of rows selected for the table and the second number indicates the number of columns. In addition to the number indicator at the bottom of the box, you see the grid boxes filled in with a different color. When you have the number of rows and columns for your table showing on the grid box, release the mouse button. PowerPoint accesses Word's table functions and displays an empty table grid on your slide (refer to fig. 8.2).

Note

It appears from the grid box that the largest table you can construct is four rows and five columns. You can increase the number of rows and columns. Simply drag the pointer down to the box indicating the number of rows and columns. PowerPoint adds another row. By continuing to drag down, you can add additional rows. By dragging the pointer past the right edge of the grid, you can add additional columns. The largest table you can create here is five rows by 13 columns. You can add additional rows and columns later.

Troubleshooting

When I click the Insert Microsoft Word Table button and either nothing happens or I get an error message, what's wrong?

You must be sure that you have version 6 or greater of Microsoft Word for Windows correctly installed on your computer. Notice that both the Windows and DOS versions of Word now have the same version numbers. You must have the Windows version.

Editing Tables

When you make changes to the structure of a table, such as adding rows and columns or adding text, formatting, charts, worksheets, pictures, or any other changes, you are editing the table. In this section you learn to enter text, edit text, and move from cell to cell. You also learn to use the Word for Windows toolbars to edit a table.

Inserting Rows and Columns

If you decide that the table you have created is too small to display the information you need, you can add additional rows and columns. When you are setting up the table format, you need to remember to include a row and/or column for row and column labels if needed.

To add rows and columns, follow these steps:

1. Add a row to your table by using one of the listed options:

   ■ Clicking the Insert Rows button on the toolbar.

   ■ From the Table menu, choose Insert Rows.

   ■ Place the mouse pointer inside of the table frame and click the right mouse button. Select the option Insert Rows from the displayed shortcut menu.

2. Add an additional column by moving the mouse pointer to the top of a column. You see the mouse pointer change to a downward-facing, black arrow, as shown in figure 8.4.

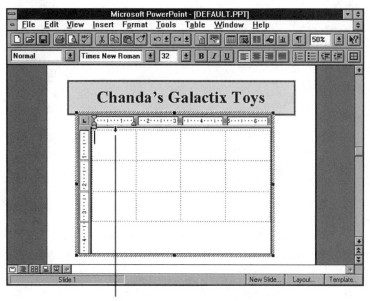

Column selector arrow

Fig. 8.4
Here you see the column selector arrow. From this point you can add additional columns to your table.

Tip
Once you have selected a column, you can use the Table, Insert Columns option to add another column.

3. Click the right mouse button and choose the Insert Columns option from the displayed shortcut menu. PowerPoint inserts another column. You can also select Table from the menu and Insert Columns from the drop-down menu.

Before you can see the new column, you may need to drag either the left or right resize handle to increase the size of the table frame. Figure 8.5 shows the new table with four rows and five columns. Notice how the table extends over the edge of the slide at this time. You can easily use your mouse to drag the table frame back onto the slide. Later in this chapter, in the section "Changing Column Width," you learn to resize your columns.

Fig. 8.5
You now see the table with both a column and a row added to it. Now that the table frame has been expanded to show all of the columns, it extends over the slide edge.

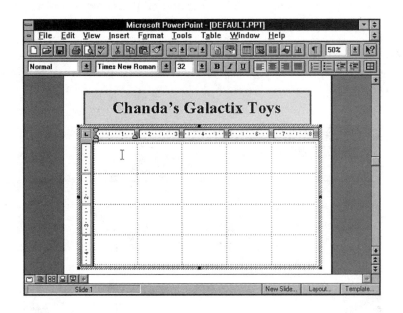

Using the Word for Windows Toolbars

When you add or edit a Microsoft Word for Windows table in PowerPoint, many of the buttons on the toolbar that were available to you are replaced by Word toolbar buttons (see fig. 8.6). Many of your menu options are also replaced by Microsoft Word for Windows menu options.

As you move the mouse pointer across the toolbar buttons, some are not available to you. You see the following message displayed in the status line at the bottom of your screen:

```
This command is not available because this document is being edited
in another application.
```

These options are again available to you after you complete your table.

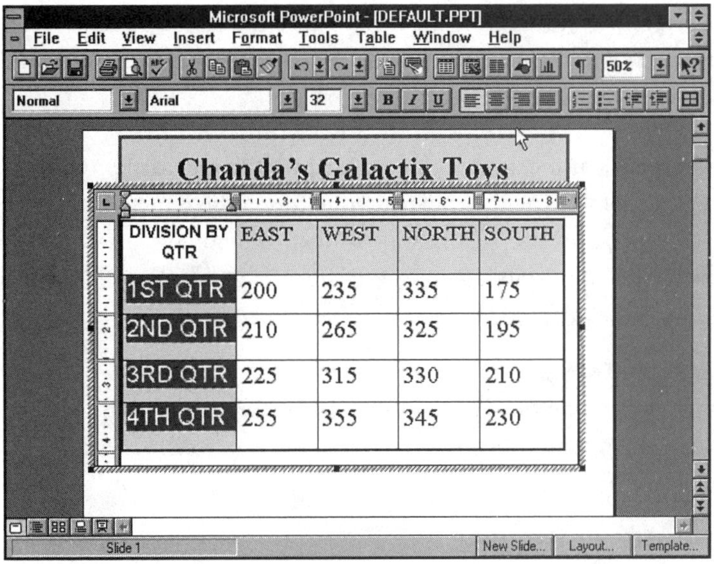

Fig. 8.6
Here you see the
Word toolbar that
you use to work
with your table.

The first toolbar contains a mixture of PowerPoint and Microsoft Word for
Windows buttons. Among the new buttons are the following:

Undo. This button enables you to undo your last action. Clicking the
down-arrow button beside the Undo button displays a list of all the
actions you have completed—starting with the most recent—since you
opened the table for use.

Redo. This button enables you to redo your last undone action. Clicking
the down-arrow button beside the Redo button displays a list box of all
the actions you have undone since you opened the table. The list begins with the most recently undone action.

AutoFormat. This option enables you to automatically format your text
or to apply a previously created style to your table.

Insert Rows. This button is used to insert a row. This option inserts a row
above the cursor's current location. For example, if you have a three
row table and want to add a new row 2, you place the cursor in the
current row 2. Click the Insert Rows button and a new row is inserted.
The old rows 2 and 3 each move down one position and are now rows 3
and 4 respectively.

Insert Microsoft Excel Worksheet. This option inserts a selected Excel worksheet at the cursor's location. This option is active only if you have Excel installed on your computer.

The second toolbar includes options similar to that included on the PowerPoint toolbar. These tools are used to format text, including options to set styles, fonts, font size, justification of text, and borders. These options are discussed in greater detail later in this chapter in the section, "Formatting Tables."

Typing Table Entries

By default, when you first create a table the cursor is located in the first cell—the upper left corner of the table. Entering text into a cell is simply a matter of typing. For the first cell type:

DIVISION BY QTR

In figure 8.7 you see the results of using the default font and font size.

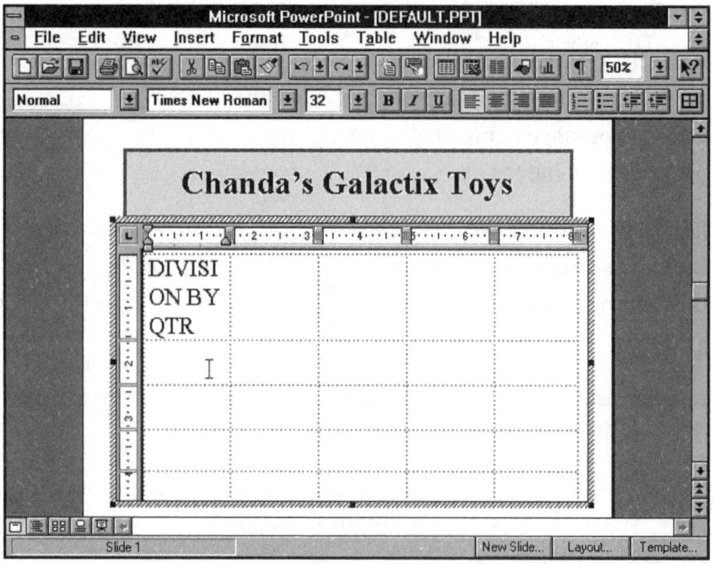

Fig. 8.7
Here you see the text entered into the first cell of the table. Notice how the text wraps to a new line and the cell height is automatically adjusted to fit the text.

Notice how the text does not go past the right cell border, but automatically wraps to the next line regardless of where the word normally breaks. You also notice how the cell height is adjusted downward to fit all the text. You learn to adjust fonts later in the section "Changing the Font Style."

Moving from Cell to Cell

You can move from cell to cell in a couple of different ways. You can always use the mouse and simply click the mouse pointer in the next cell that you want to enter text into.

You can also use the Tab key. The Tab key moves the cursor from the cell that it is currently located in to the next cell in the same row. If the cursor is in the last cell of a row, the cursor is moved to the first cell of the next row.

A third method of moving to another cell is by using the arrow keys on your keyboard.

> Pressing the right-arrow key moves the cursor to the next cell to the right.

> The down-arrow key moves the cursor to the cell immediately below the one it is currently located in.

> The up-arrow key moves the cursor to the cell above the one the cursor is located in. When the cursor reaches the first row, pressing the up-arrow key again only results in your computer beeping at you.

> The left-arrow key moves the cursor to the cell to the left. If the cursor is still located in a cell that contains text, the cursor moves one letter at a time to the left. Once the cursor reaches the beginning of the text it then moves to the next cell to the left.

Try each of these methods of moving from cell to cell and enter the following text into the indicated cells by following these steps:

1. Press the Tab key and type **EAST**.

2. Press the right-arrow key and type **WEST**.

3. Press the Tab key again and type **NORTH**.

4. Press the right-arrow key and type **SOUTH**.

5. Press the Tab key. Notice that the cursor now moves to the first cell of the next row. Type **1ST QTR**.

6. Press the down-arrow key and type **2ND QTR**.

7. Press the down-arrow key and type **3RD QTR**.

8. Press the down-arrow key and type **4TH QTR**.

Your table should now look like figure 8.8.

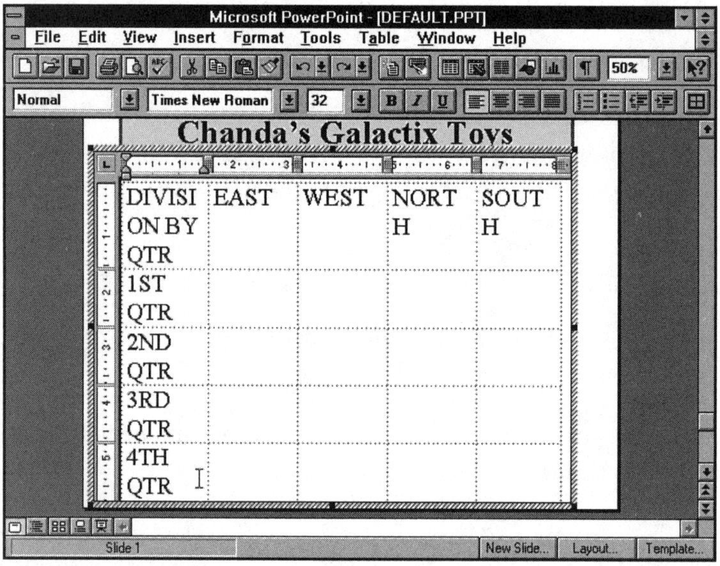

Fig. 8.8
Here you see the
completed labels
for the table.

Formatting Tables

When you start to enter information into your table, you quickly see whether
the default format settings are adequate for your needs. More often than not,
you will need to make some adjustments.

As you can see from figure 8.8, the font used for the text is too large. The text
in the first cell is broken in the wrong places, as are the words NORTH and
SOUTH.

By applying selected formatting to your text, you can make it look better,
make it easier to read, and more importantly, give the message that you are
trying to convey greater impact.

Selecting Table Entries

In order to adjust the formatting on text that has already been entered, you
must first select the table entry. You also have the capability with PowerPoint
to select an entire row, column, or the whole table. This can be especially
helpful when you want to make the same formatting changes to a row, a
column, or to the entire table.

To select the text in a single cell, follow these steps:

1. Select a single word or a cell of text by placing the mouse pointer at the beginning of the first word to be selected. Move the pointer to the left of the D in Division in the first cell. You see the mouse pointer change shape to the I-beam pointer.

2. Drag across all the text to be selected. You see the selected text highlighted in reverse video—white letters on a black background.

3. Click anywhere within the table frame to deselect the text.

Tip
You can also quickly select a single word by moving the mouse pointer on the word and double-clicking.

To select an entire row of text, follow these steps:

1. Place the cursor in the row that is to be selected. It does not matter in which cell you place the cursor, so long as the cell is located in the row that you want to select.

2. From the T**a**ble menu, choose Select **R**ow. All the text in the selected row is highlighted.

3. Click anywhere within the table frame to deselect the text.

Tip
You can also select a row of text by placing the mouse pointer at the beginning of the row and then clicking and dragging across the row.

To select an entire column of text, follow these steps:

1. Place the cursor within a cell in the column that is to be selected.

2. From the T**a**ble menu, choose Select **C**olumn. The text in the selected column is highlighted, as shown in figure 8.9.

Tip
You can also select a column of text by moving the mouse pointer to the top of the column. When the pointer changes shape to a downward pointing arrow, click once. The entire column is selected.

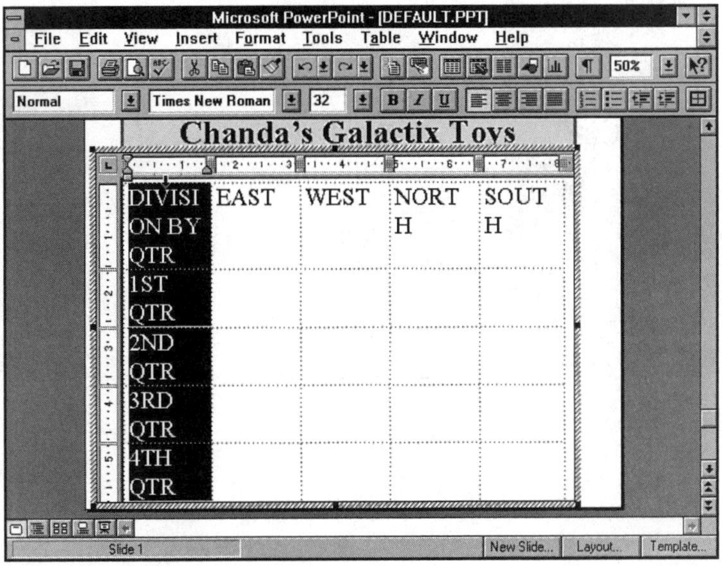

Fig. 8.9
The text in the first column of this table is selected.

Changing the Font Style

You can use any of the font styles that you have installed through the Windows Control Panel in PowerPoint. By using different fonts for the various parts of your table, you can emphasize specific parts of your information.

Some fonts are easier to read than others. You may need to experiment a little to see which of the fonts that you have available are the best for your presentation format.

To change a font style, follow these steps:

1. Select the specific text whose font is to be changed.

2. Click the down-arrow button beside the Font text box in the second toolbar at the top of your screen. You see a drop-down list box showing you the fonts that you have available for selection.

3. Scroll through the list until you find the font that you want to use and click the font name. You see the font name listed in the Font text box, and your selected text changes to the selected font. Figure 8.10 shows the selected text in the new font.

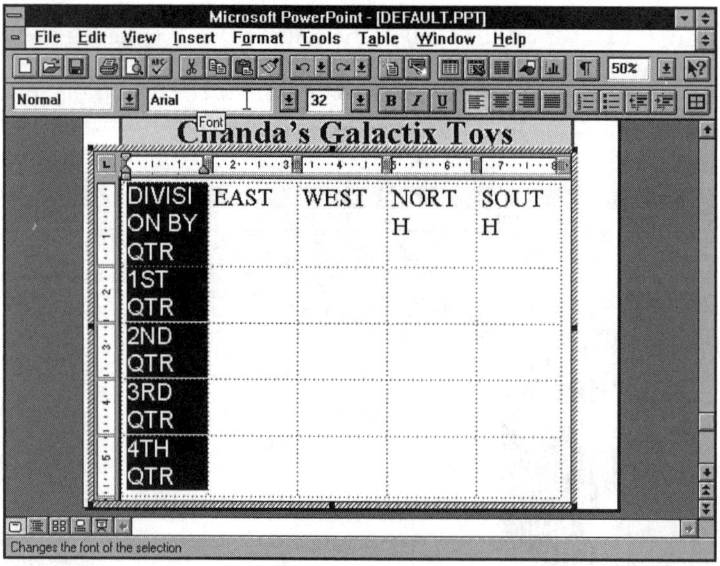

Fig. 8.10
You see the font for the selected column of text change. Notice the text remains selected until you click the mouse again.

The text remains selected until you click the mouse somewhere within the table frame. This enables you to change the font again if it is not to your liking, or to make other necessary changes to the text without selecting the same text again.

In addition to changing the font, you can apply three different attributes to a font: bold, italic, and underline. When you have selected the text, you can apply any of these attributes simply by clicking the appropriate button on the toolbar.

Changing the Font Size

In addition to changing the typeface, or font style, you can also change the sizes of many fonts. Some fonts that are installed with Windows, such as the font named LinePrinter, come in one size, 8.5 points. Others, like the Courier font, come in two sizes, 10 and 12 points. Fonts are measured by height in a system called points. There are 72 points in each inch, so if a font is 36 points, it is one-half inch high. TrueType fonts, which are designated by the double T symbol in front of the font name, are adjustable to almost any size that you may need.

Tip
Clicking the font attribute buttons before you begin to type applies that attribute to the text as you enter it.

To change the font size of your text, follow these steps:

1. Select the text whose font size you need to change. Place the cursor in any of the cells of the first row.

2. From the Table menu, choose Select **R**ow. This selects all the text in the first row of your table.

3. Click the down-arrow button beside the Font Size text box. This displays a predefined list of various font sizes available for the font that is applied to the selected text.

4. Select a font size that is a smaller number than was applied to the font. You want a smaller font than 32 points. This decreases the size of your letters, enabling you to display your words on a single line. Select 28 points for your text. Figure 8.11 shows the results of reducing your font size from 32 to 28 points.

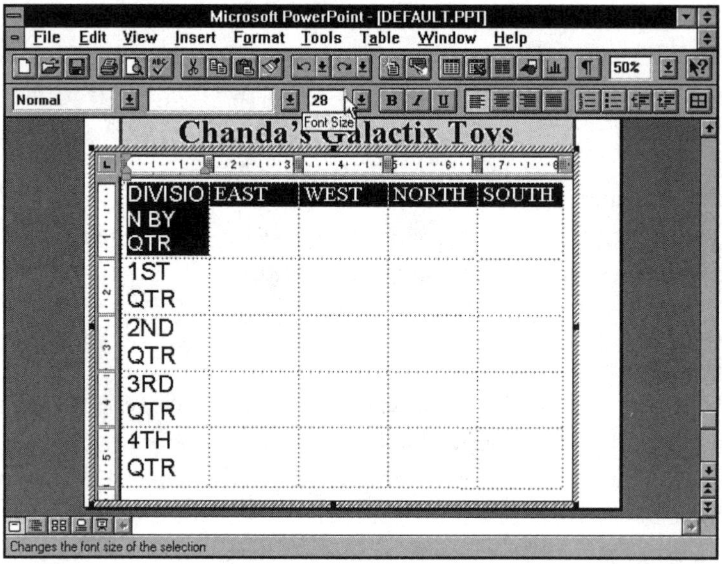

Fig. 8.11

Here you see the results of reducing the texts font size from 32 to 28 points. All the text, except that in the first cell, now fits without any unnatural breaks in the words.

5. Select the text in the first cell. Since reducing the text from 32 to 28 points was not enough to eliminate breaking the word Division, you need to reduce the font size further for this cell.

> **Note**
>
> You would not normally change the text in a single cell, because this can distract the audience from the point that you are making. For example, you would not increase the size of the word EAST in the second cell to 72 points, and leave the word NORTH as 28 points, unless you wanted to specifically draw attention to the column labeled EAST. Since the text in the first cell is a more general label for the table, and not directly associated with the other four columns (EAST, WEST, NORTH, and SOUTH), you do not have this problem.

6. Decrease the font size again for the selected text in the first cell. You may need to try several times to find the right fit for the text in the cell. You will find that 22 points is the correct size. Remember, you can select a specific font size for your text before you begin to type it.

Changing Column Width

PowerPoint enables you to easily adjust the width of selected columns or all columns in your table. This is useful when the information entered into different columns is of various lengths.

For example, you may want to make a column that contains a primary point wide and the text large and bold. The next column with the explanatory information for each point can be narrower and the text smaller. Figure 8.12 shows how different column widths can be used to draw the audience's attention to the main points of a presentation.

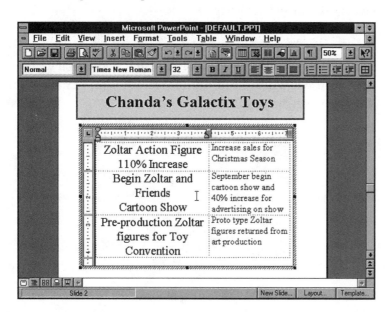

Fig. 8.12
Here you see a table with two column widths and different font sizes in each.

To adjust a single column's width in your table, follow these steps:

1. Move the mouse pointer to the column gridline on the right side of the column whose width you want to change. You see the mouse pointer change to a double-horizontal line with arrows pointing to the left and right.

2. Click the left mouse button and drag the column line to its new location. This method adjusts only the selected column border. All other columns are compressed into the space available, the table frame is not adjusted.

To adjust the width of several adjacent columns, follow these steps:

1. Move the mouse pointer to the top of the first column. When the pointer changes shape to the down-arrow column selector, click and drag across the columns to be adjusted. You see all the selected columns highlighted.

2. Double-click any of the vertical gridlines for the selected columns. PowerPoint automatically adjusts all of the columns so that they fit the longest line of data.

To automatically adjust all the columns of your table to best fit your information and the table, follow these steps:

1. To select the table, from the Table menu choose Select Table.

2. From the Table menu, choose Cell Height and **W**idth. You see the Cell Height and Width dialog box. Click the mouse pointer on the **C**olumn tab as shown in figure 8.13.

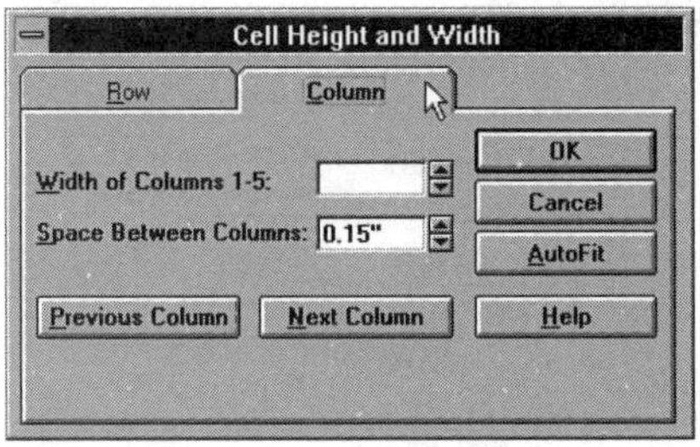

Fig. 8.13
Use the Cell Height and Width dialog box to adjust the width of all or selected columns and rows.

3. In the Cell Height and Width dialog box, make any changes you want. You can change the width of a column or the height of a row or both. When you select the **C**olumn option tab, you can make the following changes:

Width of Columns: You can specify an exact width for the selected column or table. If only a single column has been selected, the column number is displayed. Because the entire table has been selected, the display reads 1-5. You can enter any number for the width of your columns to a maximum of 22 inches.

Space Between Columns: With this option you can specify the amount of white space that remains between your columns. Again, the maximum space allowed is 22 inches.

Previous Column: This enables you to select the previous column in your table without closing the dialog box, selecting the column, and then reopening the dialog box.

Next Column: This option enables you to select the next column in your table, again without closing this dialog box and starting over.

AutoFit: This option changes the column size to best fit the longest text in the column, taking into account the size of the table frame. This option does not automatically increase the size of the table frame.

4. Choose the **A**utoFit button. Figure 8.14 shows the adjusted table.

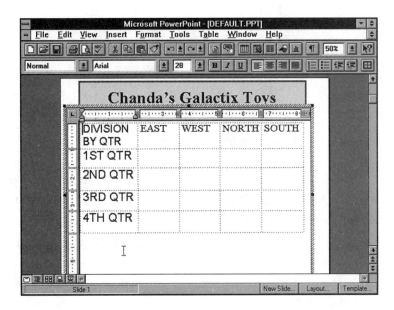

Fig. 8.14
Here you see the adjusted column widths after using the **A**utoFit option. Notice how the East and West columns are narrower than the North and South columns.

Adjusting Row Height

In addition to being able to change a column's width, you can change a row's height. The procedure for adjusting the height of a row is similar to changing the width of a column. All the individual cells of a row are the same height. Each row can have its own height.

To adjust the height of a row, follow these steps:

1. Move the mouse pointer to the vertical ruler.

2. Select the row marker for the row that you want to adjust. You see the cursor change to a vertical two-headed arrow.

3. Drag the row marker up or down the ruler. You see the row gridline move with the marker. When the row is the size that you need, release the mouse button.

Tip
Move the mouse pointer to a column marker on the horizontal ruler. Press and hold Alt+left mouse button. PowerPoint displays the actual measurements of each column on the ruler. When you release either button, the ruler reverts to normal measurements.

You can also use the Cell Height and Width dialog box to change a row or rows height. To use this dialog box, follow these steps:

1. Select the row or rows to be adjusted in height.

2. From the Table menu, choose Cell Height and **W**idth. You see the Cell Height and Width dialog box. Click the mouse pointer on the **R**ow tab, as shown in figure 8.15.

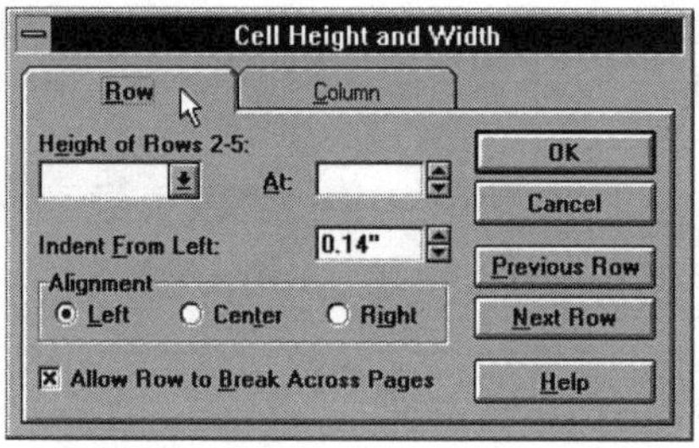

Fig. 8.15
Here you use the Cell Height and Width dialog box to adjust the height of selected rows.

3. In addition to being able to select **P**revious Row and **N**ext Row, as you were able to when selecting columns, you can choose some additional options for adjusting rows:

   H**e**ight of Rows: Select from the text box one of three options available to you. (The number beside the label indicates the number of the row or rows that are selected and will be acted upon. In figure 8.15, rows 2 through 5 are selected.)

   Auto. This option adjusts the row width automatically to fit the text that is entered.

   At Least. This option adjusts the row width to the number entered in the **A**t text box. If the contents of the row exceed this number, the row is adjusted to fit.

   Exactly. This option fixes the row height to the number entered in the **A**t text box. If the contents of the row exceed the row height, the contents are cut to fit.

   Indent **F**rom Left. Enter the distance from the left edge of the column that you want your text indented. This helps to divide your columns from each other.

Alignment. Click the appropriate alignment for your rows in relation to the slides page margins.

Allow Row to **B**reak Across Pages. When an x is placed in the box, the text in a row can be broken across a page, if necessary.

4. When you have made the necessary adjustments to the row or rows height in the dialog box, click the OK button to save and apply your changes. Your table is automatically adjusted.

Changing Cell Data Alignment

You can easily change the alignment of your text within a cell or selected cells. By simply changing the alignment of text, you can change the readability of your presentation. You have four alignment buttons available to you on the formatting toolbar.

Align Left. This button aligns your text with the left margin of the cell.

Center. This button centers the selected text within the cell.

Align Right. This buttons aligns the selected text with the right margin of the cell.

Justify. This button provides full justification of the selected text within the left and right indents. When text is justified, words may be stretched with extra space between letters so that the text fills the cell. Font size is not changed, only spacing between letters and words.

To change the alignment of text in your table, follow these steps:

1. Select the text to be aligned. For example, select the first column of text.

2. Click the Center button on the format toolbar. The selected text is immediately centered.

Adding Borders to a Table

By adding borders and shading to your table, you can help draw attention to the entire table or to selected portions of the table. You can accomplish this quite easily from within the table functions. The gridlines that are displayed are not printed, nor are they visible once you return to PowerPoint. If you want to shade cells or place lines around or within your table, you must do so now.

To add borders and shading to your table, follow these steps:

1. Click the Borders button on the Formatting toolbar. You see a new toolbar appear beneath the Formatting toolbar.

2. Select the entire table. Click the down-arrow button beside the Line Style text box. You see a drop-down list of different line styles. Select the 3pt line. It appears in the text box.

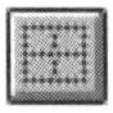

3. Click the Outside Border button. A solid 3-point border is placed around the entire table.

4. Select the Line Style drop-down list again. Choose the 1 1/2 pt line this time.

5. Click the Inside Border button. A solid 1 1/2 point border is placed inside your table around each cell. Deselect the table by clicking inside the table frame. Your table now looks like figure 8.16.

6. Select the cells that contain the division titles EAST, WEST, NORTH, and SOUTH.

7. Click the down-arrow button beside the Shading text box to display the list of shading options, and select the 20% option.

8. Select the cells in the first column, 1ST QTR through 4TH QTR, and repeat step 7. Your table now looks like figure 8.17.

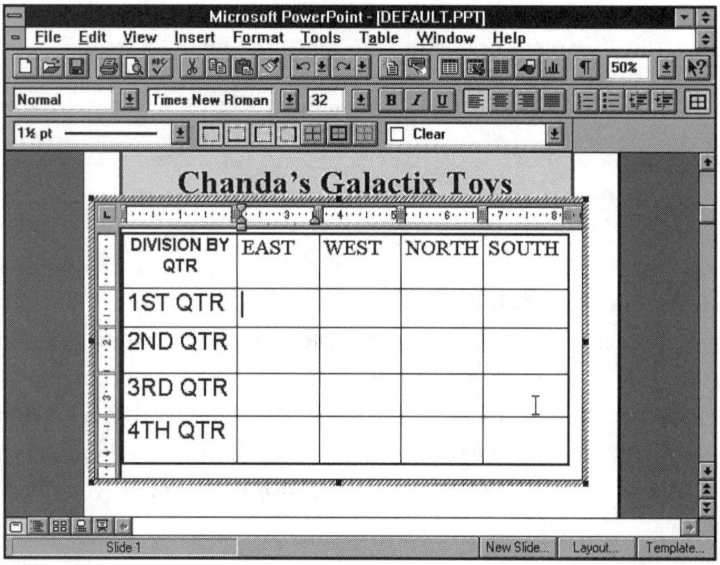

Fig. 8.16
Here you see both the inside and outside borders in this table.

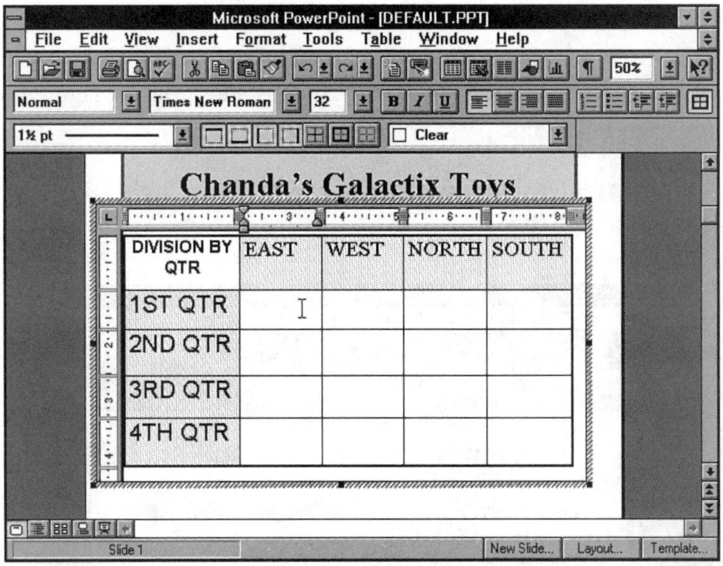

Fig. 8.17
You now see the table with shading added to selected cells that contain the labels.

Troubleshooting

When I tried to resize a column by dragging the column selector on the ruler, only one cell in one row changed size. All the rest of the cells in the column stayed the same size; what happened?

When using the column selector on the ruler, if you select a row, then only the selected row is affected when the column border is moved. You can sidestep this problem by dragging the column gridline instead of the column selector, or by deselecting the row first.

Pasting the Table Onto the Slide

After your table is complete, it is time to paste the table onto the slide. The table that you created is an embedded object. While you used Microsoft Word for Windows to create the table, it actually belongs, or is embedded, in PowerPoint. This table is not a file that you find available when you open Microsoft Word for Windows the next time.

An embedded object can be copied to a disk and then run on a computer that does not have the originating program, in this case Microsoft Word for Windows, installed on the second computer.

II

Text

To paste the table onto your slide, simply click the mouse pointer outside the table frame. After a few seconds the Microsoft Word for Windows menus and toolbars are replaced with the PowerPoint menus and toolbars. Figure 8.18 shows the completed table pasted onto the slide.

If you find that you need to edit the table at any time, simply display the slide and double-click the table.

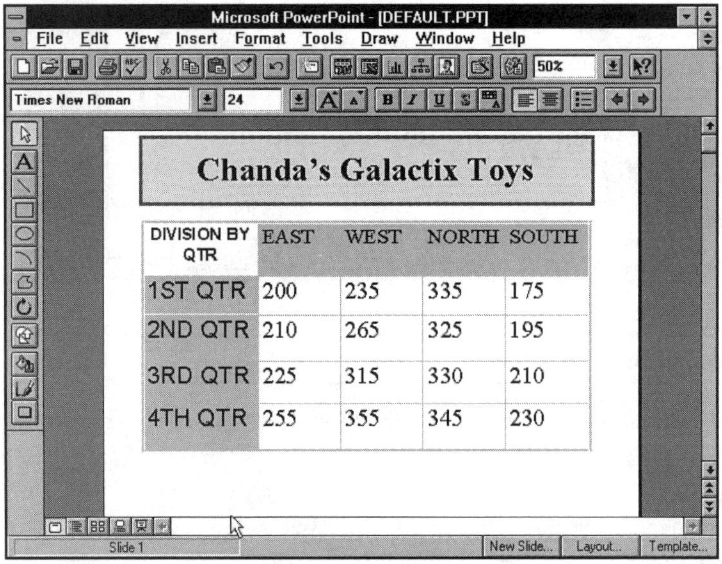

Fig. 8.18
Here you see the completed table pasted onto the PowerPoint slide.

Creating a Chart from a Table

You can use information in a table to create a chart. If your table contains labels and numbers, you can create a chart from this information. By selecting the cells to be included and then selecting the Insert Graph button on the toolbar, Microsoft Word for Windows opens Microsoft Graph. Microsoft Graph then uses the selected information to build a chart. Like the Microsoft Word for Windows table, the Microsoft chart is also an embedded object.

When you embed the chart from Microsoft Graph to the Word table, the chart is displayed below the table. You may need to do some resizing of the table frame to be sure that everything fits on your slide. See chapter 19, "Using Advanced Charting Features," for more information about charts.

From Here...

Now that you have learned to create, edit, and insert a table from Microsoft Word for Windows into your PowerPoint presentation, you are ready to learn additional features, such as charting, drawing, and creating links to other applications. Refer to the following chapters for more information about these subjects:

- Chapter 9, "Drawing Objects," shows you how to draw and place objects on your slide.

- Chapter 13, "Creating Basic Charts," shows you how to create charts using datasheets and how to customize your charts.

- Chapter 18, "Using Links to Other Applications," shows you how to take full advantage of Windows linking and embedding features.

II

Text

Part III

Drawing

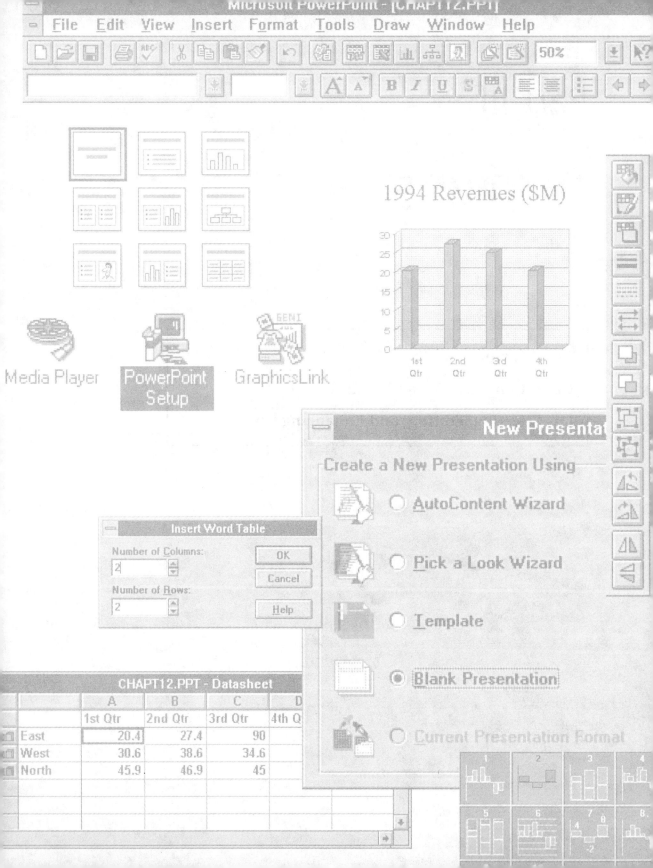

Chapter 9

Drawing Objects

When you have set the basic structure of your presentation and you know what you want to say and how you want to present your subject, it is time to take your visual effects another step forward. PowerPoint provides you with a complete set of drawing tools. You can also choose freehand drawing and use a set of AutoShapes.

With PowerPoint you have the capability to use shapes and color to emphasize a specific point or piece of information. Figures can be scaled to fit your needs, rotated, or have shadows applied to them. In this chapter, you learn to use the PowerPoint drawing tools to help you create a presentation that can inform and convince your audience.

Using PowerPoint's Drawing Tools

With PowerPoint's professional drawing tools, you can draw and revise shapes, lines, text, and pictures to create the professional presentation that you are aiming for. Each of the objects you draw for your slide is infinitely adjustable.

The PowerPoint window contains a complete set of drawing tools on the Drawing toolbar. By default, this toolbar is located along the left side of your window and has 12 tool buttons. You can add additional buttons to the toolbar at any time, move the toolbar, or cause it to be a free-floating object depending upon your needs. The twelve Drawing toolbar tools are described in table 9.1.

In this chapter, you learn to:

- Draw lines, arcs, polygons, and use AutoShapes

- Use vertical, horizontal, and 45-degree angle lines

- Draw lines, arcs, and polygons from a center point

- Use guides, grids, and edges to align objects

III

Drawing

Table 9.1	Drawing Tools	
Icon	**Tool Name**	**Usage**
	Selection Tool	Selects any object. This tool is selected by default.
	Text Tool	Enables you to enter text in a text box.
	Line Tool	Use this tool to draw a single straight line.
	Rectangle Tool	Use this tool to draw boxes or rectangles.
	Ellipse Tool	Use this tool to draw ellipses and circles.
	Arc Tool	Use this tool to draw curved lines from two selected endpoints.
	Freeform Tool	Use this tool to draw a many-sided figure. It enables you to continue to draw lines until you connect the beginning point with the endpoint.
	Free Rotate Tool	This tool enables you to rotate an object by one of the four corner points. Any object can be rotated in a full 360-degree circle.
	AutoShapes Tool	This tool displays a sub-toolbar from which you can select a predefined shape. These shapes can be manipulated as all other shapes or lines are.
	Fill On/Off	Automatically applies the default fill pattern to the selected object, or removes it.
	Line On/Off	Automatically applies the default line type to the selected line object, or removes it.
	Shadow On/Off	Automatically applies the default shadow type to the selected object, or removes it.

Drawing Basic Shapes

Many of the most complicated drawings start with the simplest shapes: the line, the arc, and the polygon. By using these objects for the basis of your drawings, you can create the emphasis that you want for the slide and your point.

To create even more complex drawings, you can combine different pieces of a drawing together to complete a single drawing.

Drawing Lines

The line is the most basic of all aspects of drawing. Lines in series compose any other object. To draw a line, follow these steps:

1. Open the slide that you want to draw on.

2. Click the Line Tool button on the Drawing toolbar.

3. Move the pointer to the slide and to the beginning point of your line. Notice how the mouse pointer changes shape to a crosshair when you cross onto the slide boundary.

4. Click to anchor the line at this point and then drag the pointer to the endpoint of your line.

5. Release the mouse button to indicate the line's endpoint, as shown in figure 9.1.

Tip

Move any object by clicking and dragging it to the desired location. As you drag, an outline of the object moves along with the mouse pointer.

Fig. 9.1

Here you see a line drawn below the slide title text. The endpoints of the line are shown by the small black squares at each end. These are also the manipulating handles for the line.

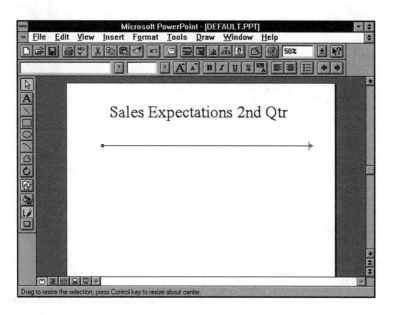

Manipulating and Moving a Line

Any PowerPoint object can be manipulated or moved to anywhere on your slide. You can quickly resize, move, or tilt a line. To adjust your line, follow these steps:

III

Drawing

1. Place the mouse pointer at the center of your line and click and hold down the mouse button. You see the solid line change to a dotted line.

2. Drag the line to its new location. Figure 9.2 shows the line moved further below the slide title.

Fig. 9.2

You see the line moved from its previous location directly underneath the title to a position closer to the middle of the slide.

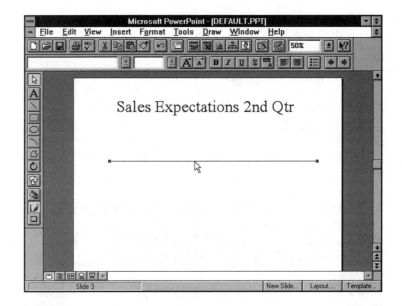

3. Click and drag one of the handles on the line.

You can extend the line by simply moving the handle in the same plane as the rest of the line. By dragging the line up or down, you can tilt the line. The opposite endpoint remains stationary throughout these movements.

Drawing an Arc

Of course, not every line is a straight line and not every item that you want to show in your slide can be illustrated by using straight lines. PowerPoint comes prepared with the capability to draw arcs. An *arc* is a curved line between two points. You have the capability to adjust the curve of the arc to fit your specific needs.

To draw an arc or curved line, follow these steps:

1. Select the Arc Tool by clicking it once.

2. Move the pointer to the place where you want to begin the arc. Click and hold the left mouse button.

3. Drag the pointer to the endpoint of your arc and release the mouse button. Your arc looks something like the one shown in figure 9.3.

4. Move the mouse pointer down to the mid-point handle on the right and drag it to the middle of your screen. Your arc has been stretched. The beginning point has remained stationary, while the endpoint has moved further to the right along the same plane.

Tip
If you used the Windows Control Panel to change the orientation of your mouse buttons, then use the right button for this operation.

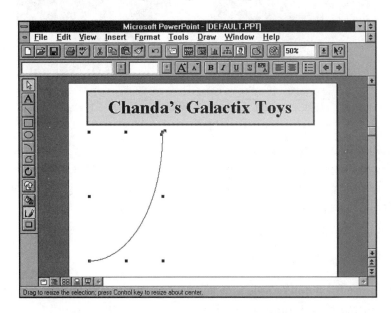

Fig. 9.3
Here you see the arc drawn on the slide. Notice the eight handles surrounding the arc. You pull or push these handles to adjust the size and curve of your arc.

> **Note**
>
> If you want to adjust the endpoints of an arc, use the handles that are located on those endpoints. To move one endpoint in a single plane, use either of the mid-point handles nearest the endpoint to be moved. The corner points opposite the arc endpoints move either one or both endpoints in two dimensions at once. Moving a corner point that also contains an arc endpoint moves only the selected endpoint in two dimensions.

Do not hesitate to experiment with your drawing. Try each of the handles to see just what it does. As you try each movement, you gain confidence in your drawing abilities. Figure 9.4 shows a series of arcs used to form a curtain effect on a slide.

Tip
Selecting an arc and then choosing from the menu **E**dit, **E**dit Arc object enables you to turn the arc line into a full or partial circle by using the current arc as the circle circumference. Simply click and drag one of the arc endpoints until your arc appears as you want.

III

Drawing

Fig. 9.4
A series of arcs was used to draw a curtain for this opening slide. Various fill patterns and colors are used to color the curtain folds.

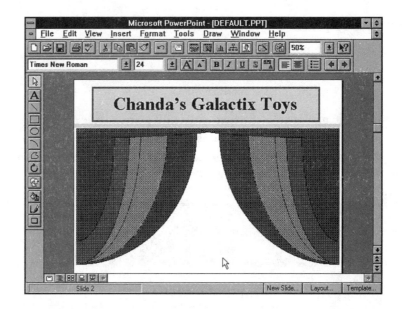

Drawing with Polygons

Polygons, or freeform shapes, can be used to draw many things. These can be either closed or open shapes. A polygon is closed when the beginning and endpoints meet. A polygon is open when the endpoints do not meet.

To draw a polygon, follow these steps:

1. Click the Freeform tool.

2. Move the pointer to the slide and click the left mouse button once to anchor the beginning point. Do not hold down the button.

> **Note**
>
> If you hold down the left mouse button or click the drag lock (if it is available on your mouse), you see the pointer shape change to a pencil. You can then draw on your slide as if you had a pencil. You may want to try this method, but it takes a very steady hand to draw successfully in this manner.

3. Move the pointer to the next corner and click the left mouse button again. This anchors the next point. You can simulate a curve by drawing many small lines together, each one a small angle from the last.

4. To finish the polygon, do either of the following:

■ Close the polygon by clicking the end drawing point on the beginning point. PowerPoint immediately changes the pointer from a crosshair to the arrow, applies the default fill pattern or color, and displays the eight resizing handles around the polygon.

■ Double-click the left mouse button or press the Enter key.

Either of these actions completes an open polygon, again displaying the eight resizing handles surrounding the polygon.

Figure 9.5 shows both an open freeform polygon and a freeform closed polygon. The one polygon is considered open because the neck has not been closed, so the beginning and endpoints do not meet.

Tip

If you are drawing a complex shape, try increasing the magnification on your slide to 200% or more so that you can easily see the smaller lines. Decrease the magnification to see your whole drawing.

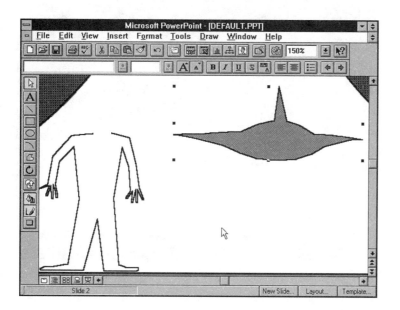

Fig. 9.5
Here you see two freeform polygons, one open and the other closed. As you can see, a fairly complex object can be quite easily drawn using a freeform shape.

Using Rectangles and Ellipses

In addition to lines, arcs, and freeform drawing, you also have access to tools that help you draw regular circles, ellipses (oblong circles), squares, and rectangles. By using these tools, you can draw a more exact figure without the potential jaggies and bumps associated with the freeform objects.

III

Drawing

To use the ellipses and rectangle tools, follow these steps:

1. Click the Ellipse tool.

2. Move the crosshair pointer to the slide. To place an ellipse, think of it as a curved rectangle. You click and hold the pointer at the position that you want to place one of the ellipse's corners.

3. Drag the pointer until the ellipse is the shape and size you want and then release the mouse button. You have an ellipse similar to that shown in figure 9.6. Remember, you can always drag the ellipse to another location or adjust its size and shape if it is not quite in the place or the size that you need.

Fig. 9.6

Here you see an ellipse used as a head for the figure drawn earlier. By using the handles on the ellipse, you can change the ellipse to a circle.

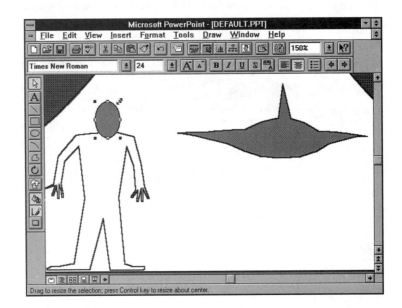

4. Click the rectangle tool.

5. Move the crosshair pointer to the position on the slide that you want to start your rectangle. A rectangle is drawn by showing PowerPoint where you want the two opposite corners placed.

6. Click and drag the pointer to the opposite corner for this rectangle and release the mouse button. Figure 9.7 shows a rectangle placed in the slide.

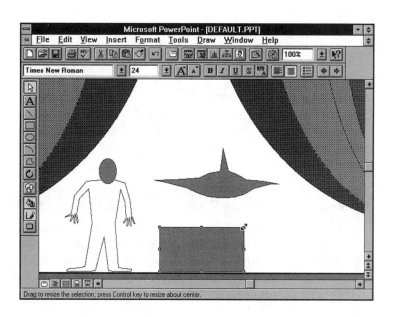

Fig. 9.7
You now see a rectangle placed on the slide. As with all other objects, you can easily adjust the placement and size of the object.

Enhancing an Object with Fills, Color, and Shadows

In addition to drawing an object, you can also enhance an object by applying colors, fill patterns, and shadows. By using color, you can make your presentation more attractive and emphasize a particular point or object. Fill patterns are useful when you must show your presentation in a non-color printed form. You can apply various fill patterns in lieu of using color. Shadows can be used to give your slide a more 3-D effect. With PowerPoint you can adjust shadows to give a greater feeling of depth.

To add fill patterns, color, and shadows to your slide, follow these steps:

1. Select an object, such as the open polygon man shape drawn earlier. Remember, an object is selected when the eight object handles are shown surrounding the object.

2. Click the right mouse button to display the object's attributes menu, which appears at the point where the mouse pointer is located.

3. Choose the Colors and Lines option from the menu. You now see the Colors and Lines dialog box appear, as shown in figure 9.8.

III

Drawing

Tip
Be sure that you have the pointer located within the object that you want to work with, not just within the rectangle of selector handles.

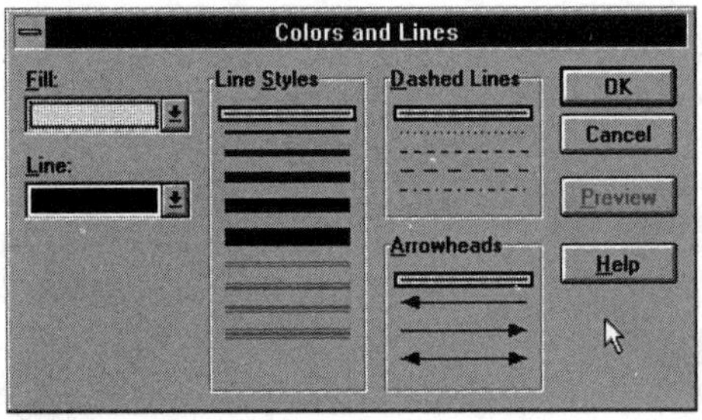

Fig. 9.8

The Colors and Lines dialog box is used to select line styles, arrowheads for lines, line colors, and fill patterns.

> **Note**
>
> Each drawn object consists of two parts. The border is the first part and it appears as a line. A rectangle's border consists of the four lines that are used to create it, while a circle is composed of a single line. The second part of an object is its interior. The attributes for each of the parts of an object are controlled from the Colors and Lines dialog box.

From the Colors and Lines dialog box you can change many of the attributes of the objects that you draw. Almost all of these options can be combined to create the specific effect that you are looking for.

4. If you want, select options for dashed lines, arrowheads, and line styles:

   Dashed Lines. Select one of the four styles of dashed lines. The chosen style is applied to the border line surrounding the selected object. The default selection is a solid line.

   Arrowheads. Select one of the three styles of arrowheads when you want to use a line to point out another object. You can choose to have an arrowhead on the left, right, or both ends of your line. The default option, again, is a solid line without arrowheads. This option is only available for an object that has two endpoints, such as a line, arc, or open polygon.

   Line **S**tyles. Choose from six solid lines of various widths and four other styles of multiple lines.

5. Use the **F**ill drop-down list and select Pattern option. From the Pattern Fill dialog box, select the fill pattern to be used (see fig. 9.9) and then click the OK button in the Pattern Fill dialog box. You see the selected pattern appear in the **F**ill box in the Colors and Lines dialog box.

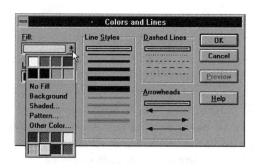

Fig. 9.9

Use the **F**ill drop-down list to select the specific type of fill option that you want to apply to your object.

From the **F**ill drop-down list, you can choose from these options:

Eight color block selections. These are the default color settings that are always available to you.

No Fill. Select this option if you do not want a fill pattern or color to be applied.

Background. Selecting this option applies the default background color or pattern to the selected object.

Shaded. This option displays the Shaded Fill dialog box. You can use this dialog box to select some specialized shading effects.

Pattern. This option displays the Pattern Fill dialog box. You select from 36 different pattern options. You can also select different background and foreground color options.

Other Color. This option displays the Other Color dialog box from which you can select from a palette of 88 colors. By clicking the **M**ore Colors button, the More Colors dialog box is displayed. You can use this dialog box to mix your own unique colors. Your options are only limited by your video graphics adapter and your monitor. When you select other colors, they are added to the eight additional color blocks at the bottom of the Fill drop-down list. When you add a second color, the first moves over a block. When you add a ninth color, the first color is dropped from the group. You can always reselect it again, but you are limited to a maximum of 16 colors on the drop-down list.

6. If you want, select an option from the **L**ine drop-down list. This list is similar to that shown by the **F**ill option. You can select a color for your

III

Drawing

line from the default block of eight colors or add additional colors by using the Other Color dialog box. You can also select the option No Line. PowerPoint shows your object without a line surrounding it.

Caution

If you create an object that has the same fill pattern or color as your slide and then select the No Line option, your object effectively becomes invisible. It is still there, but you can't see it. Only by clicking in the area that the object is in and finally clicking one of its lines will the selector box be displayed around the object.

---

7. Click the OK button in the Colors and Lines dialog box. Figure 9.10 shows you the finished result on the man shape.

Fig. 9.10
Here you can see the finished application of a pattern on a drawn object.

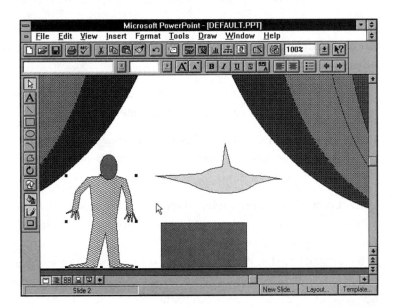

Placing a shadow behind an object adds a 3-D effect to your slide. To do so, follow these steps:

1. Select an object to apply a shadow to; for example, the closed polygon shape of the flying saucer.

2. From the **Format** menu, choose **Sh**adow from the main menu bar. You see the Shadow dialog box appear (see fig. 9.11).

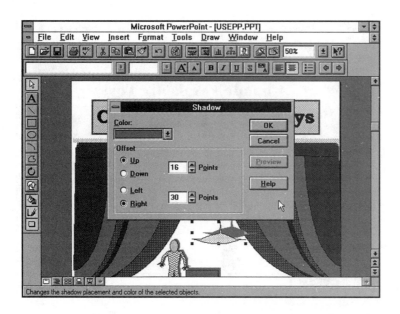

Fig. 9.11
With the Shadow
dialog box you can
select the color of
your shadow and
its placement in
relation to the
original object.

3. From the **C**olor drop-down list, select a color that is darker than your
   object and background. This list shows the eight default color blocks
   and the three options; No Shadow, Embossed, and Other Color.

   You now see that two of the radio buttons in the block labeled Offset
   are turned on and numbers placed in the two text boxes labeled Points.
   From here you control the perceived location of the light source and
   the distance of your object from the background.

4. If your light source is supposed to be coming from above and to the
   left, then your shadow should be offset down and to the right. This
   means that you should click the **D**own and **R**ight buttons.

5. To make your object appear farther from the background, increase the
   numbers in the two Points text boxes. Alternatively, decrease the numbers if you want your object to appear close to the background.

6. Click the **U**p radio button and enter the number of points that you
   want the shadow to appear from your object.

7. Click the **R**ight radio button and again enter the number of points that
   you want the shadow to appear from your object.

8. Click the OK button to apply your shadow. Figure 9.12 shows shadows
   applied to each of the objects on the slide.

Tip
Always be sure
that your shadows
all appear to come
from the same
light source, so
that all are facing
the same direction.

Tip
You can make
objects appear to
be closer or farther
away by changing
the apparent
shadow.

III

Drawing

Fig. 9.12
In this slide, you can see the effect of applying a shadow to an object.

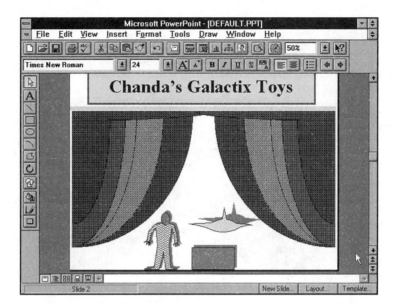

Drawing AutoShapes

PowerPoint for Windows comes equipped with a number of predefined shapes called *AutoShapes*. These shapes are fully adjustable in size and many include an additional adjusting handle. AutoShapes are included on the AutoShapes toolbar. An icon button is shown for each of the shapes. By simply clicking an AutoShape you can place it on your slide.

You have already become familiar with two AutoShapes that appear on the Drawing toolbar: the ellipse and the rectangle. The other AutoShapes are used in a similar way.

The AutoShapes toolbar has 24 additional AutoShapes available to you. Some of the other shapes include a starburst, a star, several forms of arrows, a cross, a box, a voice balloon, and others.

As with all the drawing tools, you can combine AutoShapes with each other and with freeform shapes to build complex objects. To use the AutoShapes toolbar, follow these steps:

1. Click the AutoShapes button on the Drawing toolbar. You see the AutoShapes toolbar appear. By default the AutoShapes toolbar is a floating toolbar.

2. Select the Thin Right Arrow tool and move the pointer to the slide.

3. Click the pointer to anchor the beginning point and drag to the endpoint for this object, and then release the mouse button. Your arrow should look something like figure 9.13.

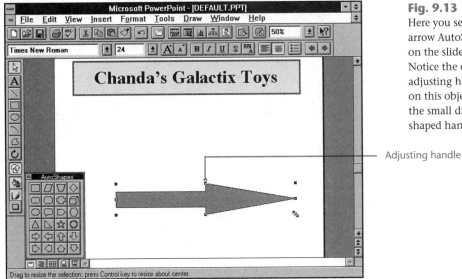

Fig. 9.13
Here you see the arrow AutoShape on the slide. Notice the extra adjusting handle on this object—the small diamond shaped handle.

Adjusting handle

4. Move the pointer to the adjusting handle and drag it forward toward the arrow's point. Figure 9.14 shows the results of using the adjusting handle. Notice that the pointer changes shape from the traditional arrow to a small arrowhead.

While not all AutoShapes have an adjusting handle, all AutoShapes do have the normal complement of eight resizing handles.

Tip
Convert the AutoShapes toolbar from a floating toolbar to a horizontal or vertical toolbar by pointing to the title bar and dragging the toolbar toward an edge of your screen. Change it back by double-clicking the toolbar.

III

Drawing

Fig. 9.14
Here you see that by using the adjusting handle on an AutoShape, you can change not only the size of a shape, but also its actual appearance.

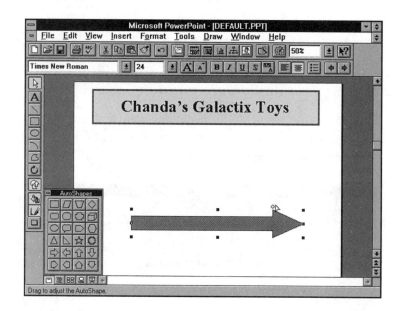

Rotating Objects

 Any object created in PowerPoint for Windows can be rotated with the Free Rotate tool. This even includes title bars and text boxes. The capability to freely rotate an object gives you a great deal of creative freedom. You are no longer limited to displaying objects and text in a single horizontal plane.

You can easily draw objects, add text if needed, and then move these objects and rotate them to suit your own requirements. To see how the Free Rotate tool is used, follow these steps:

1. Click the Seal tool from the AutoShapes toolbar. Move it to the slide and draw a large oblong shape by clicking and dragging.

2. Select the Text tool on the Drawing toolbar. Move the pointer inside the shape you have drawn and type **HUGE ONE DAY ONLY SALE**. This may fit best in three lines. You have a drawing similar to that shown in figure 9.15.

Fig. 9.15
Here you see the two objects on the slide: a drawn figure object and then a text object placed on top of the drawn object.

3. Click the Selection Tool button and move the pointer back to the slide. Draw a box that surrounds the drawn object and the text inside of it. As shown in figure 9.16, you see all the handle points for both objects displayed.

4. From the **D**raw menu, choose **G**roup. This action groups these two objects as a single object that can be manipulated together. Now when you move the drawing the text remains inside.

Tip
You may find that you need to move the drawn object to get the text to fit correctly. Generally it is easier to move the drawing than the text.

Fig. 9.16
Notice all the selector handles displayed for both the drawn and text object.

III

Drawing

5. Select the Free Rotate tool on the Drawing toolbar. Move the selector to one of the four corner handles of the group object on the slide.

6. Click and drag the object to its new location. Figure 9.17 shows the object after having been rotated.

Fig. 9.17
Here you see the figure having been rotated. Notice the rotate pointer on the slide.

Rotate pointer ──

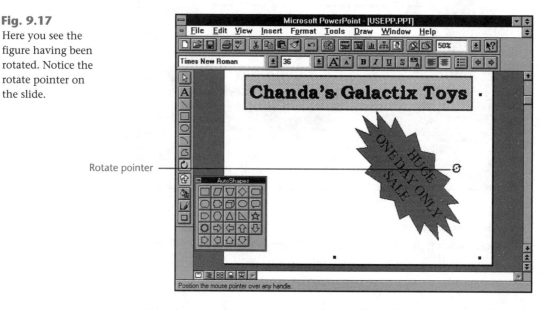

As you can see from this sequence, being able to draw an object, place text within it, group the two objects together, and then rotate them can be a very effective method of drawing attention to an idea.

Drawing Precisely

When creating a presentation, neatness counts almost as much as content. The last thing you want to do is distract your audience with sloppy drawings. The next several sections show you how to use your drawing tools in a very precise manner.

Drawing Vertical, Horizontal, and 45-Degree Angle Lines

There will be times when you do not want to freehand draw lines. You want a line that is exactly horizontal, vertical, or at a 45-degree angle, but you do not need a rectangle or right triangle for your drawing. You can easily draw such lines with PowerPoint for Windows.

To draw horizontal, vertical, and 45-degree angle lines, follow these steps:

1. Click the Line Tool button on the Drawing toolbar.

2. Move the pointer to the slide.

3. Press and hold the Shift key and click and hold the mouse button and drag your line. Figure 9.18 shows a vertical, a horizontal, and a 45-degree line drawn on the slide.

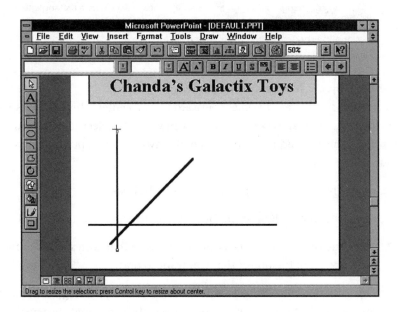

Fig. 9.18
Here you see three lines drawn on the slide, a vertical, a horizontal, and one drawn to a 45-degree angle.

Drawing Uniform Shapes

Uniform or regular shapes include squares, circles, and other shapes that can be drawn within a square. Regular shapes can include the AutoShapes buttons that you can use. You cannot turn a freeform drawn shape into a regular shape. Without PowerPoint for Windows' special capabilities to draw regular shapes, you would have to use the ellipse tool and try to approximate as closely as possible a circle, for example. Unless you have an extremely accurate eye and steady hand, this can be quite difficult.

To draw uniform shapes, follow these steps:

1. Select the Ellipse tool from the Drawing toolbar and move the pointer to the slide.

Tip
You can draw multiple objects by double-clicking the tool button. The tool remains active until you press a key or select another tool.

III

Drawing

2. Press and hold the Shift key and click and hold the mouse button, and then drag an ellipse on the slide. PowerPoint for Windows forces the shape to be a regular circle on your slide.

Note

You can also quickly turn a non-regular shape, such as an ellipse or a rectangle, into a regular shape. Simply double-click any of the resizing handles. The object changes to a regular shape: an ellipse to a circle, a rectangle to a square. Using this method always changes your shape into a regular shape along the shorter of the up/down and left/right axes.

Drawing Objects from a Center Point

You can also easily draw an object outward from a center. This can be especially helpful if you know exactly where you want an object to be placed on your slide. This technique can be used with any object except for objects drawn with the freeform tool.

To draw an object from a center point, follow these steps:

1. Select the tool to draw with, for example, select the Rectangle tool.

2. Move the pointer to the position on the slide that corresponds to the center point of the object that you want to draw.

3. Press and hold the Ctrl key and mouse button as you drag the rectangle on your slide. Notice how a mirror image of the rectangle is drawn on the opposite side of the center point as you drag the pointer. When your object is the size that you want, release the mouse button to complete the object.

Note

If, as you draw an object, you release the Ctrl key, your object will immediately be redrawn, or shifted, so that your starting point of the drawing becomes the opposite corner instead of the center point. If this is not what you want, press and continue to hold the Ctrl key again. Your drawing will again snap to the position that it had been in, with the starting point again as the center point.

Troubleshooting

I want to delete a drawing object. How do I do this?

Click the object to select it and then press the Delete key.

I made a mistake on a freeform drawing. How do I back up and correct it?

Simply press the Backspace key. This deletes the last endpoint you made. You can back up as far as you need by pressing the Backspace key. Each previous endpoint is deleted up to, but not including, the beginning point.

I want to move or resize several objects together without making them a group. Can I do this?

Yes, you can. Make sure that the Selection tool is selected. Draw a box around all the objects that you want to temporarily act upon as a group. You see each of the object's resize handles displayed. Drag any of these handles to resize all the objects together. To move all of the objects, click them and drag them to the new location.

When I try to select several objects together, I seem to miss one or another. Why?

Be sure when you draw your selection box around the objects that you completely enclose all the objects that you want to select. If you miss even a small corner of an object, it will not be included with the group.

I know that I have drawn an object and made it invisible by selecting No Fill and No Line. How do I find this object again?

Draw a selection box that surrounds the entire slide. You now see the resize handles for each object on your slide, including the invisible object. Click one of the resize handles with the right mouse button and change the line or fill type to a color. Your object can now be seen.

Tip
You can combine both the center point and regular shaped object features by pressing the Ctrl and Shift keys in combination: Ctrl+Shift+drag object.

Aligning Objects

PowerPoint for Windows has two types of methods that can be helpful in aligning your objects. One tool is called *guides* and the other is a set of *gridlines*. These tools are available to you from the menu bar.

Using Guides

To give your slides the most professional appearance possible, you may want to align some or all of your objects. The guide lines can be used to help you in this function by providing vertical and horizontal axis lines. You can move

III

Drawing

the guide lines from their origination point at the exact center of your slide. PowerPoint for Windows tells you how far from the center point you have moved the guide line. For example, you have a slide that shows an arrow and a hexagon. You want to place the center of both objects one inch below the center line of the slide.

To align both objects, follow these steps:

1. From the **V**iew menu, choose **G**uides. You see two dotted lines appear on your slide, one vertical and the other horizontal. They intersect at the exact center point of your slide, as shown in figure 9.19.

Fig. 9.19

Here you see the horizontal and vertical guide lines on the slide. The guide lines meet at the slide's center point until you move them.

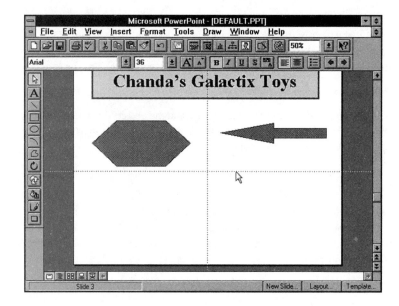

2. Click the horizontal guide line and drag the line downward. As you drag the line you see the mouse pointer replaced by the number `0.00`. As you drag the line, notice that the number increases. You also see an arrow to the right of, or beneath, the number. This arrow indicates if you are above, below, left, or right of the center point.

3. Drag the line down until you reach the point that you want to align your objects at. In this example, drag the mouse until the number reads `1.00` and then release the mouse button.

4. Now move the hexagon and then the arrow until both objects are centered on the horizontal guide line. If you move the objects slowly across

the line, you see them snapping to the guide line. Figure 9.20 shows both objects on the guide line.

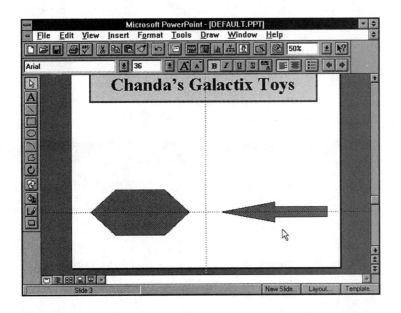

Note

If you need to align different groups of objects at different points, simply place the guide lines for the first groups and then align them. Move the guide lines for the next objects to be aligned and align them. The first objects do not move with the guide lines. Once an object has been aligned in a specific position, moving the guide lines has no further effect unless you move the object again.

5. Remove the guide lines by again choosing **G**uides from the **V**iew menu. This removes both the guide lines and the checkmark from the menu option.

Using the Grid

PowerPoint for Windows comes equipped with another alignment method called the *grid*. You can turn the grid on or off at any time. The grid consists of a series of invisible lines, both horizontal and vertical, across your slide screen. When the grid is turned on, your objects automatically snap to the closest gridline.

Tip
To see more clearly when aligning objects, increase the magnification of the slide to 100% or greater with the **Z**oom commands from the **V**iew menu or the Zoom Control on the main toolbar.

III

Drawing

Depending upon the measurement system that you have selected for PowerPoint for Windows, you have either 12 gridlines per inch or five gridlines per centimeter. To see how the grid works, use the example from the previous section on guide lines and follow these steps:

1. Increase the Zoom Control magnification to 300% and focus on the tip of the arrow. Turn on the guide lines as you learned in the previous section.

2. From the **D**raw menu, choose **S**nap to Grid.

> **Note**
>
> The Snap to Grid option is normally on by default when you first start PowerPoint. If a checkmark is displayed beside the menu option, Snap to Grid is on.

3. Select and drag the arrow upward. Notice that it does not move smoothly with the mouse pointer, but in small steps with a jerky motion.

Tip
You can temporarily override the Snap to Grid feature by pressing the Alt key as you draw your object.

4. Place the mouse pointer on the horizontal guide line and drag it up. You see the numbers change from 1.00 to 0.92 to 0.83. These are the distances from one gridline to the next. You see that the distance is not even, because 12 gridlines per inch does not work out to an exact two decimal point number.

To see how objects move without the gridlines, follow these steps:

1. From the **D**raw menu, choose **S**nap to Grid to turn off the gridlines and remove the checkmark displayed to the left of the menu option.

2. Select the horizontal guide line and drag it up again. Notice how the change in the measurement increments is as little as 0.01 inch now.

3. Select the arrow objects again. Drag it up and down the slide. Notice that the movement is now smooth and not jerky. PowerPoint for Windows is no longer snapping the object from one gridline to the next.

The gridline option is always turned on by default in PowerPoint for Windows. If you want to place objects with greater precision than that enabled by the grid, turn it off and align your objects.

From Here...

Now that you are familiar with drawing and placing objects on your slide, you are ready to add color to your drawings and add clip art to your slides. To learn to use color and clip art, refer to the following chapters:

- Chapter 10, "Adding Clip Art and Scanned Art," shows you how to use the PowerPoint for Windows ClipArt Gallery and place and add clip art pictures.

- Chapter 14, "Customizing Charts," shows you the basics about using color in charts on a slide.

- Chapter 17, "Working with Color," builds your knowledge and skills for using color to increase the impact of your presentation.

III

Drawing

Adding Clip Art and Scanned Art

PowerPoint comes with a variety of professionally drawn pictures known as clip art, which you can use in your slides. These drawings are professionally done and save you time when you need to put together a polished presentation in a hurry. PowerPoint stores these drawings in files with a .PCS extension.

PowerPoint goes further by allowing you to use pictures from other sources. For example, by using a scanner with special software, you can scan your company's logo in a bitmap (.BMP) file and include it in a presentation. You can also include pictures from other applications such as word processors, spreadsheets, or desktop publishing programs. PowerPoint is able to read over 20 different file formats currently used for storing pictures. In this chapter, you learn more about some of these formats. This chapter also discusses scanners and the use of scanned art in presentations.

Clip art is organized and accessed by using the ClipArt Gallery, a utility optionally installed with PowerPoint. In this chapter, you learn how to insert pictures onto a slide using the ClipArt Gallery. You also learn how to add and organize pictures using the ClipArt Gallery.

Using the ClipArt Gallery

There are more than 500 clip art pictures included with PowerPoint. With so many to choose from, there is a good chance you'll find one or two pictures that will work well in your presentation. If you don't find what you're

In this chapter, you learn to do the following:

- Insert clip art from the ClipArt Gallery

- Search for and organize clip art in the ClipArt Gallery

- Insert clip art from another application

- Add scanned art to a slide

III

Drawing

looking for among the clip art included with PowerPoint, you can use pictures from other applications. When you're ready to place a picture onto a slide, you do so using the ClipArt Gallery, which is discussed next.

PowerPoint's ClipArt Gallery allows you to manage a large collection of clip art organized into a number of predefined categories including business, landscapes, communications, and animals. You can also use the ClipArt Gallery to organize every picture in your collection. This includes not just what's on your hard disk, but also floppy disks as well. Like a library, the ClipArt Gallery maintains an index containing the location of each picture in the gallery. Using this method, you can keep track of a large collection of useful artwork without having to use up valuable hard disk space.

 To access the ClipArt Gallery, choose **C**lip Art from the **I**nsert menu. Alternatively, click the Insert Clip Art button on the toolbar. If you are accessing the ClipArt Gallery for the first time, notice that PowerPoint must create a clip art database that is used by the ClipArt Gallery to locate the clip art in the gallery. Before answering Yes to the prompt that appears next, keep in mind that this process could take a few minutes. Once the clip art database has been created, the ClipArt Gallery dialog box appears, as shown in figure 10.1.

Fig. 10.1
The ClipArt
Gallery dialog box.

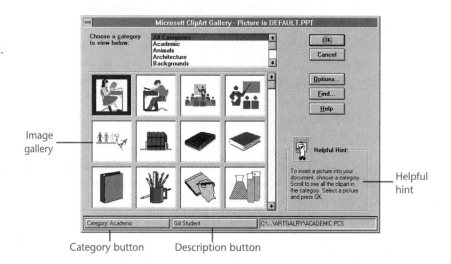

Make a selection from the Choose a **C**ategory to view below list at the top of the ClipArt Gallery to display pictures by category. The default selection is All Categories. The section just below the list is the Image Gallery, which displays pictures assigned to the current category.

At the bottom of the ClipArt Gallery dialog box are two large buttons side by side. When you select a new category, it is displayed on the left button: the Category button. If you move to another picture in the Gallery, its description is displayed on the next button to the right: the Description button. You use the Category and Description buttons to change the category name or picture description, as described later in this chapter.

Another important feature you'll find useful is the Helpful Hint section, located in the lower-right corner of the dialog box. You find Helpful Hints throughout PowerPoint in many of the major dialog boxes. They tell you how to perform the principle task associated with the current dialog box; in this case, selecting and placing a piece of clip art onto a slide. If you need additional information, choose the **H**elp button.

Placing Clip Art from the Gallery onto a Slide

You start from the ClipArt Gallery dialog box to place clip art onto a slide. Keep in mind that a presentation must be open first. Place clip art onto a slide by following these steps:

1. Display the ClipArt Gallery dialog box by choosing **C**lip Art from the **I**nsert menu, or by clicking the Insert Clip Art button on the toolbar.

2. In the ClipArt Gallery dialog box, choose a category from the Choose a **C**ategory to view below list. The default selection in the list is All Categories.

3. Scroll through the gallery of pictures in the Image Gallery and make a selection by clicking the desired picture.

4. Choose OK or press Enter.

> ### Note
> Choose Insert Picture to place clip art not found in the ClipArt Gallery onto a slide. Click the Drives box and select a new drive and then double-click a folder in the Directories box. Make your selection from the Picture Name list and then choose OK or press Enter. Either method results in the picture being placed on the current slide.

Searching for Clip Art

You can search the ClipArt Gallery for a specific picture or group of pictures. When you click the **F**ind button in the ClipArt Gallery dialog box, the Find

III

Drawing

Picture dialog box appears. The Find Picture dialog box allows you to narrow or expand your search criteria by category, text used in the picture description, file name, and file type.

To search for clip art, follow these steps:

1. Display the ClipArt Gallery dialog box by choosing **C**lip Art from the **I**nsert menu, or by clicking the Insert ClipArt button on the toolbar.

2. Choose the **F**ind button. The Find Picture dialog box appears, as shown in figure 10.2.

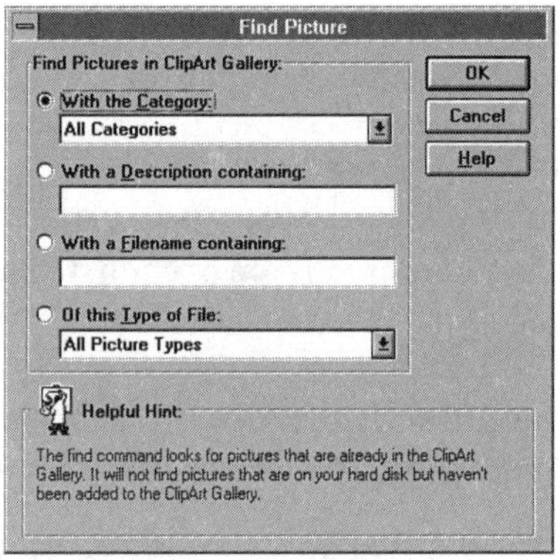

Fig. 10.2

The Find Picture dialog box, from which you can search for particular clip art.

3. From the With the **C**ategory drop-down list, choose a category. The default selection is All Categories.

4. In the With a **D**escription containing text box, type a word or partial word. Use this option to perform a search based on the text in a picture description. For example, typing the word **Jet** causes PowerPoint to search for all pictures in the gallery with this word in their descriptions. PowerPoint displays all clip art having this word in its description.

5. Optionally, in the With a **F**ilename containing text box, type a full or partial file name to further narrow the search. This option allows you to change the name or delete a category without affecting the pictures associated with the category.

6. From the Of this **T**ype of File drop-down list, select a file type. Use this option to locate pictures that are saved in a different file type than those included with the ClipArt Gallery. The default selection is All Picture Types.

7. Click OK. The ClipArt Gallery displays the pictures matching your criteria.

Managing the ClipArt Gallery

Choosing the **O**ptions button from the ClipArt Gallery dialog box causes the Options dialog box to appear (see fig. 10.3). You use the Options dialog box to manage the ClipArt Gallery—adding and deleting clip art and clip art categories. The Options dialog box divides these operations among four buttons: **R**efresh, **A**dd, **C**hange a Category, and **E**dit Picture Information. These options are described briefly in table 10.1. More details about these options are given in the sections that follow.

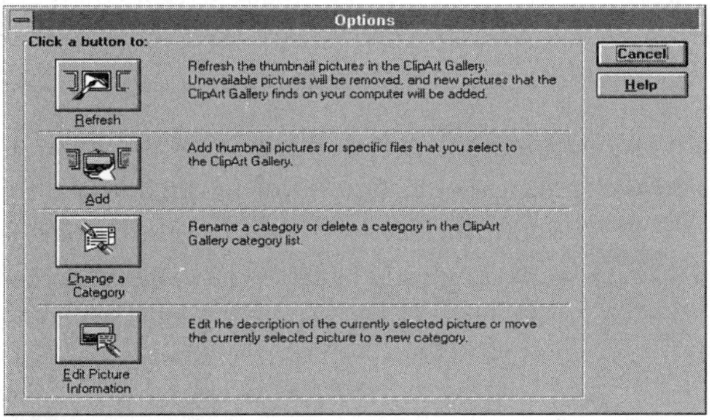

Fig. 10.3
The Options dialog box helps you manage the ClipArt Gallery.

Table 10.1   Options for Managing the ClipArt Gallery

Option	Description
Refresh	Updates the ClipArt Gallery, removing previously recorded entries that can no longer be found and adding entries for new pictures.
Add	Allows you to add a specific picture or group of pictures to the Gallery.
Change a Category	Allows you to change the name or delete a category without affecting the pictures associated with the category.
Edit Picture Information	Allows you to change the description of a picture or reassign the picture to different category.

III

Drawing

Adding Clip Art from Other Applications

You can take advantage of object linking and embedding (OLE) to add pictures, text, graphs, or tables to your presentations. Embedding inserts the object into your presentation, while linking inserts a reference to the object in your presentation.

When an object such as a graph is linked to your presentation, all copies of the object are updated whenever changes are made to the original. Use linking when you need to update several copies of the same data immediately.

Use embedding when you want to quickly make changes to an object. Because the object is actually inserted into the presentation file, there are no links to consider; you simply double-click the object and make your change in the application that appears next. Keep in mind that presentations with embedded objects take more room on your hard drive than those containing linked objects. To learn more about how to use OLE, see chapter 18, "Using Links to Other Applications."

Many Windows-based applications such as word processors and spreadsheet programs come with a variety of pictures saved in various file formats. For example, Word for Windows includes pictures that are saved in Windows Metafile (.WMF) format. Programs that enable you to create and edit images, such as desktop publishers, also allow you to optionally save images in multiple formats.

PowerPoint's ClipArt Gallery lets you add pictures from more than 19 different file formats (as shown in table 10.2) to your clip art collection. Notice that many of these file formats are native to a specific software package such as DrawPerfect or AutoCAD.

Table 10.2 File Types You Can Add to the ClipArt Gallery	
File	**Extension**
Window Bitmaps	.BMP
Windows Metafile	.WMF
HP Graphic Language	.HGL
Computer Graphic Metafile	.CGM
Encapsulated PostScript	.EPS

File	Extension
CompuServe GIF	.GIF
Tagged Image File Format	.TIF
Micrografx Designer/Draw	.DRW
PC Paintbrush	.PCX
Lotus 1-2-3 Graphics	.PIC
AutoCAD Format 2-D	.DXF
AutoCAD Plot File	.ADI
CorelDRAW!	.CDR
DrawPerfect	.WPG
HP Plotter Print File	.PLT
Kodak Photo CD	.PCD
Macintosh PICT	.PCT
Targa	.TGA
Windows DIB	.DIB

You choose the **A**dd button in the Options dialog box to search for and add one or more clip art files to the ClipArt Gallery. When you choose **A**dd, the Add ClipArt dialog box appears. Use this dialog box to select a drive, directory, and file type to locate. Files matching the specified file type are displayed in the list on the far left of the dialog box. You can click a file and choose **P**icture Preview to display the contents of the file.

To add clip art from another application to the PowerPoint ClipArt Gallery, follow these steps:

1. Display the ClipArt Gallery dialog box by choosing **C**lip Art from the **I**nsert menu, or by clicking the Insert ClipArt button on the toolbar.

2. Choose the **O**ptions button. The Options dialog box appears.

3. Choose the **A**dd button on the Options dialog box to display the Add ClipArt dialog box (shown in fig. 10.4).

III

Drawing

Fig. 10.4

The Add ClipArt
dialog box.

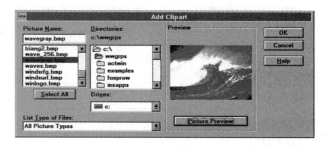

4. Click on the name of the picture in the Picture **N**ame list to select a single picture.

   To select a range of consecutive items, press the Shift key while clicking the first and last items in the group.

   To select anywhere within the list, press Ctrl while clicking various items in the list.

   To select all of the files in the list, choose the **S**elect All button.

   If you select only one picture, you can use the **P**icture Preview button to display the picture.

> **Note**
>
> If you have clip art located in other directories or another hard disk, click the Dri**v**es box and select a new drive and then double-click a folder in the **D**irectories box. Make your selections from the Picture **N**ame list by using the techniques covered in step 4.

---

5. Choose OK or press Enter.

   When more than one picture is selected, PowerPoint asks whether you want to assign each picture to a category. Answer **Y**es if you want to be prompted for a category for each picture. Otherwise, the pictures are added to the All Categories group.

6. If prompted, enter a category and description for the picture in the dialog box that appears next.

   Choose **A**dd to add the picture to the ClipArt Gallery.

   Or choose **D**on't Add to skip the picture and move on to next one.

Deleting and Renaming Categories

Choose the **C**hange a Category button from the Options dialog box to re-name or delete an existing category. The Change a Category dialog box appears, from which you can choose to rename a category or to delete a category.

When you delete a category, PowerPoint does not delete the pictures previously assigned to that category. The pictures are assigned to All Categories. To delete a category, follow these steps:

Tip

PowerPoint does not allow you to delete picture files. To do so, you must use the File Man-ager in Windows.

1. Display the ClipArt Gallery dialog box by choosing **C**lip Art from the **I**nsert menu, or by clicking the Insert ClipArt button on the toolbar.

2. Choose the **O**ptions button. The Options dialog box appears.

3. Choose the **C**hange a Category button to display the Change a Category dialog box (see fig. 10.5).

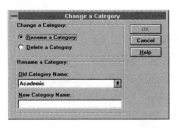

Fig. 10.5

The Change a Category dialog box, from which you can delete or rename a category.

4. In the Change a Category area of the dialog box, select **D**elete a Category.

5. Choose the category to be deleted.

6. Choose OK or press Enter. When you do so, PowerPoint prompts you for confirmation of the deletion. Choose Yes to delete the category, or No to cancel the operation.

Note

Pictures associated with a deleted category are not removed from your hard drive; they are simply added to the All Categories group.

III

Drawing

When you rename a category, all pictures that were grouped under the old category are reassigned to the new category. Follow these steps to rename a category:

1. Display the ClipArt Gallery dialog box by choosing **C**lip Art from the **I**nsert menu, or by clicking the Insert ClipArt button on the toolbar.

2. Choose the **O**ptions button to display the Options dialog box.

3. Choose the **C**hange a Category button to display the Change a Category dialog box.

4. In the Change a Category area of the dialog box, select **R**ename a Category.

5. Choose the old category name from the **O**ld Category Name drop-down list, and then type a new category name in the **N**ew Category Name text box.

6. Choose OK.

Moving Pictures to a New Category

The **E**dit Picture Information option in the Options dialog box displays the Edit Picture Information from which you can edit a picture's description or move the current picture to a new category. Another way to access the Edit Picture Information dialog box is to click the Category or Description button at the bottom of the ClipArt Gallery dialog box.

To move a picture to a new category, follow these steps:

1. Display the ClipArt Gallery dialog box by choosing **C**lip Art from the **I**nsert menu, or by clicking the Insert ClipArt button on the toolbar.

2. Choose the picture you want to move from the ClipArt Gallery.

3. Choose the Category button at the bottom of the ClipArt Gallery dialog box. The Edit Picture Information dialog box appears, as shown in figure 10.6.

> **Note**
>
> You can access the Edit Picture Information dialog box from the ClipArt Gallery dialog box by clicking the Category or Description buttons at the bottom of the dialog box.

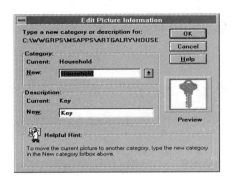

Fig. 10.6
The Edit Picture
Information dialog
box.

4. Specify a new category in the **N**ew text box in the Category area of the dialog box.

5. Choose OK or press Enter. The selected picture is moved to the specified category.

> **Note**
>
> You can use the Edit Picture Information dialog box to create a new category. Simply type a new category in the **N**ew text box and choose OK. The currently selected clip art is added to the new category.

Refreshing the ClipArt Gallery

When you choose **R**efresh, PowerPoint searches your hard drive for new clip art, optionally adding it to the ClipArt Gallery. Entries for unavailable pictures are removed from the Gallery.

Earlier in this chapter, you learned that the ClipArt Gallery records the location of each picture in your collection. You may need to move pictures located in a certain directory to a new location on your hard drive—or even to a diskette—to conserve space. When you do so, it is a good idea to update the ClipArt Gallery.

To refresh the ClipArt Gallery, follow these steps:

1. Display the ClipArt Gallery dialog box by choosing **C**lip Art from the **I**nsert menu, or by clicking the Insert ClipArt button on the toolbar.

2. Choose the **R**efresh button. The ClipArt Gallery prompts you to specify which drives to search.

III

Drawing

> **Note**
>
> Change a picture's description by choosing the Description button in the ClipArt Gallery dialog box and typing the description in the Edit Picture Information dialog box that appears next. Choose OK to complete the process. Use this feature to add description text that allows you to perform precise searches (using the Find button) based on a picture description.

3. Choose OK or press Enter to begin the operation.

4. If new art is found, PowerPoint first prompts you to ask whether you want to assign a category and description to the art. After making a choice, choose OK or press Enter to continue.

5. If prompted, enter a category and optionally enter a description.

   Choose **A**dd to add the picture to the ClipArt Gallery.

   Or choose **D**on't Add to skip the picture and move on to next one.

Entries for clip art in the Gallery that cannot be found are deleted.

Adding Scanned Art

Scanners allow you to copy a variety of important material such as company logos, drawings, photographs, and text into your computer directly from paper. There are two basic types of scanners: handheld and flatbed scanners. While flatbed scanners offer a wider range of options and features, many can cost as much as a personal computer. Handheld scanners, on the other hand, tend to be priced much lower, making them a popular accessory for a PC today.

Both types of scanners work the same way; they copy an image and save it to a file on your PC. Some flatbed scanners also allow you to scan color as well as black-and-white images. Flatbed scanners that do this make three passes over a color image using blue, red, and green light. Handheld scanners produce images that appear in shades of gray.

The software that usually comes with your scanner manages the scanning operation and also allows you to edit and print the image. Most software packages also give you more than one file format choice into which you can save the scanned image.

Placing a Scanned Image onto a Slide

Before you can place a scanned image on a slide, it must be added to the ClipArt Gallery, optionally assigning the picture to a category and giving it a description. Follow the steps given earlier in this chapter's section "Adding Clip Art from Other Applications."

To add the scanned picture to a slide, follow the steps given earlier in this chapter's section "Placing Clip Art from the Gallery onto a Slide."

Troubleshooting

I attempted to add a new image to the ClipArt Gallery by using **O***ptions,* **A***dd in the ClipArt Gallery dialog box, but there are too many files to scroll through to find the name of the image I want.*

Use the Type of File drop-down list to specify the specific file format of the file you need. If the image was created by a drawing package such as CorelDRAW!, change the File Type to CorelDRAW (.CDR).

I used PowerPoint's SETUP program to add more clip art images to my system, but when I try to access them from PowerPoint, they don't show up in the ClipArt Gallery.

To use the new images, you must let PowerPoint know where they are located on your disk drive. Use **O**ptions, then **R**efresh, in the ClipArt Gallery dialog box to scan the drive for the images. The images will be added to the ClipArt Gallery and you can add them to your slide presentations.

The ClipArt Gallery contains several categories of images that I never use. Can I delete the images to free up hard drive space?

Use the Windows File Manager to locate the PCSFILES subdirectory in the PowerPoint directory. Open the PCSFILES subdirectory and locate the files with the same names as the ClipArt Gallery *category* names that you want to remove—ANIMAL.PCS, for example. Select the file and delete it. Then, return to the ClipArt Gallery and use the Refresh command to update your changes. The images in the category you deleted will no longer be available and you gain more disk storage space.

My company has grown quickly and I have numerous divisional logo images I'd like to use in PowerPoint. I used the Add feature of the ClipArt Gallery to create a new category for the logos, but my company has gone public and changed its name. The category name I used for the images is no longer correct.

(continues)

III

Drawing

(continued)

In the ClipArt Gallery dialog box, use **O**ptions, **C**hange a Category to rename the category to match your new company name.

I mistakenly deleted a category of images in the ClipArt Gallery, and I need an image from the deleted category.

The images in the category you deleted are not gone, just relocated. The images from deleted categories are assigned to the All Categories category. Scroll through All Categories to find the images you need. To re-create the category you deleted, use the instructions about moving pictures to a new category in this chapter.

From Here...

In this chapter, you learned how to place clip art as well as other types of pictures into presentations. These are other chapters you may want to explore:

- Chapter 9, "Drawing Objects," shows you how to draw and place objects on your slide.

- Chapter 11, "Selecting, Editing, and Enhancing Objects," shows you how to edit and manipulate objects, such as clip art, in PowerPoint.

- Chapter 18, "Using Links to Other Applications," shows you how to take full advantage of Windows linking and embedding features.

Chapter 11

Selecting, Editing, and Enhancing Objects

PowerPoint handles many different types of data in a surprisingly generic way. Every data type you can possibly include in a PowerPoint presentation—charts, drawings, imported pictures, clip art, body text, organizational charts, movies, and sound—is considered an object in PowerPoint. With rare exceptions, all these data types are handled in similar ways and are manipulated and changed on slides in the same way. That's what this chapter is about: The basic mechanics of handling objects on the PowerPoint screen.

Manipulating Objects

You have probably already become acquainted with the term *placeholder* from discussions in chapters 4 and 5. A placeholder reserves space on a slide for a specific type of object. Most object types on a PowerPoint slide are contained by placeholders. Placeholders are the main tool by which various PowerPoint objects are manipulated and changed. There are seven different types of placeholders:

■ Graph placeholders	Contain charts created in Microsoft Graph
■ Organizational Chart placeholders	Contain charts created in OrgChart
■ Clip Art placeholders	Contain clip art pieces from PowerPoint's ClipArt Library

This chapter covers the following:

- ■ Selecting, deleting, and moving objects

- ■ Copying and pasting objects

- ■ Rotating and flipping objects

- ■ Applying background colors, patterns, and shading to objects

- ■ Layering and grouping objects

III

Drawing

- Table placeholders   Contain tables created in Microsoft Word

- Body Text placeholders   Contain body text for slides directly edited in PowerPoint

- Title placeholders   Contain slide title text

- Object placeholders   Contain various types of embedded and linked objects, such as sounds, movie clips, imported pictures, Excel datasheets, and other types of objects available in Windows

Figure 11.1 displays an AutoLayout slide with three different placeholders in it.

Fig. 11.1
A slide displaying three placeholders used to hold various objects.

Selected body text placeholder

Clip art placeholder

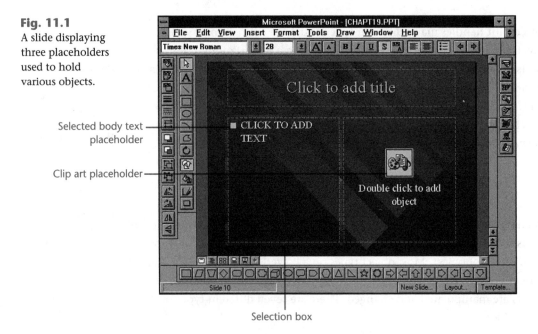

Selection box

Placeholders are the key element in this chapter. They are not in and of themselves objects, but they are capable of containing objects of various kinds.

How do you know when a placeholder or object has been selected? The Body Text placeholder in figure 11.1 has eight small boxes, or *handles*, and a selection box around its edge. When an object is selected, the eight handles indicate its selection.

Many features described in this chapter require the use of the two drawing toolbars offered as part of PowerPoint 4's standard toolbar set. To place the Drawing and Drawing+ toolbars on the PowerPoint screen (if they are not already on-screen), follow these steps:

1. From the **V**iew menu, choose **T**oolbars.

   The Toolbars dialog box appears.

2. Click in the Drawing and Drawing+ check boxes in the **T**oolbars list.

3. Choose OK or press Enter.

The Drawing and Drawing+ toolbars appear on the PowerPoint screen. You can drag them to a convenient place on the screen, if necessary.

Selecting Multiple Objects
Selecting a single object is as simple as clicking on it with the mouse.

Selecting multiple objects is done in several ways. To start, display the slide that contains the objects you want to select, as in the example shown in figure 11.2.

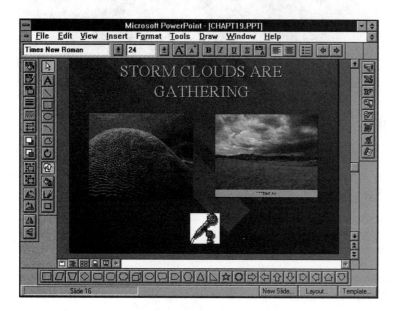

Fig. 11.2
A slide holding several different objects.

One method for selecting several objects is as follows:

1. Drag the mouse diagonally across the displayed slide from one corner to the other, drawing a "box" around the objects you want to select. Dragging across horizontally and then vertically can have the same effect, but takes a little more time.

All the objects on the slide that the mouse was dragged around are selected, as in figure 11.3.

Fig. 11.3
Selected objects after dragging the mouse.

Another method for selecting multiple objects is the following:

1. Hold down the Shift key and click on an object.

2. Holding the Shift key, click on each successive object until you have selected all the objects you want.

If you want to select all the objects in a given slide, you can also use a third method:

■ From the **E**dit menu, choose Select A**l**l.

Tip
To select all objects on a slide, press Ctrl+A when you're in Slide view.

Copying and Pasting Objects

To copy and paste any object, follow these steps:

1. Select the desired object by clicking on it with the mouse.

2. From the **E**dit menu, choose **C**opy.

3. Display the slide in which the copied object is to be pasted.

4. From the **E**dit menu, choose **P**aste. This action simply pastes a copy of the object into the currently displayed slide.

   Or, from the **E**dit menu, choose Paste **S**pecial. The Paste Special dialog box appears (see fig. 11.4).

Tip
Press Ctrl+C to copy a selected object with a keystroke.

Tip
Press Ctrl+V for a fast paste of a copied object with a keystroke.

As list showing the paste options for the object type

Paste option button

Paste Link option button

Result section showing what the results of your selection will be

Display as Icon check box

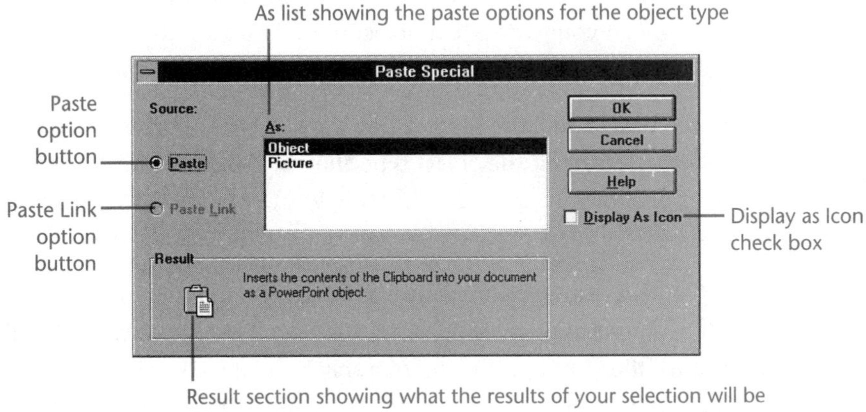

Fig. 11.4
Use the Paste Special dialog box to determine how an object is pasted.

5. Choose the object type to paste onto the slide from the **A**s list in the Paste Special dialog box.

   If your selected object is a graphic, chart, or imported picture, you can paste it either as an object or as a simple picture. If the object is of a specific type that is generated in another program, that specific object type will be displayed in the As list as well.

   If you paste your object as a plain object, it retains all the typical properties of an object of its specific type, which could be a PowerPoint object like a title text object, a chunk of body text, or just about anything else.

   For example, if the object is a bitmap Paintbrush picture, like the option shown in the **A**s list in figure 11.4, you can paste it into the slide.

III

Drawing

Then it becomes a very special object. It's not just a graphic object. It also can be edited or changed by double-clicking the picture on the slide. Then Paintbrush will come up and you can make changes to the picture. This is called creating an embedded object, and we have much more to say about this in chapter 18.

If you paste it as a picture, the pasted item is placed as a simple bitmap on the slide and the picture cannot be edited by double-clicking within PowerPoint.

The As list displays any object type that your system supports, such as a chart made in Microsoft Graph, an OrgChart, a Word table, an Excel datasheet, or any other data type that's imported from another program. If it's a plain vanilla PowerPoint object, such as a title or body text from a slide, you only see the words Object and Picture. While the program will let you paste a text object or title into a slide, it's not a good idea because the text or title becomes much harder to work with.

Notice the **P**aste and Paste **L**ink option buttons. They enable different object characteristics if the object type allows it (like the Paintbrush picture type shown in the list). Choosing **P**aste simply places the object in the slide, regardless of type.

(Paste **L**ink is a feature on which we also have much more to say, but to make it as simple as possible for now, selecting Paste **L**ink means that if you change the object in the program that created it, the change will automatically be added in your PowerPoint file without having to open PowerPoint, the presentation file, and pasting the changed picture back into the slide.)

You can display the pasted object as an icon by choosing the **D**isplay as Icon check box.

6. Choose OK or press Enter if you have used the Paste Special feature and have finished making your selections.

Rotating and Flipping Drawn and Text Objects

PowerPoint 4 allows the freeform rotation of text objects, such as titles or body text, and of objects drawn on the PowerPoint screen. Objects such as imported pictures, sound file objects, movie clips, and charts cannot be directly rotated because of their nature as objects created in other programs.

Figure 11.5 shows three different types of objects that can be rotated on a PowerPoint slide.

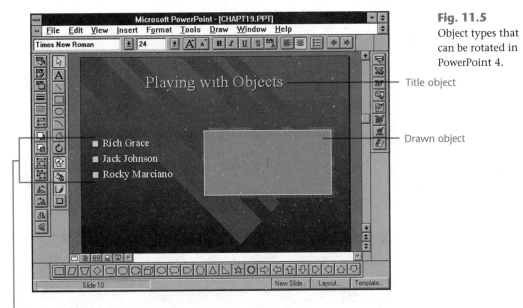

Fig. 11.5
Object types that can be rotated in PowerPoint 4.

Title object

Drawn object

Body Text object

For all three object types, the procedure for rotating is the same:

1. Click on the object you want to rotate.

2. Click the Free Rotate Tool button on PowerPoint's Drawing toolbar.

   The mouse pointer changes its shape to a pair of arrows circling each other. Also, another visual clue appears: The eight boxes around the border of the selected object turn into four, one box for each corner of the selected object.

   The status bar at the bottom of the PowerPoint screen reads:

   ```
   Position the mouse pointer over any handle.
   ```

3. Click and hold the mouse on one of the four handles of the selected object.

   The status bar at the bottom of the PowerPoint screen reads:

   ```
   Drag to rotate the selection; press Shift key to constrain
   angle
   ```

III

Drawing

4. Drag the mouse in any direction. As you do so, the status bar displays the message

```
Rotated by X degree(s);
```

describing the number of degrees around a circle by which the object has just been rotated.

5. To constrain the angle of the rotation to every 90 degrees, press and hold the Shift key while you rotate the object.

Tip
After rotating the object, click in an empty area in the slide to finish the rotation.

6. When you are finished rotating the object, click the Free Rotate Tool button again, or click on an empty part of the slide.

If you have selected and rotated all three objects in turn, the result might look like figure 11.6.

Fig. 11.6
The three objects in figure 11.5, now rotated on the slide.

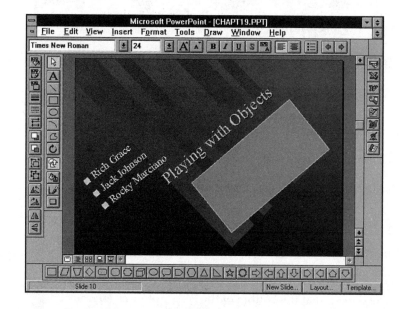

Note

It's possible to rotate more than one object at a time. Simply hold the Shift key, select the objects you want to rotate, and choose the Free Rotate Tool button. Click any selected object's handle and drag. All selected objects are rotated at the same angle.

Moving and Aligning Objects

Objects are moved according to the type of object and depending on whether the object has a color, pattern, or shading fill applied to it.

To move a text object:

1. Click the edge of the text object. Its selection box appears.

2. Drag the selection box of the object.

To move a text object or any other object that has a fill applied to it:

■ Click and drag the desired object.

To move a nontext object, such as a chart object, clip art placeholder, or other placeholder that has no fill:

■ Click and drag the edge of the desired object.

Placeholders and objects can be aligned to each other on a slide in many different ways. They can be aligned to their bottom edges, tops, left sides, or right sides. If you have two objects that you just can't seem to get lined up properly or just want a fast way to do it, here's how:

1. Select the two or more objects that you want to align to each other.

2. From the **D**raw menu, select **A**lign.

   A cascading menu, listing six different alignment options, appears (see fig. 11.7).

3. Choose the alignment option you want: Lefts (align objects' left sides), Centers (align objects to their centers), Rights (align objects' right sides), Tops (align objects' top edges), Middles (align objects to their middles), or Bottoms (align objects to their bottom edges).

III

Drawing

Fig. 11.7
The Align
options on
the Draw menu.

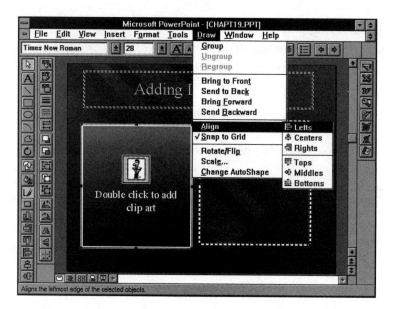

Aligning placeholders is much the same as aligning drawn objects, as discussed in chapter 9, "Drawing Objects."

Resizing Objects

Most types of objects are resized in two ways: proportionally or freely with the mouse.

> **Note**
>
> Some object types, such as imported pictures, movie clips, and charts created in Microsoft Graph, can only be resized proportionally. Other object types, such as clip art placeholders, are resized in any way that the mouse can be dragged.

Resizing is most effective with placeholders that can hold objects such as imported pictures, clip art, charts, and multimedia data types such as movie clips. Clicking and dragging a corner handle of any of those placeholders automatically resizes the object proportionally *if the object type is already inside the placeholder.* The object (and the placeholder that contains it) retains its shape regardless of its size. Holding the Shift key while resizing an object has no effect on the resizing process.

Proportionally Resizing Placeholders. Empty placeholders of any kind can be resized *proportionally* by holding the Shift key while you drag the mouse.

Doing so retains the default shape of the placeholder (usually a square or rectangle) but shrinks or enlarges it depending on the direction in which the mouse is moved.

Randomly Resizing Placeholders. An empty placeholder is resized randomly by grabbing a handle and simply dragging the mouse. The placeholder can then be reshaped and resized at will.

Resizing an empty placeholder at random does not affect the quality or proportionality of an inserted object such as a bitmap picture or clip art object; it merely affects the size of the object when it's inserted into the placeholder.

Deleting Objects

Deleting objects is a two-step process. First, the contents of the placeholder (the actual object) must be deleted, and then, if desired, the placeholder is deleted.

To delete an object, follow these steps:

1. Click on the border of the object you want to delete.

2. From the **E**dit menu, choose Cle**a**r.

   The object contents are deleted and the placeholder originally containing the object appears, selected for deletion.

3. To remove the placeholder, choose Cle**a**r or Cu**t** from the **E**dit menu; or press the Delete key.

If the object you are deleting is an object drawn with PowerPoint's drawing tools, which don't use placeholders, pressing the Delete key removes the drawn object.

Enhancing Placeholders and Objects

You can use PowerPoint 4's drawing tools to enhance object *placeholders* in much the same way as for the objects themselves. You can add line styles to placeholder borders, add color fills and shading to their backgrounds, and align them to each other for a uniform and organized appearance. Placeholders can have shadows applied to them. The colors that are applied to placeholder color fills possess the same range and availability that are offered when working with drawing, chart objects, and slide backgrounds.

III

Drawing

Framing and Shadowing Object Placeholders

Placeholders for clip art, text, titles, and other objects can have line weights and styles applied to their borders. Shadows also can be applied to placeholders to add emphasis to the presence of the object on the slide.

To add a different line style to an object placeholder, follow these steps:

1. Click the border of the desired placeholder.

2. Click the Line Style button of PowerPoint's Drawing+ toolbar.

   A drop-down list of 10 line styles and weights appears.

3. Click the desired line style or line weight.

The selected placeholder has the line style applied to its border.

Dashed lines and line styles can be combined on the same placeholder by clicking the Line Style and Dashed Lines tools on the Drawing+ toolbar in sequence while the same placeholder is selected.

Shadows can be applied to any placeholders on a slide. For example, three different placeholders containing different kinds of object data are shown in figure 11.8.

Fig. 11.8
A slide showing objects in placeholders before shadowing is applied.

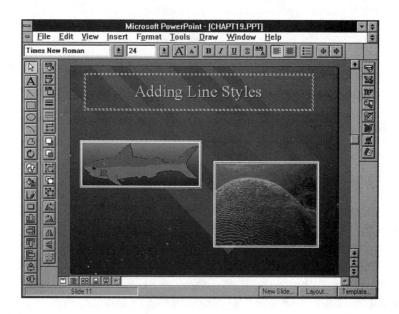

To add a shadow to a placeholder, perform the following steps:

1. Click the border of the desired placeholder.

2. Click the Apply Shadow Defaults tool on the Drawing toolbar. Or, from the Format menu, choose Shadow.

   The Shadow dialog box appears.

3. Choose from the following options to adjust and apply shadow effects:

   ■ Color   Drop-down eight-color palette that offers the basic presentation color scheme, the No Shadow option, an Embossed shadow style, and the Other Color option for adding colors from the expanded Other Color table.

   ■ Offset   Sets the offset or amount the shadow stands off from the back of the placeholder or object.

   ■ Up   Sets the shadow to project Up or Down
   Down   from the object by a specified number of points

   ■ Left   Sets the shadow to project Left or Right
   Right   from the object by a specified number of points

   For the example, an offset of eight points Down and to the Left is applied, and a color is applied that stands out more effectively against the dark slide background.

4. Choose OK or press Enter.

The result is seen in figure 11.9.

III

Drawing

Fig. 11.9
A slide showing three objects in placeholders, with the shark clip art placeholder bearing a shadow offset by eight points.

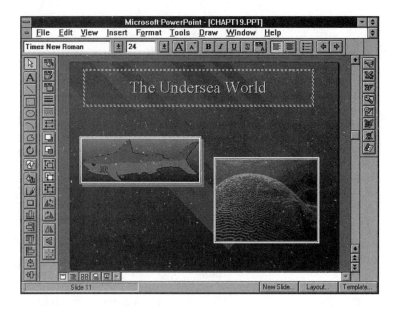

Filling, Shading, and Patterning Objects

Any placeholder or object can have a fill applied to it—a chart object, an empty placeholder for a piece of clip art, a title, a body text object—and the fill can be any style such as a solid color, a shading, or a pattern fill.

When you draw polygons and other shapes in PowerPoint, as discussed in chapter 9, "Drawing Objects," you use the same techniques for adding shading, shadows, patterns, and color fills to placeholders as you do to drawn objects. Line styles and color and shading fills can be combined to lend an attractive appearance to a placeholder, particularly if the placeholder is used for text objects such as body text and titles.

A color fill, along with a shading effect, is applied to the title text placeholder in the slide shown in figure 11.9:

1. Click on the border of the text object placeholder.

2. Click the Fill Color button in the Drawing+ toolbar.

    The drop-down color palette and option list appears (see fig. 11.10).

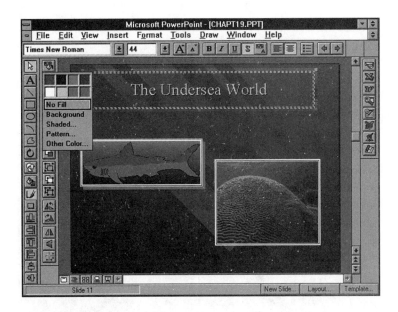

Fig. 11.10
The drop-down
color palette and
menu options list
for the Fill Color
button.

3. For the example, choose the color from the top-left corner of the palette.

   The fill color is applied to the placeholder background.

4. Click the Fill Color button in the Drawing+ toolbar.

5. From the drop-down list, choose Shaded.

   The Shaded Fill dialog box appears (see fig. 11.11).

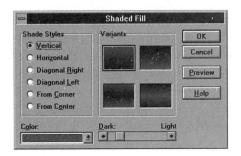

Fig. 11.11
The Shaded Fill
dialog box adds a
shaded fill to the
title placeholder.

III

Drawing

6. Choose a Shade Style (**V**ertical is the selected option button default) from the six Shade Styles option buttons.

7. Click the Dashed Lines button on the Drawing+ toolbar and select the solid line from the drop-down list to change the line style of the border to a solid line. The result resembles figure 11.12.

Fig. 11.12
The shaded fill has been applied.

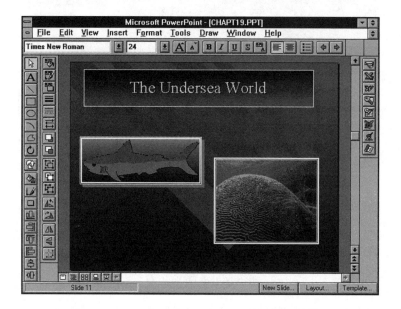

The shading has not been applied to the actual text, but to its placeholder.

Layering Objects

Object placeholders can be layered over each other, and often must be layered a certain way if objects are to be visible. Every object you place on a slide occupies its own layer. If you have three objects on a slide, or 100, each object can be Sent Backward or Brought Forward to any level.

For a simple example of object placeholder layering, figure 11.13 shows three different illustrations on a slide.

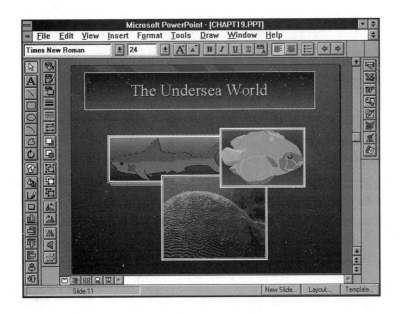

Fig. 11.13
Three graphics
objects layered
over one another.

If you want to reverse the order of the objects—with the shark on top, the
coral picture in the middle, and the tropical fish on the bottom, follow these
steps:

1. Click on the shark object.

2. Click the Bring Forward button on the Drawing+ toolbar.

   The Shark drawing is brought forward one layer, as shown in
   figure 11.14.

3. Click the Bring Forward button on the Drawing+ toolbar again.

   The shark graphic is placed on the top layer of the three layers of
   graphic objects.

4. Click on the tropical fish graphic.

5. Click the Send Backward button on the Drawing+ toolbar.

III

Drawing

Fig. 11.14

The shark graphic is brought forward one layer. The graphic is brought forward but is still partly hidden by the other graphics object.

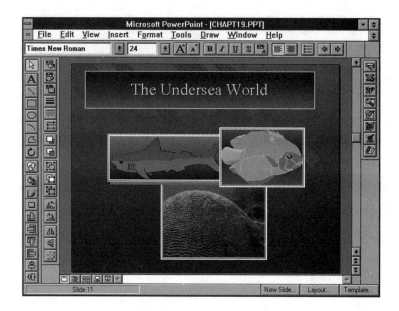

The tropical fish graphic is placed behind the Coral graphic layer, as shown in figure 11.15.

Fig. 11.15

The tropical fish graphic being Sent Backward.

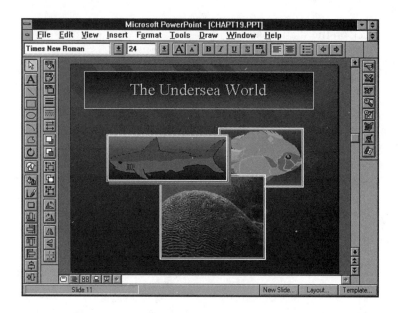

The layering example you just performed applies to any objects on a PowerPoint slide. That includes placeholders, the objects you put in those placeholders on the slide, and drawn objects. Object placeholders can be layered over each other and you can draw objects using PowerPoint's drawing tools and layer *them* over each other too.

Another common ground that placeholders and drawn objects share is the capability to be grouped together for easier moving and manipulation.

Grouping Objects

Grouping object placeholders works exactly the same way as for grouping drawn objects:

1. Shift + click on the objects on the slide that you wish to group together. You must select two or more objects.

2. Click the Group button on the PowerPoint Drawing+ toolbar.

   Or, from the **D**raw menu, choose **G**roup.

The selected objects are grouped, and a set of handles appears over the area occupied by all the selected objects.

Scaling Objects

PowerPoint's Scale feature is an easy and efficient way for users to intelligently resize pictures, charts, movie clips, and other objects on PowerPoint slides. It allows you to do several things: resize by percentages any selected object (or more than one object at a time) to be smaller or larger than its current size; resize an object to an optimum size based on the screen resolution of your slide show; or restore a resized picture or object to its original proportions.

The Scale feature resizes pictures and other objects while retaining their original proportions. You will not see any distortion of the object during resizing.

To rescale an object, follow these steps:

1. Click the object(s) you want to rescale. (You can select more than one object for rescaling by holding down the Shift key and clicking on each object in turn.)

III

Drawing

2. From the Draw menu, choose Scal**e**.

   The Scale dialog box appears.

3. In the **S**cale To text box, type a number for the percentage you want to resize the picture to. Higher numbers enlarge it, smaller numbers shrink it.

4. If you want to make sure the picture is resized back to its original size as you imported it, click the Relative to Original Picture Size check box. If this check box is selected, a scale of 100% means that the picture is resized to its original proportions.

5. If you are giving a slide show presentation and you want to size the selected object or objects to the best size for the screen when you give the actual presentation, click the Best Scale for Slide Show check box. This is especially handy for multimedia movie clips, which are discussed in more detail in chapter 21.

6. To check your scaling changes before closing the feature, you can click the Preview button and move the Scale dialog box if it happens to cover up the object.

7. When you've entered your changes, choose OK or press Enter.

Troubleshooting

When I click in a title placeholder and try to drag it, it won't move.

Placeholders can be moved by dragging them from their inside areas or from their border. If the placeholder won't move when you drag on its interior area, it's a placeholder that was originally put in your Slide Master, and consequently appears in all the slides in your presentation. This is often the case with slide title placeholders, for example. In that case, for the slide you're working in, you must click and drag on the placeholder's border to be able to move it.

I'd like to be able to move objects smoothly and make as fine an adjustment to their position as I can.

You can do several things. First, under the Draw menu, look at the Snap to Grid menu option. If a check mark is placed beside it, choose the Snap to Grid option to turn that feature off. Second, from the View menu, turn on the Ruler and the Guides by choosing both those menu options. These are the tools you need to ensure that you place your objects as accurately as possible. After that, it's mostly a matter of your good taste.

I've resized a picture and accidentally distorted it. How can I fix it?

To fix a distorted picture, first click on it to select it. Then, choose the Scal**e** command from the **D**raw menu. Click the **R**elative to Original Picture Size check box. Press Enter or choose OK. The picture will be restored to its original shape. (By the way, this process is called *restoring the aspect ratio*.)

From Here...

You have just completed a major section of this book. The last several chapters have offered instructions on many of the tools and basic techniques for working with different types of drawn objects, and this chapter wrapped up by covering the basic operations for handling and changing object placeholders.

Moving forward, the next section of this book deals with a vastly improved and enhanced area of PowerPoint 4—charting and graphing.

- Chapter 12, "Working with Datasheets," describes how to create and edit datasheets in Microsoft Graph.

- Chapter 13, "Creating Basic Charts," discusses how to create, edit, and modify basic chart types and their elements.

- Chapter 14, "Customizing Charts," shows how to change and customize charts in detail, and touches on some of the more sophisticated chart types.

- Chapter 17, "Working with Color," discusses PowerPoint's various color palettes, how to work with them, and shows more sophisticated color changing and filling techniques for various objects on slides.

- Chapter 19, "Using Advanced Charting Features," more fully discusses chart types and the powerful editing features offered in Microsoft Graph.

III

Drawing

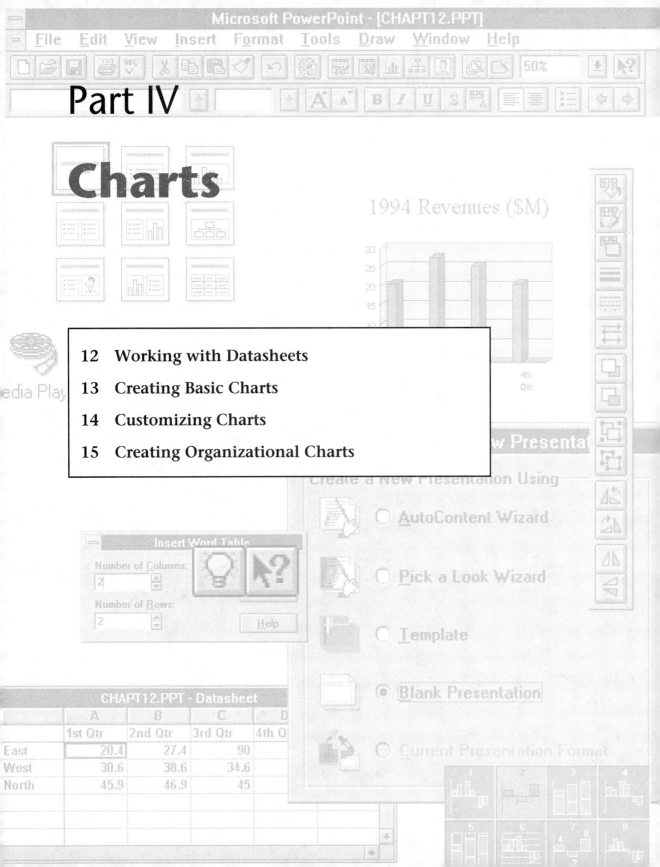

Part IV

Charts

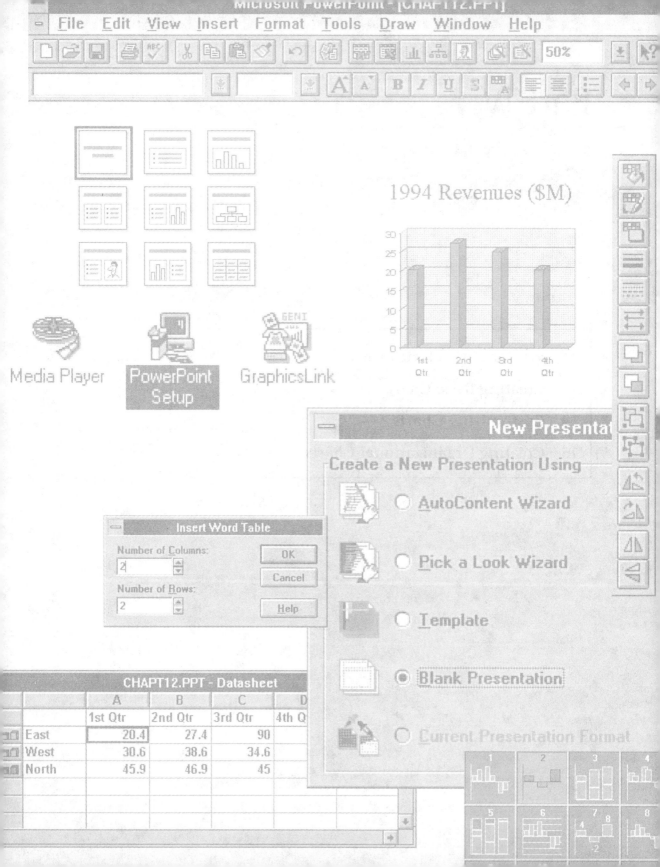

Chapter 12

Working with Datasheets

Charting is one of the key facilities in PowerPoint 4. Charts are created using rows and columns of numeric data. In PowerPoint, those rows and columns are called a *datasheet*. The process of creating and editing datasheets is the key to effective charting in PowerPoint.

This chapter starts off by discussing how datasheets are created and used. Creating datasheets is quite similar to table creation, which was discussed in previous chapters. Datasheets, however, are used solely to create charts, and are not intended for direct display on a slide. Thus, you must begin by starting up PowerPoint's Graph facilities to either create a new datasheet and chart or to edit an existing one.

Understanding PowerPoint's Charting Feature

PowerPoint 4 has undergone a major change in its charting features. To understand the profound improvement in PowerPoint's charting capabilities, you need to compare the current version with that of the previous version, PowerPoint 3.

PowerPoint 3's charting was in a program called Microsoft Graph. It was an entirely separate program, intended to be used in other Microsoft application programs such as Word for Windows as well as PowerPoint 3. It used a technique called *object linking and embedding* to place charts into PowerPoint slides. Whenever you double-clicked on a chart in PowerPoint 3 to change a chart, Microsoft Graph would pop up in a separate window from PowerPoint.

In this chapter, among many other features, you learn how to:

- Start PowerPoint's charting features

- Place data series in rows or columns

- Edit datasheets

- Work with rows and columns

- Format chart data

Object linking and embedding (called OLE) is a method for allowing application programs to share various types of data between them. It's been used for a few years as a major feature in many Windows programs.

Although PowerPoint 4 is similar to version 3, it is different in subtle but important ways. When you install PowerPoint 4, it also installs another application program—called Microsoft Graph. It too uses object linking and embedding to place charts on PowerPoint slides.

Here's where the major difference lies. When you double-click on a chart to change or edit it in PowerPoint 4, Graph does not appear in a separate window. Instead, it takes over the PowerPoint 4 screen. That's because PowerPoint and Microsoft Graph use a newer version of object linking and embedding, called OLE 2.0. It enables a feature called in-place editing, which you already used to create tables in chapter 8. If you have Microsoft Word for Windows and have used it to create tables in chapter 8, you already know that using Word to create tables also takes over the PowerPoint screen. The new version of Graph bundled with PowerPoint works exactly the same way.

That's why you don't see the name Microsoft Graph pop up when you start it to create charts for your slides. It doesn't *look* like a separate application program at all—but it is, just like Microsoft Word.

Throughout this chapter and all other chapters that talk about charting, we will thus refer to Microsoft Graph as a separate program. A final note before you start: Chapter 17 in this book talks about object linking and embedding in much greater detail.

Starting the Charting Application

To create a new datasheet and chart, follow these steps:

1. Open the presentation in which you want to embed a new chart object.

2. Display the slide on which you want to insert a chart.

3. Click the Insert Graph button on the PowerPoint toolbar.

Note

You can also create a new slide with a chart object embedded in it by clicking the New Slide button at the bottom of the PowerPoint screen and choosing a slide template with an embedded chart object. When the slide is created, a column chart icon appears in the middle of the chart object, with the caption `Double click to add chart` underneath.

The Microsoft Graph application program starts.

The Microsoft Graph standard toolbar appears at the top of the PowerPoint screen, and a new datasheet is displayed with a chart object just behind it (see fig. 12.1). The PowerPoint menu bar also changes to a new set of menus and functions.

Note

Graph's Standard toolbar offers buttons to perform many functions. Other important functions for changing the look of datasheets are available in Graph's Formatting toolbar, which by default is not displayed. Since you need this toolbar later on, from the **V**iew menu choose the **T**oolbars command and place an X in the Formatting check box in the toolbar list. Choosing OK displays the second toolbar.

Graph toolbar   Graph menu bar

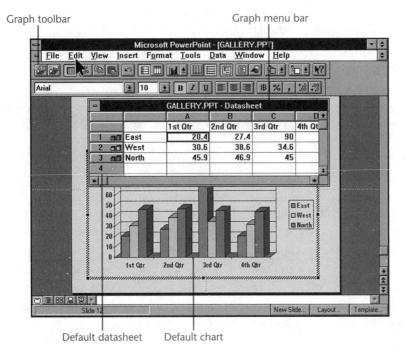

Default datasheet   Default chart

Fig. 12.1
A default datasheet and chart.

IV

Charts

Notice that the new datasheet has a set of default values that make up the sample data displayed. The chart shown just behind it is a default 3-D column chart. The following sections lead you through the process of editing the chart and choosing different types of charts to reflect the changes in your datasheet.

To modify an existing chart on a slide, follow these steps:

1. Display the slide containing the chart you want to edit.

2. Double-click the chart object.

The Graph toolbar appears. The chart is still displayed, and the datasheet from which the chart was created also appears, ready to be edited.

In many cases, the datasheet may not automatically appear. If this is the case, simply click the Datasheet button on the toolbar. (Leaving the Tooltips feature enabled will help you find it.) The datasheet appears.

Understanding Datasheets

The process of creating and editing datasheets is quite simple and closely resembles editing tables, which is described in chapter 8, "Working with Tables." The key difference is that when you are editing datasheets, they are used to create charts for display in your presentation. Unlike tables, datasheets are not displayed on slides after you edit them—they are only used to generate charts. That is why you must double-click an existing chart before the associated datasheet will appear.

> **Note**
>
> Datasheets are used to create charts. They aren't displayed on slides as tables are. They only appear when you want to insert or edit a chart.

Each rectangle containing text entries in a datasheet is called a *cell*. Some cells, such as the ones displayed on the top row and in the farthest left column of the datasheet shown in figure 12.2, are meant to hold text that is used to label each row and column in the chart. Most other cells hold data values. In many PowerPoint charts, several categories of data are compared against each other. Each category of data, in turn, is called a *data series*. In the sample datasheet in figure 12.2, the series are labeled East, West, and North.

Each series has four values, which are in turn labeled 1st Qtr, 2nd Qtr, 3rd Qtr, and 4th Qtr. The time period labels are displayed on the top row of the datasheet. Those labels are called a *measurement scale* or *timeline*.

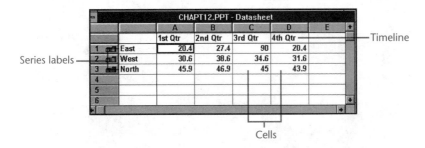

Series labels

Cells

Timeline

Fig. 12.2
A default datasheet with each key element labeled.

Each row and column is numbered, just as in a typical spreadsheet. The rows in the example are labeled 1 through 3, and the columns are labeled A through D.

Placing Data Series in Rows or Columns

An important aspect of editing charts is understanding where to place your data values for the best effect. A *data series* can be defined as a single set of values that bear a specific relationship to each other. For most charts, data values are placed in rows in the datasheet to create each series. Each successive value represents another entry for the series on the timeline represented in the chart. Notice that the PowerPoint default is to place data series in rows, as shown in figure 12.3.

Each row label has a small graphic placed next to it that indicates the chart type in which each series appears. In figure 12.3, the series label graphics indicate that 3-D columns are used and show the colors used for each series. Putting the series in rows emphasizes the timeline values (1st Qtr, 2nd Qtr, 3rd Qtr, and 4th Qtr in the default example), each of which compares the figures for East, West, and North for each quarter. Placing the data series in rows creates the best and most workable chart in most cases. This applies to almost every chart type you create. The few exceptions to this rule are discussed in later chapters.

Fig. 12.3
A default chart
with data series in
rows. Data series
are translated to
3-D column style
in the chart.

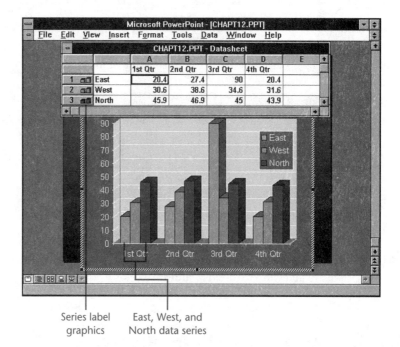

Series label
graphics

East, West, and
North data series

In some cases, however, you may want to emphasize the East, West, and
North data sets by defining the yearly quarters to be the data series rather
than the regions. The data for each quarter is broken down by columns in the
datasheet (with one value from each series for each quarter), so the data series
need to be redefined in columns.

To redefine the data series in rows to data series in columns:

1. Display the slide containing the chart you want to change.

2. Double-click the chart to select it and bring up the Graph toolbar.

3. Click the Datasheet button on the Graph toolbar to display the
   datasheet.

4. Click the By Columns button on the Graph toolbar.

Notice that the series label graphics migrate to the column labels A through
D on the datasheet. That indicates that the series labels have been transferred
to the columns. Thus, the series are now the quarters rather than the regions.

The chart also reflects these changes. Notice how the four sets of three columns in figure 12.3 have become three sets of four columns, shown in figure 12.4. Also notice how the East, West, and North labels have been placed on the axis at the bottom of the chart, replacing the original quarter labels. The data for each region is broken down in columns in the datasheet instead of the data for each quarter.

Tip
Look for the label graphics to quickly see whether the data series are organized in rows or columns.

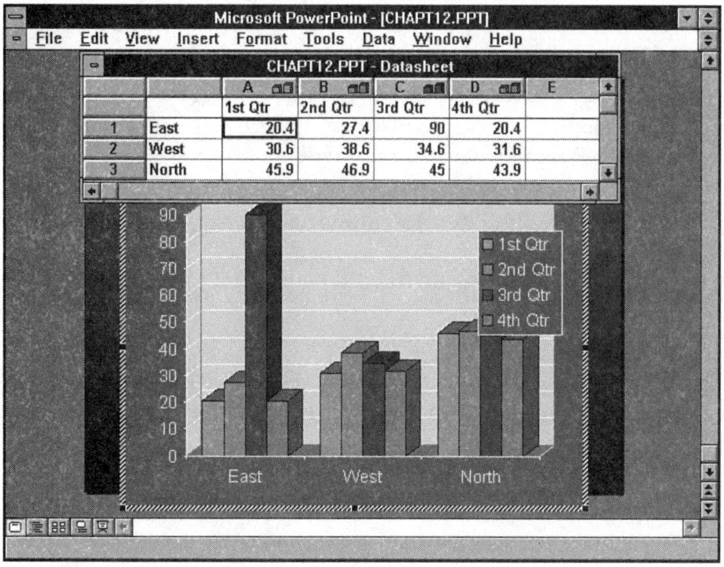

IV

Charts

Fig. 12.4
The same default chart with data series in columns. Each column is a data series that corresponds to a specific column style and color in the chart.

Editing Datasheets

In PowerPoint 4, editing a datasheet is a relatively painless process. PowerPoint's default datasheet offers a default set of data series that can either be deleted or simply typed over when you want to enter new values. There are a few generic rules to follow when editing datasheets:

- Use the arrow keys to move from one cell to another.

- To move through each successive cell in a row, press the Tab key.

- To completely remove a cell's contents, press the Del or Delete key.

- When the desired cell is selected, simply type in the new value or entry and the old one is overwritten.

Table 12.1 shows a sample data set you can enter into the datasheet. It's a fictitious listing of the market share for laser printers split between three companies over a three-year period.

Table 12.1 Market Share Datasheet	1991	1992	1993
Monolith Printers, Inc.	22.1	23.5	21.8
Massive Conglomerate, Inc.	57.1	57.3	60.2
Amalgamated Industries	20.8	19.2	18.0

To enter the data shown in table 12.1 into the datasheet, follow these steps:

1. Click the mouse once inside the cell labeled 1st Qtr in the default datasheet.

2. Type **1991**, and then press Tab or the right-arrow key to move to the cell labeled 2nd Qtr. Type **1992**, which overwrites the previous entry. Repeat the same step to enter **1993** in the next cell.

3. Press Tab or the right-arrow key again to move to the cell labeled 4th Qtr. To delete the column label, press the Del or Delete key.

> **Note**
>
> Pressing the space bar also erases the entry, but it leaves a space bar character in the datasheet cell. Pressing Backspace opens the Clear dialog box, which works just as well but imposes an extra step. The quickest way, and the safest and easiest for good datasheet editing practice, is to use the Delete key.

Tip
There are many ways to erase a cell entry. Using the Del or Delete keys is a good habit, as well as being the quickest way to get the job done.

4. Click inside the cell labeled East and type **Monolith Printers, Inc.** The original entry, as with the previous ones, is overwritten. Next, press the down-arrow key to move to the cell labeled West.

5. Repeat step 4, replacing West and North with **Massive Conglomerate, Inc.** and **Amalgamated Industries**, respectively.

6. Use the arrow keys, or click in the desired cells, to replace the default values with those in table 12.1. Remember to clear any values in the column originally labeled 4th Qtr. When you're finished, the datasheet should look like that shown in figure 12.5.

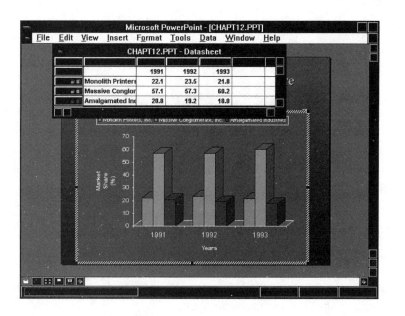

Fig. 12.5
The new datasheet
with its default
3-D column chart
displayed.

Notice that in the datasheet in the example above, the column containing
the series labels Monolith Printers, Inc., Massive Conglomerate, Inc., and
Amalgamated Industries is too narrow for the long company names; they all
override the boundaries of their cells and are not visible beyond the cell border. You learn how to solve this problem later in this chapter in the section
"Changing the Column Width."

Editing Cells

Editing a cell is quite simple, but there are a couple of generic rules to keep in
mind when doing so:

- To edit the contents of a cell without overwriting its contents, double-
  click inside the cell and then place the I-beam at the place in the cell
  text where you want to edit.

- To edit and overwrite the contents of a cell, simply click the cell once to
  select it and begin typing.

You may not want to overwrite the contents of a cell to change its contents.
Let's say, for example, that you want to change *Amalgamated Industries* to
read *Amal Ind.*

1. Double-click inside the cell labeled Amalgamated Industries. The cell contents are highlighted and the entire text "pops out" and seems to overwrite the next cell to the right. (Don't worry about this. The other cell's contents are untouched.)

2. Notice that when you pass the mouse over the highlighted cell, it turns from a cross into an I-beam for editing. Click the mouse once again at the end of the text entry you highlighted. The text insertion point blinks at the end of Amalgamated Industries.

3. Press the Backspace key until you are left with *Amalgamated Ind* in the entry, and type a period to indicate an abbreviation. With the arrow key, move the insertion point to the end of the first word and Backspace over it until the cell reads *Amal Ind.*

When editing a cell, you can also use the Del or Delete key to delete characters to the right of the text insertion point.

Copying Cells

Copying cell contents to another cell is a simple process, but there is a subtle trick to watch out for. Following these steps will help ease the process:

Tip

For efficient cell copying, click once on a datasheet cell. Then, from the **E**dit menu, choose **C**opy; or press Ctrl+C to copy its contents.

1. Select the cell you want to copy by clicking once inside it with the mouse. The cell border is bolded.

2. From the **E**dit menu, choose the **C**opy command; or press Ctrl+C.

3. Click once inside the datasheet cell to which you want to copy.

4. From the **E**dit menu, choose the **P**aste command; or press Ctrl+V.

> **Note**
>
> In many Windows software packages, you're probably used to double-clicking a word to select it before you delete it, copy it, or move it. While editing datasheets in PowerPoint 4, you are not able to do that. When you double-click a cell, the contents are highlighted, but the Ctrl+C and Ctrl+V (Cut and Paste) commands do not work. To properly copy cell contents to the Clipboard, click just once on the desired cell and perform your Copy command.

To use the right mouse button to copy a cell's contents, follow these steps:

1. Click the right mouse button on the cell you want to copy.

The Edit shortcut menu appears.

2. Choose the Copy command. The cell's contents are copied to the Clipboard. The cell's contents can now be pasted into a new cell.

Dragging and Dropping Cells

It's simple to drag and drop a cell's contents to another location in the datasheet. Just select the cell, then *click and hold the mouse over its border.* Drag the mouse to the new location on the datasheet. You can also hold down the Ctrl key while you drag, if you want to drag and drop a copy of the cell to a new location.

Troubleshooting

Even though I'm double-clicking a cell value to select it, I can't use any of the menu options on it! What's wrong?

You cannot double-click a cell to select it for many operations. Most menu options dealing with editing and formatting are ghosted. Click on it once and the menu options are available for selection.

I can't get Drag and Drop to work!

The feature may be turned off. To enable dragging and dropping of cells, from the **T**ools menu, choose **O**ptions. Several tab options will be shown. If it is not already shown, click the Datasheet Options tab. If the Cell **D**rag and Drop option is not selected, click once inside its check box to enable it, and choose OK or press Enter. You should now be able to use Drag and Drop on your datasheets.

Working with Rows and Columns

Datasheets allow editing of individual cells and their values. In PowerPoint 4, the process of editing and working with rows and columns of data has also been eased. Each cell in a datasheet can be altered, or an entire row or column, several selected rows and columns, or groups of selected cells can be copied and moved to another section of the datasheet. Columns, rows, and cells can also be selected for exclusion from a chart.

Selecting Rows and Columns

Selecting rows and columns for editing and moving is a straightforward process. Datasheets in the new PowerPoint have a series of 3-D buttons along the top and left side, each of which represents one column or one row of data. Clicking on one of these buttons automatically selects the entire row or column. All of these buttons are lettered or numbered with numbers representing rows and letters representing columns.

Use the following techniques to select rows and columns:

- To select an entire row, click the numbered button (1, 2, 3, and so on) to the left of the row you want to select. The row of data values is highlighted.

- To select an entire column, click the lettered button (A, B, C, and so on) at the top of the row. The column of data values is highlighted.

- To select more than one row or column at a time without selecting the entire chart, hold down the Shift key as you click each successive button.

- Once the row(s) or column(s) is highlighted, press Ctrl+C to copy the contents to the Clipboard.

You can also click the mouse over the first cell to be selected and drag the mouse over all the other cells you want to include in the group. The rule applies to a row of cells, a column of cells, or to any number of rows and columns in combination. All the cells selected are highlighted in black, and can then be copied and pasted into other places in the datasheet.

Clearing Rows and Columns

As you saw a bit earlier, problems can arise when you edit a datasheet. In particular, there's a right and a wrong way to delete rows and columns of data.

Simply selecting the cells to delete and pressing the Del key or Ctrl+X is not enough to remove the column. That is why there's an empty space in the chart in figure 12.6. It also explains why the label graphic is still present in column D even though there are no values in the datasheet cells in that column. PowerPoint still thinks there is a column of data in the datasheet and allocates space for it even though you erased the actual data entries.

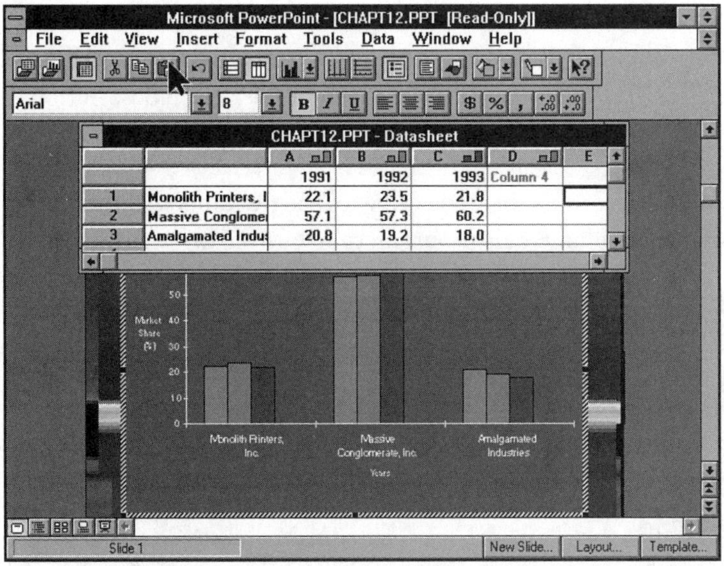

Fig. 12.6

It is not enough to simply delete the values in a column on a datasheet. The datasheet column, though it doesn't contain any values, still has a label graphic. The empty datasheet column is reflected in the chart.

An additional step needs to be taken to clean up the datasheet and remove the superfluous column space from the chart:

1. Click the column button labeled D at the top of the datasheet. The entire column is highlighted.

2. Press the Del or Delete key, or Ctrl+X for Cut.

The label graphic disappears from column D, and the accompanying chart has its empty column space removed (see fig. 12.7). What's the difference? The complete removal of the column and its contents. The same rule also applies to datasheet rows, and the process of removing them works exactly the same way.

There is another very quick way to handle the process of getting rid of the empty column by using the right mouse button:

1. With the mouse pointer (which should be in the shape of a cross) above the column button labeled D, click the right mouse button.

The entire column is selected, and the Edit shortcut menu appears.

2. Select either the Cut or Delete command from the Edit shortcut menu. The column is deleted and the chart is set to its proper appearance. Also notice that you can use either the left or the right mouse button to select the command from the shortcut menu.

You cannot select more than one cell with the right mouse button. A single cell, or a single column or row button, can be selected.

Fig. 12.7
The datasheet and column chart with the extra data column properly deleted. Notice that the label graphic has disappeared, empty columns are deleted, and the column margin still needs to be adjusted.

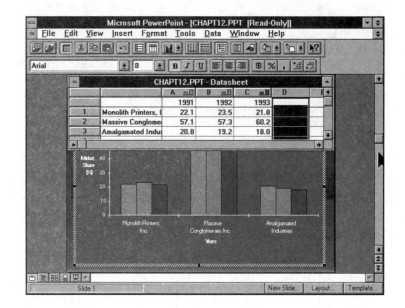

Inserting New Rows and Columns

If you discover that you need another row or column in your datasheet, it's a simple matter to add one. In fact, there are several ways to do so. Again, there are a few generic techniques that can be followed:

■ To insert a new row above any other row, click the row button (1, 2, 3, and so on) for the row above which you want to insert a new one. Then from the **I**nsert menu, choose C**e**lls.

Suppose that you want to add a new row to the top of the datasheet displayed in figure 12.7. You need to reset the chart for Series in Rows and then add the new row by following these steps:

1. Click the By Row button on the Graph toolbar. PowerPoint returns the series to the Rows in the datasheet.

2. Click the row button labeled 1. The entire datasheet row labeled Monolith Printers, Inc. is selected.

3. From the **I**nsert menu, choose **C**ells.

   A new row is inserted above the Monolith Printers, Inc. row. The datasheet row labeled Monolith Printers, Inc. moves down to row 2. You are now in the process of adding another series of data to the chart.

   Notice that the chart itself does not yet change or add any space for more columns.

4. Click the mouse in the cell above Monolith Printers, Inc. and type **Giant, Inc.** Press the right-arrow key to move to the next cell.

5. Type the values **17.1**, **15.5**, and **14.9** in columns A, B, and C respectively.

As you enter the values for the fourth series, you see that the chart adjusts to place a fourth column in each yearly group (see fig. 12.8). The new columns in the series are automatically assigned a new color in the chart, and the name Giant, Inc. is added to the legend.

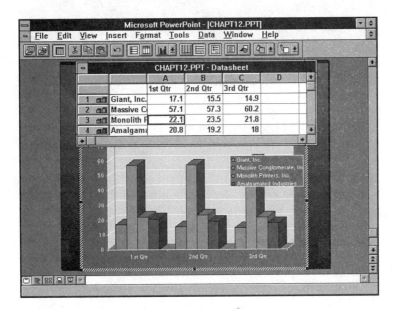

Fig. 12.8
Adding a fourth row or series to the chart.

You don't have to select an entire row in order to insert a new one:

1. With the left mouse button, click any cell in the row (except its row number) above which a new row is to be inserted.

2. From the **I**nsert menu, choose C**e**lls to display the Insert dialog box (see fig. 12.9). (Notice the ellipsis that appears in the C**e**lls option in this case, indicating the imminent appearance of the dialog box offering cell movement choices.)

Fig. 12.9
Using the Insert Cells dialog box to add a row to the datasheet.

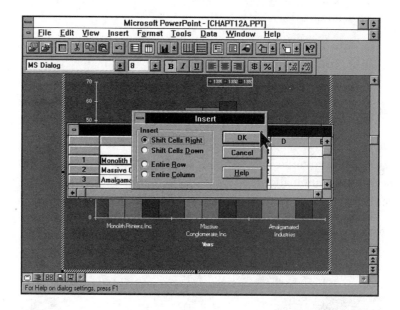

3. Choose from the following options:

   ■ Shift Cells Right enables you to shift the cell or cells you have selected to the right by one cell (or column).

   ■ Shift Cells Down enables you to shift the cell or cells you have selected down by one row.

   ■ Entire Row inserts an entire new row into the datasheet.

   ■ Entire Column inserts an entire new column into the datasheet.

   For the example, choose Entire **R**ow.

4. Choose OK or press Enter.

> **Note**
>
> The Insert dialog box appears only if you select a cell or a group of cells. If you select an entire row or column (by clicking their buttons), selecting the **Insert Cells** command automatically adds the new one.

Dragging and Dropping Rows and Columns

Graph's datasheet editor also enables you to drag and drop cells, groups of cells, rows, and columns. It's a fast rearranging feature that was not present in the previous version of Microsoft Graph.

To drag and drop one or more rows or columns, follow these steps:

1. Select the cell(s), row(s), or column(s) you want to move to a new place on the datasheet.

2. Click and hold the mouse on the border of the selected cells. Drag the cells to the new location on the datasheet. Make sure not to overwrite other datasheet elements you want to keep. If you do so accidentally, use the **E**dit **U**ndo Drag and Drop command.

Tip

To drag and drop a copy, hold the Ctrl key down while dragging to drag a copy of the selection while leaving the original in place.

Formatting Chart Data

Datasheets bear a resemblance to conventional spreadsheets because chart data can be formatted in a variety of ways. You can apply different fonts to the datasheet to change its appearance. You can change the style of numbers used in the datasheet. You can set the alignment of cell data to be left aligned, right aligned, centered, or justified. Column width can be adjusted for more readable values. Most of these operations, with one exception, do not affect the chart that you are creating with the datasheet; they are used to improve the datasheet's readability.

The only datasheet formatting specification that can alter the results of your chart display is formatting of numbers. This feature has a crucial bearing on the resulting display of your chart.

Changing the Numeric Format

Changing the numeric format of the chart is simply a matter of specifying that you want your data values to be of a specific format. Numbering systems are offered in a wide variety of formats and can be closely associated with the type of charts you are trying to create. Table 12.2 lists the numbering categories available for use in PowerPoint 4.

Table 12.2	Numbering Categories
Category	**Description**
Accounting	For "ledger sheets" and accounting charts
Currency	Adds currency signs to dollar values
Custom	No default numbers here; the user can create his or her own numbering type
Date	Formatting for various dating standards (MM/DD/YY and others)
Fraction	Used for stock quotes and Open-High-Low-Close stock charts
General	PowerPoint default; automatically adjusts numbers to most precise value
Number	Various standard number formats up to eight figures with commas
Percentage	Attaches percent signs to datasheet values
Scientific	Offers scientific notation to datasheet values
Time	Formatting for various timing standards (HH:MM:SS and others)
Text	Standard Arabic text numbers

Each category has a selection of specialized numbering types. Sometimes, if a number format is too long for the size of the cell holding the data value, the number is displayed in scientific notation. At other times, if the number is far too big to be displayed at all, it is shown as a series of hatch marks (#), in which case the column must be widened in order to properly display the data value.

Each numbering format affects the actual value in different ways. Table 12.3 shows a partial listing of samples of various number, date, and time formats.

Table 12.3	Number Formatting Examples
Type	**Result**
General	5
0	5
0.00	5.00

Type	Result
#.##0	5
#,##0.00	5.00
$#,##0_);[Red]($#.##0)	$5
$#,##0.00_);($#,##0.00)	$5.00
$#,##0.00_;[Red]$(#,##0.00)	$5.00
0%	500%
0.00%	500.00%
0.00E+00	500E+00
m/d/yy	1/5/94
d-mmm-yy	5-Jan-94
mmm-yy	Jan-94
h:mm AM/PM	12:00 AM
h:mm:ss AM/PM	12:00:00 AM
h:mm	12:00
h:mm:ss	12:00:00
md/yy h:mm	1/5/94 12:00

IV

Charts

When changing the numeric format in a datasheet, the values displayed on the Y or value measurement axis in the accompanying chart change to reflect the chosen number format.

To change the number format for one cell on a datasheet, follow these steps:

1. To quickly change the number format of a cell, click the right mouse button on the cell to select it and bring up the shortcut menu.

> **Note**
>
> You can also click once on the cell with the left mouse button to select it, and then choose the **N**umber command from the **F**ormat menu. Don't make the conventional mistake of double-clicking the cell to select it. The **N**umber menu command is ghosted and unavailable.

Tip
Use the right mouse button for speed in selecting and formatting datasheet cells, and do not double-click a cell to select it for formatting changes.

2. Choose the Number command.

The Number Format dialog box appears (see fig. 12.10).

3. Select the numbering Category, and then choose the desired numbering format.

Although many number formats are rather complex to look at, you can see their end result on the Sample line just underneath the format list. The formatting code you select is shown in the Code box. You can also customize any numbering code in the Code box by deleting or adding your own formatting characters.

4. Click the OK button.

Fig. 12.10
Changing the numbering format for selected datasheet data.

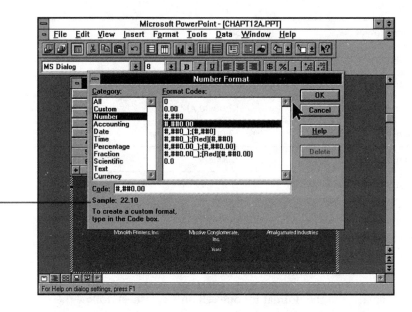

The Sample line shows the result of the chosen format

To change the numbering format for all cells in a datasheet, drag the left mouse button over the desired cells to select them. The cells are highlighted in black. Click the right mouse button over any of the selected cells and choose the Number command; or pull down the Format menu and choose the Number command.

To change the numbering format for a single row or column, simply click the row or column button to select it, and then choose the Format Number command or click the right mouse button over the selected cells.

To convert the numeric values in the sample datasheet to percentages to reflect the purpose of the chart, which is to display market share in percentages, follow these steps:

1. Select any cell in the datasheet.

2. From the Format menu, choose **N**umber to display the Format Number dialog box.

3. From the **C**ategory list, select Percentage.

4. From the **F**ormat Codes list, select the Percent numbering format you want.

5. Choose OK or press Enter.

Percent signs appear on the selected numbers in the datasheet.

Tip

Click the row or column button with the right mouse button to both select it and bring up the shortcut menu.

IV

Charts

> **Note**
>
> The Formatting toolbar contains several buttons that can be used to manipulate number formatting (see fig. 12.11). They include Currency, Percent, and Comma Style buttons, and buttons for adding significant digits to decimal numbers (from 20.3 to 20.30, for example) and subtracting them (from 20.30 to 20.3, and so on).

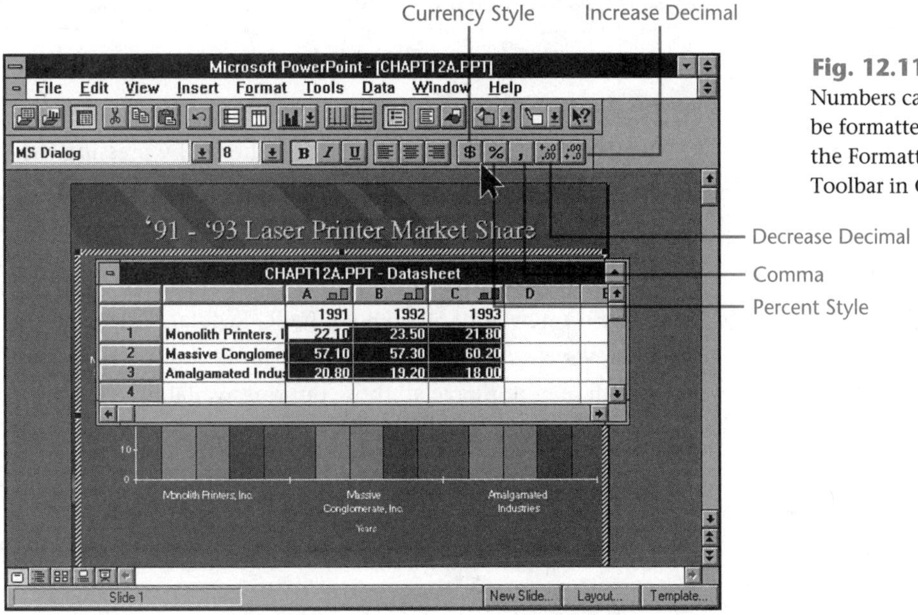

Fig. 12.11
Numbers can also be formatted using the Formatting Toolbar in Graph.

Tip
Use the Formatting toolbar's Increase Decimal and Decrease Decimal buttons to add or subtract significant digits from decimal values.

As you may have noticed by now, there are several ways to do just about any basic operation in a datasheet. Most people are used to using the left mouse button (the normally used one) to pull down menus and select options. Using the right mouse button takes a minor conceptual leap but has the potential to save time by cutting the necessary number of steps to select values and formatting menu options in half.

Changing the Font

Changing the font in a datasheet is simply a cosmetic process to improve the datasheet's appearance. Changing the font in a datasheet does not affect the display in a chart; text elements in a chart must have their fonts changed separately. With this in mind, selecting datasheet elements and changing their font works much the same way as with changing number formats.

PowerPoint 4 supports both TrueType and Adobe fonts for datasheets and charts. You can only change the font displayed on an entire datasheet; you cannot change the font or text formatting (boldface, italics, underlining, and so on) for just one cell, row, or column.

To change the fonts displayed in a datasheet, perform the following steps:

1. Click the right mouse button over any cell containing a datasheet value. The shortcut menu pops up.

2. Choose the Font command to display the Font dialog box.

3. After the dialog box opens, you can choose from the actions listed here:

   ■ Choose a new font from the Font list by clicking a name displayed on the list, or scroll down the list by pressing the down-arrow key when the insertion point is in the Font name box. Each successive font name is highlighted and displayed in the Preview window.

   ■ Choose a new Font Style: Bold, Italic, Regular, Bold Italic, or whatever is shown in the list (some fonts you install in your system may not have all those options available).

   ■ Choose a new font Size, if desired. Each size change is shown in the Preview window.

   ■ You can choose an Underline style: Single, Double, or None.

■ The displayed font **C**olor can be changed to any color available in the palette.

■ Three text **E**ffects can be selected: Stri**k**ethrough, Sup**e**rscript, or Su**b**script.

4. When the options are set properly, choose OK or press Enter.

The Formatting toolbar can also be used to add Bold, Italic, Underline, and to change the font and the font size. Also, a pull-down list is provided on the Formatting toolbar that offers quick access and selection of any available font on your system.

Changing the Column Width

Looking back at figure 12.8, you remember that the entry Massive Conglomerate, Inc. on the sample datasheet is too large for the margins of the cell in which it's entered. That's also true for the other series labels. The column width can be changed to show the entire contents of the offending cell. Individual cells cannot have their margins adjusted.

To adjust the width of a selected column, follow these steps:

1. Click the column button for the column you want to adjust.

2. From the F**o**rmat menu, choose Column **W**idth; the following options can be selected:

■ You can manually adjust the width by entering a new number value.

■ Click the **B**est Fit button for an automatic adjustment of the column to the width needed to accommodate the Massive Conglomerate, Inc. entry.

■ The Use **S**tandard Width check box can be used to adjust the column to the default width values in the datasheet.

3. Choose OK or press Enter. If you chose the **B**est Fit button, the width of the column is adjusted and the entire company name appears. Figure 12.12 shows the results of this operation.

Tip
Selecting **B**est Fit is the fastest way to adjust a column width beyond the default. You can also click and drag a column margin to adjust its width.

IV

Charts

Fig. 12.12

The fully corrected datasheet and 3-D column chart.

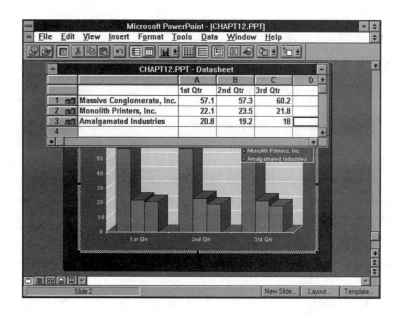

Troubleshooting

I can't drag and drop any rows or columns of data!

You're probably trying to click directly on a selected row to drag it. It won't work. Click on the row or column button to select the entire row or column, then click and drag the margin of the selected row (column). Move the mouse to the desired location on the datasheet and release the button. Drag and drop works slightly different in Graph datasheets than it does in other applications. The method also works for individual cells or blocks of cells in a datasheet, except for their method of selection.

From Here...

Now that you are familiar with working with datasheets and arranging data, you are ready to begin building PowerPoint charts. To learn how to work with charts, refer to the following chapters:

- Chapter 13, "Creating Basic Charts," builds on what you learned about datasheets in this chapter and takes you through the process of creating bar, column, pie, and other chart types from datasheet values.

- Chapter 14, "Customizing Charts," shows you how to add special elements and effects to charts.

- Chapter 19, "Using Advanced Charting Features," offers more information about powerful chart customization features.

- Many functions you saw in this chapter can be added to a customized toolbar. See chapter 22, "Customizing PowerPoint," for more information.

IV

Charts

Chapter 13

Creating Basic Charts

As noted in chapter 12, PowerPoint's charting capabilities have been greatly enhanced and more effectively integrated into the program. For native PowerPoint 4 use, a drastically enhanced charting engine has been created that offers better color scheme integration, a wider selection of chart types, greater flexibility in chart formatting, and many other features. Microsoft Graph objects from PowerPoint 3 are still supported, but any use of PowerPoint 4 quickly reveals the advantages its charting engine offers over the obsolescent Microsoft Graph program used in PowerPoint 3.

PowerPoint 4 offers sophisticated charting options that can help you convey powerful images to your viewers—or, just as easily, confuse them. The key is to make the right choices, to place just the needed information on the chart for illuminating your ideas and no more. Aside from presenting a road map of basic and essential charting features, this chapter also offers brief design tips to help ensure the most effective charting for your presentations.

Throughout this chapter, please bear in mind that Graph is a separate program from PowerPoint. Whenever you use the program to create and modify charts, the Microsoft Graph program "takes over" the PowerPoint screen and displays its own toolbars. If this issue is a little confusing, please read the first section of chapter 12, which offers a more complete description of the basic operation of Microsoft Graph.

In this chapter, you learn how to:

- Create several basic types of charts

- Learn the basics of how to select chart types for best effect

- Add and edit various chart elements, such as labels, titles, and other objects

- Change colors and patterns of various chart elements

- Add a chart onto your slide

Using Chart AutoFormats

Chart AutoFormats offer every major predefined chart type that is available in PowerPoint 4. The AutoFormat dialog box is where it all begins for high-speed chart selection.

Figure 13.1 shows the AutoFormat dialog box and its contents.

Fig. 13.1

The AutoFormat dialog box.

Formats Used buttons

Graph thumbnails

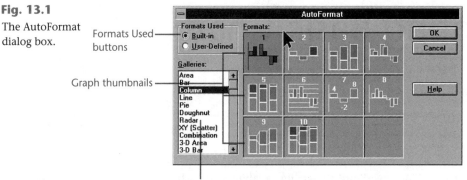

Galleries list box

To select from the greatest possible number of chart types, the AutoFormat dialog box is the key. For example, in figure 13.1, ten different types of 2-D column charts are offered, each displayed in a thumbnail picture. Each thumbnail is numbered from 1 to 10. Double-clicking any of the thumbnails containing a desired chart type changes the selected chart to the new format.

To the left of the thumbnails rests the Graph Galleries list box. Every chart category offered by PowerPoint is selected here. When a different category is selected, a different set of thumbnails appears, any of which can be selected for a new chart format. The AutoFormat chart types encompass every chart type offered in the program, and the types are listed in table 13.1:

Table 13.1	Chart AutoFormat Types	
2-D or 3-D	**Galleries Type**	**# of AutoFormats offered**
2-D	Area	5
	Bar	10
	Column	10
	Line	10
	Pie	7
	Doughnut	7
	Radar	6

2-D or 3-D	Galleries Type	# of AutoFormats offered
	XY (Scatter)	6
	Combination	6
3-D	Area	8
	Bar	5
	Column	8
	Line	4
	Pie	7
	Surface	4

To choose a chart AutoFormat, perform the following steps:

1. Double-click the chart on the PowerPoint slide to bring up Graph. (The process works either for an existing chart or a new one you just created.)

2. From the Format menu, choose AutoFormat.

   The AutoFormat dialog box appears, as shown in figure 13.1.

3. Choose a chart type from the Galleries scrollable list.

   A new set of thumbnails appears in the Formats section.

4. Click on a thumbnail that contains the desired chart type.

5. Choose OK or press Enter.

Tip
You can double-click on the desired thumbnail to select it and apply it to the chart.

There are other ways to choose chart types (including the Chart Type button on the Graph toolbar, which scrolls down an iconic list of 15 basic chart types), but AutoFormats offer the fastest access to the greatest number of options for any given chart type, and it is the option used in the charting examples in this chapter unless otherwise specified.

Also bear in mind that you are not limited to the charting choices displayed in the AutoFormat thumbnails. The Formats Used buttons (shown as **B**uilt-in and **U**ser-Defined in fig. 13.1) on the top left of the dialog box are full of implications, particularly the **U**ser-Defined button. You can create as many of your own custom chart types as you have room for in your hard disk. The process of creating custom chart types is explored in chapter 19, "Using Advanced Charting Features." In the current chapter, you stick with the built-in chart types.

Understanding the Elements of a Chart

Chart elements are simply the parts that compose a chart on a slide. Chart elements are manipulated, customized, and formatted to produce a desired visual effect. Some chart styles in the AutoFormat dialog box base their uniqueness solely on whether or not certain text labels are displayed on the chart, or whether gridlines are used on the background of a chart to aid in visual measurement. Those elements and how to work with them are the topic of discussion for the next several sections.

Knowing the basic elements of a chart is the key to effective design and customization, and will help you when you explore the chart creation and modification examples later in this chapter (and later in this book). Most chart types share the same elements and principles described in the paragraphs that follow.

The various chart elements fall into two categories: those that are common to 2-D charts, and the elements that are unique to 3-D charts.

Two-Dimensional Chart Elements

Figure 13.2 shows a sample 2-D column chart with each chart element identified.

X-axis. The horizontal axis, which is normally shown on the bottom of the chart. Each series has a single column for each increment along the x-axis. Figure 13.2 shows increments along the x-axis for the labels 1991, 1992, and 1993.

X-axis title. Identifies the x-axis and what each axis label represents. In figure 13.2, the x-axis title is Years.

X-axis labels. Labels for the increments along the x-axis. The audience uses the labels to determine what data is represented in each bar. In figure 13.2, the x-axis labels are 1991, 1992, and 1993.

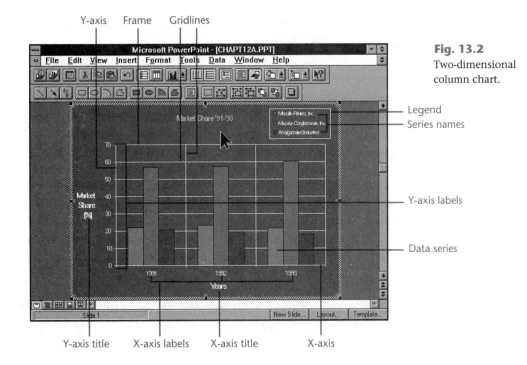

Fig. 13.2
Two-dimensional
column chart.

Y-axis. The vertical axis against which the height of each column is measured. The increments and range of the y-axis are directly based on the values in your data. The y-axis value range starts at zero or below your most negative data value, and increases to higher than your highest data value. In figure 13.2, the increments of the y-axis are evenly spaced from the bottom to the top of the range in increments of 10 from zero to 70.

Y-axis title. Helps clarify what the data values in the chart represent. In figure 13.2, the data values, and hence the columns in the chart, are shown as Share in Percentages (Share in %) for each company.

Y-axis labels. Provide a scale for measuring the heights of bars and columns. As you can see, the labels on the y-axis in figure 13.2 simply show the values of each increment, from zero to 70. The viewer compares the height of each column to the axis and labels to learn the approximate value. For example, the market share for Monolith Printers, Inc. in 1991 was just over 20 percent by visual estimate.

Tip
For most purposes, it is a good idea to limit the number of series in your chart to four or less to keep it from becoming crowded or cluttered. If you have more than four series, consider using two or more charts.

Data series. A group or set of data defined by a specific criteria, such as all the data values associated with a company. PowerPoint displays all the columns of one series in the same color and relative location in the chart. In figure 13.2, the series for Monolith Printers, Inc. appears in the first column of each group in the chart. The series for Massive Conglomerate, Inc. appears in the second position of each column group. Finally, the series for Amalgamated Industries appears in the third position, or the leftmost columns, of each group in the chart.

Legend. Provides information about the data in a chart, including the name for each series and the color for the columns (or bars, or pie slices, or whatever chart type you select). The legend in figure 13.2 indicates which series represents each company's yearly market shares and displays the color for the columns of each series.

Series names. Provide information about what the data series represent. The series names are shown in the legend of the chart. In figure 13.2, the series names are *Monolith Printers, Inc., Massive Conglomerate, Inc.,* and *Amalgamated Industries.*

Frame. Displays behind the chart and works with the y-axis as a scale with which to measure the columns in the chart. Gridlines can be added to a frame, as they are in figure 13.2.

Gridlines. Display on the frame; they extend from each axis across the frame. Gridlines displayed from the y-axis are seen behind the chart and help you measure the height and value of the column. Gridlines displayed from the x-axis help visually separate each group of yearly columns.

Tick marks. Tick marks measure each increment on a chart axis.

Three-Dimensional Chart Elements

The x- and y-axis elements just described apply to all charts you can create in Microsoft PowerPoint. X- and y-axes define 2-D charts—charts that have no visual depth. Three-dimensional charts, however, have a third axis called the *z-axis.* The z-axis helps create the depth that defines a 3-D chart. In many cases, using a 3-D chart may not be absolutely necessary, but can be used to provide visual attractiveness and impact. In other cases, using 3-D charts offers compelling advantages. The chart elements unique to 3-D charts are described in the text that follows.

Figure 13.3 shows a sample 3-D column chart with each chart element identified.

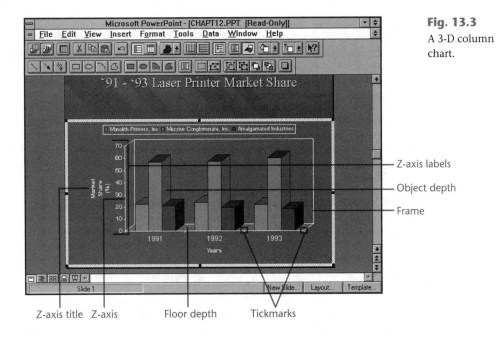

Fig. 13.3

A 3-D column chart.

Z-axis. In a 3-D chart, the z-axis is actually the vertical axis—unlike 2-D charts where the y-axis is the vertical one. Imagine a 2-D chart flopped over on its side, with the previously vertical y-axis now lying on the "floor." The z-axis is then drawn perpendicular to the plane created by the x- and y-axes. The z-axis lends depth to the chart, and is generally labeled with a series of tick-mark labels, used in turn to measure values.

Z-axis title. Identifies the z-axis and what each axis label represents. Figure 13.3 shows that the z-axis title is Market Share %.

Z-axis labels. Labels for the value increments along the z-axis, numbered from zero to 70.

Tip

The z-axis lends depth to a 3-D chart and acquires the measurement tick marks that otherwise would be on the y-axis if the chart were 2-D.

Note

In 3-D charts you normally use the x- and z-axes to provide clues about the data presented in your chart. Most 3-D charts don't provide all three axis titles or enable attachment of labels or increments to them. For that matter, adding a title to just *one* of the axes can provide all the information you need about the contents of a chart.

Object depth. Applies only to 3-D charts. Object depth is the thickness of the column or other object from the front of the chart to the back. Two-dimensional charts are flat and have no depth.

Floor depth. Applies only to 3-D charts. Floor depth gauges how deep the bottom of the chart is and shows how much room there is between each series.

Frame. Displays behind the chart and works with the y-axis as a scale with which to measure the columns in the chart. Gridlines can be added to a frame, as they are in figure 13.3.

Gridlines. Display on the frame; they extend from each axis across the frame. Gridlines displayed from the y-axis are seen behind the chart and help you measure the height and value of the column. Gridlines displayed from the x-axis help visually separate each group of yearly columns.

Tick marks. Tick marks measure each increment on a chart axis.

Choosing the Best Chart Type

In many cases, selecting a chart type is a matter of taste. Many other charting design features in this and later chapters focus on modifying and customizing charts that read effectively on-screen, but there's another issue to consider. What kinds of charts work best for different situations? Some simple guidelines are offered below that may help you when you make decisions about using basic chart types.

Bar charts are appreciated by audiences because of their visual simplicity and their common frame of reference—the size or length of horizontal bars representing the data values. When the audience walks out of the conference room, they tend to remember images of bars and how they differ in size rather than recalling specific values and percentages. The secret to effective bar charting is simplicity—providing bars in your images that can be easily seen and compared.

Use *column charts* when you have data values that you want your viewers to compare, such as the sales of different products over a period of time. Viewers can quickly see differences in values and spot trends in the data. Column charts are popular in every charting and spreadsheet program on the market. Both bar and column charts—2-D and 3-D alike—can be used to display more than one series of data.

Bar and column charts of both types can also have special sub-types, such as stacked bars and stacked columns, or 3-D column charts that place each series in its own rank, offering direct visual comparisons of values in each series while still showing their relationship to the other series in the chart.

Pie charts, on the other hand, are most effective when you are displaying one set of data values for direct comparison. For example, a pie chart is effective when you are conveying information such as a set of companies' market share in a particular business for one year. A single slice of a pie can be pulled away from the rest to lend emphasis to a value. Too many values in a pie chart can create a crowded and unreadable slide.

Line charts offer a tremendous number of options to the user. Multiple data series can easily be displayed, and line charts can be displayed in both 2- and 3-D formats. One specialized line chart type is the Stock chart, otherwise known as an Open-High-Low-Close chart. OHLC charts show the progress of a company's stock prices over a period of time. They are also unique in that a very large number of data sets can be displayed—as anyone who has seen a Dow Jones stock price history can attest.

In chapter 12, "Working with Datasheets," a datasheet was created containing fictional market-share statistics for three major laser-printer companies: Monolith Printers, Inc., Massive Conglomerate, Inc., and Amalgamated Industries. This chapter uses the same datasheet, shown in table 13.2, to step through the process of creating and customizing various basic kinds of charts within PowerPoint.

Table 13.2 Market Share Datasheet			
	1991	**1992**	**1993**
Monolith Printers, Inc.	22.1	23.5	21.8
Massive Conglomerate, Inc.	57.1	57.3	60.2
Amalgamated Industries	20.8	19.2	18.0

Using Column Charts

The options available for column charts reflect the major enhancements performed on PowerPoint's charting features. Ten different 2-D column chart types and eight different 3-D chart types are provided to the user. After you enter the data, such as that shown in table 13.2, into the datasheet, you can begin to create charts.

To create a 2-D column chart, follow these steps:

1. In the PowerPoint screen, double-click the chart object in your slide that you want to modify. Graph appears, displaying your chart for editing.

2. From the Format menu, choose AutoFormat.

   The AutoFormat dialog box appears.

3. In the Galleries list box, select Column. Clicking Column once brings a set of 10 thumbnails into the Formats section.

4. For a basic 2-D column chart type, select chart type 1 or 2. For most simple data sets, either type will do.

5. Choose OK or press Enter.

The data set in the example lends itself well to using a stacked column chart. Stacked columns can offer a fast visual glimpse of a column representing 100 percent of the market shares for each year, and each stacked column has several segments that graphically display how much is occupied by each data value. Stacked columns can also be used when you have several series of data to display.

Here's how to create a stacked column chart:

1. In the PowerPoint screen, double-click the chart object in the slide. Graph appears, displaying the chart for editing.

2. From the Format menu, choose AutoFormat.

3. In the Galleries list box, select Column. Clicking the mouse once on Column brings the set of 10 thumbnails into view.

4. For the proper 2-D stacked column chart type, select chart type 3.

5. Choose OK or press Enter.

The chart should appear similar to that in figure 13.4.

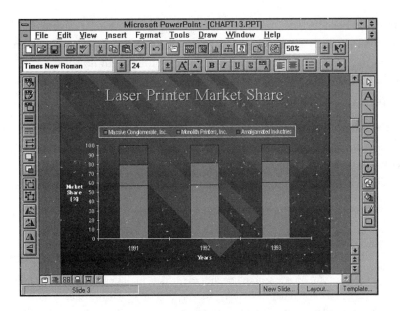

Fig. 13.4
A 2-D stacked
column chart.

In the figure, a legend has been added to provide information about the series values. For more information on adding legends to a chart, see the section "Adding and Moving a Legend" later in this chapter.

Two-dimensional column chart 9 works as well and is essentially the same type of chart, except that linking lines are added between each company value. Linking lines are used to visually separate series values in a stacked chart, providing an easier reading of values. Also notice that when you create the chart, the Massive Conglomerate, Inc. values are in the middle of the stacks, which can be visually undesirable. For this type of chart, it's more visually appealing as well as easier to read if the largest stacked column segments are placed at the bottom.

By displaying the datasheet and dragging and dropping or using a cut and paste operation of the series values (all of which is discussed in chapter 12), you can place the Massive Conglomerate, Inc. row on the *top* row of the datasheet. This has the effect of putting the Massive Conglomerate, Inc. percentages on the bottom of each stacked column, calling more effective attention to their dominance of market-share statistics.

Using Pie Charts
Pie charts are an exceptional option for comparing a set of values across series in a datasheet. For example, the market shares for the three companies

Tip
Place dominant statistics or series values on the bottom of a stacked column chart to draw attention to them. This is done by placing the series containing those numbers on the top row of the datasheet.

Monolith Printers, Inc., Massive Conglomerate, Inc., and Amalgamated Industries can easily be split up into three separate pie charts, one for each year. If you have several series of data, you have to split them up for the best effect. By using the sample datasheet, the data can be manipulated with a few simple steps to produce the desired effect.

As the datasheet stands, the series are organized in rows. Each row represents three years' market share percentages for each company. To create a pie chart with the correct numbers, set the series in columns and then set apart each set of data to create a pie chart by following these steps:

1. In PowerPoint, double-click the existing market-share chart to open it.

> **Note**
>
> Before you do any serious changes to the data in this exercise, take the time to make a backup slide containing the market-share chart you already have. You need it later in this chapter. From the **I**nsert menu, choose **N**ew Slide and then copy the chart to it. Save the file to make sure you keep its contents.

2. With the column chart displayed, click the By Column button on the Graph toolbar.

   The series indicators are transferred to columns A, B, and C of the datasheet.

3. After selecting both the B and C data columns, press Ctrl+C to copy them to the Clipboard.

4. With the B and C data columns still selected, from the **E**dit menu choose Cu**t**.

   You make the first pie chart with the contents of column A in the datasheet. For the time being, the other two series of data remain in the Clipboard until you're ready to bring them back.

5. From the F**o**rmat menu, choose **A**utoFormat. The AutoFormat dialog box appears.

6. In the **G**alleries list box, select Pie.

   Selecting Pie brings a set of seven new thumbnails into the **F**ormats section. They represent several types of pie charts, which differ largely by the types of data labels they bear and whether or not any pie slices are separated.

7. From the **F**ormats section, select chart 7.

8. Choose OK or press Enter.

   Several things have happened. Your column chart with its three series no longer exists. It's been replaced by a pie chart with one percentage for each company, representing each company's market share for 1991 (see fig. 13.5). Each pie slice has two labels: the company name, and the market share percentage.

   Also notice that a small pie has replaced the series indicator on the button for column A in the datasheet. Small pie slice graphics have been placed in the 1, 2, and 3 row buttons as well, each correctly representing a value in the pie.

9. Click once on the slide to embed the chart.

10. To retain your data for 1992 and 1993 and create charts for them, create a new slide and cut and paste each set of data to its own slide.

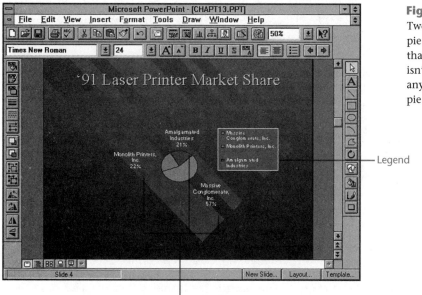

Fig. 13.5
Two-dimensional pie chart. Notice that the legend isn't needed anymore; and the pie is too small.

There are some problems with the chart as we've created it, however. First, the legend isn't needed anymore because the slice labels contain all the needed information. With this type of chart, a legend just clutters up the slide. Also, in many cases like the one illustrated here, the default pie size may be too small.

To fix these problems, follow these steps:

1. Double-click the pie chart to bring the chart back on-screen.

2. Click the legend once to select it.

3. Press the Delete key. The legend disappears.

Tip
To select a pie for moving or resizing, click just outside its contents.

4. Click once *just outside* the pie. A ghosted box should appear, showing that the pie as a whole has been selected.

5. Click on one of the corners of the *box*. Drag the mouse so that the pie is larger, and release it. You can resize it until you're comfortable with it. Notice that the labels resize with the pie automatically.

6. To move the pie, click on it. Notice that a ghosted box appears around it, showing that it's selected. Click and hold anywhere on the border of the box, and drag it until the pie is where you want it inside the chart object. The labels will come along for the ride, being moved with the chart automatically.

The pie should resemble the results shown in figure 13.6.

The exercises you just went through are only the beginning. There are many other ways to change and customize charts in PowerPoint 4, which are discussed in later chapters. In this next exercise, we assume you are already displaying the chart in Microsoft Graph, ready for editing. Before moving on, follow these steps to change the pie chart to 3-D:

1. From the F**o**rmat menu, choose **A**utoFormat.

2. In the **G**alleries list box, select 3-D Pie.

Seven new thumbnails appear in the **F**ormats section.

3. Select chart 7 to display the result shown in figure 13.7.

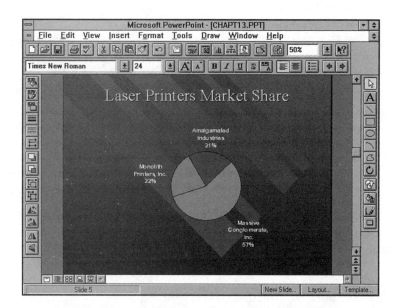

Fig. 13.6
The corrected 2-D
pie chart.

IV

Charts

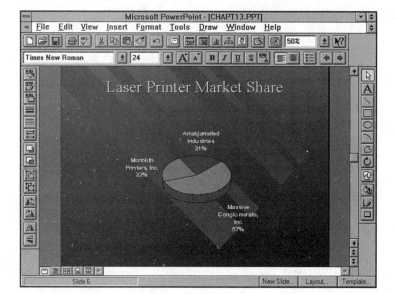

Fig. 13.7
A 3-D pie chart.

You can resize and move a 3-D pie in the same way as the 2-D pie described earlier.

Is this procedure starting to look familiar? The 2-D pie has just been transformed into a 3-D object. There are many options for chart customization that are not touched on here; they have to wait until the next chapter. Nonetheless, you can see many of the possibilities, and there's a lot of scope for experimentation.

Using Bar Charts

Bar charts are a commonly used option for presentations. In PowerPoint 4, ten different 2-D bar charts and five different 3-D bar chart types are offered. All the default bar chart types provided in Microsoft Graph are horizontal bars—so you do not have to worry about mixing up bars and columns because column chart types are always vertical.

To select and use a 2-D bar chart, follow these steps:

1. Double-click the existing market-share chart (showing all three years' worth of data) to select it for editing.

2. From the **Fo**rmat menu, choose **A**utoFormat.

3. From the **G**alleries list box, select Bar. Ten bar chart thumbnails appear, each representing a different type.

4. From the **F**ormats thumbnails, choose chart 1.

5. Choose OK or press Enter.

   The chart appears similar to that in figure 13.8, with the exception that a legend has also been added for chart readability.

6. Click the Datasheet button on the Graph toolbar to display the datasheet (see fig. 13.8). Notice that the label graphics on the row selection buttons have changed to tiny horizontal bars: one set for each data series. This provides a clue to how bar charts work. They can be slightly confusing, and the explanation for this is given in the next section.

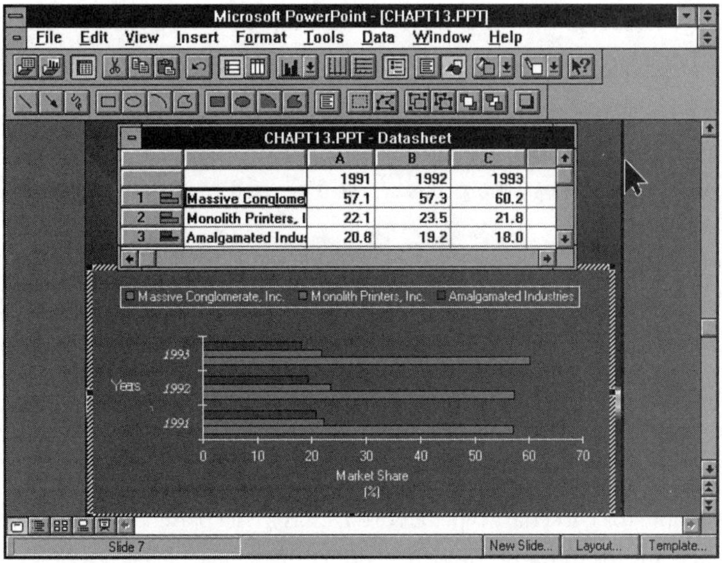

Fig. 13.8
A 2-D bar chart.

IV

Charts

The process of choosing and using a bar chart is very much the same as with other types; selecting a 3-D bar chart is as simple as the example just shown. Nonetheless, bar charts offer significant differences from other chart types, and those differences are described in the text that follows.

Why Are Bar Charts Different?

While selecting and using bar charts is as straightforward as choosing any other chart type, bar charts offer an additional level of complexity.

There are subtleties regarding bar charts that you need to be aware of to avoid confusion when using them. In bar charts, x-axis labels are displayed on the side of the chart rather than the bottom. Thus, PowerPoint displays the x-axis on the *vertical* axis, which is unique to this chart type. That's why you suddenly see the series chartic labels in a different place on the datasheet shown in figure 13.8.

However, despite its unusual position, in bar charts (as in any other chart type) the x-axis is normally used to denote categories and series labels. To understand this quickly, simply change the chart type from a 2-D column to a 2-D bar chart. You see that the position of the axis labels and titles changes to reflect the new axis positions.

Tip

Bar chart axes are not set up in the same way that other 2-D charts are.

Two-dimensional and 3-D bar charts have a few oddities that set them apart from other chart types:

■ *X-axis*. In bar charts, PowerPoint displays x-axis values on the vertical axis, shown on the side of the chart. In horizontal bar charts (as in other chart types), the x-axis can still be used to denote categories and series labels.

■ *X-axis title*. Identifies the x-axis (vertical, in this case) and what each axis label represents.

■ *X-axis labels*. Labels for the increments along the x-axis. The viewer uses the labels to determine what data is represented in each bar.

In 3-D bar graphs, the y-axis defines the *depth* of the chart. Y-axis labels are not available for this chart type. Figure 13.9 is a 3-D bar chart. The horizontal axis labels shown in figure 13.9 are actually the z-axis labels.

Fig. 13.9
A 3-D bar chart.

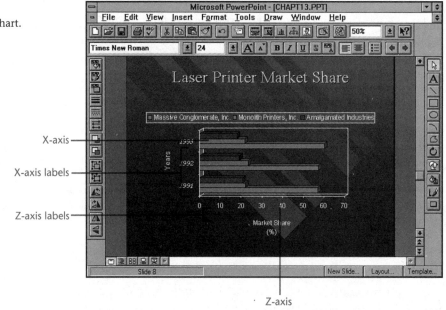

In a 3-D bar chart, the z-axis is actually the horizontal axis—unlike in 2-D bar charts where the y-axis is horizontal. Imagine a 2-D bar chart rotated 90 degrees, with the horizontal y-axis rotating 90 degrees to the "back" while still lying on the "floor." The vertical x-axis rotates in place. The z-axis is then drawn in the position previously occupied by the y-axis, perpendicular to the vertical plane created by the x- and y-axes. It is generally labeled with another series of tick-mark labels.

Three-dimensional bar charts are a special case. Notice that the z-axis also provides the scale for measuring the bars in your 3-D bar chart—as it does in every other 3-D chart in this book—it's just "lying down" in this chart type. For 3-D bar charts, the poor overworked z-axis takes a rest.

Tip

The z-axis is the axis of measurement in 3-D bar charts.

Using Other Types of Charts

PowerPoint offers a wider selection of chart types in its new version. Among them are 2-D and 3-D line charts, XY scatter charts, combination charts, doughnuts, 3-D surface, radar, and many others. A complete breakdown of all chart types and their uses is beyond the scope of this chapter and beyond the scope of this book. Brief accounts are offered of many other types, however, as you will meet some of them in chapter 19.

Line charts are an interesting and subtle option for helping your audience draw visual conclusions from your numeric data. Line charts are deceptively simple—messages can be found in line charts that may not be apparent in other types. In figure 13.10, Massive Conglomerate, Inc.'s market-share curve shows steady if unspectacular growth over the last three years. On the other hand, Amalgamated Industries is steadily losing market share to its competitors. In a line chart, this fact is driven home with emphatic clarity. This is one major advantage of a line chart—multiple messages can be conveyed with a minimum of chart clutter.

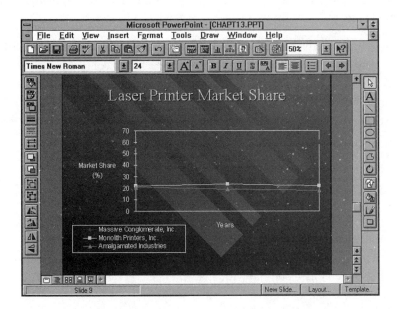

Fig. 13.10
A 2-D line chart.

XY charts are very useful when you have a large number of series that would otherwise create a very crowded bar or column chart. XY charts plot their data against two axes—the x- and y-axes—because each point, line, or sized object needs to be measured against each axis to determine its location. In figure 13.10, for example, each point on each line has a year value that ranges from 1991 to 1993, and a numeric value ranging between zero and 70. The common element across all XY charts is the requirement for two values for each data item, which are used to create and locate the graphic object denoting the series value.

In Graph, stock charts are not offered as a separate section under AutoFormats; instead, they are grouped with the line charts. Nonetheless, they are so unique and require such a different set of data that they deserve their own space in this book, and they're discussed in chapter 19. The same is true, of course, with combination charts, the building of which may be the most challenging chart-building task you will undertake.

Stock charts require different data sets from those that we used in our previous examples—one type, a High/Low/Close stock chart, requires exactly three series of data, one of which represents a series of Low stock price values, one which shows High values, and one which shows Closing values. An Open/High/Low/Close chart requires four respective series. The Open value is the price at which the stock opened trading for the given time period. The four series can be of a tremendous length; as mentioned earlier, the Dow Jones stock price poster you see in any stockbroker's office is a classic case of an OHLC chart.

Combination charts, on the other hand, can combine stock price information with profit, sales, or market-share statistics to provide a compelling picture of the overall fortunes of a company. Generally, combination charts combine columns with lines or columns with OHLC numbers. They require two distinct data sets. They are their own chart category, which we pay closer attention to in chapter 19, "Using Advanced Charting Features."

Changing Elements on a Chart

Now that you have been introduced to creating charts, it's time to take a first look at Microsoft Graph's basic chart customization features. There are quite a few elements present on even the simplest charts; by the time you finish this chapter, you'll be familiar with all of them.

Taking a close look at Graph's **F**o**r**mat menu, you begin to notice changes in
one of its menu options as you select different chart elements to edit. When
you double-click a chart on a slide to start Microsoft Graph (remember,
Graph is PowerPoint's separate charting application, even though it doesn't
look that way when you use it), the top item on the **F**o**r**mat menu is S**e**lected
Chart Area, as shown in figure 13.11.

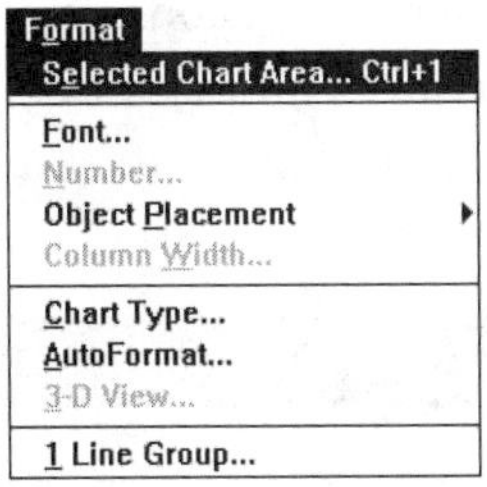

Fig. 13.11
Graph's **F**o**r**mat
menu, opening
version.

Now, after clicking the chart legend, the menu item changes to S**e**lected Legend, as shown in figure 13.12.

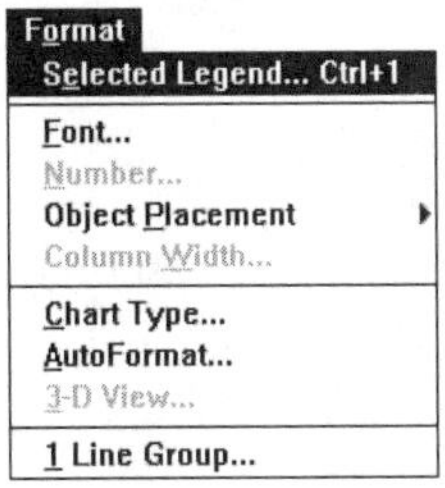

Fig. 13.12
Graph's **F**o**r**mat
menu with a
selected chart
legend.

If you press Esc and select a chart axis, the menu item changes to S**e**lected
Axis, as shown in figure 13.13.

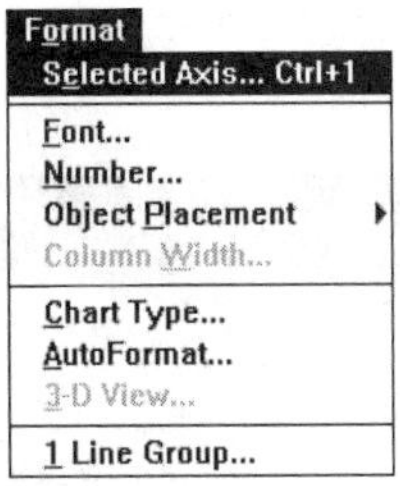

Fig. 13.13
Graph's **F**o**r**mat
menu with a
selected chart axis.

A pattern is emerging here: Whenever you decide to change a chart element and select it, the Format menu changes its top option to address the selected object.

Much earlier in this book, the structure of PowerPoint's menus was discussed. Not only are PowerPoint's menu bars replaced when different parts of the program (such as Graph) are activated, but depending on the items selected on a chart, certain menu items change too. All the element changing and formatting features are centralized on the Format Selected dynamic menu option. Therefore, you can use this menu to customize and add elements to a chart.

> **Note**
>
> Alternatively, you can use the right mouse button to help you edit chart elements. Click and hold the right mouse button on the desired chart element (axis, legend, and so on) and a shortcut menu appears offering all the formatting options that you are activating and using in other ways. The shortcut menu options work exactly the same as the options on the pull-down menu from the top of the screen. Over time, you may prefer using the right mouse button.

Selecting Objects on a Chart

Chart objects are selected in the same fashion that objects are selected on PowerPoint slides. The left and right mouse buttons work in the same fashion, offering both consistency and scope for experimenting.

Almost any object on a chart can be selected: axes, chart bars, pie slices, columns, lines, or anything else that represents a data series or data value; chart and axis titles, data points, data markers, gridlines, and legends. Many types of chart objects have similarities in formatting methods and in the ways that formatting features are accessed. In every case, a chart object must be selected before you can apply changes to it.

> **Note**
>
> There are three different ways to use the mouse with chart objects: single-clicking to select them, double-clicking to automatically bring up formatting options, or clicking with the right mouse button to bring up a shortcut menu for changing the elements.

As mentioned earlier in this book, the normal method for selecting charts and chart objects is a single click with the left mouse button. Figure 13.14 shows a 2-D pie chart with a ghosted box around it, with eight small dots called *pressure points*. The box and points indicate the object's selection. Dragging on a pressure point resizes the chart. Dragging on the border of the box allows movement of the chart along with its labels.

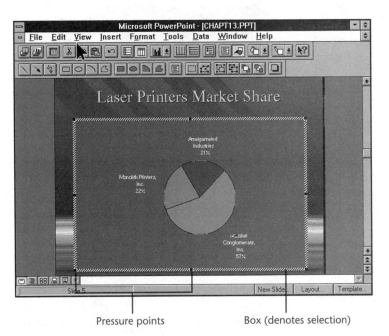

Fig. 13.14
A selected pie chart. The ghosted box denotes selection. Corners can be dragged to resize. Sides can also be dragged for moving the object. Pressure points on the corners and the middle of each side are points where the chart can be resized.

Pressure points   Box (denotes selection)

When a chart object is selected, several different things can happen. It can be formatted in various ways. Dragging a corner of many selected objects, like the pie chart just shown, resizes the object symmetrically, retaining its aspect ratio. (For some chart types, this rule doesn't apply.) Dragging a side of the box that is not a pressure point drags the object and any fonts that may be attached to it to another location in the chart.

Now, turn your attention to the numerous elements that can be added and changed within a chart.

Adding a Title to a Chart

Titles can be added to any chart to help explain its contents. They're a real help to an audience, and thus should always (or almost always) be used. To add a chart title, follow these steps:

1. Double-click the chart object to select it and bring up Microsoft Graph. The full chart object is automatically selected.

2. From the **I**nsert menu, choose **T**itles.

   The Titles dialog box appears, as shown in figure 13.15.

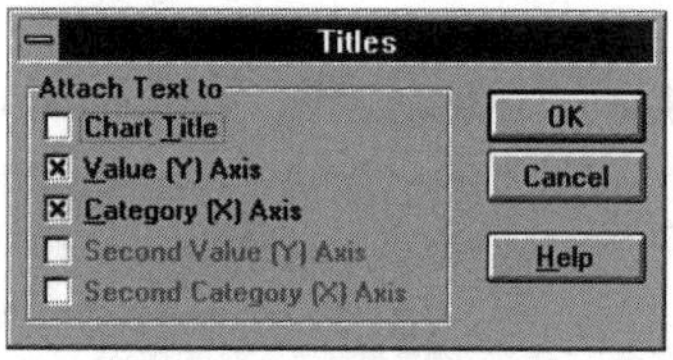

Fig. 13.15
The Titles dialog box for inserting titles in charts.

The last two title options are normally ghosted, unless you're working with combination chart types. Sometimes, particularly with pie chart types, only the Chart Title option is available. Since there are no axes of measurement in a pie chart, this stands to reason.

3. Click the Chart **T**itle check box to select that option.

4. Choose OK or press Enter.

   The word `Title` appears, currently selected.

5. Click once inside the Title object. The I-beam blinks inside the text.

6. Type a new title and then click a location outside the Title object. The new title is deselected and displayed.

Choosing Axis Line Weights and Tick Marks

Axis line weights can be changed to lend visual emphasis to an axis or to enhance its visibility. Tick marks are also offered that help the viewer to measure values and separate groups of data values into appropriate categories.

Chart types that normally display axes, such as bar, column, scatter, XY, combination, and other types, can have different line weights and tick marks applied by performing the following steps:

1. Click the desired chart axis once to select it.

   Make sure you click directly on the axis, or you may select another chart element instead.

2. From the Format menu, choose Selected Axis.

   The Format Axis dialog box appears (see fig. 13.16).

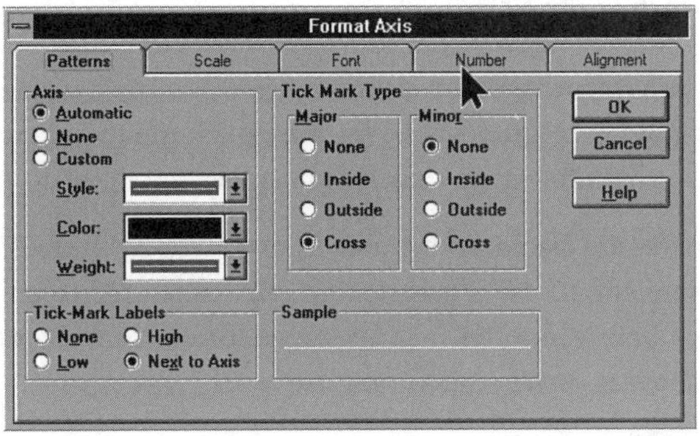

Fig. 13.16
Using the Format Axis dialog box, displaying the Patterns tab, for changing axis line weights.

3. Click the Patterns tab.

4. To change the line weight of the selected axis, click the down arrow of the **W**eight drop-down list. Several line weights are shown, with the lightest weight on top and the heaviest on the bottom. Click the desired weight to select it.

5. To assign and place labels for tick marks on the selected axis, select from the options in the Tick-Mark Labels area of the dialog box:

N**o**ne	No tick marks displayed
Low	Displays tick-mark labels
H**i**gh	Displays tick-mark labels above the chart
Ne**x**t to Axis	Places labels next to axis (for x-axis, effect is same as for Low)

6. To assign the placement and type of tick marks, choose options from the Tick Mark Type area of the dialog box. First choose either **M**ajor to assign major tick marks or Mino**r** to assign minor tick marks. Then choose from the following options:

None	Place no tick marks on the axis
Inside	Tick marks on the inside of the axis

Tip

Change the line style for the selected axis by choosing a style from the **S**tyle drop-down list. Choose a line color by choosing a color from the **C**olor drop-down list.

Outside   Tick marks on the outside of the axis

Cross   Tick marks that cross the axis

7. Choose OK or press Enter.

Tip
Minor tick marks are an important measurement tool for precise values, and are as easily selected as Major tick marks.

Tick marks are a frequently used element of good charts. Tick marks are very useful for helping to measure values on the x-axis, and to help separate categories on the y-axis for easier viewing, as can be seen in figure 13.17.

Major tick marks are placed at each major increment on the axis scale; if your scale is measured by 10, 20, 30, 40, and so on, a major increment tick mark is placed at each one. Minor tick marks are used for more precise value measurements, and show as smaller marks on the axis.

Fig. 13.17
Displaying tick marks on a column chart.

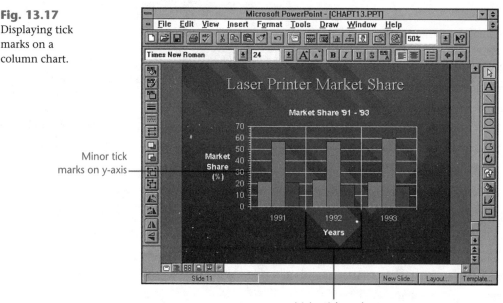

Minor tick marks on y-axis

Major tick marks

Choosing Colors and Pattern Fills for Chart Elements
Applying different colors and pattern fills is one of the most important chart customizing features you can use. While PowerPoint's built-in templates automatically assign specific colors to certain chart elements, you are not locked in to those predefined choices. Any color that is available in the current palette can be used for any chart object. Using colors is, as with many other features regarding charts, largely a matter of taste.

Generally, chart objects should have colors assigned that help them stand out from the slide background and the chart background. A pattern fill is simply a graphic pattern that is used to fill the area of an object to its borders. Colors work exactly the same way and are used to fill objects such as bars, columns, and data markers with a distinctive color that sets them apart from other data sets.

PowerPoint 4 offers substantially enhanced color and pattern options, with support for a 64-color palette (PowerPoint 3 supported only 16) in all templates and easier access to many pattern fills, which can be combined with colors to create custom effects.

There are some general rules that can be followed to make color and pattern selection easier:

■ Any object on a chart—such as a set of data markers, lines, axes, bars, pies, pie slices, fonts for chart titles, axis titles, tick-mark labels, gridlines, or chart background—can have its colors (and, usually, patterns) changed.

■ Objects are generally split into two parts for color changes: borders and areas. Borders are the outside edge of an object, which can have line weights, colors, and line styles applied to them. Areas are the interior of an object, which can be filled with colors and patterns.

■ Clicking once on any chart object selects it for color and pattern changes.

■ When a chart object is selected, the easiest way to make color and pattern changes is to use the Selected command at the top of the Format menu. When you do so, the Patterns tab automatically appears so that you can make changes.

Once you change the color or pattern of one chart object, you can do so for just about anything else by using the same methods. Suppose, for example, that you want to change the color of the chart background by following these steps:

1. Click an area of the chart that is not occupied by any other chart object.

2. From the Format menu, choose Selected Chart Area.

The Format Chart Area dialog box appears, as shown in figure 13.18, with the Patterns tab options displayed.

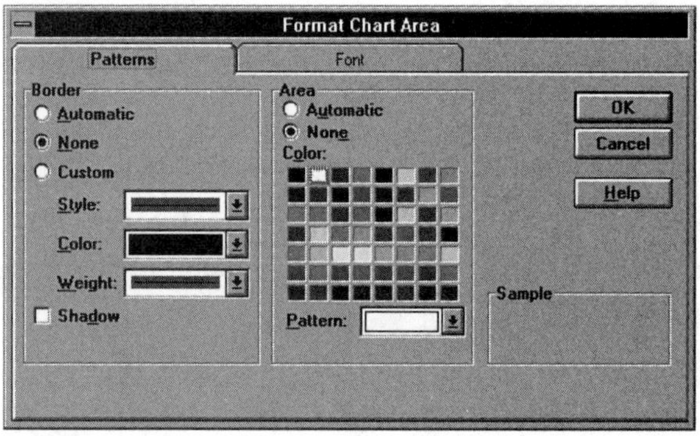

Fig. 13.18
The Patterns tab offers numerous colorizing options.

3. Select options for setting border colors for the chart object from the Border area of the dialog box:

Automatic	Default border color
None	Removes axis from display
Custom	Define custom axis settings
Style	Drop-down list to assign a new line style
Color	Drop-down list to assign a new line color
Weight	Drop-down list to assign a new line weight
Sha**d**ow	Add a shadow effect to the border of the object

Tip
Clicking any color or pattern selects it. Colors and patterns can also be mixed.

4. Select options for assigning a color fill to an object area from the Area section of the dialog box:

A**u**tomatic	Default, automatically displays default color
Non**e**	Ensures a transparent chart background or object background
C**o**lor	Select colors from the current color palette
Pattern	Pop-up box displays the color palette and a selection of 18 different pattern fills

5. To apply the color choice, choose OK or press Enter. The new color is applied to the object border or object area.

This section barely touched on the basics of handling color in PowerPoint. Palettes can be customized, new colors can be defined, mixed, and applied, and entire color schemes can be manipulated to change the look of an entire presentation. There are many associated subjects regarding color that are touched upon in later chapters.

Choosing Fonts

Using the Graph Fonts feature, you can select the type, style, size, color, and background for any fonts used in your chart. Fonts are used for many different elements on a chart, including legends, axis labels, chart titles, tick-mark labels, and comments—in fact, you can apply font changes to any chart element containing text. Any of those elements can be changed individually without affecting other elements in the chart.

To change the fonts in a chart, follow these steps:

1. Select the line, legend, axis, or other chart item containing the text you wish to change.

2. From the Format menu, choose Font.

   The Font tab appears in a dialog box, as shown in figure 13.19. In the figure, an axis has been selected, but it could be almost any other chart element.

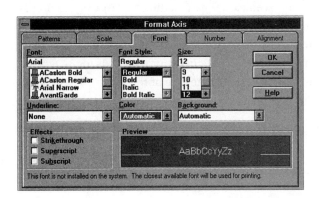

Tip

Using the Format Selected dynamic menu option for many chart objects, you can access the same font formatting options among all the other formatting option tabs available for that object type.

Fig. 13.19
Formatting the font for axis labels.

3. Choose a new font from the **F**ont list by clicking a name displayed on the list, or scroll down the list by pressing the down-arrow key when the cursor is in the **F**ont name box. Each successive font name is highlighted and displayed in the Preview window.

4. Choose a new F**o**nt Style: Bold, Italic, Regular, Bold Italic, or whatever is shown in the list (some fonts you install in your system may not have all those options available).

5. Choose a new Font **S**ize, if desired. Each size change is shown in the Preview window.

6. If you want, choose an **U**nderline style: Single, Double, or None.

7. If you want, change the displayed font **C**olor to any color available in the palette.

8. Select any of the three text Effects, if you want: ~~Strikethrough~~, Superscript, or Subscript.

9. When the options are set properly, choose OK or press Enter.

For some chart objects, another option is offered in the Font tab: Background. You can set the background color of an axis title, chart title, or the background of the chart itself to be opaque or transparent, or to use a specific color or pattern—or any combination thereof.

Adding and Editing Labels on an Axis

As you may have seen earlier with adding a chart title, adding an axis label works exactly the same way. The purpose of an axis label is different, however. It provides the identity of the axis increments—what they measure, in the case of the y-axis for most charts (or the z-axis for 3-D charts), and the categories of the data sets (in the case of the x-axis). They can thus be extremely helpful in many charting situations.

To add or edit labels on an axis, follow these steps:

Tip
Axes can have titles attached without being selected first.

1. Double-click the chart object in the slide to bring up Graph's menu and toolbar. You do not need to select an axis to add a title to it.

2. Choose **I**nsert, **T**itles to display the Titles dialog box.

3. Click either the **V**alue (Y) Axis or the **C**ategory (X) Axis check box to select it. (Or, to remove its selection, click in the check box again.)

4. Choose OK or press Enter.

The axis title appears, remaining selected on the chart.

Once you insert an axis title, it may need to be formatted with font changes, resizing, or other adjustments. You can also rotate an axis label if it interferes with the readability of tick-mark labels (an axis label longer than a few letters may very well do so, particularly on a vertical axis label). An example of an axis title that interferes with the axis tick-mark labels is shown in figure 13.20.

Tip
Axis titles can be rotated, and often should be, to avoid overwriting tick-mark labels on an axis.

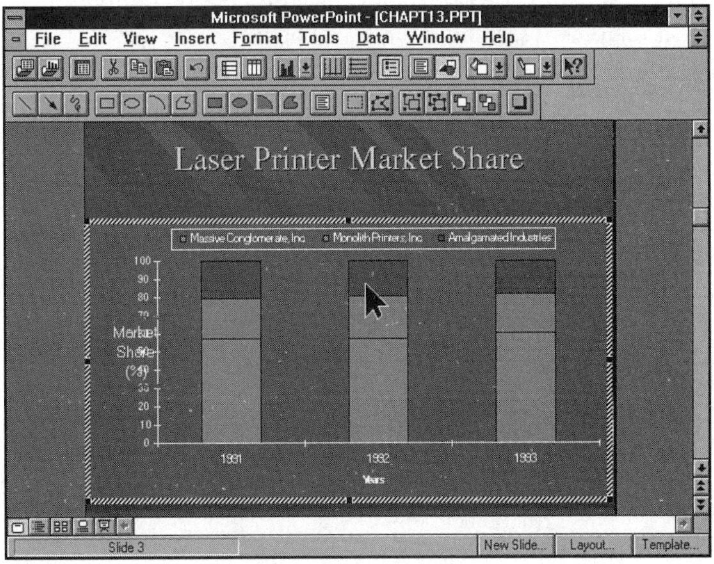

Fig. 13.20
The axis title interferes with the axis tick-mark labels.

5. With the axis title selected, choose **Fo**rmat **F**ont.

The Format Axis Title dialog box appears with the Font tab displayed.

6. If you want, select a new font type, size, style, color, and whether the background of the axis title has a color or pattern fill, or if it's transparent or opaque. In that respect, axis titles are treated just like any other objects.

7. After you choose the font settings you want, click the Alignment tab to display the options shown in figure 13.21.

Fig. 13.21
The Alignment tab
of the Format Axis
Title dialog box.

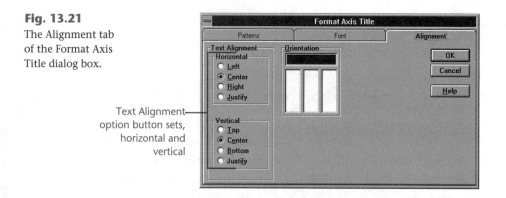

Text Alignment
option button sets,
horizontal and
vertical

8. To change the alignment of text for the axis, choose from the following options in either the Horizontal or Vertical option button lists in the Text Alignment section of the dialog box:

Horizontal

Left   Left aligns text in the object.

Center   Centers title text in the object.

Right   Right aligns title text in the object.

Justify   Justifies title text in the object.

Vertical

Top   Aligns text at the top of the object.

C**e**nter   Aligns text midway between the top and the bottom of the object.

Bottom   Aligns at the bottom edge of the object.

Justi**f**y   Vertically justifies the text in the object.

9. To rotate the axis title by 90 degrees, click one of the four icons in the Orientation area of the dialog box.

Tip
Click and drag a pressure point to resize or change the shape of a selected axis title.

Rotation can either be normal, spun 90 degrees to the left or right, or the text can be aligned with each letter below the previous one. In some ways, a rotated axis title can be very attractive on a chart.

10. Choose OK or press Enter to implement your changes.

Adding and Moving a Legend

The *legend*, the small box in your chart that is used to identify the data series, is in the upper right corner by default. But the legend can be moved to any other location on the chart. The legend can be resized, and the font displayed in the legend can be changed to any font available in your system.

Many chart styles don't automatically add a legend. Some charts, such as the labeled pie chart shown earlier in figure 13.5, don't really require it. Nonetheless, it's a simple matter to add a legend:

1. Double-click the chart you want to edit.

   The Graph toolbar and menu appears.

2. From the **I**nsert menu, choose **L**egend.

   A legend is automatically inserted into the chart showing the series names and the colors assigned to them.

   You can move the legend to any location on the chart by simply dragging it, or you can let PowerPoint find the best location for it by the following means:

3. Choose F**o**rmat, S**e**lected Legend.

   The Format Legend dialog box appears.

4. Click on the Placement tab to display the options shown in figure 13.22.

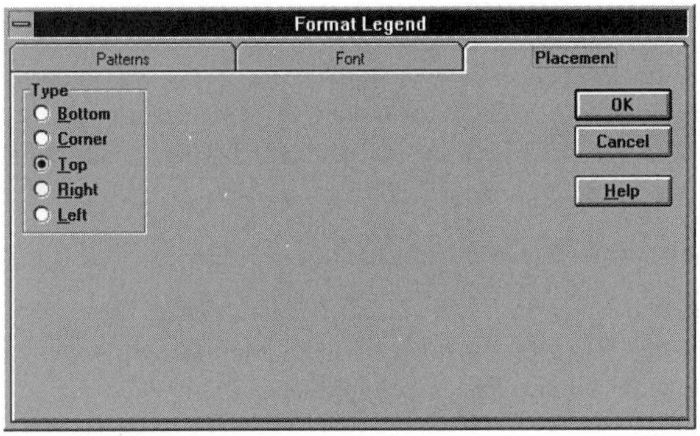

Fig. 13.22
The Format Legend dialog box with the Placement options displayed.

5. Choose from the five selectable button options: **B**ottom, **C**orner, **T**op, **R**ight, and **L**eft.

If you choose **T**op, for example, the legend is automatically formatted for a single-row legend and is placed above the center of the chart.

6. Choose OK or press Enter to execute your changes to the legend.

Note

If you should happen to click inside your legend after it's selected, you will see that one of your legend entries is selected. You can then format that entry individually just as you would any other text element in a chart.

Troubleshooting

My columns or bars are in the wrong order.

It's quite possible that your data series have been set up for Series By Columns rather than Series By Rows. Depending on how you've entered your data, your chart might look like figure 13.23.

For purposes of comparison in the chart, it's more important to ensure that each year's worth of data for all three companies is compared, rather than all three years' worth of data for each company. How do you change this? Click the By Rows button on Graph's Standard toolbar.

My axis titles still interfere with value labels on the axis.

Despite specifying a rotated axis title or a different font size for the title, you may still experience problems getting an axis title to lay properly on the chart. To fix this, click on the area holding the actual chart (the region between the x- and y-axes of the chart). Then, grab one of the pressure points on the border of the selected area and resize it to allow more space. The title moves along with the chart border.

Next, click on the axis title and then grab the border of the title and drag it. You may have to experiment a few times to get it right, but the exercise will show how many of Microsoft Graph's resizing and moving features have been made more flexible and allow for moving and resizing of any object on a chart.

I can't add titles to my pie chart.

The only title that can be added to a pie chart is a chart title. There are no axes on a pie chart—hence, you can't attach titles to them. Most pie chart types offered in the AutoFormats automatically attach percentage labels or slice labels, or both, to a chart.

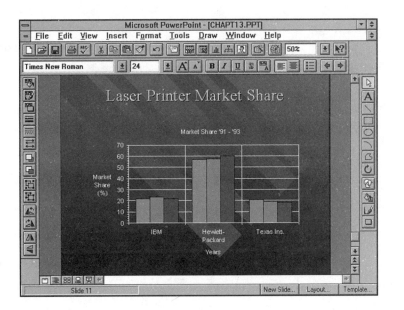

Fig. 13.23
The columns for
each company are
collected together
in this column
chart.

IV

Charts

Inserting the Chart into Your Slide

It's a simple matter to insert your completed chart into your slide. Click once anywhere outside the selected chart object. The PowerPoint main screen reappears with its menus and toolbars, and the chart is embedded on the slide.

From Here...

There are so many different ways to do so many basic tasks in PowerPoint, and in its charting facility Microsoft Graph, that it's a matter of taste as to how the user decides to use the program. Most of the basic grunt work in creating charts has been done in this chapter.

Now, with the next chapter, it's time to have a little more fun. The chart customization and alteration features of PowerPoint 4 are one of the new version's major improvements.

■ Chapter 14, "Customizing Charts," shows you how to add special elements and effects to charts.

■ Chapter 19, "Using Advanced Charting Features," offers more information about powerful chart customization features and more specialized charts.

■ Many functions you've seen in this chapter can be added to a customized toolbar. See chapter 22, "Customizing PowerPoint," for more information.

Chapter 14

Customizing Charts

With the dramatic improvements of PowerPoint 4's charting facilities, Microsoft's presentation software has come of age. When you move beyond the basic chart creation features into the areas of chart customization, color handling, and the creation and saving of custom chart types (described in depth in chapter 19), more of the true strengths of the PowerPoint 4 upgrade become apparent. This chapter builds on the basic element creation and manipulation features discussed in the previous chapter.

Customizing Chart Elements

Besides the numerous chart elements discussed in the last chapter, many other types are available that can add further effects and custom appearance to any PowerPoint chart. Most of the examples in this chapter use the same data set that was used in the previous two chapters, representing the market-share split for three fictional major companies in the laser printer business (see table 14.1).

This chapter offers new charting topics such as:

- Adding arrow pointers and colored polygons to a chart

- Chart rotation by mouse and by specified values

- Drawing various objects on a chart

- Adding colors, shading, and shadowing to drawn objects

- Understanding and applying color palettes in a chart

Table 14.1 Market Share Datasheet			
	1991	**1992**	**1993**
Monolith Printers, Inc.	22.1	23.5	21.8
Massive Conglomerate, Inc.	57.1	57.3	60.2
Amalgamated Industries	20.8	19.2	18.0

Figure 14.1 shows the Market Share datasheet represented in a typical 2-D column chart. In the sections that follow, several new types of chart elements and objects are added to the column chart to demonstrate PowerPoint's added flexibility and power.

Fig. 14.1
The Market Share
column chart.

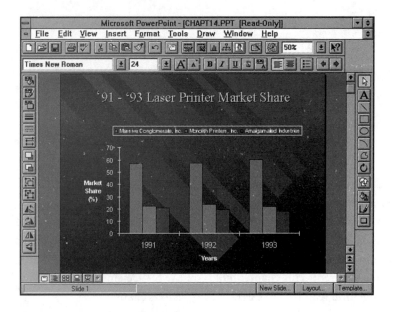

Displaying Gridlines

The column chart in figure 14.1 could benefit from a few additional touches to aid its readability. One of those touches is gridlines. *Gridlines* rest inside the vertical plane created by the x- and y-axes in 2-D charts and can provide more accurate visual measurement of data values. They can be used in conjunction with tick marks (and fill much the same function) or instead of tick marks.

Gridlines bear another similarity to tick marks because they can be specified in major and minor increments in the same way. Figure 14.2 shows the Market Share chart with the major y-axis gridlines enabled.

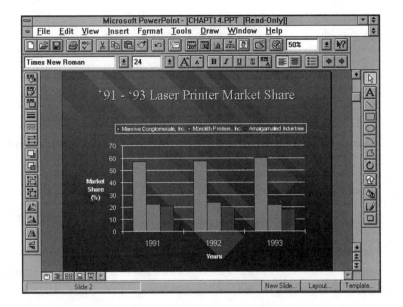

Fig. 14.2
Major y-axis
gridlines added
to a 2-D column
chart; x-axis
gridlines are
not enabled.

Notice how the gridlines intersect with the major tick marks on the y-axis.
Most chart types offer gridlines as an option, including bar, column, line,
area, and scatter charts in both 2- and 3-D formats. To add gridlines to the
Market Share chart, and to any other chart type that can use them, follow
these steps:

1. Double-click the Market Share chart to enable its editing in Graph.
   The Graph toolbar appears and the chart is automatically selected.

2. From the **I**nsert menu, choose **G**ridlines.

   The Gridlines dialog box appears, as shown in figure 14.3.

   The four options offered for 2-D chart types are for major and minor
   gridlines on the x- and y-axes. As you see shortly, it is not usually a
   good idea to go nuts on the gridlines—it's quite easy to render a chart
   almost unreadable by using too many of them.

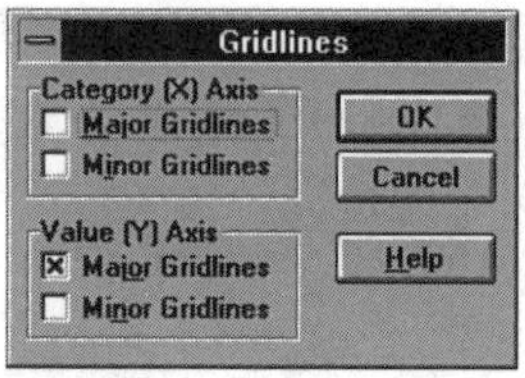

Fig. 14.3
The Gridlines
dialog box.

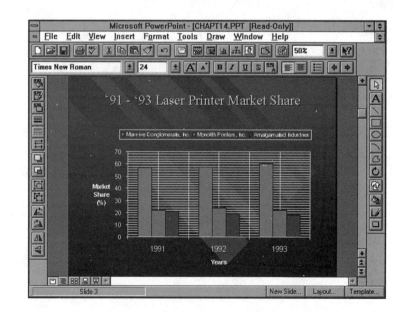

3. For the Market Share chart, choose the Major Gridlines check box for the Value (Y) Axis.

4. Choose OK or press Enter.

Your chart should now appear similar to figure 14.2.

At this point, the y-axis gridlines have changed and enhanced the readability of the column chart. The values of each column are much easier to estimate. In particular, one company—Massive Conglomerate, Inc.—is shown to have crossed the 60 percent threshold in market share in 1993, while the other two companies have either held steady or lost slight amounts of market share.

On the other hand, to demonstrate how too many gridlines can damage the readability of a chart, try enabling the major and minor x-axis gridlines along with the y-axis minor gridlines, as shown in figure 14.4.

Fig. 14.4
Major and minor
gridlines have
been added to the
x- and y-axes,
making the chart
very difficult to
read.

While the chart is still functional, there are a few risks involved with such a chart. The viewer's eye is distracted by the additional work of having to read a closely packed succession of gridlines to see the columns' values. Also, if you are working with an interlaced monitor, or displaying a slide show on a large television screen, the packed horizontal gridlines can be painful to view for both you and your audience. It is possible to use major and minor gridlines effectively on a chart, however. To do so, you may need to adjust the scale of the gridlines on your chart.

Adjusting Gridline Scales

To change the gridline scale for a chart, a few simple steps need to be followed. To adjust the y-axis gridline scale for easier reading on minor gridlines, follow these steps:

1. Click any of the y-axis gridlines displayed on the chart (whether major or minor doesn't matter).

2. From the Format menu, choose Selected Gridlines.

   The Format Gridlines dialog box appears. Two tabs are displayed in the Format Gridlines dialog box: Patterns and Scale.

3. Choose the Scale tab.

4. Choose from the following scale options for the y-axis gridlines:

   ■ Auto

Minimum:	Sets Minimum y-axis value
Maximum:	Sets Maximum y-axis value
Major Unit:	Sets the increment for each major gridline
Minor Unit:	Sets the increment for each minor gridline
Category [X] Axis Crosses At:	Sets y-axis placement where x-axis crosses the chart

   ■ Logarithmic Scale — Useful for charts that have widely ranging values

   ■ Values in **R**everse Order — Switches the Value [Y] axis increments from top to bottom or bottom to top; reverses position of x-axis

■ Category [X] Axis Crosses   Places the x-axis at the highest y-axis
at **M**aximum Value   value on the chart if the chart is
                                resized

While the sheer number of options may seem daunting, this is a place
where a lot of experimenting can be done with very little trouble. Using
only the Format Gridlines dialog box, some very sophisticated effects
can be executed on a chart—custom effects that are surprisingly simple
to create.

For the market share example, you could simply adjust the minor
gridlines to a better value. To do so, click inside the number entry box
beside the M**i**nor Unit option and type **5** to set the minor gridlines to
an increment of five ticks on the Y scale.

5. Choose OK or press Enter. The example chart is shown in figure 14.5.

Fig. 14.5
Minor gridlines
have been adjusted
to 5, maintaining
the chart's
readability while
offering more
precise value
measurement.

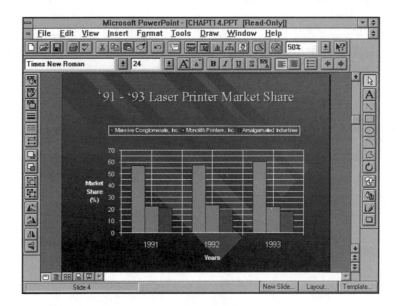

As you can see, it's quite possible to use major and minor gridlines in designing a powerful chart. Now, with the use of a proper minor gridline increment,
column values are even easier to estimate, without drowning the chart in
distracting horizontal lines.

> **Note**
>
> Chapter 19, "Using Advanced Charting Features," discusses in greater detail the use of the Gridlines dialog box to customize charts.

Displaying Data Labels

There are times when it may be helpful to an audience to see explicit data values on your chart. In the Market Share column chart shown in figure 14.1, values can be roughly estimated. While the chart is attractive, it is also somewhat minimalistic in the style it conveys. The two previous sections on gridlines discussed one method of conveying accurate visual estimates. If you do not want to provide estimations but desire to display concrete number values on your chart, you can attach data labels to your columns or other types of data markers on your chart.

To display actual values as data labels on your chart, follow these steps:

1. Click the data series marker (a column, bar, or other type of object representing a data value on the chart) to select it. All markers belonging to the same series are selected.

2. From the Format menu, choose Selected Series.

   The Format Data Series dialog box appears.

3. Choose the Data Labels tab to display the options shown in figure 14.6.

Tip
Data value labels are applied to one series at a time.

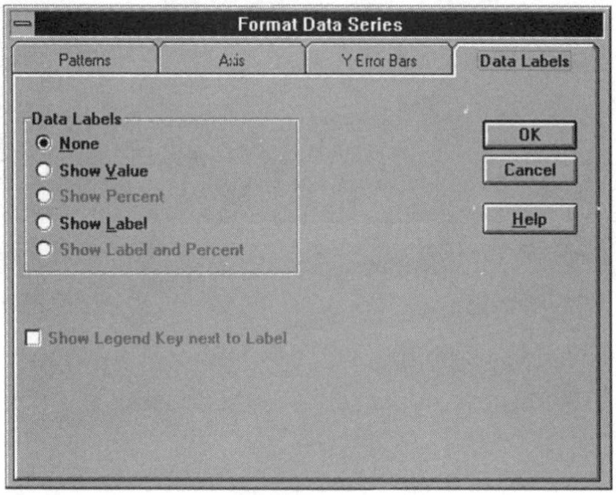

Fig. 14.6
The Format Data Series dialog box showing the Data Labels tab.

4. Choose the Show **V**alue button to display data values on the chart.

> ### Note
>
> Other options for displaying data labels are:
>
> Show Percent — Ghosted except for pie charts, displays percentage represented by pie slice
>
> Show **L**abel — Displays Category Label
>
> Show Label and Percent — Displays Value and Category Label

5. Choose OK or press Enter.

6. Repeat the same process for each data series in your chart. The end result for the Market Share column chart should resemble figure 14.7.

Fig. 14.7

The Market Share chart with data labels attached to the data series.

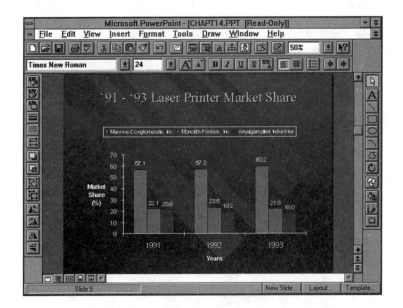

If the font for the labels is too big, you can reduce it to a more graceful size by clicking any label for each data series and choosing the **F**ont command from the Format menu. (You can also double-click any data label and the Format Data Label dialog box appears, displaying the Font tab and its contents.) Choose a new size from the Size list, and choose OK or press Enter.

In figure 14.7, gridlines aren't applied because they are unnecessary. Placing the data value labels above each column makes it crystal clear what the columns represent.

Adding Arrows

Arrows with various styles of arrowheads can be added to draw attention to an outstanding or interesting feature of the chart. After an arrow is placed, the text to be used with the arrow (if desired) must be entered in the slide view in PowerPoint.

Here's how to add an arrow:

1. Double-click the chart to edit it in Graph.

2. From the **V**iew menu, choose **T**oolbars. The Toolbars dialog box appears.

3. Select the Drawing check box in the Toolbars list to place an x in it, and choose OK or press Enter. This enables display of the Drawing toolbar while you are editing charts.

4. Click the Arrow button on the Drawing toolbar.

   As you move the mouse pointer over the chart after selecting the Arrow button, it turns into a crosshair.

5. Click and drag the mouse from the desired starting place of the arrow to the desired end point. When you release the mouse, an arrow appears (see fig. 14.8). The arrowhead is located at the point where you finished drawing the line for the arrow and released the mouse.

6. Click anywhere outside the chart to embed it into the slide.

Fig. 14.8

The Market Share
chart with an
arrow pointing to
the highest series
data value.

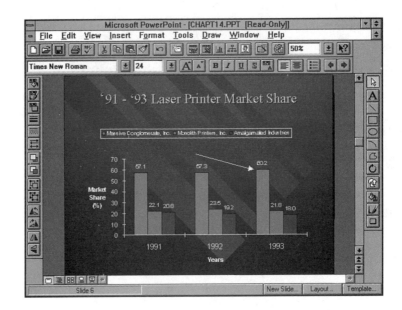

To add a caption to the arrow, follow these steps:

1. Click the Text Tool button in the PowerPoint Drawing toolbar.

2. Click the mouse in the slide where a text caption is desired. The I-beam
   appears in a new text object. Type the text you want and click outside
   the text object to embed it. The results should resemble figure 14.9.

Fig. 14.9

The Market Share
chart with an
arrow pointing to
the highest series
data value and a
caption added in
PowerPoint.

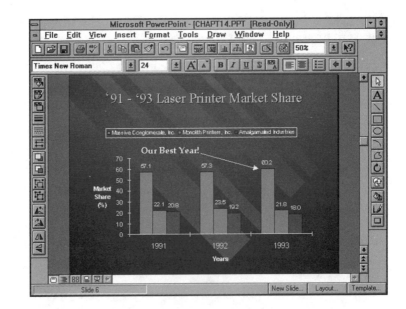

Note

Sometimes it is necessary to leave the Graphing facilities if you want to add a text caption to an arrow. This is true for any text object that isn't directly related to a series value, an axis, or any chart object that has a direct provision for a text label.

Arrows have a number of different arrowhead types available to them. To add a different arrowhead style to an existing arrow, follow these steps:

1. Double-click the embedded chart on the slide to edit it. Graph appears with its associated toolbars.

2. Click once on the arrow in the chart.

3. From the Format menu, choose Selected Object.

   The Format Object dialog box appears.

4. If it isn't already displayed, choose the Patterns tab.

5. If you want to change the line style, select from these options:

Automatic	Default, automatically displays axis
None	Removes line from display
Custom	Defines custom line style settings
Style	Drop-down list to assign a line style
Color	Drop-down list to assign a line color
Weight	Drop-down list to assign a line weight

6. If you want to change the arrowhead style, select from these options:

Sty**l**e	Drop-down list of five types for assigning an arrow head style
Wi**dth**	Drop-down list of three types for assigning a head width
Le**n**gth	Drop-down list of three types for assigning a head length

7. Choose OK or press Enter.

Tip
Double-click the mouse on the arrow to quickly display the Format Object dialog box with the Patterns tab showing.

Tip
The Sample box displays a sample of the arrow style.

Tip
Objects can now be automatically resized with the chart.

The Properties tab in the Format Object dialog box offers an interesting feature: With the Object Positioning option, the selected object can automatically be resized with the chart, or it can retain its size if the chart is shrunk or enlarged. If resizing is turned off (by selecting the Don't Size with Chart button), the selected arrow or other object stays its original size if the chart is resized. If the Size with Chart button is selected, the arrow or other object is resized to keep its aspect ratio with the rest of the chart.

Changing Axes

Chart axes can play a role in customizing a chart's appearance. Earlier in this chapter, you learned how to scale gridlines to different increments. Scaling an axis works very much the same way, which stands to reason since a gridline scale is identical to that for an axis. In 2-D charts, the x- and y-axes scales have differing properties from each other, just as the X and Y gridlines do. Each is described in turn.

Scaling Axes

Changing the scale for the x-axis involves changing the frequency that labels appear on the axis. In the Market Share column chart, for example, the x-axis categories are 1991, 1992, and 1993. Frequently, you create charts that have more than three categories on the x-axis—sometimes, you may create charts that have more x-axis categories than can be displayed practically. If, for example, you create a column chart depicting the quarterly sales of a firm for the last five years, you can have up to 20 categories on the x-axis. It isn't always necessary to display all the x-axis category labels, because sometimes it can be distracting to the viewer or chart clutter can result.

Tip
The more x-axis categories you have, the more advisable it is to limit the number of labels on that axis.

To adjust the scale for the x-axis, follow these steps:

1. Click the x-axis once to select it.

2. From the Format menu, choose Selected Axis.

   The Format Axis dialog box appears.

3. Choose the Scale tab to display the options shown in figure 14.10.

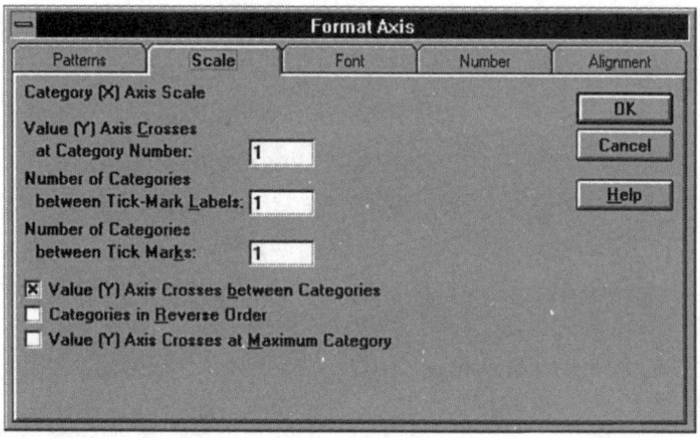

Fig. 14.10
The Format Axis
dialog box with
the Scale options
displayed.

IV

Charts

4. Select from the following Scale options for the x-axis:

- Value [Y] Axis **C**rosses at Category Number

  If set to 1, the y-axis remains in its customary position at the left side of the chart. The y-axis can be placed anywhere else, though, with major effects on the custom appearance of the chart.

- Number of Categories between Tick-Mark **L**abels

  If set to 1, this option means that each x-axis category bears a label on the chart. If set to 2, every other category is labeled. If set to 4, every fourth one is labeled, and so on.

- Number of Categories between Tick-Mar**k**s

  When this option is set to 1, every category on the x-axis has a tick mark. Setting this entry box to a higher number (such as 2) means that every other category (first, third, fifth) has a tick mark assignment on the chart for the x-axis.

■ Value [Y] Axis Crosses **b**etween Categories

Check box option enables the placement of the y-axis somewhere along the x- or Category axis, the location of which is determined by the value you enter in the Value [Y] Axis Crosses at Category Number text box.

■ Categories in **R**everse Order

Check box option sets the categories in reverse order on the x-axis.

■ Value [Y] Axis Crosses at **M**aximum Category:

Check box option places the y-axis to cross at the highest value on the x-axis, placing the y-axis on the other side of the chart.

5. When you're finished making your selections, choose OK or press Enter.

As you can see, there is a lot of room for experimentation just in this single area. Here, you can totally alter the appearance of a simple column chart.

Changing the scale for the y- or value axis is somewhat more straightforward. Here's how to change the scale for the y-axis in a 2-D chart:

1. Click the y-axis once to select it.

2. From the F**o**rmat menu, choose S**e**lected Axis.

The Format Axis dialog box appears.

3. Choose the Scale tab.

4. Select from the following Scale options for the y-axis:

■ Auto

Mi**n**imum: Sets Minimum y-axis value

Ma**x**imum: Sets Maximum y-axis value

Ma**j**or Unit: Sets the increment for each major tick mark

M**i**nor Unit: Sets the increment for each minor tick mark

- Category [X] Axis Crosses **A**t:

  Sets y-axis placement where x-axis crosses the chart (default is 0, so x-axis rests at the bottom of the chart)

- **L**ogarithmic Scale

  Useful for charts that have widely ranging values

- Values in **R**everse Order

  Switches the Value [Y] axis increments from top to bottom or bottom to top; reverses position of x-axis

- Category [X] Axis Crosses at **M**aximum Value

  Places the x-axis at the highest y-axis value on the chart

As mentioned earlier, you can do a lot of things to charts just by adjusting the axis placement and label values. While there isn't space in this chapter to do justice to all the possibilities, the examples shown in figures 14.11 and 14.12 are offered to illustrate some of the things you can do to change the appearance of even the simplest of column charts.

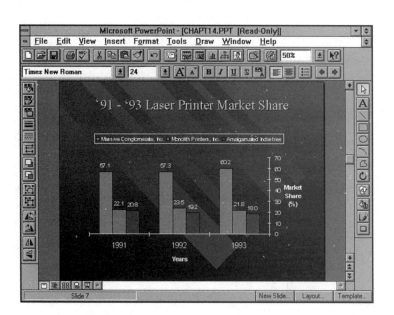

Fig. 14.11
The Market Share column chart with the Y (value) axis set to cross at the maximum value of the X (category) axis.

Fig. 14.12

The same chart, this time with the x-axis crossing halfway up the y-axis, with x- and y-axes gridlines enabled to lend some structure to the chart.

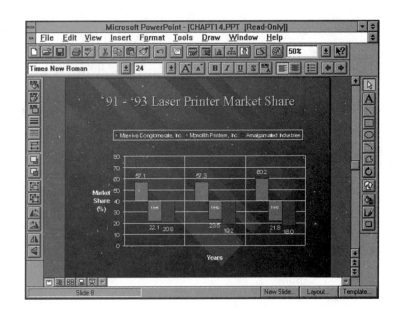

Hiding Axes

Hiding axes, thankfully, is a more straightforward process than changing the display style of axes, which is all by itself a way of designing custom charts. In figure 14.13, the y-axis and its labels have been removed from the chart, creating a pleasing minimalist effect.

Fig. 14.13

The Market Share chart with the y-axis and its tick mark labels removed.

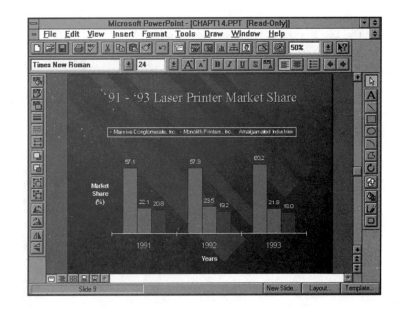

To hide the y-axis, follow these steps:

1. Click the y-axis to select it.

2. From the Format menu, choose Selected Axis.

   The Format Axis dialog box appears.

3. Click the Patterns tab if it is not already displayed.

4. To remove the y-axis from the chart display, click the **N**one button under the Axis options list.

5. Under Tick-Mark Labels, click N**o**ne. This removes the tick mark increment labels from the chart.

6. Choose OK or press Enter.

Considering that figure 14.13 already has the column values displayed above each column, it really isn't necessary to show the y-axis.

Troubleshooting

I can't add text captions to my arrows in Graph.

Unfortunately, that's not a feature in the Graph program. Once you add your arrow, you must embed the chart back into your slide and add the text caption in PowerPoint.

Some series values are too big for my chart.

You may need to use a logarithmic scale. It's a particularly handy feature to have if you have a chart in which you want to display two widely ranging sets of data, such as sales figures for an age group 10-15 years old and for an age group 60-65 years old. If you set up your age groups on the x-axis, the age groups will be so far apart on the x-axis that they will distort the chart. An x-axis logarithmic scale can be used. If one set of sales figures is an order of magnitude greater than another (one company has $10 million in sales, while another has $150 million, for example), then you can apply a logarithmic scale to the y-axis. You can even apply it to both axes if necessary. Here's how to apply a logarithmic scale to a selected axis:

1. Click the axis to be scaled.

2. From the Format menu, choose Selected Axis.

(continues)

(continued)

3. Click the Scale tab.

4. Click the Logarithmic Scale check box.

5. Choose OK or press Enter.

The selected axis is automatically adjusted to encompass the values. The data markers are also adjusted to be more proportional on the chart, while still providing for visual measurement. Notice that you can click on a gridline (if any gridlines are displayed on the desired axis) to follow the same procedure. An example of a chart using logarithmic scales is shown in Appendix B of this book.

Colorizing Charts

PowerPoint 4 has broken through some of the most grievous limitations of previous versions of the program. Perhaps one of the most important is color scheme congruence. In previous versions of PowerPoint, the Graph program did not in any way support the color palettes in the actual PowerPoint program. Graph was an entirely separate program. It turned out to be a major design flaw, because whenever you needed to edit a chart, Graph would reset the color palette to a set of default colors that had nothing to do with PowerPoint itself. Every time you used Graph, you had to painstakingly reset all the object colors in the chart to the desired values. It was a major problem, and a major drag on productivity.

 With PowerPoint 4, that has changed. In spite of the fact that Graph is still a separate program, color schemes are completely consistent between Graph and the PowerPoint application. Graph seamlessly transports the color scheme from the template in PowerPoint to its own charting facilities and conforms to those facilities whenever you create new chart elements. This, of course, doesn't mean that you can't assign your own colors to chart elements of every description. However, PowerPoint 4 now offers a much more intelligent color handling system, especially in charting.

This section begins to dig deeper into PowerPoint's enhanced color support, its improved color palettes, its method of assigning specific colors to individual chart elements, and other features.

Understanding the Basic Color Palette

PowerPoint offers an expanded color palette of 56 colors plus 18 different patterns that can be applied to chart objects (and combined with colors from the palette) in both borders and color and pattern fills, enabling you to create custom effects and aid in differentiating large numbers of series values from one another.

While this isn't the place to discuss the process of changing and customizing colors or color palettes (you simply use the palette that applies to the work you have performed so far in this book), certain colors in every color palette are assigned to specific chart and presentation elements, and understanding their respective roles is the foundation for what follows in later chapters.

To look at the color palette in Graph, perform the following steps:

1. With the chart displayed in Graph, from the **T**ools menu, choose **O**ptions.

   The Graph Options dialog box appears.

2. Choose the Color tab to display the options shown in figure 14.14.

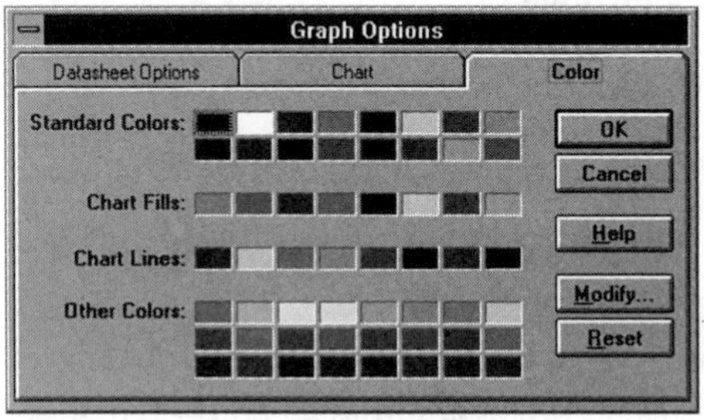

Fig. 14.14
The basic color palette, as displayed in Graph with the **T**ools **O**ptions command. The colors for the three data sets in the column chart correspond to the first three colors in the Chart Fills list.

The 56 colors in the palette are split into four specific categories:

Standard Colors:	This 16-color palette set is composed of the 16 basic colors used in the Microsoft Windows color palette.
Chart Fills:	This eight-color palette set is used for color fills in data series markers, such as the columns in the Market Share chart.
Chart Lines:	This eight-color palette set is used for the coloring of lines and borders in a chart.

Other Colors: This 24-color palette set is a group of additional colors that are "leftovers," but are also available because they are matched to the palette and template in current use.

Any of the colors in any set can be used for any other purpose, but PowerPoint's defaults are used for a reason: colors chosen for a specific set are generally the ones best suited for their assigned task. Color palettes, and the individual colors in each set, also change depending on the template that you use to create your presentation.

From the Color tab, it's possible to modify any chosen color into a new one, and a color palette that you modified and particularly like can be copied from one slide to another, allowing for consistency of custom colors in your slides.

Chapters 17 and 21 discuss the subject and uses of color in greater detail, including customizing and changing colors, the copying of palettes, and the effective use of color.

Selecting and Coloring Chart Elements

Most chart elements consist of two parts: borders and areas. Objects of these types include the following:

- Data markers such as columns, bars, and pie slices

- Drawn objects such as polygons and freeform shapes

- Floors and backgrounds of charts

Choosing color and pattern fills of object areas, or changing the line color of borders, is a generic process common to all object types. You can change the style, color, and weight of borders for a selected object, and the pattern and color for an object's area. For example, suppose that you want to change the color fill of the data markers for the Massive Conglomerate, Inc. series, which are the tallest columns in the sample chart shown in figure 14.15.

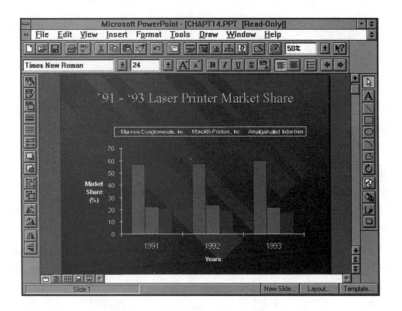

Fig. 14.15
The Market Share chart before color changes to the Massive Conglomerate series.

To change the color fill for a data series, follow these steps:

1. Double-click the chart to bring up Graph's toolbar and menus.

2. Click once on any of the data series you want to change. In the example, click any three of the columns representing Massive Conglomerate (the tallest columns in each data set). Clicking once selects the entire series.

3. From the Format menu, choose Selected Series to display the Format Data Series dialog box with the Patterns options showing (see fig. 14.16).

Fig. 14.16
The Format Data Series dialog box showing the Patterns tab.

4. If you want, change the options for displaying the chart's border:

Automatic Default, automatically displays Border

None   Removes border from object display

Custom   Defines custom border settings

Style   Drop-down list to assign a border style

Color   Drop-down list to assign a border color

Weight   Drop-down list to assign a border weight

5. To change the color of the selected area, choose from these options:

A**u**tomatic   Default, automatically displays Area in default color. Also select this option if you want to clear custom formatting and return to the defaults.

Non**e**   Removes Area from object display (in effect, makes the objects transparent)

C**o**lor   Thumbnail display of the 56-color palette. Click any color to assign it to the selected object(s).

For the example, click the third color from the left, second row down, in the C**o**lor palette. It should be a dark blue color.

6. If you want to assign a pattern to the selected area, select a pattern from the **P**attern drop-down list to assign a new Area pattern. The top-left pattern is a transparent one and shows only the color already chosen. Patterns can change the appearance of the color on a chart.

7. If you want to invert the pattern assigned in step 6, select the In**v**ert if Negative check box option. If selected, this option inverts the pattern ascribed to a series value if that value happens to be a negative number (such as a company losing money during the last quarter). Otherwise the option does not affect the colors or patterns selected.

8. Choose OK or press Enter.

The entire Massive Conglomerate series should now be redrawn in the new color. Choose **U**ndo Format Series from the **E**dit menu (or press Ctrl+Z) if you want to return to the original color.

> **Note**
>
> When changing the colors of data markers in a series, a distinction can be made between changing the color of all the markers in a series, or changing the color of a single data marker. It is a simple, but somewhat tricky step using the mouse.
>
> Click once on the series data marker you want to change. The entire series is selected. Pause for a second or two, and click *again* on the same data marker. It alone is selected this time. Then choose Selected Point from the Format menu to change the border or area of the data marker. The functions are the same as for a series.

Rotating Three-Dimensional Charts

Rotating charts is simply a fun thing to do. It's one of the fastest, most flexible ways to customize a chart and can be done easily with either the mouse or the keyboard. One limitation: It can only be done with 3-D charts. Thus, in this section, you begin to explore 3-D chart types. Before moving on to PowerPoint's chart rotation feature, convert the 2-D Market Share column chart to 3-D columns by following these steps:

1. Double-click the chart on the slide to start Graph.

2. From the Format menu, choose **A**utoFormat.

   The AutoFormat dialog box appears.

3. From the **G**alleries list box, choose 3-D Column.

   A set of eight thumbnails, each representing a 3-D column type, appears in the **F**ormats section.

4. Choose thumbnail (or chart type) 1.

5. Choose OK or press Enter (you can also double-click the thumbnail to select it and return to Graph).

6. Click outside the chart to embed the chart into the slide.

The Market Share chart should appear much as it does in figure 14.17.

Fig. 14.17
The Market Share
chart converted to
a basic 3-D column
type.

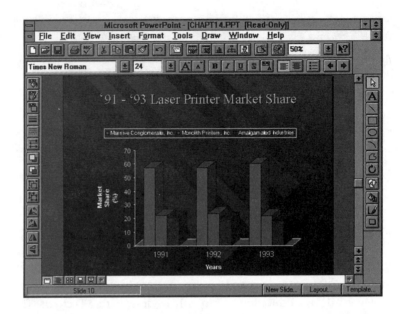

Fig. 14.17
The Market Share
chart converted to
a basic 3-D column
type.

Assigning Explicit Rotation Values to Charts

The Graph program offers flexible, powerful, and surprisingly simple methods for rotating charts to add a custom look. Many adjustments can be made, including viewing elevation, perspective adjustment, and left and right rotation values. The title of this section is no accident. It's also quite easy (almost too easy) to rotate a chart solely by using the mouse. To gain a thorough understanding of how 3-D chart rotation works, you start by assigning explicit values to change the view of your 3-D chart.

The basic 3-D column chart is a rather attractive type to begin with. Let's see what we can do to enhance it, first by using the keyboard to specify rotation values:

1. Double-click the chart to start Graph.

   The Graph toolbar appears and the chart is automatically selected.

2. From the Format menu, choose **3**-D View.

   The Format 3-D View dialog box appears, as shown in figure 14.18.

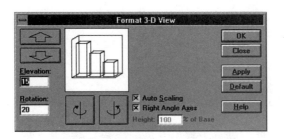

Fig. 14.18
The Format 3-D
View dialog box.

3. Choose from the options displayed for formatting 3-D chart views:

Elevation	Adjusts the view elevation (overlooking the chart). Two arrow buttons, one pointing up and one pointing down, are provided to adjust the Elevation values by increments of 5. You can, of course, also type in the number.
Rotation	Rotates the chart along the horizontal axis. Two Rotation buttons, one left rotate and one right rotate, adjust the Rotation values by increments of 5. You can also type in the number you want.
Auto **S**caling	Check box option (default enabled). Used when changing a 2-D chart to 3-D, it helps retain the size of the chart when the conversion is made.
Right Angle A**x**es	Check box option (default enabled). Controls axis orientation, showing axes at right angles to one another. If disabled, 3-D Perspective features are enabled. For an example of Right Angled A**x**es versus **P**erspective, compare figure 14.19 with figure 14.23 later in this chapter.
Height: % of Base	Text box: here is where you enter a value to adjust the perspective of your 3-D chart. If the Auto **S**caling and Right Angle A**x**es are both enabled (X's placed in their check boxes) perspective adjustments *cannot be made*, and this text box will be ghosted. Perspective is primarily used to adjust the height of your chart view. In the present example, this option is ghosted.

Tip
To restore the rotation defaults in 3-D charts, click the **D**efault button.

For the example, in the **E**levation box type a value of **30**. And in the **R**otation box type a value of **40**.

4. Choose OK or press Enter.

The Market Share 3-D column chart should resemble figure 14.19.

Fig. 14.19
The 3-D column chart with adjustments for elevation and rotation.

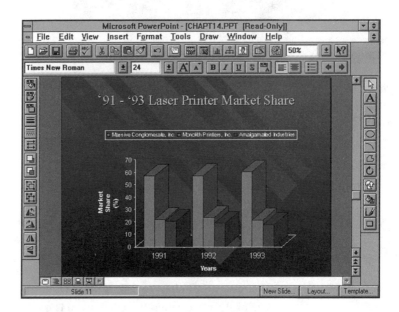

As you can see, even the minor adjustments just performed significantly change the chart's appearance. As you have seen with other charting features, there is plenty of room for experimenting here. It's one of the most powerful areas in which you can customize charts.

Rotating Charts with the Mouse

Three-dimensional rotation can also be performed with the mouse, with somewhat more unpredictable but amusing and interesting results. It's also a great convenience feature, because you can simply drag the mouse, view the results, and **U**ndo the action you just performed if the adjustment isn't to your liking; then, you can repeat the process again until you get it right, skipping the tedious but more precise process of going through the F**o**rmat **3**-D View dialog box. To rotate a 3-D chart with the mouse, follow these steps:

1. Double-click the chart to start Graph.

   The Graph toolbar appears, and the chart is automatically selected.

2. Click the mouse once within the area defined by the axes of the chart (but not on any of the data markers). The chart area is highlighted, as shown in figure 14.20.

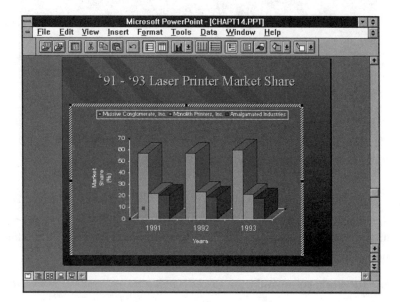

Fig. 14.20
The 3-D column chart selected for rotation with the mouse.

3. Click *and hold* the mouse on any of the pressure points on a corner of the selected chart. The mouse changes to a small crosshair.

4. Drag the mouse in any direction. The 3-D chart changes to a transparent wire-frame box, which rotates according to the movement of the mouse.

5. Release the mouse. The chart may, or may not, resemble figure 14.21.

Fig. 14.21
The 3-D column chart with an example of mouse-directed rotation.

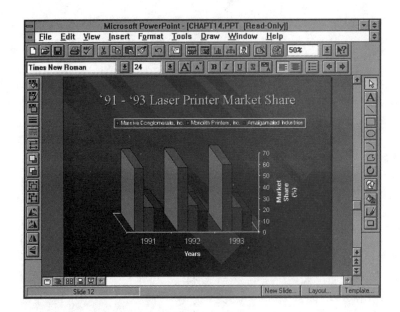

Tip
Choose the Format, **3**-D View command to check the actual values of the mouse-directed rotation.

After you wreak havoc on what was previously a perfectly respectable 3-D chart, you can check the actual rotation values by choosing the **3**-D View command from the Format menu. The Elevation and Rotation values reflect the new position created with the mouse.

Choose the **U**ndo command from the **E**dit menu if the results aren't to your liking.

Adjusting for Three-Dimensional Perspective

Three-dimensional perspective is another feature offered for those who just cannot leave a perfectly nice 3-D chart alone. Perspective is another fun adjustment to play around with, in combination with rotation and elevation. Three-dimensional Perspective changes the viewing angle from the perspective of the viewer.

To change the 3-D perspective of a chart, follow these steps:

1. Double-click the chart to start Graph.

   The Graph toolbar appears and the chart is automatically selected.

Tip
The Perspective feature is not available unless the Right Angle Axes check box is unchecked.

2. From the Format menu, choose **3**-D View.

   The Format 3-D View dialog box appears.

3. To enable the Perspective feature, click the Right Angle Axes check box to disable it. The Perspective feature pops up in the dialog box, as shown in figure 14.22.

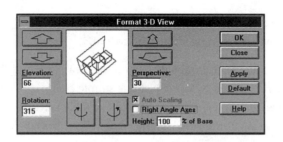

Fig. 14.22
The Format 3-D
View dialog box
after clicking Right
Angle Axes. The
Perspective feature
appears.

4. Enter a value into the **P**erspective text box. For example, type **80**.

5. Choose OK or press Enter.

Perspective has specific (and radical) effects on a 3-D chart. More perspective makes data markers at the back of a chart smaller than markers at the front of a chart, which creates a visual impression of distance to the data markers at the back. The 3-D column Market Share chart should now resemble figure 14.23.

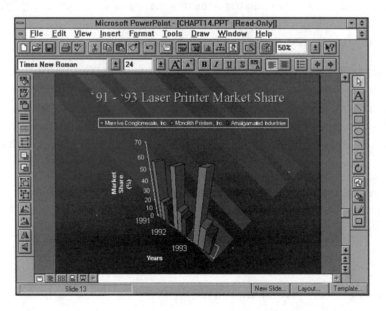

Fig. 14.23
The Market Share
chart with
perspective added.

Perspective is handy when you have a large number of data values to display because it creates a better sense of visual proportion. It also offers a remark-ably powerful way to customize any 3-D chart type that can benefit from it (3-D Pie charts are an exception to this). The perspective value that you specify in the exercise is the ratio of the front of the chart to the back of the chart, and the value can range from zero to 100.

The section you just read should give you some idea of the possibilities inherent in 3-D chart creation. By using just one simple chart type, 3-D Columns, many special effects have been used that can actually be considered new chart types and can, at the very least, provide striking visual effects in your presentation.

Drawing Shapes and Graphics on Charts

PowerPoint 4 now offers the capability to draw polygons and freeform shapes directly on a chart. Objects can be drawn quickly and efficiently, and do not require any special artistic talent to achieve an attractive effect for your charts and slides. Artwork is frequently used as a special effect to lend support and aesthetic appeal to a presentation. The new version of Graph offers a special toolbar containing all its key drawing functions, which closely resembles the Drawing toolbar used in the main PowerPoint program.

Some shape drawing features are not available in Graph. The AutoShapes toolbar, for example, is not available. Nor can you add clip art from PowerPoint's ClipArt Gallery directly to a chart. Graph's Drawing toolbar offers the capability to draw filled polygons such as ellipses, rectangles, and freehand shapes. You can also alter their color fills and borders as you would other chart objects.

Before drawing shapes and other objects on the chart, you need to make sure the Drawing toolbar is displayed in Graph.

1. With Graph displayed, from the **V**iew menu choose **T**oolbars.

   The Toolbars dialog box appears.

2. Click in the Drawing check box.

3. Choose OK or press Enter. The Drawing toolbar appears, as shown in figure 14.24.

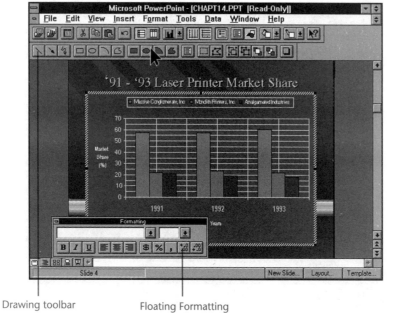

Fig. 14.24
Graph's Drawing toolbar (with the Formatting toolbar floating over the Graph screen).

IV

Charts

Drawing toolbar

Floating Formatting toolbar

Adding Ellipses, Rectangles, and Freeform Shapes to a Chart

To add an ellipse graphic object to a chart, follow these steps:

1. Double-click the chart to start Graph.

2. With the chart selected, click the Ellipse button on the Drawing toolbar.

   The mouse changes to a crosshair when it is moved over the chart object.

3. Click and drag the mouse to draw an ellipse. When you release the mouse button, an ellipse is drawn on the chart. The ellipse is transparent (without a color or pattern fill), as shown in figure 14.25.

Tip
To draw a perfect circle, hold down the Shift key while you draw the ellipse.

Fig. 14.25
An ellipse is drawn
on the chart.

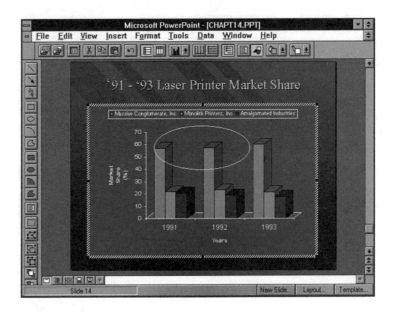

 4. To draw an ellipse with a color fill, click the Filled Ellipse button on the Drawing toolbar.

To add a rectangle graphic object to a chart, follow these steps:

1. Double-click the chart to start Graph.

2. With the chart selected, click the Rectangle button on the Drawing toolbar.

   The mouse changes to a crosshair when it is moved over the chart object.

3. Click and drag the mouse to draw a rectangle. When you release the mouse button, a rectangle is drawn on the chart. It will be transparent (without a color or pattern fill).

4. To draw a rectangle with a color fill, click the Filled Rectangle button on the Drawing toolbar.

Tip
To draw a perfect square, hold down the Shift key while you draw the rectangle.

You can see the pattern developing here. Drawing simple graphic objects is the same whether you draw a filled shape or one without a color or pattern fill.

Drawing freeform polygons is a more complex process. Freeform objects are editable: Any pressure point available on a selected freeform shape can be grabbed and moved to change the shape of the object. They can be drawn with or without color fills with the appropriate buttons, just as with other shapes on the Graph drawing toolbar.

To add a freeform polygon object to a chart, follow these steps:

1. Double-click the chart to start Graph.

2. With the chart selected, click the Freeform or Filled Freeform button on the Drawing toolbar.

   The mouse changes to a crosshair when it is moved over the chart object.

3. To draw a freeform object, click and hold the mouse and draw until the shape is the way you want.

   Before you can finish drawing the freeform shape, you have to close it.

4. *Release the mouse,* and then drag it to the point where you began drawing the shape. *Click the mouse again.* This closes the freeform shape you just drew. Otherwise, when you release the mouse button, it continues adding new segments to the shape as you move the mouse over the chart object.

   The freeform object rests on the chart, as shown in figure 14.26.

When selected, the freeform shape has a standard set of eight pressure points that can be used to resize or reshape it. The shape can be edited in detail, however, by using the following steps:

1. Select the freeform shape that you want to edit.

2. Click the Reshape button on the Drawing toolbar.

   The freeform shape acquires a large number of editable points on its border, any of which can be dragged to change the object's shape (see fig. 14.27).

3. Click and hold the mouse over the desired pressure point. Dragging the point changes the shape.

Fig. 14.26
A quick and dirty
freeform shape on
a chart.

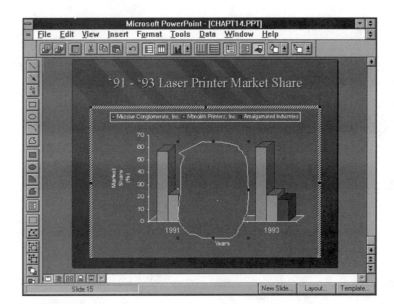

Fig. 14.27
A freeform shape
selected and
enabled for
Reshaping.

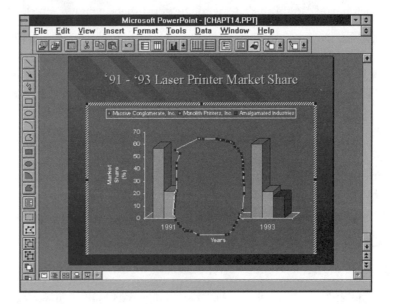

Changing Graphic Colors

Any of the shapes you draw on a chart can have their color fills or pattern
fills changed and customized. When you draw a filled shape on a chart, its
borders and areas can be changed in the same way as with any other chart
object.

To change graphic colors, follow these steps:

1. With the chart displayed in Graph, click the freeform object to select the object you want to edit.

2. From the Format menu, choose Selected Object.

   The Format Object dialog box appears, displaying the Patterns tab.

3. Select from the color fill or border line style options, as desired. These options were described in detail earlier in the chapter.

4. When the color fill or border line style is as desired, choose OK or press Enter.

Troubleshooting

Can I apply shading effects to objects drawn in Graph?

No, unfortunately, you can't. Nor can you apply shading to chart backgrounds or series markers such as bars or columns. To do so, you have to draw objects directly on the PowerPoint slide, as shading effects can only be applied there and not in Microsoft Graph. Fortunately, although Graph has a substantial set of drawing tools, PowerPoint offers a much larger set of drawing features.

I have too many columns on my 2-D bar chart, and my chart winds up looking crowded. Is there a way to fix this without deleting important values from my datasheet?

Absolutely. It requires using a feature called Format (Chart) Group. It's on the bottom of the Format menu. Choosing Format (Chart) Group is another dynamic menu option that changes according to the chart type you're dealing with.

If you have a bar chart and want to make some custom changes to it, you would choose Bar Group from the Format menu. If you wanted to customize a Column chart, the command would read Format Column Group. This holds true for any chart type.

The (Chart) Group menu command does not have a letter-based hot key; the hot key is a number. Thus, for changing bar chart characteristics, the command would read:

    1   Bar Group...

For a column chart:

    1   Column Group...

(continues)

(continued)

If you're making changes to a combination chart (one in which two different charts are combined, such as a bar/line chart), you get *two* Group commands at the bottom of the menu:

1   Bar Group...

2   Line Group...

For this example, you confine yourself to changing the overlap on a set of bars to save room on your chart. *This process can be done only for 2-D bar charts and 2-D column charts.* In so doing, you glimpse even more possibilities for chart customization.

1. With your chart displayed in Microsoft Graph, from the Format menu, choose Bar Group.

    The Format Bar Group dialog box appears.

2. Click the Options tab if it is not already displayed (see fig. 14.28).

3. In the Overlap text box, type a value of 30. As a result, 30 percent of the width of each bar is overlapped by its neighbor.

    It's also possible to set a gap between columns if you want to set them apart from each other, by using the Gap Width adjustment.

4. Choose OK or press Enter to execute your changes. Your 2-D columns are more closely grouped, resulting in a more spacious chart.

As you can see, there is much more to this feature than described here. Chapter 19 discusses the Format (Chart) Group and Format Chart Type commands in greater detail.

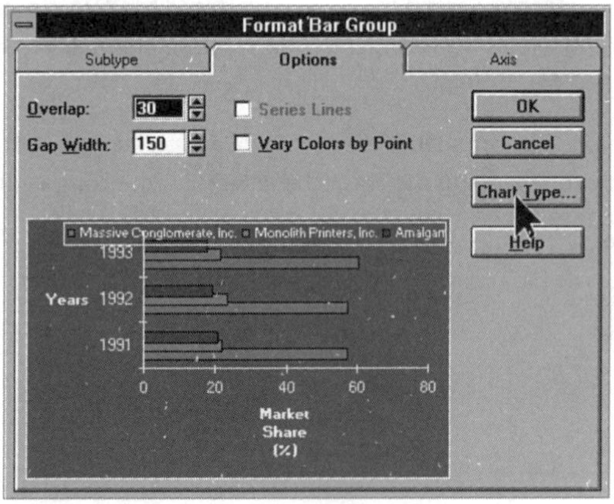

Fig. 14.28
Using the Options tab to adjust gap widths and overlapping on a bar chart.

From Here...

A book could be written just on PowerPoint's chart customization capabilities. In fact, though many subjects have been discussed here, the surface has barely been scratched. If you want to know more about associated charting and drawing subjects, take a look at the following chapters:

- Chapter 17, "Working with Color," offers a deeper discussion of basic color mechanics in PowerPoint.

- Chapter 19, "Using Advanced Charting Features," offers more information about powerful chart customization features.

- Chapter 21, "Using Advanced Color, Text, and Drawing Features," discusses in greater detail the processes of color changes, working with palettes, and advanced drawing features in PowerPoint.

Chapter 15

Creating Organizational Charts

Organizational charts are one of the many new features offered in Power-Point 4. An *organizational chart* describes the structure of a company, including company officers, assistants, departments, and employees. Organizational charts resemble nothing so much as a computer programmer's flowchart.

OrgChart is a separate application program that is bundled with PowerPoint 4. It enables you to create organizational charts as another graphical object, which can be embedded into a slide and cut and pasted to any slide in your presentation.

Understanding the Elements in an Organizational Chart

Organizational charts are quite straightforward. They're basically an organization tree of a company or department. OrgChart, however, offers many tools for creating organizational charts that can prove confusing to the user. When you bring up the OrgChart program for the first time, your screen looks like figure 15.1.

OrgChart is an application program in its own right, and you can create charts of remarkable complexity. Any element of an organizational chart can be customized with different box and line styles and color fills, and boxes of various kinds can be added with the click of a mouse.

In this chapter, you learn:

- The basic components of an organizational chart

- How to create and embed an organizational chart

- How to edit and change relationships in an organizational chart

- How to change the colors in an organizational chart

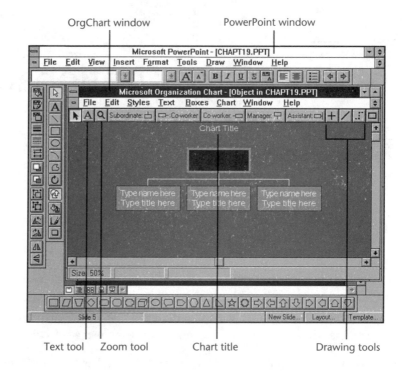

Fig. 15.1
The OrgChart program displaying one of its two chart templates.

A toolbar is located at the top of the OrgChart window, which offers the following tools:

 OrgChart's Arrow pointer tool enables you to reactivate the mouse pointer after you've used another tool in the program.

 The OrgChart Text tool enables you to type in captions and notes
anywhere on the chart window.

 The Zoom tool allows you to take a closer view at any box or section of a chart.

> **Note**
>
> OrgChart offers four levels of magnification: **S**ize to Window (F9), **5**0% of Actual (F10), **A**ctual Size (F11), and **2**00% of Actual (F12). Pressing the appropriate function key activates the appropriate Zoom level.

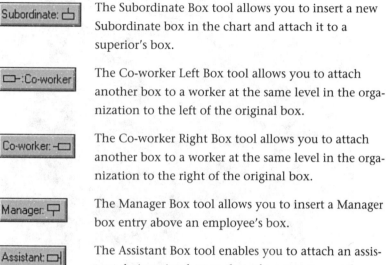 The Subordinate Box tool allows you to insert a new Subordinate box in the chart and attach it to a superior's box.

The Co-worker Left Box tool allows you to attach another box to a worker at the same level in the organization to the left of the original box.

The Co-worker Right Box tool allows you to attach another box to a worker at the same level in the organization to the right of the original box.

The Manager Box tool allows you to insert a Manager box entry above an employee's box.

The Assistant Box tool enables you to attach an assistant designation box to that of a manager or other employee's box in the chart.

 The Right Angle Line tool allows you to draw a straight line at 90 degrees, across or up and down, on the OrgChart.

 The Line tool allows you to draw a line at any angle on the OrgChart.

 The Connecting Line tool allows you to draw dashed lines between boxes in a chart to show special relationships between them.

The Box tool allows you to draw filled boxes for special entries in a chart. Drawn boxes default to the same style as the boxes in the basic template.

Figure 15.2 shows a very basic organizational chart with several important elements.

Though this is a very simple organizational chart, it combines enough elements to convey the flavor and functionality of the OrgChart application. The highest levels of management are shown as the top two boxes in the chart: the CEO and the Chief Financial Officer. Three co-workers, who are vice presidents, are ranked in a row. The VP on the far right has an assistant attached to her box, who is a separate category by herself.

Fig. 15.2
The OrgChart
program showing
several basic
elements.

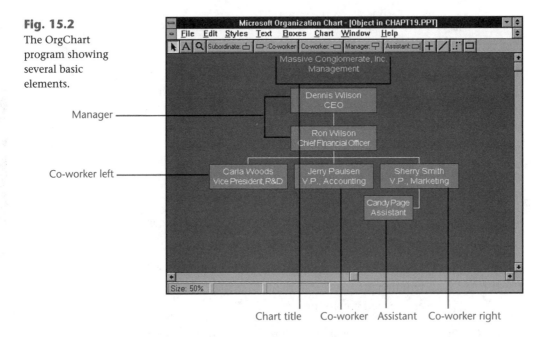

Manager ——

Co-worker left ——

Chart title   Co-worker   Assistant   Co-worker right

Creating an Organizational Chart

You start by creating a new slide from an AutoLayout that contains an
OrgChart object. To create the organizational chart, follow these steps:

1. From the **I**nsert menu, choose New **S**lide.

   The New Slide dialog box appears, displaying the AutoLayouts available.

2. Select the AutoLayout titled OrgChart.

   The new slide is displayed in PowerPoint, similar to figure 15.3.

3. Double-click the OrgChart object in the slide. The program appears
   displaying a chart template.

> **Note**
>
> When the OrgChart program appears, it is in its own window. This indicates a
> crucial difference between OrgChart and Microsoft Graph: OrgChart is an OLE
> 1.0 application program, which means that you must choose the **U**pdate
> command from the **F**ile menu when you finish editing the chart and need to
> place it back in the PowerPoint slide.

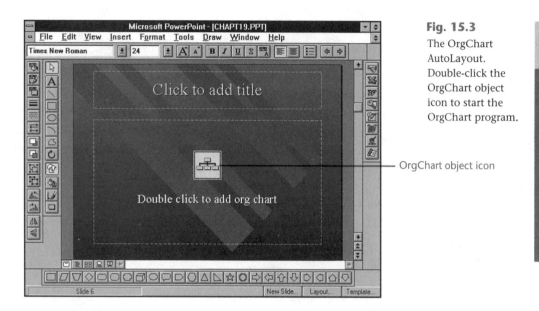

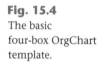

Fig. 15.3
The OrgChart
AutoLayout.
Double-click the
OrgChart object
icon to start the
OrgChart program.

OrgChart object icon

Editing an Organizational Chart

You've just created an organization chart and are now about to start editing
and adding boxes to it. To start, you reproduce the chart shown in figure 15.4
by adding a couple of boxes and editing the text entries for each box, as well
as the chart title.

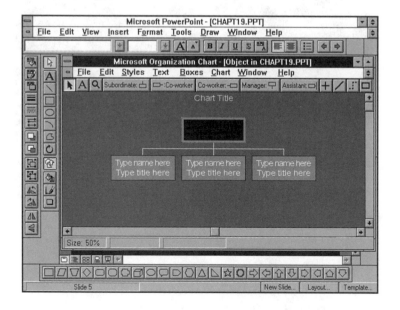

Fig. 15.4
The basic
four-box OrgChart
template.

Editing the Chart Title

To edit the title in an organizational chart, follow these steps:

1. Pass the mouse over the text object titled *Chart Title*. The mouse changes into an I-beam.

2. Click on the text object.

3. Backspace over the *Chart Title* text and type **Massive Conglomerate, Inc.**, press Enter, and type **Management**.

Adding Boxes to a Chart

To add boxes for employees to the organizational chart, follow these steps:

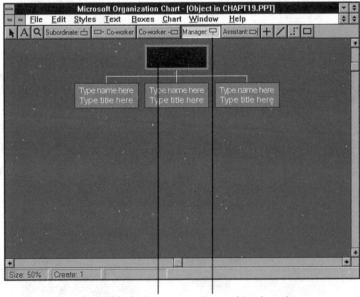

1. To add a higher manager box to the chart, click the Manager Box tool on the OrgChart toolbar.

2. Click on the Manager box in the template.

   The Manager box is filled in black, which denotes its selection and the imminent attachment of another box (see fig. 15.5). The mouse also changes shape to a small box.

Fig. 15.5
Selecting a
chart box for
attachment
of a new box.

3. Click inside the blacked-out box. A new box is added on top, as shown in figure 15.6.

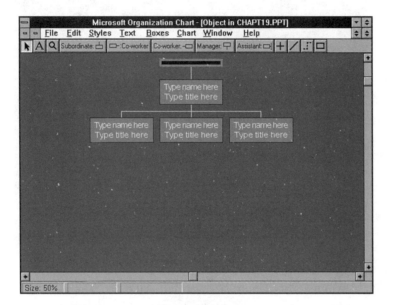

Fig. 15.6
Adding a new Manager box to the OrgChart.

The new box is blacked out in turn, indicating that it is currently selected. When a box is blacked out, it means it is selected either for editing of its text contents or to have another box attached to it.

4. Click on the bottom-right box in the OrgChart to select it.

5. Click the Assistant Box tool on the OrgChart toolbar.

Notice how the mouse pointer changes its shape again.

6. Click the mouse on the previously selected box. An Assistant box appears below it, as in figure 15.7.

You have now added all the basic elements you need for the exercise. Now, it's time to edit the text entries for each chart.

Don't be fooled by the tiny sizes of the two boxes you just added. When you select them to type in their proper text, they expand to fit. That's true for any organizational chart box.

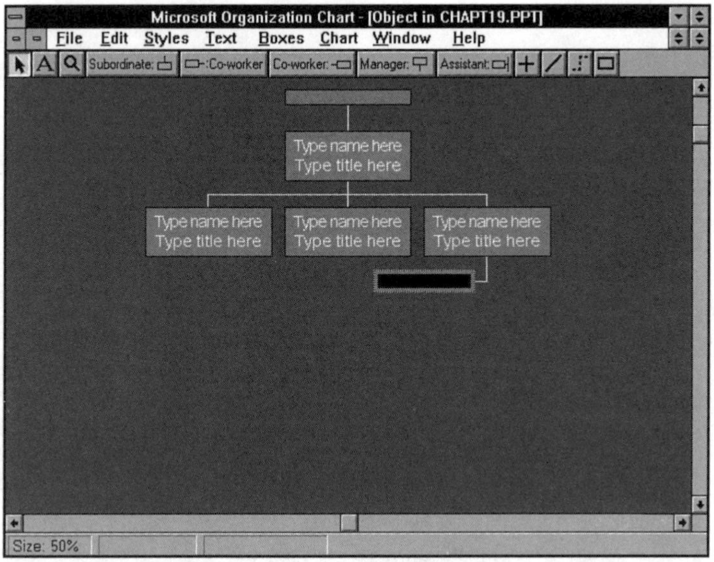

Fig. 15.7

Adding a new
Assistant box to
the OrgChart.

Editing Organizational Chart Boxes

To edit the contents of a box in an organizational chart, double-click the box. Up to four fields of information can be entered in each organizational chart box, and boxes automatically expand to accept the length of text entered.

To edit a box, follow these steps:

1. Click inside the Assistant box you just created.

   As you pass the mouse over the box, it changes into an I-beam. When you click, the box expands to its appearance shown in figure 15.8.

   All OrgChart boxes work the same way.

2. Type the name in the <Name> field of the Assistant box. For example, type **Candy Page**.

3. Press the down-arrow key.

   The next field (<Title>) in the box is highlighted.

4. Type **Assistant**.

5. Click outside the box you just edited.

6. Click on the very top box in the chart: the Manager box you previously added. It is filled in black.

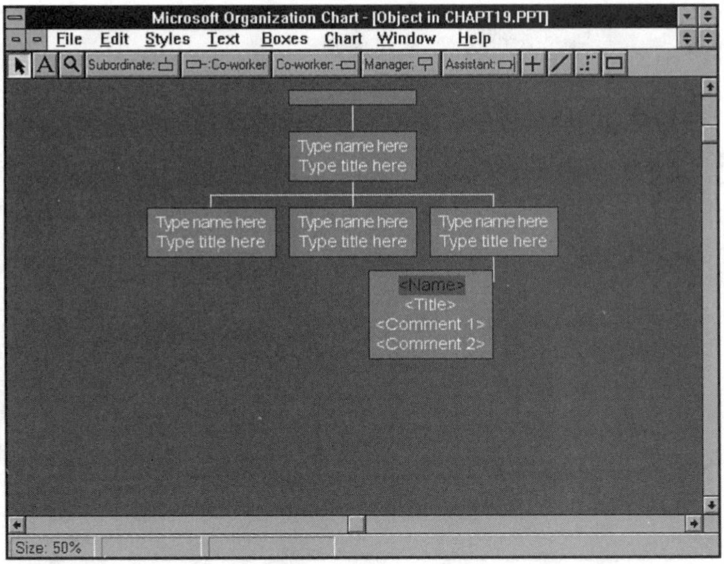

Fig. 15.8
Editing an
OrgChart box.

7. Click again on the selected top box. The box expands to display its embedded text fields. The <Name> field is automatically highlighted.

8. Type the name of the top manager. For example, type **Dennis Wilson**.

9. Press the down-arrow key. The <Title> field is highlighted.

10. Type **CEO**.

11. Click outside the box you just edited.

    The results should resemble figure 15.9.

12. Click in the box just below Dennis Wilson and then click again to edit its contents.

13. Backspace over the Type name here field and type **Ron Wilson**.

14. Press the down-arrow key and type **Chief Financial Officer**. Click outside the box. The result should look like figure 15.10.

15. For the three co-worker boxes in the chart, type the names and positions of the three vice presidents in the chain of command: **Carla Woods**, **V.P.**, **R&D**; **Jerry Paulsen**, **V.P.**, **Financial**; and **Sherry Smith**, **V.P.**, **Marketing**, from left to right, respectively.

Fig. 15.9
The partially
edited OrgChart.

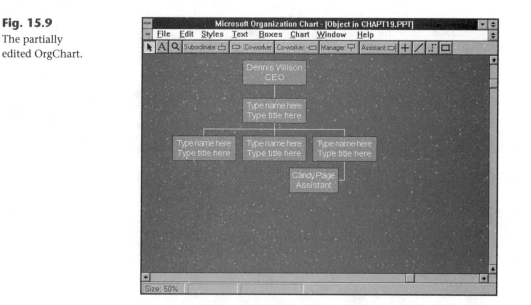

Fig. 15.10
Adding further
edits to the
OrgChart.

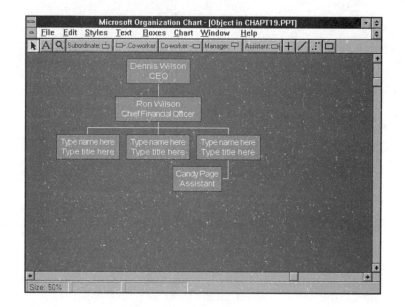

Changing the Color of Boxes and Backgrounds

Any box can be changed to reflect the special status of its occupant. You
can change both the color of the box and the background. For example,
the CEO's box can be changed to denote his level and to draw attention
to his status in the chart. To do so, follow these steps:

IV

Charts

1. Click the top box in the chart, which in the previous exercise was labeled Dennis Wilson, CEO. The box turns black.

2. From the **B**oxes menu, choose Box **C**olor. A cascading menu showing 16 color choices drops down, as shown in figure 15.11.

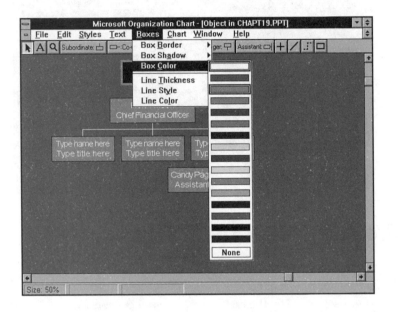

Fig. 15.11
Accessing OrgChart's Box Color menu.

3. Choose a red color or any color that stands out against the default blue background.

4. Click outside the box that you just changed.

5. To change the OrgChart background color, from the **C**hart menu, choose **B**ackground Color. Another cascading menu showing 16 color choices drops down, as shown in figure 15.12.

6. Choose a color, such as light blue, that suits your taste.

Keep in mind that the background color chosen in the OrgChart program affects the appearance of the chart in the PowerPoint slide, just like a chart created using Microsoft Graph. However, you need to choose your background color carefully to avoid clashing with your existing presentation's color scheme. You can also eliminate the background color (thus making the chart background "transparent") by choosing None from the Background Color menu.

Fig. 15.12
Accessing
OrgChart's
Background
Color menu.

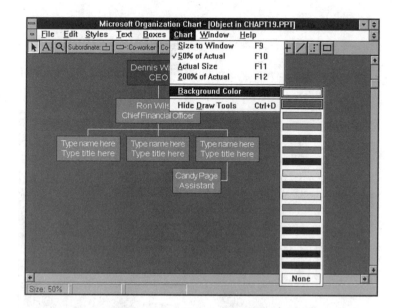

Working with the Chart Levels

When you choose to work with parts of an OrgChart, you have access to a remarkably flexible set of options for selecting various elements. OrgChart elements are denoted by the type of employees they represent and by specific sections of a more complex OrgChart.

Selecting the Levels You Want to Work with

Tip
Press Ctrl+A
to select all
elements in an
organizational
chart.

When you want to make changes to all the boxes in a certain level or levels of an organizational chart, you can use selection options to choose all those boxes at once. In OrgChart, you can execute a normal Select All command by pressing Ctrl+A, but that's just one of many options for selecting the chart levels. To see the other options for selecting chart levels, from the **E**dit menu, choose **S**elect.

A cascading menu appears with the following choices:

All	Select all chart elements without exception.
All Assistants	Select all Assistant OrgChart boxes. Assistants are a separate box type.
All Co-Managers	Select all managers of equivalent levels. Co-Managers are a specific box-and-connecting-line style that is discussed a little later.

All Managers	Select all manager OrgChart boxes.
All Non-Managers	Select all non-manager OrgChart boxes. Non-manager types include Assistants and Subordinates, both of whom have specific boxes assigned to them.
Group	Select a group of boxes.
Branch	Select a branch of an OrgChart.
Lowest Level	Select the entire lowest level of the chart.
Connecting Lines	Select all connecting lines of an OrgChart.

Tip
Press Ctrl+G to select a group of *boxes* in an organizational chart.

Tip
Press Ctrl+B to select a *branch* in an organizational chart.

You can also select more than one box on a chart by holding the Shift key while you click on each successive box.

Menu options such as All Managers, All Non-Managers, All Assistants, and Connecting Lines are exceptionally handy when you want to set those specific types of employees apart and apply a different color to them, change their font formatting, or split them into another chart.

Changing the Chart's Style

OrgChart offers an innovative feature for rearranging charts for different looks while retaining their essential structure and relationships. It's called the Styles menu. A unique feature in OrgChart, the Styles menu combines the attributes of a pull-down menu with the qualities of a button bar, as figure 15.13 shows.

Three categories of styles are offered. The Group styles are six different chart arrangements that are applied to the entire OrgChart. Clicking any of the six Group style buttons when the entire chart is selected rearranges the chart into a different style.

Selecting any box on a chart and choosing the Assistant style button changes the selected box to the Assistant style, which is denoted by a right-angled connecting line. For example, clicking on the Sherry Smith chart box and choosing the Assistant style changes her box to a new relationship with that of her supervisor, as shown in figure 15.14.

Fig. 15.13
Viewing the Styles
pull-down menu.

Assistant style button ——
Co-manager button ——

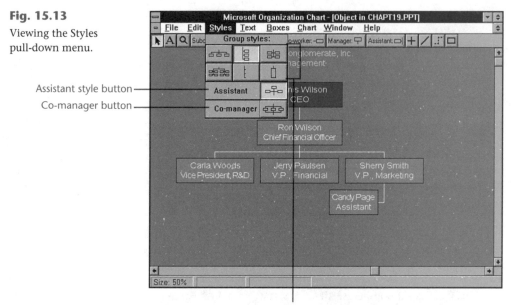

Group style buttons

Fig. 15.14
Adjusting an
Assistant box in
relation to a Vice
President.

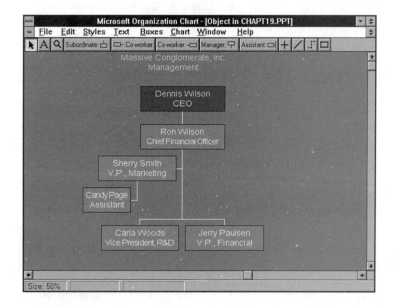

In the figure, you can see that Sherry's box has been moved to an Assistant's position relative to her supervisor. Her assistant, in turn, retains her position. The other two vice presidents, though they're located physically lower on the chart, retain their positions reporting directly to the Chief Financial Officer.

To adjust the style for an entire chart, follow these steps:

1. From the **E**dit menu, choose **S**elect, and then All.

   All the boxes in the chart are selected (blacked out).

2. From the **S**tyles menu, choose one of the six Group style buttons.

Using Styles to Create Another Level

You can see from the organizational chart you created that three vice presidents are set to be officers at the same level in the company. Yet, when you attempt to do an **E**dit, **S**elect All Co-Managers command, which would be the logical step, the selection doesn't work. The default chart doesn't create those three boxes as actual co-managers. Thus, they can't be worked with as a group of corporate officers of the same level. It's an easy problem to correct.

To create a new level in the organizational chart, follow these steps:

1. While holding down the Shift key, click on the three vice-president boxes.

2. From the **S**tyles menu, click on the very bottom chart style button on the menu, next to the label reading Co-Managers.

   The organizational chart's connecting lines change to the arrangement shown in figure 15.15. Now a Co-Manager level has been created.

Notice that the three boxes are connected on the top and the bottom. The boxes have their style changed to create a single, compact unit, as shown by the connecting lines on the bottom as well as the top, implying that the three V.P.'s are officers at exactly the same level in the corporate hierarchy. (Also notice that, as a result, the Assistant Candy Page box has been moved to a position where it is shared by all three co-manager boxes.) Now, because their style has changed, the three V.P.'s are true co-managers and can be selected as such.

Fig. 15.15

Setting the three vice presidents as true officers at the same level.

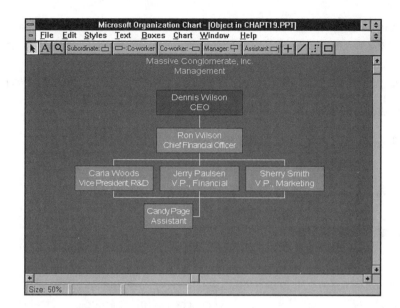

Adding Elements to a Chart with Drawing Tools

As noted earlier in this chapter, OrgChart offers a few drawing tools to aid in adding elements to a chart. Two line tools are offered for drawing solid lines between boxes.

 The Right Angle Line tool is used for one purpose: to draw horizontal or vertical lines. Regardless of the positioning of the mouse, a straight line is drawn in a vertical or horizontal direction.

 OrgChart's Line tool enables you to draw a straight line at any angle on the screen. Selecting this tool and dragging the mouse between boxes or groups draws a line at any desired angle.

 The Connecting Line tool allows you to draw dashed connecting lines between any two boxes on a chart, adding angles where necessary. For example, the CEO in the sample chart might have a special working relationship with the Marketing V.P., who may report directly to him for various business purposes, bypassing the normal chain of command. It's easy to draw a connecting line to show this relationship by following these steps:

1. Click the Connecting Line tool.

2. From the left edge of the CEO box, drag the mouse to the right and then down.

3. Drag the mouse over the box labeled Sherry Smith.

A dashed connecting line is drawn between the two boxes, as shown in figure 15.16.

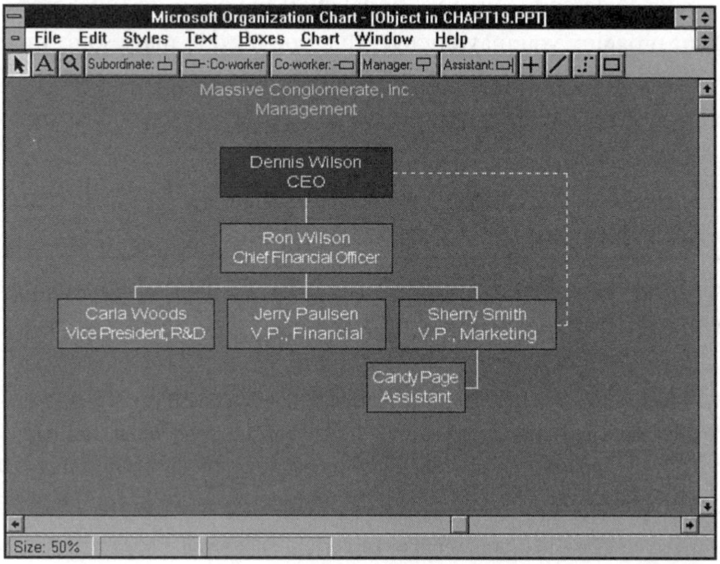

Fig. 15.16
Adding a connecting line to boxes on different levels.

Embedding an Organizational Chart

The OrgChart program, unlike Microsoft Graph, is an OLE 1.0 application. The OrgChart toolbar and menus do not appear directly in the PowerPoint window, the OrgChart program appears in its own window. After you're finished creating your OrgChart, embed it into your slide by following these steps:

1. From the File menu, choose Update (*Filename*).PPT.

(*Filename*).PPT is the name of the PowerPoint 4 file in which your OrgChart object is to be updated. Updating is the step in which the chart is actually embedded in the presentation. If the chart is as you want, you must perform this step after you create it or the chart will not be present in your presentation.

Also notice that updating is not the same as leaving the program. You can update the chart in the presentation and remain in the OrgChart program.

After updating the chart, if you want to return to the presentation:

2. From the **F**ile menu, choose E**x**it and Return to (Filename).PPT.

After you've updated the organizational chart in your slide and closed the OrgChart program, you may discover that you need to make some more edits to the chart. To do so, simply double-click the organizational chart in your PowerPoint slide. The OrgChart program reappears on-screen displaying the chart for editing.

Troubleshooting

When I double-click on the organizational chart on my slide, the OrgChart program doesn't come up.

This could be due to one of two different problems. First, you may already have OrgChart running with the chart you've tried to open. A tip-off: if the chart you click on in your slide is ghosted or grayed-out, it's already displayed in the OrgChart program. You can't reopen an organizational chart if it's already being edited in the OrgChart program.

Otherwise, the OrgChart program may be corrupted or missing from your system. Use the PowerPoint Setup program to reinstall OrgChart.

How can I add two or more subordinates to a single box on a chart?

Click the Subordinate: box tool and click on the box to which a subordinate is to be attached. Then, click the Subordinate: box tool again and click the same box to which you just added the *first* subordinate. A second subordinate box is added. You can add as many as you need to any box.

Bear in mind that this chapter is not a comprehensive discussion of the OrgChart program. In particular, organizational chart styles can be very flexible and, thus, should be handled carefully to avoid confusing your viewers.

From Here...

The last four chapters have covered the basics of charting in the PowerPoint 4 package. A number of major subjects are covered in the next several chapters, including the following:

- Chapter 16, "Printing and Other Kinds of Output," discusses how to print your presentation in monochrome and color output, how to produce overhead transparencies and slides, how to use the Genigraphics slide production service, and how to print notes pages, handouts, and outlines.

- Chapter 17, "Working with Color," offers a deeper discussion of basic color mechanics in PowerPoint.

- Chapter 19, "Using Advanced Graphing Features," offers more information about powerful graph customization features.

IV

Charts

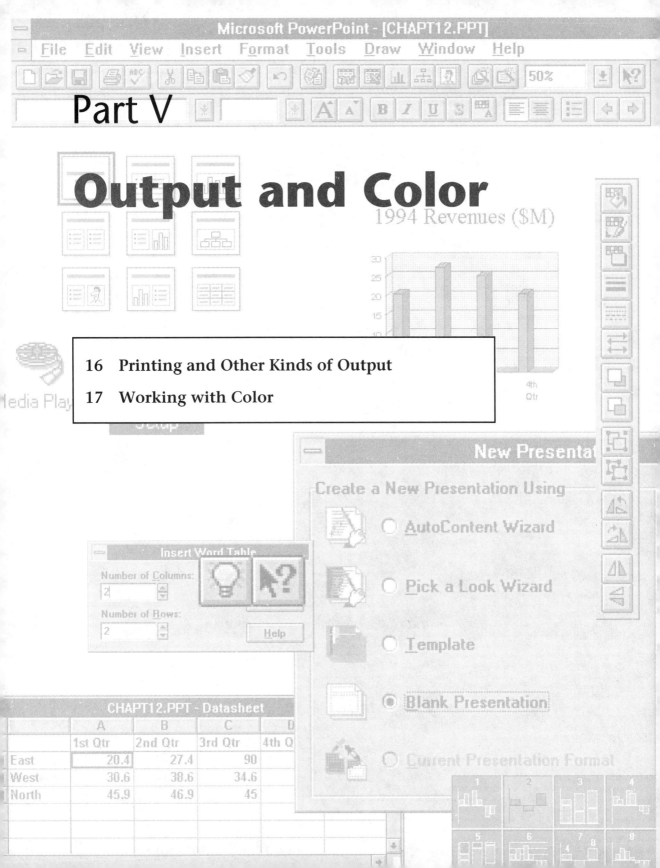

Part V

Output and Color

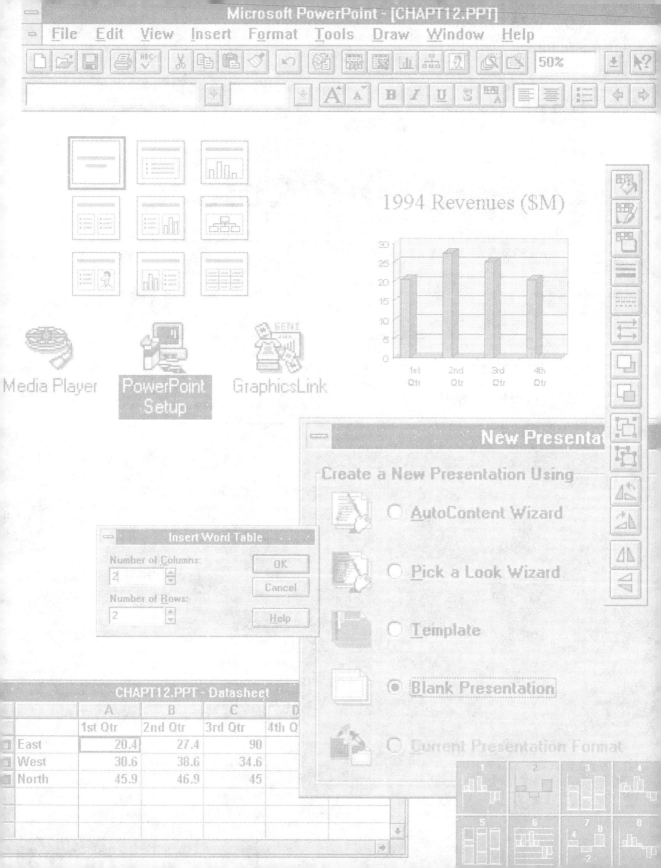

Chapter 16

Printing and Other Kinds of Output

With PowerPoint, you can produce a variety of presentation media. The simplest and cheapest, requiring no special equipment other than your printer, is to print your slides on paper. You can also print your outline, speaker's notes, and audience handouts on paper.

For a more professional-looking presentation, consider producing overhead transparencies, a computer slide show, or 35mm slides.

Choosing an Output Medium

Here are some guidelines for deciding what kind of output is best for you:

- *Overheads*. If you have a laser or inkjet printer, you can load it with transparencies that are specially made for laser printers, such as 3M Scotch Laser Printer Transparencies or 3M Inkjet Printer Transparencies (for Hewlett Packard DeskJets). You print on these transparencies as if they were paper. The result is a set of high-quality transparencies you can project by using an overhead projector.

- *Slide Show*. A slide show is an electronic presentation that utilizes your computer. Your slides fill the screen, and you can use a variety of special effects, such as timings, transitions, and builds. To display your slide show, you can use a desktop computer, but only for a small audience of, at most, three or four people. For a larger audience, you need a *projection panel*—a transparent color computer display designed to fit on top of an overhead projector.

V

Output and Color

■ *35mm Slides*. If you can fully darken the room in which you will give your presentation, you can create colorful 35mm slides by using a desktop film recorder or by sending your PowerPoint file to a service bureau. Using 35mm slides is the best choice for a large audience because you can project the slides onto a large screen. But be forewarned: You will need ample lead time. If any of the slides don't turn out or contain mistakes, you have to reshoot them and have them developed again.

Whichever output medium you choose, the process you follow to produce output is the same. First, you select the printer you want to use, and then you open the presentation you want to print. Next, you set up your slides by choosing the output media and orientation (portrait or landscape). Finally, you choose the command that starts producing output.

Setting Up Your Printer

Tip
Thanks to Windows, PowerPoint can print your slides on any Windows-compatible printer. However, you need an inkjet or laser printer to print your own overhead transparencies.

Microsoft Windows provides the information that enables PowerPoint to print with your printer. This information is stored in a file called a *printer driver*. To make use of your printer, your hard disk must contain the correct printer driver.

When you installed Microsoft Windows, the Setup program copied the correct printer driver to your hard disk. In addition, you chose a printer to serve as the *default printer,* the printer that PowerPoint uses unless you change the default printer setting.

Installing Printer Drivers with Microsoft Windows

Chances are that you have already installed your printer driver. But you may still find this section worth reading if you want to send your PowerPoint file to a graphics service bureau to make 35mm slides.

Tip
To see the current default printer setting, choose the **P**rint command from the **F**ile menu. The Printer area shows the current default printer.

Many Windows users do not realize that you can install a printer driver for a printer that is not physically connected to your system. When you select this printer while working with PowerPoint, the program uses this printer's settings and makes its special capabilities available to you. You can then save your presentation to a file, which you can transport—physically via a floppy disk, or electronically via a modem—to a graphics service bureau, which uses the printer you have selected.

You should prepare your PowerPoint file using the printer driver that the service bureau prefers. To do so, you must install this printer driver so that Windows and PowerPoint can use it.

PowerPoint comes with the printer driver and software needed to send your PowerPoint files to Genigraphics Corporation, a graphics service bureau that can transform your PowerPoint presentation into 35mm slides, 8-by-10-inch color transparencies, and 8-by-10-inch color prints. You can send your presentation to Genigraphics by mail, or, if you have a modem, you can upload your presentation using the GraphicsLink software provided with PowerPoint. You learn more about GraphicsLink elsewhere in this chapter. If you want to make use of Genigraphics' services, make sure now that the Genigraphics driver is installed by using the following procedure.

Tip
If you're using PowerPoint at home, install your office computer system's printer driver. If PowerPoint is installed on the office computer, you can save your presentation to a floppy disk, take it to the office, and print it there.

> **Note**
>
> Take some time now to call the graphics service bureau to find out which printer driver they would like you to use. For example, SlideImagers of Atlanta, Georgia (800-232-5411) prefers that you prepare and save your PowerPoint files by using the QMS ColorScript 100 driver, which is ideal for their equipment. Genigraphics Corporation requires you to print to a file using the Genigraphics driver.

To install printer drivers, follow these steps:

1. In the Program Manager, open the Main window.

2. Double-click the Control Panel icon. You see the Control Panel group (see fig. 16.1).

3. Double-click the Printers icon. You see the Printers dialog box. Click the **A**dd button to display the list of printers (see fig. 16.2).

Fig. 16.1
Use the Control Panel's Printers option to install your printer.

4. Select your printer from the printers list, and click **I**nstall.

   If your printer is not listed, check your printer's documentation to see whether you have received a *printer driver* with the printer. This is a file on a disk. Put the disk in the disk drive and, in the list of printers in the

V

Output and Color

Tip
If you want to use Genigraphics Corporation's services, make sure the Genigraphics driver is in the Installed Printers list. If it isn't, turn to the next troubleshooting section.

Printers dialog box, select the first option—Install Unlisted or Updated Printer. Then click **I**nstall. In the Install Driver dialog box, click OK and then choose your printer from the new printer list that appears. Click OK to confirm your choice and install your printer.

5. If you see a dialog box asking you to insert one of the Windows setup disks, insert the disk and click OK.

   You may not have to do this step if the printer driver has already been copied to your hard disk.

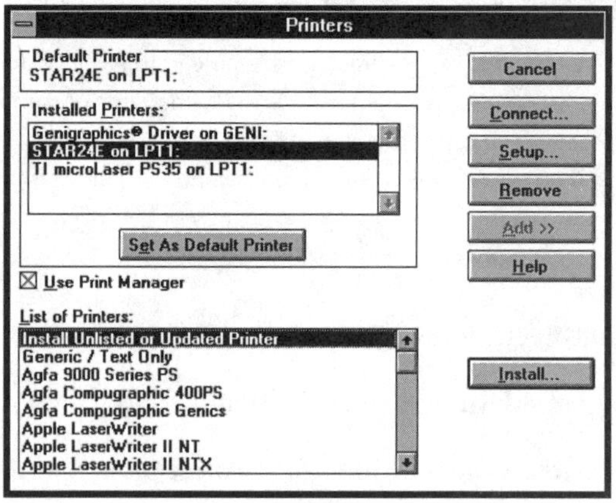

Fig. 16.2
The Printers dialog box shows the currently installed printers and lets you install additional printers.

6. With your printer selected in the Installed **P**rinters list, click **C**onnect.

7. Click the port to which you have connected your printer, and click OK.

Tip
In the Printer Setup dialog box, be sure to identify the cartridges and memory upgrades you have installed, if any. Windows cannot take advantage of these features unless you identify them here.

   Most parallel printers connect to the LPT1 port. If you're not sure, or if you have purchased a printer that connects through the serial port, read the printer installation instructions carefully—and get help if you get stuck.

8. Click **S**etup. You see the Setup dialog box for the printer you have chosen. Choose the options you want and click OK.

   What you see in this dialog box depends on which printer you've installed. With most printers, you can choose the default orientation (Portrait or Landscape) and the paper size. Depending on your printer, other options may be available.

9. Repeat steps 4 through 8 to install additional printers, if you want.

10. With your printer's name selected in the list of installed printers, click the Set As Default Printer button.

    The default printer is the one that Windows will use unless you specifically override this choice by selecting an alternate printer, as explained in the following section.

11. Click Close to close the Printers dialog box.

12. To close the Control Panel, choose **S**ettings E**x**it; press Alt+F4; or just double-click the Control menu icon.

Choosing a Printer

When you choose a printer, PowerPoint prepares and saves your presentation so that it prints as well as possible on the printer you have chosen. PowerPoint normally uses the printer driver you identified as the default printer when you used the Printers option in Windows' Control Panel; however, you may want to choose a printer other than the one physically connected to your computer system.

■ If you plan to send your PowerPoint presentation to a graphics service bureau, choose the printer driver they prefer.

■ If you plan to print your PowerPoint presentation at a different location, using a better printer (such as the one at work), choose that printer's driver.

To choose a printer driver from PowerPoint:

1. Open the presentation you want to print from a printer other than the default printer.

2. From the **F**ile menu, choose **P**rint. You can also use the Ctrl+P shortcut or click the Print icon on the toolbar. You see the Print dialog box.

    If the **P**rint option is dimmed, return to step 1 and open your presentation.

3. Choose the P**r**inter button. The Print Setup dialog box appears (see fig. 16.3).

4. In the **P**rinters list, choose the printer driver you want to use.

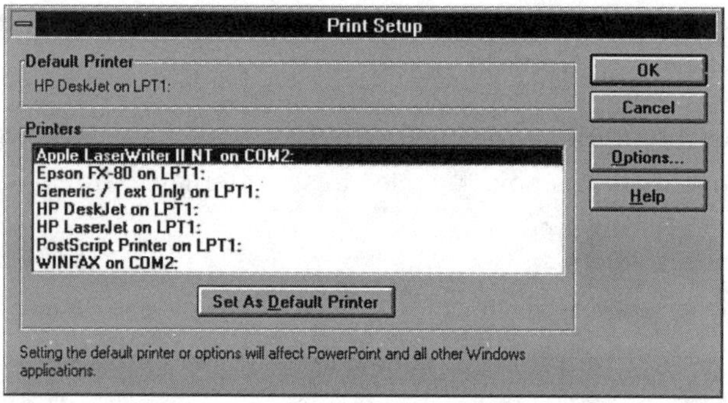

Fig. 16.3

The Print Setup dialog box lets you choose a printer driver other than the default printer.

5. Choose OK. You see the Print dialog box. The Printer area indicates the printer you have chosen.

6. Click Cancel to return to PowerPoint. (Even though you choose Cancel, PowerPoint retains the printer driver choice you made in step 4.)

Note

The printer driver choice you make affects only the *current* presentation—the one that's active when you choose **P**rint from the **F**ile menu. This choice is saved with this presentation. Your choice does not affect the printer driver setting in other PowerPoint presentations or other Windows applications.

Troubleshooting

After I printed my presentation using the Genigraphics printer driver, I can't print my other applications.

You chose the Genigraphics printer driver as the default printer driver for all your Microsoft Windows applications. Use the Printers option in the Control Panel to change this setting so that your printer is the default printer. To do so, select your printer in the Installed **P**rinters list and click the S**e**t As Default Printer button. Click Close to exit.

The Genigraphics printer driver isn't installed.

PowerPoint does not install the Genigraphics printer driver and GraphicsLink software unless you choose the Complete/Custom option when you install PowerPoint. If you did not choose the Complete/Custom option when you installed PowerPoint, you can install the Genigraphics software by using the PowerPoint Setup program on Disk 1 of your PowerPoint program disks. Run Setup as you did when you first installed the program, but choose Complete/Custom and select Install Genigraphics Driver and GraphicsLink.

Setting Up Your Slides

The next step in the output process is to set up your slides by using the Slide Setup option from the **F**ile menu. This option lets you identify your output medium (paper, on-screen slide show, or 35mm slides) as well as the orientation of slides, notes, handouts, and outlines (portrait or landscape).

To set up your slides, follow these steps:

1. If necessary, open the presentation you want to set up.

2. From the **F**ile menu, choose Slide Set**u**p. You see the Slide Setup dialog box (see fig. 16.4).

3. From the **S**lides Sized for drop-down list, choose the output medium you plan to use: letter or A4 paper, on-screen slides, 35mm slides, or custom.

Each choice comes with preset width, height, and orientation:

Option	Width	Height	Slide Orientation
Letter Paper	10in	7.5in	Landscape
A4 Paper	10.83cm	7.5cm	Landscape
On-screen slides	10in	7.5in	Landscape
35mm slides	11.25	7.5	Landscape

4. If you want, change the orientation.

In Landscape orientation, the image is wider than it is tall. In Portrait orientation, the image is taller than it is wide.

Tip
The best time to set up your slides is when you begin creating a new presentation. PowerPoint will display your new slides using the correction dimensions of the output medium you want to use.

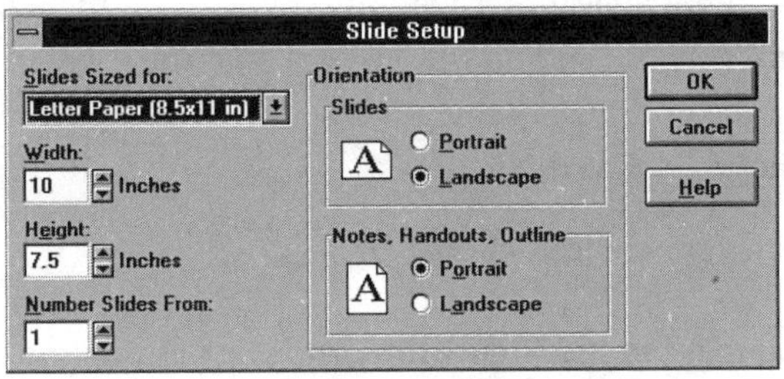

Fig. 16.4
Use the Slide Setup dialog box to identify the output medium you're using—paper, on-screen slides, 35mm slides, or custom. In addition, you can choose the orientation (portrait or landscape).

V

Output and Color

Tip
If you are planning to produce on-screen slides or 35mm slides, size your slides for the output medium you will use for your final presentation. Should you want to print drafts on paper, PowerPoint can temporarily scale the print output so that it fits on your printer's paper.

Tip
To print overhead transparencies, choose Letter or A4 in the **S**lides Sized for drop-down list and choose P**o**rtrait orientation for your slides.

Notice that you can choose one orientation for slides, and another for notes, handouts, and outlines.

The current settings—**L**andscape for slides and P**o**rtrait for notes, handouts, and outlines—are good choices for almost all purposes, with one exception: overhead transparencies. For this purpose, choose Letter or A4 paper, and choose Portrait orientation.

5. If you want, change the width and height by clicking the arrow icon next to the **W**idth and H**e**ight boxes, or type a number. If you make a change here, the **S**lides Sized for box automatically changes to the Custom option.

6. If you want to start slide numbering with a number other than 1, click the arrow icon next to the **N**umber Slides From box, or type the number.

Numbers do not appear on slides unless you insert them by using the Page N**u**mber command on the **I**nsert menu, the Page Number button on the toolbar, or the ## code. An easy way to add page numbers is to use the Pick a Look Wizard.

7. To confirm your choices, choose OK.

The choices you make in the Slide Setup dialog box affect only the presentation that is open when you choose the Slide Set**u**p command.

Caution

If you change the size or orientation of a presentation you have already created, PowerPoint adjusts the layout of each slide to produce the best possible balance. You should review each slide individually to make sure that they still look good. You may need to adjust the position of charts and text boxes.

Printing Slides, Notes, Outlines, and Handouts

Once you have chosen your printer and set up your slides, printing with PowerPoint is as simple as with any Windows application. You choose the

Print command from the File menu, select options such as the number of copies or the range of slides to be printed, and choose OK.

To print slides, outlines, notes, or handouts, follow these steps:

1. If necessary, open your presentation and set up your slides.

2. If you want to print overhead transparencies, load your printer's paper tray with laser transparencies.

Caution

If you have a laser printer, do not use heat-sensitive transparencies that are designed to be used with heat-transfer copiers. These transparencies will melt inside your printer and destroy the mechanism. Make sure you have taken the transparency from a box labeled *Laser Printer Transparencies*. If you are not sure where the transparency came from, don't use it.

Tip

If you're planning to print an outline, use Outline view to arrange your outline the way you want it to print. PowerPoint will print your outline the way it appears in Outline view.

3. From the File menu, choose Print; press Ctrl+P; or click the Printer icon in the toolbar. You see the Print dialog box (see fig. 16.5).

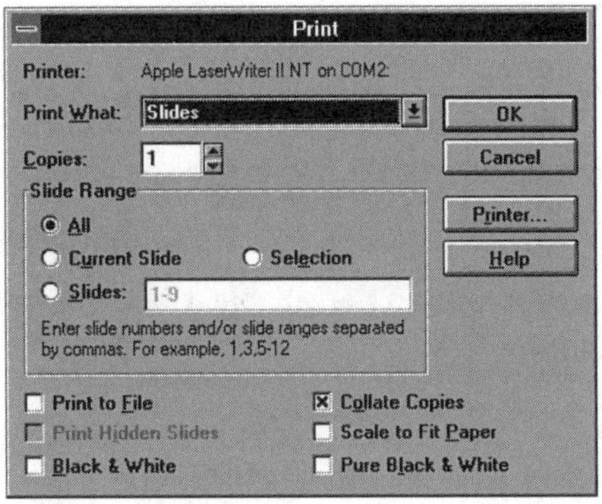

Fig. 16.5
Use the Print dialog box to print your slides, notes, outline, or handouts.

4. From the Print What drop-down list, choose the presentation component you want to print.

You may choose from Slides, Notes Pages, Handouts (2 slides per page), Handouts (3 slides per page), Handouts (6 slides per page), and Outline view. If you have incorporated builds into your presentation, you see two additional options, Slides (with builds) and Slides (without builds).

Tip

If you are printing handouts, the 3 slides per page option is a good choice. The slides are printed large enough to be easily legible, and there is space on one side of the page for your audience to take notes.

V

Output and Color

The Slides (with builds) option prints one page for each step in the build; the Slides (without builds) option prints just one page showing all the build items.

For more information, see chapter 20, "Advanced Presentation Management," for information on adding builds to your presentation.

5. If you want to print more than one copy, click the arrow icon next to the **C**opies box, or just type a number in the box.

   PowerPoint is preset to collate the pages when you are printing multiple copies. If you do not want the copies collated, deselect the C**o**llate Copies check box.

6. If you want to print only a portion of your presentation, make a choice in the Slide Range area.

   Choose C**u**rrent Slide to print the slide that is currently selected.

   To print some of the slides in your presentation (but not all), type the slides you want to print in the **S**lides box. To indicate a range of slides, type the beginning number, a hyphen, and the end number (for example, **12-15**). To indicate single slides to print, type their numbers separated by commas (for example, **2,4,7,11**). You can combine these (for example, **1,4,6-7**). If you type just one number, PowerPoint starts printing with that slide and continues to the end of the presentation.

   If you selected one or more slides before choosing **P**rint from the **F**ile menu, the Sel**e**ction option is available. Click this option to print only the selected slides.

7. If you have hidden some of the slides in your presentation but want to print them, select the Print H**i**dden Slides check box.

Tip

Select the **B**lack & White check box to print a draft quickly on a color printer.

8. If you are printing a draft, select the **B**lack & White check box to print your slides quickly in black and white (with the exception of pictures, which are printed with grays). Select Pure B**l**ack & White to print all components of your slides, including pictures, in black and white.

9. If you are printing draft copies of an on-screen or 35mm slide presentation, select the Scale to Fit **P**aper check box.

10. Choose OK.

Troubleshooting

I just printed my slides on my black-and-white printer, but they look dark and muddy and didn't photocopy very well.

Try choosing the **B**lack and White or Pure B**l**ack and White options in the Print dialog box. These options remove color fills, which are replaced by white. The **B**lack and White option turns all text to black and replaces all color fills with white, but it uses gray scale printing for some objects (such as decorative borders and clip art). The Pure B**l**ack and White doesn't print any grays except for pictures.

I just want to make a quick printout of my slides so that my assistant can double-check them. However, it's taking too long to print them. Isn't there a "Draft" printing option?

The reason it is taking so long for your slides to print is that your printer is trying to capture the colors you've used by printing gray tones. To speed up printing, choose the **B**lack and White or Pure B**l**ack and White options in the Print dialog box, as explained above.

Printing to a File

If you plan to send your PowerPoint presentation to a graphics service bureau, you may be asked to print the presentation to a file.

When you do, you should choose the printer driver that the service bureau prefers. For example, if you plan to send your file to Genigraphics Corporation, you use the Genigraphics printer driver.

To print to a PostScript file, follow these steps:

1. If necessary, open your presentation and set up your slides.

2. From the **F**ile menu, choose **P**rint; press Ctrl+P; or click the Printer icon in the toolbar. You see the Print dialog box.

3. Choose P**r**inter. You see the Print Setup dialog box, the same one you can access via the Control Panel.

4. In the **P**rinters list, select the printer driver that the graphics service bureau wants you to use.

5. Click OK to confirm your printer driver choice and return to the Print menu.

6. From the Print **W**hat drop-down list, choose Slides, if necessary.

Tip
Call the service bureau to find out which printer driver to use.

V

Output and Color

7. If you want to print only some of your slides, choose an option in the Slide Range area.

8. Select the Print to **F**ile check box. If this box is dimmed, the driver you chose is preset to print to a file.

   In the Printer area (at the top of the dialog box), the current printer changes to indicate that the output will be routed to a file rather than a port.

9. Choose OK. You see a Print Status message box informing you that PowerPoint is printing your presentation on the printer you selected; a moment later, you see the Print To File dialog box.

Tip

If you are planning to print the file to a floppy disk that you will later send to a service bureau, begin the file name by typing the disk drive (**A:** or **B:**) that contains the disk.

10. In the **O**utput File Name box, type a name for the PostScript file you are creating. Click OK to confirm the output file name and start printing the file.

If you chose the Genigraphics printer driver, you see the Genigraphics Job Instructions dialog box (see fig. 16.6) instead of the Output File Name box. This dialog box lets you specify the copies you want (35mm slides with plastic mounts, 35mm slides with glass mounts, 8-by-10-inch overheads, and/or 8-by-10-inch color prints). You can order as many of these as you like, and you can order more than one set of each. You also specify how you will send the file (via modem or diskette). If you choose the modem option, you will use the GraphicsLink software to upload your file to the nearest Genigraphics service center. Next, you specify how you want your slides returned (via express courier or mail, or hold for pickup). Finally, you type a name for your presentation in the Save **A**s box. Click OK to confirm your choices.

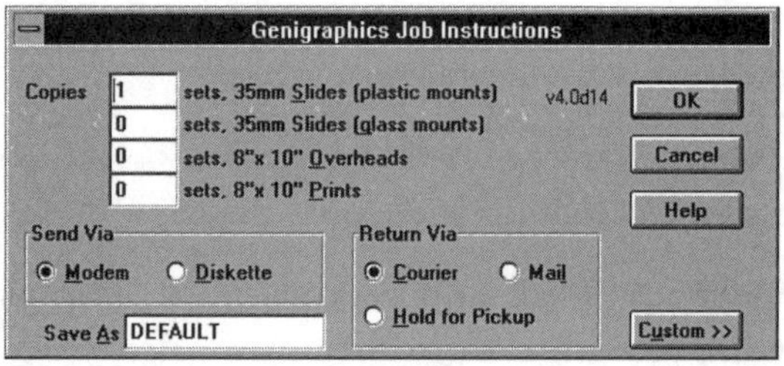

Fig. 16.6

The Genigraphics Job Instructions dialog box appears when you use the Genigraphics printer driver to print your slides to a file.

When the Genigraphics printer driver finishes printing your presentation, you see the Genigraphics Billing Information dialog box (see fig. 16.7). Using this dialog box, you specify where you want the slides, transparencies, or prints to be sent and to whom you want the charges billed. You can also specify how you want to pay for the services (Genigraphics accepts American Express, Visa, and MasterCard, in addition to Genigraphics accounts and COD). When you are finished filling out the information, click OK.

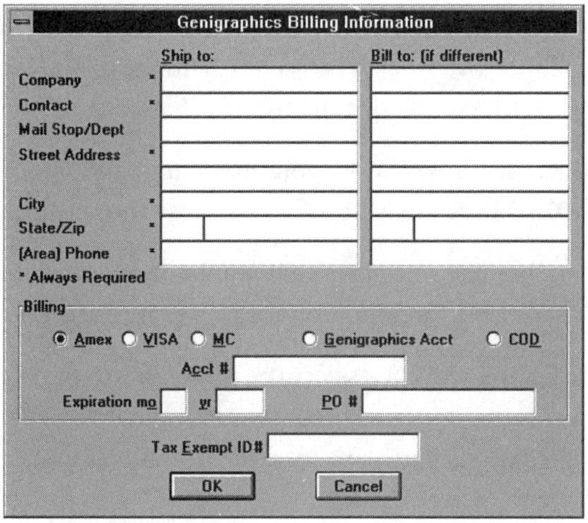

Fig. 16.7
The Genigraphics Billing Information dialog box appears after the Genigraphics printer driver finishes printing your file.

Using GraphicsLink

If your computer system is equipped with a Hayes or Hayes-compatible modem, you can use the supplied GraphicsLink software to upload your PowerPoint presentation to the nearest Genigraphics service center. There is no charge for the telephone transmission because GraphicsLink uses 800 numbers to upload your file. If you select express courier delivery and rush service, it is possible to have your slides, transparencies, or prints delivered as quickly as the next business day.

> **Note**
>
> You can use GraphicsLink with modems that are not Hayes compatible, but you will have to specify the modem initialization, dialing, and termination strings.

Tip
If you need rush processing, call your nearest Genigraphics service center before using GraphicsLink and ask about rush services. You will receive a rush confirmation code that you will need to supply using GraphicsLink.

To upload your presentation to a Genigraphics service center by using GraphicsLink, follow these steps:

1. In Program Manager, double-click the GraphicsLink program item. You will find this in the same program group that contains PowerPoint. You see the GraphicsLink dialog box (see fig. 16.8).

Tip
Before using
GraphicsLink for
the first time, you
will need the
following informa-
tion about your
modem: the port
to which it is
connected (prob-
ably COM1 or
COM2) and the
baud rate (1200,
2400, 9600,
14,400, or 19,200).
GraphicsLink is
preset to use a
2400 baud Hayes
modem connected
to COM1, but you
can change these
settings.

2. From the **F**ile menu, choose **C**ommunications Setup. The Communications Setup dialog box appears, as in figure 16.9.

3. In the **P**ort list box, choose the port to which your modem is connected
(this is probably COM1 or COM2).

4. If you are not using a 2400 baud modem, you need to change the baud
rate setting. Choose **S**ettings. You see the Settings dialog box for the
port you have selected (see fig. 16.10).

5. In the **B**aud rate list box, choose your modem's baud rate. The other
settings are OK as they are. Choose OK to close the Settings dialog box.

6. In the **D**estination list, select the Genigraphics service center to which
you want to send your presentation for processing, and choose OK.

7. In the GraphicsLink window, select the presentation that you want to
send. To select more than one presentation, hold down the Ctrl key and
click the presentations you want to send. To send all unsent presentations, choose **E**dit, Select **U**nsent.

8. Turn on your modem, if necessary.

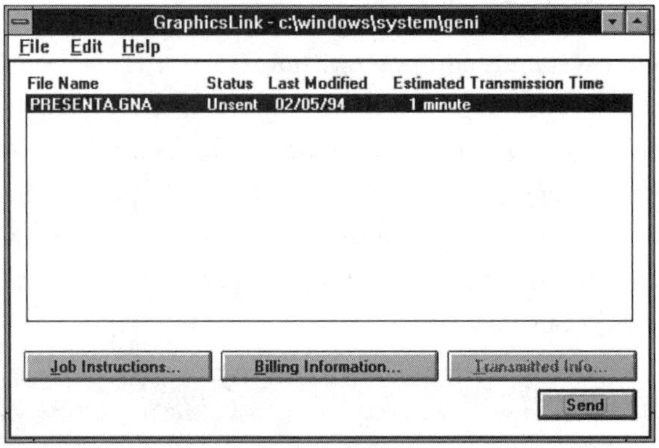

Fig. 16.8
If your computer
is equipped with a
modem, you can
send your
PowerPoint
presentation to
Genigraphics
Corporation for
rapid processing
and return.

Note

If you would like to change the job instructions, or if you want to take advan-
tage of rush services, click the **J**ob Instructions button at the bottom of the
screen. You see the same dialog box that appeared when you used the
Genigraphics printer driver to print your file. Change your order, if you want.
To supply the rush confirmation code, click Custom and type the code in the
Rush Confirmation Code box. Click OK to confirm your options.

9. Choose Send. GraphicsLink sends your presentation to the service bureau you selected.

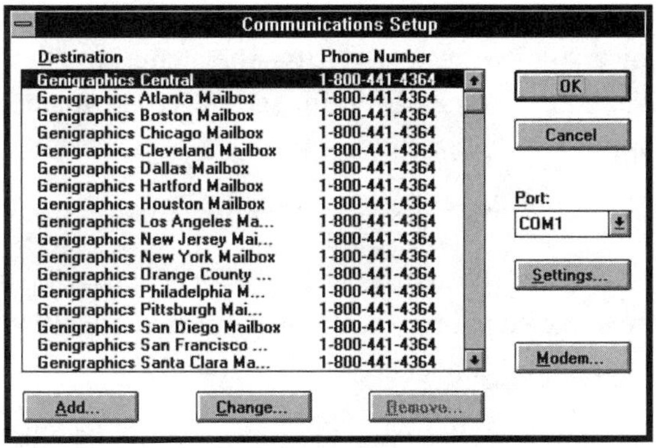

Fig. 16.9
With this GraphicsLink dialog box, you choose the Genigraphics service center that you want to process your slides, transparencies, or prints.

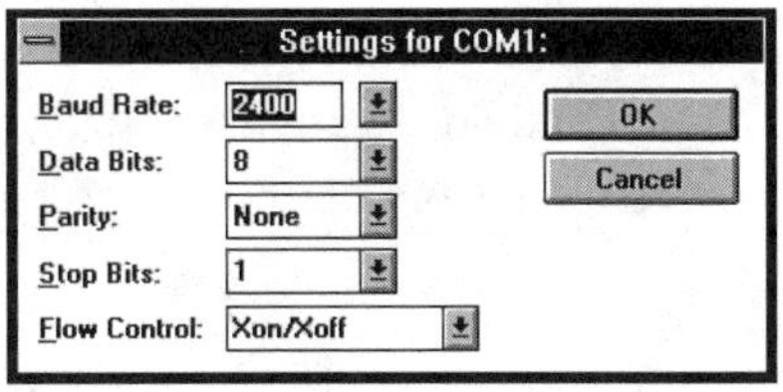

Fig. 16.10
You use this dialog box to specify your modem's baud rate.

Output and Color

Troubleshooting

I tried to send my presentation, but a dialog box appeared informing me that the transmission was unsuccessful.

GraphicsLink had trouble accessing your modem. Make sure your modem is plugged in, turned on, and connected to your computer as well as the telephone line. If GraphicsLink still can't access your modem, make sure you have selected the correct port (usually COM1 or COM2). If necessary, change the **P**ort setting in the **C**ommunications Setup dialog box.

I'm sending a big presentation file to Genigraphics and it's tying up my computer.

Just switch to another application. GraphicsLink can send your presentation in the background.

I'm trying to send my file, but Call Waiting messes up my modem and transmission ceases.

With most phone systems, you can disable Call Waiting temporarily. If you have a touch-tone phone, try pressing *70. If you then hear a dial tone, you have disabled Call Waiting for the next call. Now use GraphicsLink.

Creating a Slide Show

If you would like your presentation to feature the brilliant colors you see on your Windows display, you have two choices: 35mm slides or a slide show. In a slide show, PowerPoint's screen elements—the menus, toolbars, and scroll bars—disappear, and the first slide fills the screen. When you click the mouse, the next slide appears.

A slide show has many advantages over other presentation media:

- You need not allow substantial lead time for film development. Once you have completed your presentation with PowerPoint, you can display the slide show immediately.

- You can give a presentation in a room that cannot be fully darkened (a necessity with 35mm slides).

- You can use the mouse pointer, which is visible on-screen during the slide show, to call your audience's attention to a particular element on the slide. You can even write and draw on the screen as you give the presentation.

- You can use professional-looking effects, such as transitions and builds. These effects add variety, interest, and emphasis to your presentation.

- With PowerPoint's multimedia capabilities and a sound-equipped system, you can include sounds and movies in your presentation.

- You can rehearse your presentation until you have it just right. And you can keep making changes until the moment your presentation begins.

- If you have embedded information such as a spreadsheet into a PowerPoint slide, you can open the source spreadsheet and make changes—for example, trying a "what-if" analysis—right before your audience.

- You can give a continuous presentation, one that keeps running in an endless loop until you tell it to stop. This is a good choice for exhibits.

- You can add buttons to your slides that enable you to branch to another presentation while the slide show is in progress.

The major disadvantage of slide shows is the computer's small screen, which limits the size of your audience to three or four people. However, many organizations have projection devices that allow you to project your computer's output by means of an overhead projector. With one of these, you can present a slide show to an audience of 50 or more people.

PowerPoint's slide show capabilities are impressive and sophisticated yet extremely easy to use. You can create a simple slide show with a click of the mouse button. It is also very easy to create a continuously running slide show. As your understanding of slide shows grows, you can add special effects, such as sounds, builds, transitions, timings, branches, and movies. Chapter 20, "Advanced Presentation Management," discusses these features.

Running a Simple Slide Show

With PowerPoint, it is very easy to create a simple slide show in which slides advance when you click the mouse button.

To create a slide show using PowerPoint's default settings, follow these steps:

1. If necessary, open your presentation.

2. Switch to Slide Sorter view by clicking the Slide Sorter View button at the bottom of the window or by choosing the Slide Sorter command from the **V**iew menu.

3. Select the first slide you want to display in the slide show.

   To show all the slides, click the first slide.

4. Click the Slide Show button at the bottom of the screen.

   PowerPoint displays the first slide in your presentation.

5. To advance to the next slide, click the mouse button. You can also press the space bar, the N key, PgDn, right arrow, or down arrow to advance to the next slide.

   To write or draw on the screen with the mouse, click the Freehand Annotation tool—the pencil icon in the screen's lower corner. Click and hold down the mouse button to write or draw. When you are finished, click the pencil icon again to restore the mouse pointer. The writing or drawing you make this way is temporary; it does not affect the slide's appearance after the slide show is over.

Tip
To select the first slide quickly, press Ctrl+Home.

Tip
Rather than leaving a slide on-screen for a long time while you discuss a point, press B to black the screen. Press B again to return to your presentation.

Output and Color

V

Tip
During a slide show, click the Freehand Annotation tool (the pencil icon) to write or draw on-screen. To erase the annotation, press the E key.

Tip
Use the mouse pointer to call your audience's attention to features you want to emphasize.

6. To view all the slides in order, continue clicking the mouse button or using any of the keyboard equivalents (space bar, N, PgDn, right arrow, or down arrow). To view the previous slide, click the right mouse button or press one of these keys: Backspace, P, left arrow, up arrow, or PgUp.

   For a list of all the key and mouse commands you can use while viewing a slide show in PowerPoint, see table 16.1.

7. Continue clicking until you have seen all the slides. To stop the slide show, press Esc.

   When the slide show is finished, you see PowerPoint again.

Note

To avoid having your audience see the PowerPoint screen after you display the last slide, end your presentation with a black slide. To do so, add a blank AutoLayout slide after your last slide. From the **Fo**rmat menu, choose the Slide Back**g**round command. In the Slide Background dialog box, deselect the Display **O**bjects on Selected Slides check box. In the Shade Styles area, choose **N**one. Use the Chan**g**e Color button to change the background color to Black, click OK, and choose **A**pply.

Table 16.1   Mouse and Keyboard Commands for Slide Shows

To...	Do This...
View a list of the keys in this table	Press F1
View the next slide	Use any of these options: ■ Click the left mouse button ■ Press N ■ Press the right-arrow key ■ Press the down-arrow key ■ Press the PgDn key ■ Press the space bar
View the next slide, even if it is hidden	Press H
View the previous slide	Use any of these options: ■ Click the right mouse button ■ Press P ■ Press the left-arrow key

To...	Do This...
	■ Press the up-arrow key ■ Press the PgUp key ■ Press the Backspace key
Go to a particular slide	Type the slide number and press Enter
Return to the first slide	Hold down both mouse buttons for two seconds
Black/unblack the screen	Press B or period (.)
White/unwhite the screen	Press W or comma (,)
Show/Hide the pointer	Press A or equal (=)
Erase Freehand Annotation	Press E
Stop/Restart an automatic show	Press S or plus (+)
Stop the slide show	Press Esc ■ Press Ctrl+Break ■ Press the hyphen key (-)
Use New Time	Press T
Use Original Time	Press O
Advance on mouse click	Press M

Running a Slide Show in a Continuous Loop

At trade shows and conventions, you may have seen computers at booths that are running a continuous slide show. You can easily do the same thing with your computer and PowerPoint.

To create a continuous slide show, follow these steps:

1. If necessary, open your presentation.

2. Switch to Slide Sorter view by clicking the Slide Sorter View button at the bottom of the window or by choosing the Slide Sorter command from the **V**iew menu.

3. From the **E**dit menu, choose Select All; or use the Ctrl+A shortcut to select all the slides in your presentation.

V

Output and Color

This step is necessary because the timings you choose in step 5 affect only the slides you have selected in the Slide Sorter.

4. From the **T**ools menu, choose **T**ransition. You see the Transition dialog box (see fig. 16.11).

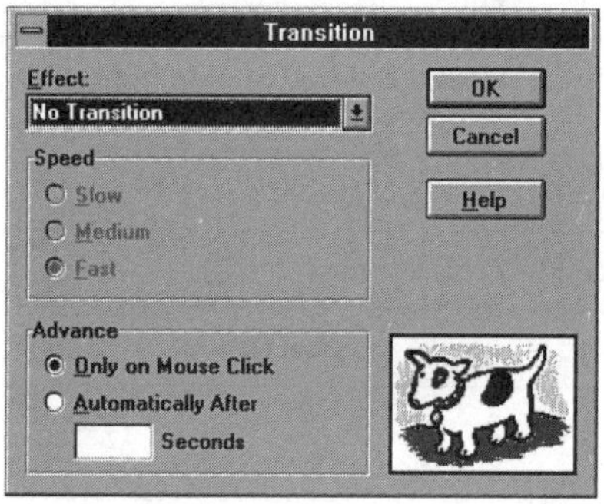

Fig. 16.11

Use the Transition dialog box to specify how long you want slides to appear during a continuous presentation.

Tip

Try displaying each slide for 15 seconds initially.

5. In the Advance area, type the number of seconds you want each slide displayed.

6. Choose OK.

7. From the **V**iew menu, choose Slide Sho**w**. You see the Slide Show dialog box (see fig. 16.12).

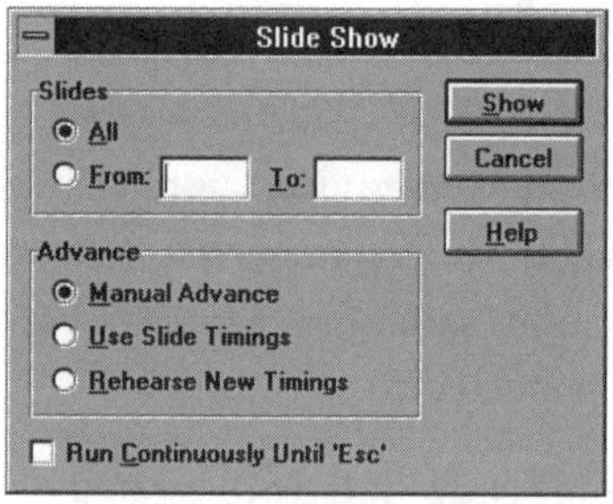

Fig. 16.12

You can use the Slide Show dialog box to create a continuously running presentation.

8. If you want to display only some of the slides, type the number of the beginning slide in the **F**rom box and the ending slide in the **T**o box.

If you type a number only in the **F**rom box, PowerPoint will display the presentation starting from the slide number you specify.

9. In the Advance area, choose **U**se Slide Timings. PowerPoint will use the automatic timing option you specified in the Transitions dialog box (step 5).

10. Select the Run **C**ontinuously Until 'Esc' check box.

11. Choose **S**how to start your slide show.

Rearranging Slides

As you preview your slide show, you may find that one or more of the slides is out of sequence. You can easily change the order of your slides by using the Slide Sorter.

To change the order of slides, follow these steps:

1. If necessary, switch to Slide Sorter view by clicking the Slide Sorter View button or choosing Sli**d**e Sorter from the **V**iew menu.

2. Click on the slide you want to move and hold down the mouse button.

   The pointer changes shape to indicate that you have enabled PowerPoint's drag-and-drop editing feature.

3. Move the pointer to the place you want the slide to appear.

   You see a dotted line showing where PowerPoint will place the slide when you release the mouse button.

4. When you have positioned the dotted line in the correct place, release the mouse button.

Viewing Slide Shows with the PowerPoint Viewer

Suppose that you want to give a presentation while traveling. A computer is available, but PowerPoint is not installed. Does this mean you can't present your slide show? No, and the credit is due to *PowerPoint Viewer,* an application included with your copy of PowerPoint. Bring with you a disk containing your presentation and PowerPoint Viewer, and you can display your presentation.

PowerPoint Viewer also comes in handy when you want to send your presentation to a computer user who does not have PowerPoint. Just include PowerPoint Viewer on the disk with your presentation.

You may duplicate PowerPoint Viewer and give it to others freely without violating the law or your software license.

Tip

To prevent viewers from disturbing the show, place the mouse and keyboard behind the computer while the show is running.

Tip

To undo any change you have just made to the slide order, immediately choose **U**ndo from the **E**dit menu or press Ctrl+Z.

V

Output and Color

Creating Disks Containing PowerPoint Viewer and Your Presentation

You need two 1.44M (high-density) floppy disks to create a portable version of your presentation, one you can take with you when traveling or that you can send to others.

To create disks that contain PowerPoint Viewer and your presentation, follow these steps:

Tip

To make a copy of a disk when you have only one high-density disk drive, open the **D**isk menu and choose **C**opy Disk in File Manager. In the Copy Disk dialog box, select the same drive letter in the Source In and Destination In boxes, and choose OK. File Manager will prompt you to insert the disks.

1. Make a copy of the PowerPoint Viewer disk included with your original PowerPoint program disks.

2. Copy your presentation to the second disk.

> **Note**
>
> If you are not sure whether the computer on which you will run your presentation has the TrueType fonts you have used, create the copy of your presentation by using the **F**ile Save **A**s command. Activate the Em**b**ed TrueType Fonts option and save your presentation to the floppy disk. PowerPoint will include the fonts you have used, and they will be available when your slide show is viewed.

Installing PowerPoint Viewer on Another Computer

PowerPoint Viewer runs too slowly from a floppy disk. For good performance, you or the person to whom you are sending your presentation must install the program and your presentation on the computer that will be used for the presentation.

Install PowerPoint Viewer and your presentation by following these steps:

1. Insert the copy you made of the PowerPoint Viewer program disk into the disk drive.

2. In Program Manager, open the **F**ile menu and choose **R**un.

3. In the Command Line box, type **a:vsetup.exe** if you inserted the disk in drive A, or type **b:vsetup.exe** if you inserted the disk in drive B. The PowerPoint Viewer Setup program will start. Click OK or press Enter.

4. The program prompts you to type the name of the directory to which you want to copy PowerPoint Viewer. The proposed name, \POWERPNT, is fine, so choose OK.

   The Setup program copies the files needed to run PowerPoint Viewer to the computer's hard disk. When the file copying is complete, click OK twice to return to Windows.

5. Insert the disk containing your presentation.

6. Use File Manager to copy your presentation from the floppy disk to the directory in which you installed PowerPoint Viewer (normally, C:\POWERPNT).

Using PowerPoint Viewer to View a Slide Show

After you have installed PowerPoint Viewer, you can display a slide show on a computer that does not have PowerPoint installed. All the features available within a PowerPoint slide show, including the special effects you may have included such as builds and transitions, are available.

To view a slide show with PowerPoint Viewer, follow these steps:

1. Start PowerPoint Viewer by double-clicking the PowerPoint Viewer icon in Program Manager.

   If you are starting PowerPoint Viewer from a floppy disk, put the disk in the drive and choose the **F**ile **R**un command in Program Manager. In the Command Line box, type **a:** or **b:** followed by **pptview.exe**, and choose OK.

   When PowerPoint Viewer starts, you see the PowerPoint Viewer dialog box, which is identical to the familiar Open dialog box that you see in most applications.

2. Use the PowerPoint Viewer dialog box to select the PowerPoint presentation you want to view, and choose Show.

3. If you want the presentation to run continuously, select the Run **C**ontinuously Until 'Esc' check box.

4. When you have selected the presentation you want to show, choose Show.

   PowerPoint Viewer runs your presentation, beginning with the first slide. All the features available in PowerPoint are available in PowerPoint Viewer, including the Freehand Annotation tool and the keyboard commands listed earlier in table 16.1.

5. At the conclusion of the slide show, you see the PowerPoint Viewer dialog box again. Choose Quit to exit.

V

Output and Color

Running Slide Shows with a Play List

By means of a *play list*—a text file containing a list of PowerPoint presentations—you can run two or more presentations consecutively as a continuous slide show. You may do this with PowerPoint or with PowerPoint Viewer.

Creating the Play List

To create the play list, you create a plain text file with any word processor or editor, such as the Windows Notepad. Simply type the file name of the first presentation you want to display, and press Enter. Then type the second presentation's file name, and press Enter. Continue until you have typed the names of all the presentations you want to include in your slide show, as in this example: SHOW1.PPT, SHOW2.PPT, and SHOW3.PPT. Save the file using the extension .LST.

Running a Play List from PowerPoint

To run a play list from PowerPoint, follow these steps:

1. From the **F**ile menu, choose **O**pen. You see the Open dialog box.

2. In the File **N**ame list box, type the name of the .LST file that contains your play list.

3. Choose OK to open the play list and start the slide show.

Running a Play List from PowerPoint Viewer

To run a play list from PowerPoint Viewer, follow these steps:

1. In Program Manager, open the **F**ile menu and choose **R**un to display the Run dialog box.

2. In the Command Line box, type the name of the .LST file.

3. Choose OK to open the play list and start the slide show.

From Here...

For more information on printing and producing output with PowerPoint, you can refer to the following chapters:

■ Chapter 2, "Getting Acquainted with PowerPoint 4," introduces the Slide Sorter.

- Chapter 3, "Quick Start: Creating a First Presentation," introduces printing.

- Chapter 17, "Working with Color," helps you design your color PowerPoint presentations for maximum effectiveness.

- Chapter 20, "Advanced Presentation Management," covers advanced slide show features such as transitions, builds, multimedia effects, hidden slides, timing, and slide show rehearsals.

- Chapter 22, "Customizing PowerPoint," shows you how to change printing default settings.

V

Output and Color

Chapter 17

Working with Color

You have already glanced at PowerPoint 4's basic color palettes in earlier chapters. In many situations, it is not enough to simply apply colors because they offer a nice appearance. Many presentation elements, such as handouts and speaker's notes, don't require color of any kind; they can be created needing little or no knowledge of color. Nonetheless, color is a very important component of slide shows, and the proper use of color can make the difference between a dull or boring presentation and one that excites, informs, and prompts a decision.

Improper use of color can also excite a negative decision. Color, if used badly, can actually create irritation in the viewer. Assigning a wrong color to text on a slide can make the text unreadable. Colors may not match properly on a slide and thus produce eye-straining effects. There are specific color combinations, on the other hand, that always seem to work because of their universal appeal and basic character. PowerPoint helps you keep your color schemes under control in some subtle but effective ways, as you see later in this chapter.

Understanding Color in PowerPoint 4

When you choose a template for use in creating a PowerPoint 4 presentation, you also make a decision on the presentation's appearance. You have a specific set of colors to work with, but that doesn't mean you cannot change them. PowerPoint allows you the flexibility to use any color you desire anywhere you want.

In this chapter, you study color more intensively and learn how to perform the following tasks, among others:

- Create new colors and place them on the palette

- Understand the relationship between template color schemes and color palettes

- Understand the 8-color and 90-color PowerPoint default palettes and how to change their colors

- Acquire techniques, tips, and tricks for effective color management

V

Output and Color

The front-line tool for working with color in PowerPoint is the drop-down palette available to you in the Fill Color tool on the Drawing+ toolbar. The tool is actually a combination of a menu list and a color palette, as seen in figure 17.1.

Fig. 17.1

The Fill Tool palette displaying several menu options, the basic 8-color palette, and some extra colors for assignment to objects.

8-color palette
4 additional colors (Up to 8 are available)

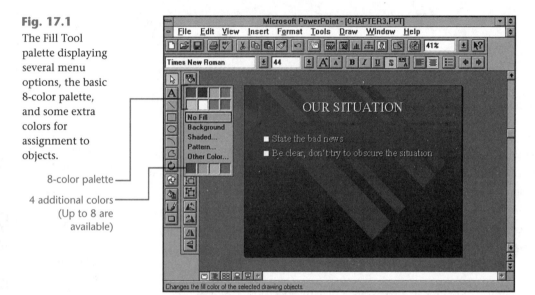

Notice the appearance of the same palette in the Font dialog box, as shown in figure 17.2, for the purpose of assigning different colors to slide text.

Fig. 17.2

The Font dialog box displaying the same color palette as for the Fill Color tool.

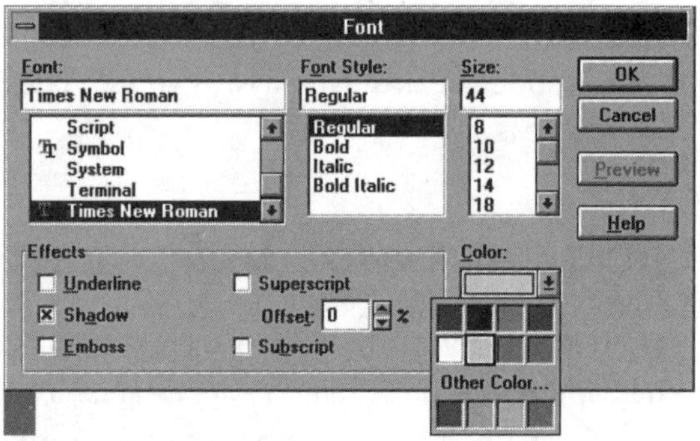

The same color set is used in several different places throughout the program.

Studying PowerPoint's Basic Color Palette

The eight-color palette you see in the preceding two figures is no accident. There is a specific reason for the placement of those eight colors. They are the eight basic colors for the entire template. Moreover, each color is assigned a specific place and is used for specific things to ensure appropriate and proper use of each color in the slide show. (Believe it or not, eight colors is usually more than enough for any slide show.)

From the Format menu, choose Slide Color Scheme. The Slide Color Scheme dialog box appears. This is where it all begins. Figure 17.3 shows its contents.

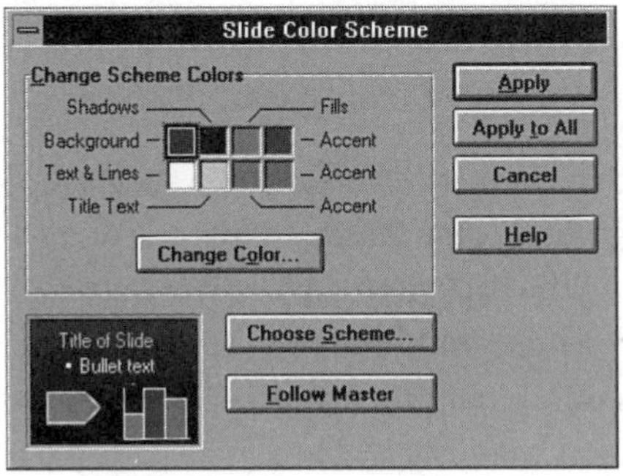

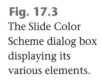

Fig. 17.3
The Slide Color Scheme dialog box displaying its various elements.

V

Output and Color

Before discussing the functions of the five buttons in the dialog box, let's dissect the eight-color basic palette shown in the dialog box. Notice that callouts are drawn in the dialog box, labeling each color. If we number the eight colors from left to right, they are listed in the dialog as described in table 17.1.

Table 17.1 The Slide Color Scheme Color Assignments	
Color #1 (Top Left)	Background color. Used to create the background fill colors for your slides.
Color #2 (Top, 2nd from Left)	The shadowing color used for text, graphic objects, and other items on your slides.
Color #3 (Top, 3rd from Left)	Default color fill from drawn objects.

(continues)

Table 17.1 Continued	
Color #4 (Top Right)	Accent color (used primarily for chart series items in the default)
Color #5 (Bottom Left)	Color assigned to body text on the slides, and to lines bordering drawn objects
Color #6 (Bottom, 2nd from Left)	Color assigned to titles on your slides
Color #7 (Bottom, 3rd from Left)	Accent color (used primarily for chart series items in the default)
Color #8 (Bottom Right)	Accent color (used primarily for chart series items in the default)

Effective color management begins with knowing the specific role of the eight colors found in the Slide Color Scheme dialog box.

You already learned in chapters 3 and 4 how a slide background color and a Slide Master's background color can be changed. Color #1 is that color. When you select a template, the background color sets the tone for the rest of the elements of your presentation. While you can change the background color at any time, bear in mind that other colors also may need to be changed to compensate. The colors that usually need to be adjusted in such a case are the Text & Lines color (Color #5) and the Title Text color (Color #6).

Also, when you select a new color scheme for your presentation, the background and text colors are the key colors selected and the other six colors are automatically assigned. You learn how to do this a little later.

The functions of the buttons in the Slide Color Scheme dialog box are described in table 17.2.

Table 17.2 The Slide Color Scheme Button Functions	
Apply button	Applies color changes to current slide and quits dialog box
Apply **t**o All button	Applies color changes to all slides and quits dialog box
Change C**o**lor button	Accesses color table and histogram to assign new colors

Choose **S**cheme button	Chooses a new color scheme (a full eight-color palette) for your presentation
Follow Master button	Resets current color scheme to that of the Slide Master color scheme (handy when you have selected a new color but don't want it after all)

You can activate the Slide Color Scheme and make your changes and color choices in three places: when viewing any slide in your presentation, when viewing the Slide Sorter, or when viewing the Slide Master.

Here's a very interesting point: While the Slide Master governs the color scheme for the overall presentation, you can use the color changing techniques you learn in this section to change the color scheme for an individual slide. Thus, one or two slides can have a completely different background color and also will likely need different text colors to match.

> **Note**
>
> A seldom-used but very intelligent way to manage multiple slide color schemes is to use the Slide Sorter view. Using the Sorter enables you to get the large view of where a different colored slide fits into the presentation. All the color changing features normally accessed in Slide view or the Slide Master can be exercised in the Sorter as well. For most of the examples in this chapter, Slide view or the Slide Master is used, but when you change the color scheme for just one slide in a presentation, Slide Sorter view is used to illustrate this principle.

Changing a Presentation's Color Scheme

Changing a color scheme should be defined as a separate process from simply changing a color. Changing a color scheme, as noted previously, requires changing two key elements: the background color and the text color.

To change the color scheme for an entire presentation, follow these steps:

1. From the **V**iew menu, choose **S**lides to change to Slide view.

   Because you are changing the color scheme for the entire presentation, it doesn't matter which slide you're currently displaying.

2. From the F**o**rmat menu, choose Slide **C**olor Scheme. The Slide Color Scheme dialog box appears.

   Do not be deceived by the title of the dialog box: A single slide or an entire presentation's color scheme can be changed here.

3. Click the Choose **S**cheme button. The Choose Scheme dialog box appears, as shown in figure 17.4.

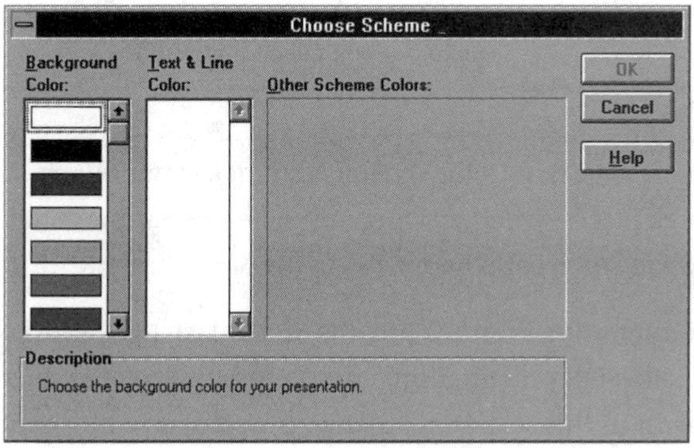

Fig. 17.4
The Choose Scheme dialog box.

There are only a few elements displayed, but they are very important for a clear understanding of how PowerPoint's color schemes work. The following list summarizes the Choose Scheme dialog box elements:

Background Color: Scrollable list of colors, one of which can be assigned as the background color for the color scheme. Ninety colors are available on the list—the same colors available on the Color Table.

Text & Line Color: This list is blank until a background color is selected. When that is done, a list of colors chosen by the program to match the background color appears. The number of colors offered varies according to the choice of the background color.

Other Scheme Colors: After choosing a text and line color, a set of four thumbnails is displayed. Each of the four thumbnails displays a different color scheme showing the choices of the other six colors made by the program for each color scheme. Clicking one of the four thumbnails selects the complete color scheme.

Notice that when the dialog appears, the **T**ext & Line Color and **O**ther Scheme Colors sections are blank.

4. Click on a **B**ackground Color. The list offers black, white, and 88 other colors.

The **T**ext & Line Color list displays a set of colors, one of which can be chosen and assigned to the text and lines slot for the color scheme. The

Text and Line list varies in the number of colors offered, depending on the background color selected. Most lists offer between eight and 12 colors.

5. Click on a **T**ext and Line color.

Some colors provide a good match for the background color and thus provide readable body text on your slides. PowerPoint makes an effort to select a group of colors that works with the background color, but colors by their very nature are mutable, and one person will see a particular color differently from another person. Some colors may not work quite as well as others. Use the thumbnails in the **O**ther Scheme Colors box to keep an eye on text color choices.

The **O**ther Scheme Colors thumbnail set appears, as shown in figure 17.5.

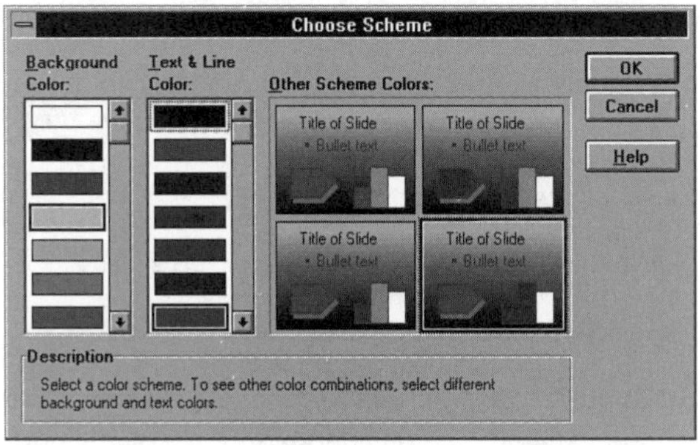

Tip

Check the text color results in the thumbnails to make sure your text color is readable against the background.

Fig. 17.5
The Choose Scheme dialog box displaying its various elements after color selections have been made.

The four thumbnails merit further examination. Instead of having to choose each additional color, you are offered a choice of four different schemes. Each scheme is displayed as a small slide thumbnail, and the various colored elements on the thumbnails display where each of the six additional colors are assigned, as shown in figure 17.6.

Within each thumbnail, the three small columns represent the three Accent colors that are automatically assigned to each scheme. The title at the top of each thumbnail reflects the new Title color. The polygon on the left side of each thumbnail shows the default fill color for drawn objects. Finally, the Shadow color is shown just behind the polygon, as a shadow, naturally.

Tip

Watch the Description area at the bottom of the Choose Scheme dialog box to provide clues about the steps you are following.

V

Output and Color

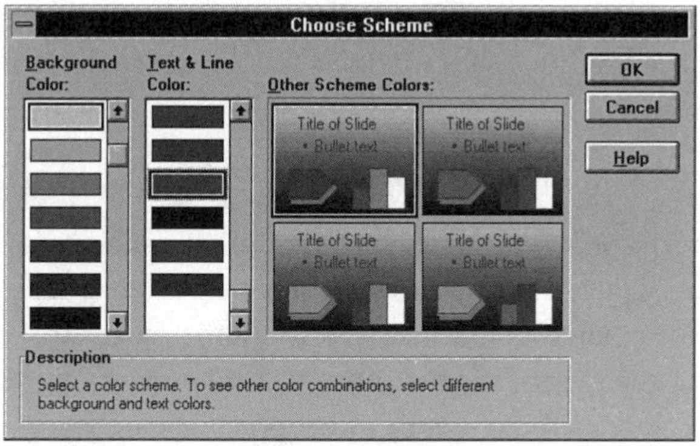

Fig. 17.6

The four color scheme thumbnails, each displaying the six additional colors for each scheme.

6. Click one of the four thumbnails to select it.

7. Choose OK or press Enter.

   The Slide Color Scheme dialog box reappears. Notice that the color scheme has changed to reflect your new choices.

8. Choose the Apply **t**o All button to apply the new color scheme to the entire presentation.

   A message pops up, reading:

   `Charts are being updated with the new color scheme`

   The Choose Scheme dialog box disappears.

   Choosing Apply **t**o All is the key to changing the entire presentation. If, when you're in Slide view, you choose only the **A**pply button, the new scheme is applied only to the currently displayed slide.

9. If the color scheme doesn't quite fit your taste when you're viewing the Slides again, choose the **U**ndo command from the **E**dit menu.

Changing a Slide's Color Scheme

The method for changing a single slide's color scheme is essentially the same as for the preceding example, which describes changing the color scheme for an entire presentation. In this example, the Slide Sorter view is used to demonstrate the utility of that feature in determining the placement of the slide containing the new color scheme. You start by displaying the Slide Sorter for the current presentation:

1. From the **V**iew menu, choose Sli**d**e Sorter.

The Slide Sorter screen appears, as shown in figure 17.7.

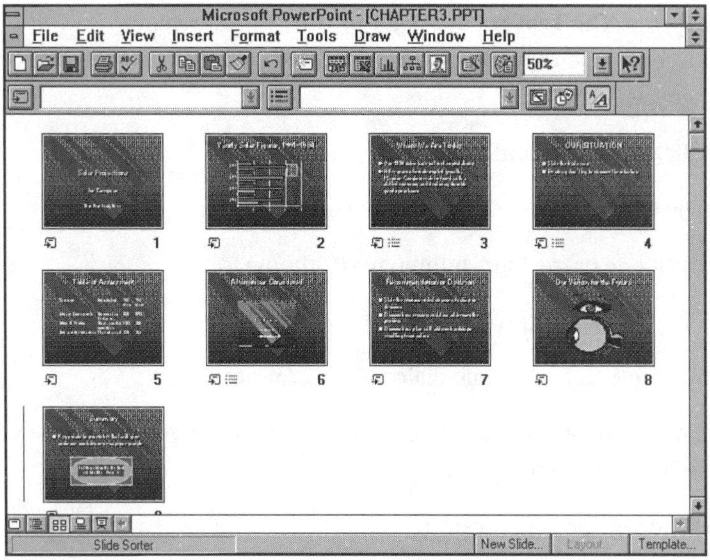

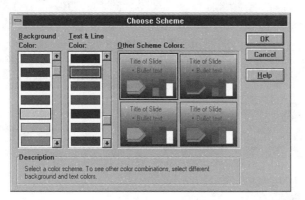

Fig. 17.7
The Slide Sorter
view displaying
the slides in the
presentation.

2. Click the slide whose color scheme you want to change.

3. From the Format menu, choose Slide Color Scheme. The Slide Color
   Scheme dialog box appears.

4. Click the Choose Scheme button. The Choose Scheme dialog box
   appears, as shown in figure 17.8.

Fig. 17.8
The Choose
Scheme dialog
box.

5. Click a Background Color. The list offers black, white, and 88 other
   colors.

The **T**ext & Line Color list now displays a set of colors, one of which can be chosen and assigned to the text and lines slot for the color scheme. The **T**ext & Line Color list varies in the number of colors offered, depending on the background color selected. Most lists offer between eight and 12 colors.

6. Click on a **T**ext and Line color.

   The **O**ther Scheme Colors thumbnail set appears.

7. Click one of the four thumbnails to choose it.

8. Choose OK or press Enter.

   The Slide Color Scheme dialog box reappears.

9. Choose the **A**pply button to apply the new color scheme to the slide selected in the Sorter.

   A message pops up, reading:

   `Charts are being updated with the new color scheme`

   The Choose Scheme dialog box disappears.

The Slide Sorter displays the new slide alongside the others, with the results resembling figure 17.9.

Fig. 17.9
The Slide Sorter showing the slide with the differing color scheme.

This slide's color scheme is different

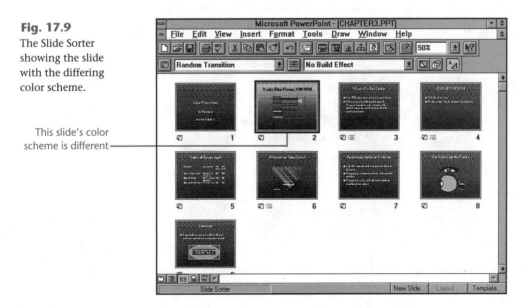

Now the slide has a different appearance, which can be an intelligent tactic to make it stand out and get the audience's attention. With a little imagination and discreet applications of color, you can ensure that your audience is never bored—and then you're halfway there.

Basic Color Theory: What Works and What Doesn't?

Modern PCs offer many temptations. Millions of colors are available to you. Almost every major software package offers a minimum of hundreds of colors in their basic palette. The quantity of colors may tempt the intrepid presentation maker into excess. PowerPoint's basic palette offers the first antidote to this possibility. Only eight colors are available in the basic palette. "Eight colors?" you may ask. "So what? I had that on my PC ten years ago!"

The crucial trick is not to please yourself. You must please your *audience*. The psychology of color is both subtle and powerful. Considering your audience and thinking ahead is what gets that crucial P.O. signed and on your desk. Consider the psychology and world view of the people who will see your presentation, and you may well get the edge you need to succeed.

Keep It Simple

The first key point, *keep it simple,* is nearly universal in any field of human endeavor, and it definitely applies to presentation design and the use of color. Drowning a slide in vibrant colors can have precisely the opposite effect from that intended. As you've just seen, PowerPoint automatically provides some levels of effective color management without intruding on the user. In most situations, it may be best to follow the guidelines and color schemes offered by the program.

Watch Your Color Schemes Carefully

The second key point: *Govern your color schemes wisely*. As you've just seen, it is possible to apply different color schemes to each slide. In most situations, this may not be a good idea. Consider that the vast majority of your slides (perhaps 70 percent) are simple text slides with bulleted lists. How do you think your audience would feel if you changed the background and text colors for every successive slide? I think *impatience* would be a kind word for it.

A corollary to this point is that shifting gears with a slide possessing a different color scheme can sometimes be a good idea, particularly if you pass between two different kinds of subject matter and you want to provide an effective transition. It can also work if you want to forcefully bring attention to a chart illustrating a crucial point during your presentation. Just don't go overboard.

Tailor Your Color Schemes to Your Audience

The third key point: Color schemes can be *tailored* to your audience. For example, if you are addressing an audience from a foreign country, try to make them feel more at home by using their national colors as a base for your presentation's color palette. How do you find this out? Check a world Atlas in either book form or in CD-ROM.

Different corporate environments can require different approaches too. In general, you may expect marketing and public relations executives to respond more warmly to a flashy and strikingly colored presentation (at least within limits) than a board of directors or upper management group of a Fortune 500 corporation. Also, company cultures vary widely regardless of the department you're addressing. Take a few minutes to do some detective work to find out a general cultural sketch of the people you are presenting to.

Watch Your Fonts and Color Schemes in Text Slides

Point four is the most specific tip: *Text slides work best with highly contrasting color schemes*. A good rule of thumb is to use yellow or light blue text against a dark background. Also, go easy on the fonts, and use conservative typefaces that are generally accepted by Corporate America, such as Times Roman, Helvetica, Garamond, and Palatino. As with colors, modern PCs offer every typeface conceived throughout the history of printing and moveable type, and it is easy to succumb to the siren song of ornate and striking typefaces for your slides. Use them very sparingly.

PowerPoint uses two different color mixing systems to help you create new colors for your palettes: Hue-Saturation-Luminance (HSL) and Red-Green-Blue (RGB). In the last section of this chapter, "Changing Palette Colors," we describe the PowerPoint color systems and how to create custom colors for your presentation.

Troubleshooting

My color schemes look crude and unattractive.

This is probably no fault of Windows, but of the video card and monitor that you use on your system. You may be running Windows in its default VGA display mode, which is 640 × 480 resolution at 16 colors. That does lend a crude appearance to even the most sophisticated of presentations. Fortunately, many Windows systems are capable of much more. You should run Windows at a minimum of 256 colors for on-screen presentations, for one thing. It's possible to display as many as 16 million colors in Windows and in PowerPoint. This lends a beautiful accuracy to color shadings and other effects within the program.

You should also consider using higher screen resolutions than 640 × 480. On-screen slide shows can look extremely sleek and readable and show much greater detail at 1024 × 768 or 1280 × 1024 screen resolution. A huge number of current video cards (also called *Windows Accelerators*, because they can also boost Windows performance) routinely support those dramatically higher resolutions. Even an 800 × 600 screen shows a dramatic improvement. Most modern Windows machines easily run 800 × 600 at 256 colors, and this is the minimum standard I recommend for pleasing visuals in PowerPoint.

Video cards usually come with a set of Windows software drivers for higher resolutions and color depths. Make sure you have access to these drivers. They make it possible to run Windows the way it should be run. Check your Windows and video card documentation for more information on video settings and how to run them.

My fonts aren't readable on-screen.

It's quite likely that you have your TrueType fonts turned off. To enable them, double-click the Control Panel application in the Windows Program Manager. Then, double-click the Fonts icon. When the Fonts dialog box appears, click the **T**rueType button. If there isn't an X inside the Enable TrueType Fonts check box, click on it. After clicking the check box to enable it, press Enter, and then press Enter again. TrueType now is running. If your fonts still aren't working right, you may need to reinstall them.

V

Output and Color

Applying Colors to Individual Objects

Unlike more generalized color schemes, applying colors to individual objects can be considered an open field of play. Essentially, for colors, shading, and pattern fills of drawn objects, you can use every color you could possibly display under Windows.

Most of the exercises in the rest of this chapter are quite straightforward. To begin, here's another look at the Drawing+ toolbar (see table 17.3). You also use some of the tools on the Drawing toolbar. To review the tools on the Drawing toolbar, refer to chapter 9, "Drawing Objects."

Table 17.3   The Drawing+ Toolbar

Button	Name	Description
	Fill Color	Drop-down list to apply a different fill color from either the eight colors offered or from a larger color palette
	Line Color	Drop-down list to apply a different line color from either the eight colors offered or from a larger color palette
	Shadow Color	Drop-down list to apply a different shadow color from either the eight colors offered or from a larger color palette
	Line Style	Drop-down list to apply a different line style (thickness or line weight, or double line)
	Dashed Lines	Drop-down list to apply a dashed line style
	Arrow Heads	Drop-down list to apply an arrowhead for either end or both ends of a line (available only if a drawn line or arc is selected)
	Bring Forward	A layering tool used to bring a selected drawn object forward over others in its area (handy when you have several drawn graphic objects piled over each other)
	Send Backward	A layering tool used to send a graphic object back down each layer when you're finished editing or changing it
	Group	Group, or collect, a number of selected drawing objects together into one selectable object (PowerPoint's ClipArt Library contains many examples of this technique)
	Ungroup	The reverse of the Group command, this tool takes one object composed of a number of drawing objects and breaks them up into their individually drawn parts (PowerPoint clip art objects can be operated on and changed in this way)
	Rotate Left	Rotate the selected drawn object by 90 degrees to the left

Button	Name	Description
![Rotate Right icon]	Rotate Right	Rotate the selected drawn object by 90 degrees to the right
![Flip Horizontal icon]	Flip Horizontal	Flip the selected drawn object by 180 degrees horizontally
![Flip Vertical icon]	Flip Vertical	Flip the selected drawn object by 180 degrees vertically

The key tools for altering colors in drawn objects are the Fill Color, Line Color, and Shadow Color tools in the Drawing+ toolbar.

Changing the Color of an Object

Figure 17.10 shows a typical slide, designed for the purpose of adding graphic objects for embellishment. Starting with this exercise, you go beyond the basic palettes offered in the drawing tools to select colors from a wider palette.

To change the color of an object, follow these steps:

1. Click the Rectangle tool on the Drawing toolbar.

2. Draw a simple rectangle on the slide that resembles figure 17.10.

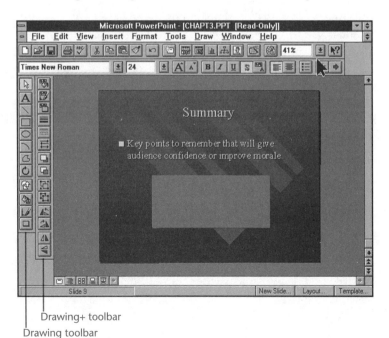

Fig. 17.10
Drawing a rectangle. The drawn object uses the default fill color from the template palette.

Drawing+ toolbar
Drawing toolbar

3. Click the rectangle to select it.

4. Click the Fill Color tool on the Drawing+ toolbar.

   The drop-down palette menu appears, as shown in figure 17.11.

Fig. 17.11
The Fill Color
palette.

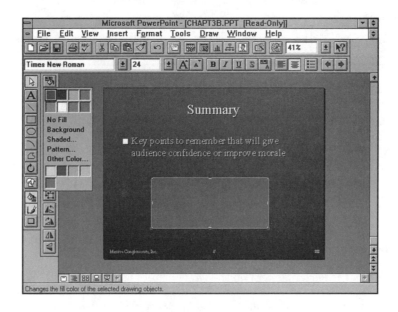

The Other Colors used, as shown in figure 17.11, are colors that have
been selected for use beyond the basic eight-color palette. You can display up to eight more colors of this type in the drop-down list. When
more "other" colors are chosen, the first color added rotates out.

> **Note**
>
> Notice that in figure 17.11, the Fill Color is highlighted in the drop-down
> palette. It corresponds to the default color applied to the selected object.

5. Click the Other Color menu option on the drop-down palette.

   The Other Color dialog box appears, as shown in figure 17.12.

   The Other Color palette (previously called the Color Table in
   PowerPoint 3) is the same palette that was briefly glanced at in
   previous chapters.

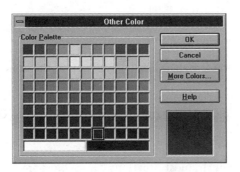

Fig. 17.12
The Other Color palette with eleven columns of colors, each spanning a range of values for one specific color. The top row shows basic hues.

The palette is arranged in 11 columns of eight swatches each. Each set of eight swatches comes under the heading of one color type, as described in table 17.4.

Table 17.4 Color Swatches in the Other Color Palette	
Color	**Column**
Gray	1
Red	2
Orange	3
Yellow-Orange	4
Yellow	5
Yellow-Green	6
Green	7
Blue-Green	8
Blue	9
Violet	10
Red-Violet	11

The rows are numbered one through eight, of course, but row #1 is on the bottom of the palette and row #8 is on top. Row #8 contains the basic hues for each color range, and rows #7 through #1 increase in intensity as you progress down the column. When you click any color swatch, its name (Red #8, Yellow #7, and so on) appears on the status bar at the bottom of the PowerPoint screen.

Two larger swatches, black and white, rest on the bottom of the palette.

6. For the current exercise, choose Blue #4. By double-clicking the swatch, you select the color and apply it to the rectangle. The Other Color dialog box disappears.

Using Shaded Color. In most situations, basic colors are adequate for any task. In others, special graphics effects, such as shading or pattern fills, can be employed for an artistic touch to a simple drawing.

To apply shading to the selected object, follow these steps:

1. Select the rectangle for color changes.

2. Click the Fill Color tool on the Drawing+ toolbar.

   The drop-down palette menu appears.

3. Choose the Shaded option from the drop-down menu.

   The Shaded Fill dialog box appears, as shown in figure 17.13.

Fig. 17.13
The Shaded Fill
dialog box.

The Shaded Fill dialog box displays a couple of options that may be familiar to you from earlier chapters: the Shade Styles option button list and the shading Variants, which displays four thumbnails showing different orientations for the same fill type. The Color button is a drop-down menu of the same type as that for the Fill Color tool, which gives you access to the basic eight-color palette and also to the Other Color palette from which you can choose any color for the background, and the **D**ark-Light slider bar, which enables you to change the brightness or darkness of the selected object.

4. Click the top-right shading Variant.

5. Choose OK or press Enter.

The result resembles figure 17.14. As you can see, it is not hard to add effects to a drawn object.

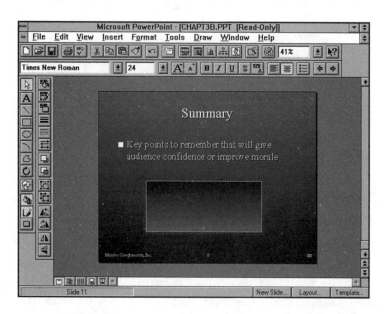

Fig. 17.14
The shaded rectangle.

Note

To add an embossed effect to a graphic, draw an ellipse or other shape on top of the rectangle (using the rectangle as a guide for your drawing cursor to ensure the ellipse is in proportion to the rectangle), change the color to the same as the rectangle, and add a shading Variant that runs in the opposite direction.

Using Pattern Fills. PowerPoint offers a selection of 36 pattern fills that can be applied to any selected object. Pattern fills are applied from the Fill Color tool's drop-down menu, and can be combined with any desired color.

To add a pattern fill to a drawn object, follow these steps:

1. Select the object for pattern filling.

2. Click the Fill Color tool on the Drawing+ toolbar.

   The drop-down palette menu appears.

3. Choose the Pattern option from the drop-down menu.

   The Pattern Fill dialog box appears, as shown in figure 17.15.

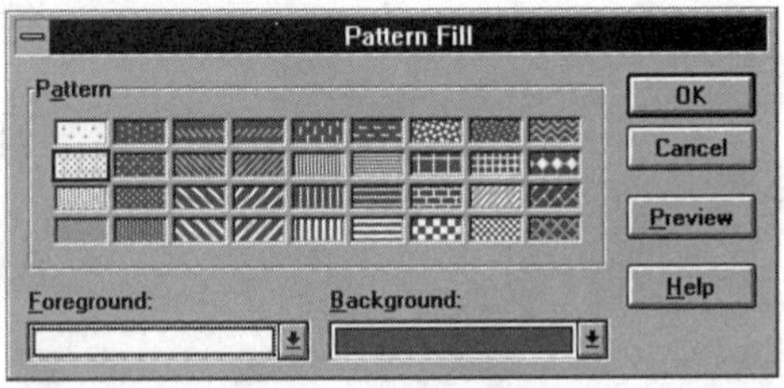

Fig. 17.15
The Pattern Fill
dialog box.

4. Choose the foreground and background colors by pulling down their respective palettes. The Other Colors dialog box can be used for each option as well.

   The foreground color is the color that the actual pattern assumes. The background color should be chosen so that the pattern stands out effectively. (In some cases, a well-chosen pattern and background color may actually resemble another color. That's an area where a lot of experimenting would be needed.)

5. Choose a pattern from the palette.

6. Click the **P**review button to view the effect of the pattern on the object before you apply it.

7. Choose OK or press Enter.

   If you select a pattern for a Shaded object, the shading is canceled and cannot be recovered or combined with the pattern fill.

Changing Line Colors

To change line colors for the selected object, follow these steps:

1. Click the Line Color tool in the Drawing+ toolbar.

The Line Color drop-down palette appears, showing the same color palette as that for the Fill Color tool (see fig. 17.16).

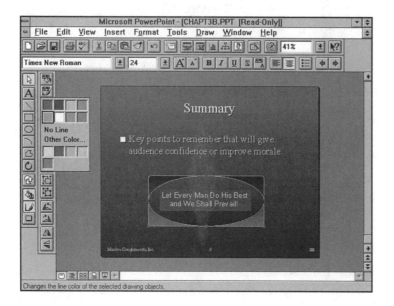

Fig. 17.16
The Line Color drop-down palette.

2. Choose any of the colors displayed or choose the Other Color option. The Other Color palette dialog box appears.

3. Choose from among the 90 color swatches in the palette (as described and shown in fig. 17.12 and table 17.3).

4. Choose OK or press Enter.

Adding a Shadow and Changing Shadow Colors

Adding a basic shadow and changing the color of a shadow is a simple process, and the latter process is almost identical to changing the color for a regular drawn object. Just make sure that the shadow color you choose is appropriate for the effect you are trying to achieve.

To quickly create an embossed shadow effect, follow these steps:

1. Click the Shadow Color tool in the Drawing+ toolbar.

   The Shadow Color drop-down menu appears, showing the same color palette as that for the Fill Color tool (see fig. 17.17)

Fig. 17.17
The Shadow
Color palette.

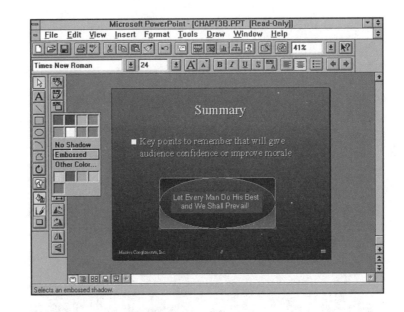

2. Choose the Embossed menu option. This places a subtle shadowing effect on the selected object, based on the same color as the selected object.

   If you select the Other Color option, you are, in effect, choosing the standard type of shadowing (not embossing), to which any typical color can be applied.

To change shadow colors for the selected object, follow these steps:

1. Click the Shadow Color tool in the Drawing+ toolbar.

2. Choose any of the colors displayed, or choose the Other Color option. The Other Color palette dialog box appears.

3. Choose from among the 90 color swatches in the palette (as described and shown in fig. 17.12 and table 17.3).

4. Choose OK or press Enter.

As you can see, once you learn the process of changing colors for one graphic element, such as a drawn object fill or line style, or shadowing, it's pretty much the same for all. The same color palettes are used and the procedures are the same. Nonetheless, PowerPoint offers more options for creating custom shadows, which you explore next.

To add a custom shadow effect to any selected graphic or text object, follow these steps:

1. Select the desired object.

2. From the Format menu, choose **Sh**adow.

   The Shadow dialog box appears (see fig. 17.18) displaying the Color drop-down list and the following options buttons for Offset:

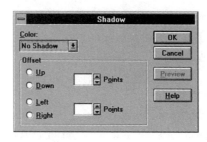

Tip
Shadows should generally be as dark or darker than the object they are laid behind.

Fig. 17.18
The Shadow dialog box.

Up: Raise the shadow offset above the object margin by the specified number of points.

Down: Lower the shadow offset below the object margin by the specified number of points.

Left: Set shadow offset to the left of the object margin by the specified number of points.

Right: Set shadow offset to the right of the object margin by the specified number of points.

The Offset option buttons specify how much shadowing to add. The up and down offsets and the left and right offsets are paired alternatives that are adjusted upward or downward by point size to lengthen or diminish the shadow.

3. Adjust the shadow to the desired level (it may take some experimenting to get it right).

4. If you want to apply a different color (different from the template default shadow color) to the shadow, click the drop-down arrow icon under the **C**olor option. The drop-down menu appears.

   The **C**olor drop-down list, shown in figure 17.19, functions the same as for the other examples in this chapter.

V

Output and Color

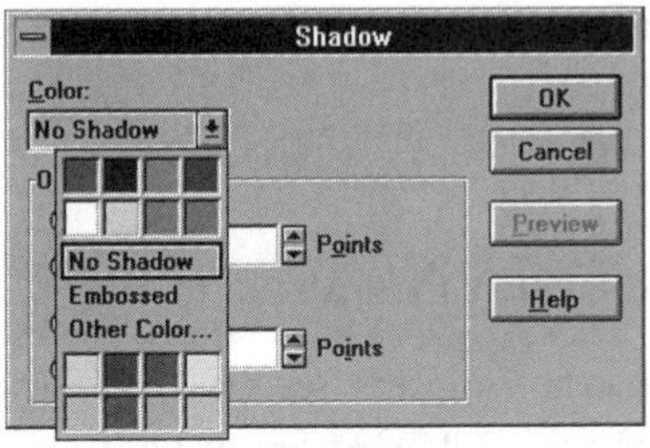

Fig. 17.19

The Shadow dialog box displaying the drop-down color menu.

5. Choose the desired color from either the drop-down palette or from the Other Color dialog box.

6. Choose OK or press Enter.

Changing the Text Color

Text objects on a slide offer two ways to work with color: change the color of the text itself or add a color fill, shading, or pattern fill to the text object background. In the first case, you are formatting the font itself; in the second, it's a matter of a simple color fill like the earlier exercises.

To change the color of title or body text on a slide, follow these steps:

1. Click and drag the mouse over the text in the text object to highlight it.

2. From the Format menu, choose Font.

   The Font dialog box appears, as shown in figure 17.20.

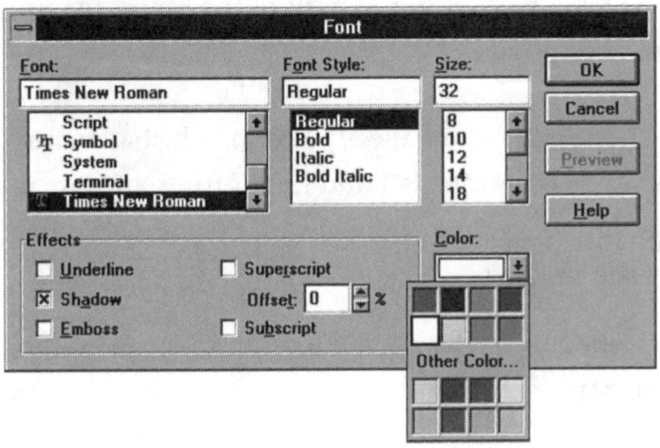

Fig. 17.20

The Font dialog box showing the drop-down color menu.

3. Click the drop-down arrow icon under the Color option. The drop-down menu appears.

4. Choose a color from the available palette colors, or choose the Other Color option and follow the steps described in the previous exercises.

5. Choose OK or press Enter.

To change the background color or fill of the text object, follow these steps:

1. Click once on the text object.

2. Click the Fill Color tool on the Drawing+ toolbar.

3. Select a color from the drop-down palette or choose the Other Color menu option. The Other Color dialog box, displaying the color palette, appears.

4. Choose a color from the palette.

5. Choose OK or press Enter.

Changing Palette Colors

The Other Color palette (refer to fig. 17.12) has another button that we haven't yet explored in detail. The **M**ore Colors button brings you to PowerPoint's deepest level of color manipulation and selection. PowerPoint's More Colors dialog box offers an extremely flexible and sensitive method for adjusting colors to a precise value (see fig. 17.21).

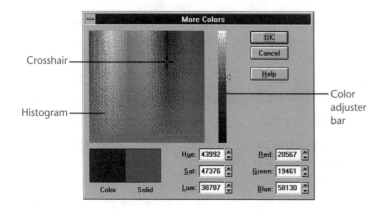

Fig. 17.21
The More Colors palette.

As noted much earlier in this chapter, PowerPoint uses two different color mixing systems for custom color creation: HSL (Hue-Saturation-Luminance) and RGB (Red-Green-Blue). How do the two color mixes work? What are the color swatches? And what is Hue-Saturation-Luminance?

Tip
You can also add shading, shadowing, and other effects to text object backgrounds, just as you can to graphic objects.

V

Output and Color

Hue	The hue is simply the color shown in the Color swatch. The hue determines the basic color, such as green, blue, orange, etc.
Saturation	Provides the basic vividness or purity of a color. More gray in a color, less saturation; less gray, more saturation.
Luminance	The degree of lightness or darkness in a color, which is created by mixing black and white in differing degrees to the color.

These three quantities are mixed together to create the colors you see in the Other Color palette, and all colors you see in PowerPoint.

HSL and RGB are very similar to each other; RGB is simply the mixture of the pure red, green, and blue brightness values to produce a mixed color. The red, green, and blue values are measured from 0 to 65,535 in PowerPoint. The HSL values are measured from 0 to 65,520. RGB, essentially, determines the brightness of the red, green, and blue *light* and is a result of the relative brightness of these three values. Think of a TV set, which uses the exact same system to produce its photo-realistic images. A TV set has three guns: red, green, and blue. Each shoots out light of their respective color. If a color gun fails in your TV set, you immediately notice the change in the color quality of your screen. The RGB color system works exactly the same way.

Tip

When you mix a color that is pleasing to you, write down the red-green-blue values so that you can reproduce the color value in other work.

Individual Red-Green-Blue and Hue-Saturation-Luminance values can be adjusted using the up- and down-arrow icons next to each text box. You can also type in specific values—in fact, whenever you create a color that pleases you or is meant to be used in other presentations, make a note of the red, green, and blue values so that you won't lose them and can quickly apply them to new jobs.

The histogram represents the entire color range supported by the VGA card or Windows accelerator in your computer. The crosshair located on the histogram is dragged by the mouse to change the color. When you do so, release the mouse; the RGB and HSL values change dynamically.

The color adjuster bar to the right of the histogram also dynamically changes to reflect the colors over which the crosshair passes. The small arrowhead on the adjuster bar is dragged to change the luminance on the selected color. Notice that when you drag the arrowhead up and down, hue and saturation values stay the same and the luminance value changes. The red, green, and blue values also change because when you change the luminance, you are also changing the quantity of "light" displayed in the color, from brighter to darker or vice versa.

The two color swatches at the bottom left of the dialog box are labeled Color and Solid. The Color swatch is simply the basic hue the color mix is based on. The Solid swatch is the actual mixed color produced when values are changed or the crosshair on the histogram is moved. It represents a color that is actually supported by your computer's display hardware. When you drag the crosshairs on the histogram, you can watch the two swatches change their color.

To add a custom color to a slide object, follow these steps:

1. Select the object to which you wish to add a custom color.

2. Click the Fill Color tool on the Drawing+ toolbar.

   The drop-down palette menu appears.

3. Choose the Other Color option. The Other Color palette dialog box appears.

4. Click one of the color swatches in the palette that most closely approximates the custom color you want to create.

5. Click the **M**ore Colors button in the dialog box. The More Colors dialog box appears.

6. Adjust the values to the level desired, or type in the Red-Green-Blue or Hue-Saturation-Luminance values desired.

7. Choose OK or press Enter.

   The Other Color dialog box shows the custom color in the thumbnail at the bottom right.

8. Choose OK or press Enter.

   The new color is applied to the selected object. The custom color has a new swatch displayed in the Other Color color set, shown in the Fill Color drop-down menu (see fig. 17.22).

Fig. 17.22
The Fill Color
palette.

The new color
swatch is
placed here

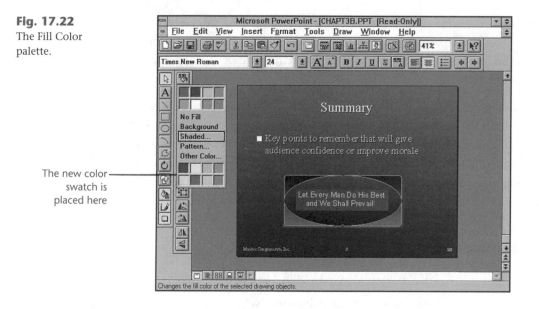

Although you clicked a color swatch in the Other Color palette to begin your custom color creation, the original palette swatch is preserved.

Clicking an object that already has a custom color fill applied (or a custom line color, shadow color, or what have you) displays the custom color in the thumbnail of the Other Color palette. Selecting the More Colors button brings up the histogram with the custom color displayed for adjustment.

Troubleshooting

I can't find all the color tools I need.

Most of the tools that are used for color fills, shading, shadowing, applying line weights and line colors, and so on are located in the Drawing+ toolbar, which is not typically displayed when you start to use PowerPoint. Use the **T**oolbars command under the **V**iew menu to make sure all the toolbars you need are displayed on-screen. The Drawing+ toolbar is enabled here.

I've screwed up my color scheme by applying the wrong color to all my slides.

You probably used the Apply **t**o All command button when you changed a color in the palette for the current slide. The trick in using the Slide **C**olor Scheme command in the F**o**rmat menu is to understand the difference between the **A**pply and Apply **t**o All buttons in the Slide Color Scheme dialog box. If you hit Apply **t**o All, you can place the new background color, object color fill, or other palette color in many places where you don't want it to be.

When this happens, the system probably takes a minute to make all the changes. The screen message Charts are being updated with the new color scheme will probably also appear.

After that's done, *before you do anything else*, make sure you choose the Undo command from the Edit menu. The screen message reappears, and your changes are undone.

From Here...

Color is a sophisticated tool, and a realm of knowledge unto itself. While you dug into some principles of color theory and techniques for using color in this chapter, you still have only glanced at the basics.

- Chapter 19, "Using Advanced Charting Features," discusses increasingly sophisticated chart types and the process of creating and saving custom chart types for use in future presentations.

- Chapter 21, "Using Advanced Color, Text, and Drawing Features," offers more tips about using color in your presentations and the process of creating a color scheme from scratch by using some of the features presented in this chapter.

V

Output and Color

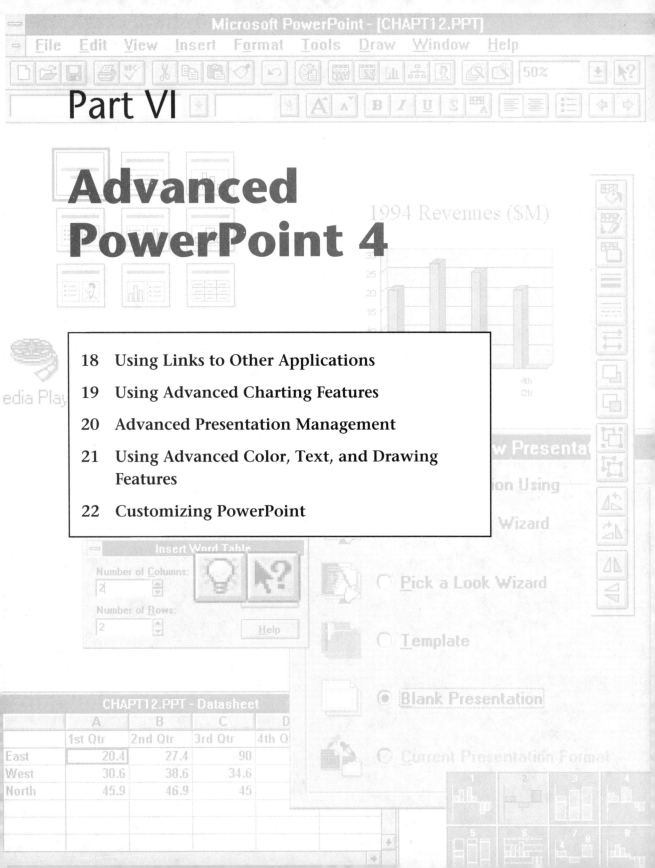

Part VI

Advanced PowerPoint 4

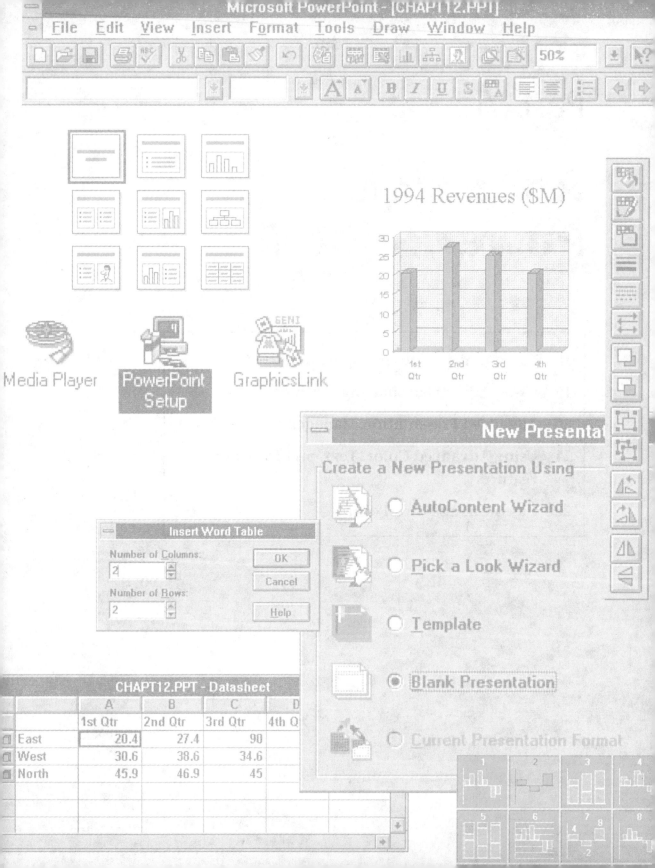

Chapter 18

Using Links to Other Applications

PowerPoint 4 offers enhanced capabilities for linking and exchanging different kinds of data from other applications to a presentation. If you change the data in the other application program, PowerPoint updates the linked data in the presentation file. The process is called Object Linking and Embedding (OLE, or Oh-Lay).

The term *object* can be quite deceptive and confusing. First of all, anything you work with in PowerPoint is an object—whether it is a simple piece of artwork, a chart created in Microsoft Graph, or a chunk of body text in a slide. Objects in a PowerPoint presentation are held in place by *placeholders*. Placeholders reserve space in the slide for the particular object type they're supposed to hold. They are resizable and moveable within the confines of the slide.

But objects aren't just items created in PowerPoint. Objects are also items that are created *in other programs*. This is where the true power of objects in PowerPoint asserts itself.

Understanding Object Linking and Embedding (OLE)

Object linking and embedding is one of Microsoft Windows most popular and powerful facilities. It enables users to combine various types of data into one document and to have instant access to any of the applications that originally created that data—without the tedious starting and restarting of

In this chapter, you learn the following:

■ To understand the two versions of object linking and embedding

■ How to link objects from other programs into your PowerPoint presentation

■ How to embed objects from other programs into your presentation

■ How to use drag and drop between files and applications in PowerPoint

VI

Advanced PowerPoint 4

programs or repetitive cutting and pasting of data into the Windows clipboard.

Tip
OLE comes in two versions: 1.0 and 2.0.

The issue of object linking and embedding is much more complicated to explain than it is to actually use. Adding complexity to the issue is the fact that there are now two types of OLE to deal with—OLE 1.0, which Windows applications have supported for a few years now, and the new OLE 2.0, also called "editing in place," that Windows applications such as Word 6 for Windows, Excel 5, and PowerPoint 4 support.

PowerPoint 4 works equally well with both types of object linking and embedding, and you learn how to take advantage of both types in this chapter. It's important to bear in mind that as flashy as OLE 2.0 is (you see why a little later), most current application programs do not support it outside of Microsoft's high-powered Word, Excel, and PowerPoint applications suite. Those other programs generally do support OLE 1.0, which has been around for awhile. Therefore, out of necessity, OLE 1.0 gets as much attention in this chapter as the new version.

The two versions of OLE can both be powerful tools for you. Though understanding them takes a little time to master, you will find the results in productivity gains and flexibility to be well worth it.

Object *linking* and object *embedding* are two different processes that have subtle but important differences. If you are using the older version of OLE (which many of your Windows applications support), double-clicking an Excel chart or spreadsheet that has been placed into a PowerPoint slide brings up the Excel program and displays the chart or spreadsheet, ready for editing. This is called editing an *embedded* object.

You can either create an embedded object from scratch or embed an existing file into your presentation. Any embedded object, whether an Excel chart, a CorelDRAW! picture, or a sound waveform, when double-clicked in PowerPoint, brings up the application program that originally created it.

Tip
Many currently released Windows applications only support OLE 1.0, so in-place editing is not available with them.

One advantage of embedding objects into your PowerPoint files is that when you bring your presentation file to another location, all the embedded objects are taken along for the ride—without having to bring all the original object files with you. All the objects are lodged and present in your PowerPoint file. (This does create a much bigger PowerPoint file, however.)

On the other hand, Excel 4.0, CorelDRAW! 4.0, and many other programs do *not* appear when attempting to edit a linked object from within PowerPoint. Linking an object in OLE 1.0 means that you have a *copy* of any picture or other things in multiple documents—say, a specific CorelDRAW! picture in five or six different PowerPoint presentations—and if you modify that picture *from within CorelDRAW!*, all your PowerPoint presentations that contain that picture are automatically updated.

Embedding, on the other hand, requires that when you modify an object in its original program, that object must be reembedded in each file that contains it, or the changes in the object will not appear in the files.

On the other hand, double-clicking a linked object from an OLE 1.0 program in PowerPoint 4.0 simply brings up the other program in a separate window. Also, to transport a PowerPoint presentation file containing linked objects, the presentation file and all the separate files containing the linked objects (CorelDRAW! and Excel files and the like) must all be transferred as a group with the presentation.

Applications that support OLE usually divide into two camps: "clients" and "servers." OLE *client* programs can accept or receive objects such as Excel charts, CorelDRAW! pictures, or other application data types, and allow double-clicking the object for use of the original program, but OLE client programs do not send objects out to other OLE-compliant programs. Desktop publishing programs are typical examples of this. On the other hand, programs such as Excel or CorelDRAW!, because they can send objects to other applications, are called OLE *servers*. Some Windows programs, like PowerPoint 4.0, support both client and server functions.

Now that those issues are settled (at least hopefully so), let's add another level of complexity to this discussion: OLE 2.0.

Tip
Linking and embedding are two very different processes. Beware!

Using OLE 2.0

PowerPoint 4 supports OLE 2.0, which enables you to edit objects from other programs in the same window without having to switch back and forth between them. Microsoft's new versions of PowerPoint (4.0), Word for Windows (6.0), and Excel (5.0) all support OLE 2.0, and future versions of applications programs from other software companies *may* also support OLE 2.0.

When using OLE 2.0, PowerPoint's menus and toolbars are temporarily replaced by those of the other application program that originally created the object. This is called *in-place editing*. You have already used this technique many times, especially in creating charts in PowerPoint, because Microsoft Graph, the program which you use for that purpose, is actually a separate application and an OLE 2.0-compliant program. Graph is an OLE server program. Every time you use Graph to create charts and paste them back onto a slide or to modify an existing chart, Graph quickly replaces PowerPoint's menus and toolbars with its own set.

Strangely enough, when you create an organizational chart, as you did in chapter 15, "Creating Organizational Charts," you use Microsoft's Organizational Chart program, which is *not* an OLE 2.0 server program. It's an OLE 1.0-compliant program.

Using Visual Editing (Editing in Place)

Embedding and linking work essentially the same way in OLE 2.0 as they do in the previous version of OLE, except that when you edit an *embedded* object on PowerPoint that originates from an OLE 2.0-compliant program, you do not see the other application program window pop up. Instead, you edit the object in its original application without leaving the PowerPoint window. *Editing in place* means, in effect, that you can have five or six application programs all using the same window, without having all six application programs open at the same time or even having any of the other ones running.

Because of the variety of applications software supporting one or more versions of OLE, and the likelihood that very few users have a complete library of OLE-compliant applications (much less OLE 2.0-compliant), the exercises in the rest of this chapter are mostly nonspecific, and teach only how to link and embed objects from other programs in a generic fashion.

Working with Other OLE 2.0 Applications

On PowerPoint's most basic level, it's easy to create and use objects from other programs. PowerPoint's Standard toolbar offers two quick tools for doing so.

PowerPoint's Insert Microsoft Word Table tool enables you to create a table using the Microsoft Word for Windows application program for embedding into a PowerPoint slide. Using this tool requires that Microsoft Word 6 for Windows be installed on your system. Using the tool does not work for version 2 or earlier versions of WinWord.

PowerPoint's Insert Microsoft Excel Worksheet tool enables you to create a typical Excel worksheet for embedding into a PowerPoint slide. Using this tool requires an installed copy of Excel 5 on your system, and earlier versions of Excel cannot be activated with this tool.

Creating an Embedded Object

Assuming that the latest version of Word is installed on your system, here is the method for how to embed objects from that program. It's a good example for two reasons: A tool is provided for fast access to the program from PowerPoint, and it provides a good demonstration of the power of OLE 2.0.

To insert a Word 6 table, make sure you're in PowerPoint's Slide view, and follow these steps:

1. Click the Insert Microsoft Word Table tool on the PowerPoint Standard toolbar.

   A drop-down 4-by-5-cell Table tool appears, as shown in figure 18.1.

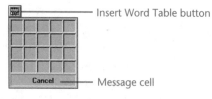

Insert Word Table button

Cancel —— Message cell

Fig. 18.1
The drop-down Table tool, which appears after clicking the Insert Word Table button.

2. Drag the mouse down and across from the top-left cell in the pop-down tool. By doing so, you are defining the number of table entries to be created in the table. As you drag, the message cell at the bottom of the table tool shows the selected table size: 3 X 3, 4 X 3, or whatever the selection is.

3. Release the mouse. After a moment, during which PowerPoint starts the Word for Windows application program, PowerPoint's toolbars and menu bar disappear and are replaced by Word's toolbars and menu bar, as shown in figure 18.2.

   The PowerPoint slide is still displayed on-screen, but the Word screen elements and a new Word table also appear on-screen.

VI

Advanced PowerPoint 4

Fig. 18.2

The PowerPoint screen showing the Microsoft Word for Windows toolbars and menu bar.

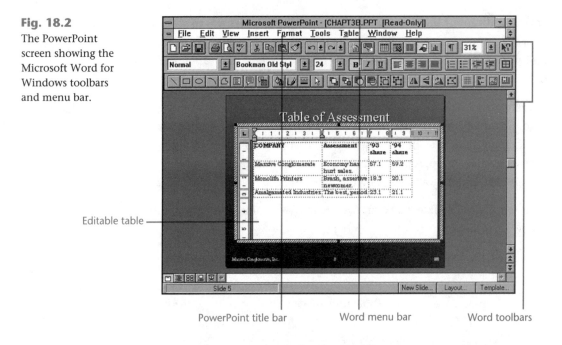

Editable table

PowerPoint title bar   Word menu bar   Word toolbars

> **Note**
>
> For more information on Word's table editing and formatting, please see Que's *Using Word Version 6 for Windows,* Special Edition, *Word for Windows Version 6 Quick Reference*, or Microsoft's documentation.

4. After editing and formatting the table, click the PowerPoint slide anywhere outside the table object you just edited and it is inserted into your slide as a text object with the color and font defaults assigned to it from within PowerPoint, as shown in figure 18.3.

The method for using Excel 5 to insert datasheet objects into a PowerPoint slide is identical to that for Word 6 except for the actual editing mechanics and data type of the program.

To insert an Excel 5 table, make sure you're in PowerPoint's Slide view, and follow these steps:

1. Click the Insert Excel Datasheet tool on the PowerPoint Standard toolbar.

   A drop-down 4-by-5-cell datasheet tool appears.

2. Drag the mouse down and across from the top left cell in the drop-down tool. By doing so, you are defining the number of rows and columns of cells to be created in the datasheet. As you drag, the message cell at the bottom of the table tool shows the selected datasheet size: 3 X 3, 4 X 3, or whatever the selection is.

3. Release the mouse. After a moment, during which PowerPoint starts the Excel 5 application program, PowerPoint's toolbars and menu bar disappear and are replaced by Excel's toolbars and menu bar.

4. After editing and formatting the table, click the PowerPoint slide anywhere outside the datasheet object you have just edited. The datasheet is inserted into your slide.

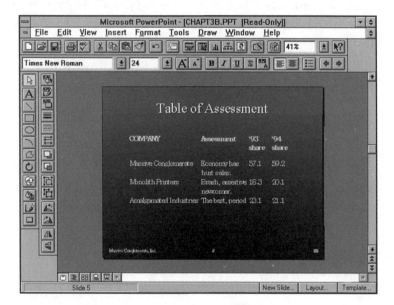

Fig. 18.3
The PowerPoint screen showing the embedded Microsoft Word for Windows table.

There is another way to create a new embedded object: by using the Insert Object command. To do so, follow these steps:

1. From the **I**nsert menu, choose **O**bject.

   The Insert Object dialog box appears, as shown in figure 18.4.

2. If not already selected, click the Create **N**ew option button.

VI

Advanced PowerPoint 4

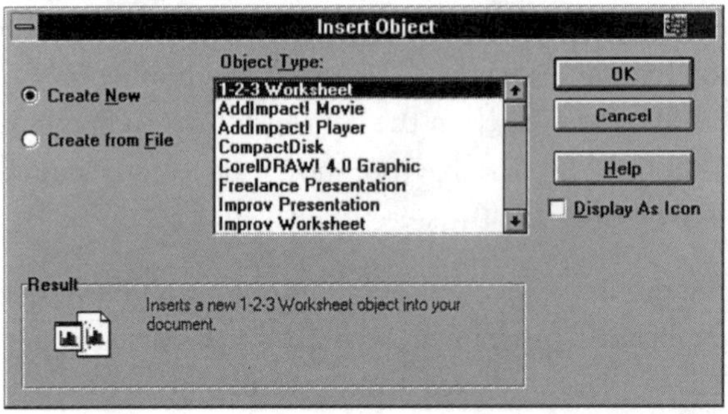

Fig. 18.4
The PowerPoint
Insert Object
dialog box.

Tip
If you are embed-
ding a new sound
file or other ob-
ject, click the
Display As Icon
check box. When
running the pre-
sentation, the
object executes.

The Object **T**ype list box in the dialog box shows the different types of objects (CorelDRAW! pictures, Excel charts and datasheets, etc.) that are available to you under Windows. The list of OLE Object types is derived from an OLE Registry list in one of Windows startup files and provides a handy reference to the specific types of files you can embed into a presentation.

3. From the Object **T**ype list box, choose the file type you want to embed.

4. Choose OK or press Enter.

   If the application program is OLE 2.0-compliant, PowerPoint's menu bar and toolbars are replaced and you can create the new object.

   If the application you selected is OLE 1.0-compliant, see the next section, "Working with OLE 1.0 Applications," for more information on how to proceed.

5. Click anywhere outside the boundaries of the object to embed it onto the PowerPoint slide.

The object has been successfully embedded.

Embedding an Existing Object File

Tip
Existing
PowerPoint 4
presentation files
can be embedded
as objects.

It is possible to bring an existing file, like an Excel spreadsheet, into a presentation as an embedded object. Instead of creating a new object from scratch, as in the previous example, any drawing, chart, or other object from a program that supports OLE can be embedded. This stands to reason, considering that an embedded object *is* the actual file created by the other program. That is why presentation files with embedded objects are so easily transported.

To embed an existing file, follow these steps:

1. Display the PowerPoint slide in which the object is to be placed.

2. From the **I**nsert menu, choose **O**bject.

The Insert Object dialog box appears, as shown in figure 18.5.

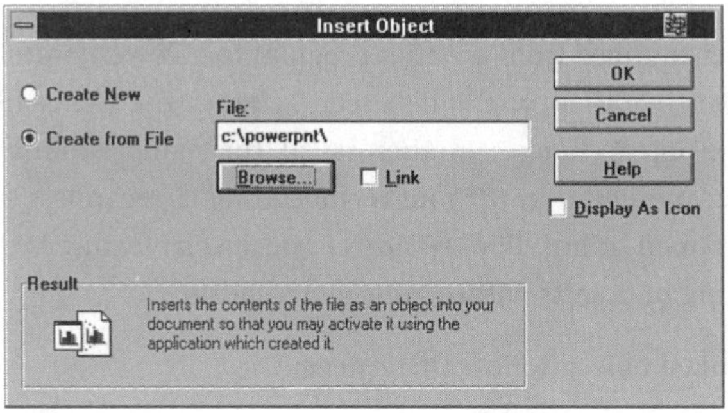

Fig. 18.5
The PowerPoint
Insert Object
dialog box
displaying options
for inserting an
existing object file.

3. Click the Create From **F**ile option button.

The Fil**e**: text box is displayed.

4. To locate the file to embed, click the **B**rowse button.

The Browse dialog box appears, as shown in figure 18.6.

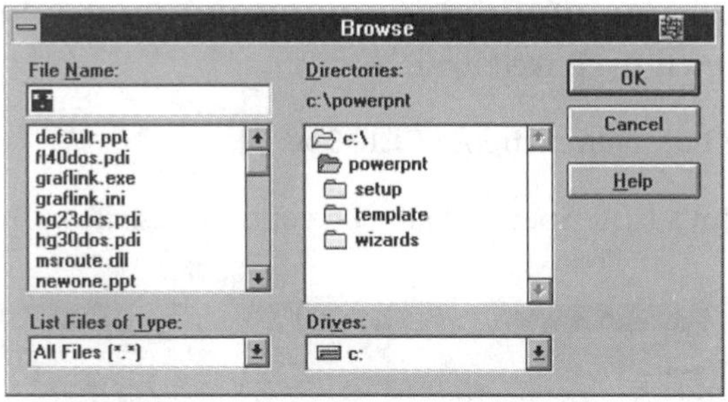

Fig. 18.6
Use the Browse
dialog box to
locate an existing
object file for
embedding.

5. By using the file, directory, and drive listings, locate the desired file.

6. Choose OK or press Enter.

The desired file name should now appear in the Fil**e**: text box.

7. Choose OK or press Enter.

The object file is embedded into the slide.

VI

Tip
An embedded
sound file, movie,
or animation
sequence auto-
matically runs in a
presentation.
Pictures and other
objects automati-
cally appear in
your slide show.

Advanced PowerPoint 4

Creating a Linked Object

Creating a link from a PowerPoint presentation to an object file of another type is as easy as copying and pasting between the programs. As noted earlier in this chapter, however, the relationship of a linked object to the OLE client program (such as PowerPoint) is different from that of an embedded one.

After an object is linked from another program to a PowerPoint 4 presentation, whenever the other program is used to change the source file for the object and the object changes are then saved, the changes to the object are shown in your presentation without reembedding it, regardless of whether PowerPoint is open or not. PowerPoint's Paste Special feature is the key to effective linking of objects within your presentation.

To create a linked object, follow these steps:

1. In the application program that was used to create the source file, open the file containing the desired object for linking.

2. Select the data in the file (the CorelDRAW! picture, Microsoft Word text, Excel chart, or whatever other type supported) that you want to link.

3. From the application's **E**dit menu, choose **C**opy.

4. Switch to the PowerPoint window and display the slide in which you want to insert the linked item.

5. From the **E**dit menu, choose Paste **S**pecial.

   PowerPoint's Paste Special dialog box appears, as shown in figure 18.7.

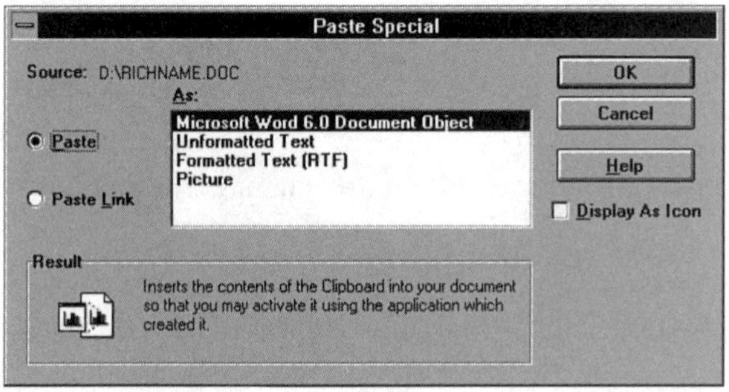

Fig. 18.7
PowerPoint's Paste Special dialog box displaying options for inserting an existing object file.

6. IMPORTANT: To enforce a link, click the Paste **L**ink option button.

In the **A**s: list, the file type that you already copied to the Windows Clipboard from the other application appears, as shown in figure 18.8.

The Results message box reads:

```
Inserts a picture of the Clipboard contents into your document.
Paste Link creates a link to the source file so that changes in
your source file will be reflected in your document.
```

This indicates a crucial point: a picture, or updatable "snapshot," of your object is created—the file is not actually placed in your presentation.

Tip
Linking places a "picture" of your linked data in the presentation, not the actual file.

7. Choose OK or press Enter.

The linked object appears on your slide.

If you double-click a linked object from inside PowerPoint, you do not see PowerPoint's menus and toolbars replaced by the other application. The other program comes up in its own window. This is the case for OLE 2.0 objects and OLE 1.0 objects when they're placed in a PowerPoint 4 file. In-place editing is not supported for linked objects.

Tip
Unlike OLE 2.0's embedding, double-clicking a linked object brings up the originating program in a *separate* window. In-place editing is not activated.

When you edit the linked object and then save it (*and saving the file is the crucial step*), the linked object is updated—even without the presentation file being open in PowerPoint. That's right—you can edit the linked item without PowerPoint being open at all, and when you save the linked object, any presentation files are automatically updated, even though they are not running. That, in a barely digestible nutshell, is how linking works.

VI

Advanced PowerPoint 4

> **Note**
>
> Here's another wrinkle. If you link an object from an OLE 1.0-compliant program like Excel 4.0 or CorelDRAW! 4.0 to a presentation in PowerPoint 4 (*an OLE 2.0-compliant program*), you can double-click the linked object and its original program comes up in a separate window. But if you link an object *between two OLE 1.0-compliant programs,* when you double-click the client program's linked object to edit it in the server program, you cannot do it. The server program does not appear.
>
> Yes. It's another exquisite twist in the tangle of OLE functions that illustrates one of the subtle differences between OLE 1.0 and 2.0. It's the way OLE *used* to work.
>
> In the end, linking works very much the same way in both versions of OLE, except that version 2.0 now enables you to edit linked objects in a separate window.

To create a link to an existing OLE 2.0 object file *from within PowerPoint*, follow these steps:

1. Display the PowerPoint slide in which the object is to be placed.

2. From the **I**nsert menu, choose **O**bject.

   The Insert Object dialog box appears.

3. Click the Create From **F**ile option button.

   The Fil**e**: text box is displayed.

4. To locate the file to embed, click the **B**rowse button.

   The Browse dialog box appears.

5. Use the Browse dialog box to locate the desired file.

6. Choose OK or press Enter.

7. Click the **L**ink check box. There should be an X inside it.

8. Choose OK or press Enter.

The linked object appears on the slide.

Working with OLE 1.0 Applications

Because most Windows applications on your hard disk are likely to support OLE 1.0, it is important to know that these programs can still play an important role in the creation of a well-rounded presentation. Many applications, though they don't support OLE 2.0, are still extremely powerful and sophisticated and may offer capabilities that Microsoft application programs cannot match. Also, those who own and use Word for Windows 2 or Excel 4 can still use these programs as vital tools in tandem with PowerPoint 4, by employing OLE 1.0 techniques to link and embed objects.

To embed a *new* OLE 1.0 object in a PowerPoint 4 slide, follow these steps:

1. Start PowerPoint 4 and open the desired presentation.

2. Minimize the PowerPoint window.

3. Start up the OLE 1.0-compliant application program, such as Excel 4.0 or CorelDRAW! 4.0, that offers the object type desired.

4. In the application program, create or open and select the drawing, datasheet, chart, or other object you want to embed.

5. From the **E**dit menu, choose **C**opy to copy the object to the Windows clipboard.

6. Minimize or close the program.

7. Maximize the PowerPoint program window.

8. From the **E**dit menu, choose Paste **S**pecial.

   PowerPoint's Paste Special dialog box appears, as shown in figure 18.9.

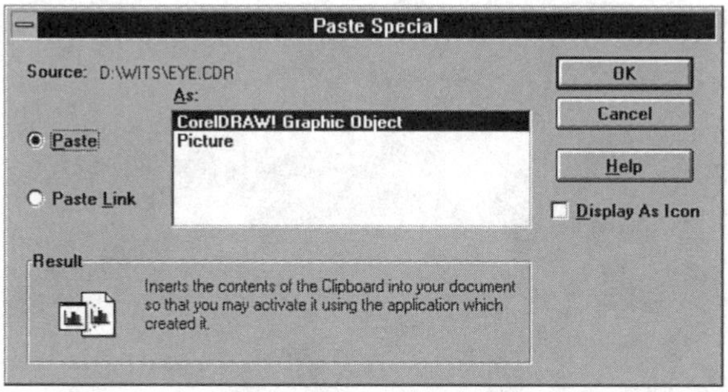

Fig. 18.9
PowerPoint's Paste Special dialog box displaying options for inserting an existing object file.

VI

Advanced PowerPoint 4

9. IMPORTANT: To embed an OLE 1.0 object, click the **P**aste option button.

In the **As**: list, the file type that you already copied to the Windows Clipboard from the other application appears, as shown in figure 18.9 (in this case, it's a CorelDRAW! 3.0 picture).

10. From the **As**: list, choose the file type you want to embed.

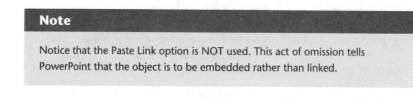

Note

Notice that the Paste Link option is NOT used. This act of omission tells PowerPoint that the object is to be embedded rather than linked.

11. Choose OK or press Enter.

The embedded object is placed into the presentation, as shown in figure 18.10.

Double-clicking the picture brings up the original application in its separate window, displaying the picture for editing. After you do so, the picture shows as ghosted on the PowerPoint slide. This is a tip-off that its originating application is running with the object file.

Fig. 18.10
The CorelDRAW! picture inserted as a linked object into PowerPoint.

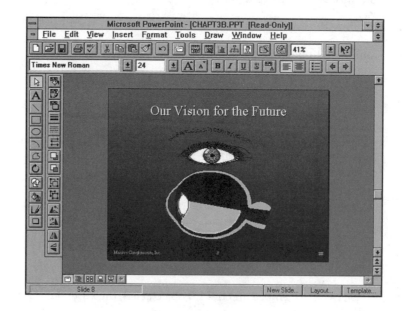

> **Note**
>
> Whenever you double-click an embedded OLE 1.0 object, the slide displays that object in a ghosted box, indicating that the object is being edited by its original program.

To modify an existing *embedded* OLE 1.0 object in PowerPoint 4, follow these steps:

1. Double-click the embedded object in the PowerPoint slide.

   The program that originally created the object appears. It is a separate Window and does not replace the PowerPoint toolbars and menus.

   Modify the object within the application program. When you're finished making your changes, save your work.

2. From the **F**ile menu of the application, choose **U**pdate.

   The program closes and the PowerPoint slide shows the changes you made to the embedded object.

> **Note**
>
> For OLE 1.0-compliant programs, when you edit and save the original object file, you must choose **U**pdate from the **F**ile menu of the original program or the changes are not placed in the presentation.

Working with Placeholders

Essentially, a placeholder is a resizeable container for objects of any description. They are interchangeable and generic. Although you can create new slides that have specified placeholders for charts, body text, organizational charts, and titles, among other things, any placeholder can be used for any purpose. By a simple trick with the mouse, a chart placeholder can be used to contain a graphics image, as in the example that follows.

To change placeholder types, follow these steps:

1. First, insert a new slide into your presentation by clicking the New Slide button and choosing an AutoLayout. Select, for example, a Graph slide, as shown in figure 18.11.

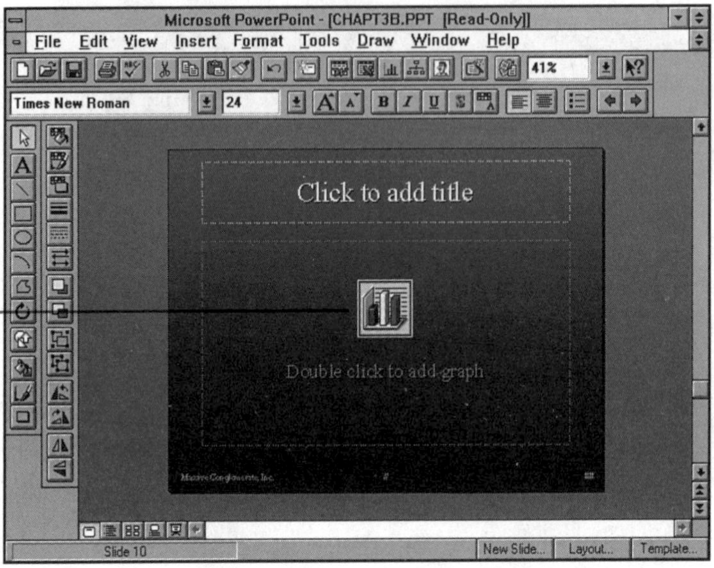

Fig. 18.11
Adding a Graph
slide to a
presentation.

Graph placeholder —

2. Click once on the outer edge of the chart placeholder to select it. Its
   highlighted border gets thicker.

3. From the **Insert** menu, choose **P**icture.

   The Insert Picture dialog box appears, as shown in figure 18.12.

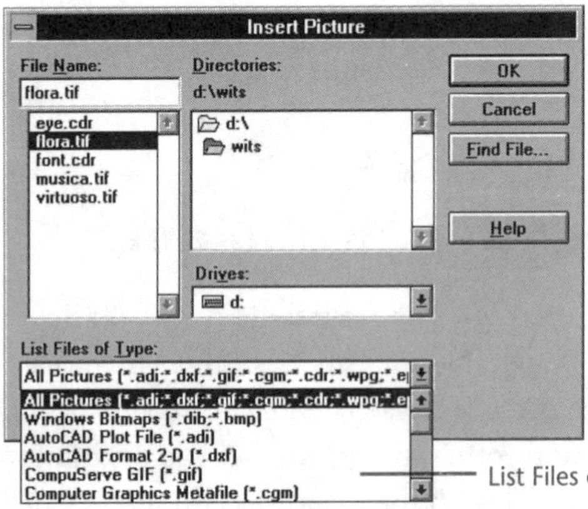

Fig. 18.12
Using the Insert
Picture dialog
box to import
a graphic.

List Files of Type drop-down list

PowerPoint supports a substantial number of graphics formats, including direct importing of CorelDRAW! files.

4. Choose the type of file to import from the List Files of **T**ype box, and
   choose the desired file from the proper drive and directory.

5. Choose OK or press Enter.

The Graph placeholder now contains a graphic, as shown in figure 18.13.

The key to the whole process of changing the placeholder type and inserting the graphic inside the placeholder is clicking the margin of the placeholder before you insert the picture or other object. If you don't, the new object is simply pasted on top of the existing placeholder. By using the placeholder, the inserted picture is automatically resized to the dimensions of the place-holder.

Tip
The Insert Picture feature also offers an easy way to link imported pictures by using the Link to File check box.

Notice in the Insert Picture dialog box that a **L**ink to File check box option is offered. This offers another simple way to link a graphic object between PowerPoint and another program.

By selecting the placeholder and choosing an option from the **I**nsert menu, a placeholder can be used to contain any object.

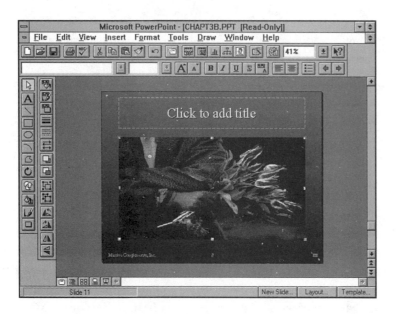

Fig. 18.13
The Graph placeholder now contains a 24-bit TIFF graphic.

Using Drag and Drop: PowerPoint's Enhancements

Among PowerPoint's most important new features is its support of enhanced drag-and-drop features. In earlier chapters of this book, you looked at the basics of drag-and-drop features—especially how to drag and drop cells

VI

Advanced PowerPoint 4

and rows or columns of data in Microsoft Graph datasheets, and text in PowerPoint slides and in Outline view. You can also drag and drop copy by simply holding down the Ctrl key when you perform the operation. There's much more to it, however.

It's possible with PowerPoint 4 to drag and drop elements between open presentation files. You can even drag and drop data between applications. Drag and drop copying is also supported between files and between apps. That particular feature is one of the key benefits available to Microsoft Office owners—those who own Microsoft Word 6 for Windows, Excel 5, and PowerPoint 4 all in the same package.

Microsoft Office owners who are reading this book should bear a few things in mind:

- Drag and drop works the same way in all levels of Windows: In a document, between documents, and between programs that support it, the keystrokes and mouse actions are the same.

- Dragging and dropping between applications dramatically slows system performance.

- Microsoft Word 6 for Windows documentation barely mentions the subject of dragging and dropping between documents in the same application, and ignores the subject of dragging and dropping between application programs. Microsoft Excel 5 for Windows documentation is flat wrong about how drag and drop works between applications. You get the right information here.

What Programs Work with Drag and Drop?

The version numbers for the programs mentioned here (Word 6 for Windows, Excel 5, and PowerPoint 4) are very important. Earlier versions of all three of these programs do not work with drag and drop in its present glory. You won't be able to drag and drop between files in the same program, or drag and drop between separate programs with earlier versions of Microsoft application programs. Only the very latest versions of the three programs included in Microsoft Office (or sold separately) work with the new drag-and-drop features.

You can certainly buy all three programs separately and obtain all the features of drag and drop among them. Buying Office simply saves you a little trouble (and possibly a little money as well).

With these caveats, the next two sections show you how to use drag and drop between PowerPoint documents and how to drag and drop a PowerPoint element from the PowerPoint program to another application (in that example, Word 6 for Windows will be used).

Dragging and Dropping Between PowerPoint Presentations

To start, make sure you have two PowerPoint 4 presentation files open and displayed, and then follow these steps:

1. Open each desired file.

2. From the **W**indow menu, choose **A**rrange All.

   The results will resemble figure 18.14. It's important that both files be displayed for drag and drop (between files) to work.

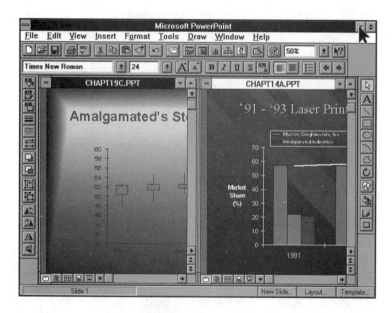

Fig. 18.14
Two presentation files open within PowerPoint.

The next step is very important. PowerPoint 4 directly supports the dragging and dropping of slides (with all the contents that the dragged slide contains) between files. *Dragging and dropping between PowerPoint files only works if both presentations are shown in Slide Sorter view.*

3. Click in each file, and for each, from the **V**iew menu, choose **Sli**de Sorter.

   The results should resemble figure 18.15.

Tip
Slide Sorter view is required for dragging and dropping of slides and their data between PowerPoint files.

VI

Advanced PowerPoint 4

Fig. 18.15
Displaying two
presentation files
in Slide Sorter
view.

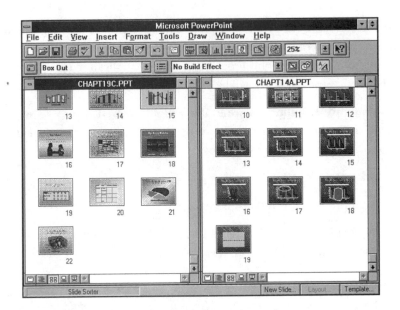

4. Click *and hold* on the desired slide in the file that you want to drag. *Drag the mouse.* As you drag, you see the mouse pointer change shape to a tiny box with a down arrow attached to it, and a bracketing arrow travels along. Move the mouse over the other presentation *to the location in its Slide Sorter where you want the slide to be dropped* (see fig. 18.16).

Fig. 18.16
Dragging and
dropping a slide.

Bracketing arrow indicates where the slide will be dropped in the other file

Mouse pointer changes shape, indicating that drag and drop is taking place

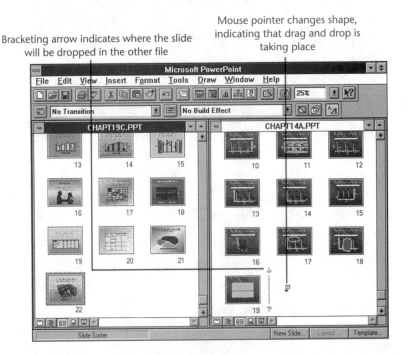

5. Release the mouse button. The slide has been dragged and dropped to the new file, as shown in figure 18.17.

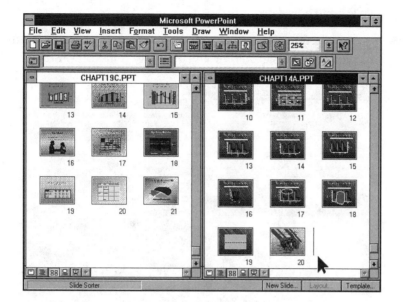

Fig. 18.17
The slide has been moved to the other file.

Does this procedure look suspiciously familiar? It's almost exactly the same as for the simple act of rearranging slides in the Slide Sorter, which was discussed in chapter 4. The major difference: the slide is moved to the other file. To retain the changes, both files must be saved by choosing **S**ave from the **F**ile menu for each file.

Note

You can also drag and drop copy slides between presentations. Simply press and hold the Ctrl key as you drag the slide thumbnail from one file's Slide Sorter to the other file.

Dragging and Dropping Between Applications

Dragging and dropping between applications is as straightforward as it is between files. Windows applications that support OLE 2.0 are the only type of program that can support drag and drop and drag and drop copy between programs; at the time of this writing the only packages that support this feature are PowerPoint 4, Excel 5, and Word 6 for Windows. Almost certainly, others will follow. In the next example, a PowerPoint file has an Excel datasheet copied to it. This can have some very interesting results, as you'll see below.

VI

Advanced PowerPoint 4

1. Display the PowerPoint file that you want to drag and drop to.

2. Next, open Microsoft Excel 5 for Windows and display a datasheet that you want to drag data from.

3. You may want to organize the two programs side by side or in another arrangement for easier viewing and dragging, as in figure 18.18.

Fig. 18.18
Excel and PowerPoint displayed for easier dragging.

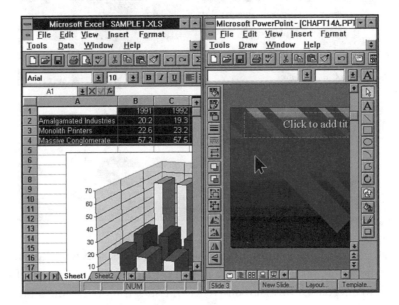

4. As shown in figure 18.18, display the PowerPoint presentation that you want to drag to. For the example, Slide view is sufficient.

5. In the Excel datasheet, select the data that you want to copy. Any selected data is highlighted.

6. Click and hold the mouse over the border of the selected data in the Excel datasheet. *Hold down the Ctrl key when you do this.*

7. Drag the mouse over to the PowerPoint window, place it over the area of the slide, and release the mouse button.

8. Figure 18.19 illustrates the result.

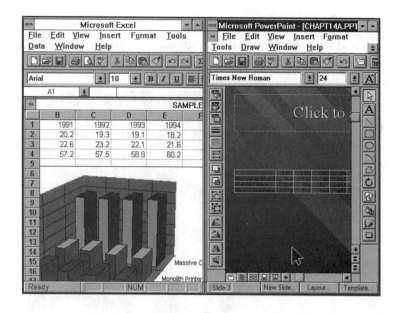

Fig. 18.19
An Excel datasheet placed in a PowerPoint slide.

The datasheet that's now in the PowerPoint slide is an Excel object. Double-clicking on the copied datasheet in the PowerPoint slide starts PowerPoint's OLE 2.0 capabililties, in which PowerPoint's menus and toolbars are replaced by those for Excel 5, and the datasheet can be edited, formatted, and resized as if you were actually using Excel. So, after the drag and drop copy is done, you're back to the process of in-place editing, which was described earlier in this chapter.

There's more. When you select the datasheet and drag and drop copy it from Excel to PowerPoint, any chart that's based on that Excel data comes along for the ride. You can drag on one of the pressure points on the new object in the PowerPoint slide to display more of its contents, as shown in figure 18.20.

You can copy and paste Excel datasheet rows and columns from the embedded Excel object into a Graph datasheet in your presentation.

This is just a basic example. As you can see, there's more to it than usually appears in advertising campaigns. Dragging and dropping between programs is not a trivial operation, and in many ways is not as efficient a use of system resources as true in-place editing. Microsoft Graph (remember, Graph is PowerPoint's charting and graphing utility) allows you to directly import Excel 5 datasheets and charts, which is a more efficient use of resources, is

Tip
It's recommended here that whenever possible, instead of executing drag and drop of Excel datasheets and charts, you simply import them into Microsoft Graph.

VI

Advanced PowerPoint 4

easier, and can take much less time. On the other hand, dragging and dropping Excel data to a Microsoft Word document can be a very appropriate and suitable use for that feature.

Fig. 18.20

As it turns out, you've dragged and dropped more than just a datasheet.

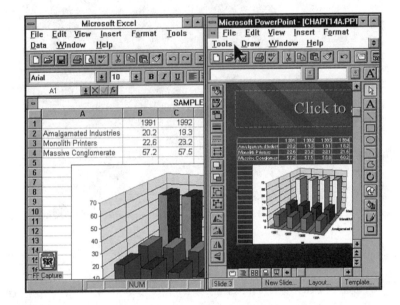

Here's another point: When you learn how to use Microsoft Graph to create charts for PowerPoint slides, you've also learned how to do the same operations in Excel 5. The two programs offer almost identical chart types and chart customization features, and their commands work in very much the same way. Excel's compelling advantages are much more powerful calculation capabilities, datasheet formatting, and much more substantial text handling and database creation features than Graph will ever support. Nonetheless, you get a leg up on Excel 5 by using Graph.

You should also notice the patterns that are emerging. In a move for ease of use, Microsoft has made sure that drag and drop copy works on all levels in the same way. Holding the Ctrl key when you drag and drop copies the selected data or object from one place to another in the same document, between documents, or between applications.

There are limits to how data can be dragged and dropped, and which views in PowerPoint that you are allowed to perform the operation. As you've seen, you can only copy slides from one presentation to another when both files are in the Slide Sorter view. You can't, for example, drag and drop a single chart from one slide to another, even if both slides are displayed in the program.

The enhanced drag-and-drop features in PowerPoint 4 (and in Microsoft Office) are a sophisticated and demanding feature, and not for the faint of heart. You should have plenty of memory and computer horsepower before you attempt such operations. There's also lots of scope for experimenting with this feature; the examples explored here are just the tip of the iceberg. Imagine what will be possible when more applications from other software publishers support drag and drop copy between them.

Troubleshooting

I can't embed Excel datasheets or Word tables in my slides.

It's very likely that you don't have the latest versions of both programs, or at least have not installed them if you have purchased Microsoft Office and not just the PowerPoint 4 application. Since Word for Windows 2 and Excel 4 do not support OLE 2.0, you cannot use PowerPoint's Insert Word Table or Insert Excel Datasheet tools with those previous-version programs for those purposes.

When I delete an object, the placeholder remains in place.

To entirely remove an object and its placeholder, you have to perform a two-step delete process. First, click the object to select it, and then delete it. Then, click the border of the placeholder and *then* delete it. There's a reason why it's done this way. You can't just create a new placeholder and put it on a slide (you must create an entire slide for that), so it's a good idea to leave it in place even if you don't want to use it. An empty placeholder does not show up on a slide show.

When I transport a bunch of linked files with a presentation, I can't get the presentation to use them when I'm at my destination and trying to give the show.

Ouch! You have run up against a bug in Microsoft's object linking and embedding 2.0 system. It turns out that unless you place the linked files in *exactly the same directory structure* at your destination computer that they were in when you created the presentation (in other words, make the same directories in the other guy's computer that are in your own and copy the linked files to them), your slide show won't find them. This winds up being a real pain, and there's no solution for this until Microsoft fixes it (and they're working on it). Until then, make notes on the location of all your linked files and reconstruct them on the destination computer system. Better yet, create and deliver your presentation on your own laptop with an external monitor, and you won't have to worry about this vexing problem.

(continues)

VI

Advanced PowerPoint 4

(continued)

I can't get OLE to work at all.

Check the Windows System subdirectory on your hard disk (normally, C:\WINDOWS\SYSTEM) for the following files:

OLECLI.DLL	(OLE 1.0 client support software)
OLESVR.DLL	(OLE 1.0 server support software)
OLE2.DLL,	(OLE 2.0 support files)
OLE2CONV.DLL	
OLE2DISP.DLL	
OLE2NLS.DLL	
OLE2PROX.DLL	

If none of these files are on your system (and especially in the C:\WINDOWS\SYSTEM directory, which is where they *must* be located), you have two choices: reinstall Windows and PowerPoint, or copy the proper compressed files (which are called OLESVR.DL_, and so on, instead of OLESVR.DLL) directly from the installation floppies of both PowerPoint and Windows to the WINDOWS\SYSTEM directory. Then use the DOS EXPAND command to decompress the files back where they belong. All files in the Windows and PowerPoint installation disks are compressed to save space, hence the underline in each file name. Use either the DOS Prompt or the Windows File Manager to do the file copying. You have to search through quite a few floppies to find the files, but it may take less time than a complete reinstall.

If you reinstall Windows, copy all your existing *.INI and *.GRP files from the Windows directory to another directory or a floppy. Those files are important and will help restore your system a lot faster.

From Here...

Despite the detailed discussion of object linking and embedding that's been offered in this chapter, there's quite a bit more about OLE that goes beyond the scope of this book. For more information on the subject, refer to Microsoft's PowerPoint 4 program documentation.

■ Chapter 19, "Using Advanced Charting Features," digs into more eso-
   teric chart types and various advanced features of chart creation, plus
   looks into the importing of charts from PowerPoint 3, the previous
   version of the program.

■ Chapter 20, "Advanced Presentation Management," discusses adding
   special effects to your presentation, and some techniques for adding
   and embedding multimedia objects such as movie clips and sounds into
   your slides.

■ Chapter 21, "Using Advanced Color, Text, and Drawing Features," helps
   you exercise some of PowerPoint 4's more advanced tools for text rotation, recoloring various objects such as clip art, and creation of new
   color schemes.

VI

Advanced PowerPoint 4

Chapter 19

Using Advanced Charting Features

Earlier in this book, three chapters were devoted to the process of creating datasheets and charts for use in PowerPoint slides. While those chapters covered a lot of ground, many features were passed by. PowerPoint 4, for example, offers many more chart types than were explained earlier, including 2-D and 3-D line charts, scatter charts, stock charts, the spectacular combination charts, 3-D area charts, and three types that are newcomers to the PowerPoint program: 3-D surface, 2-D radar, and 2-D doughnut charts. While only brief accounts can be offered here of most of the additional chart types, you learn about how these charts can be used and the reasons for using them.

Other new features that are explained in this chapter include the use of Trendlines, a chart forecasting feature that enables you to extrapolate future values from current ones for display on a chart; the capability to create and save custom chart types for future use; and importing charts and data from Microsoft Excel. We also touch briefly upon chart selection and customization commands bypassed earlier.

Understanding Alternative Chart Types

PowerPoint offers too many chart types to allow comprehensive coverage in this book. The following sections, however, give examples of many alternative chart types you might consider using.

The subjects covered in this chapter include:

- Understanding alternative chart types

- Understanding and using trendlines

- Saving custom charts and creating new default charts

- Exporting and importing charts to and from various applications

VI

Advanced PowerPoint 4

Using 2-D Line (XY) Charts

In standard charting nomenclature, line charts, area charts, scatter charts, and stock charts are all examples of XY chart types. XY charts are so named because their values are calculated against both two-dimensional axes: x and y. Unfortunately in PowerPoint, Microsoft has made the decision to split "Line" and "XY (Scatter)" charts into separate categories. There is no functional difference between them, because they are calculated the same way. This can entail confusion for the user, because there are numerous redundant chart types offered between them. It's easier, in this book, to split them into specific categories such as stock, line, and scatter chart types so that you can see the uses and subtle differences between them.

Line charts, for example, are an interesting and subtle option for helping your audience draw visual conclusions from your numeric data. Line charts are deceptively simple—messages can be found in line charts that may not be apparent in other types. In figure 19.1, you can see that a line representing Amalgamated Industries shows their market share for the last three years, for example. What you may also notice is that the market share for their products has substantially declined over the last two years. In short, Amalgamated Industries is in a recession. At the same time, at Amalgamated's expense, Massive Conglomerate, Inc. has gained market share. In a line chart, those facts are driven home with emphatic clarity. This is one major advantage of a line chart—multiple messages can be conveyed with a minimum of screen clutter.

Fig. 19.1
The Market Share data shown in a 2-D line chart.

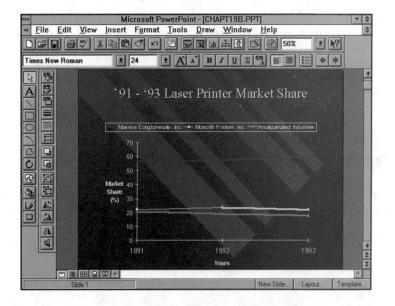

In PowerPoint 4, line charts are often called XY charts because their data is charted against two axes—the x- and y-axes—and because each point, line, or sized object needs to be measured against each axis to determine its location. In figure 19.1, for example, each point on each line has a year value that ranges from 1991 to 1993 and a numeric value ranging between 0 and 70. The common element across all XY charts is the requirement *for two values for each data item* used to create and locate the markers representing each series value.

Table 19.1 gives you the sample set of data on which the chart shown in figure 19.1 is based.

Table 19.1 Market Share Datasheet	1991	1992	1993
Massive Conglomerate, Inc.	57.1	57.3	60.2
Monolith Printers, Inc.	22.1	23.5	21.8
Amalgamated Industries	20.8	19.2	18.0

Here's how to create the chart shown in figure 19.1:

1. In PowerPoint, click the Insert Graph button on the standard toolbar. Microsoft Graph appears.

2. Select the default data in Graph's datasheet and delete it using the Clear **A**ll command from the **E**dit menu. Type the sample data set shown in table 19.1.

3. From the F**o**rmat menu, choose **A**utoFormat. The AutoFormat dialog box appears.

4. From the **G**alleries list box, choose Line.

5. Select chart #1.

6. Click the OK button.

7. Click one of the lines in the chart.

8. From the F**o**rmat menu, choose S**e**lected Series.

   The Format Data Series dialog box appears displaying the Patterns tab.

Tip

Graph's Clear command is a cascading menu offering three options: **A**ll, **C**ontents, and **F**ormats. Selecting Contents removes the data, but retains the fonts or other formatting you've applied in the selected cells for fresh data entry. Clearing Formats removes the fonts or other visual changes you've applied to datasheet numbers and labels.

VI

Advanced PowerPoint 4

9. In the Patterns Line section, choose a heavier line weight from the **W**eight drop-down list.

10. Choose OK or press Enter.

11. Follow the same procedure for the other lines in the chart.

Understanding and Using 2-D Scatter Charts

Scatter charts are a handy and useful tool when you need to display a large number of series in a chart. Lines and points are the objects that are displayed in scatter charts. (As noted earlier, there is no functional difference between a scatter and a line chart.) Points represent the actual data values in each series, and the graphic shapes used to define those points are called markers.

In many cases, you won't use lines in a chart, but simply points or data markers. Markers create the scatter chart, in which the points show their relationships to each other by the common colors or shapes of the markers. In scatter charts, the height of the points along the line represents the data values in the chart. Scatter charts are plotted against two axes—the x- and y-axes—because each point, line, or sized object needs to be measured against each axis to determine its location. (Hence, they're a type of XY chart.)

What is the reason for using a scatter chart? When you have more than four series, connecting lines may have the effect of confusing the viewer or obscuring some of the data markers on the chart. In that case, scatter charts without lines may be just the thing to display a large number of series. The nature of data markers (which are very small entities on the chart) enables the user to display almost as many series as he could want. Also, a scatter chart is suitable if you have only a few series, but also have a large number of values in each series, as is shown in table 19.2.

Table 19.2 Revised Market Share Datasheet							
	1991	**1992**	**1993**	**1994**	**1995**	**1996**	**1997**
Massive Conglomerate, Inc.	57.1	57.3	60.2	54.3	52.2	48.4	43.2
Monolith Printers, Inc.	22.1	23.5	21.8	27.0	28.7	28.4	34.7
Amalgamated Industries	20.8	19.2	18.0	18.7	19.1	23.2	22.1

Handled properly, a scatter chart can be used to bring together many disparate sets of data, such as demographic surveys of customers in the marketplace. Logarithmic scales can be used to tie together values from widely ranging statistical areas, such as surveys of different age groups.

For the next chart example, the Market Share datasheet is expanded through a few more years to provide a wider scatter chart:

1. In PowerPoint, click the Insert Graph button on the standard toolbar. Microsoft Graph appears.

2. Select the default data in Graph's datasheet and delete it using the Clear All command from the Edit menu. Type the sample data shown in table 19.2.

3. From the Format menu, choose AutoFormat. The AutoFormat dialog box appears.

4. From the Galleries list box, choose XY (Scatter).

5. Select chart #1.

6. Click the OK button.

The resulting scatter chart is shown in figure 19.2.

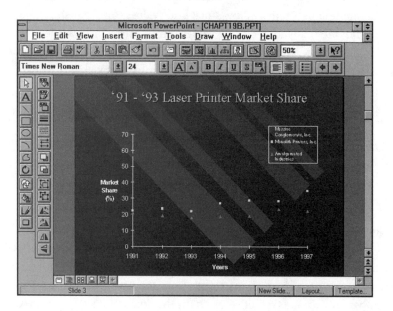

Fig. 19.2
A scatter chart using the expanded Market Share data.

VI

Advanced PowerPoint 4

Scatter chart types are quite similar to several line charts in the Gallery. Scatter chart #2, in particular, is functionally identical. Most other scatter chart types add gridlines or, in the case of scatter chart #4, a logarithmic scale is automatically added to the chart. If you had a series whose values ranged between 10 and 15, and another series that showed values of another order of magnitude (say, 100 to 150), a logarithmic scale is a good option.

Scatter chart type #6 is a smoothed line chart without data markers. The same feature can be enabled on any line chart (or scatter chart displaying lines) by enabling the **Sm**oothed Line check box option when you format lines under the Format Data Series dialog box.

Using Stock Charts

In Microsoft Graph, stock charts are not offered as a separate section under the Graph Gallery; they are, instead, grouped with the line chart type in the PowerPoint program. Nonetheless, stock charts are so unique, and require such a different set of data, that they deserve their own space in this chapter. The same is true, of course, with combination charts, the building of which may be the most challenging chart-building task you undertake. They're described in the next section.

Stock charts require different data sets from those used in previous examples—one type, a High/Low/Close stock chart, requires three series of data, one that represents a series of low stock price values, one that shows high values, and one that shows closing values. An Open/High/Low/Close chart requires four respective series. The open value is the price at which the stock opened trading for the given time period. A sample stock chart is shown in figure 19.3.

What are the elements of stock charts? Some unfamiliar element names have popped up here, and they bear some explanation.

Hi-lo lines are used to show the extent of stock price fluctuations. Hi lines extend above the up-down colored bar for each series. Lo lines extend below it.

Up-Down bars indicate the open and close values of the data series. Keep in mind that the Up-Down bar can represent a value that closes lower as well as higher; and that a high or low value and a close value can be the same: in such a case, no high or low line extends from the Up-Down bar. Up-Down bars only apply to one type of stock chart, the Open/High/Low/Close (OHLC) chart. In the High-Low-Close (HLC) chart type, a short horizontal line pointing to the right is used to indicate the closing value. Hi-lo lines are still used in HLC charts.

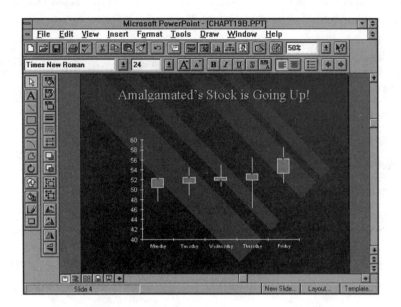

Fig. 19.3
The PowerPoint screen displaying a finished stock chart.

The open price is located on either the top or the bottom edge of the colored Up-Down bars for each trading day (or week, or year, and so on), and the open price value is measured against the y-axis. If a price went up for the time period, the open value is on the lower edge of the Up-Down bar. If it went down, it's the top edge of the bar.

The low price is located on the bottom end of the hi-lo line combination, and it's the lowest price at which the stock traded for the given time period. It is measured against the y-axis. The high price is located on the top end of the hi-lo line combination. It is the highest price level that the stock traded for during the given period, and it is measured against the y-axis. The high value is not necessarily the value that the stock closed at; if it is, no high line extends beyond the Up-Down bar.

The closing price is located on either the top edge or the bottom edge of the Up-Down bars for each trading period, and they are measured against the y-axis. The closing price is the price at which the stock rests at the end of each given trading period. A closing price data marker can be placed to clearly mark its position for each trading day. If a price went up for the time

Tip
Up-Down bars are named according to their closing value. If the value is lower, it's a Down bar. If the value is higher, it's an Up bar.

VI

Advanced PowerPoint 4

period, the closing value is on the upper edge of the Up-Down bar. If it went down, it's on the lower edge of the bar.

Table 19.3 is a simple table displaying four series of data for Massive Conglomerate, Inc. that are used for the stock chart example.

Table 19.3 Massive Conglomerate's Stock Prices for a One-Week Period				
Year	Open	High	Low	Close
Monday	50.25	52.375	47.5	51.25
Tuesday	51.25	54.5	48.75	52.25
Wednesday	52.25	55	50.5	51.75
Thursday	51.75	56.5	46.25	53.25
Friday	53.25	58.5	51.25	56.25

The values as shown in the table display what should be the typical OHLC chart data format. HLC (High-Low-Close) datasheets are also structured the same way.

Here's how to create a basic stock chart:

1. In PowerPoint, click the Insert Graph button on the standard toolbar. Microsoft Graph appears.

2. Select the default data in Graph's datasheet and delete it using the Clear All command from the Edit menu. Type the sample data set shown in table 19.3.

3. Click the By Column tool on the Graph Standard toolbar.

4. From the Format menu, choose AutoFormat. The AutoFormat dialog box appears.

5. From the Galleries list box, choose Line.

6. Select chart #9. This is the OHLC chart option.

7. Click the OK button.

   The OHLC stock chart appears, as shown in figure 19.4.

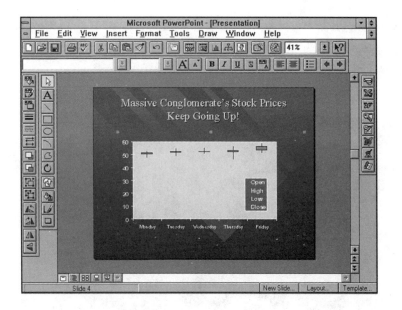

Fig. 19.4
The PowerPoint
screen displaying
the basic stock
chart.

As you can see, there are quite a few problems with the chart. The legend is in the way, the color scheme is off, and the stock values are unreadable. Except for its basic type, it in no way resembles the chart in figure 19.3. It's time to do some clean-up.

8. Click the Legend tool on the Graph toolbar to delete the legend.

9. Click on the gray area between the chart axes.

10. From the Format menu, choose Selected Plot Area.

    The Format Plot Area dialog box appears.

11. Choose the None option button inside the Patterns Area section.

12. Choose the None option button in the Patterns Border section.

    The chart area is rendered transparent, as shown in figure 19.5.

    The chart in figure 19.5, while it's already significantly improved, needs a few more minor adjustments before it resembles the final chart in figure 19.3. If you take a close look at the y-axis in figure 19.3, you see that the y-axis does not start at zero. The y-axis value range is set to display a range between 40 and 60 to give a better sense of proportion to the chart: Why have vast amounts of open space in a chart when you do not need it? Also, the color of the Open-Close boxes is set to a more visible color than the default you just created. Finally, the x-axis labels need to be displayed for each increment.

Fig. 19.5
The stock chart with the legend and chart background color deleted.

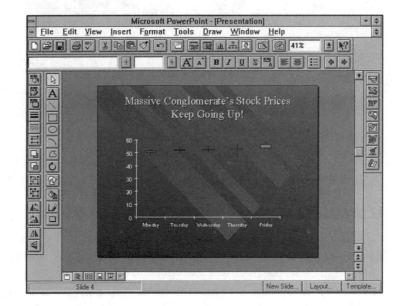

13. Click on the y-axis to select it.

14. From the Format menu, choose Selected Axis.

    The Format Selected Axis dialog box appears. Five tabs are displayed: Patterns, Scale, Font, Number, and Alignment.

15. Click the Scale tab.

16. In the Minimum text box, enter the value **40**.

17. Choose OK or press Enter.

    The y-axis scale is reset to the new values.

18. Click the x-axis.

19. From the Format menu, choose Selected Axis.

20. Click the Font tab.

21. From the **S**ize list, choose 12 to set a smaller point size.

22. From the F**o**nt Style list, choose Bold.

Tip
Double-clicking the axis has the same effect as steps 12 and 13: the axis is selected and the dialog box is brought up.

23. Choose OK or press Enter.

The axis properly displays the Day labels. At this point, the stock chart is quite serviceable, as shown in figure 19.6.

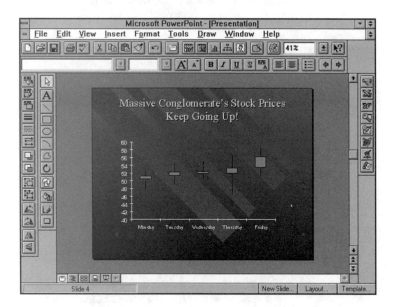

Fig. 19.6
The stock chart with the new y-axis scale and corrected x-axis labels.

The next step is to change the color of the Up-Down bars.

24. Click on any of the Up bars.

Notice that the bar for Wednesday's data is not selected. If you click Wednesday's Up-Down bar, it is the only one selected because Up bars and Down bars are treated as separate groups.

25. From the Format menu, choose Selected Up Bars.

26. Click a bright green color (or whatever color you prefer) from the Patterns Area palette.

27. Choose OK or press Enter.

28. Click the Down bar in Wednesday's chart entry.

29. From the Format menu, choose Selected Down Bars.

30. Click a bright green color (or whatever color you prefer) from the Patterns Area palette.

VI

Advanced PowerPoint 4

31. Choose OK or press Enter.

The final step is to make the closing value data markers visible.

32. In the chart, click on any place where a closing value on an Up-Down bar meets a high line. The result should appear as shown in figure 19.7.

Fig. 19.7
The stock chart with reformatted Up-Down Bar colors.

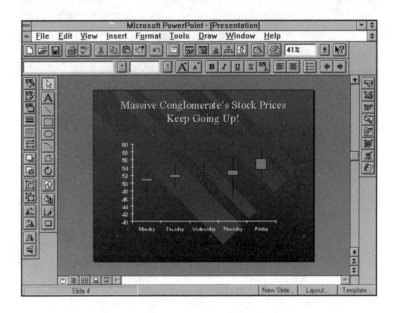

33. From the Format menu, choose Selected Series.

The Format Data Series dialog box appears.

34. Click the Patterns tab if it is not already displayed.

35. Click the Custom option button in the Patterns Marker section.

36. From the Patterns Marker Style drop-down list, choose a square marker.

37. From the Patterns Marker Foreground and Background drop-down palettes, choose a bright red color, or any color you prefer.

38. Choose OK or press Enter.

39. Click outside the chart to embed it into the slide.

As you can see, you can add some interesting touches to a stock chart. Stock charts can display a huge number of series values, as anyone who's seen a

Dow Jones stock price history chart can attest. (Appendix B shows a stock chart of this type.) HLC charts work much the same way, but discussions and examples of every chart type offered by PowerPoint are beyond the scope of this book. Nonetheless, with a little experimentation, any stock chart of either type can be customized and altered to suit your needs. They can also be added to a combination chart.

Using Combination Charts

Combination charts are an especially powerful and complex chart type that is primarily used to define and illustrate relationships between different sets of data. Combination charts can have elements of stock charts, bar charts, line charts, and column charts within them.

Combination charts combine elements from many different types of 2-D charts and enable you to plot data in two or three different ways on the same chart. Charts of this type are often used to draw relationships between, for example, gross revenues and profits, where yearly gross revenues might be shown in columns and yearly profits in a line. Powerful and informative messages can be conveyed with this chart type.

Combination or overlay charts are so named because one type of chart is overlaid on another chart. As a result, a combination chart displays, at a minimum, two y-axes and one x-axis. It's also quite possible to display two x-axes and two y-axes on the same chart. Combination charts, as you can imagine, also require a slightly different set of data than that used in previous chapters; a sample set of data is provided to build the example in this section. Combination charts, incidentally, are only available in 2-D types. Figure 19.8 shows an example of a combination chart.

Tip
Combination charts can display two x- and two y-axes on the same chart.

For combination charts, PowerPoint 4 displays x-axis values on the horizontal axis, shown on the bottom of the chart. In line charts, the x-axis is used to denote categories and series labels. Figure 19.8 shows increments along the x-axis labeled 1990, 1991, 1992, and 1993.

The y-axis is the second and vertical axis against which the numeric values of one series are measured. The increments and range of the y-axis are based on the values in your data. In figure 19.8, the y-axis is used to measure the 2-D columns in the chart, and the axis is scaled from zero to 18, in increments of two.

VI

Advanced PowerPoint 4

Fig. 19.8
A combination chart showing 2-D columns and lines.

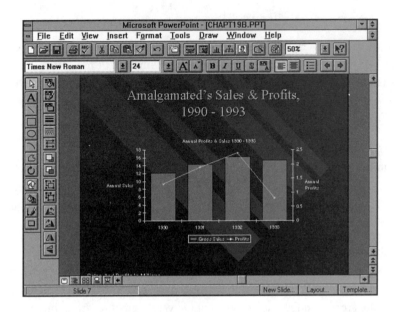

Tip
For combination or overlay charts, in many charting and applications the y-axis is also called the *Y1 axis*.

The *Y2 axis* is the third axis in your combination chart and is the basis by which your second set of data is measured. It's the second vertical axis shown on the right side of the chart. Notice that the scale of values in the Y2 axis is very different from the scale of values in the Y1 axis. In figure 19.8, the Y2 axis is scaled from zero to 2.5, in increments of 0.5. It's used to measure the line that is overlaid on the 2-D columns and it represents yearly profits.

The Y2 axis labels are used to coordinate with the legend and to describe the values on the chart that the Y2 axis measures. In figure 19.8, the label Annual Profits is attached to the Y2 axis. The legend shows that Profits are described with the yellow line and markers and thus are measured against the Y2 axis.

> **Note**
>
> In combination charts, it is a good idea to be explicit and generous with your axis labels—and to add a legend. A tremendous amount of information is conveyed in a chart of this type, and it's easy to forget a label that provides the viewer with the critical visual link to interpret the data.

You take a slightly different approach to the creation of this type of chart, because the steps required are somewhat more complex and the details must be sweated to get the chart right. Also, because of the myriad possibilities of this type of chart and space considerations, only one exercise can be used in this section. One exercise is enough, however, to illustrate the power of this chart option, its complexity, and the tremendous number of customization options available.

Table 19.4 gives you the sample set of data that figure 19.8 is based on.

Table 19.4 Massive Conglomerate's Annual Sales and Profits, 1990-1993				
	1990	**1991**	**1992**	**1993**
Gross Sales	12.2	14.3	16.2	15.4
Profits	1.3	1.9	2.4	0.8

Using this data, you create a combination chart from scratch in Microsoft Graph. The data set is deceptively simple. Many steps must be followed to properly create and customize the chart as seen in figure 19.8:

1. In PowerPoint, click the Insert Graph button on the standard toolbar. Microsoft Graph appears.

2. Select the default data in Graph's datasheet and delete it. Type the sample data set shown in table 19.4.

3. From the **Fo**rmat menu, choose **A**utoFormat. The AutoFormat dialog box appears.

4. From the **G**alleries list box, choose Combination.

5. From the **F**ormat thumbnails, choose chart type #2. It appears as a chart bearing a set of bars, a line, and two y-axes, as shown in figure 19.9.

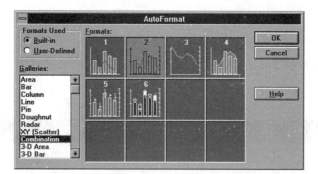

Fig. 19.9
The AutoFormat dialog box showing combination chart options.

VI

Advanced PowerPoint 4

6. Choose OK or press Enter.

A rough combination chart appears, as shown in figure 19.10.

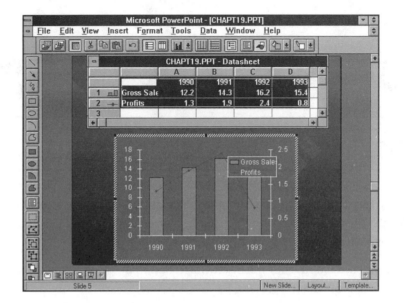

Now, you change some colors.

7. Double-click any of the Gross Sales columns.

The Format Data Series dialog box appears.

8. In the Patterns Area section of the dialog box, click a desired color in the palette, choosing a color that stands out clearly against your slide background without being too strident (against the blue diagonal slide background, a more subdued blue, violet, or magenta hue might be suitable).

9. Choose OK or press Enter.

10. Double-click the Profits line in the combination chart.

The Format Data Series dialog box reappears.

> **Note**
>
> Despite the wildly different appearance of the series on the chart, formatting either of them is much the same procedure. The only real difference is the type of marker that is used: lines or columns, in the current example.

11. In the Patterns Line section of the dialog box, choose the Custom option button.

12. From the Patterns Line **C**olor drop-down list of the dialog box, choose a bright yellow color.

13. In the Patterns Marker section of the dialog box, choose the Custom option button.

14. In the Patterns Marker **F**oreground and **B**ackground drop-down lists of the dialog box, choose a bright yellow color.

15. Choose OK or press Enter.

16. To make the axis fonts more proportional to the chart (they're a little large in the default), double-click the Y1 axis (the y-axis on the left of the chart).

The Format Axis dialog box appears.

17. Click the Font tab.

18. From the **S**ize list, choose 12 to set a smaller point size.

19. From the F**o**nt Style list, choose Bold.

20. Choose OK or press Enter.

21. Follow steps 17-21 for all three axes on the chart.

22. To make the legend more proportional in size to the rest of the chart, double-click the legend.

The Format Legend dialog box appears.

23. Click on the Placement tab.

24. From the Placement Type list, choose the **B**ottom option button.

25. Click the Font tab.

26. From the **S**ize list, choose 12 to set a smaller point size.

27. From the F**o**nt Style list, choose Bold.

28. Choose OK or press Enter.

Now, you add the y-axis labels.

29. Click the Y (Y1) axis to select it.

30. From the **I**nsert menu, choose **T**itles.

The Titles dialog box appears.

31. Choose the **V**alue (Y) Axis and Second Value (**Y**) Axis check boxes. xs should appear in both of them.

32. Choose OK or press Enter.

33. If the font for the axis titles is a little too big, choose **F**ont from the F**o**rmat menu, and choose 12 Point Bold for all the axis titles in turn.

34. Click the OK button.

A Y appears next to the left-hand Y (or Y1) axis. An X2 appears above the chart at the position of the (undisplayed) X2 axis. A Y2 appears alongside the Y2 axis to the right of the chart.

Tip

As noted, the second y-axis in a combination or overlay chart is also called the Y2 axis. When Graph puts the Y2 in the title entry, it is leaving you a clue about what axis you are adding a title to.

35. Click the mouse on the y-axis label to select it, and once inside the label to activate the I-beam.

36. Delete the Y and type **Annual Sales**. To save room, place a carriage return between *Annual* and *Sales*. (In some situations, *Sales* may automatically move to a second line.)

37. Click the mouse on the Y2 axis label to select it, and once inside the label to activate the insertion point.

38. Delete the Y2 and type **Annual Profits**. To save room, place a carriage return between *Annual* and *Profits*. (In some situations, *Profits* may automatically move to a second line.)

You may need to resize the chart to compensate for any overwriting of titles and axis labels.

As you can see, it takes quite a few steps to create an effective combination chart. Hang in there, you're almost done. To add a chart title:

39. From the **I**nsert menu, choose **T**itles.

40. Click the Chart **T**itle check box.

41. Click the OK button.

The word Title appears over the chart.

42. Click the mouse in the Chart **T**itle text object that appears over the chart, delete *Title*, and type **Annual Profits & Sales**.

As a final step, make the line thicker in the chart to make it more visible.

43. Double-click the line.

The Format Data Series dialog box appears, displaying the Patterns tab.

44. In the Patterns Line section, choose a heavier line weight from the **W**eight drop-down list.

45. Choose OK or press Enter.

46. Click outside the chart object to embed the finished chart in your slide. The chart should look similar to figure 19.11.

Tip
Don't make your line weight too heavy. It may damage the visual attractiveness of the chart.

Fig. 19.11
A finished column-line combination chart.

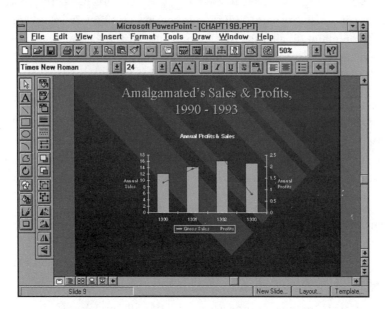

As you can see, it takes some work to properly build a readable, useful combination chart. It's necessary to strike a balance between conveying all the information required to deliver your message and avoiding cluttering up your slide. That's why gridlines aren't used in this chart—they would only confuse the viewer.

VI

Advanced PowerPoint 4

> ### Note
>
> When you create your combination chart, take a look at the left margin of the spreadsheet holding your series data. You see a white dot next to the Profits series row. That white dot is the *overlay chart indicator*. It indicates that the Profits data series forms the overlay chart, which, in this case, is a line chart with markers.

Given your experience with customizing bar and column charts and your recent work with line and stock charts, it should be clear that combination charts have an almost frightening number of choices available. They require more work than other types, but their rewards are greater, because they can convey a great amount of information that would otherwise require two or three charts to depict.

There's more. You don't have to use the AutoFormats to change the appearance of combination charts. You can use the Format Chart Type and Format Group commands to alter the overlays in your chart. A section near the end of this chapter, "Customizing Combination Charts," describes these techniques in more detail.

Using 2-D Radar Charts

Radar charts are often also called "spider" charts, because their general shape is like that of a spider's web. Radar charts are best used when you need to show multiple variables, such as ratings in different areas, performance levels of entities such as employees or corporate divisions, or progress in a project or other endeavor.

Radar charts require at least three categories and one series of data. They can also be somewhat perplexing to understand at first glance. Figure 19.12 shows a radar chart generated with the basic default labels and series names provided by PowerPoint.

The row labels are shown in the legend and the column labels in the datasheet are used to label each spoke. The rows represent the three series of data, and each series is shown as a geometric shape whose appearance is determined by the position of each series value on the spokes.

Radar charts are best viewed when the series are arranged to provide maximum visibility to as many series values as possible. This means that the series must be "stacked" like pancakes with the smallest shape on top, the next largest below that, and the largest on the bottom. If they aren't, entire series can be hidden from view and thus from analysis by the audience.

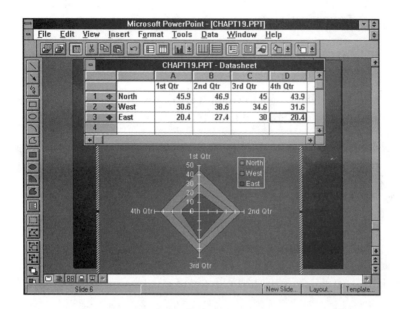

Fig. 19.12
A simple radar
chart using
PowerPoint default
series names and
colors.

> **Note**
>
> In figure 19.12, the series are arranged in such a way that all the series values can be measured along the spokes. Look closely at the datasheet in the figure. The East data set, which is on the top of the chart stack, is on the third row of the datasheet. Notice also that its values are consistently less than those of the next datasheet row up, the West row. Radar charts may require rearranging of chart values to get the best effect.

A standard datasheet can usually be made to work well with a radar-type chart; the key is to arrange your series for best visibility. Otherwise, axes and axis labels, series markers, gridlines, and other elements of radar charts can be selected and customized much as any other chart.

The Market Share datasheet in table 19.5 is well suited to a simple radar chart.

Table 19.5 Market Share Datasheet

	1991	1992	1993
Massive Conglomerate, Inc.	57.1	57.3	60.2
Monolith Printers, Inc.	22.1	23.5	21.8
Amalgamated Industries	20.8	19.2	18.0

To create a simple radar chart, follow these steps:

1. In PowerPoint, click the Insert Graph button on the standard toolbar. Microsoft Graph appears.

2. Select the default data in Graph's datasheet and delete it. Type the sample data set shown in table 19.5.

3. From the Format menu, choose **A**utoFormat. The AutoFormat dialog box appears.

4. From the **G**alleries list box, choose Radar.

5. Select chart #2. This option is a radar chart without gridlines.

6. Click the OK button.

The radar chart appears, as shown in figure 19.13.

Fig. 19.13
A simple radar chart using the Market Share data.

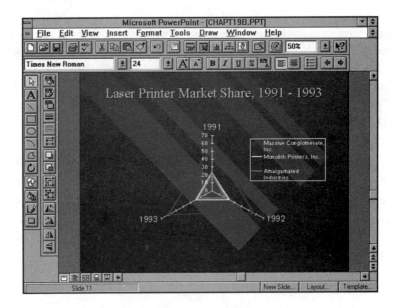

Tip
Radar charts can benefit greatly from somewhat heavier line weights.

The end result, given the relative sparseness of the chart, can be rather striking and visually attractive. Radar charts are also well suited for displaying a substantially greater number of series and data values than are given in this example. Up to six or eight data series can be accommodated in a radar chart without difficulty. They're worth considering for an offbeat and striking accent to your data—if you can ensure that your series values will be visible.

Using 2-D Doughnut Charts

Doughnut charts offer many of the same attributes of pie charts, which were described in chapters 13 and 14. The main difference between pie charts and doughnuts is the obvious visual one: the center of a doughnut chart is hollowed out. There is one more difference: unlike a pie chart, it's possible to display more than one series in a doughnut chart. Each series has its own doughnut, one inside of another.

Otherwise, a doughnut chart provides much the same function that a pie chart does: to display the division of a finite quantity, such as a year's market share, from *one* series of data. The use of a doughnut chart is mainly a stylistic decision. A data series is provided in table 19.6 for use in building a doughnut chart.

Table 19.6 Market Share Datasheet	
	1991
Massive Conglomerate, Inc.	57.1
Monolith Printers, Inc.	22.1
Amalgamated Industries	20.8

1. In PowerPoint, click the Insert Graph button on the standard toolbar. Microsoft Graph appears.

2. Select the default data in Graph's datasheet and delete it. Type the sample data set shown in table 19.6.

3. From the **F**ormat menu, choose **A**utoFormat. The AutoFormat dialog box appears (see fig. 19.14).

4. From the **G**alleries list box, choose Doughnut.

5. From the **F**ormats thumbnails, choose chart type #1. It appears as a simple doughnut chart.

6. Choose OK or press Enter.

7. If the doughnut appears to be all one color, click on the chart (to select it) and then click the By Column tool on the Graph toolbar. The three series values should split the doughnut up properly.

Fig. 19.14
The AutoFormat dialog box showing doughnut chart options.

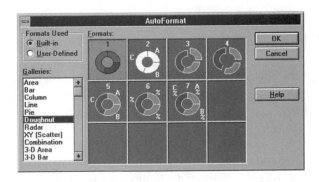

8. From the **I**nsert menu, choose **D**ata Labels.

   The Data Labels dialog box appears.

9. Choose the Show **P**ercent option button.

10. Choose OK or press Enter.

The doughnut chart should resemble figure 19.15.

Fig. 19.15
A doughnut chart displaying a legend and percentage labels.

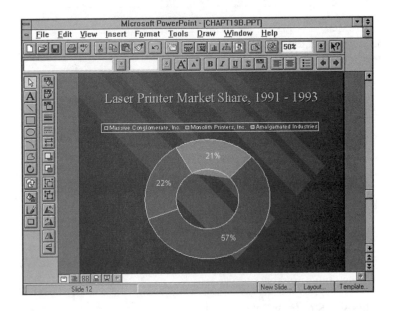

Tip
Doughnut slices, just like pie slices, can be pulled away from the chart.

The use of doughnut charts is quite straightforward—a 3-D doughnut type is not even available. They're a good substitute for pie charts if you want to break the monotony of a long series of chart slides.

Using 3-D Surface Charts

3-D surface charts are new to PowerPoint; they are a more specialized chart type that is generally not suited for many of the conventional business tasks used by other charts in this chapter. 3-D surface charts closely resemble topo-graphic maps—in fact, given enough series of data, you could actually con-struct a topographic map with geological data in PowerPoint.

Surface charts are used to show surface variations established over two or more evenly spaced values. Those evenly spaced values are the X and Y values in your chart, and there must be a minimum of two series of data and two categories of values to form a surface chart. The z-axis values in the chart determine the "topography" of the chart's surface. Using the laser printer market share datasheet, with a few minor chart adjustments, a fairly typical 3-D surface chart can be created, as shown in figure 19.16.

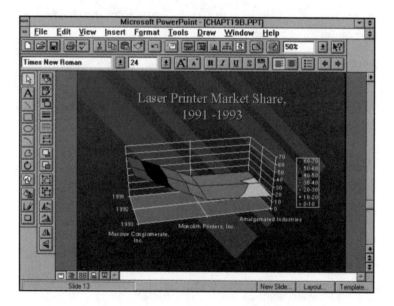

Fig. 19.16

A 3-D surface chart.

3-D surfaces are a chart type that can greatly benefit from the use of major gridlines on each axis. The 1991, 1992, and 1993 categories are arranged on the x-axis and the series labels are displayed on the y-axis. The major gridlines for all axes are displayed on the chart, which greatly aids readability on an already difficult chart.

Each series label has a tick mark and a major gridline assigned to it to help show the values of each series as they move across the chart. Based on the surface altitudes, the chart assigns colors to each value range. On first glance this can be confusing—what values do the colors signify? They actually don't signify any series values—just surface transitions from one series to another. The surface traverses up several ranges of altitude, for example, between the Monolith Printers series on the y-axis and the Massive Conglomerate series.

The surface is much flatter between the Amalgamated Industries series and Monolith Printers, reflecting the much closer range in values between them. While the 3-D surface chart reflects the dominance of Massive Conglomerate in this market, there are a number of other chart types that can be made to better serve the message of the market share data. There is great scope for creativity and experimenting with this chart type, however. The chart in figure 19.16 shows a few adjustments, such as 3-D rotation, that have been made to render the chart's values more readable. The following example helps you create that chart:

1. In PowerPoint, click the Insert Graph button from the standard toolbar. Microsoft Graph appears.

2. Select the default data in Graph's datasheet and delete it. Type the sample data set shown in table 19.5.

3. From the **F**ormat menu, choose **AutoFormat**. The AutoFormat dialog box appears.

4. From the **G**alleries list box, choose 3-D Surface.

5. From the **F**ormat thumbnails, choose chart type #1.

6. Choose OK or press Enter.

7. From the **F**ormat menu, choose **3**-D View.

   The Format 3-D View dialog box appears, as shown in figure 19.17.

8. In the **E**levation text box, enter the value **25**.

9. In the **R**otation text box, enter the value **75**.

10. In the **P**erspective text box, enter the value **30**.

11. Choose OK or press Enter.

    Now, gridlines are added to the chart.

12. From the **I**nsert menu, choose **G**ridlines.

    The Gridlines dialog box appears.

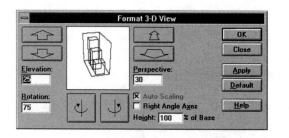

Fig. 19.17
The Format 3-D
View dialog box.

13. Click the Major Gridlines check boxes in the Category (X) Axis, Series (Y) Axis, and Value (Z) Axis dialog box sections.

14. Choose OK or press Enter.

15. To relocate the legend to a more convenient place, click the legend.

16. From the Format menu, choose Selected Legend.

17. Click the Placement tab.

18. Click the **R**ight option button under the Type option list to place the legend on the left side of the chart.

19. Choose OK or press Enter.

The surface chart should resemble that in figure 19.16.

Surface charts can be heavily customized, and you just had a small taste of that in the preceding example. While they're a very specialized chart type, surface charts are also very attractive and if they're chosen properly for the subject matter, they can be a striking addition to a slide show.

Comparing 3-D Area and 3-D Line Charts

3-D area and 3-D line charts are two more options that you should consider for your slide shows. Both types are readily adaptable to the same kinds of data and can deliver the same message; the use of one over another is generally a matter of taste. Area charts simply fill the areas below the lines with colors or patterns, but the values defined are the same. 3-D lines and areas are easily customized in much the same way that other 3-D charts are—for different chart depths, rotated views and different perspectives, gap widths between 3-D lines, different gridlines, and more.

Lines are generally easier to see in three dimensions than in 3-D area charts because you don't run the risk of hiding substantial areas behind other ones.

VI

Advanced PowerPoint 4

Viewers see lines somewhat more distinctly, as separate series at different depths within the chart. Nonetheless, 3-D areas offer other advantages, such as a greater physical presence in the chart, particularly when one area is much greater than the others. Figure 19.18 displays such a chart.

Fig. 19.18

A 3-D area chart displaying the Laser Printer Market Share data.

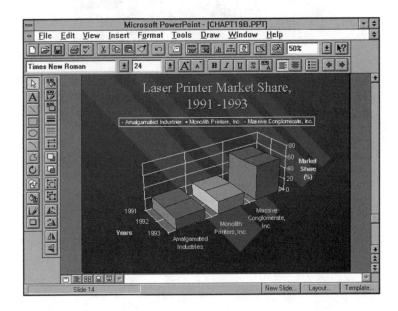

To get to this point, quite a few things may need to be adjusted beyond the basic chart. The rows of data in the chart datasheet may need to be rearranged to ensure that the largest area is in the "back" of the chart. The 3-D viewing angle may need to be adjusted for better area visibility. Axis label fonts may need to be readjusted.

Given the numerous similarities between 3-D area and 3-D line charts, one exercise should be adequate to reveal the possibilities inherent in both chart types. Use the data in table 19.7 to complete the next set of steps.

Table 19.7   Market Share Datasheet

	1991	1992	1993
Massive Conglomerate, Inc.	57.1	57.3	60.2
Monolith Printers, Inc.	22.1	23.5	21.8
Amalgamated Industries	20.8	19.2	18.0

1. In PowerPoint, click the Insert Graph button on the standard toolbar. Microsoft Graph appears.

2. Select the default data in Graph's datasheet and delete it using the Cle**a**r **A**ll command from the **E**dit menu. Type the sample data set shown in table 19.7.

3. From the F**o**rmat menu, choose **A**utoFormat.

   The AutoFormat dialog box appears.

4. From the **G**alleries list, choose 3-D Area. Eight thumbnails appear in the **F**ormats area.

5. Choose Chart #6.

Note

3-D area chart types #5, #6, and #7 are all quite similar, except for the gridlines that are displayed as their default. Also, several stacked area charts are offered that vary according to their use of gridlines, labels, and other chart elements.

---

6. Choose OK or press Enter.

   The chart appears, as shown in figure 19.19.

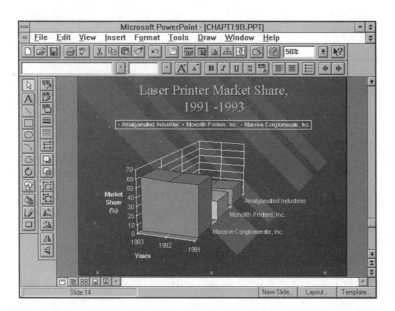

Fig. 19.19

A basic 3-D area chart displaying the Laser Printer Market Share data. Notice that fonts are out of proportion, areas are hidden, and the viewing angle could stand adjustment.

VI

Advanced PowerPoint 4

7. Click the y-axis—the axis bearing the company names.

8. From the Format menu, choose Selected Axis.

The Format Axis dialog box appears.

9. Click the Font tab.

10. Choose a 12 Point Regular font size.

11. Choose OK or press Enter. All three series labels should appear.

12. Follow steps 7-11 for the x-axis.

13. Click the Datasheet tool to display the Market Share datasheet, if it isn't already visible.

To ensure visibility for all the area values, the rows need to be in reverse order with Amalgamated, the series with the smallest values, in the top row, and Massive Conglomerate, the series with the largest values, in the third or bottom row.

14. Drag and drop edit each series (by clicking the row button and dragging each row to its new position—make sure you don't erase any other rows) until Amalgamated is on top, Monolith is in the second row, and Massive Conglomerate is in the third row of the datasheet. Cutting and pasting also works just as well.

The chart results in a better view of the respective areas, as shown in figure 19.20.

15. From the Format menu, choose **3**-D View.

The Format 3-D View dialog box appears.

16. In the **E**levation text box, enter the value **25**.

17. In the **R**otation text box, enter the value **55**.

18. If the **P**erspective feature is not displayed, click the Right Angle A**x**es check box. The x should be removed, displaying the **P**erspective feature in the dialog box. If the **P**erspective feature is already displayed, proceed to the next step.

19. In the **P**erspective text box, enter the value **30**.

For many charts, you need to play with the 3-D values to get it right. Also, don't forget that you can rotate a 3-D chart with the mouse.

20. Choose OK or press Enter.

With the end result of this chart, as shown in figure 19.21, you can see that it closely resembles another chart type—3-D columns.

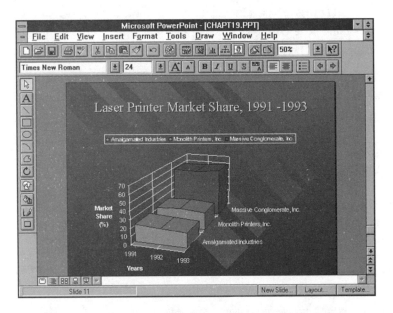

Fig. 19.20
The 3-D area chart displaying the rearranged Market Share data.

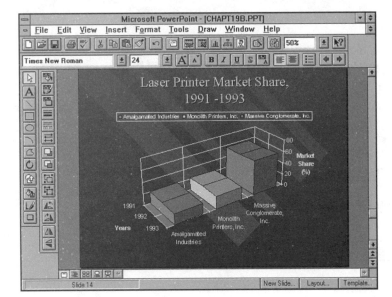

Fig. 19.21
The 3-D area chart displayed after changing its 3-D view.

VI

Advanced PowerPoint 4

In the end, PowerPoint's chart types, plus the many customizing features that are available, offer myriad ways to deliver a chart-based message to your audience. There are other alternatives, however. If you're used to creating your charts and datasheets in Excel, it's quite easy to import them into your presentation and entirely bypass having to create charts in PowerPoint at all. (That procedure is described a little later in this chapter in the section "Importing Excel Charts.")

You can also adopt a preferred chart as a new default type. That procedure is described in the section titled "Creating a New Default Chart," also a little later in this chapter.

Troubleshooting

I can't get my stock charts to display properly.

The key to correct stock charting is two-fold: having the correct number of series, and displaying your series By Columns on the datasheet. An OHLC (Open-High-Low-Close) stock chart must have four series, one each for the Open, High, Low, and Close data sets, and an HLC (High-Low-Close) chart must have three series. When your data series are properly entered, click the By Column button on Graph's Standard toolbar.

My scatter chart data markers are almost invisible on-screen.

This proves to be a difficult problem only because you have to do some work with the chart's color scheme (and very likely its slide as well) to make your scatter chart markers more visible. On many occasions, a scatter chart will need a different color scheme from the rest of the presentation because of the difficulty of making the markers visible.

A good rule of thumb is to use bold, bright primary colors for scatter chart markers, and to use a dark background color on the slide. First, click on the scatter markers, each series in turn, and choose Format Selected Data Series. Change the marker colors to reflect your needs (making sure, of course, that each marker series is a different color). If you must use gridlines (which can be a good idea with a scatter chart) use black for their color to ensure that your markers show up. Then select a dark color for your slide background.

An example of the use of these techniques for a scatter chart appears in Appendix B of this book.

Creating a New Default Chart

Using a preferred chart as a default chart format has a number of advantages. First, it prevents the necessity of reentering the same set of data for a series of charts using the same datasheet, or even the tedium of clearing and pasting data between slides.

Second, every formatting specification you desire can be included in the default format, including axes, axis labels, types of gridlines, line weights, fonts attached to labels, colors, and anything else having to do with chart formatting.

To create a new default chart, follow these steps:

1. If you're pleased with your current chart layout and want to use it as the new default format, make sure all the formatting changes are made that you want included in the new default.

2. From the **T**ools menu, choose **O**ptions.

   The Graph Options dialog box appears, as shown in figure 19.22.

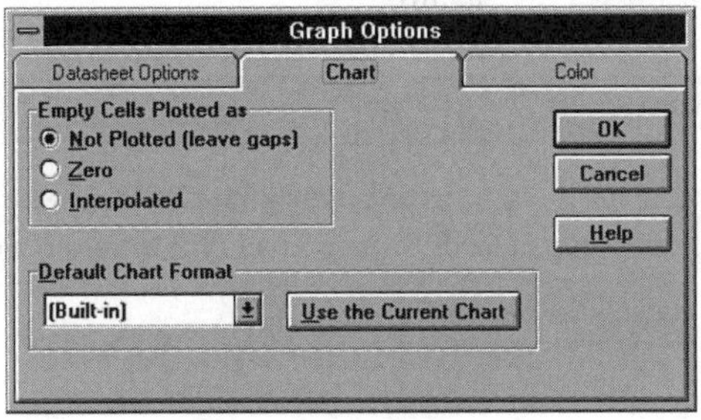

Fig. 19.22

The Graph Options dialog box showing the Chart tab options.

3. Click the Chart tab.

   Here, an entire list of new charts can be added for new default chart types. Under the **D**efault Chart Format list, the Graph default is called "Built-In."

4. Under the **D**efault Chart Format section of the dialog box, choose the **U**se the Current Chart button.

   The Add Custom AutoFormat dialog box appears, as shown in figure 19.23.

Fig. 19.23
Using the Add
Custom
AutoFormat dialog
box to specify a
new Graph
default.

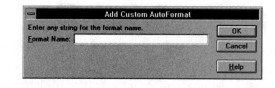

> **Note**
>
> The name of the dialog box, Add Custom AutoFormat, should give you a clue
> about another PowerPoint feature—the capability to save your charts as spe-
> cial user-defined types for use in Graph AutoFormats. A section later in this
> chapter discusses using the Add Custom AutoFormat feature to show your
> special charts for use in creating new ones.

5. In the **F**ormat Name text box, type the desired chart name (make it an
   easily understood name that won't get mixed up with other chart
   types).

6. Choose OK or press Enter.

7. Choose OK or press Enter again.

> **Note**
>
> The new default chart type is placed as an entry in the Windows text file GRAPH.INI.
> Whenever Graph is started up, it loads the new chart type from this file as the default
> format.

Exporting a PowerPoint Chart to Other Applications

Though PowerPoint cannot directly export chart objects to other applications, it's possible to save a slide as a bitmap picture for display in other programs. It's a straightforward process, and it's described in the following steps:

1. Display the slide that you want to export as a bitmap picture.

2. From the **F**ile menu, choose Save **A**s (see fig. 19.24).

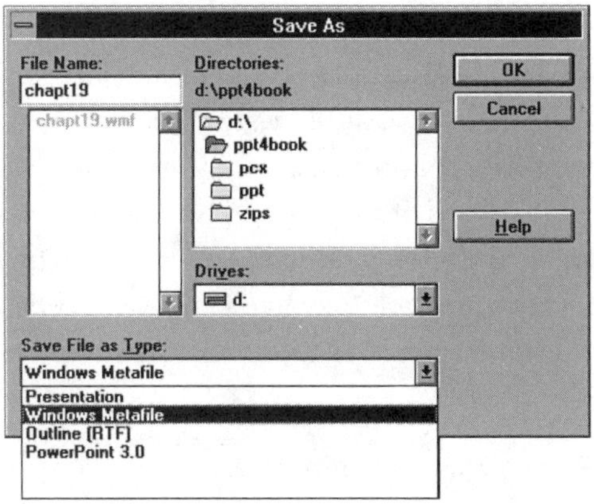

Fig. 19.24
Using the Save As dialog box to export a slide as a picture file.

3. In the File **N**ame text box, type the desired name for the file, of eight characters or less.

4. Choose the **D**irectories and Dri**v**es under which the file can be saved.

5. In the Save File as **T**ype drop-down list, choose Windows Metafile.

6. If you want the fonts to be included in the picture, click the Em**b**ed TrueType Fonts check box.

7. Choose OK or press Enter.

The slide is saved as a picture, or "screen shot," to be viewed or placed in a different application.

Tip
Windows Metafile picture files have the extension *.WMF.

Importing Data and Charts

PowerPoint 4 offers direct ways to import data and charts from Microsoft Excel. Versions 4.0 and 5.0 of Excel are supported, and although PowerPoint has a closer relationship to Excel 5.0 in terms of object linking and embedding capabilities, you can still include Excel 4.0 charts and datasheets. Chapter 18, "Using Links to Other Applications," describes how to work with object linking and embedding for use between PowerPoint and other applications such as Excel 5.0. This short section describes the direct importing of data and charts from Excel files.

VI

Advanced PowerPoint 4

Importing Data

Importing Excel or Lotus 1-2-3 datasheets can be an extremely handy feature for PowerPoint users. You may want to create your own charts in PowerPoint but have most of your data committed in datasheets from another program. Importing them can save tons of work. Doing so requires only that you be in PowerPoint's Graphing application. A good way to start is by displaying a PowerPoint default chart and datasheet in a new Graph slide. With the default chart and datasheet displayed in Microsoft Graph (*not in PowerPoint*), follow these steps:

1. From the **E**dit menu, choose **I**mport Data.

   The Import Data dialog box appears, as shown in figure 19.25.

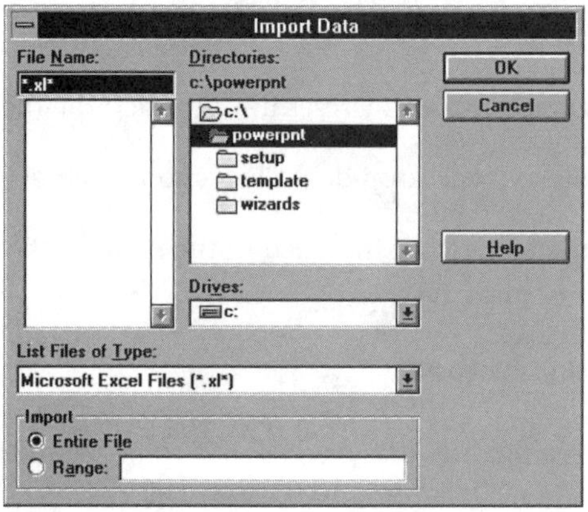

Fig. 19.25

Using the Import Data dialog box in Graph to import an Excel datasheet.

2. In the List Files of **T**ype drop-down list, choose the desired file type. Excel files are shown as (*.xl*) and Lotus 1-2-3 files are shown as (*.wk*).

3. Choose the **D**irectories and Dri**v**es under which the file can be located.

4. In the File **N**ame list, click the desired file name to select it and display it in the text box.

5. Choose OK or press Enter.

   A message box appears asking whether you want to overwrite the existing data.

6. Choose the Yes button.

The Excel data is displayed in the Graph datasheet.

Importing Excel Charts

Importing Excel charts can also be useful for PowerPoint users. You may want to create your own charts in Excel because you're used to that program, and your data may be committed to datasheets in that program. Importing them is simple and doing so requires only that you be in PowerPoint's Graphing application. A good way to start is by displaying a PowerPoint default chart and datasheet in a new Graph slide. With the default chart and datasheet displayed in Graph (not in PowerPoint), follow these steps:

1. From the **E**dit menu, choose **I**mport C**h**art.

    The Import Chart dialog box appears, as shown in figure 19.26.

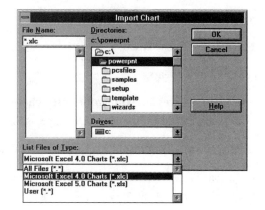

Fig. 19.26
Importing an Excel chart using Graph's Import Chart feature.

2. In the List Files of **T**ype drop-down list, choose the desired file type. Excel 4.0 files are shown as (*.xlc) and Excel 5.0 chart files are shown as (*.xls).

3. Choose the **D**irectories and Dri**v**es under which the file can be located.

4. In the File **N**ame list, click the desired file name to select it and display it in the text box.

5. Choose OK or press Enter.

    A message box appears asking whether you want to overwrite the existing chart.

6. Choose the Yes button.

The Excel chart is displayed in Graph, available for changing and editing in Graph's normal modes.

VI

Advanced PowerPoint 4

Importing Charts from PowerPoint 3

If you've built up a library of presentations and charts created in PowerPoint 3, you're in luck. It's a very simple matter to import charts from the previous version of the program into PowerPoint 4.

Essentially, all you have to do is load the old-format presentation into the PowerPoint program. Once you've done so, double-clicking on a chart in a slide automatically converts the old Microsoft Graph charts to the new version. The major difference between the versions of Graph, of course, is that the older version uses OLE 1.0, while the current version uses OLE 2.0, or in-place editing. Graph data is converted automatically, invisible to the user. Here's how the procedure is done:

1. Start the PowerPoint program.

2. From the **F**ile menu, choose **O**pen.

   The Open dialog box appears.

Tip

PowerPoint 3 files also have the file extension .PPT.

3. From the File **N**ame, Dri**v**es and **D**irectories lists, choose the PowerPoint 3 file you want to load and then choose OK or press Enter.

   After a moment, the program displays a message box reading:

   ```
   This presentation uses File Format 80. It will be converted to
   Format 102 and opened as Read-Only.
   ```

4. Choose OK or press Enter.

5. When the file is opened, use the File Save As command to save the opened file as a new PowerPoint 4 format file (you will not be able to overwrite the old one — the program will not let you).

6. When that's done, double-click on a chart in the presentation. The conversion is done.

There's an alternative method that saves a few steps: by using the Slides From File command from the **I**nsert menu under PowerPoint.

1. With your presentation displayed in PowerPoint, from the **I**nsert menu, choose Slides from **F**ile.

   The Insert File dialog box appears.

2. From the File **N**ame, Dri**v**es and **D**irectories lists, choose the PowerPoint 3 file you want to load and then choose OK or press Enter.

The slides from the PowerPoint 3 file (or PowerPoint 4 file, for that matter) are automatically converted and inserted into your presentation. You will not even see a screen message regarding file formats, but you may see a `Charts are being updated to the new color scheme` message for a moment as the computer does its work.

Saving Custom Chart Types for Later Use

Earlier in this chapter, you learned how to create a new default chart. Now, a similar procedure can be used to create new AutoFormats. Doing so enables you to re-use powerful new chart formats for any appropriate chart. Some exercises in this chapter required 40 or more steps to complete. Such a complex chart is a perfect candidate for a new AutoFormat.

There are actually two different ways to perform this task. One is to use the same procedure as for defining a default chart. The other way is simpler and more efficient. The easier procedure is described first:

1. Display the chart, in Microsoft Graph, that you want to make a new AutoFormat for.

2. From the Format menu, choose **A**utoFormat. The AutoFormat dialog box appears.

3. Under the Formats Used section of the dialog box, click the **U**ser-Defined option button.

4. Click the Custo**m**ize button.

   The User-Defined AutoFormats dialog box appears, similar to figure 19.27.

Tip
You can delete any AutoFormat you previously defined here.

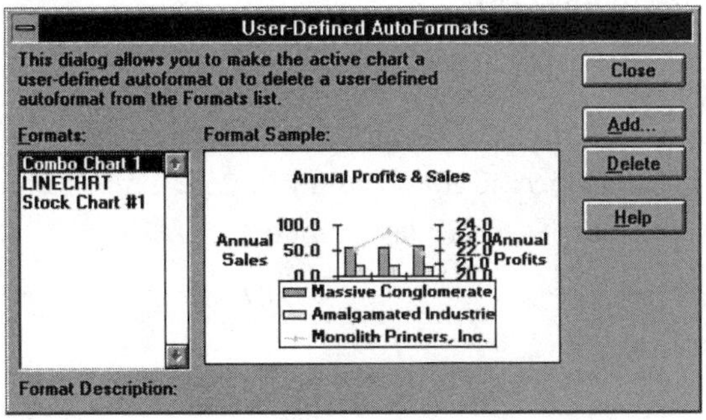

Fig. 19.27
The User-Defined AutoFormats dialog box showing the existing user-defined formats and a sample of the new type to be added.

VI

Advanced PowerPoint 4

5. Click the **A**dd button.

6. The Add Custom AutoFormat dialog box appears, as shown in figure 19.28.

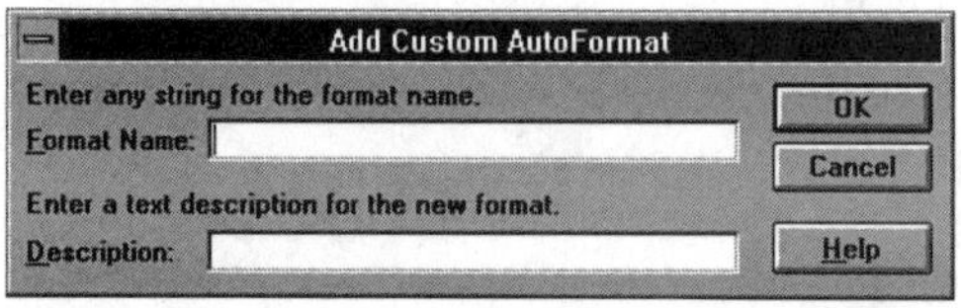

Fig. 19.28

The Add Custom AutoFormat dialog box, where the name and description of the new AutoFormat is entered.

7. In the **F**ormat Name text box, type the desired chart name (make it an easily understood name that won't be confused with other chart types).

8. Type a description in the **D**escription text box, if desired (it is not required).

9. Choose OK or press Enter.

10. Click the Close button or press Enter.

The AutoFormat has been added to the User-Defined list.

Now, check on your chart type to see its place in the AutoFormat selections.

Tip

If you're pleased with your current chart layout and want to save it as a new AutoFormat, make sure all the formatting changes are made that you want included in the new chart type.

11. From the F**o**rmat menu, choose **A**utoFormat.

The AutoFormat dialog box appears.

12. Under the Formats Used section of the dialog box, click the **U**ser-Defined button.

13. Under the **F**ormats list, click the chart type you want. The dialog box displays a sample chart.

14. Choose OK or press Enter.

The AutoFormat you previously defined is applied to the chart. Notice that all the proper text formatting and chart elements are exactly where they should be. Bear in mind that specific chart types you define may also require a certain number of data series to display properly.

Customizing Combination Charts

PowerPoint offers other features to customize and change combination charts (and, for that matter, any chart type), by using two commands that haven't been discussed very much until now: the Format Chart Type command and the Format Group command. Neither command is particularly difficult and both offer another dimension to the conventional use of AutoFormats, which you've relied on for most of the charting examples in this book.

Both commands allow you to change the type of data markers that are applied to any data series in your chart. For example, if you have a combination chart that uses a line and an area, the area can be quickly converted to a set of 2-D columns. A chart of any type can be converted to any other type.

The Format Chart Type command and the Format Group command are closely interrelated, and they can both be accessed from one another (see fig. 19.29 and fig. 19.30).

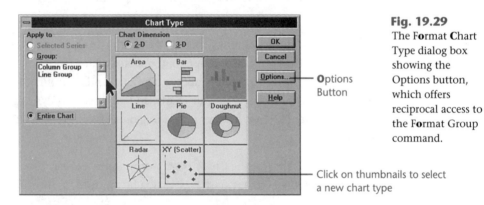

Fig. 19.29
The Format Chart Type dialog box showing the Options button, which offers reciprocal access to the Format Group command.

Options Button

Click on thumbnails to select a new chart type

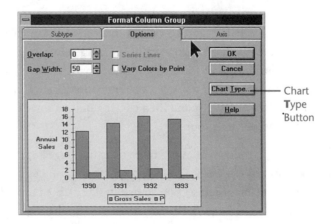

Fig. 19.30
The Format Group dialog box showing its Chart Type button, which offers reciprocal access to the Format Group command.

Chart Type Button

VI

Advanced PowerPoint 4

As you may recall from the final troubleshooting section in chapter 14, the Format Group menu option is a dynamic one that changes based on the chart type you select (see fig. 19.31).

Fig. 19.31
The Format menu showing two Group commands (because the chart used is a combination chart).

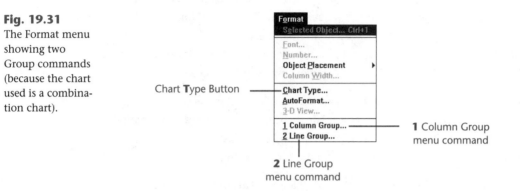

Chart **T**ype Button

1 Column Group menu command

2 Line Group menu command

You see two Group commands on the Format menu only if you're using a combination chart. Otherwise, only one Group command is shown on the menu.

If you click on the **1** Column Group or **2** Column Group menu commands, you bring up the Format Column Group or Format Line Group dialog box, each of which bears three tabs: Subtype, Options, and Axis. All of them are used to add custom effects to your charts, and all three tabs dynamically change to offer different features depending on the chart type that's currently selected.

In all cases, clicking on the Chart **T**ype button in the Format Group dialog box brings up the Format Chart Type dialog box in turn, as shown in figure 19.30.

This is the place where you can change the chart type that's applied to the current chart or selected series (or a Group) in a combination chart. A Group is a group of data series used to create a chart, and a single series is obviously one set of data markers of the same color in the chart. You can have up to two groups in a chart, which results in a combination chart. Clicking on one of the groups in the Group list and then clicking on a thumbnail changes the chart type for the selected group.

It isn't as hard as it sounds. Be aware that you can change any chart to a 2-D or 3-D type (by choosing the **2**-D or **3**-D option button under the Format Chart Type Chart Dimension section shown in fig. 19.29), but you cannot apply 3-D chart types to groups in a combination chart. The other group will be erased from view in the chart.

Click on a thumbnail in the Format Chart Type dialog box to change the chart type for the selected chart or group. It's a great way to experiment with various combinations and chart styles.

Using Trendlines to Do Forecasting

Trendlines are a useful tool for forecasting and illustrating trends in your charts. You can apply trendlines to most 2-D chart types; they're very useful for 2-D column charts, but they can be applied to bar, scatter, line, and area charts as well. In fact, they can be applied to any chart type in the XY category. They can also be used with a combination chart, and in such a chart a trendline can be applied to each group. They cannot, however, be applied to an OHLC or HLC stock chart. You see a 2-D column chart used generically in the examples shown here.

Trendlines are a tool for forecasting possible future trends in your data. While they're simple to use, the concept behind trendlines is not. The theory behind trendlines is an idea called *regression analysis*. Without getting too technical, regression analysis is the basis for using your datasheet statistics to create the trendline. The math behind creating trendlines is not trivial, and you can choose between six different mathematical models to create your trendline.

Linear

Polynomial

Logarithmic

Exponential

Power

Moving Average

Depending on the nature of your datasheet numbers, you may need to try two or three math models to get the most accurate trendline. How can you tell if a trendline is accurate? Check the R-Squared value. All the calculation methods listed above yield a final value between 0 and 1. The closer a

Tip
Use the Format Chart Type and Format Group commands to experiment with combination chart types.

VI

Advanced PowerPoint 4

trendline's R-Squared value is to 1, the more accurate it is for the purposes of your chart. If it's closer to 0, the less accurate its trend calculations will be.

Please note that many details are beyond the scope of this book; Graph's On-Line Help on this subject (which is best found by using the Search for Help On feature) is highly recommended for users who need more detail than can feasibly be provided here.

You can apply a trendline in the following steps:

1. Display your 2-D column chart in Microsoft Graph.

2. Click on the data series (a set of columns of a specific color) to which you want to add a trendline.

3. From the **I**nsert menu, choose **T**rendline.

    The Format Trendline dialog box appears, as shown in figure 19.32.

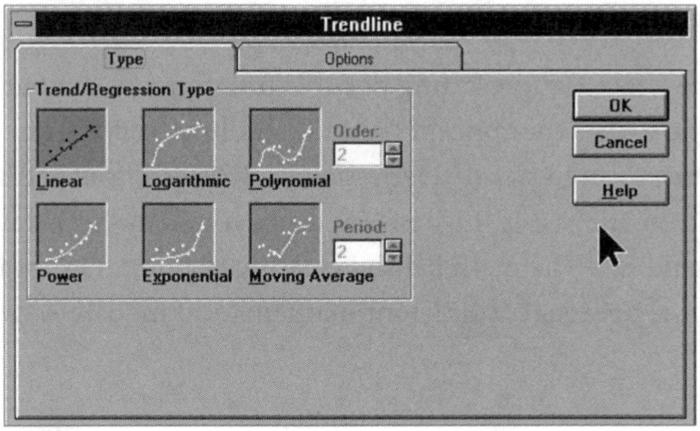

Fig. 19.32

The Format Trendline dialog box showing the six types of trendlines that can be added to your chart.

4. Six thumbnails are displayed showing the various trendline types that can be applied: **L**inear, **L**ogarithmic, **P**olynomial, Po**w**er, E**x**ponential, or **M**oving Average. Click on any of them (it may take some experimenting to get the best trendline type for your chart).

    You can add a name for your trendline and set other options for the trendline, such as displaying the R-Squared value.

5. Click the Options tab (see fig. 19.33).

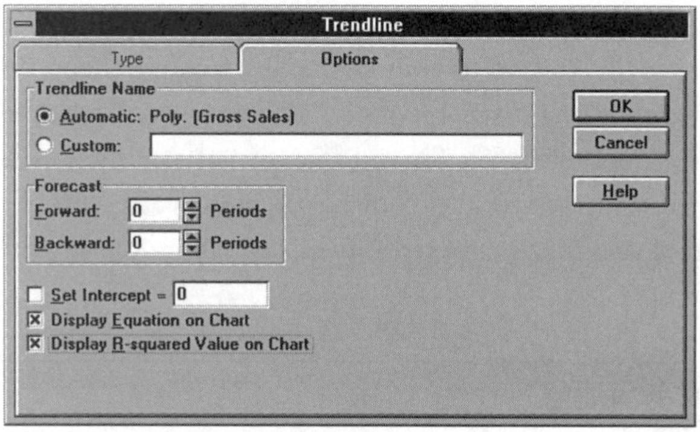

Fig. 19.33
Using the Format
Trendlines Option
tab to add a name
and display the R-
Squared value of
the trendline.

> **Note**
>
> You need at least four series values to display the R-Squared value of your trendline to determine its accuracy.

6. To display the R-Squared value for your trendline, click in the Display **R**-Squared value on Chart check box.

7. To display the formula used to create the trendline, click the Display **E**quation on Chart check box.

> **Note**
>
> The use of trendlines also offers a forecasting feature in which you can extrapolate from the data in your chart to a user-specified number of time periods based on the time periods reflected in your chart. Doing so extends your trendline beyond the scope provided by your basic chart. You can forecast backward or forward on your chart trendline. This feature is also called goal seeking.

8. To add forecasting to your chart, under the Forecast section of the Trendlines Options dialog box, type a value in the **F**orward Periods or **B**ackward Periods text box or use the mouse to increment them to a desired value. Both **F**orward and **B**ackward forecasting can be used at one time.

9. The Trendline name is automatically added, or you can add your own by typing it into the **C**ustom text box.

10. Choose OK or press Enter.

VI

Advanced PowerPoint 4

By using trendlines, you can add a sophisticated element of forecasting and statistical trend illustration to your charts. It's recommended that you have some understanding of mathematics (or know someone who does) so that you can make the best choice for accurate forecasts. Nonetheless, displaying the R-Squared value is a good expedient for a quick assessment of the accuracy of each of the six types of trendlines, though it does require some experimenting.

Troubleshooting

How can I get all my axis tick mark labels to display properly? Some of them are erased when I display the chart.

Oftentimes, Graph does not display all your axis tick mark labels because the font that's assigned to the axis is too large. When that happens, sometimes labels overrun each other, and the Graph program tends to drop some of them. To fix this, reduce the font size by clicking on the offending axis and choosing the Format Font command.

Sometimes you run into the same problem in a 3-D chart. The cure for this is two-fold: change the font size and adjust the 3-D Rotation values in the ways described in this chapter.

Can I create combination charts using 3-D types, say a 3-D column chart combined with a 2-D Line?

No. It's not possible to combine a 3-D chart to create a combination chart type. The other chart type will automatically be erased. Your series data in the datasheet will not be removed, but Graph will not display it in combination.

Also, if you play around with the Format Chart Type command as described a little earlier in this chapter, you will find it's possible to combine a 2-D pie chart with, say, a line chart, but the results will be almost meaningless and you'll have a very hard time trying to define the relationship between such a combination of types. Nonetheless, the scope for experimentation is so great that even with a trial-and-error process, you may find combinations no one has thought of, and with customizing features even be able to pull them off.

From Here...

Despite the extensive looks at PowerPoint 4's powerful charting capabilities, there is much that has been skipped or glossed over due to simple space considerations. An entire book could be devoted to PowerPoint's charting features alone. Hopefully, ample information has been provided to you for further explorations of charting. There are some advanced topics remaining to be discussed in the following chapters:

■ Chapter 20, "Advanced Presentation Management," shows you how to add special transition effects and their timing to a presentation, along with the use of multimedia effects such as sound bites and video clips.

■ Chapter 21, "Using Advanced Color, Text, and Drawing Features," shows how to add special effects to slide text, text rotation, tricks with color, and the creation of new color schemes.

■ Many functions you've seen in this chapter can be added to a customized toolbar. See chapter 22, "Customizing PowerPoint," for more information.

Chapter 20

Advanced Presentation Management

PowerPoint 4, along with previous versions, offers many special effects that can be added to slide shows. No presentation, particularly if it includes special multimedia elements such as video and audio clips, is complete without a set timing structure that enables the user to seamlessly integrate various elements without unwanted foul-ups during the actual show. Even if you have never conducted a public talk in your life, PowerPoint's transition, timing, and rehearsal features can help you appear as a Norman Vincent Peale. For effective presentation management, you need to understand and use PowerPoint's rehearsal features.

Setting Transition Styles and Transition Timing

When you run a slide show, it's quite simple to flip from one slide to the next on-screen—it's the typical 35mm slide show metaphor. It's just as easy, however, to provide graceful transitions between slides that add a more sophisticated effect with minimal trouble on your part. Transition styles can be assigned for any or all slides in your presentation with a few mouse clicks.

A *transition style* is the style in which a slide appears and disappears in an on-screen presentation. The concept is analogous to a slow fade or a "peeling" of the screen during a movie or a fancy video effect applied to a screen message during a football game. It's a quick "segue" to the next slide in your presentation. PowerPoint 4 offers 46 different transition styles that can be applied to

You learn about the following PowerPoint 4 features in this chapter:

- How to create transitions between slides

- How to rehearse and set timings for events in your presentation

- How to integrate multimedia elements into your presentation

VI

Advanced PowerPoint 4

any slide in your presentation. Styles include vertical and horizontal blinds, in which segments of the slide are revealed to the viewer; Box In and Box Out, in which the information on the next slide appears to "implode" or "explode" onto the screen; Checkerboard Across and Checkerboard Down, in which the contents of the next slide appear in a checkerboard pattern; and Cover Left, Up, Down, Left-Up, Right-Up, Left-Down, and Right-Down, in which the slide is assigned a direction from which it appears to be plopped down on top of the previous one. There are, of course, many more.

When you rehearse a presentation, you're actually in the process of setting the timing for all the events in your presentation—when each slide appears, when text points in a list appear on-screen, and so on. Effective use of timing in a presentation, particularly in a long and complex one, is a vital tool in preventing your audience from losing interest in your ideas.

Knowing the timing of your slide show also points out the importance of the other parts of your presentation—the outlines, speaker's notes, and handouts that are discussed in chapter 7. With a few extra minutes of preparation, all these tools can be used to deliver your message intelligently and cogently.

Setting a Transition Style on a Slide

Tip

Slide transitions can be assigned in any PowerPoint View mode.

You can assign a transition to a slide in any PowerPoint view: Slide view, Notes Pages, Outline, and in the Slide Sorter (see fig. 20.1). Although all views offer the same method for assigning effects, the Slide Sorter has advantages because its thumbnail display of all the slides enables you to keep visual track of all the slides to which you have assigned effects, and to interact with the entire presentation in a way that other views don't permit. Slides can be dragged and dropped in the Sorter to a different order, for example. You use the Slide Sorter view to assign transition effects for the examples in this chapter.

Another solid advantage of using the Slide Sorter to apply transitions and other effects is its display of small Transition icons underneath each slide thumbnail indicating when a transition effect has been applied to a selected slide, as shown in figure 20.1. The icons do not appear if a slide has not had an effect applied to it.

Slide Sorter toolbar Build button PowerPoint standard toolbar

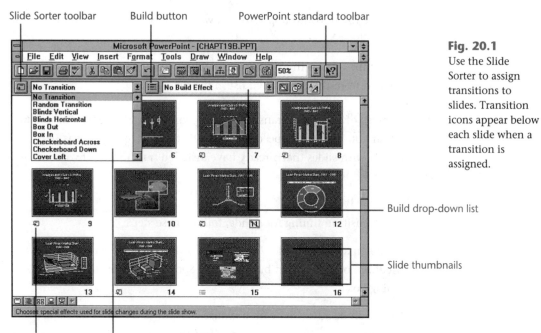

Fig. 20.1
Use the Slide Sorter to assign transitions to slides. Transition icons appear below each slide when a transition is assigned.

Build drop-down list

Slide thumbnails

Transition icon Transition drop-down list

To assign transitions to slides in Slide Sorter view, follow these steps:

1. Open the desired presentation in PowerPoint.

2. From the **V**iew menu, choose Sli**d**e Sorter.

    The Slide Sorter appears, as in figure 20.1.

3. Click once on the slide that you want to assign a transition.

4. Click the Transition button on the Slide Sorter toolbar to display the Transition dialog box, as shown in figure 20.2.

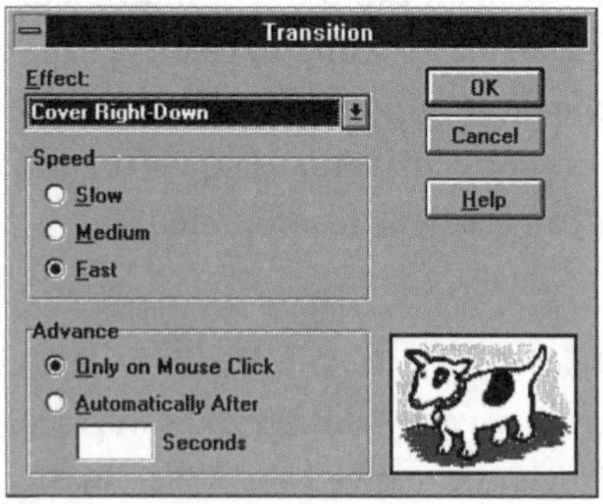

Tip
For a fast transition assignment, choose an effect from the Transition drop-down list. A transition icon appears below the chosen slide.

VI

Advanced PowerPoint 4

Fig. 20.2
Use the Transition dialog box to assign specific timings and advance specifications.

5. Choose the transition options you want. (These are described in text that follows.)

Remember: As on the Slide Sorter toolbar, a transition effect can be applied from the drop-down list in the dialog box.

An advantage of using the Transition dialog box in the Slide Sorter or in Slide view is that you can assign speeds and specific timings to transitions. This can be done with slides that already have assigned transitions, or with newly assigned ones.

Setting Transition Timing

To set the transition timing for a slide, follow these steps:

1. To assign a different speed to your transition, click on either the **S**low, **M**edium, or **F**ast option button in the Speed section of the Transition dialog box.

   Slides can be advanced with a mouse click, or you can set the slide to advance automatically after a specified time.

Tip
Select all your slides and choose a transition if you want to do this quickly. The transition you choose is applied to every slide.

2. Select an option for advancing your slides:

   ■ If you want the slide transition to advance on your prompting, click the **O**nly on Mouse Click option button.

   ■ To set a custom slide timing, click on the **A**utomatically After __ Seconds option button and enter the desired length in seconds (before the next slide appears) in the text box.

Managing Multimedia Effects

The last few years have seen an explosion of multimedia effects and applications in the PC market. A few meaningful results have come of this wave of new technology; the most important additions to the roster of computer-based media are full-motion video and CD-quality sound. Both of these additional data types can easily be incorporated into your PowerPoint presentation.

Understanding Video

Video comes from any of several sources: you can place a video-capture board into your computer, such as Creative Labs' Video Blaster or Intel's Smart

Video, and hook up a portable video camera or a VCR to it, and you instantly have new video clips to play with. You can also buy video clips on CD-ROM, which is a safe bet to avoid copyright infringements.

Several software standards have emerged for the use of video on your Windows PC; the most important being Apple's QuickTime for Windows, Intel's Indeo video, and Microsoft's Video for Windows. All of them cooperate in supporting a specific video file standard. Generally, video is placed into a small window on-screen, as figure 20.3 shows.

Fig. 20.3
A video clip displayed by using Windows Media Player.

Recording video clips on your PC is an expensive business; video typically chews up hard disk space at an astonishing speed. Also, unless you run your Windows screen at VGA resolution (640X480), you can have some difficulty viewing your video clips; for most video recording products, the largest video capture screen is 320X240 pixels, and video clips are normally played back at that resolution (hence the window in figure 20.3). If you run PowerPoint at 1024X768 or 1280X1024 screen resolution (which in many ways is very desirable), the video clip is roughly the size of a postage stamp. However, there are ways to avoid this problem when running a presentation.

PowerPoint 4 uses the Windows Media Player as its tool for playing video clips that are integrated into your presentation. A clip can be played on a prompt by the user during the presentation, or the clip can be set to play automatically during the slide show, once or in a continuous loop.

> **Note**
>
> When you load video clips as objects into PowerPoint, they normally have the file extension *.AVI. That's the Video for Windows file standard.

VI

Advanced PowerPoint 4

A copy of the Windows Media Player is bundled with the PowerPoint 4 package. Several features of the Media Player can be used to ease the process of playing video and sound clips during a presentation. In fact, for efficient placement of a video clip on your PowerPoint presentation, it's necessary to use the features of the Video Player. Later in this chapter, you learn about the techniques for proper manipulation of video and sound clips in your slides. The next section deals with the placement of video clips in your presentation.

Inserting Video Clips

Tip

In the Slide Sorter, double-click the slide in which you want to insert a video clip. The slide is displayed in **S**lides view.

You can insert video clips into any slide of your presentation. Doing so is a straightforward process. To insert video clips and other objects, you must be in PowerPoint's **S**lides view. Follow these steps:

1. If you're still in the Slide Sorter, from the **V**iew menu, choose **S**lides.

2. Choose the slide to insert the video clip into with the Slide Changer.

3. From the **I**nsert menu, choose **O**bject.

   The Insert Object dialog box appears (see fig. 20.4).

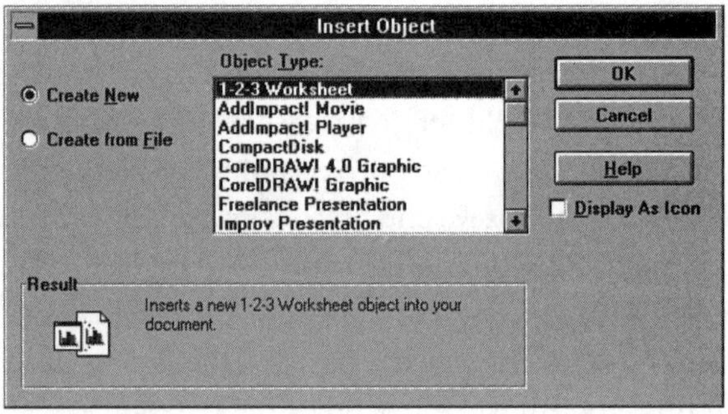

Fig. 20.4

The Insert Object dialog box listing the various types of files you can load as Objects into your presentation.

4. In the Object **T**ype list box, choose Media Clip.

   The Windows Media player program appears (see fig. 20.5). From this program, you must load the video file that is to be inserted into your slide.

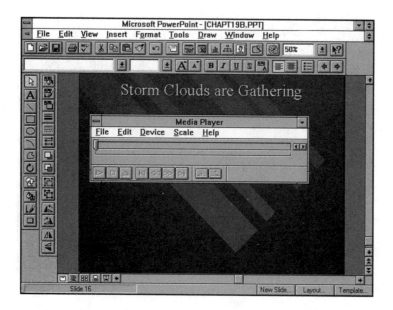

Fig. 20.5
The Media Player
program, which
pops up over your
PowerPoint screen
during the process
of loading a video
clip.

5. From the Media Player **F**ile menu, choose **O**pen.

   The Media Player's Open dialog box appears. It's a standard File Open-style dialog box. The List Files of **T**ype drop-down list displays the media file types that can be loaded by the program.

6. Locate the proper drive and directory that contain your video file, and choose the .AVI file you want to insert.

7. Choose OK or press Enter.

   The Media Player is still displayed. Before quitting and returning to PowerPoint, the object must be updated in the presentation.

8. From the Media Player's **F**ile menu, choose **U**pdate.

9. From the Media Player's **F**ile menu, choose E**x**it; or press Alt+F4.

   The new video clip appears as an icon on the slide, as shown in figure 20.6.

   The video object can be resized and moved around the slide like any other object on-screen.

Fig. 20.6
A PowerPoint slide displaying the video clip object.

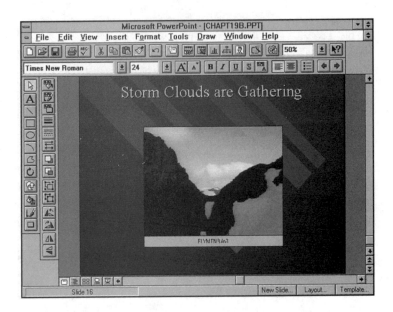

10. To preview the video, double-click it. A movie window pops up on-screen, as shown in figure 20.7, and the clip runs.

Fig. 20.7
Previewing the video. Click the Maximize icon for a full-screen movie display.

Notice the Play and Pause buttons on the movie screen. At any time during the video playback, you can click the Pause button to stop the video. Clicking the Play button resumes the paused clip. When the clip is finished, its window disappears and you return to the PowerPoint screen.

11. To display the movie on the entire screen, click the Maximize icon on the movie window.

Tip

If you maximize the movie screen, it will not close after the clip runs. You must double-click its Control icon or press Alt+F4.

There are other options for controlling and playing video clips and other multimedia data types. They are discussed a little later in this chapter.

Understanding Sound

Sound is another, somewhat touchier media. Many dozens of sound cards are available, most of which allow the recording of voice, sound, and music at almost CD-quality levels; most products are more effective on paper than they are in the real world. Sound recording (which is called *sampling*) can require as much as 10M of hard disk space for one minute of sound. Generally, for presentation purposes, such a sound file is impractical. It's more feasible to add lesser quality sound files, or sounds of a much shorter duration of time, to a presentation.

Most higher-quality sound cards support six different recording formats:

Card Size	Frequency	Sound Quality
8-bit	11Khz	Poorest quality, smallest files
	22Khz	
	44Khz	
16-bit	11Khz	
	22Khz	
	44 Khz	CD-Quality sound, largest files

The 8-bit and 16-bit specifications refer to the kind of sound card and the number of bits allocated to each segment of sound recording: an 8-bit or 16-bit ISA bus card, for example. The Sound Blaster Pro is an 8-bit sound card, and the Pro Audio Spectrum, Sound Blaster 16, and Turtle Beach Multisound

VI

Advanced PowerPoint 4

cards (just to name a few) are 16-bit ISA cards. Using 16-bit means substantially higher quality sound.

In fact, for most applications there is absolutely no need to use CD-quality sound. 16-bit 22Khz or 8-bit 44Khz sound—or even 8-bit 22Khz—is more than adequate for most presentation needs. Also, if you intend to include higher-quality sound files in your presentation, make sure the system you deliver the presentation on has sound capabilities of its own, or your extra work will go for nothing.

The Windows Media Player program sound file standard has the *.WAV (for Waveform) file extension. These are the files you should seek for inclusion in your multimedia presentations.

Inserting Sound Files

Adding sound files to your presentation works in much the same way as for video clips. Here's how to add sound files:

1. From the **I**nsert menu, choose **O**bject.

   The Insert Object dialog box appears (refer to fig. 20.4). The Insert Object dialog box lists the various types of files you can load as Objects into your presentation.

2. In the Object **T**ype list box, choose Media Clip. (Yes, it's the same object type.)

   The Windows Media player program appears (refer to fig. 20.5). From this program, you must load the video file that is to be inserted into your slide. The Media Player program pops up over your PowerPoint screen during the process of loading a video clip.

3. From the Media Player **F**ile menu, choose **O**pen.

   The Media Player's Open dialog box appears. It's a standard File Open-style dialog box. The List Files of **T**ype drop-down list displays the media file types that can be loaded by the program.

4. Locate the proper drive and directory that contains your sound file, and choose the .WAV file you want to insert.

5. Choose OK or press Enter.

   The Media Player is still displayed. Before quitting and returning to PowerPoint, the object must be updated in the presentation.

6. From the Media Player's **F**ile menu, choose **U**pdate.

7. From the Media Player's **F**ile menu, choose E**x**it or press Alt+F4.

The new sound file object appears as an icon on the slide, as shown in figure 20.8.

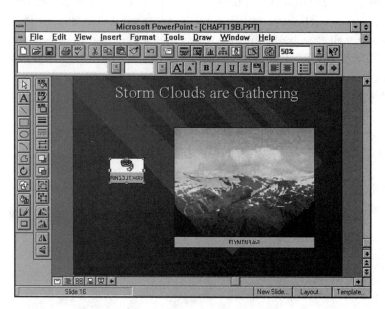

The sound object can be resized and moved around the slide like any other object on-screen.

8. To preview the sound bite, double-click it. The Media Player pops up, and the audio is played.

> **Note**
>
> If you want to embed the entire sound file into the slide, choose the Create from **F**ile option button in the Insert Object dialog box. The Object **T**ype list disappears, replaced by a File text box and a **B**rowse button that enables you to search for the exact location of your sound file. When you've located your *.WAV file, choose OK or press Enter. The sound file is embedded into your slide. The same is true of video files.

For more features and information on how to manipulate and trigger video and sound objects, see the next section.

VI

Advanced PowerPoint 4

Using the Play Settings Feature to Trigger Multimedia Events

PowerPoint 4 offers a simple but powerful way to manage the timing and triggering of multimedia elements in your presentation by using the Play Settings command.

It's easy to apply timing to multimedia events in your presentation. It's also a handy, or even essential, feature if you're not interested in clicking the mouse to control all aspects of your slide show when you deliver it. As with other timing events in your presentation, it's a matter of specifying a time delay with a couple of mouse clicks and typing a value into a dialog box. To do so, follow these steps:

1. Click on the desired video or sound object.

2. From the **T**ools menu, choose Pla**y** Settings.

   The Play Settings dialog box appears (see fig. 20.9).

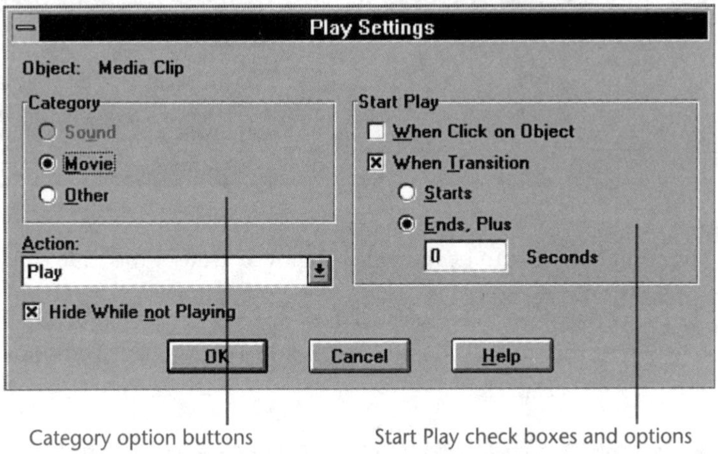

Fig. 20.9
Using
PowerPoint's Play
Settings feature to
set the triggering
of multimedia
events.

Play Settings
Object: Media Clip

Category
- ○ Sound
- ● Movie
- ○ Other

Action:
Play

☒ Hide While not Playing

Start Play
- ☐ When Click on Object
- ☒ When Transition
  - ○ Starts
  - ● Ends, Plus
    - 0 Seconds

[OK] [Cancel] [Help]

Category option buttons   Start Play check boxes and options

3. Choose from the options in the dialog box. For the object types discussed in this chapter, both sound and video are called Media Clips. The options displayed in this dialog box are described in the following listing:

   ■ Category   Specify object category for settings

   So**u**nd   Sound file (*.WAV)

   Movie   Video clip (*.AVI)

   Other   Other objects such as animations

■ Start Play   Specify how to play an object during a presentation

When Click   Tell the program to play the object when it's
on Object   double-clicked on by the presenter

When   Play the object at a specific time after the slide
Transition   appears

Starts   Play object immediately when the slide appears

Ends, Plus   Specify a time delay after the slide (0) appears
Seconds

To set Play Settings for a sound object, click the So**u**nd option button.
For a video object, click the **M**ovie option button.

4. To trigger a multimedia event in your slide manually, click the **W**hen
Click on Object check box. If the When **T**ransition check box is still
selected, click on it to remove the x.

5. To set an automatic triggering of the multimedia event in your slide
show, choose the When **T**ransition check box. You can elect to start the
event immediately after the slide is displayed (by choosing the **S**tarts
button) or to set a predetermined time delay with the **E**nds, Plus (0)
Seconds option button and text box.

6. Choose OK or press Enter.

> **Note**
>
> If you have two or more multimedia objects in a slide, different timings can be
> assigned to each so that they trigger in sequence. A sound bite can be set to
> trigger two or three seconds after the start of a video clip, so that they run
> more or less simultaneously.

Multimedia objects are a fun way to dress up a slide, but don't go overboard
with them. Many products, disk-based and particularly on CD-ROM, are
available that provide libraries of stock video footage and sound files that can
be used freely. When you are importing video clips and sounds, and especially if you're recording your own sound files and video, remember: don't
use copyrighted material. You may be held liable for expensive royalties, or

Tip
When you cut and
paste multimedia
objects that have
Play Settings ap-
plied to them, the
settings migrate
with the objects.

Tip
To hide multime-
dia effects on an
otherwise crowded
slide, choose the
Hide While **n**ot
Playing check box
in the Play Set-
tings dialog.

VI

Advanced PowerPoint 4

even criminal prosecution, if the unlikely chance occurs that you are caught using someone else's artistic or intellectual property to spice up your slide show.

Tips for Control of Multimedia Objects in Your Presentations

PowerPoint bundles a copy of the Media Player and installs it along with the main program. The Media Player is an OLE Server program, and it is the key component for assuring efficient use of video and sound files in your PowerPoint presentation. Although you can set timings for the multimedia events in PowerPoint, many aspects of controlling multimedia objects in your presentation must still be executed in the Media Player. The basic placement of the multimedia objects in your slide is not enough to guarantee the desirable effect. You may need to make some adjustments to provide a cleaner and more sophisticated effect. You do this by using the Media Player.

Managing Video Effects

The Media Player allows you to set a number of options for how your video clip is going to be played in your slide show. To start, figure 20.10 shows the Media Player displayed, with a typical video clip.

Fig. 20.10
Using the Media Player to edit multimedia objects.

Media Player

Video clip window

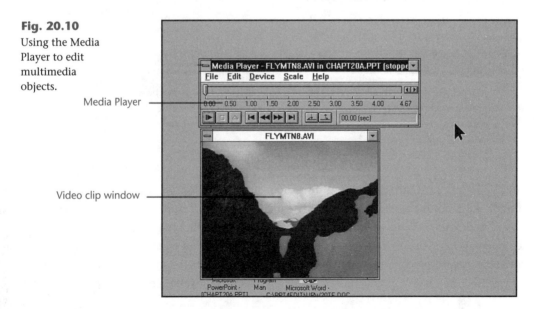

The procedures described here can be applied to objects that have already been embedded in a slide or they can be used when you place a new multimedia object. In the current example, they are applied to an existing object.

1. Click on the embedded video object to select it.

2. From the **E**dit menu in PowerPoint, choose Media Clip **O**bject, and then **E**dit.

   After a moment, the Media Player appears displaying the video clip in a separate window.

   There are a number of options that can be set for more efficient execution of video clips in a slide show. A set of Video Playback options is available under the **D**evice **C**onfigure menu option in the Media Player. Another set of check box options is available under Media Player's **E**dit menu in the **O**ptions dialog box. The check box options under **E**dit **O**ptions include features for automatic rewind and auto repeat of video clips, and several OLE object options including the capability to play videos with or without a border, a file name caption, a playback toolbar, and others.

3. From the **D**evice menu in the Media Player, choose **C**onfigure.

   The Video Playback Options dialog box appears (see fig. 20.11).

Tip
Click the right mouse button on top of an audio file icon or a movie clip. The shortcut menu pops up. Choose Edit Media Clip Object from the shortcut menu, and the Media Player appears, ready for editing.

Fig. 20.11
The Device Configure command in the Media Player brings up the Video Playback Options dialog box.

■ Video Mode: The Video Mode section offers two option buttons that are mutually exclusive; if one is selected the other is automatically disabled. Here, you can choose whether to run the video clip **F**ull Screen or in a **W**indow. In either case, the selection you choose causes the video clip to run accordingly during the slide show in PowerPoint.

VI

Advanced PowerPoint 4

Window: If you select the **W**indow option button, the clip plays inside its own window on top of the slide.

Full Screen: If you select the **F**ull Screen option button, when you run the slide show, the video clip automatically opens into a full-screen view and plays through its sequence. When it's done, the clip disappears and the slide show resumes.

- **Z**oom by 2: In either case, if you also click the **Z**oom by 2 check box, the video clip is magnified by a factor of 2. This is an especially handy feature if you're playing the video in a window and you're running Windows at a higher resolution, because it eliminates the "postage stamp" visual effect that a small video window acquires at higher resolutions. If this check box is enabled for a full-screen video clip display, the effect is somewhat less pleasing because the video becomes more grainy and loses some detail.

- **S**kip Video Frames if Behind: The **S**kip Video Frames if Behind box, if enabled, allows a more efficient playback when the system is recovering video frames off the disk. If the video playback runs ahead of the disk fetching of the next frames, it simply skips some of the missing video frames to minimize the "jumping" effect of the playback.

- **I**nformation: A scrollable list offering a description of the video clip: its duration in time, its length in frames, the name of the .AVI file, its type, number of frames per second playback, and other information.

4. When you're finished making your Video Playback options, choose OK or press Enter. A considerable number of playback options are also offered in the **E**dit **O**ptions dialog box.

5. From the **E**dit menu in Media Player, choose **O**ptions. The Options dialog box appears.

Fig. 20.12
Using the Edit Options command in the Media Player to set more playback options.

A substantial number of other playback options are offered here:

■ **A**uto Rewind: Sets the video clip to rewind to the beginning after playback (it's not done automatically, so the check box must be enabled before this can happen).

■ Auto **R**epeat: Sets the video clip to repeat in an endless loop until the presenter or user interrupts it with a mouse click during the presentation.

■ OLE Object: A selection of options for defining how the video clip appears when it is played back in the OLE client application (in this case, PowerPoint 4).

Cap**t**ion: Enabling this check box displays a caption showing the file name of the video clip during playback in the presentation. For most situations, this may not be desirable, because it distracts from the actual content of the slide.

Border around object: Enabling this check box displays a window border around the video clip when it's played. Disabling it does not affect the playing of the clip, but a border is not added during playback.

Play in Client Document: This option is highly recommended if you want a seamless appearance of the video clip in your PowerPoint slide show (or, for that matter, any OLE client application that uses video clips). Enabling this check box allows the direct playing of the clip in the slide show, without the appearance of the Media Player application during playback.

Control Bar on Playback: Enabling this check box displays a control bar on the video clip, which offers the standard Play and Pause buttons pictured in figure 20.7. The control bar buttons can be clicked on during the playback of the video in the slide show.

Dither Picture to VGA Colors: Resets the color palette of the video clip to the basic VGA 16-color palette under Windows. You won't need to do this if you're running Windows in a 256-color or higher display mode. Also, the average video clip will look horrible in the 16-color VGA palette, so avoid this unless there's no alternative.

6. After making your Options selections, choose OK or press Enter.

7. Finally, choose **E**xit from the **E**dit menu.

The features described in the two commands (**E**dit **O**ptions and **D**evice **C**onfigure) offer a wide variety of options to the user. Despite the fact that they're used in the Media Player and not in PowerPoint, they have a direct effect on how the video clip appears in your presentation. For example, figure 20.13 shows a PowerPoint slide using a video clip that has been arranged to rest on top of a piece of clip art.

Fig. 20.13
A PowerPoint 4 slide with an embedded video clip and audio clip.

Video clip is embedded and layered on top of a piece of clip art

Audio clip is shown with a Media Player icon

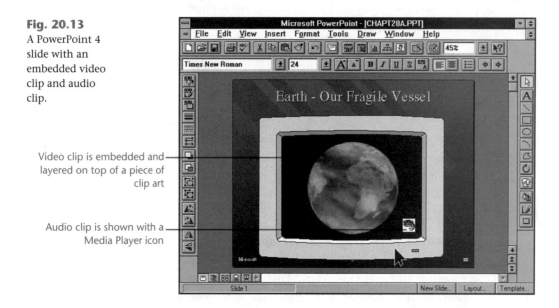

The intended effect of the slide is to show the video clip as if it were being displayed on a monitor screen. When the slide show is started and the slide containing the video appears, the video remains in place and executes directly inside the area encompassed by the clip art.

This is easily done, but how?

In the Media Player's **D**evice **C**onfigure Video Playback Options dialog box, make sure the **W**indow option button in the Video mode section is chosen. Leave the **Z**oom by 2 check box vacant.

In the Media Player's **E**dit **O**ptions dialog box, all the check box options should be vacant except **P**lay in Client Document.

Setting these options in the Media Player ensures a seamless appearance of the video clip in your slide show.

Managing Audio Effects

The Media Player is also used as an OLE server for sound files, and you can use the program to set up sound files for proper playback in PowerPoint slide shows in much the same way. The options available are less extensive than those for video, but they are still very handy for good management of sound-based multimedia effects.

For this example, the assumption is made that you're changing the settings of a sound file that's already been inserted into the presentation.

1. On the PowerPoint slide, click on the embedded sound file (it's shown as a Media Player icon) to select it.

2. From the **E**dit menu in PowerPoint, choose Media Clip **O**bject, and then **E**dit.

    After a moment, the Media Player appears showing its tools and control bar and the name of the sound file that's currently selected.

3. From the **D**evice menu in the Media Player, choose **C**onfigure.

    The MCI Waveform Driver Setup dialog box appears with a slider bar as shown in figure 20.14.

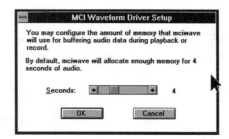

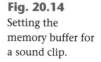

Fig. 20.14
Setting the memory buffer for a sound clip.

VI

Advanced PowerPoint 4

Notice that the dialog box has changed its contents and its title from the previous exercise, which dealt with video objects. Instead of offering a few check box and option buttons for video playback, a single slider bar is shown. It allows you to set the amount of system memory (called a *memory buffer*) that will be used to hold the sound file while it's being played.

As you move the slider bar back and forth, the amount of memory is set by the number of seconds of audio. The value is automatically set to an optimum value when you load the sound file. If you set the amount of memory to be much less than the duration of the sound file, the file still plays, but it may not play as efficiently.

4. When you're finished setting the audio memory, choose OK or press Enter.

A substantial number of playback options are also offered in the **E**dit **O**ptions dialog box. They are mostly the same options as those used for video clips.

5. From the **E**dit menu in Media Player, choose **O**ptions. The Options dialog box appears.

- Auto Rewind: Sets the sound file to rewind to the beginning after playback (it's not done automatically, so the check box must be enabled before this can happen).

- Auto **R**epeat: Sets the sound file to repeat in an endless loop until the presenter or user interrupts it with a mouse click during the presentation.

- OLE Object: A selection of options for defining how the sound file will appear on-screen when it is played back in the OLE client application.

    Cap**t**ion: Enabling this check box displays a caption showing the file name of the audio file during playback in the presentation. For most situations, this may not be desirable, because it distracts from the actual content of the slide.

    Border around object: Enabling this check box displays a window border around the audio clip when it's played. (At least, the option is offered for a sound file, but in practice you won't see a border even if this check box option is enabled for a sound file.)

    Play in Client Document: This option is highly recommended if you want a seamless playing of the sound in your PowerPoint slide show. Enabling this check box allows the direct playing of the sound file in the slide show, without the appearance of the Media Player application during playback.

Control Bar on Playback: Enabling this check box will display a sound file control bar while the sound file is played. The control bar buttons can be clicked on during the playback of the video in the slide show. They include a Play button, a Pause button, and a slider bar for advancing or reversing back through the sound file sequence.

The **D**ither Picture to VGA Colors option is ghosted for sound files, which seems natural, considering it applies to video and not audio.

6. When you're finished making your sound playback choices, choose OK or press Enter.

7. Finally, choose E**x**it from the **E**dit menu.

Multimedia is at best an inexact science on the PC. It's a good idea to stick to the most standard hardware and software you can when using multimedia objects in your presentations. Although PowerPoint's support for multimedia is somewhat scanty, some experimenting with the features described in this section will help you master the techniques you need to make your presentations come alive.

Troubleshooting

I can't access the Configure command on the Device menu in Media Player when I edit a video clip.

That's because you don't have the right video driver enabled in the Media Player. The Media Player uses the Microsoft Video for Windows MCI driver, which can be loaded from the Windows Control Panel with the Drivers program. If the driver is already loaded, it should appear on the Device menu in the Media Player. If it doesn't, use the Drivers program in the Windows Control Panel to load it. See your Windows user's manual for more information if necessary.

My video or sound clip doesn't play during my presentation.

You very likely haven't brought the sound files (.WAV) or video files (.AVI) with you when you transported the presentation file. Unfortunately, you must. PowerPoint is supposed to embed the multimedia object into your presentation, but the program doesn't do as good a job as it could. Make sure you bring all your multimedia objects with you when you deliver your presentation.

(continues)

VI

Advanced PowerPoint 4

(continued)

Another tip: When you embed video and audio files into your presentation, make sure you bring them from your hard disk and not a CD-ROM. You need to think ahead on this issue, because the host computer on which you deliver your presentation may not have a CD-ROM drive. The safest bet is to place your multimedia object files (*.AVI and *.WAV) on the root directory of your C:\ drive before you embed them into your presentation. In other words, copy the desired files from the CD-ROM (if that's where they originate from) to the hard disk.

Then, when you bring the presentation and its multimedia object files in to the other site, you can be assured that the presentation will find them, because you can place the object files in the C:\ drive of the host computer. Every Windows PC known to Man has a C:\ drive, so you'll be safe in knowing that your presentation will find the files when it needs them. If necessary, consult your DOS manual for more information on copying files. The odds are, you won't have to, because if you've gotten this far in the book, you're probably a very knowledgeable user already.

Hiding Slides

PowerPoint 4 offers the capability to hide one or more slides in a presentation. Hidden slides are especially useful if you have created a large presentation that contains elements for several different audiences—some of whom may not need to see parts of the same slide show.

Creating Hidden Slides

Tip
To hide multiple slides with a single Hide Slide command, hold the Shift key as you click on each slide in the Slide Sorter and then execute the Hide command (see fig. 20.15).

Slides can be hidden when you are in Slide view or in the Slide Sorter. The Slide Sorter is recommended for this operation because it's easy to keep track of the slides on which you perform this operation.

To create hidden slides in a presentation, follow these steps:

1. Display the presentation in Slide Sorter view.

2. Click on the slide to be hidden during the presentation.

3. From the **T**ools menu, choose **H**ide Slide.

   Or, click the Hide Slide button on the Slide Sorter toolbar.

The slide number at the bottom has a box icon stamped over it, signifying that it is hidden when the slide show is run. The hidden slide is skipped automatically.

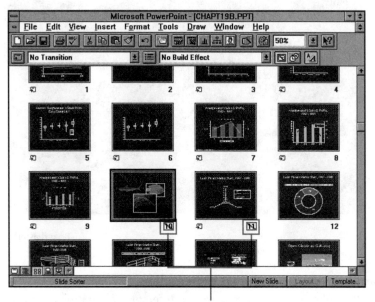

Fig. 20.15
The Slide Sorter with several hidden slides.

Slide numbers are boxed out

If you change your mind about a hidden slide, simply execute the Hide Slide command again.

Displaying Hidden Slides

During a presentation, it may become necessary to display a hidden slide for an unanticipated reason. The procedure is a simple one and can be done during the slide show. Figure 20.16 below supplies the clue.

1. Run the slide show.

2. When a slide appears during the slide show, move the mouse. If the slide after the current one is a hidden slide, an asterisk icon will appear at the bottom right corner.

By moving the mouse on-screen, the asterisk icon is displayed. The mouse must be moved by the presenter for the icon to appear. The icon can then be clicked on for the next, otherwise hidden, slide to appear.

VI

Advanced PowerPoint 4

Fig. 20.16
A slide in a slide show displaying an icon in the bottom right corner indicating the next slide is hidden. The boxed asterisk icon indicates that the next slide is hidden.

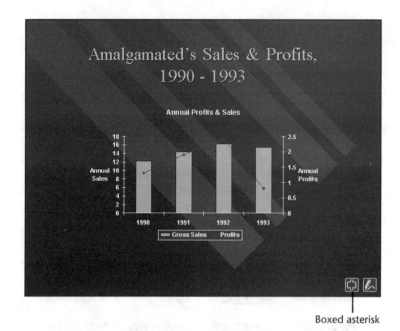

Boxed asterisk

Branching Between Different Presentations

PowerPoint 4 offers branching between different presentations. It's a feature that offers greater flexibility for the presentation content that you want to display to the audience. Audiences may want to examine several angles of the same issue, such as studying a marketing plan in one slide show, scrutinizing the budget for that plan in a branch off one of the first slides, or seeing another branch if they want to see an assessment of competing companies' strategies. One slide can have several branches attached to it.

Branching to another PowerPoint 4 presentation is done by embedding it as an object, just like a sound file or video clip. To branch to another presentation, follow these steps:

1. Display your presentation in Slide view.

2. Display the slide from which you want to branch.

3. From the **I**nsert menu, choose **O**bject.

   The Insert Object dialog box appears. The Insert Object dialog box lists the various types of files you can load as Objects into your presentation.

   Follow the next steps *precisely* to carry out the procedure properly.

4. In the Object **T**ype list box, choose *MS PowerPoint 4.0 Presentation.* (Yes, it's considered an object type.)

5. Click the Create from **F**ile option button.

The Object **T**ype list disappears, replaced by a Fil**e** text box and a **B**rowse button that allows you to search for the exact location of your presentation file.

6. Click the **B**rowse button to search for the specific file for embedding.

7. When the file is displayed in the Fil**e** text box, choose OK.

A presentation object is displayed in your slide, as shown in figure 20.17.

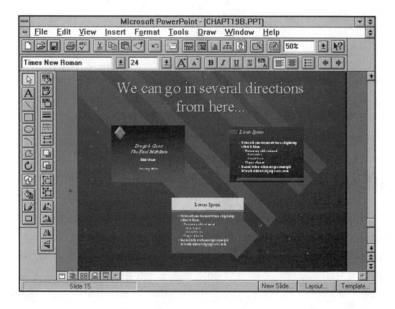

Fig. 20.17
A slide showing several embedded PowerPoint presentations, any of which can be double-clicked or triggered to move to the new branch.

If you embed another PowerPoint presentation, all its assigned timings and special effects are included—just as if it were a stand-alone presentation. Individual slides can also be embedded.

Also consider the other possibilities: if you're a user of Lotus Freelance, or if you produce presentations or elements from Excel, Lotus 1-2-3 for Windows, or Lotus Improv, or other presentation programs, their files can be embedded in the same way.

A simpler method of linking presentations is to load slides from another presentation into the current one. It's analogous to the Merge Files command in a word processor: You can merge the slides from one presentation with those of another.

To load the contents of a second slide show into the current one, follow these steps:

1. Display the slide after which the new slides are to be inserted.

2. From the **I**nsert menu, choose Slides from **F**ile.

   The Insert File dialog box appears, which is identical to the Open dialog box under the **F**ile menu.

3. Locate the desired presentation file.

4. Choose OK or press Enter.

The entire contents of the second presentation are merged with the current one. The presentation slides that have just been merged adopt the template of the current presentation, but any builds or transition effects or Object timings and triggerings translate intact.

Building Text Effects

The wording of this section head, "Building Text Effects," is important. Text elements in your slides can have a feature applied to them called *builds*. Builds are similar to the transition styles described earlier in this chapter, except that they're applied to text objects. Individual build effects are applied to individual items in a bulleted list, or assigned to an entire selected bulleted list or text object at once. There are some disappointing restrictions on build effects, however:

- You cannot apply build effects to Slide titles

- You cannot apply build effects to drawn, clip art, or any object other than a body text object

- In a bulleted list, you cannot apply one build effect to one bullet item, and then another build effect to a second or third bullet item

As with transitions, builds can be applied to slides in either Slide view or the Slide Sorter. For this example, the Slide Sorter is used. Figure 20.18 shows a Slide Sorter displaying several slides to which builds have been added.

Build button   Build drop-down list

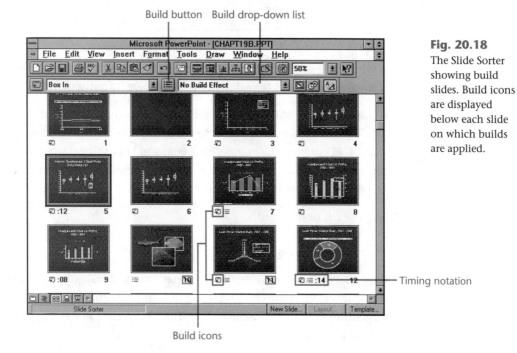

Fig. 20.18
The Slide Sorter showing build slides. Build icons are displayed below each slide on which builds are applied.

Timing notation

Build icons

Builds are normally applied to text slides—slides that contain a bulleted list as their main component. They're called build slides for this reason. Sometimes they are also termed Progressive Transition slides. Regardless of the semantics, here is how to create them:

1. Display the current presentation in the Slide Sorter.

2. Click the slide to which a build is to be added.

3. Click the Build button on the Slide Sorter toolbar.

   The Build dialog box appears (see fig. 20.19).

4. Click the **B**uild Body Text check box if it is not already enabled.

   This has the effect of making the current slide a build slide, regardless of its contents. Although the slide may contain no body text at all, the build is attached to the slide. *Non-text objects in the slide are not affected.*

Tip
Build effects can *only be applied to body text*—but builds can be assigned to any slide.

VI

Advanced PowerPoint 4

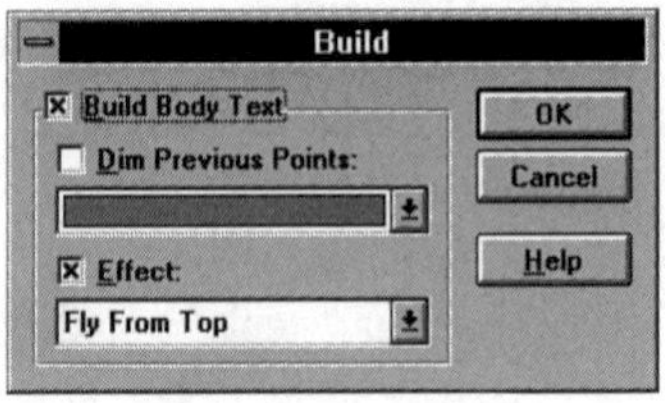

Fig. 20.19

The Build dialog box.

5. In the **E**ffect drop-down list, choose from the various effects offered. They closely parallel the effects offered for slide transitions.

6. To dim previous bulleted items in the body text (have them fade out when you are ready to move on to the next point in your argument), click the **D**im Previous Points check box, and choose a color to block them out from the drop-down list. Colors are applied in the same way as with other PowerPoint elements that use color, such as color fills.

7. Choose OK or press Enter.

The chosen build effect is assigned to the slide.

If the build is applied to body text in a bulleted list, each bullet item reveals itself in sequence using the chosen build effect. In the Sorter, a small icon appears denoting the slide as a build slide. The icon is the same as the graphic on the Build button on the Slide Sorter toolbar.

Rehearsing Your Presentation

Now that you have learned about transitions, builds, multimedia events (at least, the basics thereof), and merging and branching presentations, it's time for the finishing touch: rehearsing presentation timing and events. PowerPoint's rehearsing tools are among the best in its field.

Rehearsing is a vital step in creating an effective slide show. It's also much simpler than it sounds. Why is it important? When you apply build and transition effects, and include numerous multimedia elements, it's important to keep control of the timing of all the various elements to—simply put—keep yourself from messing up in front of your audience. Rehearsing is another tool that puts you in control, and with speaker's notes, handouts, and outlines, is one that should not be neglected.

Looking back at figure 20.19, notice that a callout points to some numeric entries under certain slides. Those numbers indicate the number of seconds that elapse in which that specific slide is displayed during the presentation.

Here's a quick course on how to rehearse your presentation:

1. Display the first slide in your presentation.

2. From the **V**iew menu, choose Slide Sho**w**.

The Slide Show dialog box appears (see fig. 20.20).

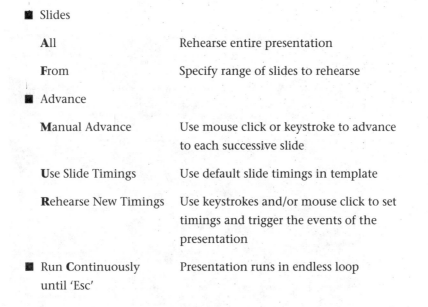

Fig. 20.20
Beginning the rehearsal with the Slide Show dialog box.

3. Choose from the rehearsal options:

■ Slides

All	Rehearse entire presentation
From	Specify range of slides to rehearse

■ Advance

Manual Advance	Use mouse click or keystroke to advance to each successive slide
Use Slide Timings	Use default slide timings in template
Rehearse New Timings	Use keystrokes and/or mouse click to set timings and trigger the events of the presentation

■ Run **C**ontinuously until 'Esc' — Presentation runs in endless loop

VI

Advanced PowerPoint 4

To rehearse slide and element timings (builds, etc.), choose the **Re**-hearse New Timings option button.

4. Choose **S**how or press Enter.

The slide show starts, and a timer is displayed at the bottom of the screen, showing elapsed seconds. Click the mouse, or press the spacebar or Enter to trigger each successive event in the slide show. You can press Esc at any time to stop and go back to the PowerPoint screen.

Remember that when you rehearse a presentation, you're rehearsing all the events that compose it—builds, multimedia event triggerings, and the length of time that each slide is displayed.

Annotating Slides

While you're conducting a slide show, you might find it handy to emphasize points, like a teacher at a chalkboard. PowerPoint 4 offers an easy way to do this.

When you run a slide show, you see a small marker pen icon on the bottom right corner of the screen, as shown in figure 20.21.

Fig. 20.21
Annotating to
emphasize slide
elements during a
show. Click the
marker pen icon
during a show to
draw on a slide to
emphasize a point.

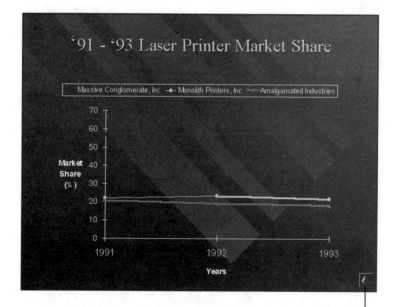

Marker pen icon

Click on the icon while in the slide show. Drag the mouse across the screen. You can draw circles around items, and draw arrows to point to slide elements, as shown in figure 20.22.

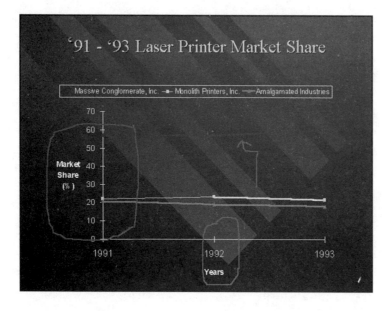

Fig. 20.22
Annotating during a slide show.

To move on to the next slide, or the next event in the current slide, press the space bar or Enter.

From Here...

Many tools for effective presentation management are presented in this chapter. Some subjects, such as multimedia objects, have been extensively discussed, but out of necessity many detailed touches have been left out. Exploring the features described in this chapter should give a much stronger feel for how an entire presentation is tied together, and how the many parts can fit into a whole.

- Chapter 21, "Using Advanced Color, Text, and Drawing Features," shows how to add special effects to slide text, text rotation, tricks with color, and the creation of new color schemes.

- Many functions covered in this chapter can be added to a customized toolbar. See chapter 22, "Customizing PowerPoint," for more information.

Chapter 21

Using Advanced Color, Text, and Drawing Features

It's a truism that no matter how powerful an application program is, the day will probably never come when one program can perform every task that a user needs to get a job done. This is true even of PowerPoint 4, and as useful and flexible as it is for presentations, it can never hurt to expand on PowerPoint's capabilities to add sizzle and pop to your slides.

There are many powerful and inexpensive tools that PowerPoint users can take advantage of for brilliant presentations. This chapter introduces you to a few of them.

Tips for Using Colors and Patterns Effectively

As you've seen in several earlier chapters in this book, color is an important tool for creating successful presentations. Color provides many elements in a presentation beyond making pretty pictures. Color can add emphasis to items in a slide and lend balance to a slide's appearance when required.

The understandable impulse is to use numerous color mixes to break up the monotony of a long presentation. In most situations, that impulse should be resisted. For a series of slides, color can lend unity to an overall presentation concept.

Essentially, this chapter is a grab bag of various advanced topics:

- Tips for using colors and patterns effectively

- Importing special color palettes

- Tips on shading effects

- Handling fonts

- Tips on table creation

- Using outside clip art applications

Why learn more about how color works? Slide and chart readability can be aided greatly by the proper use of color. Thus, colors should be carefully chosen when building a color scheme. In black-and-white overheads, shades of gray and patterns aid in readability and must be chosen even more carefully.

Colors and patterns can be used to direct attention to important points, data, graphics, or chart elements in a slide. In color printouts or overheads, a bold and striking color can be applied to the most important series for emphasis. Lighter shades of the same color can be applied to the other series in a chart. For on-screen presentations, light or bright colors can be used for emphasis. For black-and-white overheads and slides, the most important series should be shown in the darkest pattern.

A good rule of thumb for text slides (which constitutes the majority of the slides you make) is to use color rather than text style for emphasizing lines or values in text.

Understanding good color relationships can be very useful in creating a successful presentation. Warm colors, such as red, orange, and yellow, draw the eye's attention, offering more visual punch and activity. Cooler colors, such as greens, blues, and violets, provide rest for the eye. They can be used for backgrounds to set off areas of warmer colors, such as a movie clip depicting a bright outdoors scene.

Tip

Avoid red-green color combinations because a substantial portion (almost 10%) of the population is red-green color-blind.

Colors also have *complementary relationships*. Color complements demonstrate that certain colors get along with each other most effectively, regardless of their essential character. That's why dark blue and yellow have such a frequent use in presentations. On a color wheel, for example, the colors of the rainbow are drawn, each occupying a segment of the wheel. Colors that are located on opposite sides of the wheel from each other are complements.

Blue, of course, is a more restful color than yellow, yet the two different colors mesh quite well. They are located directly opposite to one another on the color wheel. Light greens and violets and reds and light blues are also complementary color combinations. Such combinations please the eye when used properly. Generally, one of the complements is used in a larger area (such as a slide background) or with a higher saturation, while the other color is used to accent, such as colorizing text.

Another phenomenon in using color is the idea of a *split complement*, which expands on the range of complementary colors for a more subtle effect. For example, on the color wheel, light green is located next to yellow. It's a *split complement* color that can be used well with a dark blue, which is normally the complement of yellow. Thus, a complementary color can have a color substitute that is adjacent to it in the color range but still works as a combination, offering a subtly new look. The color templates offered in PowerPoint 4 universally follow the concepts of using complementary colors and split complements for their color schemes.

The simple use of complementary colors is not always enough. Physiological and psychological changes take place in people when they're exposed to certain colors. People are capable of finding a room that's painted a blue color to be colder in temperature than a room painted in a mild peach color, even if both rooms are the same temperature. Red is known as a color that can raise the tension of the viewer, or even raise his blood pressure.

By the same token, if you have large areas of complementary colors (or split complementary colors) bordering on each other, the effect is visually disturbing and annoying. It's an effect known as *simultaneous contrast* and should be avoided. It happens, for example, if you have an area of a bright red color and one of a bright green color bordering on each other. The contrast leaps out at you and is hard to look at.

Note

To avoid the problem of simultaneous contrast, a good technique is to place a black, gray, or white border around the surrounded color object. An even better technique is to avoid having two large areas of complementary colors present. You can also lower the saturation of each color to produce a milder effect.

With some basic tips for good color relationships behind you, it's time to take a closer look at PowerPoint's color mixing system.

Understanding PowerPoint's Color Matching Systems

While chapter 17 discussed color and PowerPoint in some detail, understanding the attributes of color in PowerPoint needs some further explanation.

As seen earlier, PowerPoint relies on two color mixing schemes for color creation: RGB and HSL. They are more than sufficient for any color work in a presentation and touch upon several basic concepts and definitions of color. As used in PowerPoint, the two color mixing systems cooperate with each other, and when one mix is adjusted, the other adjusts to match. The two color models are mathematically identical.

As you've seen in earlier chapters, the Red-Green-Blue color model defines how much of each of the three colors is added to the mix in order to arrive at the final color. PowerPoint provides an unusually generous scale for mixing RGB-based colors, with the range for each color being from zero to 65,535 in *brightness* values. The brighter each of the three colors are, the closer the mix is to white—the brightest possible color. If all three values (red, green, and blue) are zero, the end color is black.

The Hue is the basic color of the mix—red, green, blue, yellow, or any of the other basic colors in the spectrum. Saturation and Luminance affect the actual purity and brightness of the color, respectively. Luminance actually represents the effect of *light* on the color, and is also shown when you adjust the brightness values of the red, green, and blue mix. The more saturated a color is, the more purity it displays.

The More Colors dialog box provides several important tools for creating new colors and for understanding exactly how color works in the program (see fig. 21.1).

Fig. 21.1
Viewing the More
Colors dialog box.

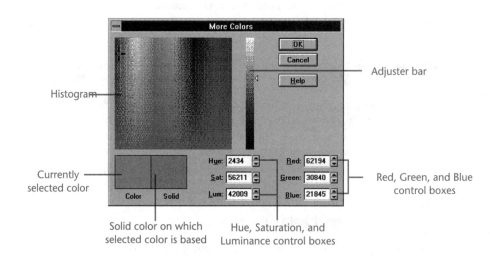

Notice in the histogram that at its bottom edge, gray predominates. The colors grow brighter at the top of the histogram, reaching their highest intensity at the top edge. Histogram colors diminish in intensity at the bottom. The color *hues* change from the left edge to the right in the histogram.

If you change the value in the **Hu**e control box (by clicking and holding the up- or down-arrow icons or typing in a new value), the cross-hair in the histogram moves to the left or right. Movement in either direction changes the color.

Saturation is adjusted from top to bottom. If you change the value in the **S**at control box, the crosshair in the histogram adjusts straight up or down. If the crosshair moves down, the color is less vivid and less intense, with more gray mixed in.

Notice that when you adjust the saturation, the **R**ed, **G**reen, and **B**lue values in the control boxes to the right all adjust simultaneously. Depending on the hue that is currently selected, the RGB values may adjust up or down when the saturation is changed. For example, if you have a blue hue selected, and you adjust the saturation down, the Red and Green values increase while the Blue value decreases. This varies, of course, depending on the hue.

Also, when you adjust the Saturation, you can watch the color intensity slowly change on the adjacent bar (the bar with the arrowhead that Luminance is adjusted with).

The **L**um (Luminance) control box does not affect the position of the crosshair. Instead, the arrowhead alongside the adjuster bar to the right of the histogram moves up or down along the bar. Drag the arrowhead up or down to adjust the luminance—brightness. If the arrowhead moves down, the brightness of the color is decreasing.

Keep in mind that when you make adjustments to any values, you may not see results of color adjusting on the monitor. This relates to the color range that can be displayed by your video card under Windows. If you're running Windows in 256-color mode, the colors you can specify are much less substantial than in other video display modes, which PowerPoint 4 supports for the first time.

Understanding PowerPoint's True Color Support

The More Colors dialog box is the perfect place to explain what *true color* support means for the PowerPoint 4 user. If you're using a video card that supports 16 million colors in 640×480 resolution, 800×600 resolution, or even 1024×768 resolution, you can use true color on your screen.

PowerPoint's histogram looks markedly different. Color contrasts are much smoother and the adjuster bar is one continuously darkening band of color.

When using true color display modes, the two color thumbnails displayed at the bottom left of the dialog box—Color and Solid—consistently display the same color when color mixing values are adjusted. When you're using true color modes on your PC, the display is capable of displaying the exact color that your eye normally sees (unless, of course, you're color-blind to some degree).

Conversely, if you normally run in 256-color mode, the Color and Solid thumbnails are almost always different, because the selected color cannot be adjusted as finely in that video mode. Otherwise, the HSL and RGB color mixing adjustments work exactly the same way. In true color display modes, they can simply be adjusted much more precisely.

When you use true color display modes in PowerPoint, you don't just have access to many more colors and the opportunity to adjust them more precisely. The visual results of your presentation (especially if you use an on-screen slide show) can be much richer. Color shading and patterns are more subtle and attractive. Color dithering is eliminated (the practice of mixing a color with dots and patterns of other colors to create new ones to compensate for a more limited display color palette). Photo-realistic pictures can also be imported into a slide or template and will look more realistic (while substantially increasing the size of your presentation file).

> **Note**
>
> The terms *true color*, *16 million colors*, and *24-bit color* all describe the same thing. When you're using 24-bit color, it means that your video card uses 24 bits of data to determine the color value of each pixel on-screen. That's why when you're using 256 colors on the screen display, it's often referred to as *8-bit mode* because only eight bits of data are used by the video to define each pixel's color. It's less sophisticated for viewing, but often much faster for daily work.

Importing Pantone Color Palettes

Pantone is an important company in the field of color publishing. In brief, Pantone created an industry standard color system, which is widely used by desktop publishers, magazine designers, and anyone who uses color artwork in professionally published documents. This color system is called the

Pantone Matching System©, or PMS. Since then, Pantone has expanded its influence in the computer arena to the point where a very large number of major graphics programs on both the PC and Macintosh (such as Quark XPress and Aldus PageMaker, Aldus Freehand and CorelDRAW!, and Micrografx Designer) directly support it. Probably the most popular *spot color* standard anywhere, it provides a precise method of identifying colors in any publishing or photographic project—including color slides.

PowerPoint, while using Red-Green-Blue and Hue-Saturation-Luminance color changes, does not use some of the other industry-standard color schemes that many service bureaus and color-separation companies employ as a vital part of their production. Why? This is understandable, given that PowerPoint is not a desktop publishing or precision drawing program, and the concepts of spot color and process color (in both of which Pantone is a crucial standard and that are also crucial aspects of color desktop publishing) are largely unnecessary for presentations. Nonetheless, the inquiring user can easily expand his or her color horizons beyond the options offered by PowerPoint.

Pantone has recently stepped forward with a powerful and friendly utility that allows you to export special Pantone color palettes to PowerPoint and many other packages. Pantone's ColorUp software is a simple color palette exporting utility that offers up to 256 custom colors for use in your PowerPoint slides—every color that conforms to the standards set by the company and is used and adhered to by every service bureau worth its salt. It's available at most local software stores. The results can take a lot of the guesswork out of color palette creation.

ColorUp provides over 1,500 color palettes selectable for use in PowerPoint. Each color in the program uses a Pantone industry standard name, which is readily recognized by service bureaus anywhere. The palettes are organized by the background colors you choose in the program, and the other colors in the palette are organized around the background color for the best and most compatible mixes. Each background color, furthermore, has four or five dif-ferent color palettes available, any of which can be chosen for your use. Pantone exports the palettes in an actual PowerPoint file, with the extension .PPT. Output types must be defined in ColorUp in the same way as for PowerPoint, and the same types are supported: 35mm slides, on-screen presentations, overhead transparencies, and paper (see fig. 21.2).

VI

Advanced PowerPoint 4

Fig. 21.2
Pantone ColorUp's
screen.

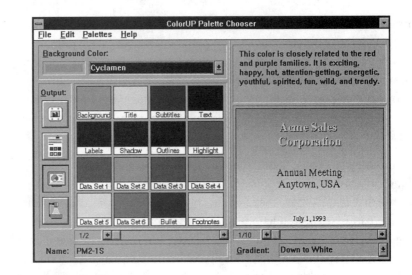

All that's required to apply a Pantone palette in your existing presentation is to open your presentation in PowerPoint, choose the **P**resentation Template command from the F**o**rmat menu, and load the new file exported from ColorUp.

> **Note**
>
> There are a couple of minor glitches that crop up when using ColorUp with PowerPoint 4. The main one is that the current version of ColorUp directly supports PowerPoint versions 2 and 3 but not version 4. Because of this, you may get a PowerPoint 4 error message stating:
>
> ```
> The template is missing a master title or body. The corresponding
> slide objects will not be changed.
> ```
>
> Though it is a problem (particularly in the Slide Master), it doesn't affect the actual application of colors to any element in your presentation—charts, titles, body text, and any other object that uses PowerPoint palette colors from the original template are automatically changed. Thus, don't use a Pantone-exported color template to create a new presentation—simply apply the template to an existing presentation.

Once you import the palette and apply it to your presentation, the colors can be handled in exactly the same way as normal PowerPoint colors. A thoughtful feature in ColorUp is the program's easy cross-referencing of its special hues to RGB and HSL color values, so you need never be confused about the colors you apply to your presentation.

Another very valuable resource offered in the ColorUp package is Pantone's Color Explorer, which is a useful and comprehensive on-line guide to color theory and how to mix colors for the best effect. Of all the add-on programs available for use with PowerPoint, ColorUp is perhaps the most valuable.

Using Adobe Fonts

If you've ever worked in publishing, and if you've worked with computers extensively, you've probably heard of Adobe. As Pantone is to color, Adobe certainly is to fonts and typefaces on small computers. Adobe Systems was the inventor of the Postscript language for laser printers; it's very widely used today. A massive library of computer fonts has been created by Adobe and a host of imitators; among those, of course, are the TrueType fonts you've been using throughout this book.

Adobe fonts can be used for slide titles, body text, and outlining in the same ways as Microsoft's conventional TrueType fonts. Adobe fonts are special because they are the standard for service bureaus, particularly in the publishing realm. Thus, many professionals prefer them for computing tasks.

Almost invariably, when you send any kind of file to a service bureau for output, they ask for Adobe fonts to be used in your files. That's partly because Adobe font *names* are accepted as the standard names for typefaces (TrueType fonts usually have imitative names but can't be named identically because of copyright restrictions and most places don't bother to have them in-house) and also because most companies consider TrueType a technically inferior standard, which it is. TrueType is a low-cost competitor to Adobe, but realistically it doesn't compete with professional-quality Adobe fonts. They're aimed at the average Windows user who really doesn't want to bother with the issue of building a font library but wants to produce good-looking output without having to resort to a service bureau or who wants to avoid spending money on more expensive Adobe fonts.

Adobe fonts are also installed in laser printers; many people probably have a Postscript laser printer on their desk. Those who don't can use another alternative, called Adobe Type Manager. Adobe Type Manager, or ATM, is a high-quality font control program that allows your Windows machine to display and print industry-standard Adobe fonts whether or not you have a Postscript-type printer. Most Windows users have either ATM or TrueType, or both, on their systems. TrueType, of course, is included with every copy of Windows. PowerPoint also comes with a small selection of TrueType fonts.

> **Note**
>
> If you use Adobe fonts in your presentation, you have to bring them along with the presentation when you deliver it to the service bureau for output.

The advantage of using Adobe fonts is the comfort of knowing you're using industry standard, professional-quality fonts. The disadvantage of using Adobe is that you can *embed* TrueType fonts into a presentation, but the same cannot be done with Adobe fonts. There is no feature provision for that in PowerPoint 4, hence the note above. Keep this in mind.

Using Alternative Table Editing Techniques

Instead of building table creation features into PowerPoint 4, Microsoft elected to enable users to take advantage of Microsoft Word 6 for Windows to build complex row-column tables. However, there's one hitch: if you don't own Word 6 for Windows, there's no way to make use of PowerPoint's OLE 2.0 features to embed a table from Word for Windows 6 into a slide.

The same is true if you don't own Microsoft Excel 5. PowerPoint 4 offers a tool for editing and inserting row/column datasheets using Excel 5. The process, as with Word 6 for Windows, uses OLE 2.0. PowerPoint does not offer a native method for editing and creating datasheets for display in a slide—even Graph's datasheets are used only to create charts and cannot be directly displayed in the program. Essentially, you can only take full advantage of PowerPoint's table creation and datasheet creation tools if you also own Word 6 and Excel 5.

Fortunately, there are many alternatives. Almost every Windows user has at least one major word processing program, such as Lotus' Ami Pro, WordPerfect for Windows, or half a dozen other alternatives available in the Windows market, including older versions of Word for Windows. The same is true of spreadsheet programs, and many users own programs such as Lotus' 1-2-3 for Windows, Improv, or Borland's Quattro Pro for Windows.

If you own Ami Pro, Lotus Improv, an older version of Excel or Word, or WordPerfect for Windows, you can easily use any of the programs to create a table or datasheet. In so doing, you're using object linking and embedding. All the programs mentioned above support OLE 1.0, which is easily sufficient for your needs, thus the steps below are relatively generic:

Tip
Use the **O**bject command from PowerPoint's **I**nsert menu to help create a new datasheet or table object with other Windows programs.

1. From PowerPoint's **I**nsert menu, choose **O**bject.

2. When the dialog box appears, choose the appropriate program object type from the Object **T**ype list.

3. If you're creating a new table or datasheet, click the Create **N**ew option button; if you want to use an existing file, click the Create from **F**ile option button.

4. Choose OK or press Enter. If you're creating a new datasheet or table, the program that you use to create the new object appears, ready for editing. If you're creating the object from an existing word processing or spreadsheet file, the table or datasheet pops up on your current slide. Double-clicking the new object brings up its originating program for editing.

Creating Tables Directly in PowerPoint

Simple tables can be created directly on the PowerPoint slide. Though typing in and editing a simple table on a slide is fairly inflexible and doesn't offer the formatting capabilities of a sophisticated word processor like Word, WordPerfect, or Ami Pro, there are a few advantages:

- There's no need to run another application program.

- All of PowerPoint's basic editing tools are available, including line spacing, text formatting, and ruler tab setting.

- Because you're typing in unformatted text for your table, it's considered just another PowerPoint object. Background coloring and shading can be applied, as well as shadowing and text colors.

When you want to create a table directly in PowerPoint, follow these steps:

1. In PowerPoint's Slide view, display the slide where you want to write your table.

2. From the **V**iew menu, choose **R**uler.

   PowerPoint's Ruler is a valuable tool for creating tables on a slide.

3. Click the Text button on the Drawing toolbar.

4. Type your tabular data. Press the Tab key between each field of data. At the end of each table row, press Enter.

   As you enter your data, the Ruler changes its appearance to reflect the growth of the table, as shown in figure 21.3.

Fig. 21.3
Editing a
simple table on a
PowerPoint slide.

Tab stop tool ————

Ruler ————

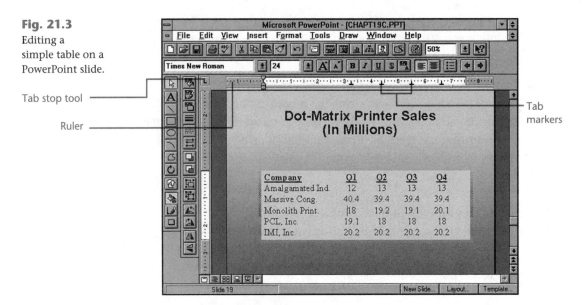

Tab markers

You can use four different types of tab stops in a table format: Left, Right, Center, and Center with Leader. The Tab Stop tool in the top left corner of the document window (adjacent to both rulers) allows you to cycle between the four tab types to select the one you want.

5. To add tab stop formatting on columns in a table, click the mouse in any text item in the desired column. Do not select any text, because then tabs cannot be set.

6. Click the Tab Stop tool to select the tab style you want.

7. Click the mouse inside the top ruler to place the tab markers. The entire column adjusts. Figure 21.4 shows the same table with four center tab markers used to align the values.

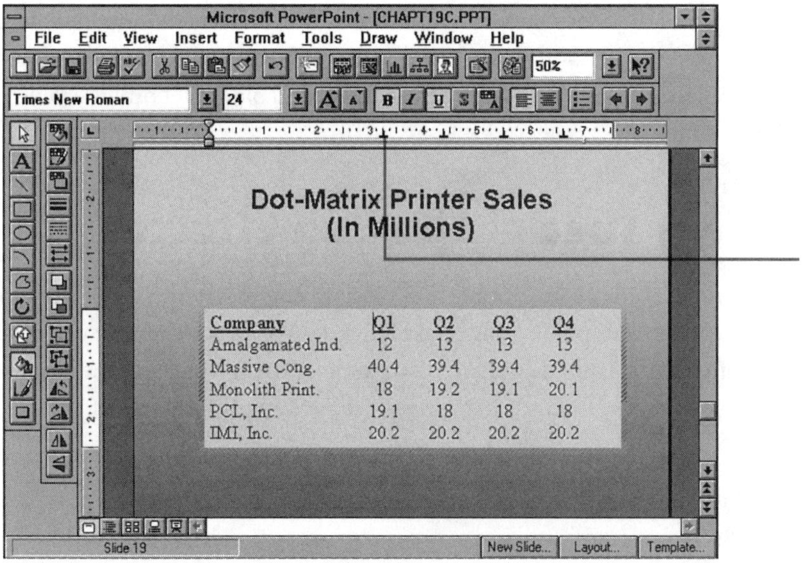

Fig. 21.4
Setting tab stops
on a simple table
in PowerPoint;
center tab markers
have been placed.

Center tab markers

Colors can also be set for borders of a table because it is just another text object. A top row of labels can be boldfaced and underlined. Fill colors can also be set, lending a bit more emphasis to a table (see fig. 21.5).

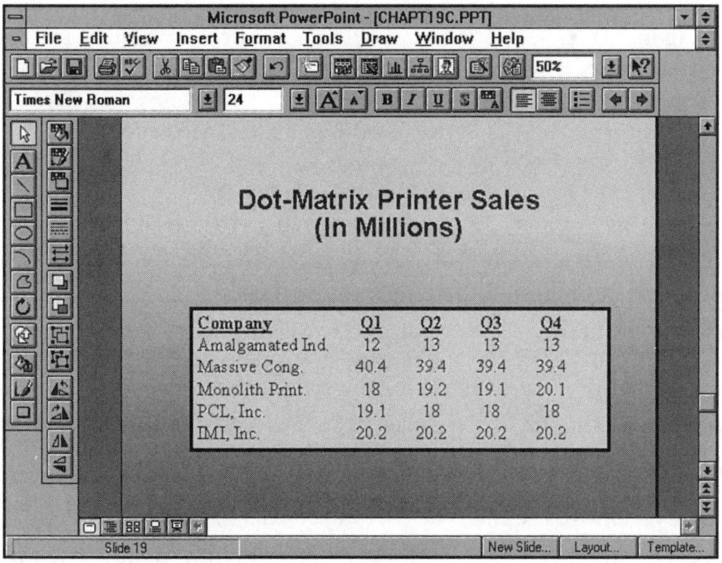

Fig. 21.5
Adding a border
and color fill to
the table, with
boldfacing and
underlining for
a top row of
value labels.

VI

Advanced PowerPoint 4

Unfortunately, there's no provision for adding borders to individual table cells. Because the table you're keystroking onto the slide is only a simple text object, there's no easy way to structure a table with borders around each value.

Using Special Shading Effects

PowerPoint offers some interesting shading effects beyond those used for most of the examples in this book. In all, PowerPoint offers 22 specific shading effects that can be applied to one slide or to all slides in a presentation. First, let's review briefly what's involved in changing shading effects.

You can change shading effects for one or more slides by using the Slide Background command under the Format menu. Shading styles are split into six discrete Variant categories:

Vertical	4 Styles (shading is oriented vertically)
Horizontal	4 Styles (shading is oriented across the slide)
Diagonal Right	4 Styles (shading is oriented from left to right diagonally)
Diagonal Left	4 Styles (shading is oriented from right to left diagonally)
From Corner	4 Styles (shading effect is directed from a corner of the slide)
From Title	2 Styles (shading radiates from slide title)

One of the most interesting shading styles is the From Title variant set. In and of itself, the style is quite distinctive, as shown in figure 21.6.

When you change the size of a title on a slide that has this type of shading variant applied, the shading changes its shape to conform to the new title size, as shown in figure 21.7.

Wherever you move the title, the shading adjusts to match. The From Title shading style should be used sparingly because it tends to draw attention to the title, which can be a detriment to the clarity of the message conveyed in the slide. Nonetheless, the effect is very striking, because the eye is also drawn downward to the object below the title, in a spotlight effect.

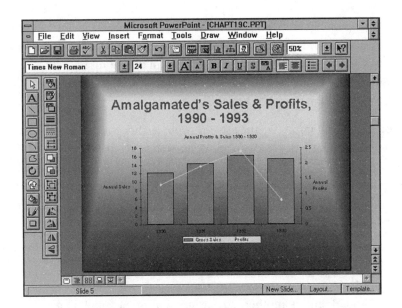

Fig. 21.6
The From Title Shading variant, which lends a distinctive emphasis to a slide title and to its overall appearance.

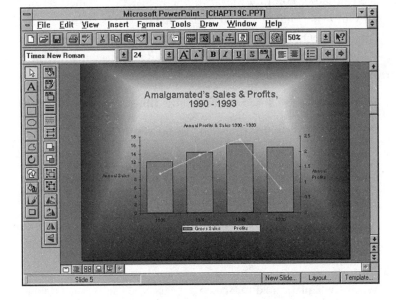

Fig. 21.7
The shading variant adjusts to conform to the new title size.

Looking at Other Clip Art Options

Lotus SmartPics is a handy alternative and add-on to PowerPoint's ClipArt Library. It's a utility that functions as an OLE 1.0 server for a reasonably large library of clip art, most of which is of good quality. The program comes with

2,000 pieces of clip art, arranged into about two dozen image libraries, primarily oriented toward the business world. Using SmartPics couldn't be simpler. Simply select the picture you want to copy from the thumbnails displayed in the SmartPics window, select the Copy button, and close the program. Go back to PowerPoint, and select **P**aste.

If you decide you don't like the artwork, double-click the picture and SmartPics pops back up, ready to go. When you select another piece of clip art, choose **U**pdate from the **F**ile menu. The new art is embedded into your slide and SmartPics closes. It's an easy way to expand on the clip art library supplied with PowerPoint, and a good way to make use of OLE in your system.

Using the Equation Editor

The Equation Editor is another separate application program, or *applet,* that is provided with PowerPoint for the creation and insertion of mathematical equations into your slides. If you're a math major, this is a program that you'll appreciate. Only a short section describing its basic features can be offered here, but if you are knowledgeable about advanced math topics, Equation Editor has a lot to offer.

1. From PowerPoint's **I**nsert menu, choose **O**bject.

2. When the dialog box appears, choose Microsoft Equation 2.0 from the Object **T**ype list.

   The Equation Editor toolbar and menus appear, as shown in figure 21.8 (Equation Editor is an OLE 2.0 application).

   An editing area in white surrounded by a grayed border also appears, displaying a blinking insertion point. This is where you edit your equation.

   When the Equation Editor screen appears, you can immediately begin entering your equation.

3. For the current example, type **27**.

   Now, you enter a template. The Editor's toolbar is divided into two sets of tools. The top row of buttons on the toolbar is a set of Symbol

Palettes used to enter mathematical value symbols, and the second or bottom row of buttons is a set of Template Palettes that are used to insert mathematical templates for fractions, matrices, integrals, brackets of various types, and other elements of math equations.

Whenever you click on an Equation Editor button on its toolbar, a drop-down list of symbols attached to the button type appears. For example, the figure 21.9 shows the template list attached to the Fraction and Radical Templates symbol button.

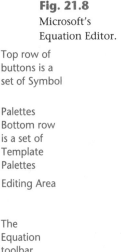

Tip

The crucial feature of the Equation Editor is its toolbar, which is split into two rows: Symbol Palettes on the top row and Template Palettes on the bottom row.

Fig. 21.8

Microsoft's Equation Editor.

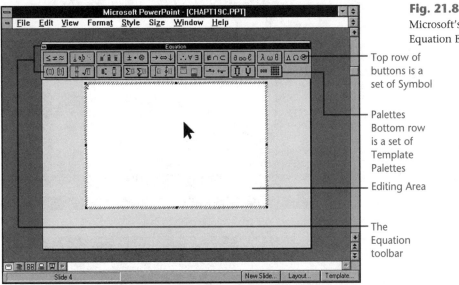

Top row of buttons is a set of Symbol

Palettes Bottom row is a set of Template Palettes

Editing Area

The Equation toolbar

4. Click the Fraction and Radical Templates button as shown in the figure above. (It's the second button from the left in the bottom row of the toolbar.) This toolbar button offers formatting for fractions, radicals, and long division.

5. To add a fraction symbol to your equation, you can click on any of several template buttons on the drop-down list.

Each button on every drop-down list is actually a template for formatting numbers with mathematical symbols. When you choose a fraction template, it's inserted into your equation. Fraction templates automatically contain two placeholders for numbers that you can type in to finish the mathematical expression.

VI

Advanced PowerPoint 4

6. Type a number in the top half of the fraction template, press the down arrow key to advance the insertion point to the bottom of the fraction template, and type another number.

The results appear somewhat like figure 21.10.

Fig. 21.9
Equation Editor's toolbar buttons offer lists of selectable math symbols.

Fraction Templates

Radical Templates

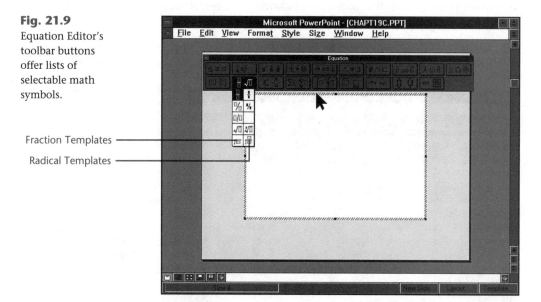

Fig. 21.10
Applying a fraction template.

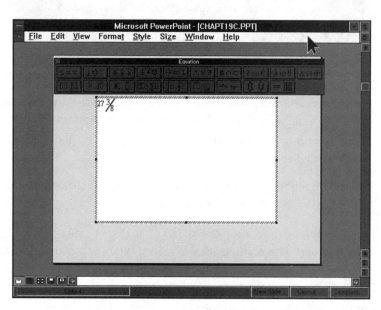

The fraction template has been applied and numbers have been added to create the fraction.

7. To add a multiplication sign or other operator to your equation, click the Operator Symbols button on the Equation Editor toolbar (it's the fourth button from the left on the top row). Choose the multiplication symbol from the drop-down list. The multiplication symbol is inserted into the equation.

8. Type **32**.

9. Click the Fraction and Radical Templates button again and add another fraction template. Type in the desired numbers.

The results should resemble figure 21.11.

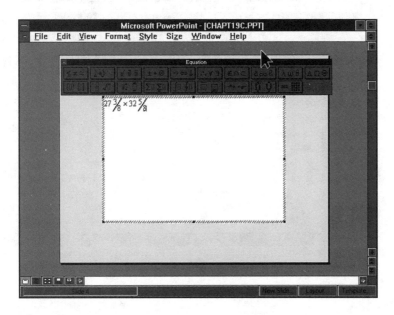

Fig. 21.11
Completing a simple equation.

There's a great deal more about Equation Editor that cannot be explained in this book; Equation Editor is, in fact, a powerful and complex application program all by itself, and a book could be written about this subject alone. The last steps in this exercise show you how to resize the equation to a larger font.

VI

Advanced PowerPoint 4

10. Drag the mouse to select the equation text.

11. From the Size menu in the Equation Editor, choose Define.

The Sizes dialog box appears. This is where you define the default point sizes for the fonts in your equations—for the full-size font in the equation, subscript and superscript fonts, the point size of mathematical symbols, and the point size of math subsymbols.

12. In the Full text box, enter **40pt**.

13. Choose OK or press Enter.

The results will appear similar to figure 21.12.

Fig. 21.12
Enlarging the equation for greater readability on the slide.

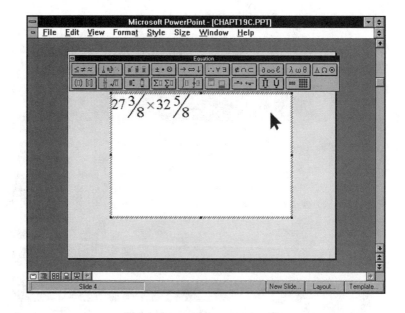

14. Click anywhere outside the editing area in the Editor to embed the equation into the slide.

15. To edit the equation again, simply double-click on the equation object. The Editor appears, displaying the equation for further work.

Troubleshooting

I can't get the Equation Editor to start up. It's not listed in the Insert Object dialog box.

You probably didn't install it. Fortunately, it's easy to do by using the PowerPoint 4 Setup program and choosing to install components that weren't previously installed in your computer. Double-click the PowerPoint Setup icon in the Windows Program Manager, choose the Add/Remove button when the Setup screen appears, and follow the instructions from there.

What can I do to ensure an effective black-and-white or gray-scale presentation?

Colors don't always translate well into gray-scale or black-and-white. A good practice is to use more pattern fills in your objects to help visually distinguish them. This is particularly useful for laptop users.

Believe it or not, the vast majority of PowerPoint users rely on either overhead transparencies or black-and-white handouts for their presentations. According to Microsoft, only 2-3 percent of PowerPoint users employ on-screen slide shows for their work. You'll probably be dealing with the issue of using gray scales on a frequent basis. That's why Microsoft provides a large selection of black-and-white overhead templates in the program, along with color slides and overhead transparencies.

When I double-click on the table or datasheet created with a non-Microsoft application, it doesn't come up.

That's probably because you linked the file, instead of embedding it. Programs like WordPerfect for Windows, Ami Pro, Quattro Pro, and others (including the older but still very useful Microsoft Excel 4.0) use OLE 1.0. This means you can still embed and link objects from these programs in your slides, but if you link an object in a PowerPoint slide from one of these programs, double-clicking on the object may not bring up the other program. You must then open the other program separately, do your edits, and then Update the Link.

However, many OLE 1.0 programs appear if you double-click on a linked object originally created in them that is in a PowerPoint 4.0 slide. Microsoft's OLE 2.0 allows you to do that with programs that support it. Check to make sure the other application program is still installed properly.

From Here...

Congratulations! From the simple to the complex, all the chapters up to this have covered many important issues about creating your own presentations.

You are now very likely to have a lot of your coworkers asking you how to use features of the PowerPoint 4 application program. Go forth and wow the corporate masses!

- Chapter 22, "Customizing PowerPoint," the final chapter in this book, discusses how to customize PowerPoint's user interface.

- Chapters 13, 14, and 19 discuss charting and graphing from the simple to the complex.

- Chapter 17, "Working with Color," digs into many of PowerPoint's color handling features.

- Chapter 18, "Using Links to Other Applications," discusses object linking and embedding issues in more detail.

- Chapter 20, "Advanced Presentation Management," discusses special effects, presentation rehearsing, and adding multimedia elements.

Chapter 22

Customizing PowerPoint

PowerPoint allows you to change your work environment to suit your needs. You can change toolbars: adding, removing, or rearranging their contents. You can even create your own custom toolbar. Default settings associated with your presentations, such as color and text, may also be changed. When you finish customizing PowerPoint, you can save changes and apply them to future presentations.

> **Note**
>
> For the instructions in this chapter, it is assumed that PowerPoint 4.0 has been installed in the C:\POWERPNT directory. If you have installed PowerPoint in a different directory, please substitute your directory's name in the following examples.

Understanding PowerPoint's Defaults

Defaults are initial settings used by PowerPoint that can be changed at any time. If you've used other Windows applications such as Word for Windows, then you're already aware of the advantage of defaults: they allow you to start using the product immediately to create results. In the case of Word for Windows, you can create a document without first choosing the page size, layout, or other important settings. In PowerPoint, these settings cover all aspects associated with creating, viewing, and outputting a presentation. Specifically these are:

- Printing defaults

- Viewing defaults

- Text editing defaults

In this chapter, you learn to do the following:

- Change PowerPoint's defaults

- Create custom toolbars

- Modify existing toolbars

- Change PowerPoint's default editing options

- Set PowerPoint to prompt for summary information

- Color defaults

- Object defaults

- Options defaults

> **Note**
>
> Defaults allow you to get up to speed quickly. Until you get comfortable with PowerPoint, create your presentations using the default settings.

Because you don't have to assign default settings before creating your first presentation, you can get acquainted with PowerPoint's commands at your own pace. It's good idea to do so before changing default settings. PowerPoint's defaults are saved in a file called DEFAULTS.PPT. Later on in this chapter, you learn how to change this file.

Printing Defaults

Any printer installed in Windows may be used by PowerPoint. Printer settings are determined by the type of printer currently selected for use in PowerPoint. To determine which printer is currently selected, choose **P**rint from the **F**ile menu, or press Ctrl+P. The Print dialog box appears displaying the selected printer at the top of the dialog box (see fig. 22.1).

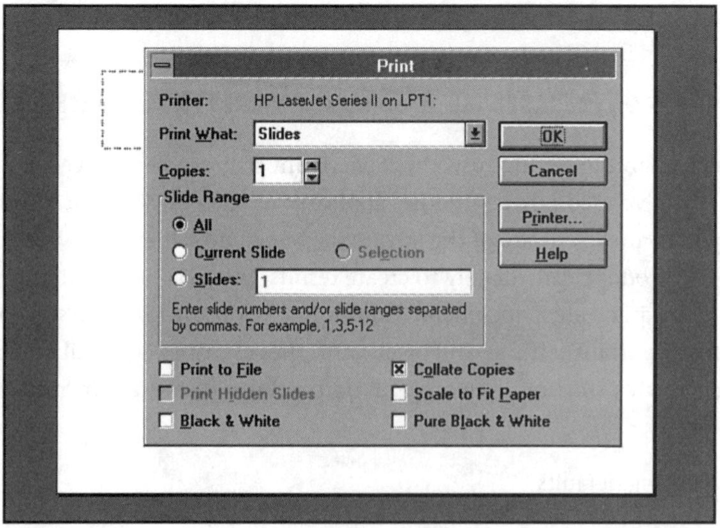

Fig. 22.1
The Print dialog box with the selected printer shown at the top.

To view the current printing defaults, choose the P**r**inter button (see fig. 22.2).

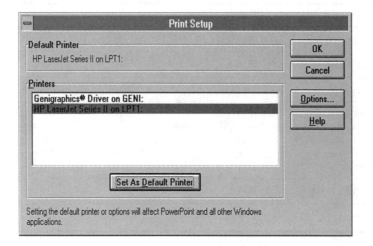

Fig. 22.2
The Print Setup dialog box.

If you want to change the default printer, select the new printer name from the **P**rinters list, and choose the Set As **D**efault Printer button. The Default Printer section of the dialog box displays your change after you choose the Set As **D**efault button.

Viewing Defaults

PowerPoint allows you to switch between four presentation views. The Slide view is scaled to 50 percent initially. The Slide Master has a centered title at the top, set in Times New Roman 44 Normal (if available). The Notes Master centers a reduced 50 percent scaled down slide at the top of the notes page. The Outline Master displays a blank outline page, scaled down to 33 percent of its full size. The default handout page contains no text or objects.

Text Editing Defaults

Title objects in PowerPoint have a default text style of Times New Roman 44 Regular while body object text uses Times New Roman 32 Regular. Initially text is centered. Text boxes receive the Adjust Object Size to Fit Text feature.

To change the default text editing settings, change the text size and style as desired. Then follow one of the two methods described in the next sections to save the default settings.

Tip
You can also change the default printer from Windows. See chapter 16, "Printing and Other Kinds of Output," to learn how.

VI

Advanced PowerPoint 4

Color Defaults

The following eight colors are available in the default color scheme:

Area	Color
Background	WHITE
Lines & Text	BLACK
Shadows	GRAY 5
Title Text	BLACK
Fill	BLUE 5
Accents	GREEN 4
Accents	RED 8
Accents	GRAY 6

To change the default color scheme settings, select new color schemes by using the Color Scheme option on the Format menu. Then, follow one of the two methods described in the next sections to save the default settings.

> **Note**
>
> To change the color scheme of a slide, see chapter 17, "Working with Color."

Object Defaults

Drawn objects are transparent (not opaque), framed in black, filled with white, and unshadowed. The default line style is the thinnest line in the menu, without arrowheads.

To change the default object setting, change select new object attributes and follow one of the two methods described in the next sections to save the default settings.

Changing PowerPoint Defaults

PowerPoint defaults for all presentations are stored in the DEFAULT.PPT file. You can save default settings for all future presentations or for only the current presentation.

To save new default settings for all future presentations, follow these steps:

1. Open a new presentation and use the commands on the F**o**rmat menu (**F**ont, Slide Lay**o**ut, Slide Back**g**round, and Slide **C**olor Scheme) to select the setting you want to change.

    Or, open an existing presentation that contains the settings you want to use as defaults.

2. When all settings are correct, choose Save **A**s from the **F**ile menu. The Save **A**s dialog box appears.

3. In the File Name box, type DEFAULT.PPT and click OK to save the file. The next time you open or create a presentation, your settings will be the defaults.

To save setting default settings for only the current presentation, follow these steps:

1. Select the Arrow button on the Drawing toolbar. Doing so ensures that no objects or text in the active presentation are selected.

2. Use the commands on the F**o**rmat menu (**F**ont, Slide Lay**o**ut, Slide Back**g**round, and Slide **C**olor Scheme) to select the settings you want to change.

    Because you change the settings without selecting text or an object first, PowerPoint automatically saves the new settings as defaults for the active presentation.

Customizing Toolbars

PowerPoint allows you to display, modify, and create toolbars to suit your needs. Specifically, you can:

- Add or remove buttons from any of the supplied toolbars

- Rearrange the buttons on toolbars

- Create a custom toolbar

> **Note**
>
> You must have a mouse to modify toolbars or create custom toolbars. Refer to chapter 2, "Getting Acquainted with PowerPoint 4," for instructions on how to display toolbars.

Adding and Removing Buttons on the Toolbar

To add a button to a toolbar, follow these steps:

1. Click the toolbar area using the right mouse button, and then choose Customize from the shortcut menu, or choose **C**ustomize from the **T**ools menu. The Customize Toolbars dialog box appears, as shown in figure 22.3.

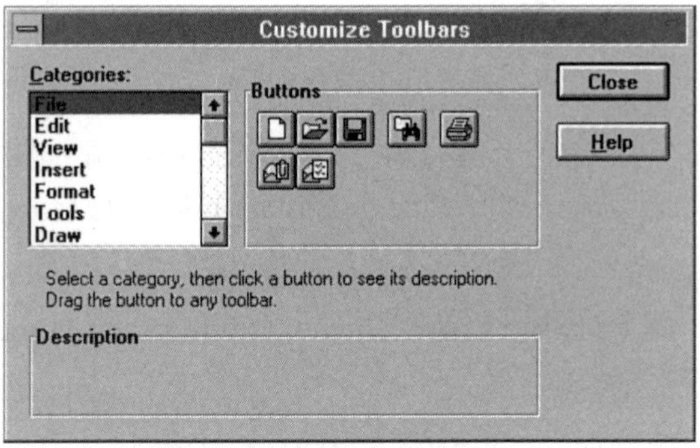

Fig. 22.3

The Customize Toolbars dialog box.

2. Select a button category from the **C**ategories list. Notice that each selection determines the items shown in the Buttons area in the dialog box.

3. Select the desired button and then drag and drop it onto the toolbar.

4. Add more buttons by repeating steps 2 through 3.

To remove buttons from a toolbar, follow these steps:

1. Click the toolbar area using the right mouse button, and then choose Customize from the shortcut menu, or choose **C**ustomize from the **T**ools menu. The Customize Toolbars dialog box appears.

2. Drag the button you want to remove from its toolbar. As you drag, the button's outline follows the mouse pointer.

3. Release the mouse button when the button is no longer on the toolbar.

Tip

You can add the same button to more than one toolbar. If you find that you're using a particular button frequently, add it to the Drawing toolbar as well as the Standard toolbar. Next time you need to access the button, you can click the one that is closest.

4. Remove more buttons by repeating steps 2 and 3. You can close the Customize Toolbars dialog box once you have finished removing buttons.

Rearranging the Contents of a Toolbar

You may wish to organize buttons in groups by inserting spaces between buttons or simply move a button to a new location on the toolbar. To move a button on a toolbar, follow these steps:

1. Move the mouse pointer to the toolbar you want to modify, click the right mouse button, and choose Customize. The Customize Toolbars dialog box appears.

2. While the Customize Toolbars dialog box is on-screen, move the mouse pointer to the toolbar and drag the button to its new location on the toolbar.

3. Release the mouse button to complete the operation.

To group tools together, do the following:

1. Move the mouse pointer to the toolbar you want to modify, click the right mouse button, and choose Customize. The Customize Toolbars dialog box appears.

2. While the Customize Toolbars dialog box is on-screen, move the mouse pointer to the toolbar and click the button at the end where you want to insert a space.

3. Drag the button to the right and release the mouse button to complete the operation. A space should exist between the dragged button and the button to its left.

Creating a Custom Toolbar

Create your own toolbar by following these steps:

1. Click **V**iew on the menu bar and choose **T**oolbars. The Toolbars dialog box appears (see fig. 22.4).

2. Click on the Custom setting and choose OK to close the dialog box. An empty custom menu appears on-screen.

Tip

When you remove a button from a toolbar, it's not gone forever. You can always put it back by following the steps for adding buttons to toolbars.

Tip

Toolbars may slow down PowerPoint, especially if you are using Windows with just 4M of RAM. To increase performance, remove all toolbars and create and display a custom toolbar.

Tip

It is helpful to group like tools together. Use the default groupings of tools on toolbars as an example. For example, on the Drawing toolbar, all the drawing related buttons are grouped together, the text button is by itself, and the Fill and Shadow buttons are grouped near the bottom of the toolbar.

VI

Advanced PowerPoint 4

> ### Note
>
> There are several ways to display the Customize Toolbars dialog box. You can display the dialog box by choosing **C**ustomize from the **T**ools menu, or by choosing **T**oolbars on the **V**iew menu and then clicking **C**ustomize in the dialog box that appears.

Fig. 22.4
The Custom
dialog box.

3. Move the mouse pointer to the empty Custom toolbar, click the right mouse button, and choose Customize from the shortcut menu. The Customize Toolbars dialog box appears.

4. Select a button category from the **C**ategories list. Notice that each selection determines the items shown in the Buttons area in the dialog box.

5. Select the desired button and drag and drop it onto the Custom toolbar.

6. Add more buttons by repeating steps 3 through 5.

> ### Note
>
> As you create and customize toolbars, you may find it helpful to "float" the toolbar on the PowerPoint screen. To "float" a toolbar, drag it away from the top or sides of the screen until its outline changes to a rectangular shape. Release mouse button to place to the toolbar.

Troubleshooting

I can't see some of the buttons on a toolbar when the toolbar is placed on the sides of the screen.

Change the toolbar to a "floating" toolbar by dragging the toolbar near the center of the screen until its shape changes to a rectangle.

I accidentally removed a button from a toolbar.

Select **T**ools, **C**ustomize to display the Customize Tools dialog box. Select the name of the toolbar missing the button from the Categories list. Locate the missing button and drag it to the toolbar on the PowerPoint screen.

I wanted to remove a button from a toolbar by dragging it, but I just selected the button.

Display the Customize Tools dialog box by clicking the right mouse button while the pointer is on the toolbar. You can now drag the button to remove it.

I tried to swap the position of two buttons on a toolbar, but I just get additional space between the two buttons.

Make sure you drag the button past the center of the adjacent button. Be careful not to drag the button off the toolbar, you'll remove it completely.

Changing PowerPoint Options

In addition to defaults associated with presentations, you can set preferences by using the Options dialog box shown in figure 22.5. You can set options for editing, spelling, viewing, saving, and some general items. Choose **O**ptions from the **T**ools menu to display the Options dialog box. All nine options in this dialog box are enabled by default. To disable an option, simply choose it. The options are described briefly in table 22.1, and then in more detail in the sections that follow.

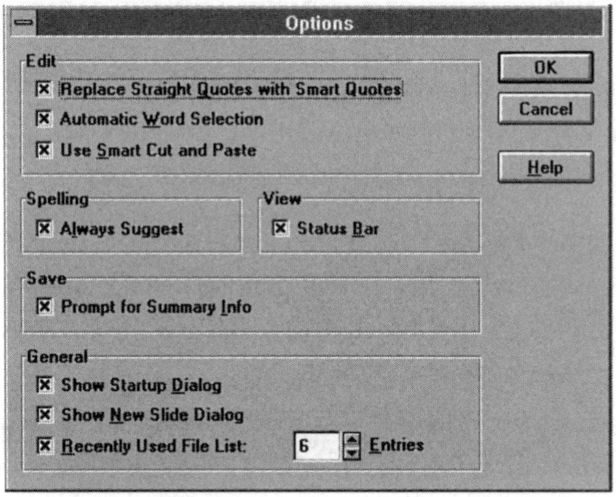

Fig. 22.5
The Options dialog box.

VI

Advanced PowerPoint 4

Table 22.1   Options in the Options Dialog Box

Option	Result
Replace Straight **Q**uotes with Smart Quotes	Replaces straight quotes with Smart Quotes that curve in the appropriate direction to either open or close the quote.
Automatic **W**ord Selection	Selects text a complete word at a time as you drag. Turning off this option causes words to be selected one character at a time.
Use **S**mart Cut and Paste	Text pasted from the clipboard is pasted with appropriate spaces between words.
A**l**ways Suggest	Always suggests an alternative word when encountering a spelling error.
Status **B**ar	Displays the Status Bar.
Prompt for Summary **I**nfo	Always prompts for summary information when saving a presentation for the first time.
Show Startup **D**ialog	Displays the Startup dialog box when you start PowerPoint.
Show **N**ew Slide Dialog	Displays the New Slide dialog box when you start PowerPoint.
Recently Used File List	Displays a list of recently used files on the File menu. You can specify the maximum number of files to be displayed in the Entries box.

Replace Straight Quotes with Smart Quotes

Smart quotes are special characters used by typesetters. This option is enabled by default in the English version of PowerPoint.

When Smart Quotes are enabled, double " and single ' straight quote marks you type are replaced with single ' and double " Smart Quotes, respectively. Also, existing quotes are not affected; any existing quotes must be changed manually after enabling Smart Quotes.

Note

The Smart Quotes feature also controls apostrophes to make sure they curve in the proper direction.

Automatic Word Selection

Marking this option enables the Automatic Word Selection feature of PowerPoint. Automatic word selection causes entire words to be highlighted as you drag the I-beam pointer into the word. This feature is helpful if you tend to re-word titles or bullet text frequently. If this option is not marked, the letters of words will be highlighted one at a time.

Use Smart Cut and Paste

When Smart Cut and Paste is enabled, PowerPoint pastes text from the clipboard with some intelligence. That is, PowerPoint adds or removes the necessary spaces between words as needed. To illustrate this feature, consider the following sentence:

"The quick fox jumped over the lazy dog's back."

Now suppose you have copied the word *brown* from another sentence onto the clipboard. With Smart Cut and Paste disabled, pasting the word directly after the word *quick* would yield the following:

"The quickbrown fox jumped over the lazy dog's back."

With Smart Cut and Paste enabled, pasting the word after quick yields:

"The quick brown fox jumped over the lazy dog's back."

The feature added a space after quick to make the sentence read properly. The feature will also remove extra spaces between words, as necessary.

Spelling

When Always Suggest is enabled, the Spelling dialog box always suggests an alternative when a misspelled word is encountered.

Status Bar

Select the Status **B**ar option to remove the status bar from the bottom of the screen. If you are using the minimum memory configuration in Windows, removing the status bar may increase performance.

> **Caution**
>
> Disabling the Status Bar option makes you rely more on your memory. If you have difficulty remembering which slide you're on, or how to perform a procedure, turn the status bar back on.

Tip

If you have difficulty selecting individual letters of a word, try turning off the Automatic Word Selection feature and editing the text again.

VI

Advanced PowerPoint 4

Prompt for Summary Info

The Prompt for Summary Info option, which is enabled by default, displays the Summary Info dialog box whenever you save a file for the first time. You can disable this option and access the Summary Info dialog box whenever you want by choosing Summary Info from the File menu. Use this dialog box to enter descriptive information about your presentation.

Whenever a file is saved for the first time, PowerPoint prompts you for descriptive notes or summary information that make finding the presentation easier later on.

> **Note**
>
> You can add summary information anytime to a presentation. To do so, first make sure the presentation is open and choose Summary Info from the File menu to display the Summary Info dialog box. Type descriptive text in the fields (up to 255 characters) and then choose OK.

General Options

Enabling the Show Startup Dialog option displays PowerPoint's startup dialog box each time you start PowerPoint. The startup dialog box gives you options for creating new presentations and for opening existing presentations. If you become proficient at locating and using options such as the AutoContent Wizard and the Pick a Look Wizard, you'll speed your startup process by disabling the Show Startup Dialog feature.

Enabling the Show New Slide Dialog feature displays a New Slide dialog box each time you start PowerPoint—if you're not using the AutoContent or Pick A Look Wizards to begin your presentations. The New Slide dialog box allows you to choose the layout of the tiles and text of your slides.

If you frequently use the same set of files, the Recently Used File List option will save you time. By default, PowerPoint displays the last four files that were opened and closed at the bottom of the File menu. Select the Recently Used File List option to hide the list, or adjust the number of files displayed on the list by specifying a different number in the Entries box.

Troubleshooting

I wanted to select a few letters in a title by dragging across them, but each time I try, the entire word selects.

Turn off the Automatic Word Selection option under **T**ools, **O**ptions.

Each time I paste a word into a line of text, I have to delete or add spaces.

Turn on the Use Smart Cut and Paste option under **T**ools, **O**ptions.

I find it irritating that the Summary Info dialog box appears every time you save a file.

Disable the Prompt for Summary Info option under **T**ools, **O**ptions.

From Here...

In this chapter, you explored PowerPoint's defaults and customization options. Refer to chapters throughout this book for more details about the many PowerPoint features mentioned here. After you've used PowerPoint for awhile, you may want to come back to this chapter to customize the program to best meet your needs.

Other chapters you may want to review again now are:

- Chapter 2, "Getting Acquainted with PowerPoint 4," gives you more information about the various toolbars and how to display them.

- Chapter 16, "Printing and Other Kinds of Output," tells how to choose a default printer with Windows.

VI

Advanced PowerPoint 4

Installing PowerPoint 4 for Windows

Because PowerPoint runs only under Windows, Windows must be installed and running on your PC before you can install PowerPoint 4. If you haven't installed Windows, do so before you continue. Please refer to your Windows documentation for the Windows installation instructions.

System Requirements

PowerPoint 4's base requirements are:

> Windows 3.1 or higher
>
> (PowerPoint 4 also runs under Windows for Workgroups 3.11 and Windows NT)
>
> 386-33 or higher
>
> 4M of RAM
>
> 15M of disk space (40M *strongly* recommended)
>
> VGA or higher video card and monitor

A full installation of PowerPoint occupies 40M of disk space. Given the depth and richness of the program's feature set, there shouldn't be any big surprise about this.

System Recommendations

For serious work with PowerPoint 4, you should have 8M of RAM in your PC. Particularly when you begin adding movies and sound clips to your slide show, your presentation files can get very large in a very short period of time. Adding photo-realistic pictures or a lot of bitmapped images also rapidly expands a presentation file. Every slide you add to a slide show also expands the size of the file.

Also, reserve about 10M in a permanent swap file under Windows. Anything larger is unnecessary and in fact can slow your system down by forcing the machine to perform too many unnecessary writes to your hard disk. That process is called *thrashing*. A Windows swap file is actually used as a form of memory in your system; it's called *virtual memory,* and Windows uses it to store excess data that won't fit in system RAM. To check your virtual memory settings, use the 386 Enhanced program in the Windows Control Panel.

Given the size of the PowerPoint program on your hard disk, a large, fast hard disk and controller is a very good idea. Hard drive prices have recently been going through the floor; stores in Southern California have been selling 340M hard drives for $200. IDE and SCSI (Small Computer Systems Interface) are the accepted current standards; anything else is not worth bothering with.

A 386-33 or 386-40 CPU is adequate to run PowerPoint 4; nonetheless, if you don't want finger-drumming screen updates while working with the program, a 486SX-25 system is really the baseline. Fortunately, prices are plummeting. The same goes for your video card and monitor.

Choosing the video system for your computer is probably the most sensitive and difficult part of building or choosing a PC, particularly if you plan to run Windows beyond VGA resolution (and PowerPoint can look really snappy at higher resolutions). A high-quality monitor and Windows accelerator card can go a very long way toward making your PowerPoint work sessions far more productive and enjoyable. Many companies make quality monitors; among them but not limited to them are NEC, Sony, Mitsubishi, Nanao, MAG, and Viewsonic. Among the best video card makers are companies such as ATI, Diamond, Orchid, Number Nine, Hercules, and Cardinal Technologies. Spending a little more for better video quality is something you'll never regret.

Copying Source Disks

Before installing PowerPoint, it's a very good idea to make a backup set of your PowerPoint installation disks in case anything goes wrong. Keep the original disks in a safe place and use the copies to do your installation. (Don't worry, it's legal.) You can do this in two ways: by running the Windows File Manager or by executing an MS-DOS command. Both methods are described in the text that follows.

For either method, you need 12 to 14 high-density 3 1/2-inch diskettes to perform a complete copy of the PowerPoint installation disks. Label the target disks (the disks on which the copies are being made) something like *PowerPoint Disk 1*, *PowerPoint Disk 2*, and so on, until the entire set is accounted for.

To use the Windows File Manager to perform the disk copy, use the **C**opy Disk command from the **D**isk menu. Follow the instructions on-screen.

To perform a disk copy at the DOS prompt, follow these steps:

1. At the DOS prompt, type:

   diskcopy a: a:

   or:

   diskcopy b: b:

   and press Enter.

   MS-DOS displays this message:

   ```
   Insert source diskette in drive A:

   Press any key when ready...
   ```

2. Insert the original PowerPoint Disk 1 into the floppy disk drive and press any key.

   After a short time another message appears:

   ```
   Insert target diskette in drive A:

   Press any key when ready...
   ```

3. Place the first target disk into the floppy drive and press any key.

   DOS copies files onto this disk. For each disk, unless you are running MS-DOS 6.2, DOS prompts you to change the source and target disks several times because of the large number of files involved. Fortunately, DOS 6.2, in a long overdue feature, offers a single-pass DISKCOPY command. It works the same way as above.

   When the disk is finished with its copying, you see the following message:

   ```
   Copy another diskette (Y/N)?
   ```

4. Press Y to indicate Yes, and repeat the steps above to copy the rest of the PowerPoint installation disks. When you finish the last diskette, type N to tell Diskcopy to stop.

You can now use the working copies to install PowerPoint 4, which is explained in the next section.

Installing PowerPoint

As mentioned earlier, you must have Windows 3.1 installed and running before you install PowerPoint. Make sure that your computer is turned on and ready to run before starting installation.

During the installation process, you are asked to choose the type of installation you want. You can choose one of the following:

- The *Complete* installation installs PowerPoint and all its support files, including Equation Editor and the Clip Art library. It occupies 35-40M of disk space.

- The *Custom* installation should only be chosen if you need to conserve disk space, because you make decisions as to what to install and what to leave out.

- The *Minimal* installation installs only those files that are needed to run Microsoft PowerPoint. Programs such as the Equation Editor, WordArt, the ClipArt Library, Cue Cards, Wizards, and numerous other shared components and features are left out, but can be installed later at any time.

Follow these steps to install PowerPoint:

1. If you are not yet in Windows, start Windows by typing **win** at the DOS prompt.

   The Windows Program Manager appears on-screen. If it isn't open (it does happen), double-click the Program Manager icon at the bottom of your computer screen.

2. Insert the PowerPoint Installation Disk 1 (your working copy) into your floppy disk drive.

3. From the Program Manager **F**ile menu, choose **R**un; or press Alt+F and then R.

4. Type **a:\setup** or **b:\setup** in the command line box, and press Enter or click the OK button.

   A Welcome screen appears.

5. Click the Continue button, type your name and company, and click Continue again. A message appears: `Please wait while Setup copies its working files to your hard disk.`

   After a moment, the Program Manager screen disappears and is replaced by the Microsoft PowerPoint Setup screen.

6. Choose an installation option: Install Complete, Custom, or Minimum.

   If you need to clear some more disk space for the program, click the Exit Setup button.

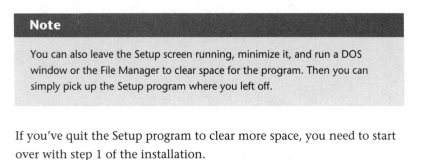

Note

You can also leave the Setup screen running, minimize it, and run a DOS window or the File Manager to clear space for the program. Then you can simply pick up the Setup program where you left off.

If you've quit the Setup program to clear more space, you need to start over with step 1 of the installation.

Setup also tells you how much disk space you need and how much is available during the course of installation.

7. Follow the automated instructions during the process. You need to swap disks numerous times during the process. The program prompts you every time you need to do so.

A final note: If you later need to make changes in your PowerPoint setup, it isn't necessary to perform the entire installation again, particularly if you installed PowerPoint in its minimum configuration or left out many components during a custom installation. After you install PowerPoint, an Installation Maintenance setup mode is available, by simply running Setup again after you install PowerPoint. This enables you to add other PowerPoint components to your system or to remove the entire program if you desire.

Gallery of
Presentation Examples

High-Low-Close Stock Chart

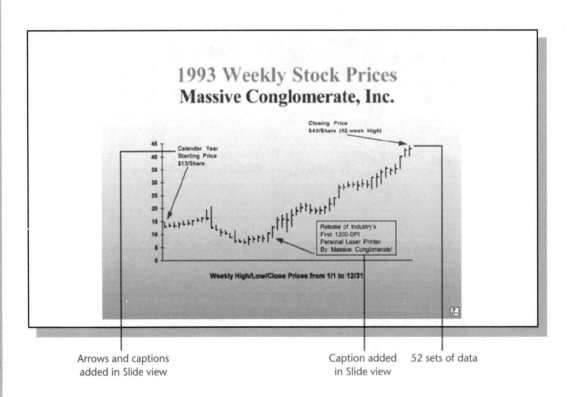

Arrows and captions
added in Slide view

Caption added
in Slide view

52 sets of data

Line-Column Combination Chart

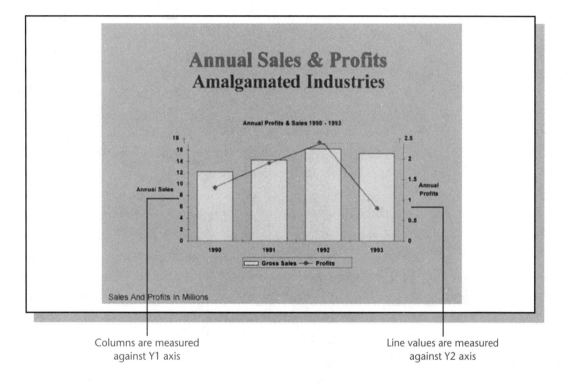

Columns are measured
against Y1 axis

Line values are measured
against Y2 axis

Combination Chart—Same Contents, Different Charting from Preceding Chart

Sales are now
shown by an area

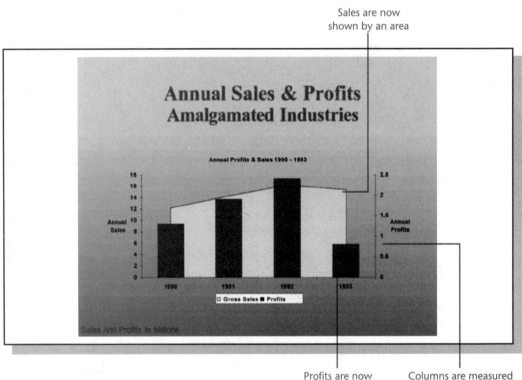

Profits are now
shown by columns

Columns are measured
against Y2 axis

Another Combination Chart—This Time Showing Annual Sales (Columns) and Stock Prices

High-Low-Close markers
with markers crossing

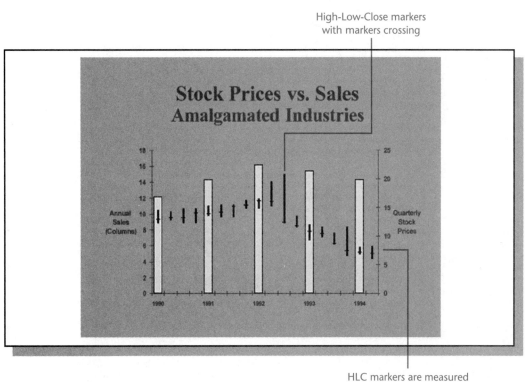

HLC markers are measured
against Y2 axis

Simple Text Slide with Clip Art

3-D Line Chart

Elevation of 5   Perspective of 30

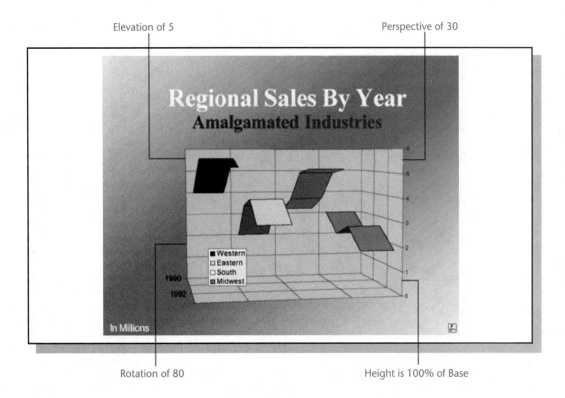

Rotation of 80   Height is 100% of Base

2-D Scatter Chart

Logarithmic scale
applied to y-axis

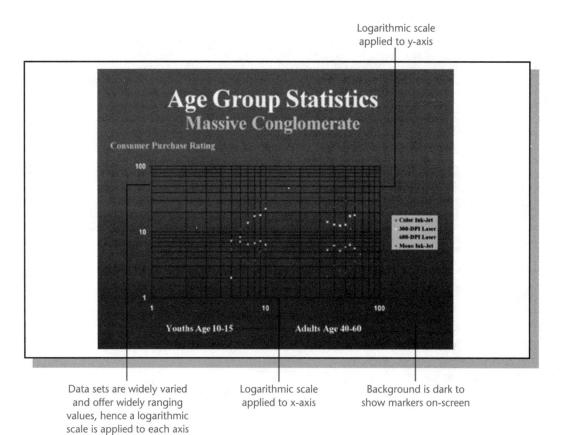

Data sets are widely varied
and offer widely ranging
values, hence a logarithmic
scale is applied to each axis

Logarithmic scale
applied to x-axis

Background is dark to
show markers on-screen

A Table Created with Word 6 for Windows

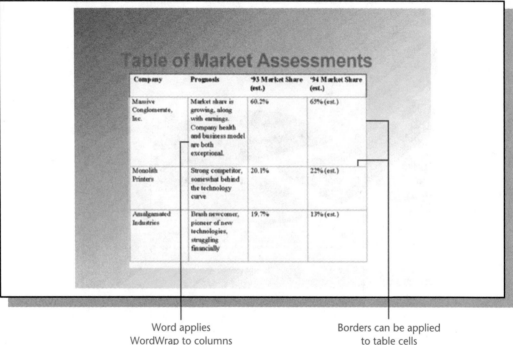

Word applies
WordWrap to columns
and cell text

Borders can be applied
to table cells

3-D Pie Chart

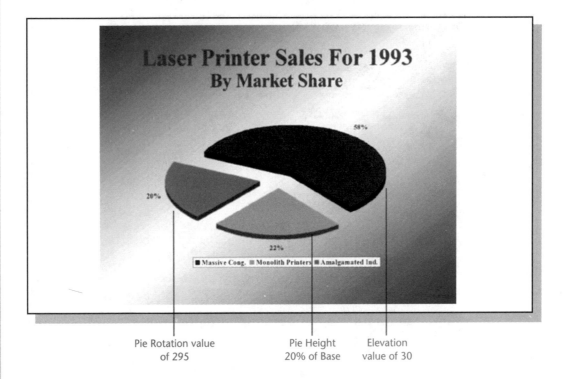

Pie Rotation value of 295

Pie Height 20% of Base

Elevation value of 30

Custom 3-D Column Chart

Elevation
value of 25

Major gridlines
in all 3 axes

Darkened chart walls
show off columns

Perspective
value of 30

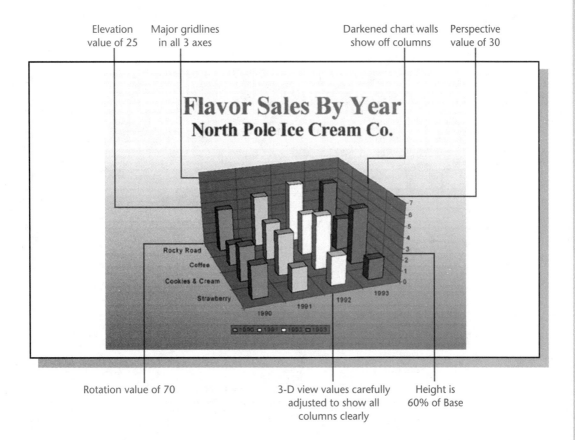

Rotation value of 70

3-D view values carefully
adjusted to show all
columns clearly

Height is
60% of Base

3-D Surface Chart

Legend (shows
"altitude" values)

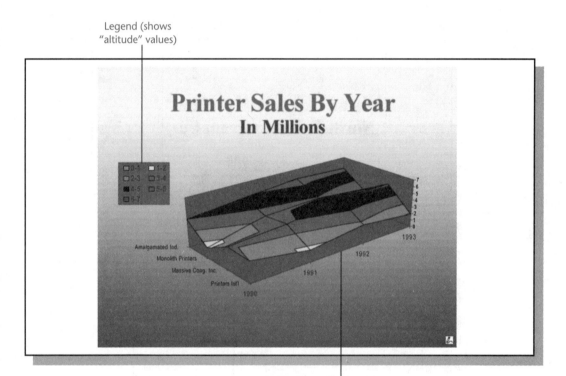

A wide range of values
creates a greater surface

Multimedia

Clip art piece   .AVI video file (will play
in-place with proper
Media Player settings)

Index

O

Q

R